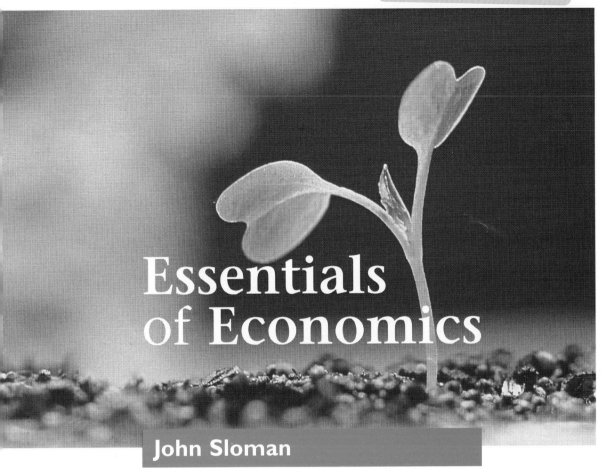

Essentials of Economics

John Sloman

PRENTICE HALL EUROPE

LONDON   NEW YORK   TORONTO   SYDNEY   TOKYO
SINGAPORE   MADRID   MEXICO CITY   MUNICH   PARIS

First published 1998 by
Prentice Hall Europe
Campus 400, Maylands Avenue
Hemel Hempstead
Hertfordshire, HP2 7EZ
A division of Simon & Schuster International Group

Typeset in 10pt Stone serif
by Goodfellow and Egan Ltd, Cambridge

Printed and bound in Great Britain
by Martins the Printers Ltd, Berwick upon Tweed

Library of Congress Cataloguing-in-Publication Data

Available from the publisher

British Library Cataloging in Publication Data

A catalogue record for this book is available from
the British Library

ISBN 0-13-356254-9

1 2 3 4 5 02 01 00 99 98

Contents

Detailed contents

Preface

To the student

Welcome to this introduction to economics. Whether you are planning to study economics beyond this level, or whether this will be your only exposure to this fascinating subject, I hope that you will find the book enjoyable and that it will give you some insight into the economy in which you live and the economic forces which shape all our lives.

Although you have probably never studied the subject before, you will almost certainly know quite a lot of economics already. After all, you make economic decisions virtually every day of your life. Every time you go shopping, you will be acting as an 'economist': deciding what to buy with your limited amount of money. And it is not just with decisions about buying that we act as economists. How much to work (something that students are increasingly forced to do nowadays), how much to study, even how much time to devote to various activities during the course of the day, are all, in a way, *economic* choices.

To satisfy us as consumers, goods and services have to be produced. We will therefore study the behaviour of firms and what governs the decisions that they make. How will the decisions of big businesses differ from those of small firms? How will the degree of competition affect the extent to which we gain or lose from the activities of firms?

We will also look at some of the big economic issues that face us all as members of society at the end of the twentieth century. Despite huge advances in technology, and despite the comfortable lives led by many people in the industrialised world, we still suffer from unemployment, poverty and inequality, and in many countries (the UK included) the gap between rich and poor has grown wider; our environment is polluted; our economy still goes through periodic recessions; our growing affluence as consumers is increasingly bought at the expense of longer hours at work and growing levels of stress. So what can be done about these problems? This book seeks not only to analyse these problems but also to examine the sorts of policies that governments pursue in their attempt to address them.

The book is designed with one overriding aim: to make this exciting and highly relevant subject as clear to understand as possible. To this end, the book has a number of important features:

- A direct and straightforward written style; short paragraphs to aid rapid comprehension. The aim all the time is to provide maximum clarity.
- Summaries at the end of each section (rather than each chapter). This provides a very useful means of revising and checking your understanding.
- Definitions of all technical terms placed in the margin on the same page as the term is used. The term itself is highlighted in the text.

- A comprehensive index, including reference to all defined terms. This enables you to look up a definition as required and to see it used in context.
- Plentiful use of up-to-date examples to illustrate the arguments. This helps to bring the subject alive and puts it in context.
- A careful use of colour to guide you through the text and make the structure easy to follow.
- Review questions at the end of each chapter for either individual or class use.
- Answers given at the end of the book to all odd-numbered questions. These questions will be helpful for self-testing, while the even-numbered ones can be used for class testing.
- Many boxes (typically four per chapter) providing case studies, news items, applications, or elaborations of the text.

Good luck with your studies, and have fun. Perhaps this will be just the beginning for you of a lifelong interest in economic issues and the economy.

To tutors

This book is an abridged version of my *Economics* (third edition). Some passages have been directly transcribed, while others have been extensively rewritten in order to provide a consistent coverage of the 'essentials' of economics.

The book is designed specifically for one-semester courses in introductory economics. There are 12 chapters (6 micro and 6 macro), each providing about a week's worth of reading. The book is also ideal for year-long courses which are designed for those not going on to specialise in economics, or where economics is only a subsidiary component at level 2.

Naturally, in a one-semester course, or in courses for non-specialists, tutors cannot hope to cover all the principles of economics. Thus some things have had to go. The book does not cover indifference curves or isoquants. The analysis of costs is developed with only an informal reference to production functions. Distribution theory is confined to the determination of wage rates. In macroeconomics, ISLM analysis has been left out, as have some of the more advanced debates in monetary and exchange rate theory. In addition, many passages have been simplified to reflect the nature of courses on which the book is likely to be used. The result is a book that is approximately half the length of *Economics* (third edition).

The book is also ideal for the new economics A-level syllabuses of the various boards and for courses, such as HND, where the economic environment component is part of a larger module.

I hope that your students will find this an exciting and interesting text that is relevant to today's issues.

Supplements

There are various additional items that are available to tutors:

- **Answer pack.** This includes answers to all the even-numbered questions and to all the questions in boxes.

- **Workshop sheets.** With increasing class sizes, workshops are an efficient, effective and interesting way for students to learn. Together with my colleague, Sue Hatt, I have been running workshops with up to 300 students for several years. The feedback from students has been very positive. Students are told the topic (or chapter) to prepare, and are then presented with a workshop sheet when they enter the lecture theatre. In pairs, they work at these questions, one or two at a time. The tutors come round to check on progress (this is an effective means of using postgraduate teaching assistants). Then the lecturer goes through the question(s) at the front. The students then do another one or two questions, and so on. Three or four rounds like this can be completed in an hour.

  Twelve workshop sheets are available to tutors using this book: one for each chapter.
- **Masters of lecture plans and diagrams** that can be copied onto acetate and used for projection in lectures. The lecture plans are available in both electronic form (Word and WordPerfect formats) and hard copy.
- **PowerPoint® slideshows** in full colour of lecture plans with key diagrams incorporated.
- **PowerPoint® slideshows** in full colour of the main models, with diagrams built up in sequence, often from tables. These are easy to use and show how models are developed, how equilibria are derived and the effect of shifts in curves.
- **Test bank.** This is available in a Windows- or DOS-based format. It is made up of 3000 questions which tutors can access to compose their own tests. Although this was designed for use with *Economics* (third edition), it is very flexible and allows tutors to select questions by type, topic and level of difficulty. This user-friendly software comes with a full set of instructions.

All the above are available as separate items or together on a compact disk.

Acknowledgements

Writing books is a very time-consuming and often frustrating exercise and requires a good deal of support from everyone around you.

My wife Alison in particular has been brilliant. Without her total commitment to the project, her advice, forbearance and good humour, the book would never have been completed. Thanks also to all my family and friends. As always, they seem remarkably understanding.

The whole team at Prentice Hall has been excellent. Tony Johnston, who, as editor, has seen the project through from its inception, has been great to work with as both a colleague and friend. I've really valued his encouragement, ideas and good sense. Many thanks Tony. Also, particular thanks to Alison Stanford in production for her patience and good humoured efficiency, to Clare Grist Taylor for managing the project, to Derek Moseley in editorial, Jane Mackarell in marketing and Simon Allen in sales.

Thanks too to Chris Bessant, who, as copy editor, has made the task of producing the final manuscript as painless as possible.

A special thank you to colleagues at the University of Western Australia, where I spent two months in 1997, and especially to Pamela Statham, for trying out and commenting on the PowerPoint slides. Their suggestions have been very valuable. Finally, many thanks to all my colleagues and friends at the University of the West of England, and particularly to Mark Sutcliffe, who, as collaborator and co-author on other books, continues to feed me good suggestions and puts up with my moaning.

chapter one

Markets, demand and supply

You may never have studied economics before, and yet when you open a newspaper what do you read? – a report from 'our economics correspondent'. Turn on the television news and what do you see? – an item on the state of the economy. Talk to friends and often the topic will turn to the price of this or that product, or whether you have got enough money to afford to do this or that.

The fact is that economics affects our daily lives. Continually we are being made aware of local, national and international economic issues: whether it be price increases, interest rate changes, fluctuations in exchange rates, unemployment, economic recessions or balance of payments problems.

We are also continually faced with economic problems and decisions of our own. What should I buy in the supermarket? Should I save up for a summer holiday, or spend more on day-to-day living? Should I go to university, or should I try to find a job now?

So just what is economics about? In this chapter we will attempt to answer this question and to give you some insights into the subject you will be studying by using this book.

We will also look at the ways in which different types of economy operate: from the centrally planned economies of the former communist countries, to the free-market economies of most of the world today. We will ask just how do 'markets' work?

The economic problem

What is economics all about?

Many people think that economics is about *money*. Well, to some extent this is true. Economics has a lot to do with money: with how much money people are paid; how much they spend; what it costs to buy various items; how much money firms earn; how much money there is in total in the economy. But despite the large number of areas in which our lives are concerned with money, economics is more than just the study of money.

It is concerned with the following:

Definitions

Production
The transformation of inputs into outputs by firms in order to earn profit (or meet some other objective).

Consumption
The act of using goods and services to satisfy wants. This will normally involve purchasing the goods and services.

Factors of production (or resources)
The inputs into the production of goods and services: labour, land and raw materials, and capital.

Labour
All forms of human input, both physical and mental, into current production.

Land (and raw materials)
Inputs into production that are provided by nature: e.g. unimproved land and mineral deposits in the ground.

Capital
All inputs into production that have themselves been produced: e.g. factories, machines and tools.

- The production of goods and services: how much the economy produces; what particular combination of goods and services; how much each firm produces; what techniques of production they use; how many people they employ.
- The consumption of goods and services: how much the population as a whole spends (and how much it saves); what the pattern of consumption is in the economy; how much people buy of particular items; what particular individuals choose to buy; how people's consumption is affected by prices, advertising, fashion and other factors.

But we still have not quite got to the bottom of what economics is about. What is the crucial ingredient for a problem to be an *economic* one? The answer is that there is one central problem faced by all individuals and all societies. From this one problem stem all the other economic problems we shall be looking at throughout this book.

This central economic problem is the problem of *scarcity*. This applies not only in Ethiopia and the Sudan, but also in Britain, the USA, Japan, France and all other countries of the world. For an economist, scarcity has a very specific definition. Let us examine that definition.

The problem of scarcity

Ask people if they would like more money, and the vast majority would answer 'Yes'. They want more money so that they can buy more goods and services; and this applies not only to poor people but also to most wealthy people too. The point is that human wants are virtually unlimited.

Yet the means of fulfilling human wants are limited. At any one time the world can produce only a limited amount of goods and services. This is because the world has got only a limited amount of resources. These resources, or factors of production as they are often called, are of three broad types:

- Human resources: labour. The labour force is limited both in number and in skills.
- Natural resources: land and raw materials. The world's land area is limited, as are its raw materials.
- Manufactured resources: capital. Capital consists of all those inputs that have themselves had to have been produced in the first place. The world has a limited stock of capital: a limited supply of factories, machines,

transportation and other equipment. The productivity of capital is limited by the state of technology.

So here is the reason for scarcity: human wants are virtually unlimited, whereas the resources available to satisfy these wants *are* limited. We can thus define scarcity as 'the excess of human wants over what can actually be produced'.

Of course, we do not all face the problem of scarcity to the same degree. A poor person unable to afford enough to eat or a decent place to live will hardly see it as a 'problem' that a rich person cannot afford a second Rolls-Royce. But economists do not claim that we all face an *equal* problem of scarcity. In fact this is one of the major issues economists study: how resources are *distributed*, whether between different individuals, different regions of a country or different countries of the world.

But given that people, both rich and poor, want more than they can have, this will cause them to behave in certain ways. Economics studies that behaviour. It studies people at work, producing the goods that people want. It studies people as consumers buying the goods they themselves want. It studies governments influencing the level and pattern of production and consumption. In short, it studies anything to do with the process of satisfying human wants.

Demand and supply

We said that economics is concerned with consumption and production. Another way of looking at this is in terms of *demand* and *supply*. It is quite likely that you already knew that economics had something to do with demand and supply. In fact, demand and supply and the relationship between them lie at the very centre of economics. But what do we mean by the terms, and what is their relationship with the problem of scarcity?

Demand is related to wants. If goods and services were free, people would simply demand whatever they wanted. Such wants are virtually boundless: perhaps limited only by people's imagination. *Supply*, on the other hand, is limited. It is related to resources. The amount firms can supply depends on the resources and technology available.

Given the problem of scarcity, given that human wants exceed what can actually be produced, *potential* demands will exceed *potential* supplies. Society therefore has to find some way of dealing with this problem. Somehow it has got to try to match demand and supply. This applies at the level of the economy overall: *aggregate* demand will need to be balanced against *aggregate* supply. In other words, total spending in the economy will need to balance total production. It also applies at the level of individual goods and services. The demand and supply of cabbages will need to balance, as will the demand and supply of video recorders, cars, houses and bus journeys.

But if potential demand exceeds potential supply, how are *actual* demand and supply to be made equal? Either demand has to be curtailed, or supply has to be increased, or a combination of the two. Economics studies this process. It studies how demand adjusts to available supplies, and how supply adjusts to consumer demands.

Definition

Scarcity
The excess of human wants over what can actually be produced to fulfil these wants.

Dividing up the subject

Economics is traditionally divided into two main branches – *macroeconomics* and *microeconomics*, where 'macro' means big, and 'micro' means small.

Macroeconomics is concerned with the economy as a whole. It is thus concerned with **aggregate demand** and **aggregate supply**. By 'aggregate demand' we mean the total amount of spending in the economy, whether by consumers, by customers outside the country for our exports, by the government, or by firms when they buy capital equipment or stock up on raw materials. By 'aggregate supply' we mean the total national output of goods and services.

Microeconomics is concerned with the individual parts of the economy. It is concerned with the demand and supply of *particular* goods and services and resources: cars, butter, clothes and haircuts; electricians, secretaries, blast furnaces, computers and oil.

Macroeconomics

Because things are scarce, societies are concerned that their resources should be used as *fully as possible*, and that over time their national output should *grow*.

The achievement of growth and the full use of resources is not easy, however, as witness the periods of high unemployment and stagnation that have occurred from time to time throughout the world (for example, in the 1930s, the early 1980s and the early 1990s). Furthermore, attempts by government to stimulate growth and employment have often resulted in inflation and balance of payments crises. Even when societies do achieve growth, it is often short lived. Economies have often experienced cycles, where periods of growth alternate with periods of stagnation, such periods varying from a few months to a few years.

Macroeconomics, then, studies the determination of national output and its growth over time. It also studies the problems of recession, unemployment, inflation, the balance of international payments and cyclical instability, and the policies adopted by governments to deal with these problems.

Macroeconomic problems are closely related to the balance between aggregate demand and aggregate supply.

If aggregate demand is *too high* relative to aggregate supply, inflation and balance of payments deficits are likely to result.

- Inflation refers to a general rise in the level of prices throughout the economy. If aggregate demand rises substantially, firms are likely to respond by raising their prices. After all, if demand is high they can probably still sell as much as before (if not more) even at the higher prices, and thus make more profits. If firms in general put up their prices, inflation results.
- (Current account) balance of payments deficits[1] are the excess of imports over exports. If aggregate demand rises, people are likely to buy more imports. In other words, part of the extra expenditure will go on Japanese videos, German cars, French wine, etc. Also if inflation is high,

[1]The current account excludes investments and financial movements into and out of the country. Such movements are called the 'capital account' (see Chapter 12).

Definitions

Macroeconomics
The branch of economics that studies economic aggregates (grand totals): e.g. the overall level of prices, output and employment in the economy.

Aggregate demand
The total level of spending in the economy.

Aggregate supply
The total amount of output in the economy.

Microeconomics
The branch of economics that studies individual units: e.g. households, firms and industries. It studies the interrelationships between these units in determining the pattern of production and distribution of goods and services.

Rate of inflation
The percentage increase in the level of prices over a twelve-month period.

home-produced goods will become uncompetitive with foreign goods. We are likely, therefore, to buy more foreign imports, and people abroad are likely to buy fewer of our exports.

If aggregate demand is *too low* relative to aggregate supply, unemployment and recession may well result.

- A **recession** is where output in the economy declines: in other words, growth becomes negative. A recession is associated with a low level of consumer spending. If people spend less, shops are likely to find themselves with unsold stocks. As a result they will buy less from the manufacturers, which in turn will cut down on production.
- **Unemployment** is likely to result from cutbacks in production. If firms are producing less, they will need to employ fewer people.

Macroeconomic *policy*, therefore, tends to focus on the balance of aggregate demand and aggregate supply. It can be demand-side policy, which seeks to influence the level of spending in the economy. This in turn will affect the level of production, prices and employment. Or it can be supply-side policy. This is designed to influence the level of production directly: for example, by trying to create more incentives for workers or businesspeople.

Microeconomics

Microeconomics and choice
Because resources are scarce, choices have to be made. There are three main categories of choices that must be made in any society.

- *What* goods and services are going to be produced and in what quantities, given that there are not enough resources to produce all the things people desire? How many cars, how much wheat, how much insurance, how many pop concerts, how many coats, etc. will be produced?
- *How* are things going to be produced, given that there is normally more than one way of producing things? What resources are going to be used and in what quantities? What techniques of production are going to be adopted? Will cars be produced by robots or by assembly-line workers? Will electricity be produced from coal, oil, gas, nuclear fission, renewable resources or a mixture of these?
- *For whom* are things going to be produced? In other words, how is the nation's income going to be distributed? After all, the higher your income, the more you can consume of the nation's output. What will be the wages of farm workers, printers, cleaners and accountants? How much will pensioners receive? How much of the nation's income will go to shareholders or landowners?

All societies have to make these choices whether they be made by individuals, by groups or by the government. These choices can be seen as *micro*economic choices, since they are concerned not with the *total* amount of national output, but with the *individual* goods and services that make it up: what they are, how they are made, and who gets the incomes to buy them.

Definitions

Current account balance of payments
Exports of goods and services minus imports of goods and services. If exports exceed imports, there is a 'current account surplus' (a positive figure). If imports exceed exports, there is a 'current account deficit' (a negative figure).

Recession
A period where national output falls for a few months or more.

Unemployment
The number of people who are actively looking for work but are currently without a job. (Note that there is much debate as to who should officially be counted as unemployed.)

Demand-side policy
Government policy designed to alter the level of aggregate demand, and thereby the level of output, employment and prices.

Supply-side policy
Government policy that attempts to alter the level of aggregate supply directly.

Choice and opportunity cost

Choice involves sacrifice. The more food you choose to buy, the less money you will have to spend on other goods. The more food a nation produces, the less resources there will be for producing other goods. In other words, the production or consumption of one thing involves the sacrifice of alternatives. This sacrifice of alternatives in the production (or consumption) of a good is known as its opportunity cost.

If the workers on a farm can produce either 1000 tonnes of wheat or 2000 tonnes of barley, then the opportunity cost of producing 1 tonne of wheat is the 2 tonnes of barley forgone. The opportunity cost of buying a textbook is the new pair of jeans you also wanted that you have had to go without. The opportunity cost of working overtime is the leisure you have sacrificed.

Rational choices

Economists often refer to rational choices. By this is simply meant the weighing-up of the *costs* and *benefits* of any activity, whether it be firms choosing what and how much to produce, workers choosing whether to take a particular job or to work extra hours, or consumers choosing what to buy.

Imagine you are doing your shopping in a supermarket and you want to buy a bottle of wine. Do you spend a lot of money and buy a top-quality French wine, or do you buy a cheap eastern European one instead? To make a rational (i.e. sensible) decision, you will need to weigh up the costs and benefits of each alternative. The top-quality wine may give you a lot of enjoyment, but it has a high opportunity cost: because it is expensive, you will need to sacrifice quite a lot of consumption of other goods if you decide to buy it. If you buy the cheap bottle, however, although you will not enjoy it so much, you will have more money left over to buy other things: it has a lower opportunity cost.

Thus rational decision making, as far as consumers are concerned, involves choosing those items that give you the best value for money: i.e. the *greatest benefit relative to cost*.

The same principles apply to firms when deciding what to produce. For example, should a car manufacturer open up another production line? A rational decision will again involve weighing up the benefits and costs. The benefits are the revenues the firm will earn from selling the extra cars. The costs will include the extra labour costs, raw material costs, costs of component parts, etc. It will be profitable to open up the new production line only if the revenues earned exceed the costs entailed: in other words, if it adds to profit.

In the more complex situation of deciding which model of car to produce, or how much of each model, the firm must weigh up the relative benefits and costs of each: i.e. it will want to produce the most profitable product mix.

Marginal costs and benefits

In economics we argue that rational choices involve weighing up marginal costs and marginal benefits. These are the costs and benefits of doing a little bit more or a little bit less of a given activity. They can be contrasted with the *total* costs and benefits of the activity.

Definitions

Opportunity cost
The cost of any activity measured in terms of the best alternative forgone.

Rational choices
Choices that involve weighing up the benefit of any activity against its opportunity cost.

Marginal costs
The additional costs of doing a little bit more (or *I unit* more if a unit can be measured) of an activity.

Marginal benefits
The additional benefits of doing a little bit more (or *I unit* more if a unit can be measured) of an activity.

Take a familiar example. What time will you set the alarm clock to go off tomorrow morning? Let us say that you have to leave home at 8.30. Perhaps you will set the alarm for 7.00. That will give you plenty of time to get up and get ready, but it will mean a relatively short night's sleep. Perhaps then you will decide to set it for 7.30 or even 8.00. That will give you a longer night's sleep, but much more of a rush in the morning to get ready.

So how do you make a rational decision about when the alarm should go off? What you have to do is to weigh up the costs and benefits of *additional* sleep. Each extra minute in bed gives you more sleep (the marginal benefit) but gives you more of a rush when you get up (the marginal cost). The decision therefore is based on the costs and benefits of *extra* sleep, not on the *total* costs and benefits of a whole night's sleep.

This same principle applies to rational decisions made by consumers, workers and firms. For example, the car firm we were considering just now will weigh up the marginal costs and benefits of producing cars: in other words, it will compare the costs and revenue of producing *additional* cars. If additional cars add more to the firm's revenue than to its costs, it will be profitable to produce them.

The social implications of choice

Microeconomics does not just study how choices are made. It also looks at their consequences. Under certain conditions the consequences may be an efficient allocation of the nation's resources.

There are, however, a whole series of possible problems that can arise from the choices that people make, whether they are made by individuals, by firms or by the government. These problems include such things as inefficiency, waste, inequality and pollution.

Take the case of pollution. It might be profitable for a firm to tip toxic waste into a river. But what is profitable for the firm will not necessarily be 'profitable' for society. There may be serious environmental consequences of the firm's actions (see Box 1.2).

Illustrating economic issues: the circular flow of goods and incomes

The process of satisfying human wants involves producers and consumers. The relationship between them is two-sided and can be represented in a flow diagram (see Figure 1.1).

The consumers of goods and services are labelled 'households'. Some members of households, of course, are also workers, and in some cases are the owners of other factors of production too, such as land. The producers of goods and services are labelled 'firms'.

Firms and households are in a twin 'demand and supply' relationship with each other.

First, in the top half of the diagram, households demand goods and services, and firms supply goods and services. In the process, exchange takes place. In a money economy (as opposed to a barter economy, firms exchange goods and services for money. In other words, money flows from households to firms in the form of consumer expenditure, while goods and services flow the other way – from firms to households.

Definition

Barter economy
An economy where people exchange goods and services directly with one another without any payment of money. Workers would be paid with bundles of goods.

BOX 1.1 *The opportunity costs of studying economics*

What are you sacrificing?

You may not have realised it, but you probably consider opportunity costs many times a day. The reason is that we are constantly making choices: what to buy, what to eat, what to wear, whether to go out, how much to study and so on. Each time we make a choice to do something, we are in effect rejecting doing some alternative. This alternative forgone is the opportunity cost of our action.

Sometimes the opportunity costs of our actions are the direct monetary costs we incur. Sometimes it is more complicated.

Take the opportunity costs of your choices as a student of economics.

Buying a textbook costing £17.95

This does involve a direct money payment. What you have to consider is the alternatives you could have bought with the £17.95. You then have to weigh up the benefit from the best alternative against the benefit of the textbook.

 What might prevent you from making the best decision?

Coming to classes

You may or may not be paying your own course fees. Even if you are, there is no extra (marginal) monetary cost in coming to classes once the fees have been paid. You will not get a refund by skipping classes!

So are the opportunity costs zero? No: by coming to classes you are *not* working in the library; you are *not* having an extra hour in bed; you are *not* sitting drinking coffee with friends, and so on. If you are making a rational decision to come to classes, then you will consider such possible alternatives.

 If there are several other things you could have done, is the opportunity cost the sum of all of them?

Revising for an economics exam

Again, the opportunity cost is the best alternative to which you could have put your time. This might be revising for some *other* exam. You will probably want to divide your time

FIGURE 1.1
Circular flow of goods and incomes

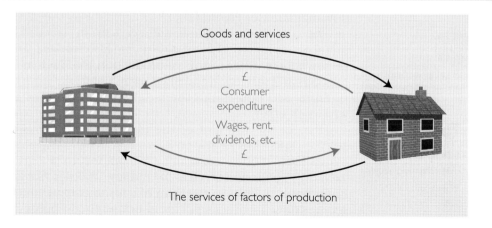

Goods and services

£
Consumer
expenditure

Wages, rent,
dividends, etc.
£

The services of factors of production

sensibly between your subjects. A *sensible* decision is not to revise economics on any given occasion if you will gain a greater benefit from revising for another subject. In such a case the (marginal) opportunity cost of revising economics exceeds the (marginal) benefit.

Choosing to study at university or college

What are the opportunity costs of being a student in higher education?

At first it might seem that the costs would include the following:

- Tuition fees.
- Books, stationery, etc.
- Accommodation expenses.
- Transport.
- Food, entertainment and other living expenses.

But adding these up does *not* give the *opportunity* cost. The opportunity cost is the *sacrifice* entailed by going to university or college *rather* than doing something else. Let us assume that the alternative is to take a job that has been offered. The correct list of opportunity costs of higher education would include:

- Books, stationery, etc.
- *Additional* accommodation and transport expenses over what would have been incurred by taking the job.
- Wages that would have been earned in the job *less* any student grant received.

Tuition fees paid by you (as opposed to your parents or anyone else).

Q3 Why is the cost of food not included?

Q4 Make a list of the benefits of higher education.

Q5 Is the opportunity cost to the individual of attending higher education different from the opportunity costs to society as a whole?

This coming together of buyers and sellers is known as a **market** – whether it be a street market, a shop, an auction, a mail-order system or whatever. Thus we talk about the market for apples, the market for oil, for cars, for houses, for televisions and so on.

Second, firms and households come together in the market for factors of production. This is illustrated in the bottom half of the diagram. This time the demand and supply roles are reversed. Firms demand the use of factors of production owned by households – labour, land and capital. Households supply them. Thus the services of labour and other factors flow from households to firms, and in exchange firms pay households money – namely, wages, rent, dividends and interest. Just as we referred to particular goods markets, so we can also refer to particular factor markets – the market for bricklayers, for secretaries, for hairdressers, for land, etc.

Definition

Market
The interaction between buyers and sellers.

BOX 1.2 *Green economics*

....

Taking account of environmental costs

People have become concerned by a number of environmental problems in recent years. These include the following:

- *Acid rain.* This is caused by sulphur and nitrogen emissions from power stations, industry and cars. It has been blamed for *Waldsterben* (forest death) in Central Europe and the contamination of many lakes and streams, with the death of fish and plant life.
- *The greenhouse effect.* This is caused by carbon dioxide and other gases emitted again by power stations, various industries and cars. The fear is that these gases will cause a heating of the earth's atmosphere. This will lead to climatic changes which will affect food production. It will also lead to a raising of sea levels and flooding as parts of the polar ice caps melt.
- *Depletion of the ozone layer.* This is caused by the use of CFC gases in aerosols, refrigerators and the manufacture of polystyrene foam. The ozone layer protects us from harmful ultraviolet radiation from the sun. A depletion of this layer could lead to increased skin cancer.
- *Nuclear radiation.* The fear is that accidents or sabotage at nuclear power stations could cause dangerous releases of radiation. The disposal of nuclear waste is another environmental problem.
- *Land and river pollution.* The tipping of toxic waste into the ground or into rivers can cause long-term environmental damage. Soils can be poisoned; rivers and seas can become polluted. It is not just industry that is to blame here. Sewage pollutes rivers and seas. Nitrogen run-off and slurry from farming are also major pollutants.

It was not until the late 1960s and early 1970s that the 'environment' became more firmly part of the political agenda in most European countries. It was largely a response not only to the spectacular growth of the western economies, but also to the continued and extensive industrialisation of the Eastern bloc countries such as Poland and the former USSR.

'Green groups' sprang up round Europe. These groups realised that, if economic growth was to be sustained, then environmental damage could grow at an alarming rate.

The problems such groups have encountered in attempting to change attitudes and economic strategies have been immense. Certain governments have been reluctant to enter international environmental agreements, perceiving them to be against their national interest. The agreement to cut sulphur dioxide emissions from power stations is one example.

There is thus a circular flow of incomes. Households earn incomes from firms, and firms earn incomes from households. The money circulates. There is also a circular flow of goods and services, but in the opposite direction. Households supply factor services to firms, which then use them to supply goods and services to households.

This flow diagram can help to show the distinction between micro and macroeconomics.

The costs of pollution abatement are high, especially in the short run. As long as these short-run costs are greater than the perceived costs of continuing pollution, then industry and government will continue to incur them. The consequences of this, however, could be devastating and far more costly in the long run, in both a financial and an environmental sense.

What can economists say about the causes of these environmental problems? They have three common features:

- *Ignorance*. It is often not for many years that the nature and causes of environmental damage are realised. Take the case of aerosols. It was not until the 1980s that scientists connected their use to ozone depletion.
- *The polluters do not pay*. The costs of pollution are rarely paid by the polluters. Economists call such costs *external* costs. Because polluters rarely pay to clean up their pollution or compensate those who suffer, they frequently ignore the problem.
- *Present gains for future costs*. The environmental costs of industrialisation often build up slowly and do not become critical for many years. The benefits of industrialisation, however, are more immediate. Thus governments, consumers and industry are frequently prepared to continue with various practices and leave future generations to worry about their environmental consequences. The problem is therefore a reflection of the importance that people attach to the present relative to the future.

Environmentalists recognise these problems and try through the political process and various pressure groups, such as Friends of the Earth and Greenpeace, to reduce people's ignorance and to change their attitudes.

They stress the need for clean technologies, for environmentally sound growth and for greater responsibility by industry, consumers and government alike. Policies, they argue, should prevent problems occurring and not merely be a reaction to them once they are nearing crisis point. If growth is to be sustainable into the long term, with a real increase in the quality of life, then current growth must not be at the expense of the environment.

 Should all polluting activities be banned? Could pollution ever be justified? Explain your answer.

Microeconomics is concerned with the composition of the circular flow: *what* combinations of goods makes up the goods flow; *how* the various factors of production are combined to produce these goods; *for whom* the wages, dividends, rent and interest are paid out.

Macroeconomics is concerned with the total size of the flow and what causes it to expand and contract.

Summary

1. The central economic problem is that of scarcity. Given that there is a limited supply of factors of production (labour, land and capital), it is impossible to provide everybody with everything they want. Potential demands exceed potential supplies.
2. The subject of economics is usually divided into two main branches, macroeconomics and microeconomics.
3. Macroeconomics deals with aggregates such as the overall levels of unemployment, output, growth and prices in the economy.
4. Microeconomics deals with the activities of individual units within the economy: firms, industries, consumers, workers, etc. Because resources are scarce, people have to make choices. Society has to choose by some means or other *what* goods and services to produce, *how* to produce them and *for whom* to produce them. Microeconomics studies these choices.
5. Rational choices involve weighing up the marginal benefits of each activity against its marginal opportunity costs. If the marginal benefit exceeds the marginal cost, it is rational to choose to do more of that activity.
6. The circular flow of goods and incomes shows the interrelationships between firms and households in a money economy. Firms and households come together in markets. In goods markets, firms supply goods and households demand goods. In the process, money flows from households to firms in return for the goods and services that the firms supply. In factor markets, firms demand factors of production and households supply them. In the process, money flows from firms to households in return for the services of the factors that households supply.

Economic systems

How do countries differ in the way their economies are organised?

All societies are faced with the problem of scarcity. They differ considerably, however, in the way they tackle the problem. One important difference between societies is in the degree of government control of the economy.

At the one extreme lies the completely planned or command economy, where all the economic decisions are taken by the government.

At the other extreme lies the completely free-market economy. In this type of economy there is no government intervention at all. All decisions are taken by individuals and firms. Households decide how much labour and other factors to supply, and what goods to consume. Firms decide what goods to produce and what factors to employ. The pattern of production and consumption that results depends on the interactions of all these individual demand and supply decisions.

In practice, all economies are a mixture of the two. It is therefore the *degree* of government intervention that distinguishes different economic systems. Thus in the former communist countries of eastern Europe, the government played a large role, whereas in the United States, the government plays a much smaller role.

Definition

Centrally planned or command economy
An economy where all economic decisions are taken by the central authorities.

It is nevertheless useful to analyse the extremes in order to put the different mixed economies of the real world into perspective.

We start by having a brief look at the command economy. Then for the rest of this chapter we will see how a free-market economy operates. In subsequent chapters we will examine the various ways in which governments intervene in market economies: i.e. we will look at the various forms of mixed market economy.

The command economy

The command economy is usually associated with a socialist or communist economic system, where land and capital are collectively owned. The state plans the allocation of resources at three important levels:

- It plans the allocation of resources between current consumption and investment for the future. By sacrificing some present consumption and diverting resources into investment, it could increase the economy's growth rate.

  The amount of resources it chooses to devote to investment will depend on its broad macroeconomic strategy: the importance it attaches to growth as opposed to current consumption.

- At a microeconomic level it plans the output of each industry and firm, the techniques that will be used and the labour and other resources required by each industry and firm.

  In order to ensure that the required inputs are available, the state would probably conduct some form of input–output analysis. All industries are seen as users of *inputs* from other industries and as producers of *output* for consumers or other industries. For example, the steel industry uses inputs from the coal and iron-ore industries and produces output for the vehicle and construction industries. Input–output analysis shows, for each industry, the sources of all its inputs and the destination of all its output. By its use the state attempts to match up the inputs and outputs of each industry so that the planned demand for each industry's product is equal to its planned supply.

- It plans the distribution of output between consumers. This will depend on the government's aims. It may distribute goods according to its judgement of people's *needs*; or it may give more to those who produce more, thereby providing an *incentive* for people to work harder.

  It may distribute goods and services directly (for example, by a system of rationing); or it may decide the distribution of money incomes and allow individuals to decide how to spend them. If it does the latter, it may still seek to influence the pattern of expenditure by setting appropriate prices: low prices to encourage consumption, and high prices to discourage consumption.

Assessment of the command economy

With central planning, the government could take an overall view of the economy. It could direct the nation's resources in accordance with specific national goals.

High growth rates could be achieved if the government directed large amounts of resources into investment. Unemployment could be largely

Definitions

Free-market economy
An economy where all economic decisions are taken by individual households and firms and with no government intervention.

Mixed economy
An economy where economic decisions are made partly by the government and partly through the market.

Mixed market economy
A market economy where there is some government intervention.

Input–output analysis
This involves dividing the economy into sectors where each sector is a user of inputs from and a supplier of outputs to other sectors. The technique examines how these inputs and outputs can be matched to the total resources available in the economy.

BOX 1.3 *The rise and fall of planning in the former Soviet Union*

Early years

The Bolsheviks under the leadership of Lenin came to power in Russia with the October revolution of 1917. The Bolsheviks, however, were opposed by the White Russians and civil war ensued.

During this period of *War Communism*, the market economy was abolished. Industry and shops were nationalised; workers were told what jobs to do; there were forced requisitions of food from peasants to feed the towns; the money economy collapsed as rampant inflation made money worthless; workers were allocated goods from distribution depots.

With the ending of the civil war in 1921, the economy was in bad shape. Lenin embarked on a *New Economic Policy*. This involved a return to the use of markets. Smaller businesses were returned to private hands, and peasants were able to sell their food rather than having it requisitioned. The economy began to recover.

Lenin died in 1924 and Stalin came to power.

The Stalinist system

The Soviet economy underwent a radical transformation from 1928 onwards. The key features of the Stalinist approach were collectivisation, industrialisation and central planning.

Collectivisation of agriculture

Peasant farms were abolished and replaced by large-scale collective farms where land was collectively owned and worked. Collectivisation initially caused massive disruption and famine, with peasants slaughtering their animals rather than giving them up to the collective. People died in their thousands. Despite an initial fall in output, more food was provided for the towns, and many workers left the land to work in the new industries.

In addition to the collective farms, state farms were established. These were owned by the state and were run by managers appointed by the state. Workers were paid a wage rather than having a share in farm income.

Both collective and state farms were given quotas of output that they were supposed to deliver for which the state would pay a fixed price.

Industry and central planning

A massive drive to industrialisation took place. To achieve this a vast planning apparatus was developed. At the top was *Gosplan*, the central planning agency. This prepared five-year plans and annual plans.

The five-year plans specified the general direction in which the economy was to move. The annual plans gave the details of just what was to be produced and with what resources for some 200 or so key products. Other products were planned at a lower level – by various industrial ministries or regional authorities.

The effect was that all factories were given targets that had to be achieved. It was the task of the planning authorities to ensure that the targets were realistic: that there were sufficient resources to meet the targets. The system operated without the aid of the price mechanism and the profit motive. The main incentive was the *bonus*: bonuses were paid to managers and workers if targets were achieved.

The Stalinist system remained with only minor changes until the 1980s. In the early years, very high growth rates were achieved; but this was at a cost of low efficiency. The poor flow of information from firms to the planners led to many inconsistencies in the plans. The targets were often totally unrealistic, and as a result there were frequent shortages and sometimes surpluses. With incentives purely geared to meeting targets, there was little product innovation and goods were frequently of poor quality and finish.

The limits of planning

Although most resources were allocated through planning, there were nevertheless some goods that were sold in markets. Any surpluses above their quota that were produced by collective farms could be sold in collective farm markets (street markets) in the towns. In addition, the workers on collective farms were allowed to own their own small private plots of land, and they too could sell their produce in the collective farm markets.

A large 'underground economy' flourished in which goods were sold on the black market and in which people did second 'unofficial' jobs (e.g. as plumbers, electricians or garment makers).

Gorbachev's reforms

Stalin died in 1953. The planning system, however, remained largely unchanged until the late 1980s.

During the 1970s growth had slowed down and by the time Gorbachev came to power in 1985 many people were pressing for fundamental economic reforms. Gorbachev responded with his policy of *perestroika* (economic reconstruction), which among other things included the following:

- Making managers more involved in preparing their own plans rather than merely being given instructions.
- Insisting that firms cover their costs of production. If they could not, the state might refuse to bale them out and they could be declared bankrupt. The aim of this was to encourage firms to be more efficient.
- Improving the incentive system by making bonuses more related to genuine productivity. Workers had come to expect bonuses no matter how much or how little was produced.
- Organising workers into small teams or 'brigades' (typically of around 10–15 workers). Bonuses were then awarded to the whole brigade according to its productivity. The idea was to encourage people to work more effectively together.
- Stringent checks on quality by state officials and the rejection of substandard goods.
- Allowing one-person businesses and co-operatives (owned by the workers) to be set up.
- A greater willingness by the state to raise prices if there were substantial shortages.

These reforms, however, did not halt the economic decline. What is more there was now an unhappy mix of planning and the market, with people unclear as to what to expect from the state. Many managers resented the extra responsibilities they were now expected to shoulder and many officials saw their jobs threatened. Queues lengthened in the shops and people increasingly became disillusioned with *perestroika*.

Following the failed coup of 1991, in which hard-line communists had attempted to reimpose greater state control, and with the consequent strengthening of the position of Boris Yeltsin, the Russian president and the main advocate of more radical reforms, both the Soviet Union and the system of central planning came to an end.

Russia embarked upon a radical programme of market reforms in which competition and enterprise were intended to replace state central planning. The Stalinist system now appears to be but a fading memory.

avoided if the government carefully planned the allocation of labour in accordance with production requirements and labour skills. National income could be distributed more equally or in accordance with needs. The social repercussions of production and consumption (e.g. the effects on the environment) could be taken into account, provided the government was able to predict these effects and chose to take them into account.

In practice, these goals could be achieved only at considerable social and economic cost. The reasons are as follows:

- The larger and more complex the economy, the greater the task of collecting and analysing the information essential to planning, and the more complex the plan. Complicated plans are likely to be costly to administer and involve cumbersome bureaucracy.
- If there is no system of prices, or if prices are set arbitrarily by the state, planning is likely to involve the inefficient use of resources. It is difficult to assess the relative efficiency of two alternative techniques that use different inputs, if there is no way in which the value of those inputs can be ascertained. For example, how can a rational decision be made between an oil-fired and a coal-fired furnace if the prices of oil and coal do not reflect their relative scarcity?
- It is difficult to devise appropriate incentives to encourage workers and managers to be more productive without a reduction in quality. For example, if bonuses are given according to the quantity of output produced, a factory might produce shoddy goods, since it can probably produce a larger quantity of goods by cutting quality. To avoid this problem, a large number of officials may have to be employed to check quality.
- Complete state control over resource allocation would involve a considerable loss of individual liberty. Workers would have no choice where to work; consumers would have no choice what to buy.
- The government might enforce its plans even if they were unpopular.
- If production is planned, but consumers are free to spend money incomes as they wish, then there will be a problem if consumer wishes change. Shortages will occur if consumers decide to buy more, and surpluses will occur if they decide to buy less.

Most of these problems were experienced in the former USSR and the other Eastern bloc countries, and were part of the reason for the overthrow of their communist regimes (see Box 1.3).

The free-market economy

Free decision making by individuals

The free-market economy is usually associated with a pure capitalist system, where land and capital are privately owned. All economic decisions are taken by households and firms, which are assumed to act in their own self-interest. The following assumptions are usually made:

- Firms seek to maximise profits.
- Consumers seek to get the best value for money from their purchases.
- Workers seek to maximise their wages relative to the human cost of working in a particular job.

It is also assumed that individuals are free to make their own economic choices; consumers are free to decide what to buy with their incomes; workers are free to choose where and how much to work; firms are free to choose what to sell and what production methods to use.

The resulting supply and demand decisions of firms and households are transmitted to each other through their effect on *prices*.

The price mechanism

The price mechanism works as follows. Prices respond to *shortages* and *surpluses*. Shortages cause prices to rise. Surpluses cause prices to fall.

If consumers decide they want more of a good (or if producers decide to cut back supply), demand will exceed supply. The resulting shortage will cause the price of the good to *rise*. This will act as an incentive to producers to supply more, since production will now be more profitable. It will discourage consumers from buying so much. *Price will continue rising until the shortage has thereby been eliminated.*

If, on the other hand, consumers decide they want less of a good (or if producers decide to produce more), supply will exceed demand. The resulting surplus will cause the price of the good to *fall*. This will act as a disincentive to producers, who will supply less, since production will now be less profitable. It will encourage consumers to buy more. *Price will continue falling until the surplus has thereby been eliminated.*

The same analysis can be applied to factor markets. If the demand for a particular type of labour exceeded its supply, the resulting shortage would drive up the wage rate (i.e. the price of labour), thus reducing firms' demand for that type of labour and encouraging more workers to take up that type of job. Wages would continue rising until demand equalled supply: until the shortage was eliminated.

Likewise if there were a surplus of a particular type of labour, the wage would fall until demand equalled supply.

The effect of changes in demand and supply

How will the price mechanism respond to changes in consumer demand or producer supply? After all, the pattern of consumer demand changes. For example, people may decide they want more mountain bikes and fewer racers. Likewise the pattern of supply also changes. For example, changes in technology may allow the mass production of microchips at lower cost, while the production of hand-built furniture becomes relatively expensive.

In all cases of changes in demand and supply, the resulting changes in *price* act as both *signals* and *incentives*.

A change in demand. A rise in demand is signalled by a rise in price. This then acts as an incentive for firms to produce more of the good: the quantity supplied rises. What in effect is happening is that the high prices of these goods relative to their costs of production are signalling that consumers are willing to see resources diverted from other uses. But this is just what firms do. They do divert resources from goods with lower prices relative to costs (and hence lower profits) to those goods that are more profitable.

Definition

The price mechanism
The system in a market economy whereby changes in price in response to changes in demand and supply have the effect of making demand equal to supply.

A fall in demand is signalled by a fall in price. This then acts as an incentive for firms to produce less: such goods are now less profitable to produce. Thus the quantity supplied falls.

A change in supply. A rise in supply is signalled by a fall in price. This then acts as an incentive for consumers to buy more: the quantity demanded rises. A fall in supply is signalled by a rise in price. This then acts as an incentive for consumers to buy less: the quantity demanded falls.

The interdependence of markets

The interdependence of goods and factor markets. A rise in demand for a good will raise its price and profitability. Firms will respond by supplying more. But to do this they will need more inputs. Thus the demand for the inputs will rise, which in turn will raise the price of the inputs. The suppliers of inputs will respond to this incentive by supplying more. This can be summarised as follows:

1. Goods market
   - Demand for the good rises.
   - This creates a shortage.
   - This causes the price of the good to rise.
   - This eliminates the shortage by choking off some of the demand and encouraging firms to produce more.
2. Factor market
   - The increased supply of the good causes an increase in the demand for factors of production (i.e. inputs) used in making it.
   - This causes a shortage of those inputs.
   - This causes their prices to rise.
   - This eliminates their shortage by choking off some of the demand and encouraging the suppliers of inputs to supply more.

Goods markets thus affect factor markets.

It is common in economics to summarise an argument like this by using symbols. It is a form of shorthand. Figure 1.2 summarises this particular sequence of events.

FIGURE 1.2
The price mechanism: the effect of a rise in demand

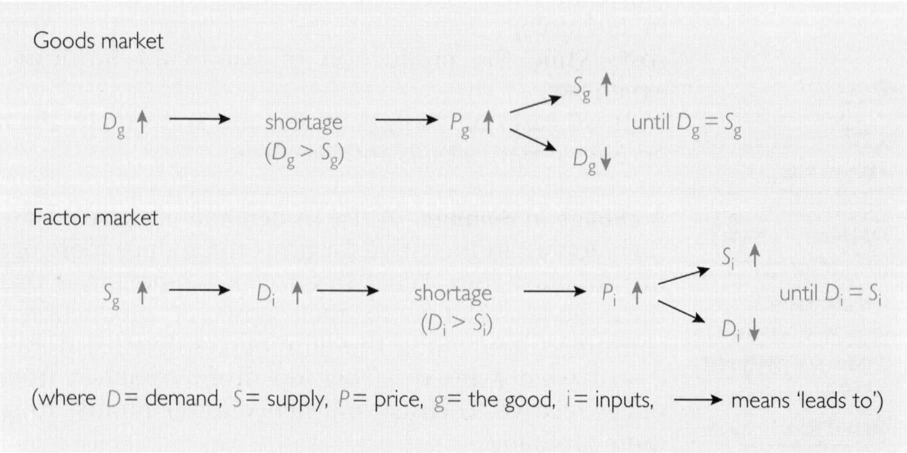

Goods market

$D_g \uparrow \longrightarrow$ shortage $\longrightarrow P_g \uparrow$ $\begin{cases} S_g \uparrow \\ D_g \downarrow \end{cases}$ until $D_g = S_g$
$(D_g > S_g)$

Factor market

$S_g \uparrow \longrightarrow D_i \uparrow \longrightarrow$ shortage $\longrightarrow P_i \uparrow$ $\begin{cases} S_i \uparrow \\ D_i \downarrow \end{cases}$ until $D_i = S_i$
$(D_i > S_i)$

(where D = demand, S = supply, P = price, g = the good, i = inputs, $\longrightarrow$ means 'leads to')

Interdependence exists in the other direction too: factor markets affect goods markets. For example, the discovery of raw materials will lower their price. This will lower the costs of production of firms using these raw materials and increase the supply of the finished goods. The resulting surplus will lower the price of the good, which will encourage consumers to buy more.

The interdependence of different goods markets. A rise in the price of one good will encourage consumers to buy alternatives. This will drive up the price of alternatives. This in turn will encourage producers to supply more of the alternatives.

Interdependence and the public interest. Even though all individuals are merely looking to their own self-interest in the free-market economy, they are in fact being encouraged to respond to the wishes of others through the incentive of the price mechanism. It is often claimed that this is a major advantage of a free-market economy. We will be examining this claim in subsequent chapters.

Competitive markets

For the rest of this chapter we will examine the working of the price mechanism in more detail. We will look first at demand, then at supply, and then we will put the two together to look at the determination of price.

The markets we will be examining are highly competitive markets, with many firms competing against each other. In economics we call this perfect competition. This is where consumers and producers are too numerous to have any control over prices: they are price takers.

In the case of consumers, this means that they have to accept the prices as given for the things that they buy. On most occasions this is true. For example, when you get to the supermarket checkout you cannot start haggling with the checkout operator over the price of a can of beans or a tub of margarine.

In the case of firms, perfect competition means that producers are too small and face too much competition from other firms to be able to raise prices. Take the case of farmers selling wheat. They have to sell it at the current market price. If individually they try to sell at a higher price, no one will buy, since purchasers of wheat (e.g. flour millers) can get all the wheat they want at the market price.

Of course, many firms *do* have the power to choose their prices. This does not mean that they can simply charge whatever they like. They will still have to take account of overall consumer demand and their competitors' prices. Ford, when setting the price of its Escort cars, will have to ensure that they remain competitive with Astras, Golfs, 306s, etc. Nevertheless, most firms have some flexibility in setting their prices: they have a degree of 'market power'.

If this is the case, then why do we study *perfect* markets, where firms are price takers? One reason is that they provide a useful approximation to the real world and give us many insights into how a market economy works. Many markets do function very similarly to the markets we shall be describing.

Another is that perfect markets provide an ideal against which to compare the real world. It is often argued that perfect markets benefit the

Definitions

Perfect competition (preliminary definition)
A situation where the consumers and producers of a product are price takers. (There are other features of a perfectly competitive market; these are examined in Chapter 4.)

Price taker
A person or firm with no power to be able to influence the market price.

consumer, whereas markets dominated by big business may operate against the consumer's interests. For example, the consumer may up end paying higher prices in a market dominated by just a few firms than in one operating under perfect competition.

Summary

1. The economic systems of different countries vary according to the extent to which they rely on the market or the government to allocate resources.
2. At the one extreme, in a command economy, the state makes all the economic decisions. It plans how many resources to allocate for present consumption and how many for investment for future output. It plans the output of each industry, the methods of production it will use and the amount of resources it will be allocated. It plans the distribution of output between consumers.
3. A command economy has the advantage of being able to address directly various national economic goals, such as rapid growth and the avoidance of unemployment and inequality. A command economy, however, is likely to be inefficient: a large bureaucracy will be needed to collect and process information; prices and the choice of production methods are likely to be arbitrary; incentives may be inappropriate; shortages and surpluses may result.
4. At the other extreme is the free-market economy. In this economy, decisions are made by the interaction of demand and supply. Price changes act as the mechanism whereby demand and supply are balanced. If there is a shortage, prices will rise until the shortage is eliminated. If there is a surplus, price will fall until that is eliminated.
5. For the rest of this chapter we will be studying perfect markets. These are markets where both producers and consumers are price takers.

Demand

How much will people buy of any item?

The relationship between demand and price

The headlines announce, 'Major crop failures in Brazil and East Africa: coffee prices soar.' Shortly afterwards you find that coffee prices have doubled in the shops. What do you do? Presumably you will cut back on the amount of coffee you drink. Perhaps you will reduce it from, say, six cups per day to two. Perhaps you will give up drinking coffee altogether.

This is simply an illustration of the general relationship between price and consumption: *when the price of a good rises, the quantity demanded will fall*. This relationship is known as the law of demand. There are two reasons for this law:

- People will feel poorer. They will not be able to afford to buy so much of the good with their money. The purchasing power of their income (their *real income*) has fallen. This is called the income effect of a price rise.

• The good will now be dearer relative to other goods. People will thus switch to alternative or 'substitute' goods. This is called the substitution effect of a price rise.

Similarly, when the price of a good falls, the quantity demanded will rise. People can afford to buy more (the income effect), and they will switch away from consuming alternative goods (the substitution effect).

Therefore, returning to our example of the increase in the price of coffee, we will not be able to afford to buy as much as before, and we will probably drink more tea, cocoa, fruit juices or even water instead.

The amount by which the quantity demanded falls will depend on the size of the income and substitution effects.

The size of the income effect depends primarily on the proportion of income spent on the good. Thus the more coffee we buy in the first place, the more likely we will be forced to cut down on the amount we buy if the price goes up. In other words, the bigger the proportion of income spent on the good, the bigger will be the effect of a price rise on people's real income, and the more they will reduce the quantity they demand.

The size of the substitution effect depends primarily on the number and closeness of substitute goods. Thus if you are quite happy to drink tea instead of coffee, a rise in the price of coffee will cause you to cut your consumption of coffee considerably, and correspondingly to increase your consumption of tea.

A word of warning: be careful about the meaning of the words quantity demanded. They refer to the amount consumers are willing and able to purchase at a given price over a given time period (for example, a week, or a month, or a year). They do *not* refer to what people would simply *like* to consume. You might like to own a luxury yacht, but your demand for luxury yachts will almost certainly be zero at the current price.

The demand curve

Consider the hypothetical data in Table 1.1. The table shows how many kilos of potatoes per month would be purchased at various prices.

Columns (2) and (3) show the demand schedules for two individuals, Tracey and Darren. Column (4), by contrast, shows the total market demand schedule. This is the total demand by all consumers. To obtain the market demand schedule for potatoes, we simply add up the quantities demanded at each price by *all* consumers: i.e. Tracey, Darren and anyone else that demands potatoes. Notice that we are talking about demand *over a period of time* (not at a *point* in time). Thus we would talk about daily demand, or weekly demand, or annual demand or whatever.

The demand schedule can be represented graphically as a demand curve. Figure 1.3 shows the market demand curve for potatoes corresponding to the schedule in Table 1.1. The price of potatoes is plotted on the vertical axis. The quantity demanded is plotted on the horizontal axis.

Point *E* shows that at a price of 20p per kilo, 100 000 tonnes of potatoes are demanded each month. When the price falls to 16p we move down the

Definitions

Income effect The effect of a change in price on quantity demanded arising from the consumer becoming better or worse off as a result of the price change.

Substitution effect The effect of a change in price on quantity demanded arising from the consumer switching to or from alternative (substitute) products.

Quantity demanded The amount of a good that a consumer is willing and able to buy at a given price over a given period of time.

Demand schedule for an individual A table showing the different quantities of a good that a person is willing and able to buy at various prices over a given period of time.

Market demand schedule A table showing the different total quantities of a good that consumers are willing and able to buy at various prices over a given period of time.

TABLE I.I *The demand for potatoes (monthly)*

	Price (pence per kg) (1)	Tracey's demand (kg) (2)	Darren's demand (kg) (3)	Total market demand (tonnes: 000s) (4)
A	4	28	16	700
B	8	15	11	500
C	12	5	9	350
D	16	1	7	200
E	20	0	6	100

FIGURE 1.3
Market demand curve for potatoes (monthly)

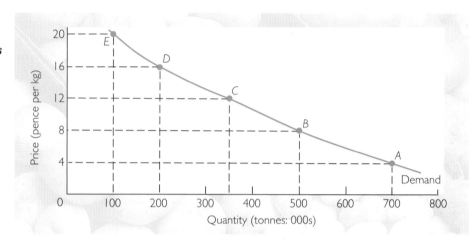

curve to point *D*. This shows that the quantity demanded has now risen to 200 000 tonnes per month. Similarly, if price falls to 12p we move down the curve again to point *C*: 350 000 tonnes are now demanded. The five points on the graph (*A–E*) correspond to the figures in columns (1) and (4) of Table 1.1. The graph also enables us to read off the likely quantities demanded at prices other than those in the table.

A demand curve could also be drawn for an individual consumer. Like market demand curves, individuals' demand curves generally slope downward from left to right: the lower the price of a product, the more is a person likely to buy.

Two points should be noted at this stage:

- In textbooks, demand curves (and other curves too) are only occasionally used to plot specific data. More frequently they are used to illustrate general theoretical arguments. In such cases, the axes will simply be price and quantity, with the units unspecified.
- The term demand 'curve' is used even when the graph is a straight line! In fact, when using demand curves to illustrate arguments we frequently draw them as straight lines – it's easier.

Other determinants of demand

Price is not the only factor that determines how much of a good people will buy. Demand is also affected by the following:

Definition

Demand curve
A graph showing the relationship between the price of a good and the quantity of the good demanded over a given time period. Price is measured on the vertical axis; quantity demanded is measured on the horizontal axis. A demand curve can be for an individual consumer or group of consumers, or more usually for the whole market.

Tastes. The more desirable people find the good, the more they will demand. Tastes are affected by advertising, by fashion, by observing other consumers, by considerations of health and by the experiences from consuming the good on previous occasions.

The number and price of substitute goods (i.e. competitive goods). The higher the price of substitute goods, the higher will be the demand for this good as people switch from the substitutes. For example, the demand for coffee will depend on the price of tea. If tea goes up in price, the demand for coffee will rise.

The number and price of complementary goods. Complementary goods are those that are consumed together: cars and petrol, shoes and polish, fish and chips. The higher the price of complementary goods, the fewer of them will be bought and hence the less the demand for this good. For example, the demand for electricity will depend on the price of electrical goods. If the price of electrical goods goes up, so that fewer are bought, the demand for electricity will fall.

Income. As people's incomes rise, their demand for most goods will rise. Such goods are called normal goods. There are exceptions to this general rule, however. As people get richer, they spend less on inferior goods such as cheap margarine, and switch to better quality goods.

Distribution of income. If national income were redistributed from the poor to the rich, the demand for *luxury* goods would rise. At the same time, as the poor got poorer they might have to turn to buying inferior goods, whose demand would thus rise too.

Expectations of future price changes. If people think that prices are going to rise in the future, they are likely to buy more now before the price does go up.

To illustrate these six determinants, let us look at the demand for butter:

- Tastes: if it is heavily advertised, demand is likely to rise. If on the other hand there is a cholesterol scare, people may demand less for health reasons.
- Substitutes: if the price of margarine goes up, the demand for butter is likely to rise as people switch from one to the other.
- Complements: if the price of bread goes up, people will buy less bread and hence less butter to spread it on.
- Income: if people's income rises, they may well turn to consuming butter rather than margarine or feel that they can afford to spread butter more thickly on their bread.
- Income distribution: if income is redistributed away from the poor, they may have to give up consuming butter and buy cheaper margarine instead, or simply buy less butter and be more economical with the amount they use.
- Expectations: if it is announced in the news that butter prices are expected to rise in the near future, people are likely to buy more now and stock up their freezers while current prices last.

Definitions

Substitute goods
A pair of goods which are considered by consumers to be alternatives to each other. As the price of one goes up, the demand for the other rises.

Complementary goods
A pair of goods consumed together. As the price of one goes up, the demand for both goods will fall.

Normal good
A good whose demand rises as people's incomes rise.

Inferior good
A good whose demand falls as people's incomes rise.

FIGURE I.4
An increase in demand

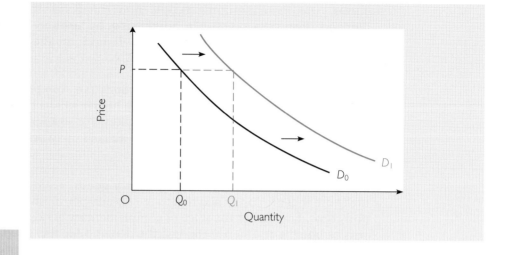

Ceteris paribus
Latin for 'other things being equal'. This assumption has to be made when making deductions from theories.

Change in demand
The term used for a shift in the demand curve. It occurs when a determinant of demand *other* than price changes.

Change in the quantity demanded
The term used for a movement along the demand curve to a new point. It occurs when there is a change in price.

Movements along and shifts in the demand curve

A demand curve is constructed on the assumption that 'other things remain equal' (sometimes known by the Latin term *ceteris paribus*. In other words, it is assumed that none of the determinants of demand, other than price, changes. The effect of a change in price is then simply illustrated by a movement along the demand curve: for example, from point *B* to point *D* in Figure 1.3 when the price of potatoes rises from 8p to 16p per kilo.

What happens, then, when one of these other determinants does change? The answer is that we have to construct a whole new demand curve: the curve shifts. If a change in one of the other determinants causes demand to rise – say, income rises – the whole curve will shift to the right. This shows that at each price, more will be demanded than before. Thus in Figure 1.4 at a price of *P*, a quantity of Q_0 was originally demanded. But now, after the increase in demand, Q_1 is demanded. (Note that D_1 is not necessarily parallel to D_0.)

If a change in a determinant other than price causes demand to fall, the whole curve will shift to the left.

To distinguish between shifts in and movements along demand curves, it is usual to distinguish between a change in *demand* and a change in the *quantity demanded*. A shift in demand is referred to as a change in demand, whereas a movement along the demand curve as a result of a change in price is referred to as a change in the quantity demanded.

Summary

1. **When the price of a good rises, the quantity demanded per period of time will fall. This is known as the 'law of demand'. It applies both to individuals' demand and to the whole market demand.**
2. **The law of demand is explained by the income and substitution effects of a price change.**

3. The relationship between price and quantity demanded per period of time can be shown in a table (or 'schedule') or as a graph. On the graph, price is plotted on the vertical axis and quantity demanded per period of time on the horizontal axis. The resulting demand curve is downward sloping (negatively sloped).
4. Other determinants of demand include tastes, the number and price of substitute goods, the number and price of complementary goods, income, the distribution of income and expectations of future price changes.
5. If price changes, the effect is shown by a movement along the demand curve. We call this effect 'a change in the quantity demanded'.
6. If any other determinant of demand changes, the whole curve will shift. We call this effect 'a change in demand'. A rightward shift represents an increase in demand; a leftward shift represents a decrease in demand.

Supply

How much of any item will firms want to produce?

Supply and price

Imagine you are a farmer deciding what to do with your land. Part of your land is in a fertile valley. Part is on a hillside where the soil is poor. Perhaps, then, you will consider growing vegetables in the valley and keeping sheep on the hillside.

Your decision will depend to a large extent on the price that various vegetables will fetch in the market and likewise the price you can expect to get from sheep and wool. As far as the valley is concerned, you will plant the vegetables that give the best return. If, for example, the price of potatoes is high, you will probably use a lot of the valley for growing potatoes. If the price gets higher, you may well use the whole of the valley, perhaps being prepared to run the risk of potato disease. If the price is very high indeed, you may even consider growing potatoes on the hillside, even though the yield per hectare is much lower there.

In other words, the higher the price of a particular crop, the more you are likely to grow in preference to other crops. This illustrates the general relationship between supply and price: *when the price of a good rises the quantity supplied will also rise*. There are three reasons for this:

- As firms supply more, they are likely to find that beyond a certain level of output costs rise more and more rapidly.

  In the case of the farm we have just considered, once potatoes have to be grown on the hillside, the costs of producing them will increase. Also if the land has to be used more intensively, say by the use of more and more fertilisers, again the costs of producing extra potatoes are likely to rise quite rapidly. It is the same for manufacturers. Beyond a certain level of output, costs are likely to rise rapidly as workers have to be paid overtime and as machines approach capacity working. If higher output

Table 1.2 *The supply of potatoes (monthly)*

	Price of potatoes (pence per kg)	Farmer X's supply (tonnes)	Total market supply (tonnes: 000s)
a	4	50	100
b	8	70	200
c	12	100	350
d	16	120	530
e	20	130	700

involves higher costs of production, producers will need to get a higher price if they are to be persuaded to produce extra output.

- The higher the price of the good, the more profitable it becomes to produce. Firms will thus be encouraged to produce more of it by switching from producing less profitable goods.
- Given time, if the price of a good remains high, new producers will be encouraged to set up in production. Total market supply thus rises.

The first two determinants affect supply in the short run. The third affects supply in the long run. We distinguish between short-run and long-run supply in Chapter 2 (page 59).

The supply curve

The amount that producers would like to supply at various prices can be shown in a **supply schedule**. Table 1.2 shows a monthly supply schedule for potatoes, both for an individual farmer (farmer X) and for all farmers together (the whole market).

The supply schedule can be represented graphically as a **supply curve**. A supply curve may be an individual firm's supply curve or a market curve (i.e. that of the whole industry).

Figure 1.5 shows the *market* supply curve of potatoes. As with demand curves, price is plotted on the vertical axis and quantity on the horizontal axis. Each of the points *a–e* corresponds to a figure in Table 1.2. Thus, for example, a price rise from 12p per kilo to 16p per kilogram will cause a movement along the supply curve from point *c* to point *d*: total market supply will rise from 350 000 tonnes per month to 530 000 tonnes per month.

Not all supply curves will be upward sloping (positively sloped). Sometimes they will be vertical, or horizontal, or even downward sloping. This will depend largely on the time period over which firms' response to price changes is considered. This question is examined in Chapter 2 in the section on the elasticity of supply (section 2.3) and in more detail in Chapters 3 and 4.

Other determinants of supply

Like demand, supply is not simply determined by price. The other determinants of supply are as follows:

Definitions

Supply schedule
A table showing the different quantities of a good that producers are willing and able to supply at various prices over a given time period. A supply schedule can be for an individual producer or group of producers, or for all producers (the market supply schedule).

Supply curve
A graph showing the relationship between the price of a good and the quantity of the good supplied over a given period of time.

FIGURE 1.5
Market supply curve of potatoes (monthly)

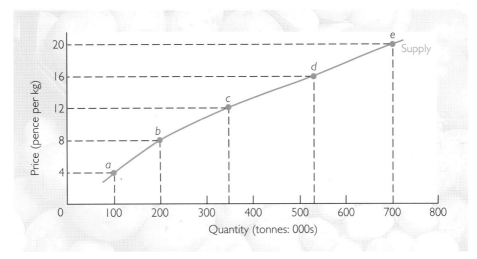

The costs of production. The higher the costs of production, the less profit will be made at any price. As costs rise, firms will cut back on production, probably switching to alternative products whose costs have not risen so much.

The main reasons for a change in costs are:

- Change in input prices: costs of production will rise if wages, raw material prices, rents, interest rates or any other input prices rise.
- Change in technology: technological advances can fundamentally alter the costs of production. Consider, for example, how the microchip revolution has changed production methods and information handling in virtually every industry in the world.
- Organisational changes: various cost savings can be made in many firms by reorganising production.
- Government policy: costs will be lowered by government subsidies and raised by various taxes.

The profitability of alternative products (substitutes in supply). If some alternative product (a substitute in supply) becomes more profitable to supply than before, producers are likely to switch from the first good to this alternative. Supply of the first good falls. Other goods are likely to become more profitable if:

- their prices rise;
- their costs of production fall.

For example, if the price of carrots goes up, or the cost of producing carrots comes down, farmers may decide to produce more carrots. The supply of potatoes is therefore likely to fall.

The profitability of goods in joint supply. Sometimes when one good is produced, another good is also produced at the same time. These are said to be goods in joint supply. An example is the refining of crude oil to produce petrol. Other grade fuels will be produced as well, such as diesel and paraffin. If more petrol is produced, due to a rise in demand, then the supply of these other fuels will rise too.

Substitutes in supply
These are two goods where an increased production of one means diverting resources away from producing the other.

Goods in joint supply
These are two goods where the production of more of one leads to the production of more of the other.

Nature, 'random shocks' and other unpredictable events. In this category we would include the weather and diseases affecting farm output, wars affecting the supply of imported raw materials, the breakdown of machinery, industrial disputes, earthquakes, floods and fire, etc.

The aims of producers. A profit-maximising firm will supply a different quantity from a firm that has a different aim, such as maximising sales.

Expectations of future price changes. If price is expected to rise, producers may temporarily reduce the amount they sell. Instead they are likely to build up their stocks and release them on to the market only when the price does rise. At the same time they may plan to produce more, by installing new machines, or taking on more labour, so that they can be ready to supply more when the price has risen.

To illustrate some of these determinants, let us consider the example of butter. What would cause the supply of butter to rise?

- A reduction in the costs of producing butter. This could be caused, say, by a reduction in the price of nitrogen fertiliser. This would encourage farmers to use more fertiliser, which would increase grass yields, which in turn would increase milk yields per hectare. Alternatively, new technology may allow more efficient churning of butter. Or again, the government may decide to give subsidies to farmers to produce more butter.
- A reduction in the profitability of producing cream or cheese. If these products become less profitable, due say to a reduction in their price, due in turn to a reduction in consumer demand, more butter is likely to be produced instead.
- An increase in the profitability of skimmed milk. If consumers buy more skimmed milk, then an increased supply of skimmed milk is likely to lead to an increase in the supply of butter and other cream products, since they are jointly produced with skimmed milk.
- If weather conditions are favourable, grass yields and hence milk yields are likely to be high. This will increase the supply of butter and other milk products.
- If butter producers expect butter prices to rise in the future, they may well decide to release less on to the market now and put more into frozen storage until the price does rise.

Movements along and shifts in the supply curve

The principle here is the same as with demand curves. The effect of a change in price is illustrated by a movement along the supply curve: for example, from point *d* to point *e* in Figure 1.5 when price rises from 16p to 20p. Quantity supplied rises from 530 000 to 700 000 tonnes per month.

If any other determinant of supply changes, the whole supply curve will shift. A rightward shift illustrates an increase in supply. A leftward shift illustrates a decrease in supply. Thus in Figure 1.6, if the original curve is S_0, the curve S_1 represents an increase in supply (more is supplied at each price),

Definitions

Change in the quantity supplied
The term used for a movement along the supply curve to a new point. It occurs when there is a change in price.

Change in supply
The term used for a shift in the supply curve. It occurs when a determinant *other* than price changes.

FIGURE 1.6
Shifts in the supply curve

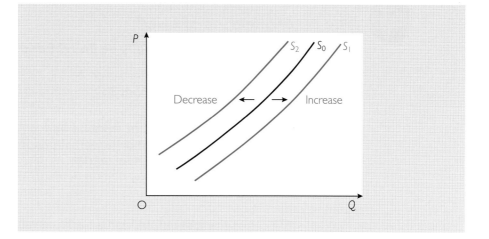

whereas the curve S_2 represents a decrease in supply (less is supplied at each price).

A movement along a supply curve is often referred to as a change in the quantity supplied, whereas a shift in the supply curve is simply referred to as a change in supply.

Summary

1. When the price of a good rises, the quantity supplied per period of time will usually also rise. This applies both to individual producers' supply and to the whole market supply.
2. There are two reasons in the short run why a higher price encourages producers to supply more: (a) they are now willing to incur higher costs per unit associated with producing more; (b) they will switch to producing this product away from now less profitable ones. In the long run there is a third reason: new producers will be attracted into the market.
3. The relationship between price and quantity supplied per period of time can be shown in a table (or schedule) or as a graph. As with a demand curve, price is plotted on the vertical axis and quantity per period of time on the horizontal axis. The resulting supply curve is upward sloping (positively sloped).
4. Other determinants of supply include the costs of production, the profitability of alternative products, the profitability of goods in joint supply, random shocks and expectations of future price changes.
5. If price changes, the effect is shown by a movement along the supply curve. We call this effect 'a change in the quantity supplied'.
6. If any determinant *other* than price changes, the effect is shown by a shift in the whole supply curve. We call this effect 'a change in supply'.
   A rightward shift represents an increase in supply; a leftward shift represents a decrease in supply.

I.5 The determination of price

How much of any item will actually be bought and sold and at what price?

Equilibrium price and output

We can now combine our analysis of demand and supply. This will show how the actual price of a product and the actual quantity bought and sold are determined in a free and competitive market.

Let us return to the example of the market demand and market supply of potatoes, and use the data from Tables 1.1 and 1.2. These figures are given again in Table 1.3.

What will be the price and output that actually prevail? If the price started at 4p per kilogram, demand would exceed supply by 600 000 tonnes ($A-a$). Consumers would be unable to obtain all they wanted and would thus be willing to pay a higher price. Producers, unable or unwilling to supply enough to meet the demand, will be only too happy to accept a higher price. The effect of the shortage, then, will be to drive up the price. The same would happen at a price of 8p per kilogram. There would still be a shortage; price would still rise. But as the price rises, the quantity demanded falls and the quantity supplied rises. The shortage is progressively eliminated.

What would happen if the price started at a much higher level: say at 20p per kilogram? In this case supply would exceed demand by 600 000 tonnes ($e-E$). The effect of this surplus would be to drive the price down as farmers competed against each other to sell their excess supplies. The same would happen at a price of 16p per kilogram. There would still be a surplus; price would still fall.

In fact, only one price is sustainable. This is the price where demand equals supply: namely 12p per kilogram, where both demand and supply are 350 000 tonnes. When supply matches demand the market is said to clear. There is no shortage and no surplus.

This price, where demand equals supply, is called the equilibrium price. By equilibrium we mean a point of balance or a point of rest: in other words, a point towards which there is a tendency to move. In Table 1.3, if the price starts at other than 12p per kilogram, there will be a tendency for it to move towards 12p. The equilibrium price is the only price at which producers' and consumers' wishes are mutually reconciled: where the producers' plans to supply exactly match the consumers' plans to buy.

Definitions

Market clearing
A market clears when supply matches demand, leaving no shortage or surplus.

Equilibrium price
The price where the quantity demanded equals the quantity supplied: the price where there is no shortage or surplus.

Equilibrium
A position of balance. A position from which there is no inherent tendency to move away.

TABLE I.3 *The market demand and supply of potatoes (monthly)*

Price of potatoes (pence per kg)	Total market demand (tonnes: 000s)	Total market supply (tonnes: 000s)
4	700 (A)	100 (a)
8	500 (B)	200 (b)
12	350 (C)	350 (c)
16	200 (D)	530 (d)
20	100 (E)	700 (e)

FIGURE 1.7
The determination of market equilibrium (potatoes: monthly)

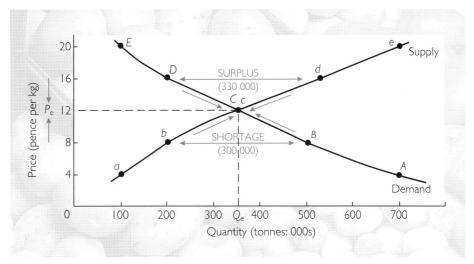

Demand and supply curves

The determination of equilibrium price and output can be shown using demand and supply curves. Equilibrium is where the two curves intersect.

Figure 1.7 shows the demand and supply curves of potatoes corresponding to the data in Table 1.3. Equilibrium price is P_e (12p) and equilibrium quantity is Q_e (350 000 tonnes).

At any price above 12p, there would be a surplus. Thus at 16p there is a surplus of 330 000 tonnes ($d-D$). More is supplied than consumers are willing and able to purchase at that price. Thus a price of 16p fails to clear the market. Price will fall to the equilibrium price of 12p. As it does so, there will be a movement along the demand curve from point D to point C, and a movement along the supply curve from point d to point c.

At any price below 12p, there would be a shortage. Thus at 8p there is a shortage of 300 000 tonnes ($B-b$). Price will rise to 12p. This will cause a movement along the supply curve from point b to point c and along the demand curve from point B to point C.

Point Cc is the equilibrium: where demand equals supply.

Movement to a new equilibrium

The equilibrium price will remain unchanged only so long as the demand and supply curves remain unchanged. If either of the curves shifts, a new equilibrium will be formed.

A change in demand

If one of the determinants of demand changes (other than price), the whole demand curve will shift. This will lead to a movement *along* the *supply* curve to the new intersection point.

For example, in Figure 1.8, if a rise in consumer incomes led to the demand curve shifting to D_2, there would be a shortage of $h-g$ at the original price P_{e_1}. This would cause price to rise to the new equilibrium P_{e_2}. As it did so, there would be a movement along the supply curve from point g to

FIGURE 1.8
Effect of a shift in the demand curve

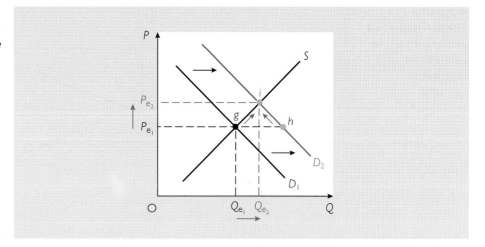

point *i*, and along the new demand curve (D_2) from point *h* to point *i*. Equilibrium quantity would rise from Q_{e_1} to Q_{e_2}.

The effect of the shift in demand, therefore, has been a movement *along* the supply curve from the old equilibrium to the new: from point *g* to point *i*.

A change in supply

Likewise, if one of the determinants of supply changes (other than price), the whole supply curve will shift. This will lead to a movement *along* the *demand* curve to the new intersection point.

For example, in Figure 1.9, if costs of production rose, the supply curve would shift to the left: to S_2. There would be a shortage of *g – j* at the old price of P_{e_1}. Price would rise from P_{e_1} to P_{e_3}. Quantity would fall from Q_{e_1} to Q_{e_3}. In other words, there would be a movement along the demand curve from point *g* to point *k*, and along the new supply curve (S_2) from point *j* to point *k*.

To summarise: a shift in one curve leads to a movement along the other curve to the new intersection point.

Sometimes a number of determinants might change. This may lead to a shift in *both* curves. When this happens, equilibrium simply moves from the point where the old curves intersected to the point where the new ones intersect.

FIGURE 1.9
Effect of a shift in the supply curve

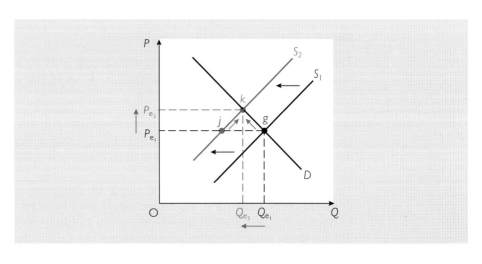

Summary

1. If the demand for a good exceeds the supply, there will be a shortage. This will lead to a rise in the price of the good.
2. If the supply of a good exceeds the demand, there will be a surplus. This will lead to a fall in the price.
3. Price will settle at the equilibrium. The equilibrium price is the one that clears the market: the price where demand equals supply.
4. If the demand or supply curve shifts, this will lead either to a shortage or to a surplus. Price will therefore either rise or fall until a new equilibrium is reached at the position where the supply and demand curves *now* intersect.

The free-market economy

How well does it serve us?

Advantages of a free-market economy

The fact that a free-market economy functions automatically is one of its major advantages. There is no need for costly and complex bureaucracies to co-ordinate economic decisions. The economy can respond quickly to changing demand and supply conditions.

When markets are highly competitive, no one has great power. Competition between firms keeps prices down and acts as an incentive to firms to become more efficient. The more firms there are competing, the more responsive they will be to consumer wishes.

The more efficiently firms can combine their factors of production, the more profit they will make. The more efficiently workers work, the more secure will be their jobs and the higher their wages. The more carefully consumers decide what to buy, the greater the value for money they will receive.

Thus people pursuing their own self-interest through buying and selling in competitive markets helps to minimise the central economic problem of scarcity, by encouraging the efficient use of the nation's resources in line with consumer wishes. From this type of argument, the following conclusion is often drawn by defenders of the free market:

'The pursuit of private gain results in the social good.' This is obviously a highly significant claim and has profound moral implications.

Problems with a free-market economy

In practice, however, markets do not achieve maximum efficiency in the allocation of scarce resources, and governments feel it necessary to intervene to rectify this and other problems of the free market. The problems of a free market are as follows:

- Competition between firms is often limited. A few giant firms may dominate an industry. In these cases they may charge high prices and

BOX 1.4

The UK housing market

The home buyer's big dipper

If you are thinking of buying a house sometime in the future, then you may well follow the fortunes of the housing market with some trepidation. In the late 1980s there was a housing price explosion in the UK: in fact, between 1984 and 1989 house prices *doubled*. In 1984 the average price of a house was £30952; by 1989 it was £61163. If similar increases were to occur again, many people might find that owning a home of their own remains just a dream.

UK house prices (all houses, all buyers)

House prices since the early 1980s

The diagram shows what happened to house prices in the period 1983 to 1996. The line graph shows the rapid house price inflation up to 1989. It reached a peak in 1988, when average house prices rose by 23.3 per cent in that one year alone.

The two sets of bars show the index of house prices and the index of average earnings, based on 1983 = 100. To interpret these, consider the position in 1985. The house price index was 117.0. This means that house prices were 17 per cent higher than in 1983. The index of average earnings was 113.9. This means that average earnings were 13.9 per cent higher than in 1983. By its peak in 1989, the house price index had risen to 224.3, whereas the index of average earnings was only 160.1

In their rush to buy a house before prices rose any further, many people in this period borrowed as much as they were able. Building societies and banks at that time had plenty of money to lend and were only too willing to do so. Many people, therefore, took out very large mortgages. In 1983 the average new mortgage was 2.08 times average annual earnings. By 1989 this figure had risen to 3.44.

After 1989 there followed a period of *falling* prices. From 1990 to 1995, house prices fell by 12.2 per cent. By mid-1995, the index of house prices was only 197.0 and had been overtaken by the index of average earnings, which stood at 221.8.

Many people now found themselves in a position of *negative equity*. This is the situation where the size of their mortgage is greater than the value of their house. In other words, if they sold their house, they would end up still owing money! For this reason many people found that they could not move house.

Then in 1996, house prices began to recover. Was this good news or bad news? For those trapped in negative equity, it was good news. It was also good news for old people who wished to move into a retirement home and who had a house to sell. It was bad news for the first-time buyer, however! As we shall see in many parts of this book, what is good news for one person is often bad news for another.

The determinants of house prices

House prices are determined by demand and supply. If demand rises (i.e. shifts to the right) or if supply falls (i.e. shifts to the left), the equilibrium price of houses will rise. Similarly, if demand falls or supply rises, the equilibrium price will fall.

So why did house prices rise so rapidly in the 1980s, only to fall in the early 1990s? The answer lies primarily in changes in the *demand* for housing. Let us examine the various factors that affected the demand for houses.

Incomes (actual and anticipated). The second half of the 1980s was a period of rapidly rising incomes. The economy was experiencing an economic `boom'. Many people wanted to spend their extra incomes on housing: either buying a house for the first time, or moving to a better one. What is more, many people thought that their incomes would continue to grow, and were thus prepared to stretch themselves financially in the short term by buying an expensive house, confident that their mortgage payments would become more and more affordable over time.

The early 1990s, by contrast, was a period of recession, with rising unemployment and much more slowly growing incomes. People had much less confidence about their ability to afford large mortgages.

The desire for home ownership. Mrs Thatcher put great emphasis on the virtues of home ownership: a home-owning democracy. Certainly, the mood of the age was very much that it was desirable to own one's own home. This fuelled the growth in demand in the 1980s.

The cost of mortgages. During the second half of the 1980s, mortgage interest rates were generally falling. This meant that people could afford larger mortgages, and thus afford to buy more expensive houses. In 1989, however, this trend was reversed. Mortgage interest rates were now rising. Many people found it difficult to maintain existing payments, let alone to take on a larger mortgage.

The availability of mortgages. In the late 1980s, mortgages were readily available. Banks and building societies were prepared to accept smaller deposits on houses, and to grant mortgages of $3^1/_2$ times a person's annual income, compared with $2^1/_2$ times in the early 1980s. In the early 1990s, however, banks and building societies were more cautious about granting mortgages. They were aware that, with falling house prices, rising unemployment and the growing problem of negative equity, there was a growing danger that borrowers would default on payments.

Speculation. In the 1980s, people generally believed that house prices would continue rising. This encouraged people to buy as soon as possible, and to take out the biggest mortgage possible, before prices went up any further. There was also an effect on supply. Those with houses to sell held back until the last possible moment in the hope of getting a higher price. The net effect was a rightward shift in the demand curve for houses and a leftward shift in the supply curve. The effect of this speculation, therefore, was to help bring about the very effect that people were predicting (see section 2.5).

In the early 1990s, the process was reversed. People thinking of buying houses held back, hoping to buy at a lower price. People with houses to sell tried to sell as quickly as possible before prices fell any further. Again the effect of this speculation was to aggravate the fall in prices.

What of the future?

In 1996, house prices began to rise again. Whether the late 1990s and early 2000s will be another period of rapidly rising prices depends very much on the factors listed above. If the economy booms, if interest rates remain low, if mortgages are readily available, and if people believe that prices will continue to rise, there may well be another boom in house prices. It is unlikely, however, that the boom will be as great as in the late 1980s. Political parties are only too well aware of the dangers of allowing too much money to be available for mortgages too cheaply.

 Draw supply and demand diagrams to illustrate what was happening to house prices (a) in the second half of the 1980s; (b) in the early 1990s.

 Are there any factors on the *supply* side that influence house prices?

make large profits. Rather than merely responding to consumer wishes, they may attempt to persuade consumers by advertising. Consumers are particularly susceptible to advertisements for products that are new to them and of which they have little knowledge.

- Lack of competition and high profits may remove the incentive for firms to be efficient.
- Power and property may be unequally distributed. Those who have power and/or property (e.g. big business, unions, landlords) will gain at the expense of those without power and property.
- The practices of some firms may be socially undesirable. For example, a chemical works may pollute the environment.
- Some socially desirable goods would simply not be produced by private enterprise. What firm would build and operate a lighthouse, unless it were paid for by the government?
- A free-market economy may lead to macroeconomic instability. There may be periods of recession with high unemployment and falling output, and other periods of rising prices.
- Finally, there is the ethical objection that a free-market economy, by rewarding self-interested behaviour, may encourage selfishness, greed, materialism and the acquisition of power.

We shall be examining these various problems in more detail in later chapters.

The mixed economy

Because of the problems of both free-market and command economies, all real-world economies are a mixture of the two systems. The economies of the former communist bloc all used the market mechanism to some extent. All market economies involve some degree of government intervention.

Definition

Relative price
The price of one good compared with another (e.g. good x is twice the price of good y).

In mixed market economies, the government may control the following:

- **Relative prices** of goods and inputs, by taxing or subsidising them or by direct price controls.
- Relative incomes, by the use of income taxes, welfare payments or direct controls over wages, profits, rents, etc.
- The pattern of production and consumption, by the use of legislation (e.g. making it illegal to produce unsafe goods), by direct provision of goods and services (e.g. education and defence), by taxes and subsidies or by nationalisation.
- The macroeconomic problems of unemployment, inflation, lack of growth and balance of payments deficits, by the use of taxes and government expenditure, the control of bank lending and interest rates, the direct control of prices and incomes, and the control of the foreign exchange rate.

Just how the government intervenes, and what the effects of the various forms of intervention are, will be examined in detail in later chapters.

The relative merits of alternative mixtures of government and the market depend on the weight attached to various political and economic goals: goals such as liberty, equality, efficiency in production, the fulfilling of consumer wishes, economic growth and full employment. No one type of mixed market economy is likely to be superior in all respects.

Summary

1. A free-market economy functions automatically, and if there is plenty of competition between producers, this can help to protect consumers' interests.
2. In practice, however, competition may be limited; there may be great inequality; there may be adverse social and environmental consequences; there may be macroeconomic instability.
3. All real-world economies are some mixture of the market and government intervention. Governments intervene in market economies in various ways in order to correct the failings of the free market. The degree and form of government intervention depend on the aims of governments and the nature of the problems they are attempting to tackle.

Questions

1. Imagine that you won millions of pounds on the National Lottery. Would your 'economic problem' be solved?

2. Assume that in a household one parent currently works full time and the other stays at home to look after the family. How would you set about identifying and calculating the opportunity costs of the second parent now taking a full-time job? How would such calculations be relevant in deciding whether it is worth taking that job?

3. In what way does specialisation reduce the problem of scarcity?

4. Would redistributing incomes from the rich to the poor reduce the overall problem of scarcity?

5. Assume that oil begins to run out and that extraction becomes more expensive. Trace through the effects of this on the market for oil and the market for other fuels.

6. This question is concerned with the supply of oil for central heating. In each case consider whether there is a movement along the supply curve (and in which direction) or a shift in it (and whether left or right).
   (a) New oil fields start up in production.
   (b) The demand for central heating rises.
   (c) The price of gas falls.
   (d) Oil companies anticipate an upsurge in demand for central heating oil.
   (e) The demand for petrol rises.
   (f) New technology decreases the costs of oil refining.
   (g) All oil products become more expensive.

7. The weekly demand and supply schedules for t-shirts (in millions) in a free market are as follows:

Price (£)	8	7	6	5	4	3	2	1
Quantity demanded	6	8	10	12	14	16	18	20
Quantity supplied	18	16	14	12	10	8	6	4

   (a) What is the equilibrium price and quantity?
   (b) Assume that changes in fashion cause the demand for t-shirts to rise by 4 million at each price. What will be the new equilibrium price and quantity? Has equilibrium quantity risen as much as the rise in demand? Explain why or why not.
   (c) Now plot the data in the table on a graph and mark the equilibrium. Also plot the new data corresponding to (b) and mark the new equilibrium.

8. On separate demand and supply diagrams for bread, sketch the effects of the following: (a) a rise in the price of wheat; (b) a rise in the price of butter and margarine; (c) a rise in the price of rice, pasta and potatoes. In each case, state your assumptions.

9. For what reasons might the price of foreign holidays rise? In each case identify whether these are reasons affecting demand, or supply (or both).

10. If both demand and supply change, and if we know which direction they have shifted but not how much, why is it that we will be able to predict the direction in which *either* price *or* quantity will change, but not both? (Clue: consider the four possible combinations and sketch them if necessary: (a) *D* left, *S* left; (b) *D* right, *S* right; (c) *D* left, *S* right; (d) *D* right, *S* left.)

11. What will happen to the equilibrium price and quantity of butter in each of the following cases? You should state whether demand or supply (or both) have shifted and in which direction. (In each case assume *ceteris paribus*.)
    (a) A rise in the price of margarine.
    (b) A rise in the demand for yoghurt.
    (c) A rise in the price of bread.
    (d) A rise in the demand for bread.
    (e) An expected rise in the price of butter in the near future.
    (f) A tax on butter production.
    (g) The invention of a new, but expensive, process for removing all cholesterol from butter, plus the passing of a law which states that all butter producers must use this process.

chapter two

Markets in action

In this chapter we explore the working of markets in more detail. We start by examining one of the most important concepts in the whole of economics – that of *elasticity* (sections 2.1–2.4).

A bumper harvest may seem like good news for farmers: after all, they will be able to sell more. But is it good news? Although they will sell more, the effect of the increased supply will be to drive down the price – and that's bad news for farmers! So will the increased sales (the good news) be enough to compensate for the reduction in price (the bad news)? Will farmers end up earning more or less from their bumper harvest? It all depends on just how much the price falls, and this depends on the *price elasticity of demand* for their produce. This is a measure of how *responsive* demand is to a change in price.

It is not just the responsiveness of *demand* that is important in determining the functioning of markets. It is also the responsiveness of *supply*. Why, do you think, do some firms respond to a rise in price by producing a lot more, whereas others only produce a little more? Is it simply because of different technologies? We will discover just what influences the price elasticity of supply in section 2.3.

The chapter closes by looking at what happens if governments set about *controlling* prices. Why will shortages occur if the government sets the price too low, or surpluses if it sets it too high? When might governments feel that it is a good idea to fix prices?

Price elasticity of demand

How responsive is demand to a change in price?

When the price of a good rises, the quantity demanded will fall. That much is fairly obvious. But in most cases we will want to know more than this. We will want to know just *how much* the quantity demanded will fall. In other words, we will want to know how *responsive* demand is to a rise in price.

Take the case of two products: oil and cauliflowers. In the case of oil, a rise in price is likely to result in only a slight fall in the quantity demanded. If people want to continue driving, they have to pay the higher prices for fuel. A few may turn to riding bicycles, and some people may try to make fewer journeys, but for most people, a rise in the price of petrol and diesel will make little difference to how much they use their cars.

In the case of cauliflowers, however, a rise in price may lead to a substantial fall in the quantity demanded. The reason is that there are alternative vegetables that people can buy. Many people, when buying vegetables, are very conscious of their prices and will buy whatever is reasonably priced.

We call the responsiveness of demand to a change in price the price elasticity of demand. If we know the price elasticity of demand for a product, we can predict the effect on price and quantity of a shift in the *supply* curve for that product. For example, we can predict the effect of the bumper harvest that we considered at the beginning of the chapter.

Figure 2.1 shows the effect of a shift in supply with two quite different demand curves (D and D'). Curve D' is more elastic than curve D. In other words, for any given change in price, there will be a larger change in quantity demanded along curve D' than along curve D.

Assume that initially the supply curve is S_1, and that it intersects with both demand curves at point *a*, at a price of P_1 and a quantity of Q_1. Now supply shifts to S_2. What will happen to price and quantity? In the case of the less elastic demand curve D, there is a relatively large rise in price (to P_2) and a relatively small fall in quantity (to Q_2): equilibrium is at point *b*. In the case of the more elastic demand curve D', however, there is only a relatively

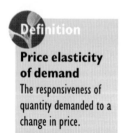

Definition

Price elasticity of demand
The responsiveness of quantity demanded to a change in price.

FIGURE 2.1
Market supply and demand

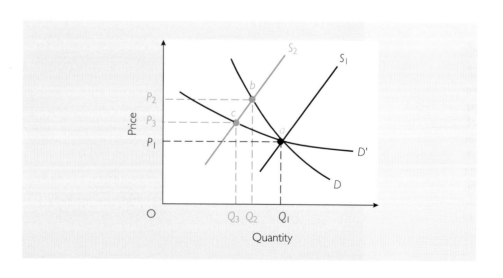

small rise in price (to P_3) but a relatively large fall in quantity (to Q_3): equilibrium is at point c.

Measuring the price elasticity of demand

We saw from Figure 2.1 that if we plot two demand curves on the same diagram, the flatter curve will be more elastic than the steeper one. But looking at a curve's slope gives us only a very rough indication of elasticity. It is important to have a much more precise measure.

What we want to compare is the size of the change in quantity demanded with the size of the change in price. But given that price and quantity are measured in different units, the only sensible way we can do this is to use percentage or proportionate changes. This gives us the following formula for the price elasticity of demand ($P\varepsilon_D$) for a product: percentage (or proportionate) change in quantity demanded divided by the percentage (or proportionate) change in price. Putting this in symbols gives:

$$P\varepsilon_D = \frac{\%\Delta Q_D}{\%\Delta P}$$

where ε is the Greek epsilon and is the symbol we use for elasticity, and Δ is the capital Greek delta and is the symbol we use for a 'change in'.

Thus if a 40 per cent rise in the price of oil caused the quantity demanded to fall by a mere 10 per cent, the price elasticity of oil over this range would be:

$$-10\%/40\% = -0.25$$

On the other hand, if a 5 per cent fall in the price of cauliflowers caused a 15 per cent rise in the quantity demanded, the price elasticity of demand for cauliflowers over this range would be:

$$15\%/-5\% = -3$$

Cauliflowers have a more elastic demand than oil, and this is shown by the figures. But just what do these two figures show? What is the significance of minus 0.25 and minus 3?

Interpreting the figure for elasticity

The use of proportionate or percentage measures:
Elasticity is measured in proportionate or percentage terms for the following reasons:

- It allows comparison of changes in two qualitatively different things, and thus which are measured in two different types of unit: i.e. it allows comparison of *quantity* changes with *monetary* changes.
- It avoids the problem of what size units to use. For example, an increase from £2 to £4 is 2 price units. An increase from 200 pence to 400 pence is 200 price units. By measuring this change in proportionate or percentage terms the same result is obtained whichever price unit is used, thus avoiding the problems of a merely apparent difference in price change.

Definition

Formula for price elasticity of demand ($P\varepsilon_D$)
The percentage (or proportionate) change in quantity demanded divided by the percentage (or proportionate) change in price: $\%\Delta Q_D \div \%\Delta P$.

- It is the only sensible way of deciding *how big* a change in price or quantity is. Take a simple example. An item goes up in price by £1. Is this a big increase or a small increase? We can answer this only if we know what the original price was. If a can of beans goes up in price by £1, that is a huge price increase. If, however, the price of a house goes up by £1, that is a tiny price increase. In other words, it is the percentage or proportionate increase in price that we look at in deciding how big a price rise it is.

The sign (positive or negative)

Demand curves are generally downward sloping. This means that price and quantity change in opposite directions. A *rise* in price (a positive figure) will cause a *fall* in the quantity demanded (a negative figure). Similarly a *fall* in price will cause a *rise* in the quantity demanded. Thus when working out price elasticity of demand we either divide a negative figure by a positive figure, or a positive figure by a negative. Either way, we end up with a negative figure.

The value (greater or less than 1)

If we now ignore the negative sign and just concentrate on the value of the figure, this tells us whether demand is elastic or inelastic.

Elastic (ε > 1). This is where a change in price causes a proportionately larger change in the quantity demanded. In this case the value of elasticity will be greater than 1, since we are dividing a larger figure by a smaller figure.

Inelastic (ε < 1). This is where a change in a price causes a proportionately smaller change in the quantity demanded. In this case elasticity will be less than 1, since we are dividing a smaller figure by a larger figure.

Unit elastic (ε = 1). Unit elasticity is where price and quantity demanded change by the same proportion. This will give an elasticity equal to 1, since we are dividing a figure by itself.

Determinants of price elasticity of demand

The price elasticity of demand varies enormously from one product to another. Table 2.1 gives some examples. But why do some products have a highly elastic demand, whereas others have a highly *in*elastic demand? What determines price elasticity of demand?

The number and closeness of substitute goods. This is the most important determinant. The more substitutes there are for a good, and the closer they are, the more will people switch to these alternatives when the price of the good rises: the greater, therefore, will be the price elasticity of demand.

Returning to our examples of oil and cauliflowers, there is no close substitute for oil and thus demand is relatively inelastic. There are plenty of alternatives to cauliflowers, however, and thus demand is relatively elastic. Of course, the closeness is very often in the mind of the consumer. Some people may have a particular fondness of cauliflowers. For them demand will be less

Definitions

Elastic demand
Where quantity demanded changes by a larger percentage than price. Ignoring the negative sign, it will have a value greater than 1.

Inelastic demand
Where quantity demanded changes by a smaller percentage than price. Ignoring the negative sign, it will have a value less than 1.

Unit elastic demand
Where quantity demanded changes by the same percentage as price. Ignoring the negative sign, it will have a value equal to 1.

TABLE 2.1 *Estimates of price and income elasticity of demand for the USA*

Product	Price elasticity of demand	Income elasticity of demand
Food	−0.21	+0.28
Medical services	−0.22	+0.22
Housing		
Rental	−0.18	+1.00
Owner occupied	−1.20	+1.20
Electricity	−1.14	+0.61
Cars	−1.20	+3.00
Beer	−0.26	+0.38
Wine	−0.88	+0.97
Cigarettes	−0.35	+0.50
Transatlantic air travel	−1.30	+1.40
Imports	−0.58	+2.73

Source: W. Nicholson, *Microeconomic Theory: Basic principles and extensions*, 6th edition (Dryden Press, 1995), p. 219.

elastic than for people who are not fussy whether they eat cauliflowers, cabbages, broccoli, or any other vegetable.

Similar arguments apply to particular brands of a product. The price elasticity of demand for a particular brand of a product will probably be fairly high. If its price goes up, people can simply switch to another brand: there is a large substitution effect. By contrast, the demand for a product in *general* will normally be pretty inelastic. If the price of food in general goes up, demand for food will fall only slightly. People will buy a little less, since they cannot now afford so much: this is the *income* effect of the price rise. But there is no alternative to food that can satisfy our hunger: there is therefore virtually no *substitution* effect.

The proportion of income spent on the good. The higher the proportion of our income that is spent on a good, the more we will be forced to cut consumption when its price rises: the bigger will be the income effect and the more elastic will be the demand.

Thus salt has a very low elasticity of demand. This is because we spend such a tiny fraction of our income on salt, that we would find little difficulty in paying a relatively large percentage increase in its price: the income effect of a price rise would be very small. By contrast, there will be a much bigger income effect when a major item of expenditure rises in price. For example, if mortgage interest rates rise (the 'price' of loans for house purchase), people may have to cut down substantially on their demand for housing, being forced to buy somewhere smaller and cheaper, or to live in rented accommodation.

The time period. When price rises, people may take a time to adjust their consumption patterns and find alternatives. The longer the time period after a price change, then, the more elastic the demand is likely to be.

To illustrate the effect of time on the price elasticity of demand, let us return to our example of oil. Between December 1973 and June 1974 the price of crude oil quadrupled, which led to similar increases in the prices of petrol and central heating oil. Over the next few months, there was only a very small reduction in the consumption of oil products. Demand was highly inelastic. Motorists had no alternative fuel to which they could turn. All they could do was to cut the number of journeys (not easy to do for many people) and try to drive their cars more economically. Likewise, those with oil-fired central heating could not suddenly burn gas or coal in their boilers. All they could do was to turn their heating down.

Over time, however, as the higher oil prices persisted, new fuel-efficient cars were developed and many people switched to smaller cars. Similarly, people switched to gas or solid fuel central heating, and spent more money insulating their houses to save on fuel bills. Demand was thus much more elastic in the long run.

Summary

1. Price elasticity of demand is a measure of the responsiveness of demand to a change in price.
2. It is defined as the proportionate (or percentage) change in quantity demanded divided by the proportionate (or percentage) change in price. Given that demand curves are downward sloping, price elasticity of demand will have a negative value.
3. If quantity changes proportionately more than price, the figure for elasticity will be greater than 1 (ignoring the sign): demand is elastic. If the quantity changes proportionately less price, the figure for elasticity will be less than 1 (again, ignoring the sign): demand is inelastic. If quantity and price change by the same proportion, the elasticity has a value of (minus) 1: demand is unit elastic.
4. Demand will be more elastic the greater the number and closeness of substitute goods, the higher the proportion of income spent on the good and the longer the time period that elapses after the change in price.

Price elasticity of demand and total consumer expenditure

How much do we spend on a good at a given price?

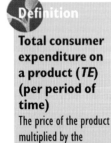

Definition

Total consumer expenditure on a product (*TE*) (per period of time)
The price of the product multiplied by the quantity purchased: *TE* = *P* × *Q*.

One of the most important applications of price elasticity of demand concerns its relationship with the total amount of money that consumers spend on a product. Total consumer expenditure (*TE*) is simply price times quantity purchased.

$$TE = P \times Q$$

For example, if consumers buy 3 million units (*Q*) at a price of £2 per unit (*P*), they will spend a total of £6 million (*TE*). This is shown graphically in Figure 2.2 as the area of the shaded rectangle. But why? The area of a rectangle is simply its height multiplied by its length. But *TE* is simply price (the height of the shaded rectangle) multiplied by quantity (the length of the rectangle).

FIGURE 2.2
Total expenditure

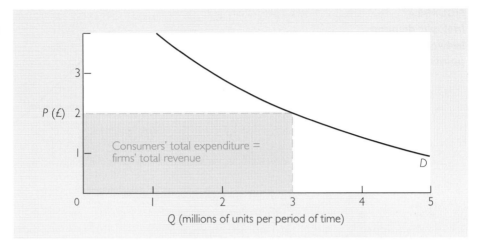

Total consumer expenditure will be the same as the total revenue (*TR*) received by firms from the sale of the product (before any taxes or other deductions).

What will happen to consumer expenditure (and hence firms' revenue) if there is a change in price? The answer depends on the price elasticity of demand.

Elastic demand

As price rises so quantity demanded falls, and vice versa. When demand is elastic, quantity demanded changes proportionately more than price. Thus the change in quantity has a bigger effect on total consumer expenditure than does the change in price. For example, when the price rises, there will such a large fall in consumer demand that *less* will be spent than before. This can be summarised as follows:

- *P* rises; *Q* falls proportionately more; therefore *TE* falls.
- *P* falls: *Q* rises proportionately more; therefore *TE* rises.

In other words, total expenditure changes in the same direction as *quantity*.

This is illustrated in Figure 2.3. Demand is elastic between points *a* and *b*. A rise in price from £4 to £5 causes a proportionately larger fall in quantity

Definition

**Total revenue
(*TR*) (per period
of time)**
The total amount received by firms from the sale of a product, before the deduction of taxes or any other costs. The price multiplied by the quantity sold.
$TR = P \times Q$.

FIGURE 2.3
*Elastic demand
between two
points*

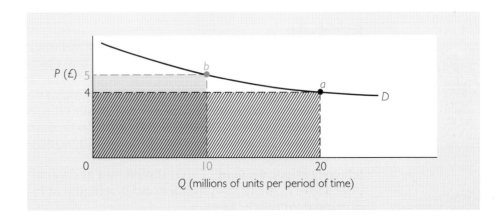

FIGURE 2.4
*Inelastic demand
between two
points*

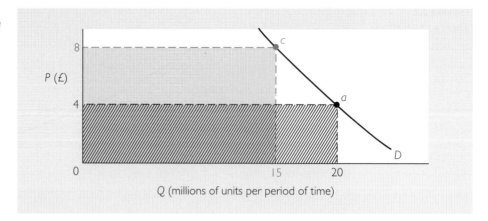

demanded: from 20 million to 10 million. Total expenditure *falls* from £80 million (the striped area) to £50 million (the blue shaded area).

When demand is elastic, then, a rise in price will cause a fall in total consumer expenditure and thus a fall in the total revenue that firms selling the product receive. A reduction in price, however, will result in consumers spending more, and hence firms earning more.

Inelastic demand

When demand is inelastic, it is the other way around. Price changes proportionately more than quantity. Thus the change in price has a bigger effect on total consumer expenditure than does the change in quantity. To summarise the effects:

- *P* rises; *Q* falls proportionately less; therefore *TE* rises.
- *P* falls; *Q* rises proportionately less; therefore *TE* falls.

In other words, total consumer expenditure changes in the same direction as *price*.

This is illustrated in Figure 2.4. Demand is inelastic between points *a* and *c*. A rise in price from £4 to £8 causes a proportionately smaller fall in quantity demanded: from 20 million to 15 million. Total expenditure *rises* from £80 million (the striped area) to £120 million (the blue shaded area).

In this case, firms' revenue will increase if there is a rise in price, and fall if there is a fall in price.

Special cases

Figure 2.5 shows three special cases: (a) a totally inelastic demand ($P\varepsilon_D = 0$), (b) an infinitely elastic demand ($P\varepsilon_D = -\infty$) and (c) a unit elastic demand ($P\varepsilon_D = -1$).

Totally inelastic demand. This is shown by a vertical straight line. No matter what happens to price, quantity demanded remains the same. It is obvious that the more the price rises, the bigger will be the level of consumer expenditure. Thus in Figure 2.5(a) consumer expenditure will be higher at P_2 than at P_1.

Infinitely elastic demand. This is shown by a horizontal straight line. At any price above P_1 in Figure 2.5(b) demand is zero. But at P_1 (or any price below) demand is 'infinitely' large.

BOX 2.1 *Shall we put up our price?*
....
Competition, price and revenue

When you buy a can of drink on a train, or an ice-cream in the cinema, or a bottle of wine in a restaurant, you may well be horrified by its price. How can they get away with it?

The answer is that these firms are *not* price takers. They can choose what price to charge. We will be examining the behaviour of such firms in Chapter 4, but here it is useful to see how price elasticity of demand can help to explain their behaviour.

Take the case of the can of drink on the train. If you are thirsty, and if you haven't brought a drink with you, then you will have to get one from the train's bar, or go without. There is no substitute. What we are saying here is that the demand for drink on the train is inelastic at the normal shop price. This means that the train operator can put up the price of its drinks, and food too, and earn *more* revenue.

Generally, the less the competition a firm faces, the lower will be the elasticity of demand for its products, since there will be fewer substitutes (competitors) to which consumers can turn. The lower the price elasticity of demand, the higher the price the firm charges is likely to be.

When there is plenty of competition, it is quite a different story. Petrol stations in the same area may compete fiercely in terms of price. One station may hope that by reducing its price by 1p, or even 0.1p, per litre below that of its competitors, it can attract customers away from them. With a highly elastic demand, a small reduction in price may lead to a substantial increase in their revenue. The problem is, of course, that when they *all* reduce prices, no firm wins. No one attracts customers away from the others! In this case it is the customer who wins.

Q1 Why may a restaurant charge very high prices for wine and bottled water and yet quite reasonable prices for food?

Q2 Why are clothes with designer labels so much more expensive than 'own brand' clothes from a chain store, even though they may cost a similar amount to produce?

This seemingly unlikely demand curve is in fact relatively common for an *individual producer*. In a perfect market, as we have seen, firms are small relative to the whole market (like the small-scale grain farmer). They have to accept the price as given by supply and demand in the *whole market*, but at that price they can sell as much as they produce. (Demand is not *literally* infinite, but as far as the farmer is concerned it is.) In this case, the more the individual farmer produces, the more revenue will be earned. In Figure 2.5(b), more revenue is earned at Q_2 than at Q_1.

Unit elastic demand. This is where price and quantity change in exactly the same proportion. Any rise in price will be exactly offset by a fall in quantity, leaving total revenue unchanged. In Figure 2.5(c) the striped area is exactly equal to the blue shaded area: in both cases total revenue (i.e. total expenditure) is £800.

You might have thought that a demand curve with unit elasticity would be a straight line at 45° to the axes. Instead it is a curve called a *rectangular hyperbola*. The reason for its shape is that the proportionate *rise* in quantity

BOX 2.2 *The measurement of elasticity*
....

We have defined price elasticity as the percentage or proportionate change in quantity demanded divided by the percentage or proportionate change in price. But how, in practice, do we measure these changes for a specific demand curve?

A common mistake that students make is to think that you can talk about the elasticity of a *whole curve*. The mistake here is that in most cases the elasticity will vary along the length of the curve.

Different elasticities along different portions of a demand curve

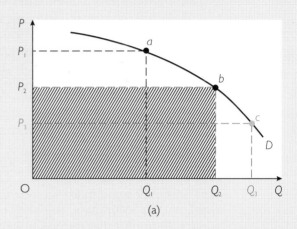

(a)

Take the case of the demand curve illustrated in Figure (a). Between points *a* and *b*, total expenditure rises ($P_2Q_2 > P_1Q_1$): demand is thus elastic between these two points. Between points *b* and *c*, however, total revenue falls ($P_3Q_3 < P_2Q_2$). Demand here is inelastic.

Normally, then, we can refer to the elasticity only of a *portion* of the demand curve, not of the *whole* curve. There are, however, two exceptions to this rule.

The first is when the elasticity just so happens to be the same all the way along a curve, as in the three special cases illustrated in Figure 2.5. The second is where two curves are drawn on the same diagram, as in Figure 2.1 (see page 42). Here we can say that demand curve *D* is less elastic than demand curve *D'* at any given price. Note, however, that each of these two curves will still have a different elasticity along its length.

Although we cannot normally talk about the elasticity of a whole curve, we can nevertheless talk about the elasticity between any two points on it. Remember the formula we used was:

$$\frac{\% \text{ or proportionate } \Delta Q}{\% \text{ or proportionate } \Delta P} \quad (\text{where } \Delta \text{ means 'change in'})$$

The way we measure a *proportionate* change in quantity is to divide that change by the level of Q: i.e. $\Delta Q/Q$. Similarly, we measure a proportionate change in price by dividing that change by the level of P: i.e. $\Delta P/Q$. Price elasticity of demand can thus now be rewritten as:

$$\frac{\Delta Q}{Q} \div \frac{\Delta P}{P}$$

But just what value do we give to P and Q? Consider the demand schedule given in the table and graphed in Figure (b). What is the elasticity of demand between points m and n? To answer this we need to identify ΔQ and Q, and ΔP and P. Let us start with quantity.

Measuring elasticity using the arc method

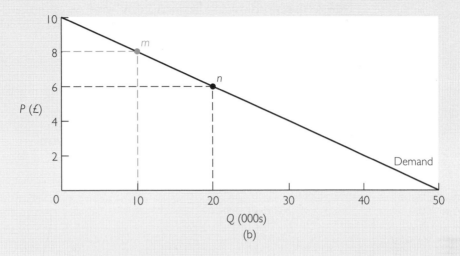

Q (000s)

(b)

P(£)	Q(000s)
8	10
6	20
4	30
2	40

Quantity

The difference in quantity (ΔQ) between 10 (point m) and 20 (point n) is 10.

$$\Delta Q = 10$$

But what is the *proportionate* change in Q ($\Delta Q/Q$). Is it 10/10, taking $Q = 10$ (point m) as the base from which to measure the change in Q? Or is it 10/20, taking $Q = 20$ (point n)? To avoid this problem the average of the two quantities is used: in other words, the mid-point between them:

$$Q = 15 \text{ i.e } \frac{(10 + 20)}{2}$$

$$\therefore \frac{\Delta Q}{Q} = \frac{10}{15}$$

Price

The difference in price between 8 (point m) and 6 (point n) is 2.

$$\Delta P = 2$$

The *proportionate* change in P is found in the same way as the proportionate change in Q. The base price is taken as the mid-point between the two prices:

$$P = 7 \text{ i.e. } \frac{(8 + 6)}{2}$$

$$\therefore \frac{\Delta P}{P} = \frac{-2}{7}$$

Elasticity

Now we have worked out figures for ΔQ, Q, ΔP and P, we can proceed to work out elasticity. Using the *average (or 'mid-point') formula*, price elasticity of demand is given by

$$\frac{\Delta Q}{\text{average } Q} \div \frac{\Delta P}{\text{average } P}$$

In our example this would give the following elasticity between *m* and *n*:

$$10/15 \div -2/7 = -7/3 = -2.33$$

Since 2.33 is greater than 1, demand is elastic between *m* and *n*.

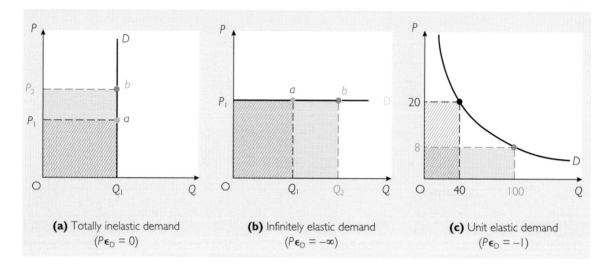

(a) Totally inelastic demand
$(P\epsilon_D = 0)$

(b) Infinitely elastic demand
$(P\epsilon_D = -\infty)$

(c) Unit elastic demand
$(P\epsilon_D = -1)$

FIGURE 2.5
(a) Totally inelastic demand ($P\epsilon_D$) (b) Infinitely elastic demand ($P\epsilon_D = \infty$) (c) Unit elastic demand ($P\epsilon_D = -1$)

must equal the proportionate *fall* in price (and vice versa). As we move down the demand curve, in order for the *proportionate* change in both price and quantity to remain constant there must be a bigger and bigger *absolute* rise in quantity and a smaller and smaller absolute fall in price. For example, a rise in quantity from 200 to 400 is the same proportionate change as a rise from 100 to 200, but its absolute size is double. A fall in price from £5 to £2.50 is the same percentage as a fall from £10 to £5, but its absolute size is only half.

Summary

1. **The total expenditure on a product is found by multiplying the quantity sold by the price of the product.**
2. **When demand is price elastic, a rise in price will lead to a reduction in total expenditure on the good and hence a reduction in the total revenue of producers.**
3. **When demand is price inelastic, a rise in price will lead to an increase in total expenditure on the good and hence an increase in the total revenue of producers.**

Price elasticity of supply ($P\varepsilon_S$)

How responsive is supply to a change in price?

When price changes, there will be not only a change in the quantity demanded, but also a change in the quantity *supplied*. Frequently we will want to know just how responsive quantity supplied is to a change in price. The measure we use is the price elasticity of supply.

Figure 2.6 shows two supply curves. Curve S_2 is more elastic between any two prices than curve S_1. Thus, when price rises from P_1 to P_2 there is a larger increase in quantity supplied with S_2 (namely, Q_1 to Q_3) than there is with S_1 (namely, Q_1 to Q_2). For any shift in the demand curve there will be a larger change in quantity supplied and a smaller change in price with curve S_2 than with curve S_1. Thus the effect on price and quantity of a shift in the demand curve will depend on the price elasticity of supply.

The formula for the price elasticity of supply ($P\varepsilon_S$) is: the percentage (or proportionate) change in quantity supplied divided by the percentage (or proportionate) change in price. Putting this in symbols gives:

$$P\varepsilon_S = \frac{\%\Delta Q_S}{\%\Delta P}$$

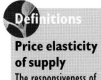

Definitions

Price elasticity of supply
The responsiveness of quantity supplied to a change in price.

Formula for price elasticity of supply (arc method)
ΔQ_S/average Q_S ÷ ΔP/average P.

In other words, the formula is identical to that for the price elasticity of demand, except that quantity in this case is quantity *supplied*. Thus if a 10 per cent rise in price caused a 25 per cent rise in the quantity supplied, the price elasticity of supply would be:

$$25\%/10\% = 2.5$$

and if a 10 per cent rise in price caused only a 5 per cent rise in the quantity, the price elasticity of supply would be:

$$5\%/10\% = 0.5$$

In the first case, supply is elastic ($P\varepsilon_S > 1$); in the second it is inelastic ($P\varepsilon_S < 1$). Notice that, unlike the price elasticity of demand, the figure is

FIGURE 2.6
Effect of price elasticity of supply on price and quantity

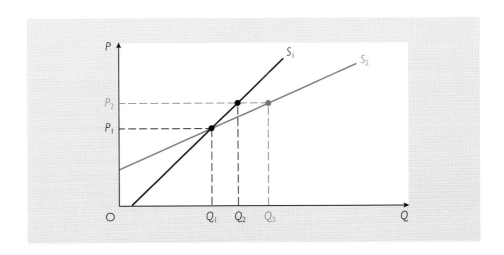

BOX 2.3 *Advertising and its effect on the demand curve*

How to increase sales and price

When we are told that brand X will make us more beautiful, enrich our lives, wash our clothes whiter, give us get-up-and-go, give us a new taste sensation or make us the envy of our friends, just what are the advertisers up to? 'Trying to sell the product', you may reply. In fact there is a bit more to it than this. Advertisers are trying to do two things:

- Shift the product's demand curve to the right.
- Make it less price elastic.

This is illustrated in the diagram.

Effect of advertising on the demand curve

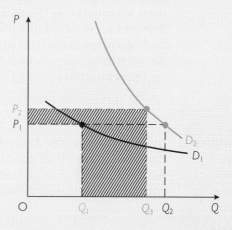

D_1 shows the original demand curve with price at P_1 and sales at Q_1. D_2 shows the curve after an advertising campaign. The rightward shift allows an increased quantity (Q_2)

positive (assuming that the supply curve is upward sloping). This is because price and quantity supplied change in the *same* direction.

The determinants of price elasticity of supply

The amount that costs rise as output rises. The less the additional costs of producing additional output, the more will firms be encouraged to produce for a given price rise: the more elastic will supply be.

Supply is thus likely to be elastic if firms have plenty of spare capacity, if they can readily get extra supplies of raw materials, if they can easily switch away from producing alternative products and if they can avoid having to introduce overtime working (at higher rates of pay). If all these conditions hold, costs will be little affected by a rise in output and supply will be relatively elastic. The less these conditions apply, the less elastic will supply be.

to be sold at the original price. If the demand is also made highly inelastic, the firm can also raise its price and still have a substantial increase in sales. Thus in the diagram, price can be raised to P_2 and sales will be Q_3 – still substantially above Q_1. The total gain in revenue is shown by the shaded area.

How can advertising bring about this new demand curve?

Shifting the demand curve to the right

This will occur if the advertising brings the product to more people's attention and if it increases people's desire for the product.

Making the demand curve less elastic

This will occur if the advertising creates greater brand loyalty. People must be led to believe (rightly or wrongly) that competitors' brands are inferior. This will allow the firm to raise its price above that of its rivals with no significant fall in sales. There will only be a small substitution effect because consumers have been led to believe that there are no close substitutes.

(Q1) Think of some advertisements which deliberately seek to make demand less elastic.

(Q2) Imagine that 'Sunshine' sunflower margarine, a well-known brand, is advertised with the slogan, 'It helps you live longer'. What do you think would happen to the demand curve for a supermarket's *own* brand of sunflower margarine? Consider both the direction of shift and the effect on elasticity. Will the elasticity differ markedly at different prices? How will this affect the pricing policy and sales of the supermarket's own brand?

Time period

- Immediate time period. Firms are unlikely to be able to increase supply by much immediately. Supply is virtually fixed, or can vary only according to available stocks. Supply is highly inelastic. In Figure 2.7, S_i is drawn with $P\varepsilon_S = 0$. If demand increases to D_2, supply will not be able to respond. Price will rise to P_2. Quantity will remain at Q_1. Equilibrium will move to point *b*.
- Short run. If a slightly longer time period is allowed to elapse, some inputs can be increased (e.g. raw materials) while others will remain fixed (e.g. heavy machinery). Supply can increase somewhat. This is illustrated by S_s. Equilibrium will move to point *c* with price falling again, to P_3, and quantity rising to Q_3.
- Long run. In the long run, there will be sufficient time for all inputs to be increased and for new firms to enter the industry. Supply, therefore,

FIGURE 2.7
*Supply in
different time
periods*

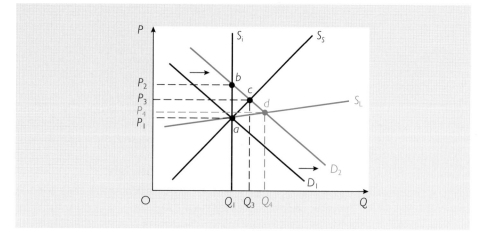

is likely to be highly elastic. This is illustrated by curve S_L. Long-run equilibrium will be at point *d* with price falling back even further, to P_4, and quantity rising all the way to Q_4. In some circumstances the long-run supply curve may even slope downward. (See the section on economies of scale in Chapter 3.)

Summary

1. **Price elasticity of supply measures the responsiveness of supply to a change in price. It has a positive value.**
2. **Supply will be more elastic the less costs per unit rise as output rises and the longer the time period.**

2.4 Other elasticities

How does demand respond to changes in income and to changes in the price of other goods?

Income elasticity of demand

So far we have looked at the responsiveness of demand and supply to a change in price. But price is just one of the determinants of demand and supply. In theory, we could look at the responsiveness of demand or supply to a change in *any* one of their determinants. We could have a whole range of different types of elasticity of demand and supply. In practice there are just two other elasticities that are particularly useful to us, and both are demand elasticities.

The first is the **income elasticity of demand** ($Y_{\varepsilon D}$). This measures the responsiveness of demand to a change in consumer incomes (Y).[1] It enables us to predict how much the demand curve will shift for a given change in income. The **formula for the income elasticity of demand** is: the

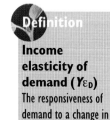

Definition

Income elasticity of demand ($Y_{\varepsilon D}$)
The responsiveness of demand to a change in consumer incomes.

[1] Note that we use the letter Y rather than the letter I to stand for 'income'. This is normal practice in economics. The reason is that the letter I is used for 'investment'.

percentage (or proportionate) change in demand divided by the percentage (or proportionate) change in income. Putting this in symbols gives:

$$Y\varepsilon_D = \frac{\%\Delta Q_D}{\%\Delta Y}$$

In other words, the formula is identical to that for the price elasticity of demand, except that we are dividing the change in demand by the change in *income* that caused it rather than by a change in price. Thus if a 2 per cent rise in income caused an 8 per cent rise in a product's demand, then its income elasticity of demand would be:

$$8\%/2\% = 4$$

Formula for income elasticity of demand
The percentage (or proportionate) change in demand divided by the percentage (or proportionate) change in income: $\%\Delta Q_D \div \%\Delta Y$.

Normal goods
Goods whose demand increases as consumer incomes increase. They have a positive income elasticity of demand. Luxury goods will have a higher income elasticity of demand than more basic goods.

Inferior goods
Goods whose demand *decreases* as consumer incomes increase. Such goods have a negative income elasticity of demand.

Cross-price elasticity of demand
The responsiveness of demand for one good to a change in the price of another.

Determinants of income elasticity of demand

Degree of 'necessity' of the good. In a developed country, the demand for luxury goods expands rapidly as people's incomes rise, whereas the demand for basic goods, such as bread, rises only a little. Thus items such as cars and foreign holidays have a high income elasticity of demand, whereas items such as potatoes and bus journeys have a low income elasticity of demand.

The demand for some goods actually decreases as income rises. These are *inferior goods* such as cheap margarine. As people earn more, so they switch to butter or better quality margarine. Unlike normal goods, which have a positive income elasticity of demand, inferior goods have a negative income elasticity of demand.

The rate at which the desire for a good is satisfied as consumption increases. The more quickly people become satisfied, the less their demand will expand as income increases.

The level of income of consumers. Poor people will respond differently from rich people to a rise in their incomes. For example, for a given rise in income, poor people may buy a lot more butter, whereas rich people may buy only a little more.

Income elasticity of demand is an important concept to firms considering the future size of the market for their product. If the product has a high income elasticity of demand, sales are likely to expand rapidly as national income rises, but may also fall significantly if the economy moves into recession.

Cross-price elasticity of demand ($C\varepsilon_{D_{ab}}$)

This is often known by its less cumbersome title of cross elasticity of demand. It is a measure of the responsiveness of demand for one product to a change in the price of another (either a substitute or a complement). It enables us to predict how much the demand curve for the first product will shift when the price of the second product changes. For example, knowledge of the cross elasticity of demand for Coca-Cola to the price of Pepsi would allow Coca-Cola to predict the effect on its own sales if the price of Pepsi were to change.

The **formula for the cross-price elasticity of demand** ($C\varepsilon_{D_{ab}}$) is: the percentage (or proportionate) change in demand for good a divided by the percentage (or proportionate) change in price of good b. Putting this in symbols gives:

$$C\varepsilon_{D_{ab}} = \frac{\%\Delta Q_{D_a}}{\%\Delta P_b}$$

If good b is a *substitute* for good a, a's demand will *rise* as b's price rises. For example, the demand for pork will rise as the price of beef rises. In this case, cross elasticity will be a positive figure. For example, if the demand for butter rose by 2 per cent when the price of margarine (a substitute) rose by 8 per cent, then the cross elasticity of demand for butter with respect to margarine would be:

$$2\%/8\% = 0.25$$

If good b is *complementary* to good a, however, a's demand will *fall* as b's price rises and thus as the quantity of b demanded falls. In this case, cross elasticity of demand will be a negative figure. For example, if a 4 per cent rise in the price of bread led to a 3 per cent fall in demand for butter, the cross elasticity of demand for butter with respect to bread would be:

$$-3\%/4\% = -0.75$$

The major determinant of cross elasticity of demand is the closeness of the substitute or complement. The closer it is, the bigger will be the effect on the first good of a change in the price of the substitute or complement, and hence the greater the cross elasticity – either positive or negative.

Firms will wish to know the cross elasticity of demand for their product when considering the effect on the demand for their product of a change in the price of a rival's product or of a complementary product. These are vital pieces of information for firms when making their production plans.

Another example of the usefulness of the concept of cross elasticity of demand is in the field of international trade and the balance of payments. A government will wish to know how a change in domestic prices will affect the demand for imports. If there is a high cross elasticity of demand for imports (because they are close substitutes for home-produced goods), and if prices at home rise due to inflation, the demand for imports will rise substantially, thus worsening the balance of payments.

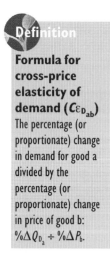

Definition

Formula for cross-price elasticity of demand ($C\varepsilon_{D_{ab}}$)
The percentage (or proportionate) change in demand for good a divided by the percentage (or proportionate) change in price of good b: $\%\Delta Q_{D_a} \div \%\Delta P_b$.

FIGURE 2.8
Response of supply to an increase in demand

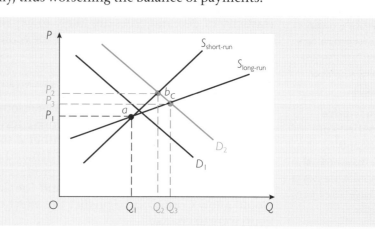

Summary

1. Income elasticity of demand measures the responsiveness of demand to a change in income. For normal goods it has a positive value; for inferior goods it has a negative value.
2. Demand will be more income elastic the more luxurious the good and the less rapidly demand is satisfied as consumption increases.
3. Cross-price elasticity of demand measures the responsiveness of demand for one good to a change in the price of another. For substitute goods the value will be positive; for complements it will be negative.
4. The cross-price elasticity will be more elastic the closer the two goods are as substitutes or complements.

Markets and adjustment over time

How do markets respond over the longer term to a change in demand or supply?

The full adjustment of price, demand and supply to a situation of disequilibrium will not be instantaneous. It is necessary, therefore, to analyse the time path which supply takes in responding to changes in demand, and which demand takes in responding to changes in supply.

Short-run and long-run adjustment

As we have already seen, the price elasticities of demand and supply vary with the time period under consideration. The reason is that producers and consumers take time to respond to a change in price. The longer the time period, the bigger the response, and thus the greater the elasticity of demand and supply.

This is illustrated in Figures 2.8 and 2.9. In both cases, as equilibrium moves from points *a* to *b* to *c*, there is a large short-run price change (P_1 to

FIGURE 2.9
Response of demand to an increase in supply

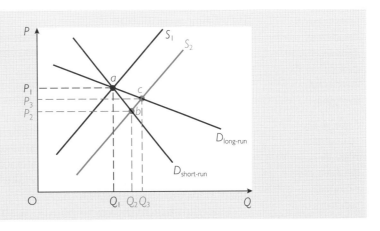

P_2) and a small short-run quantity change (Q_1 to Q_2), but a small long-run price change (P_1 to P_3) and a large long-run quantity change (Q_1 to Q_3).

Speculation

In a world of shifting demand and supply curves, prices do not stay the same. Sometimes they go up; sometimes they come down. If prices are likely to change in the foreseeable future, this will affect the behaviour of buyers and sellers *now*. If, for example, it is now December and you are thinking of buying a new winter coat, you might decide to wait until the January sales, and in the meantime make do with your old coat. If, on the other hand, when January comes you see a new summer dress in the sales, you might well buy it now and not wait until the summer for fear that the price will have gone up by then. Thus a belief that prices will go up will cause people to buy now; a belief that prices will come down will cause them to wait.

The reverse applies to sellers. If you are thinking of selling your house and prices are falling, you will want to sell it as quickly as possible. If, on the other hand, prices are rising sharply, you will wait as long as possible so as to get the highest price. Thus a belief that prices will come down will cause people to sell now; a belief that prices will go up will cause them to wait.

This behaviour of looking into the future and making buying and selling decisions based on your predictions is called **speculation**. Speculation is often based on current trends in price behaviour. If prices are currently rising, people may then try to decide whether they are about to peak and go back down again, or whether they are likely to go on rising. Having made their prediction, they will then act on it. This speculation will thus affect demand and supply, which in turn will affect price. Speculation is commonplace in many markets: the stock exchange, the foreign exchange market and the housing market are three examples.

Speculation tends to be **self-fulfilling**. In other words, the actions of speculators tend to bring about the very effect on prices that speculators had anticipated. For example, if speculators believe that the price of ICI shares is about to rise, they will buy more ICI shares. But by doing this they will ensure that the price *will* rise. The prophecy has become self-fulfilling.

Speculation can either help to reduce price fluctuations or aggravate them: it can be stabilising or destabilising.

Definitions

Speculation
Where people make buying or selling decisions based on their anticipations of future prices.

Self-fulfilling speculation
The actions of speculators tend to cause the very effect that they had anticipated.

Stabilising speculation
Where the actions of speculators tend to reduce price fluctuations.

Stabilising speculation
Speculation will tend to have a **stabilising** effect on price fluctuations when suppliers and/or demanders believe that a change in price is only *temporary*.

An initial fall in price. In Figure 2.10 demand has shifted from D_1 to D_2; equilibrium has moved from point *a* to point *b*, and price has fallen to P_2. How do people react to this fall in price?

Given that they believe this fall in price to be only temporary, suppliers *hold back*, expecting prices to rise again: supply shifts from S_1 to S_2. After all, why supply now when, by waiting, they could get a higher price?

Buyers *increase* their purchases, to take advantage of the temporary fall in price. Demand shifts from D_2 to D_3.

The equilibrium moves to point *c*, with price rising back towards P_1.

FIGURE 2.10
Stabilising speculation: initial price fall

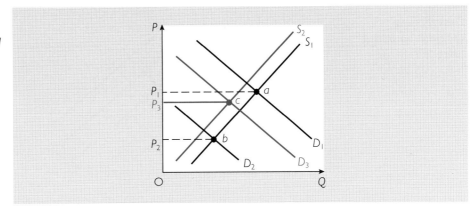

An initial rise in price. In Figure 2.11 demand has shifted from D_1 to D_2. Price has risen from P_1 to P_2.

Suppliers bring their goods to market now, before price falls again. Supply shifts from S_1 to S_2. Demanders, however, hold back until price falls. Demand shifts from D_2 to D_3. The equilibrium moves to point c, with price falling back towards P_1.

A good example of stabilising speculation is that which occurs in agricultural commodity markets. Take the case of wheat. When it is harvested in the autumn there will be a plentiful supply. If all this wheat were to be put on the market, the price would fall to a very low level. Later in the year, when most of the wheat would have been sold, the price would then rise to a very high level. This is all easily predictable.

So what do farmers do? The answer is that they speculate. When the wheat is harvested they know price will tend to fall, and so instead of bringing it all to market they put a lot of it into store. The more price falls, the more they will put into store *anticipating that the price will later rise*. But this holding back of supplies prevents prices from falling. In other words, it stabilises prices.

Later in the year, when the price begins to rise, they will gradually release grain on to the market from the stores. The more the price rises, the more they will release on to the market *anticipating that the price will fall again by the time of the next harvest*. But this releasing of supplies will again stabilise prices by preventing them rising so much.

FIGURE 2.11
Stabilising speculation: initial price rise

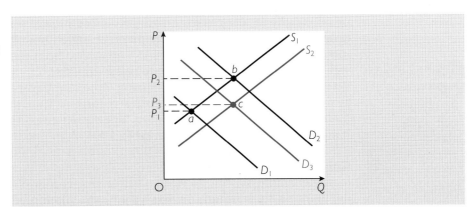

FIGURE 2.12
*Destabilising
speculation: initial
price fall*

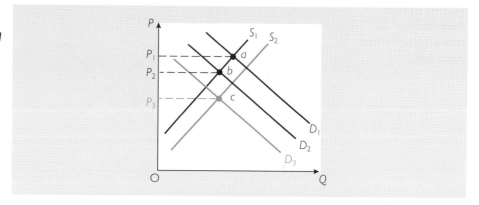

Rather than the farmers doing the speculation, it could be done by grain merchants. When there is a glut of wheat in the autumn, and prices are relatively low, they buy wheat on the grain market and put it into store. When there is a shortage in the spring and summer they sell wheat from their stores. In this way they stabilise prices just as the farmers did when they were the ones that operated the stores.

Destabilising speculation

Speculation will tend to have a destabilising effect on price fluctuations when suppliers and/or buyers believe that a change in price heralds similar changes to come.

An initial fall in price. In Figure 2.12 demand has shifted from D_1 to D_2 and price has fallen from P_1 to P_2. This time, believing that the fall in price heralds further falls in price to come, suppliers sell now before the price does fall. Supply shifts from S_1 to S_2. And demanders wait: they wait until price does fall further. Demand shifts from D_2 to D_3.

Their actions ensure that the price does fall further: to P_3.

An initial rise in price. In Figure 2.13 a price rise from P_1 to P_2 is caused by a rise in demand from D_1 to D_2. Suppliers wait until the price rises further. Supply shifts from S_1 to S_2. Demanders buy now before any further rise in price. Demand shifts from D_2 to D_3. As a result, the price continues to rise: to P_3.

Box 1.4 examined the housing market. In this market, speculation is frequently destabilising. Assume that, after a long period of relatively stable or falling prices, people see house prices beginning to move upward. This might be the result of increased demand brought about by a cut in mortgage interest rates or by a recovery of the economy from recession. People may well believe that the rise in house prices signals a recovery in the housing market and that prices will go on rising. Potential buyers will thus try to buy as soon as possible before prices rise any further. This increased demand (as in Figure 2.13) will thus lead to even bigger price rises. This is precisely what happened in the UK housing market in 1996–7

Definition

Destabilising speculation
Where the actions of speculators tend to make price movements larger.

Conclusion

In some circumstances, then, the action of speculators can help keep price fluctuations to a minimum (stabilising speculation). This is most likely

FIGURE 2.13
Destabilising speculation: initial price rise

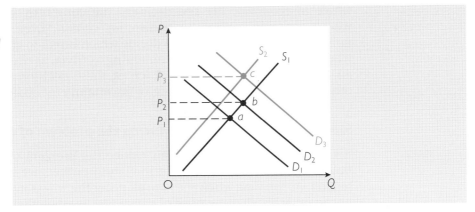

when markets are relatively stable in the first place, with only moderate underlying shifts in demand and supply.

In other circumstances, however, speculation can make price fluctuations much worse. This is most likely in times of uncertainty, when there are significant changes in the determinants of demand and supply. Given this uncertainty, people may see price changes as signifying some trend. They then 'jump on the bandwagon' and do what the rest are doing, and further fuel the rise or fall in price.

Dealing with uncertainty and risk

When price changes are likely to occur, buyers and sellers will try to anticipate them. Unfortunately on many occasions no one can be certain just what these price changes will be. Take the case of stocks and shares. If you anticipate that the price of, say, BP shares is likely to go up substantially in the near future, you may well decide to buy some now and then sell them later after the price has risen. But you cannot be certain that they will go up in price: they may fall instead. If you buy the shares, therefore, you will be taking a gamble.

Now gambles can be of two types. The first is where you know the odds. Let us take the simplest case of a gamble on the toss of a coin. Heads you win; tails you lose. You know that the odds of winning are precisely 50 per cent. If you bet on the toss of a coin, you are said to be operating under conditions of **risk**. *Risk is when the probability of an outcome is known.* Risk itself is a measure of the *variability* of an outcome. For example, if you bet £1 on the toss of a coin, such that heads you win £1 and tails you lose £1, then the variability is –£1 to +£1.

The second form of gamble is the more usual. This is where the odds are not known or are known only roughly. Gambling on the stock exchange is like this. You may have a good idea that a share will go up in price, but is it a 90 per cent chance, an 80 per cent chance or what? You are not certain. Gambling under these sort of conditions is known as operating under **uncertainty**. *This is when the probability of an outcome is not known.*

You may well disapprove of gambling and want to dismiss people who engage in it as foolish or morally wrong. But 'gambling' is not just confined to horses, cards, roulette and the like. Risk and uncertainty pervade the

Risk
When an outcome may or may not occur, but its probability of occurring is known. It is a measure of the variability of that outcome.

Uncertainty
When an outcome may or may not occur and its probability of occurring is not known.

whole of economic life and decisions are constantly having to be made whose outcome cannot be known for certain. Even the most morally upright person will still have to decide which career to go into, whether and when to buy a house, or even something as trivial as whether or not to take an umbrella when going out. Each of these decisions and thousands of others are made under conditions of uncertainty (or occasionally risk).

Stock holding as a way of reducing the problem of uncertainty

A simple way that suppliers can reduce the problem of uncertainty is by holding stocks. Take the case of the wheat farmers we saw in the previous section. At the time when they are planting the wheat in the spring, they are uncertain as to what the price of wheat will be when they bring it to market. If they keep no stores of wheat, they will just have to accept whatever the market price happens to be at harvest time. If, however, they have storage facilities, they can put the wheat into store if the price is low and then wait until it goes up. Alternatively, if the price of wheat is high at harvest time, they can sell it straight away. In other words, they can wait until the price is right.

Although the keeping of stocks will substantially reduce uncertainty, it can never eliminate it. The farmer when planting the wheat cannot know just how good a harvest it will be. If it is a very good harvest, the market price is likely to remain low for a long time after the harvest, since farmers generally have full barns and are all anxious to sell the moment prices begin to rise. Also there is the problem that storage costs money. Thus the farmer must weigh up the possible benefits in terms of higher prices of waiting longer before selling against the additional storage costs involved.

A market in information

One way of reducing uncertainty is to buy information. For example, you might take advice on shares from a stock broker, or buy a copy of a consumer magazine, such as *Which?* The buying and selling of information in this way helps substantially to reduce uncertainty.

Better information can also, under certain circumstances, help to make any speculation more stabilising. With poor information, people are much more likely to be guided by rumour or fear, which could well make speculation destabilising as people 'jump on the bandwagon'. If people generally are better informed, however, this is likely to make prices go more directly to a long-run stable equilibrium.

Summary

1. **A complete understanding of markets must take into account the time dimension.**
2. **Given that producers and consumers take a time to respond fully to price changes, we can identify different equilibria after the elapse of different lengths of time. Generally, short-run supply and demand tend to be less price elastic than long-run supply and demand. As a result, any shifts in D**

or *S* curves tend to have a relatively bigger effect on price in the short run and a relatively bigger effect on quantity in the long run.

3. People often anticipate price changes and this will affect the amount they demand or supply. This speculation will tend to stabilise price fluctuations if people believe that the price changes are only temporary. However, speculation will tend to destabilise these fluctuations (i.e. make them more severe) if people believe that prices are likely to continue to move in the same direction as at present (at least for some time).

4. Many economic decisions are taken under conditions of risk or uncertainty. Uncertainty over future prices can be tackled by holding stocks. When prices are low, the stocks can be built up. When they are high, stocks can be sold. Uncertainty can be reduced by buying information.

Markets where prices are controlled

What happens if the government fixes prices?

At the equilibrium price, there will be no shortage or surplus. The equilibrium price, however, may not be the most *desirable* price. The government, therefore, may prefer to keep prices above or below the equilibrium price.

If the government sets a minimum price above the equilibrium (a price floor), there will be a surplus: $Q_s - Q_d$ in Figure 2.14. Price will not be allowed to fall to eliminate this surplus.

If the government sets a maximum price below the equilibrium (a price ceiling), there will be a shortage: $Q_d - Q_s$ in Figure 2.15. Price will not be allowed to rise to eliminate this shortage.

Setting a minimum (high) price

The government sets **minimum prices** to prevent them falling below a certain level. It may do this for various reasons:

- To protect producers' incomes. If the industry is subject to supply fluctuations (e.g. crops, due to fluctuations in weather) and if industry

Definition

Minimum price
A price floor set by the government or some other agency. The price is not allowed to fall below this level (although it is allowed to rise above it).

FIGURE 2.14
Minimum price: price floor

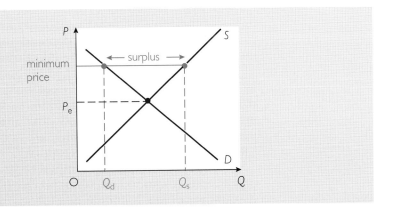

FIGURE 2.15
Maximum price: price ceiling

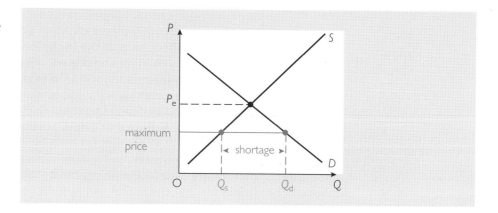

demand is price inelastic, prices are likely to fluctuate severely. Minimum prices will prevent the fall in producers' incomes that would accompany periods of low prices.

- To create a surplus (e.g. of grains), particularly in periods of plenty, which can be stored in preparation for possible future shortages.
- In the case of wages (the price of labour), minimum wages legislation can be used to prevent workers' incomes from falling below a certain level.

There are various methods the government can use to deal with the surpluses associated with minimum prices.

- The government could buy the surplus and either store it, destroy it or sell it abroad in other markets.
- Supply could be artificially lowered by restricting producers to particular quotas. In Figure 2.14, supply could therefore be reduced to Q_d.
- Demand could be raised by advertising, by finding alternative uses for the good, or by cutting down on substitute goods (e.g. by imposing taxes or quotas on substitutes, such as imports).

One of the problems with minimum prices is that firms with surplus on their hands may try to evade the price control and cut their prices. It is possible that the minimum price was not set by the government, but by an agreement between firms in an attempt to keep their profits up. Here too, there is the temptation for individual firms to break the agreement and undercut their rivals. (Note that in cases where firms can choose what prices to charge, simple supply and demand analysis needs to be replaced by a more sophisticated analysis. This is examined in Chapter 4.)

Another problem is that high prices may cushion inefficiency. Firms may feel less need to find more efficient methods of production and cut their costs if their profits are being protected by the high price. Also the high price may discourage firms from producing alternative goods which they could produce more efficiently or which are in higher demand, but which nevertheless have a lower (free-market) price.

One of the best-known examples of governments fixing high minimum prices is the Common Agricultural Policy (CAP) of the European Union. This is examined in Box 2.4.

Setting a maximum (low) price

The government sets maximum prices to prevent them rising above a certain level. This will normally be done for reasons of fairness. In wartime, or times of famine, the government may set maximum prices for basic goods so that poor people can afford to buy them.

The resulting shortages, however, create further problems. If the government merely sets prices and does not intervene further, the shortages will lead to the following:

- Allocation on a 'first come, first served' basis. This is likely to lead to queues developing, or firms adopting waiting lists. Queues were a common feature of life in eastern European countries where governments kept prices below the level necessary to equate demand and supply. In recent years, as part of their economic reforms, they have allowed prices to rise. This has had the obvious benefit of reducing or eliminating queues, but at the same time it has made life very hard for those on low incomes.
- Firms deciding which customers should be allowed to buy: for example, giving preference to regular customers.

Neither of the above may be considered to be fair. Certain needy people may be forced to go without. Therefore, the government may adopt a system of rationing. People could be issued with a set number of coupons for each item rationed. Alternatively, if many goods were rationed, people could be allocated a certain number of 'points'. This system operated in the UK during the Second World War. Each consumer received a number of points every four weeks to spend as desired. Each rationed product in the points system was given a points value, calculated so as to reflect the expected demand in relation to supply. Thus luxury goods, such as canned salmon, had high points values, whereas cereals had low values.

A major problem with maximum prices is likely to be the emergence of black markets, where customers, unable to buy enough in legal markets, may well be prepared to pay very high prices: prices above P_e in Figure 2.15.

Another problem is that the maximum prices reduce the quantity produced of an already scarce commodity. For example, artificially low prices in a famine are likely to reduce food supplies: if not immediately, then at the next harvest, because of less being sown. In many developing countries, governments control the price of basic foodstuffs in order to help the urban poor. The effect, however, is to reduce incomes for farmers, who are then encouraged to leave the land and flock into the ever growing towns and cities.

To minimise these types of problem the government may attempt to reduce the shortage by encouraging supply: by drawing on stores, by direct government production, or by giving subsidies or tax relief to firms. Alternatively, it may attempt to reduce demand: by the production of more alternative goods (e.g. home-grown vegetables in times of war) or by controlling people's incomes.

Definitions

Maximum price
A price ceiling set by the government or some other agency. The price is not allowed to rise above this level (although it is allowed to fall below it).

Rationing
Where the government restricts the amount of a good that people are allowed to buy.

Black markets
Where people ignore the government's price and/or quantity controls and sell illegally at whatever price equates illegal demand and supply.

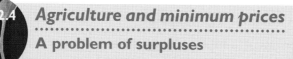

Agriculture and minimum prices

A problem of surpluses

Governments in many countries intervene in agricultural markets. The problem of fluctuating prices, dependency on foreign food imports, and the maintenance of farmers' and farm workers' incomes are but a few of the reasons for such intervention. The form that government intervention takes varies, from a series of subsidies or tax reliefs, to the more formal fixing of high minimum prices.

The fixing of high minimum prices has been the main policy used by the European Union in its Common Agricultural Policy (CAP). Here the Intervention Boards of the EU buy up any surpluses that result at a given 'intervention' price, usually set above the equilibrium.

The EU system of high prices in foodstuffs where the EU is self-sufficient

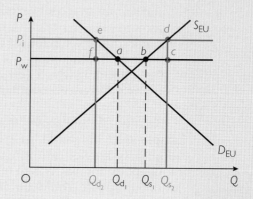

The effects of this system are illustrated in the diagram. Assume that the EU demand is D_{EU}. Assume also that the world price is P_w. This will be the equilibrium price, since any surplus at P_w (i.e. $b - a$) will be exported at that price. Thus before intervention, EU demand is Q_{d_1} and EU supply is Q_{s_1}.

Now assume that the EU sets an intervention price of P_i. Given that this is above the equilibrium (world) price, there will be a surplus of $d - e$ (i.e. $Q_{s_2} - Q_{d_2}$). This will be bought by the appropriate Intervention Board. The cost to the EU of buying this surplus is shown by the total shaded area ($edQ_{s_2}Q_{d_2}$: i.e. the surplus multiplied by the intervention price). Unless the food is thrown away or otherwise disposed of, there will obviously then be the additional costs of storing this food: costs which have been very high in some years as wine 'lakes' and grain and dairy 'mountains' have built up.

An alternative to storing the food is for the Boards to sell the surpluses on the world market. In this case, the net cost to the Intervention Boards would only be area $edcf$. Alternatively, export subsidies could be paid to farmers who sell on world markets to bring the amount they receive up to the intervention price.

The justifications for such a policy are that: it assures food supplies (i.e. it encourages countries to be self-sufficient in food); it stabilizes prices; and, by increasing farmers' incomes, it encourages them to invest in agriculture, which, in turn, results in a growth in agricultural productivity.

The CAP has been criticised, on a number of counts:

- Food surpluses are a costly waste of scarce resources. 'Guarantee' expenditure, as it is called, accounts for around half of the total EU budget (in the past it has been as high as three-quarters). This amounts to ECU110 (approximately £85) per annum per head of the EU population.
- Although food prices are kept high generally, some are kept much higher above free-market prices than others. The effect is to cause a misallocation of resources within agriculture.
- It has increased inequalities within agriculture. The bigger the farm, the bigger its output, and therefore the bigger the benefit the farmer receives from high prices. Similarly, richer agricultural regions of the EU receive more support than poorer ones.
- By raising food prices it penalises the poor, who spend a larger proportion of their income on food than do the rich.
- It has had harmful effects on the environment. By encouraging increased output, the CAP has encouraged the destruction of hedgerows and wildlife, and the increased use of chemical fertilisers and pesticides. Many of these chemicals have caused pollution.
- EU food surpluses 'dumped' on to world markets have had a doubly damaging effect on agriculture in developing countries: (a) exporters of foodstuffs find it very difficult to compete with subsidised EU exports; (b) farmers in developing countries who are producing for their domestic market find that they cannot compete with cheap imports of food.

Agriculture in the developing world thus declines. Farmers' incomes are too low to invest in the land. Many migrate to the overcrowded cities and become slum dwellers in shanty towns, with little or no paid employment. The neglect of agriculture can then lead to famines if there is poor rainfall in any year. Calls are then made for European (and North American) food surpluses to be used for emergency aid: the same food surpluses that contributed to the problem in the first place!

Q1 One of the reforms to the CAP has been to reduce intervention prices and to compensate farmers for the resulting lost income by paying them grants ('income support') unrelated to current output. What, do you think, are the merits of this reform?

Summary

1. The government may fix minimum or maximum prices. If a minimum price is set above the equilibrium price, a surplus will result. If a maximum price is set below the equilibrium price, a shortage will result.
2. Minimum prices are set as a means of protecting the incomes of suppliers or creating a surplus for storage in case of future reductions in supply. If the government is not deliberately trying to create a surplus, it must decide what to do with it.
3. Maximum prices are set as a means of keeping prices down for the consumer. The resulting shortage will cause queues, waiting lists or the restriction of sales by firms to favoured customers. Alternatively, the government could introduce a system of rationing. If it does, then black markets are likely to arise. This is where goods are sold illegally above the maximum price.

Questions

1. Draw a diagram with two supply curves, one steeply sloping and one gently sloping. Ensure that the two curves cross. Draw a demand curve through the point where they cross and mark the equilibrium price and quantity. Now assume that the demand curve shifts to the right. Show how the shape of the supply curve will determine just what happens to price and quantity.

2. Which of the following will have positive signs and which will have negative ones? (a) price elasticity of demand; (b) income elasticity of demand (normal good); (c) income elasticity of demand (inferior good); (d) cross elasticity of demand (with respect to changes in price of a substitute good); (e) cross elasticity of demand (with respect to changes in price of a complementary good); (f) price elasticity of supply.

3. Demand for oil might be relatively elastic over the longer term, and yet it could still be observed that over time people consume more oil (or only very slightly less) despite rising oil prices. How can this apparent contradiction be explained?

4. How might a firm set about making the demand for its brand less elastic?

5. Assuming that a firm faces an inelastic demand and wants to increase its total revenue, in what direction should it change its price? Is there any limit to which it should go on changing its price in this direction?

6. Why are both the price elasticity of demand and the price elasticity of supply likely to be greater in the long run?

7. Which are likely to have the highest cross elasticity of demand: two brands of coffee, or coffee and tea? Explain.

8. Redraw each of Figures 2.10–2.13, only this time assume that it was an initial shift in supply that caused price to change in the first place.

9. What are the advantages and disadvantages of speculation from the point of view of (a) the consumer; (b) firms?

10. Give some examples of decisions you have taken recently that were made under conditions of uncertainty. With hindsight do you think you made the right decisions?

11. Assume that the (weekly) market demand and supply of tomatoes are given by the following figures:

Price (£ per kilo)	4.00	3.50	3.00	2.50	2.00	1.50	1.00
Q_d (000 kilos)	30	35	40	45	50	55	60
Q_s (000 kilos)	80	68	62	55	50	45	38

   (a) What are the equilibrium price and quantity?
   (b) What will be the effect of the government fixing a minimum price of (i) £3.00 per kilo; (ii) £1.50 per kilo?
   (c) Suppose that the government paid tomato producers a subsidy of £1.00 per kilo. (i) Give the new supply schedule. (ii) What will be the new equilibrium price? (iii) How much will this cost the government?
   (d) Alternatively, suppose that the government guaranteed tomato producers a price of £2.50 per kilo. (i) How many tomatoes would it have to buy in order to ensure that all the tomatoes produced were sold? (ii) How much would this cost the government?
   (e) Alternatively, suppose it bought all the tomatoes produced at £2.50. (i) At what single price would it have to sell them in order to dispose of the lot? (ii) What would be the net cost of this course of action?

12. Think of two things that are provided free. In each case, identify when and in what form a shortage might occur. In what ways are/could these shortages be dealt with? Are they the best solution to the shortages?

13. Think of some examples where the price of a good or service is kept below the equilibrium. In each case consider the advantages and disadvantages of the policy.

chapter three

The supply decision

So far we have assumed that supply curves are generally upward sloping: that a higher price will encourage firms to supply more. But just how much will firms choose to supply at each price? It depends largely on the amount of profit they will make. If a firm can increase its profits by producing more, it will normally do so.

Profit is made by firms earning more from the sale of goods than they cost to produce. A firm's total profit ($T\Pi$) is thus the difference between its total sales revenue (TR) and its total costs of production (TC). In order then to discover how a firm can maximise its profit or even get a sufficient level of profit, we must first consider what determines costs and revenue.

In sections 3.1 and 3.2 we examine short-run and long-run costs respectively. Over the short run a firm will be limited in what inputs it can expand. For example, a manufacturing company might be able to use more raw materials, or possibly more labour, but it will not have time to open up another factory. Over the long run, however, a firm will have much more flexibility. It can, if it chooses, expand the whole scale of its operations.

In section 3.3 we turn to the revenue side and see how a firm's revenue varies with output. Finally, section 3.4 puts revenue and cost together to see how profit is determined. In particular, we shall see how profit varies with output and how the point of maximum profit is found.

3.1 Short-run costs

How do a firm's costs vary with output over the short term?

The cost of producing any level of output will depend on the amount of inputs used and the price the firm must pay for them. Let us first focus on the quantity of inputs used.

Short-run and long-run changes in production

If a firm wants to increase production, it will take time to acquire a greater quantity of certain inputs. For example, a manufacturer can use more electricity by turning on switches, but it might take a long time to obtain and install more machines, and longer still to build a second or third factory.

If, then, the firm wants to increase output in a hurry, it will only be able to increase the quantity of certain inputs. It can use more raw materials, more fuel, more tools and possibly more labour (by hiring extra workers or offering overtime to its existing workforce). But it will have to make do with its existing buildings and most of its machinery.

The distinction we are making here is between **fixed factors** and **variable factors**. A *fixed* factor is an input that cannot be increased within a given time period (e.g. buildings). A *variable* factor is one that can.

The distinction between fixed and variable factors allows us to distinguish between the short run and the long run.

The short run. The short run is a time period during which at least one factor of production is fixed. In the short run, then, output can be increased by only using more variable factors. For example, if a shipping line wanted to carry more passengers in response to a rise in demand, it could possibly accommodate more passengers on existing sailings if there were space. It could possibly increase the number of sailings with its existing fleet, by hiring more crew and using more fuel. But in the short run it could not buy more ships: there would not be time for them to be built.

The long run. The long run is a time period long enough for all inputs to be varied. Given long enough, a firm can build a second factory and install new machines.

The actual length of the short run will differ from firm to firm. It is not a fixed period of time. Thus if it takes a farmer a year to obtain new land, buildings and equipment, the short run is any time period up to a year and the long run is any time period longer than a year. On the other hand, if it takes a shipping company three years to obtain an extra ship, the short run is any period up to three years and the long run is any period longer than three years.

For the remainder of this section we will concentrate on *short-run* production and costs. We will look at the long run in section 3.2.

Production in the short run: the law of diminishing returns

Production in the short run is subject to *diminishing returns*. You may well have heard of 'the law of diminishing returns': it is one of the most famous

Definitions

Fixed factor
An input that cannot be increased in supply within a given time period.

Variable factor
An input that *can* be increased in supply within a given time period.

Short run
The period of time over which at least one factor is fixed.

Long run
The period of time long enough for *all* factors to be varied.

of all 'laws' of economics. To illustrate how this law underlies short-run production let us take the simplest possible case where there are just two factors: one fixed and one variable.

Take the case of a farm. Assume that the fixed factor is land and the variable factor is labour. Since the land is fixed in supply, output per period of time can be increased only by increasing the amount of workers employed. But imagine what would happen as more and more workers crowded on to a fixed area of land. The land cannot go on yielding more and more output indefinitely. After a point the additions to output from each extra worker will begin to diminish.

We can now state the **law of diminishing (marginal) returns**. It says that: when increasing amounts of a variable factor are used with a given amount of a fixed factor, there will come a point when each extra unit of the variable factor will produce less extra output than the previous unit. Box 3.1 is a case study illustrating the law of diminishing returns.

Costs and inputs

Having looked at the background to costs in the short run, we now turn to examine short-run costs themselves. We will be examining how costs change as a firm changes the amount it produces. Obviously, if it is to decide how much to produce, it will need to know just what the level of costs will be at each level of output.

A firm's costs of production will depend on the factors of production it uses. The more factors it uses, the greater its costs will be. More precisely, this relationship depends on two elements:

- The productivity of the factors. The greater their productivity, the smaller will be the quantity of them that is needed to produce a given level of output, and hence the lower will be the cost of that output.
- The price of the factors. The higher their price, the higher will be the costs of production.

In the short run, some factors are fixed in supply. Their total costs, therefore, are fixed, in the sense that they do not vary with output. Rent on land is a **fixed cost**. It is the same whether the firm produces a lot or a little.

The total cost of variable factors, however, does vary with output. The cost of raw materials is a **variable cost**. The more that is produced, the more raw materials are used and therefore the higher is their total cost.

Total cost

The **total cost** (*TC*) of production is the sum of the *total variable costs* (*TVC*) and the *total fixed costs* (*TFC*) of production.

$$TC = TVC + TFC$$

Consider Table 3.1 and Figure 3.1. They show the total costs for an imaginary firm for producing different levels of output (*Q*). Let us examine each of the three cost curves in turn.

Definitions

Law of diminishing (marginal) returns
When one or more factors are held fixed, there will come a point beyond which the extra output from additional units of the variable factor will diminish.

Fixed costs
Total costs that do not vary with the amount of output produced.

Variable costs
Total costs that do vary with the amount of output produced.

Total cost
The sum of total fixed costs and total variable costs: *TC = TFC + TVC.*

BOX 3.1

Diminishing returns in the bread shop

Is the baker using his loaf?

Just up the road from where I live is a bread shop. Like many others, I buy my bread there on a Saturday morning. Not surprisingly, Saturday morning is the busiest time of the week for the shop and as a result it takes on extra assistants.

During the week only one assistant serves the customers, but on a Saturday morning there used to be five serving. But could they serve five times as many customers? No, they could not. There were diminishing returns to labour.

The trouble is that certain factors of production in the shop are fixed:

- The shop is a fixed size. It gets very crowded on Saturday morning. Assistants sometimes have to wait while customers squeeze past each other to get to the counter, and with five serving, the assistants themselves used to get in each other's way.
- There is only one cash till. Assistants frequently had to wait while other assistants used it.
- There is only one pile of tissue paper for wrapping the bread. Again the assistants often had to wait.

The fifth and maybe even the fourth assistant ended up serving very few extra customers. I am still going to the same bread shop and they still have only one till and one pile of tissue paper. But now only three assistants are employed on a Saturday! The shop, however, is just as busy.

 How would you advise the baker as to whether he should (a) employ *four* assistants on a Saturday; (b) extend his shop, thereby allowing more customers to be served on a Saturday morning?

Total fixed cost (*TFC*)

In our example, total fixed cost is assumed to be £12. Since this does not vary with output, it is shown by a horizontal straight line.

Total variable cost (*TVC*)

With a zero output, no variable factors will be used. Thus $TVC = 0$. The *TVC* curve, therefore, starts from the origin.

The shape of the *TVC* curve follows from the law of diminishing returns. Initially, *before* diminishing returns set in, *TVC* rises less and less rapidly as more variable factors are added. For example, in the case of a factory with a fixed supply of machinery, initially as more workers are taken on, the workers can do increasingly specialist tasks and make a fuller use of the capital equipment. With this increasing productivity, so *TVC* will rise less and less quickly.

As output is increased beyond point *m* in Figure 3.1, diminishing returns set it. Given that extra workers (the extra variable factors) are producing less and less extra output, the extra units of output they do produce will be

TABLE 3.1 *Total costs for firm X*

Output (Q)	TFC (£)	TVC (£)	TC (£)
0	12	0	12
1	12	10	22
2	12	16	28
3	12	21	33
4	12	28	40
5	12	40	52
6	12	60	72
7	12	91	103
.	.	.	.
.	.	.	.
.	.	.	.

FIGURE 3.1
Total costs for firm X

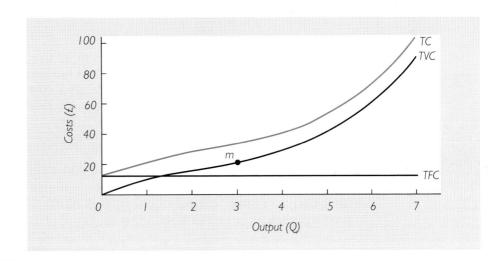

Definitions

Average (total) cost
Total cost (fixed plus variable) per unit of output: $AC = TC/Q = AFC + AVC$.

Average fixed cost
Total fixed cost per unit of output: $AFC = TFC/Q$.

Average variable cost
Total variable cost per unit of output: $AVC = TVC/Q$.

costing more and more in terms of wage costs. Thus *TVC* rises more and more rapidly. The *TVC* curve gets steeper.

Total cost (TC)
Since $TC = TVC + TFC$, the *TC* curve is simply the *TVC* curve shifted vertically upwards by £12.

Average and marginal cost

Average cost (*AC*) is cost per unit of production.

$$AC = TC/Q$$

Thus if it cost a firm £2000 to produce 100 units of a product, the average cost would be £20 for each unit (£2000/100).

Like total cost, average cost can be divided into the two components, fixed and variable. In other words, average cost equals average fixed cost (*AFC = TFC/Q*) plus average variable cost (*AVC = TVC/Q*).

$$AC = AFC + AVC$$

Marginal cost (*MC*) is the *extra* cost of producing *one more unit*: that is, the rise in total cost per one unit rise in output.

$$MC = \frac{\Delta TC}{\Delta Q}$$

To explain this formula, consider the following two examples.

Example 1

A firm is currently producing 100 units of output at a cost of £2000. It now increases its output to 101 units and its total cost rises to £2030. It has thus incurred an extra cost of £30 to produce this 101st unit. Thus the marginal cost of the 101st unit is £30.

Putting these figures into the formula gives:

$$MC = \frac{\Delta TC}{\Delta Q} = \frac{(£2030 - £2000)}{101 - 100} = \frac{£30}{1}$$

But why do we have to divide the rise in cost by 1? In cases like this, where output can be increased one unit at a time, it is obviously not necessary to divide the rise in cost by the rise in output. Marginal cost is simply the rise in costs of producing that extra unit. There are cases, however, where output can only be increased in batches …

Example 2

Assume that a firm is currently producing 1 000 000 boxes of matches a month. It now increases output by 1000 boxes (another batch): $\Delta Q = 1000$. Assume that, as a result, total costs rise by £40: $\Delta TC = £40$. What is the cost of producing *one* more box of matches? It is:

$$MC = \frac{\Delta TC}{\Delta Q} = \frac{£40}{1000} = 4p$$

(Note that all marginal costs are variable, since, by definition, there can be no extra fixed costs as output rises.)

Given the *TFC*, *TVC* and *TC* for each output, it is possible to derive the *AFC*, *AVC*, *AC* and *MC* for each output using the above definitions. For example, using the data of Table 3.1, Table 3.2 can be constructed.

What will be the shapes of the *MC*, *AFC*, *AVC* and *AC* curves? These are illustrated in Figure 3.2.

Marginal cost (MC). The shape of the *MC* curve follows directly from the law of diminishing returns. Initially, in Figure 3.2, as more of the variable factor is used, extra units of output cost less than previous units. *MC* falls. This corresponds to the portion of the *TVC* curve in Figure 3.1 to the left of point *m*.

Beyond a certain level of output, diminishing returns set in. This is shown as point *x* in Figure 3.2 and corresponds to point *m* in Figure 3.1. Thereafter *MC* rises. Additional units of output cost more and more to produce, since they require ever increasing amounts of the variable factor.

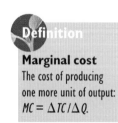

Definition

Marginal cost
The cost of producing one more unit of output: $MC = \Delta TC / \Delta Q$.

TABLE 3.2 *Total, average and marginal costs for firm X*

Output (Q) (units)	TFC (£)	AFC (TFC/Q) (£)	TVC (£)	AVC (TVC/Q) (£)	TC (TFC+TVC) (£)	AC (TC/Q) (£)	MC (ΔTC/ΔQ) (£)
0	12	–	0	–	12	–	
							10
1	12	12	10	10	22	22	
							6
2	12	6	16	8	28	14	
							5
3	12	4	21	7	33	11	
							7
4	12	3	28	7	40	10	
							12
5	12	2.4	40	8	52	10.4	
							20
6	12	2	60	10	72	12	
							31
7	12	1.7	91	13	103	14.7	

FIGURE 3.2
Average and marginal costs

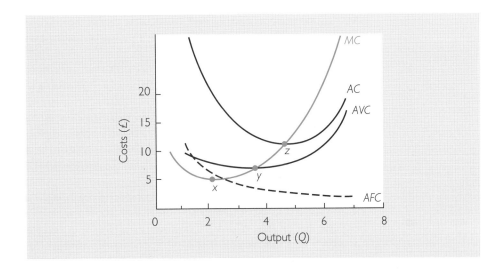

Average fixed cost (AFC). This falls continuously as output rises, since *total* fixed costs are being spread over a greater and greater output.

Average (total) cost (AC). The shape of the *AC* curve depends on the shape of the *MC* curve. As long as new units of output cost less than the average, their production must pull the average cost down. That is, if *MC* is less than *AC*, *AC* must be falling. Likewise, if new units cost more than the average, their production must drive the average up. That is, if *MC* is greater than *AC*, *AC* must be rising. Therefore, the *MC* curve crosses the *AC* curve at its minimum point (point *z* in Figure 3.2).

Average variable cost (AVC). Since *AVC* = *AC* – *AFC*, the *AVC* curve is simply the vertical difference between the *AC* and the *AFC* curves. Note that as *AFC* gets less, the gap between *AVC* and *AC* narrows. Since all marginal costs are variable (by definition, there are no marginal *fixed* costs), the same relationship holds between *MC* and *AVC* as it did between *MC* and *AC*. That is, if *MC* is less than *AVC*, *AVC* must be falling, and if *MC* is greater than *AVC*, *AVC* must be rising. Therefore, as with the *AC* curve, the *MC* curve crosses the *AVC* curve at its minimum point (point *y* in Figure 3.2).

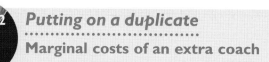

BOX 3.2 *Putting on a duplicate*

Marginal costs of an extra coach

A few years ago I had to travel to London by coach and decided to book my seat early in case the coach was full. 'There is no need to do that,' I was told, 'because we will always put on an extra coach if there is not enough room on the first.'

Was this an example of 'irrational' behaviour on the part of the coach company? What was the cost of providing me with a seat on that second coach? Would the company have made a loss on my custom?

Let us assume that the cost of putting on a second coach to London holding 50 passengers is £500. *When deciding whether to put on the coach*, what is the marginal cost that the firm must take into account? The answer is that it depends on how many people travel on it. Remember that the formula for marginal cost is $\Delta TC/\Delta Q$. If I have the coach to myself ($\Delta Q = 1$), the marginal cost will be £500. In other words, the coach company is having to pay an extra £500 to let me have a seat. Clearly it will be making a loss by putting on that extra coach.

If, however, 50 people use the second coach, the marginal cost of providing the extra seats is only £10 per seat: $\Delta TC/\Delta Q = £500/50 = £10$. Presumably, with a full coach, the company will make a profit.

Once it has had to put on a second coach and has thus incurred the extra £500 cost, the marginal cost of extra passengers on that coach will be zero. In other words, the marginal cost of the first passenger is £500; thereafter there are no extra costs to be incurred (except maybe for a little extra fuel to cope with the extra weight) until a third coach is put on.

If, then, the question is *whether* to put on a second coach, and if all the company is thinking about is its short-term profits, the marginal cost it will look at is the marginal cost per passenger on it: i.e. $\Delta TC/\Delta Q$. If, however, it has already put on that second coach and it has vacant seats, the marginal cost of taking one more passenger (say, a person arriving at the coach station at the last minute and wanting to buy a ticket on the coach) will be virtually zero.

 Why may it still make economic sense for the company to put on a coach for just one or two passengers, rather than turning them away?

Recently I again had to travel to London by coach. This time I was advised to book in case the coach was full! Was the coach company being more sensible now?

Summary

1. **Production in the short run is subject to diminishing returns. As greater quantities of the variable factor(s) are used, so each additional unit of the variable factor will add less to output than previous units: i.e. output will rise less and less rapidly.**

BOX 3.3 *The relationship between averages and marginals*

In this chapter we have just examined the concepts of *average* and *marginal* cost. We shall be coming across several other average and marginal concepts later on. It is useful at this stage to examine the general relationship between averages and marginals. In all cases there are three simple rules that relate them.

To illustrate these rules, consider the following example.

Imagine a room with ten people in it. Assume that the *average* age of those present is 20. Now if a 20-year-old enters the room (the *marginal* age), this will not affect the average age. It will remain at 20. If a 56-year-old now comes in, the average age will rise: not to 56, of course, but to 23. This is found by dividing the sum of everyone's ages (276) by the number of people (12). If then a child of 10 were to enter the room, this would pull the average age down.

From this example we can derive the three universal rules about averages and marginals:

- If the marginal equals the average, the average will not change.
- If the marginal is above the average, the average will rise.
- If the marginal is below the average, the average will fall.

Q1 A cricketer scores the following number of runs in five successive innings:

Innings:	1	2	3	4	5
Runs:	20	20	50	10	0

These can be seen as the marginal number of runs from each innings. Calculate the total and average number of runs after each innings. Show how the average and marginal scores illustrate the three rules above.

2. **With some factors fixed in supply in the short run, their total costs will be fixed with respect to output. In the case of variable factors, their total cost will increase as more output is produced and hence as more of them are used.**

3. **Total cost can be divided into total fixed and total variable cost. Total variable cost will tend to increase less rapidly at first as more is produced, but then, when diminishing returns set in, it will increase more and more rapidly.**

4. **Marginal cost is the cost of producing one more unit of output. It will probably fall at first (corresponding to the part of the *TVC* curve where the slope is getting shallower), but will start to rise as soon as diminishing returns set in.**

5. **Average cost, like total cost, can be divided into fixed and variable costs. Average fixed cost will decline as more output is produced. The reason is that the total fixed cost is being spread over a greater and greater number of units of output. Average variable cost will tend to decline at first, but once the marginal cost has risen above it, it must then rise. The same applies to average cost.**

Long-run costs

How do a firm's costs vary with output over the longer term?

Production in the long run: the scale of production

In the long run, *all* factors of production are variable. There is time for the firm to build a new factory (maybe in a different part of the country), to install new machines, to use different techniques of production, and in general to combine its inputs in whatever proportion and in whatever quantities it chooses.

If a firm were to double all of its inputs – something it could do in the long run – would it double its output? Or will output more than double or less than double? We can distinguish three possible situations:

Constant returns to scale. This is where a given percentage increase in inputs will lead to the *same* percentage increase in output.

Increasing returns to scale. This is where a given percentage increase in inputs will lead to a *larger* percentage increase in output.

Decreasing returns to scale. This is where a given percentage increase in inputs will lead to a *smaller* percentage increase in output.

Notice the terminology here. The words 'to scale' mean that *all* inputs increase by the same proportion. Decreasing returns to *scale* are therefore quite different from diminishing *marginal* returns (where only the *variable* factor increases). The differences between marginal returns to a variable factor and returns to scale are illustrated in Table 3.3.

In the short run, input 1 is assumed to be fixed in supply (at 3 units). Output can be increased only by using more of the variable factor (input 2). In the long run, however, both input 1 and input 2 are variable.

In the short-run situation, diminishing returns can be seen from the fact that output increases at a decreasing rate (25 to 45 to 60 to 70 to 75) as input 2 is increased. In the long-run situation, the table illustrates increasing returns to scale. Output increases at an *increasing* rate (15 to 35 to 60 to 90 to 125) as both inputs are increased.

TABLE 3.3 *Short-run and long-run increases in output*

Short run			Long run		
Input 1	Input 2	Output	Input 1	Input 2	Output
3	1	25	1	1	15
3	2	45	2	2	35
3	3	60	3	3	60
3	4	70	4	4	90
3	5	75	5	5	125

Economies of scale

The concept of increasing returns to scale is closely linked to that of economies of scale. A firm experiences economies of scale if costs per unit of output fall as the scale of production increases. Clearly, if a firm is getting increasing returns to scale from its factors of production, then as it produces more it will be using smaller and smaller amounts of factors per unit of output. Other things being equal, this means that it will be producing at a lower average cost.

There are a number of reasons why firms are likely to experience economies of scale. Some are due to increasing returns to scale; some are not.

Specialisation and division of labour. In large-scale plants, workers can do more simple, repetitive jobs. With this specialisation and division of labour less training is needed; workers can become highly efficient in their particular job, especially with long production runs; there is less time lost in workers switching from one operation to another; and supervision is easier. Workers and managers can be employed who have specific skills in specific areas.

Indivisibilities. Some inputs are of a minimum size. They are indivisible. The most obvious example is machinery. Take the case of a combine harvester. A small-scale farmer could not make full use of one. They only become economical to use, therefore, on farms above a certain size. The problem of indivisibilities is made worse when different machines, each of which is part of the production process, are of a different size. For example, if there are two types of machine, one producing 6 units a day, the other packaging 4 units a day, a minimum of 12 units per day will have to be produced, involving two production machines and three packaging machines, if all machines are to be fully utilised.

The 'container principle'. Any capital equipment that contains things (e.g. blast furnaces, oil tankers, pipes, vats, etc.) will tend to cost less per unit of output the larger its size. The reason has to do with the relationship between a container's volume and its surface area. A container's cost will depend largely on the materials used to build it and hence roughly on its *surface area.* Its output will depend largely on its *volume.* Large containers have a bigger volume relative to surface area than do small containers. For example, a container with a bottom, top and four sides, with each side measuring 1 metre, has a volume of 1 cubic metre and a surface area of 6 square metres (6 surfaces of 1 square metre each). If each side were now to be doubled in length to 2 metres, the volume would be 8 cubic metres and the surface area 24 square metres (6 surfaces of 4 square metres each). Thus an eightfold increase in capacity has been gained at only a fourfold increase in the container's surface area, and hence an approximate fourfold increase in cost.

Greater efficiency of large machines. Large machines may be more efficient in the sense that more output can be gained for a given amount of inputs. For example, only one worker may be required to operate a machine

Definitions

Economies of scale
When increasing the scale of production leads to a lower cost per unit of output.

Specialisation and division of labour
Where production is broken down into a number of simpler, more specialised tasks, thus allowing workers to acquire a high degree of efficiency.

Indivisibilities
The impossibility of dividing a factor into smaller units.

whether it be large or small. Also, a large machine may make more efficient use of raw materials.

By-products. With production on a large scale, there may be sufficient waste products to enable them to make some by-product.

Multi-stage production. A large factory may be able to take a product through several stages in its manufacture. This saves time and cost moving the semi-finished product from one firm or factory to another. For example, a large cardboard-manufacturing firm may be able to convert trees or waste paper into cardboard and then into cardboard boxes in a continuous sequence.

All the above are examples of plant economies of scale. They are due to an individual factory or workplace or machine being large. There are other economies of scale that are associated with the *firm* being large – perhaps with many factories.

Organisational economies. With a large firm, individual plants can specialise in particular functions. There can also be centralised administration of the firms. Often, after a merger between two firms, savings can be made by rationalising their activities in this way.

Spreading overheads. There are some expenditures that are only economic when the *firm* is large, such as research and development: only a large firm can afford to set up a research laboratory. This is another example of indivisibilities, only this time at the level of the firm rather than the plant. The greater the firm's output, the more these overhead costs are spread.

Financial economies. Large firms may be able to obtain finance at lower interest rates than small firms. They may be able to obtain certain inputs cheaper by buying in bulk. (These are examples of economies of scale which are *not* the result of increasing returns to scale.)

Diseconomies of scale

When firms get beyond a certain size, costs per unit of output may start to increase. There are several reasons for such diseconomies of scale:

- Management problems of co-ordination may increase as the firm becomes larger and more complex, and as lines of communication get longer. There may be a lack of personal involvement by management.
- Workers may feel 'alienated' if their jobs are boring and repetitive, and if they feel an insignificantly small part of a large organisation. Poor motivation may lead to shoddy work.
- Industrial relations may deteriorate as a result of these factors and also as a result of the more complex interrelationships between different categories of worker.
- Production-line processes and the complex interdependencies of mass production can lead to great disruption if there are hold-ups in any one part of the firm.

Definitions

Plant economies of scale
Economies of scale that arise because of the large size of the factory.

Rationalisation
The reorganising of production (often after a merger) so as to cut out waste and duplication and generally to reduce costs.

Overheads
Costs arising from the general running of an organisation, and only indirectly related to the level of output.

Diseconomies of scale
Where costs per unit of output increase as the scale of production increases.

External economies of scale
Where a firm's costs per unit of output decrease as the size of the whole *industry* grows.

FIGURE 3.3
Alternative long-run average cost curves
(a) Economies of scale
(b) Diseconomies of scale
(c) Constant costs

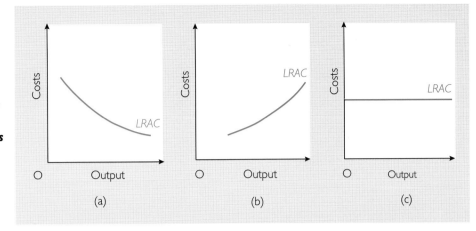

Industry's infrastructure
The network of supply agents, communications, skills, training facilities, distribution channels, specialised financial services, etc. that supports a particular industry.

External diseconomies of scale
Where a firm's costs per unit of output increase as the size of the whole industry increases.

Long-run average cost curve
A curve that shows how average cost varies with output on the assumption that *all* factors are variable. (It is assumed that the least-cost method of production will be chosen for each output.)

Whether firms experience economies or diseconomies of scale will depend on the conditions applying in each individual firm.

The size of the whole industry

As an *industry* grows in size, this can lead to external economies of scale for its member firms. This is where a firm, whatever its own individual size, benefits from the *whole industry* being large. For example, the firm may benefit from having access to specialist raw material or component suppliers, labour with specific skills, firms that specialise in marketing the finished product, and banks and other financial institutions with experience of the industry's requirements. What we are referring to here is the industry's infrastructure: the facilities, support services, skills and experience that can be shared by its members.

The member firms of a particular industry might, however, experience external diseconomies of scale. For example, as an industry grows larger, this may create a growing shortage of specific raw materials or skilled labour. This will push up their prices, and hence the firms' costs.

Long-run average costs

Since there are no fixed factors in the long run, there are no long-run fixed costs. For example, the firm may rent more land in order to expand its operations. Its rent bill therefore goes up as it expands its output. All costs, then, in the long run are variable costs.

Long-run average cost (*LRAC*) curves can take various shapes. If the firm experiences economies of scale, its *LRAC* curve will fall as the scale of production increases (diagram (a) in Figure 3.3). This, after all, is how we define economies of scale: namely, a reduction in average costs as the scale of production increases. If diseconomies of scale predominate, the *LRAC* curve will rise (diagram (b)). Alternatively, if the firm experiences neither economies nor diseconomies of scale, the *LRAC* curve will be horizontal (diagram (c)).

It is often assumed that as a firm expands, it will initially experience economies of scale and thus face a downward-sloping *LRAC* curve. After a point, however, all such economies will have been achieved and thus the

FIGURE 3.4
A typical long-run average cost curve

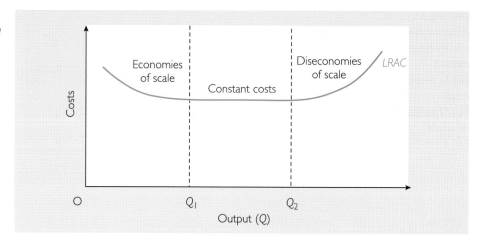

curve will flatten out. Then, possibly after a period of constant *LRAC*, the firm will get so large that it will start experiencing diseconomies of scale and thus a rising *LRAC*. At this stage, production and financial economies begin to be offset by the managerial problems of running a giant organisation.

The effect of this is to give a ∪-shaped or saucer-shaped curve, as in Figure 3.4.

Assumptions behind the long-run average cost curve

There are three key assumptions that we make when constructing long-run average cost curves:

Factor prices are given. At each level of output it is assumed that a firm will be faced with a given set of factor prices. If factor prices *change*, therefore, both short- and long-run cost curves will shift. Thus an increase in wages would shift the curves upwards.

It may be the case, however, that factor prices will be different at *different* levels of output. For example, one of the economies of scale that many firms enjoy is the ability to obtain bulk discount on raw materials and other supplies. In such cases the curve does *not* shift. The different factor prices are merely experienced at different points along the curve, and are reflected in the shape of the curve. Factor prices are still given for any particular level of output.

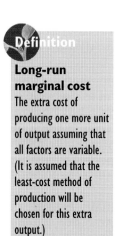

Definition

Long-run marginal cost
The extra cost of producing one more unit of output assuming that all factors are variable. (It is assumed that the least-cost method of production will be chosen for this extra output.)

The state of technology and factor quality are given. These are assumed to change only in the *very* long run (see below, page 88). If a firm gains economies of scale, it is because it is being able to exploit *existing* technologies and make better use of the existing availability of factors of production.

Firms choose the least-cost combination of factors for each output. The assumption here is that firms operate efficiently: that they choose the cheapest possible way of producing any level of output.

Long-run marginal costs

The relationship between long-run average and long-run marginal cost curves is similar to that between short-run average and marginal cost curves.

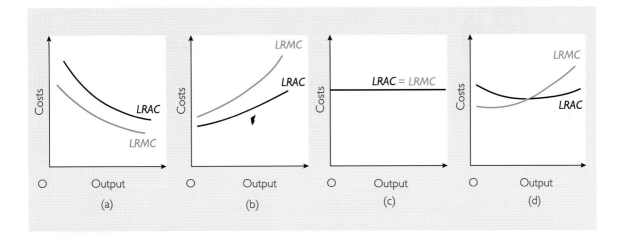

FIGURE 3.5
The relationship between long-run average and marginal costs
(a) Economies of scale
(b) Diseconomies of scale
(c) Constant costs
(d) Initial economies of scale, then diseconomies of scale

If there are economies of scale (diagram (a) in Figure 3.5), additional units of output will add less to costs than the average. The *LRMC* curve must be below the *LRAC* curve and thus pulling the average down as output increases. If there are diseconomies of scale (diagram (b)), additional units of output will cost more than the average. The *LRMC* curve must be above the *LRAC* curve, pulling it up. If there are no economies or diseconomies of scale, so that the *LRAC* curve is horizontal, any additional units of output will cost the same as the average and thus leave the average unaffected (diagram (c)).

The relationship between long-run and short-run average cost curves

Take the case of a firm which has just one factory and faces a short-run average cost curve illustrated by $SRAC_1$ in Figure 3.6.

In the long run, it can build more factories. If it thereby experiences economies of scale (due, say, to savings on administration), each successive factory will allow it to produce with a new lower *SRAC* curve. Thus with two factories it will face curve $SRAC_2$; with three factories curve $SRAC_3$, and so on. Each *SRAC* curve corresponds to a particular amount of the factor that is

FIGURE 3.6
Constructing long-run average cost curves from short-run average cost curves

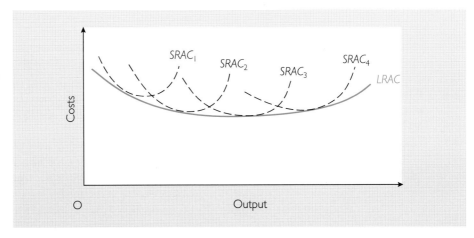

BOX 3.4 *Minimum efficient scale*
....
The extent of economies of scale in practice

One of the most important studies of economies of scale was made in the late 1980s by C. F. Pratten.[1] Pratten found strong evidence that many firms, especially in manufacturing, experienced substantial economies of scale.

In a few cases long-run average costs fell continuously as output increased. For most firms, however, they fell up to a certain level of output and then remained constant.

There are two methods commonly used to measure the extent of economies of scale. The first involves identifying a *minimum efficient scale (MES)*. The *MES* is the size beyond which no significant additional economies of scale can be achieved: in other words, the point where the *LRAC* curve flattens off. In Pratten's studies he defined this level as the minimum scale above which any possible doubling in scale would reduce average costs by less than 5 per cent (i.e. virtually the bottom of the *LRAC* curve). In the diagram *MES* is shown at point *a*.

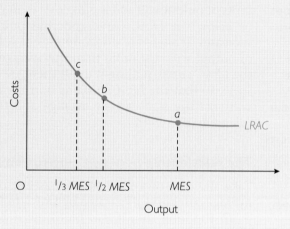

The *MES* can be expressed in terms either of an individual factory or of the whole firm. Where it refers to the minimum efficient scale of an individual factory, the *MES* is known as the *minimum efficient plant size (MEPS)*.

The *MES* can then be expressed as a percentage of the total size of the market or of total domestic production. The table shows *MES* for various plants and firms. The first column shows *MES* as a percentage of total UK production. The second column shows *MES* as a percentage of total EU production.

Expressing *MES* as a percentage of total output gives an indication of how competitive the industry could be. In some industries (such as shoes and tufted carpets), economies of scale were exhausted (i.e. *MES* was reached) with plants or firms that were still small relative to total UK production and even smaller relative to total EU production. In such industries there would be room for many firms and thus scope for considerable competition.

In other industries, however, even if a single plant or firm were large enough to produce the whole output of the industry in the UK, it would still not be large enough to experience the full potential economies of scale: the *MES* is greater than 100 per cent. Examples include factories producing cellulose fibres, and car manufacturers. In such industries there is no possibility of competition. In fact, as long as the *MES* exceeds 50 per

Product	MES as % of production		% additional cost at $\frac{1}{2}$ MES
	UK	EU	
Individual plants			
Cellulose fibres	125	16	3
Rolled aluminium			
semi-manufactures	114	15	15
Refrigerators	85	11	4
Steel	72	10	6
Electric motors	60	6	15
TV sets	40	9	9
Cigarettes	24	6	1.4
Ball-bearings	20	2	6
Beer	12	3	7
Nylon	4	1	12
Bricks	1	0.2	25
Tufted carpets	0.3	0.04	10
Shoes	0.3	0.03	1
Firms			
Cars	200	20	9
Lorries	104	21	7.5
Mainframe			
computers	> 100	n.a.	5
Aircraft	100	n.a.	5
Tractors	98	19	6

Sources: C. F. Pratten (1988); M. Emerson, *The Economics of 1992* (Oxford University Press, 1988).

cent there will not be room for more than one firm large enough to gain full economies of scale. In this case the industry is said to be a *natural monopoly*. As we shall see in the next few chapters, when competition is lacking, consumers may suffer by firms charging prices considerably above costs.

The second way of measuring the extent of economies of scale is to see how much costs would increase if production were reduced to a certain fraction of *MES*. The normal fractions used are $\frac{1}{2}$ or $\frac{1}{3}$ *MES*. This is illustrated in the diagram. Point *b* corresponds to $\frac{1}{2}$ *MES*; point *c* to $\frac{1}{3}$ *MES*. The greater the percentage by which *LRAC* at point *b* or *c* is higher than at point *a*, the greater will be the economies of scale to be gained by producing at *MES* rather than at $\frac{1}{2}$ *MES* or $\frac{1}{3}$ *MES*. For example, in the table there are greater economies of scale to be gained from moving from $\frac{1}{2}$ *MES* to *MES* in the production of electric motors than in cigarettes.

The main purpose of Pratten's study was to determine whether the creation of a large internal EU market with no trade barriers by the end of 1992 would significantly reduce costs and increase competition. The table suggests that in all cases, other things being equal, the EU market is large enough for firms to gain the full economies of scale *and* for there to be enough firms for the market to be competitive.

fixed in the short run: in this case, the factory. (There are many more *SRAC* curves that could be drawn between the ones shown, since factories of different sizes could be built or existing ones could be expanded.)

From this succession of short-run average cost curves we can construct a long-run average cost curve. This is shown in Figure 3.6. This is known as the envelope curve, since it envelops the short-run curves.

Long-run cost curves in practice

Firms do experience economies of scale. Some experience continuously falling *LRAC* curves, as in Figure 3.3(a). Others experience economies of scale up to a certain output and thereafter constant returns to scale.

Evidence is inconclusive on the question of diseconomies of scale. There is little evidence to suggest the existence of *technical* diseconomies, but the possibility of diseconomies due to managerial and industrial relations problems cannot be ruled out.

Some evidence on economies of scale in the UK is considered in Box 3.4.

Postscript: Decision making in different time periods

We have distinguished between the short run and the long run. Let us introduce two more time periods to complete the picture. The complete list then reads as follows.

Very short run (immediate run). All factors are fixed. Output is fixed. The supply curve is vertical. On a day-to-day basis a firm may not be able to vary output at all. For example, a flower seller, once the day's flowers have been purchased from the wholesaler, cannot alter the amount of flowers available for sale on that day. In the very short run, all that may remain for a producer to do is to sell an already produced good.

Short run. At least one factor is fixed in supply. More can be produced, but the firm will come up against the law of diminishing returns as it tries to do so.

Long run. All factors are variable. The firm may experience constant, increasing or decreasing returns to scale. But although all factors can be increased or decreased, they are of a fixed *quality*.

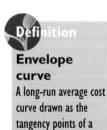

Definition

Envelope curve
A long-run average cost curve drawn as the tangency points of a series of short-run average cost curves.

Very long run. All factors are variable, *and* their quality and hence productivity can change. Labour productivity can increase as a result of education, training, experience and social factors. The productivity of capital can increase as a result of new inventions (new discoveries) and innovation (putting inventions into practice).

Improvements in factor quality will reduce costs and thus shift the short- and long-run cost curves downwards.

Just how long the 'very long run' is will vary from firm to firm. It will depend on how long it takes to develop new techniques, new skills or new work practices.

It is important to realise that decisions *for* all four time periods can be made *at* the same time. Firms do not make short-run decisions *in* the short run and long-run decisions *in* the long run. They can make both short-run and long-run decisions today. For example, assume that a firm experiences an increase in consumer demand and anticipates that it will continue into the foreseeable future. It thus wants to increase output. Consequently, it makes the following four decisions *today*.

- *(Very short run)* It accepts that for a few days it will not be able to increase output. It informs its customers that they will have to wait. It may temporarily raise prices to choke off some of the demand.
- *(Short run)* It negotiates with labour to introduce overtime working as soon as possible, to tide it over the next few weeks. It orders extra raw materials from its suppliers. It launches a recruitment drive for new labour so as to avoid paying overtime longer than is necessary.
- *(Long run)* It starts proceedings to build a new factory. The first step may be to discuss requirements with a firm of consultants.
- *(Very long run)* It institutes a programme of research and development and/or training in an attempt to increase productivity.

Although we distinguish these four time periods, it is the middle two we are primarily concerned with. The reason for this is that there is very little the firm can do in the *very* short run. And in the *very* long run, although the firm will obviously want to increase the productivity of its inputs, it will not be in the position to make precise calculations of how to do it. It will not know precisely what inventions will be made, or just what will be the results of its own research and development.

Summary

1. **In the long run, a firm is able to vary the quantity it uses of all factors of production. There are no fixed factors and hence no long-run fixed costs.**
2. **If it increases all factors by the same proportion, it may experience constant, increasing or decreasing returns to scale.**
3. **Economies of scale occur when costs per unit of output fall as the scale of production increases. This can be due to a number of factors, some of which are directly due to increasing (physical) returns to scale. These include the benefits of specialisation and division of labour, the use of**

larger and more efficient machines, and the ability to have a more integrated system of production. Other economies of scale arise from the financial and administrative benefits of large-scale organisations.

4. When constructing long-run cost curves it is assumed that factor prices are given, that the state of technology is given and that firms will choose the least-cost method of production for each given output.

5. The *LRAC* curve can be downward sloping, upward sloping or horizontal, depending in turn on whether there are economies of scale, diseconomies of scale or neither. Typically *LRAC* curves are drawn as ∪-shaped (sometimes with a flat bottom), or as ∟-shaped. As output expands, initially there are economies of scale. When these are exhausted the curve will become flat. When the firm becomes very large it may begin to experience diseconomies of scale. If this happens, the *LRAC* curve will begin to slope upward again.

6. The long-run marginal cost curve will be below the *LRAC* curve when *LRAC* is falling, above it when *LRAC* is rising and equal to it when *LRAC* is neither rising nor falling.

7. An envelope curve can be drawn which shows the relationship between short-run and long-run average cost curves. The *LRAC* curve envelops the short-run *AC* curves: it is 'tangential' to them (i.e. just touches them).

8. Four distinct time periods can be distinguished. In addition to the short- and long-run periods, we can also distinguish the very-short- and very-long-run periods. The very short run is when all factors are fixed. The very long run is where not only the quantity of factors but also their quality is variable (as a result of changing technology, etc.).

Revenue

How does a firm's revenue vary with its level of sales?

Remember that we defined a firm's total profit (*TΠ*) as its total revenue minus its total costs of production.

$$TΠ = TR - TC$$

In the last two sections we have looked at costs in some detail. We must now turn to the revenue side of the equation. As with costs, we distinguish between three revenue concepts: total revenue (*TR*), average revenue (*AR*) and marginal revenue (*MR*).

Total, average and marginal revenue

Definition

Total revenue
A firm's total earnings from a specified level of sales within a specified period: $TR = P \times Q$.

Total revenue (*TR*)
Total revenue is the firm's total earnings per period of time from the sale of a particular amount of output (*Q*).

For example, if a firm sells 1000 units (*Q*) per month at a price of £5 each (*P*), then its monthly total revenue will be £5000: in other words, £5 × 1000 (*P* × *Q*). Thus:

$$TR = P \times Q$$

Average revenue (AR)

Average revenue is the amount that the firm earns per unit sold. Thus:

$$AR = TR/Q$$

So if the firm earns £5000 (*TR*) from selling 1000 units (*Q*), it will earn £5 per unit. But this is simply the price! Thus:

$$AR = P$$

(The only exception to this is when the firm is selling its products at different prices to different consumers. In this case *AR* is simply the (weighted) average price.)

Marginal revenue (MR)

Marginal revenue is the extra total revenue gained by selling one more unit (per time period). So if a firm sells an extra 20 units this month compared with what it expected to sell, and in the process earns an extra £100, then it is getting an extra £5 for each extra unit sold: *MR* = £5. Thus:

$$MR = \Delta TR/\Delta Q$$

We now need to see how each of these three revenue concepts (*TR*, *AR* and *MR*) varies with output. We can show this relationship graphically in the same way as we did with costs.

The relationship will depend on the market conditions under which a firm operates. A firm which is too small to be able to affect market price will have different-looking revenue curves from a firm which is able to choose the price it charges. Let us examine each of these two situations in turn.

Revenue curves when price is not affected by the firm's output

Average revenue
Total revenue per unit of output. When all output is sold at the same price, average revenue will be the same as price: $AR = TR/Q = P$.

Marginal revenue
The extra revenue gained by selling one more unit per period of time: $MR = \Delta TR/\Delta Q$.

Price taker
A firm that is too small to be able to influence the market price.

Average revenue

If a firm is very small relative to the whole market, it is likely to be a **price taker**. That is, it has to accept the price given by the intersection of demand and supply in the whole market. But, being so small, it can sell as much as it is capable of producing at that price. This is illustrated in Figure 3.7.

The left-hand diagram shows market demand and supply. Equilibrium price is £5. The right-hand diagram looks at the demand for an individual firm which is tiny relative to the whole market. (Look at the difference in the scale of the horizontal axes in the two diagrams.)

Being so small, any change in its output will be too insignificant to affect the market price. It thus faces a horizontal demand 'curve' at this price. It can sell 200 units, 600 units, 1200 units or whatever without affecting this £5 price.

Average revenue is thus constant at £5. The firm's average revenue curve must therefore lie along exactly the same line as its demand curve.

Marginal revenue

In the case of a horizontal demand curve, the marginal revenue curve will be the same as the average revenue curve, since selling one more unit at a constant price (*AR*) merely adds that amount to total revenue. If an extra unit is sold at a constant price of £5, an extra £5 is earned.

FIGURE 3.7
Deriving a firm's
AR and MR:
price-taking firm
(a) The market
(b) The firm

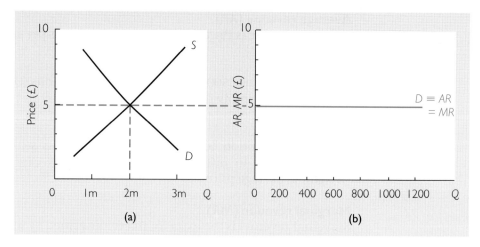

(a)   (b)

Total revenue
Table 3.4 shows the effect on total revenue of different levels of sales with a constant price of £5 per unit.

As price is constant, total revenue will rise at a constant rate as more is sold. The *TR* 'curve' will therefore be a straight line through the origin, as in Figure 3.8.

Revenue curves when price varies with output

The three curves (*TR*, *AR* and *MR*) will look quite different when price does vary with the firm's output.

If a firm has a relatively large share of the market, it will face a downward-sloping demand curve. This means that if it is to sell more, it must lower the price. But it could also choose to raise its price. If it does so, however, it will have to accept a fall in sales.

Average revenue
Remember that average revenue equals price. If, therefore, the price has to be reduced to sell more output, average revenue will fall as output increases.

Table 3.5 gives an example of a firm facing a downward-sloping demand curve. The demand curve (which shows how much is sold at each price) is given by the first two columns.

TABLE 3.4 Deriving total revenue: the firm is a price taker

Quantity (units)	Price ≡ AR = MR(£)	TR (£)
0	5	0
200	5	1000
400	5	2000
600	5	3000
800	5	4000
1000	5	5000
1200	5	6000
.	.	.

FIGURE 3.8
Total revenue curve for a price-taking firm

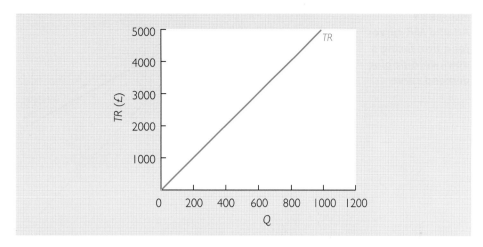

Note that, as in the case of a price-taking firm, the demand curve and the *AR* curve lie along exactly the same line (see Figure 3.9). The reason for this is simple: *AR = P*, and thus the curve relating price to quantity (the demand curve) must be the same as that relating average revenue to quantity (the *AR* curve).

Marginal revenue

When a firm faces a downward-sloping demand curve, marginal revenue will be less than average revenue, and may even be negative. But why?

If a firm is to sell more per time period, it must lower its price (assuming it does not advertise). This will mean lowering the price not just for the extra units it hopes to sell, but also for those units it would have sold had it not lowered the price.

Thus the marginal revenue is the price at which it sells the last unit, *minus* the loss in revenue it has incurred by reducing the price on those units it could otherwise have sold at the higher price. This can be illustrated with Table 3.5.

Assume that price is currently £7. Two units are thus sold. The firm now wishes to sell an extra unit. It lowers the price to £6. It thus gains £6 from the sale of the third unit, but loses £2 by having to reduce the price by £1 on the two units it could otherwise have sold at £7. Its net gain is therefore £6 − £2 = £4. This is the marginal revenue: it is the extra revenue gained by the firm from selling one more unit.

TABLE 3.5 Revenues for a firm facing a downward-sloping demand curve

Q (units)	P = AR (£)	TR (£)	MR (£)
1	8	8	
			6
2	7	14	
			4
3	6	18	
			2
4	5	20	
			0
5	4	20	
			−2
6	3	18	
			−4
7	2	14	
.	.	.	.

FIGURE 3.9
AR and MR curves for a firm facing a downward-sloping demand curve

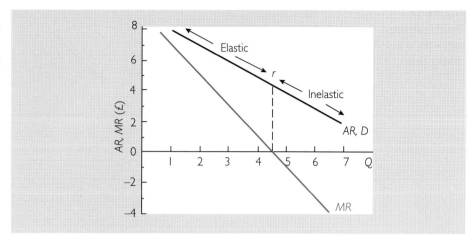

There is a simple relationship between marginal revenue and *price elasticity of demand*. Remember from Chapter 2 (page 47) that if demand is price elastic, a *decrease* in price will lead to a proportionately larger increase in the quantity demanded and hence to an *increase* in revenue. Marginal revenue will thus be positive. If, however, demand is inelastic, a decrease in price will lead to a proportionately smaller increase in sales. In this case the price reduction will more than offset the increase in sales and as a result revenue will fall. Marginal revenue will be negative.

If, then, marginal revenue is a positive figure (i.e. if sales per time period are 4 units or less in Figure 3.9), the demand curve will be elastic at that quantity, since a rise in quantity sold (as a result of a reduction in price) would lead to a rise in total revenue. If, on the other hand, marginal revenue is negative (i.e. at a level of sales of 5 or more units in Figure 3.9), the demand curve will be inelastic at that quantity, since a rise in quantity sold would lead to a *fall* in total revenue.

Thus the demand (*AR*) curve of Figure 3.9 is elastic to the left of point *r* and inelastic to the right.

Total revenue

Total revenue equals price times quantity. This is illustrated in Table 3.5. The *TR* column from Table 3.5 is plotted in Figure 3.10.

Unlike the case of a price-taking firm, the *TR* curve is not a straight line. It is a curve that rises at first and then falls. But why? As long as marginal revenue is positive (and hence demand is price elastic), a rise in output will raise total revenue. However, once marginal revenue becomes negative (and hence demand is inelastic), total revenue will fall. The peak of the *TR* curve will be where *MR* = 0. At this point the price elasticity of demand will be equal to –1.

Shifts in revenue curves

We saw in Chapter 1 that a change in *price* will cause a movement along a demand curve. It is similar with revenue curves, except that here the causal connection is in the other direction. Here we ask what happens to revenue

FIGURE 3.10
Total revenue for a firm facing a downward-sloping demand curve

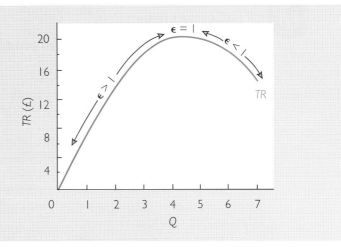

when there is a change in the firm's *output*. Again the effect is shown by a movement along the curves.

The effect of a change in any *other* determinant of demand, such as tastes, income or the price of other goods, will shift the demand curve. By affecting the price at which each level of output can be sold, there will be a shift in all three revenue curves. An increase in revenue is shown by a vertical shift upward; a decrease by a shift downward.

Summary

1. Total revenue (*TR*) is the total amount a firm earns from its sales in a given time period. It is simply price times quantity: $TR = P \times Q$.
2. Average revenue (*AR*) is total revenue per unit: $AR = TR/Q$. In other words, $AR = P$.
3. Marginal revenue is the extra revenue earned from the sale of one more unit per time period: $MR = \Delta TR / \Delta Q$.
4. The *AR* curve will be the same as the demand curve for the firm's product. In the case of a price taker, the demand curve and hence the *AR* curve will be a horizontal straight line and will also be the same as the *MR* curve. The *TR* curve is an upward-sloping straight line from the origin.
5. A firm that faces a downward-sloping demand curve must obviously also face the same downward-sloping *AR* curve. The *MR* curve will also slope downwards, but will be below the *AR* curve and steeper than it. The *TR* curve will be an arch shape starting from the origin.
6. When demand is price elastic, marginal revenue will be positive and the *TR* curve will be upward sloping. When demand is price inelastic, marginal revenue will be negative and the *TR* curve will be downward sloping.
7. A change in output is represented by a movement along the revenue curves. A change in any other determinant of revenue will shift the curves up or down.

3.4 Profit maximisation

How much output should a firm produce if it wants to maximize its profit?

We are now in a position to put costs and revenue together to find the output at which profit is maximised, and also to find out how much that profit will be.

There are two ways of doing this. The first and simpler method is to use total cost and total revenue curves. The second method is to use marginal and average cost and marginal and average revenue curves. Although this method is a little more complicated (but only a little!), it is more useful when we come to compare profit maximising under different market conditions (see Chapter 4).

We will look at each method in turn. In both cases we will concentrate on the short run: namely, that period in which one or more factors are fixed in supply. In both cases we take the case of a firm facing a downward-sloping demand curve.

Short-run profit maximisation: using total curves

Table 3.6 shows the total revenue figures from Table 3.5. It also shows figures for total cost. These figures have been chosen so as to produce a *TC* curve of a typical shape.

Total profit (*TΠ*) is found by subtracting *TC* from *TR*. Check this out by examining the table. Where *TΠ* is negative, the firm is making a loss. Total profit is maximised at an output of 3 units: namely, where there is the greatest gap between total revenue and total costs. At this output, total profit is £4 (£18 − £14).

The *TR*, *TC* and *TΠ* curves are plotted in Figure 3.11. The size of the maximum profit is shown by the arrows.

Short-run profit maximisation: using average and marginal curves

Table 3.7 is based on the figures in Table 3.6.

TABLE 3.6 *Total revenue, total cost and total profit*

Q (units)	TR (£)	TC (£)	TΠ (£)
0	0	6	−6
1	8	10	−2
2	14	12	2
3	18	14	4
4	20	18	2
5	20	25	−5
6	18	36	−18
7	14	56	−42
.	.	.	.

FIGURE 3.11
Finding maximum profit using totals curve

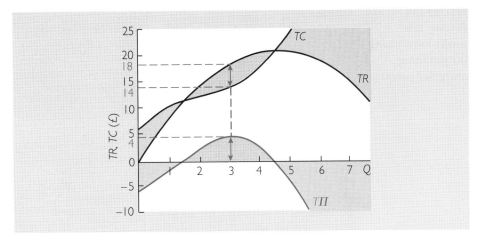

Finding the maximum profit a firm can make is a two-stage process. The first stage is to find the profit-maximising output. To do this we use the *MC* and *MR* curves. The second stage is to find out just how much profit is at this output. To do this we use the *AR* and *AC* curves.

Stage 1: Using marginal curves to arrive at the profit-maximising output
There is a very simple **profit-maximising rule**: if profits are to be maximised, *MR must equal MC*. From Table 3.7 it can be seen that *MR = MC* at an output of 3. This is shown as point *e* in Figure 3.12.

But why are profits maximised when *MR = MC*? The simplest way of answering this is to see what the position would be if *MR* did not equal *MC*.

Referring to Figure 3.12, at a level of output below 3, *MR* exceeds *MC*. This means that by producing more units there will be a bigger addition to revenue (*MR*) than to cost (*MC*). Total profit will *increase*. As long as MR *exceeds MC, profit can be increased by increasing production.*

At a level of output above 3, *MC* exceeds *MR*. All levels of output above 3 thus add more to cost than to revenue and hence *reduce* profit. As long as MC *exceeds MR, profit can be increased by cutting back on production.*

Profits are thus maximised where *MC = MR*: at an output of 3. This can be confirmed by reference to the *TΠ* column in Table 3.7.

Definition

Profit-maximising rule
Profit is maximised where marginal revenue equals marginal cost.

TABLE 3.7 Revenue, cost and profit

Q (units)	P = AR (£)	TR (£)	MR (£)	TC (£)	AC (£)	MC (£)	TΠ (£)	AΠ (£)
0	9	0		6	–		−6	–
			8			4		
1	8	8		10	10		...	−2
			...			2		
2	7	14		12	...		2	1
			4			2		
3	6	18		14	4²/₃		4	1 1/3
			2			4		
4	5	20		18	4¹/₂		2	1/2
			0			7		
5	4	20		25	5		−5	−1
			−2			...		
6	3	18		36	...		...	...
			...			20		
7	2	14		56	8		−42	−6
.	.	.	.	.	.	.	.	.

FIGURE 3.12
Finding the profit-maximising output using marginal curves

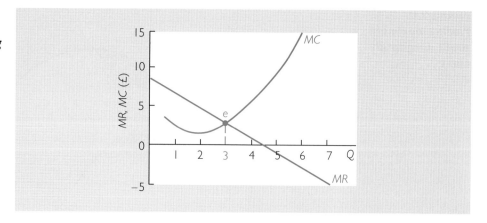

Students worry sometimes about the argument that profits are maximised when $MR = MC$. Surely, they say, if the last unit is making no profit, how can profit be at a *maximum*? The answer is very simple. If you cannot *add* anything more to a total, the total must be at the maximum. Take the simple analogy of going up a hill. When you cannot go any higher, you must be at the top.

Stage 2: Using average curves to measure the size of the profit

Once the profit-maximising output has been discovered, we now use the average curves to measure the *amount* of profit at the maximum. Both marginal and average curves corresponding to the data in Table 3.7 are plotted in Figure 3.13.

First, average profit ($A\Pi$) is found. This is simply $AR - AC$. At the profit-maximising output of 3, this gives a figure for $A\Pi$ of £6 – £4^2/$_3$ = £1^1/$_3$. Then total profit is obtained by multiplying average profit by output:

$$T\Pi = A\Pi \times Q$$

This is shown as the shaded area. It equals £1^1/$_3$ × 3 = £4. This can again be confirmed by reference to the $T\Pi$ column in Table 3.7.

Some qualifications

Long-run profit maximisation

Assuming that the AR and MR curves are the same in the long run as in the short run, long-run profits will be maximised at the output where MR equals the *long-run MC*. The reasoning is the same as with the short-run case.

The meaning of 'profit'

One element of cost is the opportunity cost (see page 6) to the owners of the firm of being in business. This is the minimum return that the owners must make on their capital in order to prevent them from eventually deciding to close down and perhaps move into some alternative business. It is a *cost* since, just as with wages, rent, etc., it has to be covered if the firm is to continue producing. This opportunity cost to the owners is sometimes known as **normal profit**, and is *included in the cost curves*.

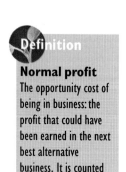

Definition

Normal profit
The opportunity cost of being in business: the profit that could have been earned in the next best alternative business. It is counted as a cost of production.

FIGURE 3.13
*Measuring the
maximum profit
using average
curves*

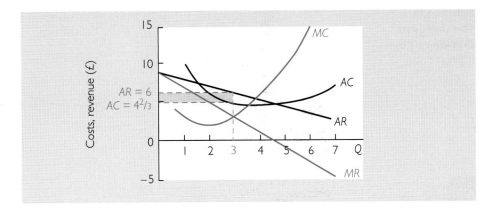

Definitions

**Supernormal
profit**
(also known as pure
profit, economic profit,
abnormal profit,
producer's surplus or
simply profit) The
excess of total profit
above normal profit.

**Short-run shut-
down point**
Where the *AR* curve is
tangential to the *AVC*
curve. The firm can only
just cover its variable
costs. Any fall in revenue
below this level will
cause a profit-
maximising firm to shut
down immediately.

Normal profit is the profit that the owners could have earned in the next best alternative business. If they can earn more than normal profit, they will prefer to stay in this business. If they earn less than normal profit, then after a time they will consider leaving and using their capital for some other purpose.

Given that normal profits are included in costs, any profit that is shown diagrammatically (e.g. the shaded area in Figure 3.13) must therefore be over and above normal profit. It is known by several alternative names: supernormal profit, pure profit, economic profit, abnormal profit, producer's surplus (or sometimes simply profit). They all mean the same thing: the excess of profit over normal profit.

Loss minimising

It may be that there is no output at which the firm can make a profit. Such a situation is illustrated in Figure 10.8: the *AC* curve is above the *AR* curve at all levels of output.

In this case, the output where *MR* = *MC* will be the loss-minimising output. The amount of loss at the point where *MR* = *MC* is shown by the shaded area in Figure 3.14.

Whether or not to produce at all

The short run. Fixed costs have to be paid even if the firm is producing nothing at all. Rent has to be paid, business rates have to be paid, etc.

FIGURE 3.14
*Loss-minimising
output*

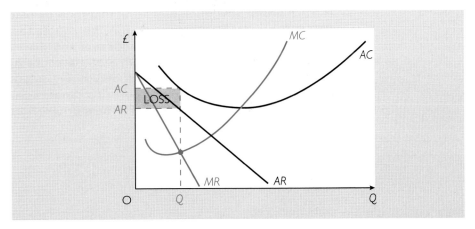

FIGURE 3.15

The short-run shut-down point

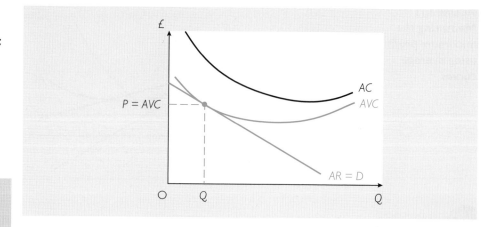

Long-run shut-down point
Where the *AR* curve is tangential to the *LRAC* curve. The firm can just make normal profits. Any fall in revenue below this level will cause a profit-maximising firm to shut down once all costs have become variable.

Providing, therefore, that the firm is more than covering its *variable* costs, it can go some way to paying off these fixed costs and therefore will continue to produce.

It will shut down if it cannot cover its variable costs: that is, if the *AVC* curve is above, or the *AR* curve is below, that illustrated in Figure 3.15. This situation is known as the short-run shut-down point.

The long run. All costs are variable in the long run. If, therefore, the firm cannot cover its long-run average costs (which include normal profit), it will close down. The long-run shut-down point will be where the *AR* curve is tangential to (i.e. just touches) the *LRAC* curve.

Summary

1. **Total profit equals total revenue minus total cost. By definition, then, a firm's profits will be maximised at the point where there is the greatest gap between total revenue and total cost.**
2. **Another way of finding the maximum-profit point is to find the output where marginal revenue equals marginal cost. Having found this output, the level of maximum profit can be found by finding the average profit (*AR* – *AC*) and then multiplying it by the level of output.**
3. **Normal profit is the minimum profit that must be made to persuade a firm to stay in business in the long run. It is counted as part of the firm's costs. Supernormal profit is any profit over and above normal profit.**
4. **For a firm that cannot make a profit at any level of output, the point where *MR* = *MC* represents the loss-minimising output.**
5. **In the short run, a firm will close down if it cannot cover its variable costs. In the long run, it will close down if it cannot make normal profits.**

Questions

1. Up to roughly how long is the short run in the following cases?
   (a) A mobile disco firm.
   (b) Electricity power generation.
   (c) A small grocery retailing business.
   (d) 'Superstore Hypermarkets plc'.
   In each case specify your assumptions.

2. Given that there is a fixed supply of land in the world, what implications can you draw from the law of diminishing returns about the effects of an increase in world population for food output per head?

3. The following are some costs incurred by a shoe manufacturer. Decide whether each one is a fixed cost or a variable cost or has some element of both.
   (a) The cost of leather.
   (b) The fee paid to an advertising agency.
   (c) Wear and tear on machinery.
   (d) Business rates on the factory.
   (e) Electricity for heating and lighting.
   (f) Electricity for running the machines.
   (g) Basic minimum wages agreed with the union.
   (h) Overtime pay.
   (i) Depreciation of machines as a result purely of their age (irrespective of their condition).

4. What economies of scale is a large department store likely to experience?

5. Why are many firms likely to experience economies of scale up to a certain size and then diseconomies of scale after some point beyond that?

6. Name some industries where external economies of scale are gained. What are the specific external economies in each case?

7. Examine Figure 3.3 (on page 85). What would (a) the firm's long-run total cost curve, and (b) its long-run marginal cost curve look like in each of these three cases?

8. Under what circumstances is a firm likely to experience a flat-bottomed *LRAC* curve?

9. Draw a downward-sloping demand curve. Now put in scales of your own choosing for both axes. Read off various points on the demand curve and use them to construct a table showing price and quantity. Use this table to work out the figures for a marginal revenue column. Now use these figures to draw an *MR* curve.

10. Copy Figures 3.9 and 3.10 (which are based on Table 3.5). Now assume that incomes have risen and that, as a result, two more units per time period can be sold at each price. Draw a new table and plot the

resulting new *AR*, *MR* and *TR* curves on your diagrams. Are the new curves parallel to the old ones? Explain.

11. What can we say about the slope of the *TR* and *TC* curves at the maximum-profit point? What does this tell us about marginal revenue and marginal cost?

12. From the information given in the following table, construct a table like Table 3.7.

Q	0	1	2	3	4	5	6	7
P	12	11	10	9	8	7	6	5
TC	2	6	9	12	16	21	28	38

Use your table to draw diagrams like Figures 3.11 and 3.13. Use these two diagrams to show the profit-maximising output and the level of maximum profit. Confirm your findings by reference to the table you have constructed.

13. Normal profits are regarded as a cost (and are included in the cost curves). Explain why.

14. What determines the size of normal profit? Will it vary with the general state of the economy?

15. A firm will continue producing in the short run even if it is making a loss, providing it can cover its variable costs. Explain why. Just how long will it be willing to continue making such a loss?

16. The price of pocket calculators and digital watches fell significantly in the years after they were first introduced, and at the same time demand for them increased substantially. Use cost and revenue diagrams to illustrate these events. Explain the reasoning behind the diagram(s) you have drawn.

chapter four

Market structures

As we saw in section 3.4, a firm's profits are maximised where its marginal cost equals its marginal revenue: *MC = MR.* But we will want to know more than this.

What determines the *amount* of profit that a firm will make? Will its profits be large, or just enough for it to survive, or so low that it will be forced out of business? Will the price charged to the consumer be high or low? And, more generally, will the consumer benefit from the decisions a firm makes?

The answers to these questions depend on the amount of *competition* that a firm faces. A firm in a highly competitive environment will behave quite differently from a firm facing little or no competition. In particular, a firm facing competition from many other firms will have very little, if any, command over prices. Normally, under these circumstances, we would expect the consumer to gain: the competition will tend to keep prices down.

Even if a firm faces only one or two rivals, competition *might* be quite intense. Firms might put a lot of effort into producing more efficiently or into developing new or better products in order to gain a larger share of the market. They may, however, collude with each other to keep prices up.

In this chapter we look at different types of market and how well they serve the consumer.

The degree of competition

How much competition does a firm face?

As we saw in section 3.4, a firm's profits are maximised where its marginal cost equals its marginal revenue: $MC = MR$. But we will want to know more than this.

- What determines the *amount* of profit that a firm will make? Will profits be large, or just enough for the firm to survive, or so low that it will be forced out of business?
- Will the firm produce a high level of output or a low level?
- Will it be producing efficiently?
- Will the price charged to the consumer be high or low?
- And, more generally, will the consumer benefit from the decisions a firm makes?

The answers to all these questions depend on the amount of *competition* that a firm faces. A firm in a highly competitive environment will behave quite differently from a firm facing little or no competition.

It is traditional to divide industries into categories according to the degree of competition that exists between the firms within the industry. There are four such categories.

At one extreme is **perfect competition** where there are very many firms competing. Each firm is so small relative to the whole industry that it has no power to influence price. It is a price taker. At the other extreme is **monopoly**, where there is just one firm in the industry, and hence no competition from *within* the industry. In the middle come **monopolistic competition**, where there are quite a lot of firms competing and where there is freedom for new firms to enter the industry, and **oligopoly**, where there are only a few firms and where entry of new firms is restricted.

To distinguish more precisely between these four categories, the following must be considered:

- The freedom with which firms can enter the industry. Is entry free or restricted? If it is restricted, just how great are the barriers to the entry of new firms?
- The nature of the product. Do all firms produce an identical product, or do firms produce their own particular brand or model or variety?
- The degree of control the firm has over price. Is the firm a price taker or does it have the freedom to choose its price, and if it does, how will changing its price affect its profits? What we are talking about here is the nature of the demand curve it faces. How elastic is it? If the firm puts up its price, will it lose (a) all its sales (a horizontal demand curve), or (b) a large proportion of its sales (a relatively elastic demand curve), or (c) just a small proportion of its sales (a relatively inelastic demand curve)?

Table 4.1 shows the differences between the four categories.

The market structure under which a firm operates will determine its behaviour. Firms under perfect competition will behave quite differently

Definitions

Perfect competition
A market structure where there are many firms; where there is freedom of entry into the industry; where all firms produce an identical product; and where all firms are price takers.

Monopoly
A market structure where there is only one firm in the industry.

Monopolistic competition
A market structure where, like perfect competition, there are many firms and freedom of entry into the industry, but where each firm produces a differentiated product and thus has some control over its price.

Oligopoly
A market structure where there are few enough firms to enable barriers to be erected against the entry of new firms.

TABLE 4.1 *Features of the four market structures*

Type of market	Number of firms	Freedom of entry	Nature of product	Examples	Implication for demand curve for firm
Perfect competition	Very many	Unrestricted	Homogeneous (undifferentiated)	Cabbages, carrots (these approximate to perfect competition)	Horizontal. The firm is a price taker
Monopolistic competition	Many/several	Unrestricted	Differentiated	Plumbers, restaurants	Downward sloping, but relatively elastic. The firm has some control over price
Oligopoly	Few	Restricted	1. Undifferentiated or 2. Differentiated	1. Cement 2. Cars, electrical appliances	Downward sloping, relatively inelastic but depends on reactions of rivals to a price change
Monopoly	One	Restricted or completely blocked	Unique	British Gas (in many parts of Britain), local water company	Downward sloping, more inelastic than oligopoly. The firm has considerable control over price

from firms that are monopolists, which will behave differently again from firms under oligopoly or monopolistic competition.

This behaviour (or 'conduct') will in turn affect the firm's performance: its prices, profits, efficiency, etc. In many cases it will also affect other firms' performance: *their* prices, profits, efficiency, etc. The collective conduct of all the firms in the industry will affect the whole industry's performance.

Economists thus see a causal chain running from market structure to the performance of that industry.

Structure → Conduct → Performance

First we shall look at the two extreme market structures: perfect competition and monopoly (sections 4.2 and 4.3). Then we shall turn to look at the two intermediate cases of monopolistic competition and oligopoly (sections 4.4 and 4.5).

These two intermediate cases are sometimes referred to collectively as imperfect competition. The vast majority of firms in the real world operate under imperfect competition. It is still worth studying the two extreme cases, however, because they provide a framework within which to understand the real world. Some industries tend more to the competitive extreme, and thus their performance corresponds to some extent to perfect competition. Other industries tend more to the other extreme: for example, when there is one dominant firm and a few much smaller firms. In such cases their performance corresponds more to monopoly.

Definition

Imperfect competition
The collective name for monopolistic competition and oligopoly.

Summary

1. There are four alternative market structures under which firms operate. In ascending order of firms' market power, they are: perfect competition, monopolistic competition, oligopoly and monopoly.
2. The market structure under which a firm operates will affect its conduct and its performance.

4.2 Perfect competition

What happens when there are very many firms all competing against each other? Is this good for us as consumers?

The theory of perfect competition illustrates an extreme form of capitalism. In it, firms are entirely subject to market forces. They have no power whatsoever to affect the price of the product. The price they face is that determined by the interaction of demand and supply in the whole *market*.

Assumptions

The model of perfect competition is built on four assumptions:

- There is *a very large number of firms* in the industry. As a result, the individual firm produces an insignificantly small portion of total industry supply, and therefore will not affect price. The firm is thus a price taker. It faces a *horizontal demand 'curve'*.
- There is complete *freedom of entry* of new firms into the industry. Existing firms are unable to stop new firms setting up in business. Setting up a business takes time, however. Freedom of entry, therefore, applies in the long run.
- All firms produce an *identical product*. (The product is 'homogeneous'.) There is therefore no branding or advertising.
- Producers and consumers have *perfect knowledge* of the market. That is, producers are fully aware of prices, costs and market opportunities. Consumers are fully aware of price, quality and availability of the product.

These assumptions are very strict. Few, if any, industries in the real world meet these conditions. Certain agricultural markets are perhaps closest to perfect competition. The market for certain fresh vegetables, such as potatoes, is an example. A potato grower is likely to face competition from so many others that he or she cannot affect the market price of any given variety of potatoes; there is freedom for farmers to set up in business growing potatoes; for any variety and grade of potatoes, each farmer produces a virtually identical product (potatoes are not branded by grower); knowledge of the market by both producers and consumers is very good.

The short-run equilibrium of the firm

The determination of price, output and profit in the short run under perfect competition can best be shown in a diagram.

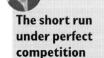

Definition

The short run under perfect competition
The period during which there is too little time for new firms to enter the industry.

FIGURE 4.1
Short-run equilibrium of industry and firm under perfect competition (a) Industry (b) Firm

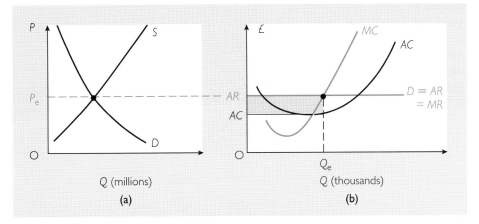

Figure 4.1 shows a short-run equilibrium for both industry and a firm under perfect competition. Both parts of the diagram have the same scale for the vertical axis. The horizontal axes have totally different scales, however. For example, if the horizontal axis for the firm were measured in, say, thousands of units, the horizontal axis for the whole industry might be measured in millions or tens of millions of units, depending on the number of firms in the industry.

Let us examine the determination of price, output and profit in turn.

Price
The price is determined in the industry by the intersection of demand and supply. Being a price taker, the firm faces a horizontal demand (or average revenue) 'curve' at this price. It can sell all it can produce at the market price (P_e), but nothing at a price above P_e.

Output
The firm will maximise profit where marginal cost equals marginal revenue ($MR = MC$), at an output of Q_e. Note that, since the price is not affected by the firm's output, marginal revenue will equal price (see page 93). The reason is that the firm is not having to reduce its price in order to sell more. An extra unit produced will therefore earn its full price for the firm. Thus the firm's MR 'curve' and AR 'curve' (= demand 'curve') are the same horizontal straight line.

Profit
If the average cost (AC) curve (which includes normal profit) dips below the average revenue (AR) 'curve', the firm will earn supernormal profit. Supernormal profit per unit at Q_e is the vertical difference between AR and AC at Q_e. Total supernormal profit is the shaded rectangle in Figure 4.1.

The long-run equilibrium of the firm

In the long run, if typical firms are making supernormal profits, new firms will be attracted into the industry. Likewise, if existing firms can make supernormal profits by increasing the scale of their operations, they will do so, since all factors of production are variable in the long run.

Definition

The long run under perfect competition
The period of time which is long enough for new firms to enter the industry.

FIGURE 4.2
*Long-run
equilibrium under
perfect
competition
(a) Industry
(b) Firm*

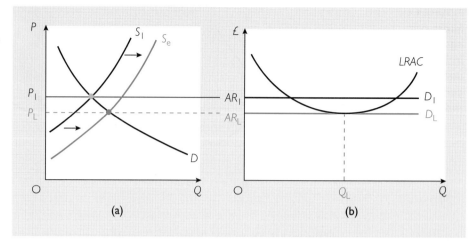

The effect of the entry of new firms and/or the expansion of existing firms is to increase industry supply. This is illustrated in Figure 4.2.

The industry supply curve shifts to the right. This in turn leads to a fall in price. Supply will go on increasing, and price falling, until firms are making only normal profits. This will be when price has fallen to the point where the demand 'curve' for the firm just touches the bottom of its long-run average cost curve. Q_L is thus the long-run equilibrium output of the firm, with P_L the long-run equilibrium price.

Since the *LRAC* curve is tangential to (i.e. just touching) all possible short-run *AC* curves (see section 3.2), the full long-run equilibrium will be as shown in Figure 4.3 where:

$$LRAC = AC = MC = MR = AR$$

The incompatibility of perfect competition and substantial economies of scale

Why is perfect competition so rare in the real world – if it even exists at all? One important reason for this has to do with economies of scale.

In many industries, firms may have to be quite large if they are to experience the full potential economies of scale. But perfect competition requires

FIGURE 4.3
*Long-run
equilibrium of the
firm under perfect
competition*

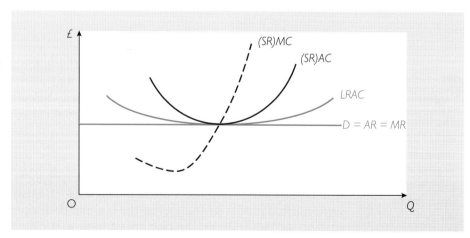

there to be *many* firms. Firms must therefore be small under perfect competition: too small in most cases for economies of scale.

Once a firm expands sufficiently to achieve economies of scale, it will usually gain market power. It will be able to undercut the prices of smaller firms, which will thus be driven out of business. Perfect competition is destroyed.

Perfect competition could exist in any industry, therefore, only if there were no (or virtually no) economies of scale.

Summary

1. The assumptions of perfect competition are: a very large number of firms, complete freedom of entry, a homogeneous product and perfect knowledge of the good and its market by both producers and consumers.
2. In the short run, there is not time for new firms to enter the market, and thus supernormal profits can persist. In the long run, however, any supernormal profits will be competed away by the entry of new firms.
3. The short-run equilibrium for the firm will be where the price, as determined by demand and supply in the market, is equal to marginal cost. At this output the firm will be maximising profit.
4. The long-run equilibrium will be where the market price is just equal to firms' long-run average cost.
5. There can be no substantial economies of scale to be gained in a perfectly competitive industry. If there were, the industry would cease to be perfectly competitive as the large, low-cost firms drove the small, high-cost ones out of business.

Monopoly

What happens when there is only one firm in the market? Do we as consumers suffer?

What is a monopoly?

This may seem a strange question, because the answer seems obvious. A monopoly exists when there is only one firm in the industry.

But whether an industry can be classed as a monopoly is not always clear. It depends how narrowly the industry is defined. For example, Courtaulds has a monopoly on certain types of fabric, but it does not have a monopoly on fabrics in general. The consumer can buy alternative fabrics to those supplied by Courtaulds. A rail company may have a monopoly over rail services between two cities, but it does not have a monopoly over public transport between these two cities. People can travel by coach or air. They could also use private transport.

To some extent, the boundaries of an industry are arbitrary. What is more important for a firm is the amount of monopoly *power* it has, and that depends on the closeness of substitutes produced by rival industries. In many countries, there is a monopoly supplier of electricity. As such it has virtually no rivals in supplying energy for lighting and running many domestic appliances, but in the case of supplying fuel for heating it may have serious rivals in the form of gas, oil and coal.

Barriers to entry

In order for a firm to maintain its monopoly position, there must be barriers to the entry of new firms. As we shall see, barriers also exist under oligopoly, but in the case of monopoly they must be high enough to block the entry of new firms. Barriers can be of various forms.

Economies of scale. If the monopolist's costs go on falling significantly up to the output that satisfies the whole market, the industry may not be able to support more than one producer. This case is known as natural monopoly. It is particularly likely if the market is small. For example, two bus companies might find it unprofitable to serve the same routes, each running with perhaps only half-full buses, whereas one company with a monopoly of the routes could make a profit.

Even if a market could support more than one firm, a new entrant is unlikely to be able to start up on a very large scale. Thus the monopolist that is already experiencing economies of scale can charge a price below the cost of the new entrant and drive it out of business. If, however, the new entrant is a firm already established in another industry, it may be able to survive this competition.

Product differentiation and brand loyalty. If a firm produces a clearly differentiated product, where the consumer associates the product with the brand, it will be very difficult for a new firm to break into that market. This barrier can occur even though the market is potentially big enough for two firms each gaining all the available economies of scale. In other words, the problem for the new firm is not in being able to produce at low enough costs, but in being able to produce a product sufficiently attractive to consumers who are loyal to the familiar brand.

Lower costs for an established firm. An established monopoly is likely to have developed specialised production and marketing skills. It is more likely to be aware of the most efficient techniques and the most reliable and/or cheapest suppliers. It is likely to have access to cheaper finance. It is thus operating on a lower cost curve. New firms would therefore find it hard to compete and would be likely to lose any price war.

Ownership of, or control over, key factors of production. If a firm governs the supply of vital inputs (say, by owning the sole supplier of some component part), it can deny access to these inputs to potential rivals.

Ownership of, or control over, wholesale or retail outlets. Similarly, if a firm controls the outlets through which the product must be sold, it can prevent potential rivals from gaining access to consumers.

Definition

Natural monopoly
A situation where long-run average costs would be lower if an industry were under monopoly than if it were shared between two or more competitors.

Legal protection. The firm's monopoly position may be protected by patents on essential processes, by copyright, by various forms of licensing (allowing, say, only one firm to operate in a particular area) and by tariffs (i.e. customs duties) and other trade restrictions to keep out foreign competitors.

Mergers and takeovers. The monopolist can put in a takeover bid for any new entrant. The sheer threat of takeovers may discourage new entrants.

Aggressive tactics. An established monopolist can probably sustain losses for longer than a new entrant. Thus it could start a price war, mount massive advertising campaigns, offer attractive after-sales service, introduce new brands to compete with new entrants, and so on.

Intimidation. The monopolist may resort to various forms of harassment, legal or illegal, to drive a new entrant out of business.

Equilibrium price and output

Since there is, by definition, only one firm in the industry, the firm's demand curve is also the industry demand curve.

Compared with other market structures, demand under monopoly tend to be less elastic at each price. The monopolist can raise its price and consumers have no alternative firm to turn to within the industry. They either pay the higher price, or go without the good altogether.

Unlike the firm under perfect competition, the monopoly firm is thus a 'price maker'. It can choose what price to charge. Nevertheless, it is still constrained by its demand curve. A rise in price will reduce the quantity demanded. This is illustrated in Figure 4.4.

As with firms in other market structures, a monopolist will maximise profit where $MR = MC$. In Figure 4.4 profit is maximised at Q_m. The super-normal profit obtained is shown by the shaded area.

These profits will tend to be larger the less elastic is the demand curve (and hence the steeper is the MR curve), and thus the bigger is the gap between MR and price (AR). The actual elasticity will depend on whether

FIGURE 4.4
Profit maximising under monopoly

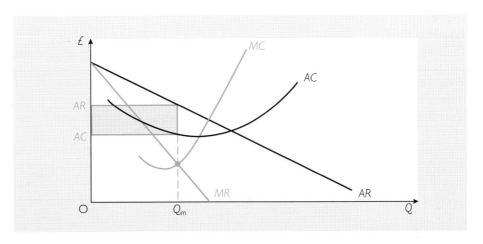

reasonably close substitutes are available in *other* industries. The demand for a rail service will be much less elastic (and the potential for profit greater) if there is no bus service to the same destination.

Since there are barriers to the entry of new firms, a monopolist's super-normal profits will not be competed away in the long run. The only difference, therefore, between short-run and long-run equilibrium is that in the long run the firm will produce where *MR = long-run MC*.

Monopoly versus perfect competition: which best serves the public interest?

Because it faces a different type of market environment, the monopolist will produce a quite different output and at a quite different price from a perfectly competitive industry.

Let us compare the two.

Short-run price and output. Figure 4.5 compares the profit-maximising position for an industry under monopoly with that under perfect competition. Note that we are comparing the monopoly with the whole *industry* under perfect competition. That way we can assume, for sake of comparison, that they both face the same demand curve. We also assume for the moment that they both face the same cost curves.

The monopolist will produce Q_1 at a price of P_1. This is where $MC = MR$. If the same industry were under perfect competition, however, it would produce at Q_2 and P_2 – a higher output and a lower price. But why? The reason for this is that for each of the firms in the industry – and it is at this level that the decisions are made – marginal revenue is the same as price. Remember that the *firm* under perfect competition faces a perfectly elastic demand (*AR*) curve, which also equals *MR* (see Figure 4.1). Thus producing where $MC = MR$ also means producing where $MC = P$. When *all* firms under perfect competition do this, price and quantity in the *industry* will be given by P_2 and Q_2 in Figure 4.5.

In the short run, therefore, it would seem (other things being equal) that perfect competition better serves the consumer's interest than does monopoly.

FIGURE 4.5
Equilibrium of the industry under perfect competition and monopoly: with the same MC curve

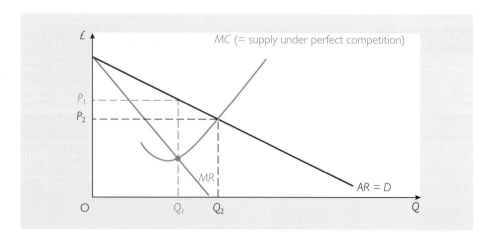

Long-run price and output. Under perfect competition, freedom of entry eliminates supernormal profit and forces firms to produce at the bottom of their *LRAC* curve. The effect, therefore, is to keep long-run prices down. Under monopoly, however, barriers to entry allow profits to remain supernormal in the long run. The monopolist is not forced to operate at the bottom of the *AC* curve. Thus, other things being equal, long-run prices will tend to be higher, and hence output lower, under monopoly.

Thus, again, it would *seem* that perfect competition better serves the consumer's interests. But this assumes that the cost curves will be the *same* under both perfect competition and monopoly. Let us, therefore, turn to costs.

Costs under monopoly. The sheer survival of a firm in the long run under perfect competition requires that it uses the most efficient known technique, and develops new techniques wherever possible. The monopolist, however, sheltered by barriers to entry, can still make large profits even if it is not using the most efficient technique. It has less incentive, therefore, to be efficient. For this reason, costs may be *higher* under monopoly (another criticism of monopoly).

On the other hand, the monopoly may be able to achieve substantial economies of scale due to larger plant, centralised administration and the avoidance of unnecessary duplication (e.g. a monopoly water company would eliminate the need for several sets of rival water mains under each street). If this results in an *MC* curve substantially below that of the same industry under perfect competition, the monopoly may even produce a *higher* output at a *lower* price.

Another reason why a monopolist may operate with lower costs is that it can use part of its supernormal profits for research and development and investment. It may not have the same *incentive* to become efficient as the perfectly competitive firm which is fighting for survival, but it may have a much greater ability to become efficient than has the small firm with limited funds.

Although a monopoly faces no competition in the goods market, it may face an alternative form of competition in financial markets. A monopoly, with potentially low costs, which is currently run inefficiently, is likely to be subject to a takeover bid from another company. This competition for corporate control, as it is called, may thus force the monopoly to be efficient in order to prevent being taken over.

Innovation and new products. The promise of supernormal profits, protected perhaps by patents, may encourage the development of new (monopoly) industries producing new products. It is this chance of making monopoly profits that encourages many people to take the risks of going into business.

Definition

Competition for corporate control
The competition for the control of companies through takeovers.

Potential competition or potential monopoly? The theory of contestable markets

Potential competition
In recent years, economists have developed the theory of contestable markets. This theory argues that what is crucial in determining price and

BOX 4.1

Competition in the pipeline?
....
Monopoly in the supply of gas

Some of the best examples of monopoly in the UK are the privatised utilities such as telecommunications, water and gas. The government, recognising the dangers of high prices and high profits under monopoly, has attempted to introduce competition in various parts of these industries. But in other parts there is no competition: they remain monopolies.

This mixture of competition and monopoly is well illustrated in the UK market for gas. There are three parts to this market: production; storage and distribution; and supply to customers. In production there is considerable competition, with several companies operating in the North Sea. In storage and distribution, however, there is a monopoly. TransCo International owns the expensive gas pipelines and storage facilities. TransCo was formed in 1996 when British Gas (BG) was split into two parts. The other part, British Gas Energy, is involved in supply to the customer. In supply, the market has been gradually opened up to competition.

First, businesses which used large amounts of gas were allowed to buy from alternative suppliers. Initially competitors to BG could only supply customers consuming more than 25 000 therms per year (the typical household consumes about 600 therms). By 1993 this limit had been reduced to 2000 therms, by which time BG's share of the industrial gas market had fallen to 41 per cent (from virtually 100 per cent in 1990).

Then the market for domestic consumers was opened up to competition. In 1996 competitors to BG Energy were allowed to supply the far south-west of England. This was a trial in preparation for opening up the whole of the British domestic market by 1998.

But how do gas suppliers compete, given that TransCo has a monopoly of the pipelines? The answer is that TransCo is required to allow companies to use its pipelines. It charges them a rent for this service. Producers' supply is metered in; the gas used by companies supplying consumers is metered out. This enables the producing companies to charge the customer-supplying companies, and enables TransCo to work out the amount of rent to charge. Typically this accounts for about 40 per cent of the average household bill.

output is not whether an industry is *actually* a monopoly or competitive, but whether there is the real *threat* of competition.

If a monopoly is protected by high barriers to entry – say, that it owns all the raw materials – then it will be able to make supernormal profits with no fear of competition.

If, however, another firm *could* take over from it with little difficulty, it will behave much more like a competitive firm. The threat of competition has a similar effect to actual competition.

As an example, consider a catering company that is given permission by a factory to run its canteen. The catering company has a monopoly over the supply of food to the workers in that factory. If, however, it starts charging high prices or providing a poor service, the factory could offer the running of the canteen to an alternative catering company. This threat may force the original catering company to charge 'reasonable' prices and offer a good service.

One reason for splitting BG was the worry that it would charge very high rents to its competitors, thereby giving itself an unfair advantage. In other words, it would use its monopoly in one part of the industry to prevent fair competition in another part.

One solution to this monopoly problem would be for the government to regulate the size of the rent and to insist that BG charged itself the same rent as its competitors. This was the policy in the early 1990s. OFGAS, the regulatory agency set up by the government at the time of privatisation in 1986, attempted to get BG to charge all customers, including itself, the same rent. After the split, TransCo remains regulated to prevent it using its monopoly power to charge excessive rents or to discriminate unfairly between users of its pipelines.

In addition to being responsible for the safety of the gas system, TransCo operates as a 'supplier of last resort'. For example, if there is an upsurge in demand as a result of the weather turning colder, and there is an immediate need to find new supplies in order to avoid households being cut off, TransCo will come into the market and buy gas on behalf of the supplier, thereby ensuring that there is sufficient gas to meet consumer needs. The price it charges to the suppliers is based on the market price for gas: a price that fluctuates daily with demand and supply.

With TransCo's rental charges firmly and fairly regulated, many of the new potential entrants into the gas supply industry are claiming that they will be able to offer domestic consumers savings of anywhere between 10 per cent and 15 per cent on their current bills. We shall see!

Q1 What possible *advantages* to the consumer could there be in (a) TransCo having a monopoly over gas pipelines; (b) BG Energy remaining a monopoly in the supply of gas to domestic households?

Q2 How would suppliers react if TransCo charged a very high price for providing gas on a last resort basis?

Perfectly contestable markets

A market is **perfectly contestable** when the costs of entry and exit by potential rivals are zero, and when such entry can be made very rapidly. In such cases, the moment the possibility of earning supernormal profits occurs, new firms will enter, thus driving profits down to a normal level. The sheer threat of this happening, so the theory goes, will ensure that the firm already in the market will (a) keep its prices down, so that it just makes normal profits, and (b) produce as efficiently as possible, taking advantage of any economies of scale and any new technology. If the existing firm did not do this, entry would take place, and potential competition would become actual competition.

Contestable markets and natural monopolies

So why in such cases are the markets not *actually* perfectly competitive? Why do they remain monopolies?

Definition

Perfectly contestable market
A market where there is free and costless entry and exit.

The most likely reason has to do with economies of scale and the size of the market. To operate on a minimum efficient scale, the firm may have to be so large relative to the market that there is only room for one such firm in the industry. If a new firm does come into the market, then one or other of the two firms will not survive the competition. The market is simply not big enough for both of them.

If, however, there are no entry or exit costs, new firms will be perfectly willing to enter even though there is only room for one firm, provided they believe that they are more efficient than the existing firm. The existing firm, knowing this, will be forced to produce as efficiently as possible and with only normal profit.

The importance of costless exit

Setting up in a new business usually involves large expenditures on plant and machinery. Once this money has been committed, it becomes fixed costs. If these fixed costs are no higher than those of the existing firm, then the new firm could win the battle. But, of course, there is always the risk that it might lose.

But does losing the battle really matter? Can the firm not simply move to another market?

It does matter if there are substantial costs of exit. This will be the case if the capital equipment cannot be transferred to other uses – for example, a new blast furnace constructed by a new rival steel company. In this case, these fixed costs are known as **sunk costs**. The losing firm is left with capital equipment it cannot use. The firm may therefore be put off entering in the first place. The market is not perfectly contestable, and the established firm can make supernormal profit.

If, however, the capital equipment can be transferred, the exit costs will be zero (or at least very low), and new firms will be more willing to take the risks of entry. For example, a rival coach company may open up a service on a route previously operated by only one company, and where there is still only room for one operator. If the new firm loses the resulting battle, it can still use the coaches it has purchased. It simply uses them for a different route. The cost of the coaches is not a sunk cost.

Costless exit, therefore, encourages firms to enter an industry, knowing that, if unsuccessful, they can always transfer their capital elsewhere.

The lower the exit costs, the more contestable the market. This implies that firms already established in other similar markets may provide more effective competition against monopolists, since they can simply transfer capital from one market to another. For example, studies of airlines in the USA show that entry to a particular route may be much easier for an established airline, which can simply transfer planes from one route to another.

Contestability and the consumer's interests

The more contestable the market, the more will a monopoly be forced to act like a firm under perfect competition. If, therefore, a monopoly operates in a perfectly contestable market, it might bring the 'best of both worlds' for the consumer. Not only will it be able to achieve low costs through economies of scale, but also the potential competition will keep profits and hence prices down.

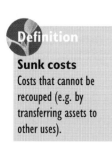

Definition

Sunk costs
Costs that cannot be recouped (e.g. by transferring assets to other uses).

Summary

1. A monopoly is where there is only one firm in an industry. In practice it is difficult to determine where a monopoly exists because it depends on how narrowly an industry is defined.
2. Barriers to the entry of new firms will normally be necessary to protect a monopoly from competition. Such barriers include economies of scale (making the firm a natural monopoly or at least giving it a cost advantage over new (small) competitors), control over supplies of inputs or over outlets, patents or copyright, and tactics to eliminate competition (such as takeovers or aggressive advertising).
3. Profits for the monopolist will be maximised (as for other firms) where *MC = MR*.
4. If demand and cost curves are the same in a monopoly and a perfectly competitive industry, the monopoly will produce a lower output and at a higher price than the perfectly competitive industry.
5. On the other hand, any economies of scale will, in part, be passed on to consumers in lower prices, and the monopolist's high profits may be used for research and development and investment, which in turn may lead to better products at possibly lower prices.
6. Potential competition may be as important as actual competition in determining a firm's price and output strategy.
7. The threat of this competition is greater the lower are the entry and exit costs to and from the industry. If the entry and exit costs are zero, the market is said to be *perfectly* contestable. Under such circumstances an existing monopolist will be forced to keep its profits down to the normal level if it is to resist entry of new firms. Exit costs will be lower, the lower are the sunk costs of the firm.

4.4 Monopolistic competition

What happens if there are quite a lot of firms competing, but each firm tries to attract us to its particular product or service?

Very few markets in practice can be classified as perfectly competitive or as a pure monopoly. The vast majority of firms do compete with other firms, often quite aggressively, and yet they are not price takers: they do have some degree of market power. Most markets, therefore, lie between the two extremes of monopoly and perfect competition, in the realm of 'imperfect competition'. As we saw in section 4.1, there are two types of imperfect competition: namely, monopolistic competition and oligopoly.

Monopolistic competition is nearer to the competitive end of the spectrum. It can best be understood as a situation where there are a lot of firms competing but where each firm does nevertheless have some degree of market power (hence the term 'monopolistic' competition): each firm has some discretion as to what price to charge for its products.

Assumptions of monopolistic competition

- There is *quite a large number of firms*. As a result each firm has an insignificantly small share of the market, and therefore its actions are unlikely to affect its rivals to any great extent. What this means is that each firm in making its decisions does not have to worry how its rivals will react. It assumes that what its rivals choose to do will *not* be influenced by what it does.

    This is known as the assumption of independence. (As we shall see later, this is not the case under oligopoly. There we assume that firms believe that their decisions *do* affect their rivals, and that their rivals' decisions will affect them. Under oligopoly we assume that firms are *inter*dependent.)

- There is *freedom of entry* of new firms into the industry. If any firm wants to set up in business in this market, it is free to do so.

In these two respects, therefore, monopolistic competition is like perfect competition.

- Unlike perfect competition, however, each firm produces a product or provides a service in some way different from its rivals. As a result it can raise its price without losing all its customers. Thus its demand curve is downward sloping, albeit relatively elastic given the large number of competitors to which customers can turn. This is known as the assumption of product differentiation.

    Petrol stations, restaurants, hairdressers and builders are all examples of monopolistic competition.

    A typical feature of monopolistic competition is that, although there are many firms in the industry, there is only one firm in a particular location. This applies particularly in retailing. There may be many greengrocers in a town, but only one in a particular street. In a sense, therefore, it has a local monopoly. People may be prepared to pay higher prices there for their vegetables to avoid having to go elsewhere.

Equilibrium of the firm

Short run

As with other market structures, profits are maximised at the output where $MC = MR$. The diagram will be the same as for the monopolist, except that the AR and MR curves will be more elastic. This is illustrated in Figure 4.6(a). As with perfect competition, it is possible for the monopolistically competitive firm to make supernormal profit in the short run. This is shown as the shaded area.

Just how much profit the firm will make in the short run depends on the strength of demand: the position and elasticity of the demand curve. The further to the right the demand curve is relative to the average cost curve, and the less elastic the demand curve is, the greater will be the firm's short-run profit. Thus a firm whose product is considerably differentiated from its rivals may be able to earn considerable short-run profits.

Long run

If typical firms are earning supernormal profit, new firms will enter the industry in the long run. As new firms enter, they will take some of the

---

Definitions

Independence (of firms in a market)
Where the decisions of one firm in a market will not have any significant effect on the demand curves of its rivals.

Product differentiation
Where one firm's product is sufficiently different from its rivals' to allow it to raise the price of the product without customers all switching to the rivals' products. A situation where a firm faces a downward-sloping demand curve.

FIGURE 4.6
Equilibrium of the firm under monopolistic competition
(a) Short run
(b) Long run

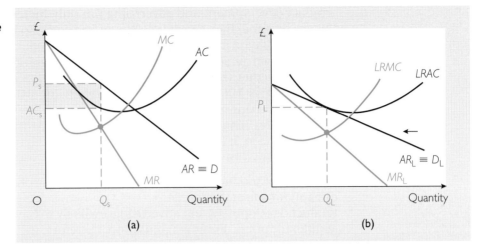

(a)

(b)

customers away from the existing firms. The demand for the existing firms will therefore fall. Their demand (*AR*) curve will shift to the left, and will continue doing so as long as supernormal profits remain and thus new firms continue entering.

Long-run equilibrium will be reached when only normal profits remain: when there is no further incentive for new firms to enter. This is illustrated in Figure 4.6(b). The firm's demand curve settles at D_L, where it is tangential to the firm's *LRAC* curve. Output will be Q_L: where $AR_L = LRAC$. (At any other output, *LRAC* is greater than *AR* and thus less than normal profit would be made.)

Non-price competition

One of the biggest problems with the simple model in Figure 4.6 is that it concentrates on price and output decisions. In practice, the profit-maximising firm under monopolistic competition will also need to decide the exact variety of product to produce and how much to spend on advertising it. This will lead the firm to take part in non-price competition.

Non-price competition involves two major elements: product development and advertising.

The major aims of *product development* are to produce a product that will sell well (i.e. one in high or potentially high demand) and that is different from rivals' products (i.e. has an inelastic demand due to lack of close substitutes). In the case of shops or other firms providing a service, 'product development' will take the form of attempting to provide a service which is better than, or at least different from, that of rivals: personal service, late opening, certain lines stocked, etc.

The major aim of *advertising* is to sell the product. This can be achieved not only by informing the consumer of the product's existence and availability, but also by deliberately trying to persuade consumers to purchase the good. Like product development, successful advertising will both increase demand and also make the firm's demand curve less elastic, since it stresses the specific qualities of this firm's product over its rivals' (see Box 2.3).

Definition

Non-price competition
Competition in terms of product promotion (advertising, packaging, etc.) or product development.

Product development and advertising not only increase a firm's demand and hence revenue, they also involve increased costs. So how much should a firm advertise, say to maximise profits?

For any given price and product, the optimal amount of advertising is where the revenue from *additional* advertising (MR_A) is equal to its cost (MC_A). As long as $MR_A > MC_A$, additional advertising will add to profit. But extra amounts spent on advertising are likely to lead to smaller and smaller increases in sales. Thus MR_A falls, until $MR_A = MC_A$. At that point no further profit can be made. It is at a maximum.

Two problems arise with this analysis:

- The effect of product development and advertising on demand will be difficult for a firm to forecast.
- Product development and advertising are likely to have different effects at different prices. Profit maximisation, therefore, will involve the more complex choice of the optimum combination of price, type of product, and level and variety of advertising.

Monopolistic competition and the public interest

Comparison with perfect competition

It is often argued that monopolistic competition leads to a less efficient allocation of resources than perfect competition.

Figure 4.7 compares the long-run equilibrium positions for two firms. One firm is under perfect competition and thus faces a horizontal demand curve. It will produce an output of Q_1 at a price of P_1. The other is under monopolistic competition and thus faces a downward-sloping demand curve. It will produce the lower output of Q_2 at the higher price of P_2. A crucial assumption here is that a firm would have the *same* long-run average cost (*LRAC*) curve in both cases. Given this assumption, we can make the following two predictions about monopolistic competition:

- Less will be sold and at a higher price.
- Firms will not be producing at the least-cost point.

By producing more than their profit-maximising level of output, firms would move to a lower point on their *LRAC* curve. Thus firms under monopolistic competition are said to have **excess capacity**. In Figure 4.7 this excess capacity is shown as $Q_1 - Q_2$. In other words, monopolistic competition is

FIGURE 4.7
Long-run equilibrium of the firm under perfect and monopolistic competition

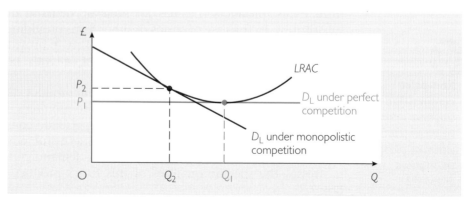

Definition

Excess capacity (under monopolistic competition)
In the long run firms under monopolistic competition will produce at an output below their minimum-cost point.

typified by quite a large number of firms (e.g. petrol stations), all operating at less than optimum output, and thus being forced to charge a price above that which they could charge if they had a bigger turnover. How often have you been to a petrol station and had to queue for the pumps?

So how does this affect the consumer? Although the firm under monopolistic competition may charge a higher price than under perfect competition, the difference may be very small. Although the firm's demand curve is downward sloping, it is still likely to be highly elastic due to the large number of substitutes. Furthermore, the consumer may benefit from monopolistic competition by having a greater variety of products to choose from. Each firm may satisfy some particular requirement of particular consumers.

Comparison with monopoly
The arguments are very similar here to those when comparing perfect competition and monopoly.

On the one hand, freedom of entry for new firms and hence the lack of long-run supernormal profits under monopolistic competition are likely to help keep prices down for the consumer and encourage cost saving. On the other hand, monopolies are likely to achieve greater economies of scale and have more funds for investment and research and development.

Summary

1. Monopolistic competition occurs where there is free entry to the industry and quite a large number of firms operating independently of each other, but where each firm has some market power as a result of producing differentiated products or services.
2. In the short run, firms can make supernormal profits. In the long run, however, freedom of entry will drive profits down to the normal level. The long-run equilibrium of the firm is where the (downward-sloping) demand curve is tangential to the long-run average cost curve.
3. The long-run equilibrium is one of excess capacity. Given that the demand curve is downward sloping, its tangency point with the *LRAC* curve will not be at the bottom of the *LRAC* curve. Increased production would thus be possible at *lower* average cost.
4. In practice, supernormal profits may persist into the long run: firms have imperfect information; entry may not be completely unrestricted; firms may use non-price competition to maintain an advantage over their rivals.
5. Monopolistically competitive firms, because of excess capacity, may have higher costs, and thus higher prices, than perfectly competitive firms, but consumers may gain from a greater diversity of products.
6. Monopolistically competitive firms may have fewer economies of scale than monopolies and conduct less research and development, but the competition may keep prices lower than under monopoly. Whether there will be more or less choice for the consumer is debatable.

4.5 Oligopoly

What happens if there are just a few firms that dominate the market? Will there be fierce competition between them, or will there be a 'cosy' relationship where we as consumers end up paying higher prices?

Oligopoly occurs when just a few firms between them share a large proportion of the industry.

There are, however, significant differences in the structure of industries under oligopoly and similarly significant differences in the behaviour of firms. The firms may produce a virtually identical product (e.g. metals, chemicals, sugar, petrol). Most oligopolists, however, produce differentiated products (e.g. cars, soap powder, cigarettes, electrical appliances). Much of the competition between such oligopolists is in terms of the marketing of their particular brand. Marketing practices may differ considerably from one industry to another.

The two key features of oligopoly

Despite the differences between oligopolies, there are two crucial features that distinguish oligopoly from other market structures.

Barriers to entry

Unlike firms under monopolistic competition, there are various barriers to the entry of new firms. These are similar to those under monopoly (see page 112). The size of the barriers, however, will vary from industry to industry. In some cases entry is relatively easy, whereas in others it is virtually impossible.

Interdependence of the firms

Because there are only a few firms under oligopoly, each firm will have to take account of the others. This means that they are mutually dependent: they are interdependent. Each firm is affected by its rivals' actions. If a firm changes the price or specification of its product, for example, or the amount of its advertising, the sales of its rivals will be affected. The rivals may then respond by changing their price, specification or advertising. No firm can therefore afford to ignore the actions and reactions of other firms in the industry.

It is impossible, therefore, to predict the effect on a firm's sales of, say, a change in its price without first making some assumption about the reactions of other firms. Different assumptions will yield different predictions. For this reason there is no single generally accepted theory of oligopoly. Firms may react differently and unpredictably.

Competition and collusion

Oligopolists are pulled in two different directions:

* The interdependence of firms may make them wish to *collude* with each other. If they can club together and act as if they were a monopoly, they could jointly maximise industry profits.

Definition

Interdependence (under oligopoly) One of the two key features of oligopoly. Each firm will be affected by its rivals' decisions. Likewise its decisions will affect its rivals. Firms recognise this interdependence. This recognition will affect their decisions.

FIGURE 4.8
Profit-maximising cartel

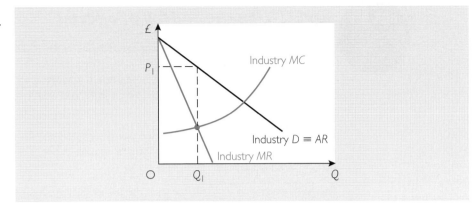

- On the other hand, they will be tempted to *compete* with their rivals to gain a bigger share of industry profits for themselves.

These two policies are incompatible. The more fiercely firms compete to gain a bigger share of industry profits, the smaller these industry profits will become! For example, price competition will drive down the average industry price, while competition through advertising will raise industry costs. Either way, industry profits are likely to be reduced.

Sometimes firms will collude. Sometimes they will not. First we will examine **collusive oligopoly** (both open and tacit), and then **non-collusive oligopoly**.

Equilibrium of industry under collusive oligopoly

When firms under oligopoly engage in collusion, they may agree on prices, market share, advertising expenditure, etc. Such collusion will reduce the uncertainty they face. It will reduce the fear of engaging in competitive price cutting or retaliatory advertising, both of which could reduce total industry profits.

A formal collusive agreement is called a **cartel**. The cartel will maximise profits if it acts like a monopoly: if the members behave as if they were a single firm. This is illustrated in Figure 4.8.

The total market demand curve is shown with the corresponding market *MR* curve. The cartel's *MC* curve is the horizontal sum of the *MC* curves of its members. Profits are maximised at Q_1 where $MC = MR$. The cartel must therefore set a price of P_1 (at which Q_1 will be demanded).

Having agreed on the cartel price, the members may then compete against each other using *non-price competition*, to gain as big a share of resulting sales (Q_1) as they can.

Alternatively, the cartel members may somehow agree to divide the market between them. Each member would be given a **quota**. The sum of all the quotas must add up to Q_1. If the quotas exceeded Q_1, either there would be output unsold if price remained fixed at P_1, or the price would fall.

But if quotas are to be set by the cartel, how will it decide the level of each individual member's quota? The most likely method is for the cartel to divide the market between the members according to their current market share. That is the solution most likely to be accepted as 'fair'.

BOX 4.2

OPEC – the rise and fall of a cartel
The history of the world's most famous cartel

OPEC is probably the best known of all cartels. It was set up in 1960 by the five major oil-exporting countries: Saudi Arabia, Iran, Iraq, Kuwait and Venezuela. Its stated objectives were as follows:

- The co-ordination and unification of the petroleum policies of member countries.
- The organisation of means to ensure the stabilisation of prices, eliminating harmful and unnecessary fluctuations.

The years leading up to 1960 had seen the oil-producing countries increasingly in conflict with the international oil companies, which extracted oil under 'concessionary agreement'. Under this scheme, oil companies were given the right to extract oil in return for royalties. This meant that the oil-producing countries had little say over output and price levels.

Despite the formation of OPEC in 1960, it was not until 1973 that control of oil production was effectively transferred from the oil companies to the oil countries, with OPEC making the decisions on how much oil to produce and thereby determining its oil revenue. By this time OPEC consisted of thirteen members.

OPEC's pricing policy over the 1970s consisted of setting a market price for Saudi Arabian crude (the market leader), and leaving other OPEC members to set their prices in line with this: a form of dominant 'firm' price leadership.

As long as demand remained buoyant, and was price inelastic, this policy allowed large price increases with consequent large revenue increases. In 1973/4, after the Arab–Israeli war, OPEC raised the price of oil from around $3 per barrel to over $12. The price was kept at roughly this level until 1979. And yet the sales of oil did not fall significantly.

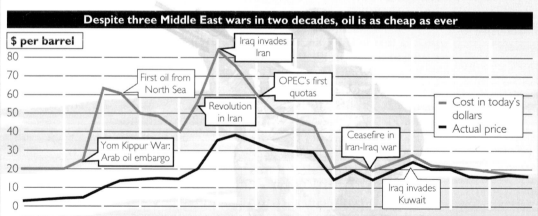

Sources: *The Observer* (12 September 1993); *OECD Economic Outlook* (OECD).

After 1979, however, following a further increase in the price of oil from around $15 to $40 per barrel, demand did fall. This was largely due to the recession of the early 1980s (although this recession was in turn largely caused by governments' responses to the oil price increases).

Faced by declining demand, OPEC after 1982 agreed to limit output and allocate production quotas in an attempt to keep the price up. A production ceiling of 16 million barrels per day was agreed in 1984.

The cartel was beginning to break down, however, due to the following:

• The world recession and the resulting fall in the demand for oil.
• Growing output from non-OPEC members.
• 'Cheating' by some OPEC members which exceeded their quota limits.

With a glut of oil, OPEC could no longer maintain the price. The 'spot' price of oil (the day-to-day price at which oil was trading on the open market) was falling, as the graph shows.

The trend of lower oil prices was reversed in the late 1980s. With the world economy booming, the demand for oil rose and along with it the price. Then in 1990 Iraq invaded Kuwait and the Gulf War ensued. With the cutting off of supplies from Kuwait and Iraq, the supply of oil fell and there was a sharp rise in its price.

But with the ending of the war and the recession of the early 1990s, the price rapidly fell again. Today the price of crude oil stands at about $16 per barrel, which in 1973 prices is only about $2.50! However, OPEC still dominates world production, and fresh moves to revive oil prices were made by re-establishing oil quotas.

Oil prices, however, have continued to fall. On the demand side, the development of energy-saving technology plus increases in fuel taxes have led to a relatively slow growth in consumption. On the supply side, the growing proportion of output supplied by non-OPEC members, plus the adoption in 1994 of a relatively high OPEC production ceiling of 24$^1/_2$ million barrels per day, has meant that supply has more than kept pace with demand.

The problem for OPEC is how to constrain output, given the unwillingness of non-OPEC members to adopt quotas and given the chronic tendency of some OPEC members, such as Venezuela and Nigeria, to cheat by producing more than their quota. Typically production by OPEC has been some 1 million barrels per day over the production ceiling.

Q1 What conditions facilitate the formation of a cartel? Which of these conditions were to be found in the oil market in (a) the early 1970s; (b) the mid-1980s?

Q2 Could OPEC have done anything to prevent the long-term decline in real oil prices since 1981?

Q3 Many oil analysts are predicting a rapid decline in world oil output from the late 1990s as world reserves are depleted. What effect is this likely to have on OPEC's behaviour?

In many countries, cartels are illegal – being seen by the government as a means of driving up prices and profits, and thereby as being against the public interest. Where open collusion is illegal, firms may simply break the law, or get round it. Alternatively, firms may stay within the law, but still *tacitly* collude by watching each other's prices and keeping theirs similar. Firms may tacitly 'agree' to avoid price wars or aggressive advertising campaigns.

Tacit collusion

One form of tacit collusion is where firms set the same price as an established leader. The leader may be the largest firm: the firm which dominates the industry. This is known as dominant firm price leadership. Alternatively, the price leader may simply be the one that has emerged over time as the most reliable one to follow: the one that is the best barometer of market conditions. This is known as barometric firm price leadership.

Dominant firm price leadership. How does the leader set the price? This depends on the assumptions it makes about its rivals' reactions to its price changes. If it assumes that rivals will simply follow it by making exactly the same percentage price changes up or down, then a simple model can be constructed. This is illustrated in Figure 4.9, which assumes that the leader has approximately 50 per cent of the market at any given price.

The leader will maximise profits where its marginal revenue is equal to its marginal cost. It knows its current position on its demand curve (say, point *a*). It then estimates how responsive its demand will be to industry-wide price changes and thus constructs its demand and *MR* curves on that basis. It then chooses to produce Q_L at a price of P_L: at point *l* on its demand curve (where $MC = MR$). Other firms then follow that price. Total market demand will be Q_T, with followers supplying that portion of the market not supplied by the leader: namely, $Q_T - Q_L$.

There is one problem with this model. That is the assumption that the followers will want to maintain a constant market share. It is possible that if the leader raises its price, the followers may want to supply more at this new price. On the other hand, the followers may decide merely to maintain their market share for fear of invoking retaliation from the leader, in the form of price cuts or an aggressive advertising campaign.

Barometric firm price leadership. A similar exercise can be conducted by a barometric firm. Although the firm is not dominating the industry, its price will be followed by the others.

It merely tries to estimate its demand and *MR* curves – assuming, again, a constant market share – and then produces where $MR = MC$ and sets price accordingly.

In practice, which firm is taken as the barometer will frequently change. Whether we are talking about oil companies, car producers or banks, any firm may take the initiative in raising prices. If the other firms are merely waiting for someone to take the lead – say, because costs have risen – they will all quickly follow suit. For example, if one of the bigger building societies or banks raises its mortgage rates by 1 per cent, then this is likely to stimulate the others to follow suit.

Definitions

Tacit collusion
Where oligopolists take care not to engage in price cutting, excessive advertising or other forms of competition. There may be unwritten 'rules' of collusive behaviour such as price leadership.

Dominant firm price leadership
Where firms (the followers) choose the same price as that set by a dominant firm in the industry (the leader).

Barometric firm price leadership
Where the price leader is the one whose prices are believed to reflect market conditions in the most satisfactory way.

FIGURE 4.9
A price leader aiming to maximise profits for a given market share

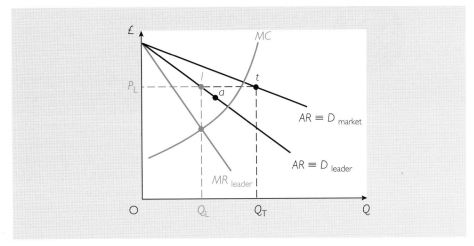

Other forms of tacit collusion

An alternative to having an established leader is for there to be an established set of simple 'rules of thumb' that everyone follows. One such example is **average cost pricing**. Here producers, instead of equating MC and MR, simply add a certain percentage for profit on top of average costs. Thus, if average costs rise by 10 per cent, prices will automatically be raised by 10 per cent. This is a particularly useful rule of thumb in times of inflation, when all firms will be experiencing similar cost increases.

Another rule of thumb is to have certain **price benchmarks**. Thus clothes may sell for £9.95, £14.95, £19.95, etc. (but not £12.31, £16.42 or £20.04). If costs rise, then firms simply raise their price to the next benchmark, knowing that other firms will do the same.

Rules of thumb can also be applied to advertising (e.g. you do not criticise other firms' products, only praise your own); or to the design of the product (e.g. lighting manufacturers tacitly agreeing not to bring out an everlasting light bulb).

Definitions

Average cost pricing
Where a firm sets its price by adding a certain percentage for (average) profit on top of average cost.

Price benchmark
A price which is typically used. Firms, when raising a price, will usually raise it from one benchmark to another.

Factors favouring collusion

Collusion between firms, whether formal or tacit, is more likely when firms can clearly identify with each other or some leader and when they trust each other not to break agreements. It will be easier for firms to collude if the following conditions apply:

- There are only very few firms and hence they are well known to each other.
- They are not secretive with each other about costs and production methods.
- They have similar production methods and average costs, and will thus be likely to want to change prices at the same time and by the same percentage.
- They produce similar products and can thus more easily reach agreements on price.
- There is a dominant firm.

BOX 4.3 *Oligopoly in electrical goods*

A case of collusion?

In the UK, the Office of Fair Trading (OFT) is the official body that investigates and reports on suspected cases of anti-competitive practices. If the OFT suspects that firms are abusing a monopoly/oligopoly position (for example, when a manufacturer refuses to supply retailers that discount its products, or when firms deliberately sell at a loss in part of the market in order to undercut the price of a new entrant), then it can refer such firms to the Monopolies and Mergers Commission (MMC). The MMC will conduct an investigation, and the government will decide whether to take action.

If firms are operating as a cartel, then the OFT can refer them to the Restrictive Practices Court to justify their agreement. If they cannot convince the Court that the cartel is in the public interest, the agreement must be terminated.

In the mid-1990s the OFT gathered evidence suggesting that manufacturers of electrical goods were putting pressure on retailers by refusing to supply discount warehouses and seeking to maintain a high retail price in the leading nationwide stores, such as Dixons, Comet and Argos, as well as in department stores such as John Lewis, Debenhams and the House of Fraser.

A survey conducted by the *Sunday Times*[1] supported these findings, and showed that there was virtually no difference in the prices charged for major brands of electrical appliances in the different shops. For example, in the case of a Sony colour television (KV25F2), the highest price was found in Harrods, but this was only 1p more than the price

Prices of leading brands of electrical goods

Item	Dixons	Argos	John Lewis	Comet	Currys	Harrods	USA
Sony PlayStation	£197.00	£196.50	£197.00	£197.00	£197.00	£200.00	£120
Sega Saturn	£197.00	£197.00	£196.00	£197.00	£196.00	–	£120
Sony TV (KV25F2)	£699.99	–	£699.99	£699.99	£699.99	£700.00	£361
Pentax Espio (140 Zoom)	£299.99	£299.00	£299.99	–	–	£299.95	£198
Kenwood mini hi-fi UD205	£329.99	£329.95	–	–	£329.99	–	£180
Sharp Viewcam VLE34 8 mm	£599.99	£599.00	–	£599.99	£599.99	–	£421
Psion P/organiser 3a 2MB	£329.99	£329.99	£329.00	–	£329.99	£329.00	£361
Phillips TV/Video 14PV162	£379.99	£379.99	–	–	£379.99	–	£211
Aiwa CD/tape player CSD ES60	£130.00	£129.99	–	£129.99	£129.99	–	£77

– indicates not stocked or not available.

Source: *Sunday Times*, 17 November 1996.

- There are significant barriers to entry and thus there is little fear of disruption by new firms.
- The market is stable. If industry demand or production costs fluctuate wildly, it will be difficult to make agreements, partly due to difficulties in predicting

in any other store! As an interviewee remarked to the *Sunday Times* journalist, 'If you have to pay the same in Argos and Harrods, I'd rather go to Harrods and get a posh carrier bag.' So much for the 'price promise' made by various leading stores: namely, that if you can purchase the item cheaper elsewhere, they will refund the difference.

The table shows the prices for nine leading brands of electrical goods. Apart from the similarity in prices between the six shops in the table, what is also revealing is that eight of the items were sold at much lower prices in the USA, where there is more competition.

But why don't the retail stores put pressure on the manufacturers to enable them to sell the items at a discount? The answer is that it is not in their interests. It would seem that the retailers are tacitly colluding to keep their prices up. The last thing they want is to start undercutting each other and end up with a price war.

Tacit collusion is possible for two reasons. The first is that there are relatively few electrical retailers, and the main ones in most towns are national companies. In fact, the two largest, Dixons and Currys, are one and the same company. The second reason is that the manufacturers, by refusing to supply independent discount warehouses, are restricting the amount of competition that the chain stores face.

There seems, therefore, to be a 'cosy' relationship between manufacturers and retailers, where, for their own sake, each group is keen not to upset the apparent collusion taking place by the other.

But what of the OFT? Was it prepared to allow such practices to continue? It asked the MMC to look at the supply and pricing of eight categories of goods, including televisions, hi-fi systems, games machines, camcorders and videos. The provisional view of the MMC was that these appeared to be cases of 'complex monopolies' (i.e. where monopoly power was exercised in different ways and involved several different companies, including both manufacturing and retail). The MMC also claimed that because of this complexity the full investigation would take time.

Q1 If two or more companies sell at the same price, is this necessarily evidence of collusion?

Q2 In 1996 and 1997, Esso ran its 'Price Watch' campaign, whereby it promised that its petrol stations would match the lowest supermarket petrol prices within a three-mile radius. One of the effects of this was to drive some of the 'cut-price' independent petrol retailers, which could not compete in this price war, out of the market. Esso admitted that it was selling petrol below cost. Was Esso's campaign in the motorist's interests?

[1] *Sunday Times*, 17 November 1996, p. 11.

and partly because agreements may frequently have to be amended. There is a particular problem in a declining market where firms may be tempted to undercut each other's price in order to maintain their sales.

- There are no government measures to curb collusion.

Non-collusive oligopoly: the breakdown of collusion

In some oligopolies, there may only be a few (if any) factors favouring collusion. In such cases, the likelihood of price competition is greater.

Even if there is collusion, there will always be the temptation for individual oligopolists to 'cheat', by cutting prices or by selling more than their allotted quota. The danger, of course, is that this would invite retaliation from the other members of the cartel, with a resulting price war. Price would then fall and the cartel could well break up in disarray.

When considering whether to break a collusive agreement, even if only a tacit one, a firm will ask: (1) 'How much can we get away with without inviting retaliation?' and (2) 'If a price war does result, will we be the winners? Will we succeed in driving some or all of our rivals out of business and yet survive ourselves, and thereby gain greater market power?'

The position of rival firms, therefore, is rather like that of generals of opposing armies or the players in a game. It is a question of choosing the appropriate *strategy*: the strategy that will best succeed in outwitting your opponents. The strategy a firm adopts will, of course, be concerned not just with price but also with advertising and product development.

The firm's choice of strategy will depend on (a) how it thinks its rivals will react to any price changes or other changes it makes; (b) its willingness to take a gamble. Economists have developed game theory, which examines the best strategy a firm can adopt for each assumption about its rivals' behaviour.

Non-collusive oligopoly: game theory

The simplest case is where there are just two firms with identical costs, products and demand. They are both considering which of two alternative prices to charge. Table 4.2 shows typical profits they could each make.

Let us assume that at present both firms (X and Y) are charging a price of £2 and that they are each making a profit of £10 million, giving a total industry profit of £20 million. This is shown in the top left-hand box (A).

Now assume they are both (independently) considering reducing their price to £1.80. In making this decision they will need to take into account what their rival might do, and how this will affect them. Let us consider X's position. In our simple example there are just two things that its rival, firm Y, might do. Either Y could cut its price to £1.80, or it could leave its price at £2. What should X do?

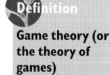

Definition

Game theory (or the theory of games)
The study of alternative strategies that oligopolists may choose to adopt, depending on their assumptions about their rivals' behaviour.

TABLE 4.2 *Profits for firms A and B at different prices*

		X's price	
		£2	£1.80
Y's price	£2	**A** £10m each	**B** £5m for Y £12m for X
	£1.80	**C** £12m for Y £5m for X	**D** £8m each

One alternative is to go for the *cautious* approach and think of the worst thing that its rival could do. If X kept its price at £2, the worst thing for X would be if its rival Y cut its price. This is shown by box C: X's profit falls to £5 million. If, however, X cut its price to £1.80, the worst outcome would again be for Y to cut its price, but this time X's profit only falls to £8 million. In this case, then, if X is cautious, it will *cut its price to £1.80*. Note that Y will argue along similar lines, and if it is cautious, it too will cut its price to £1.80. This policy of adopting the safer strategy is known as maximin. Following a maximin strategy, the firm will opt for the alternative that will *maxi*mise its *min*imum possible profit.

An alternative strategy is to go for the optimistic approach and assume that your rivals react in the way most favourable to you. Here the firm will go for the strategy that yields the highest possible profit. In X's case this will be again to cut price, only this time on the optimistic assumption that firm Y will leave its price unchanged. If firm X is correct in its assumption, it will move to box B and achieve the maximum possible profit of £12 million. This strategy of going for the maximum possible profit is known as maximax: Note that again the same argument applies to Y. Its maximax strategy will be to cut price and hopefully end up in box C.

Given that in this 'game' *both* approaches, maximin and maximax, lead to the *same* strategy (namely, cutting price), this is known as a dominant strategy game.

But, given that both X and Y will be tempted to reduce prices, they will end up earning a lower profit (£8 million profit each in box D) than if they had charged the higher price (£10 million profit each in box A). Thus collusion, rather than a price war, would have benefited both, and yet both would be tempted to cheat and cut prices. This is known as the prisoners' dilemma. An example is given in Box 4.4.

More complex games with no dominant strategy

More complex 'games' can be devised with more than two firms, many alternative prices, differentiated products and various forms of non-price competition (e.g. advertising). In such cases, the cautious (maximin) strategy may suggest a different policy (e.g. do nothing) from the high-risk (maximax) strategy (e.g. cut prices substantially).

In complex and changing situations, firms may alter their tactics in the light of new circumstances. Thus in some cases firms may compete hard for a time (in price or non-price terms) and then realise that maybe no one is winning. Firms may then jointly raise prices and reduce advertising. Later, after a period of tacit collusion, competition may break out again. This may be sparked off by the entry of a new firm, by the development of a new product design, by a change in market demand, or simply by one or more firms no longer being able to resist the temptation to 'cheat'. In short, the behaviour of particular oligopolists may change quite radically over time.

Non-collusive oligopoly: the kinked demand curve

Even when there is no collusion, prices under oligopoly can often remain stable, with little apparent price competition. One explanation for this is

Definitions

Maximin
The strategy of choosing the policy whose worst possible outcome is the least bad.

Maximax
The strategy of choosing the policy which has the best possible outcome.

Dominant strategy game
Where the *same* policy is suggested by different strategies.

Prisoners' dilemma
Where two or more firms (or people), by attempting independently to choose the best strategy for whatever the other(s) are likely to do, end up in a worse position than if they had co-operated in the first place.

BOX 4.4 *The prisoners' dilemma*

Game theory is not just relevant to economics. A famous non-economic example is the prisoners' dilemma.

Nigel and Amanda have been arrested for a joint crime of serious fraud. Each is interviewed separately and given the following alternatives:

- First, if they say nothing, the court has enough evidence to sentence both to a year's imprisonment.
- Second, if either Nigel or Amanda alone confesses, he or she is likely to get only a three-month sentence but the partner could get up to ten years.
- Third, if both confess, they are likely to get three years each.

What should Nigel and Amanda do?

		Amanda's alternatives	
		Not confess	Confess
Nigel's alternatives	Not confess	**A** Each gets 1 year	**C** Nigel gets 10 years / Amanda gets 3 months
	Confess	**B** Nigel gets 3 months / Amanda gets 10 years	**D** Each gets 3 years

that oligopolists often face a **kinked demand curve**. This will occur when two conditions hold:

- If an oligopolist cuts its price, its rivals will feel forced to follow suit and cut theirs, to prevent losing customers to the first firm.
- If an oligopolist raises its price, however, its rivals will *not* follow suit since, by keeping their prices the same, they will thereby gain customers from the first firm.

On these assumptions, each oligopolist will face a demand curve that is *kinked* at the current price and output (see Figure 4.10). A rise in price will lead to a large fall in sales as customers switch to the now lower-priced rivals. The firm will thus be reluctant to raise its price. Demand is relatively elastic above the kink. On the other hand, a fall in price will bring only a modest increase in sales, since rivals lower their prices too and therefore customers do not switch. The firm will thus also be reluctant to reduce its price. Demand is relatively inelastic below the kink. Thus oligopolists will be reluctant to change prices at all.

Definition

Kinked demand theory
The theory that oligopolists face a demand curve that is kinked at the current price: demand being significantly more elastic above the current price than below. The effect of this is to create a situation of price stability.

Let us consider Nigel's dilemma. Should he confess in order to get the short sentence (the maximax strategy)? This is better than the year he would get for not confessing. There is, however, an even better reason for confessing. Suppose Nigel doesn't confess but, unknown to him, Amanda does confess. Then Nigel ends up with the long sentence. Better than this is to confess and to get no more than three years: this is the safest (maximin) strategy.

Amanda is in the same dilemma. The result is simple. When both prisoners act selfishly by confessing, they both end up in position D with relatively long prison terms. Only when they collude will they end up in position A with relatively short prison terms, the best combined solution.

Of course the police know this and will do their best to prevent any collusion. They will keep Nigel and Amanda in separate cells and try to persuade each of them that the other is bound to confess.

Thus the choice of strategy depends on:

- Nigel's and Amanda's risk attitudes: i.e. are they 'risk lovers' or 'risk averse'?
- Nigel's and Amanda's estimates of how likely the other is to own up.

Q1 How would Nigel's choice of strategy be affected if he had instead been involved in a joint crime with Jeremy, Pauline, Diana and Dave, and they had all been caught?

Q2 Can you think of any other non-economic examples of the prisoners' dilemma?

The possibility of having a kinked demand curve is not the only reason why firms may be reluctant to change prices. Changing prices will involve modifying price lists, working out new revenue predictions and revaluing stocks of finished goods; it may also upset customers.

FIGURE 4.10
Kinked demand for a firm under oligopoly

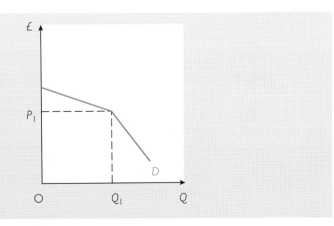

Oligopoly and the consumer

If oligopolists act collusively and jointly maximise industry profits, they will in effect be acting together as a monopoly. In such cases, prices may be very high. This is clearly not in the best interests of consumers.

Furthermore, in two respects, oligopoly may be more disadvantageous than monopoly:

* Depending on the size of the individual oligopolists, there may be less scope for economies of scale to mitigate the effects of market power.
* Oligopolists are likely to engage in much more extensive advertising than a monopolist.

These problems will be less, however, if oligopolists do not collude, if there is some degree of price competition and if barriers to entry are weak.

Also the power of oligopolists in certain markets may to some extent be offset if they sell their product to other powerful firms. Thus oligopolistic producers of baked beans or soap powder sell a large proportion of their output to giant supermarket chains which can use their market power to keep down the price at which they purchase these products. This phenomenon is known as countervailing power.

In some respects, oligopoly has *advantages* to society over other market structures:

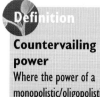

Definition

Countervailing power
Where the power of a monopolistic/oligopolistic seller is offset by powerful buyers which can prevent the price from being pushed up.

* Oligopolists, like monopolists, can use part of their supernormal profit for research and development. Unlike monopolists, however, oligopolists will have a considerable *incentive* to do so. If the product design is improved, this may allow the firm to capture a larger share of the market, and it may be some time before rivals can respond with a similarly improved product. If, in addition, costs are reduced by technological improvement, the resulting higher profits will enable the firm to withstand better a price war should one break out.
* Non-price competition through product differentiation may result in greater choice for the consumer. Take the case of stereo equipment. Non-price competition has led to a huge range of different products of many different specifications, each meeting the specific requirements of different consumers.

It is difficult to draw any general conclusions, since oligopolies differ so much in their performance.

Summary

1. **An oligopoly is where there are just a few firms in the industry and barriers to the entry of new firms. Firms recognise their mutual dependence.**
2. **Oligopolists will want to maximise their joint profits. This will tend to make them collude to keep prices high. On the other hand, they will want the biggest share of industry profits for themselves. This will tend to make them compete.**

3. **Whether they compete or collude depends on the conditions in the industry. They are more likely to collude if there are few of them; if they are open with each other; if they have similar products and cost structures; if there is a dominant firm; if there are significant entry barriers; if the market is stable; and if there is no government legislation to prevent collusion.**

4. **Collusion can be open or tacit.**

5. **A formal collusive agreement is called a 'cartel'. A cartel aims to act as a monopoly. It can set price and leave the members to compete for market share, or it can assign quotas. There is always a temptation for cartel members to 'cheat' by undercutting the cartel price if they think they can get away with it and not trigger a price war.**

6. **Tacit collusion can take the form of price leadership. This is where firms follow the price set by either a dominant firm in the industry or one seen as a reliable 'barometer' of market conditions. Alternatively, tacit collusion can simply involve following various rules of thumb such as average cost pricing and benchmark pricing.**

7. **Non-collusive oligopolists will have to work out a price strategy. This will depend on their attitudes towards risk and on the assumptions they make about the behaviour of their rivals. Game theory examines various strategies that firms can adopt when the outcome of each is not certain. They can adopt a low-risk 'maximin' strategy of choosing the policy that has the least-bad worst outcome, or a high-risk 'maximax' strategy of choosing the policy with the best possible outcome, or some compromise.**

8. **Because firms are likely to face a kinked demand curve, they are likely to keep their prices stable unless there is a large shift in costs or demand.**

9. **Whether consumers benefit from oligopoly depends on the particular oligopoly and how competitive it is; whether there is any countervailing power; whether the firms engage in extensive advertising and of what type; whether product differentiation results in a wide range of choice for the consumer; and how much of the profits are ploughed back into research and development. Since these conditions vary substantially from oligopoly to oligopoly, it is impossible to state just how well or how badly oligopoly in general serves the consumer's interest.**

4.6 Price discrimination

In what situations will firms be able to charge different prices to different consumers? How will we as consumers benefit or lose from the process?

Definition

Price discrimination
Where a firm sells the same product at different prices.

Up to now we have assumed that a firm will sell its output at a single price. Sometimes, however, firms may practise price discrimination. This is where consumers are grouped into two or more independent markets and a separate price is charged in each market. Examples include different-priced seats on buses for adults and children, different prices for the same seats on

FIGURE 4.11
Third-degree price discrimination

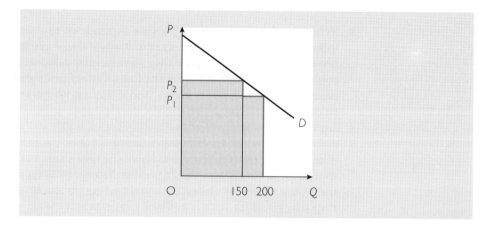

FIGURE 4.11
Third-degree price discrimination

aircraft (depending on when they are booked), and different prices charged for the same product in different countries or different parts of the same country. (There are other forms of price discrimination, but this – known as 'third-degree price discrimination' – is the most common.)

Conditions necessary for price discrimination to operate

As we shall see, a firm will be able to increase its profits if it can engage in price discrimination. But under what circumstances will it be able to charge discriminatory prices? There are three conditions that must be met:

- The firm must be able to set its price. Thus price discrimination will be impossible under perfect competition, where firms are price takers.
- The markets must be separate. Consumers in the low-priced market must not be able to resell the product in the high-priced market. For example, children must not be able to resell a half-priced child's cinema ticket for use by an adult.
- Demand elasticity must differ in each market. The firm will charge the higher price in the market where demand is less elastic, and thus less sensitive to a price rise.

Advantages to the firm

Price discrimination will allow the firm to earn a higher revenue from any given level of sales. Figure 4.11 represents a firm's demand curve. If it is to sell 200 units without price discrimination, it must charge a price of P_1. The total revenue it earns is shown by the grey area. If, however, it can practise price discrimination by selling 150 of those 200 units at the higher price of P_2, it will gain the blue area in addition to the grey area.

Another advantage to the firm of price discrimination is that it may be able to use it to drive competitors out of business. If a firm has a monopoly in one market (e.g. the home market), it may be able to charge a high price due to its relatively inelastic demand, and thus make high profits. If it is under oligopoly in another market (e.g. the export market), it may use the high profits in the first market to subsidise a very low price in the oligopolistic market, thus forcing its competitors out of business.

FIGURE 4.12
Profit-maximising output under third-degree price discrimination
(a) Market X
(b) Market Y
(c) Total (markets X + Y)

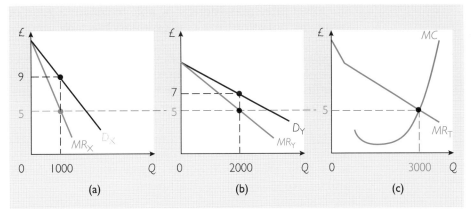

Large bus companies in the UK have been accused of doing this. They use the profits made from the high fares on routes where they face no competition to subsidise fares on routes where they do face competition, often from a small rival attempting to break into the market. The aim is to drive the small company out of business. Sometimes on these routes, the large company charges fares which are below cost (thereby making a temporary loss on these routes). This practice is known as **predatory pricing**.

Profit-maximising prices and output

Assuming that the firm wishes to maximise profits, what discriminatory prices should it charge and how much should it produce? Assume that a firm sells an identical product in two separate markets X and Y with demand and *MR* curves as shown in Figure 4.12.

Diagram (c) shows the *MC* and *MR* curves for the firm as a whole. This *MR* curve is found by adding the amounts sold in the two markets at each level of *MR* (in other words, the horizontal addition of the two *MR* curves). Thus, for example, with output of 1000 units in market X and 2000 in market Y, making 3000 in total, revenue would increase by £5 if one extra unit were sold, whether in market X or Y.

Total profit is maximised where *MC* = *MR*: i.e. at an output of 3000 units in total. This output must then be divided between the two markets so that *MC* is equal to *MR* in each market: i.e. *MC* = *MR* = £5 in each market. *MR* must be the same in both markets, otherwise revenue could be increased by switching output to the market with the higher *MR*.

The profit-maximising price in each market will be given by the relevant demand curve. Thus, in market X, 1000 units will be sold at £9 each, and in market Y, 2000 units will be sold at £7 each. Note that the higher price is charged in the market with the less elastic demand curve.

Price discrimination and the consumer

No clear-cut decision can be made over the desirability of price discrimination from the point of view of the consumer. Some people will benefit from it; others will lose. Those paying the higher price will probably feel that price discrimination is unfair to them. On the other hand, those charged

Definition

Predatory pricing
Selling at a price below average variable cost in order to drive competitors from the market.

the lower price may thereby be able to obtain a good or service they could otherwise not afford: e.g. concessionary bus fares for old-age pensioners.

Competition. As explained above, a firm may use price discrimination to drive competitors out of business. On the other hand, it might use its profits from its high-priced market to break into another market and withstand a possible price war. Competition is thereby increased.

Profits. Price discrimination raises a firm's profits. This could be seen to be against the interests of the consumer, especially if the average price of the product is raised. On the other hand, the higher profits may be reinvested and lead to lower costs in the future.

Summary

1. Price discrimination is where a firm sells the same product at different prices in different markets.
2. Price discrimination allows the firm to earn a higher revenue from a given level of sales.
3. The profit-maximising output is where the firm's *MC* is equal to the overall *MR* (found by adding horizontally the *MR* curves in each of the separate markets). This is then divided between the markets by selling that amount in each market where *MC* = *MR*, at a price given by the demand curve in each market.
4. Some people will gain from price discrimination; others will lose. It is likely to be particularly harmful when it is used as a means of driving competitors from the market (predatory pricing).

Questions

1. A perfectly competitive firm faces a price of £14 per unit. It has the following short-run cost schedule:

Output	0	1	2	3	4	5	6	7	8
TC (£)	10	18	24	30	38	50	66	91	120

(a) Copy the table and put in additional rows for average cost and marginal cost at each level of output. (Enter the figures for marginal cost in the space between each column.)
(b) Plot *AC*, *MC* and *MR* on a diagram.
(c) Mark the profit-maximising output.
(d) How much (supernormal) profit is made at this output?
(e) What would happen to the price in the long run if this firm were typical of others in the industry? Why would we need to know information about long-run average cost in order to give a precise answer to this question?

2. If the industry under perfect competition faces a downward-sloping demand curve, why does an individual firm face a horizontal demand curve?

3. On a diagram similar to Figure 4.2, show the long-run equilibrium for both firm and industry under perfect competition. Now assume that the demand for the product falls. Show the short-run and long-run effects.

4. If supernormal profits are competed away under perfect competition, why will firms have an incentive to become more efficient?

5. Is it a valid criticism of perfect competition to argue that it is incompatible with economies of scale?

6. As an illustration of the difficulty in identifying monopolies, try and decide which of the following are monopolies: British Telecom; your local evening newspaper; British Gas; the village post office; the Royal Mail; Interflora; the London Underground; ice-creams in the cinema; Guinness; food sold in a train buffet car; Tipp-Ex; the board game 'Monopoly'.

7. Try this brain teaser. A monopoly would be expected to face an inelastic demand. After all, there are no direct substitutes. And yet, if it produces where $MR = MC$, MR must be positive, and demand must therefore be *elastic*. Therefore the monopolist must face an elastic demand! Can you solve this conundrum?

8. For what reasons would you expect a monopoly to charge (a) a higher price, and (b) a lower price than if the industry were operating under perfect competition?

9. In which of the following industries are exit costs likely to be low: (a) steel production; (b) market gardening; (c) nuclear power generation; (d) specialist financial advisory services; (e) production of fashion dolls; (f) production of a new drug; (g) contract catering; (h) mobile discos; (i) car ferry operators? Are these exit costs dependent on how narrowly the industry is defined?

10. Think of three examples of monopolies (local or national) and consider how contestable their markets are.

11. Think of ten different products or services and estimate roughly how many firms there are in the market. You will need to decide whether 'the market' is a local one, a national one or an international one. In what ways do the firms compete in each of the cases you have identified?

12. Assume that a monopolistically competitive industry is in long-run equilibrium. On a diagram like Figure 4.6, show the effect of a fall in demand on a firm's price and profit in (a) the short run and (b) the long run.

13. Imagine there are two types of potential customer for jam sold by a small food shop. The one is the person who has just run out and wants some now. The other is the person who looks in the cupboard, sees that the pot of jam is less than half full and thinks, 'I will soon need some more.' How will the price elasticity of demand differ between these two customers?

14. Why may a food shop charge higher prices than supermarkets for 'essential items' and yet very similar prices for delicatessen items?

15. Firms under monopolistic competition generally have spare capacity. Does this imply that if, say, half of the petrol stations were closed down, the consumer would benefit? Explain.

16. Will competition between oligopolists always reduce total industry profits?

17. In which of the following industries is collusion likely to occur: bricks, beer, margarine, cement, crisps, washing powder, blank audio or video cassettes, carpets?

18. Devise a box diagram like that in Table 4.1, only this time assume that there are three firms each considering the two strategies of keeping price the same or reducing it by a set amount. Is the game still a 'dominant strategy game'?

19. Which of the following are examples of effective countervailing power?
    (a) Power stations buying coal from British Coal.
    (b) A large factory hiring a photocopier from Rank Xerox.
    (c) Marks and Spencer buying clothes from a garment manufacturer.
    (d) A small village store (but the only one for miles around) buying food from a wholesaler.
    Is it the size of the purchasing firm that is important in determining its power to keep down the prices charged by its suppliers?

20. If a cinema could sell all its seats to adults in the evenings at the end of the week, but only a few on Mondays and Tuesdays, what price discrimination policy would you recommend to the cinema in order for it to maximise its weekly revenue?

21. Think of two examples of price discrimination. In what ways do the consumers gain or lose? What information would you need to be certain in your answer?

chapter five

Wages and the distribution of income

Why do pop stars, footballers and stockbrokers earn such large incomes? Why, on the other hand, do cleaners, hospital porters and workers in clothing factories earn very low incomes?

The explanation for differences in wages lies in the working of labour markets. In the first part of the chapter we will consider how labour markets operate. In particular, we will focus on the determination of wage rates in different types of market: ones where employers are wage takers, ones where they can choose the wage rate, and ones where wage rates are determined by a process of collective bargaining.

In section 5.4 we ask the more general question of why some people are rich and others poor, and consider the degree of inequality in our society: a society which includes the super rich, with their luxury yachts and their villas abroad, and people living in slum conditions, with not enough to feed and clothe themselves or their children properly: a society where people begging in the streets are an all too familiar sight.

The chapter closes with a consideration of what can be done to reduce inequality. Is the solution to tax the rich very heavily so that the money can be redistributed to the poor? Or might this discourage people from working so hard? Would it be better, then, to focus on benefits and increase the support for the poor?

Labour market trends

How has the pattern of employment changed in recent years?

The labour market has undergone great change in recent years. Advances in technology, changes in the pattern of output, a need to be competitive in international markets and various social changes have all contributed to changes in work practices and in the structure and composition of the workforce. Major changes include the following:

- A shift from agricultural and manufacturing to service-sector employment. Figure 5.1 reveals that employment in agriculture has been falling over a long historical period. The fall in manufacturing employment, however, has been more recent, starting in the 1960s and gathering pace through the 1970s, 1980s and 1990s. By contrast, employment in the service industries has grown steadily since 1946. In fact since 1979, it has expanded by over 3 million jobs.
- A rise in part-time employment, and a fall in full-time employment (see Figure 5.2). In 1971 approximately one in six workers in the UK was part time; by 1997 this had risen to almost one worker in three. The fall in full-time employment closely mirrors the decline in manufacturing, where jobs were more likely to be on a full-time basis. At the same time, the growth in part-time work reflects the growth in the service sector, where many jobs are part time. Since 1979 part-time employment has risen by over 1.8 million.
- A rise in female participation rates. Women now constitute approximately half of the paid labour force. The rise in participation rates is strongly associated with the growth in the service sector and the creation of part-time positions. Over 45 per cent of all female workers, about 5 million, are in part-time work.
- A rise in the proportion of workers employed on fixed-term contracts, or on a temporary or casual basis. Many firms nowadays prefer to employ

FIGURE 5.1
Employment in different sectors of the UK economy

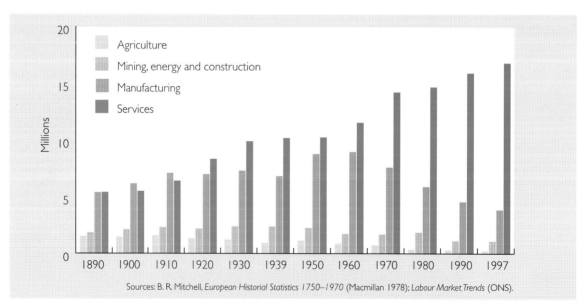

Sources: B. R. Mitchell, *European Historical Statistics 1750–1970* (Macmillan 1978); *Labour Market Trends* (ONS).

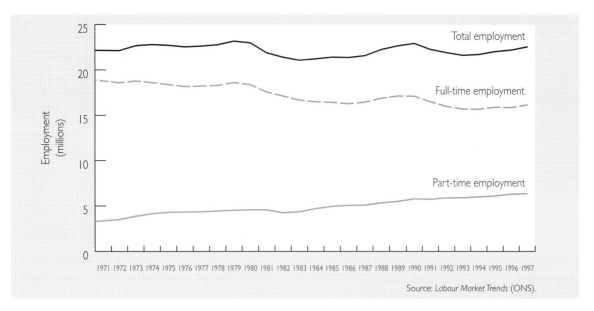

Source: *Labour Market Trends* (ONS).

FIGURE 5.2
The growth of part-time employment

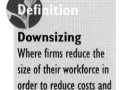

Downsizing
Where firms reduce the size of their workforce in order to reduce costs and thereby increase profits.

only their core workers/managers on a permanent ('continuing') basis. They feel that it gives them more flexibility to respond to changing market conditions to have the remainder of their workers employed on a short-term basis, and, perhaps, to make use of agency staff or to contract out work.

- **Downsizing.** It has become very fashionable in recent years for companies to try to 'trim' the numbers of their employees in order to reduce costs. There is now, however, a growing consensus that the process may have gone too far. The cost of reducing its workforce may be that a company loses revenue: if it cuts back on people who had been employed in marketing its products, or in developing new products or in ensuring that quality is maintained, then it is likely to lose market share. It might reduce unit costs, but total profits could nevertheless fall, not rise.

Summary

Major changes in the UK labour market over recent years include: a movement towards service-sector employment; a rise in part-time working; a growth in female employment levels; a rise in the proportion of temporary, short-term contract and casual employment; downsizing.

Wage determination in a perfect market
Why are some people paid higher wage rates than others?

Perfect labour markets

When looking at the market for labour, it is useful to make a similar distinction to that made in goods markets: the distinction between perfect and

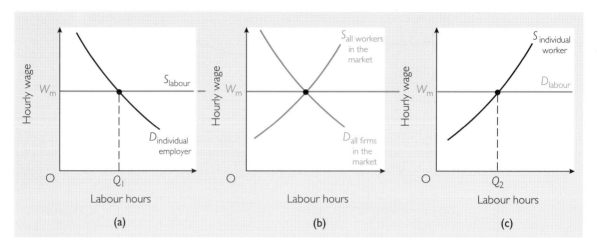

(a)   (b)   (c)

FIGURE 5.3
*A perfectly
competitive
labour market*
*(a) Individual
employer*
(b) Whole market
*(c) Individual
worker*

imperfect markets. That way we can gain a clearer understanding of the effects of power, or lack of it, in the labour market. Although in practice few labour markets are totally perfect, many do at least approximate to it.

The assumptions of perfect labour markets are similar to those of perfect goods markets. The main one is that everyone is a **wage taker**. In other words, neither employers nor employees have any economic power to affect wage rates. This situation is not uncommon. Small employers are likely to have to pay the 'going wage rate' to their employees, especially where the employee is of a clear category, such as an electrician, a bar worker, a secretary or a porter. As far as employees are concerned, being a wage taker means not being a member of a union and therefore not being able to use collective bargaining to push up the wage rate.

The other assumptions of a perfect labour market are as follows:

- Freedom of entry. There are no restrictions on the movement of labour. For example, workers are free to move to alternative jobs or to areas of the country where wage rates are higher. There are no barriers erected by, say, unions, professional associations or the government. Of course, it takes time for workers to change jobs and maybe to retrain. This assumption therefore applies only in the long run.
- Perfect knowledge. Workers are fully aware of what jobs are available at what wage rates and with what conditions of employment. Likewise employers know what labour is available and how productive that labour is.
- Homogeneous labour. It is usually assumed that, in perfect markets, workers of a given category are identical in terms of productivity. For example, it would be assumed that all bricklayers are equally skilled and motivated.

Definition

Wage taker
An employer (or employee) who is unable to influence the wage rate.

Wage rates and employment under perfect competition are determined by the interaction of the market demand and supply of labour. This is illustrated in Figure 5.3(b).

Generally it would be expected that the supply and demand curves slope the same way as in goods markets. The higher the wage rate paid for a certain type of job, the more workers will want to do that job. This gives an upward-sloping supply curve of labour. On the other hand, the higher the wage rate that employers have to pay, the less labour they will want to employ. Either they will simply produce less output, or they will substitute other factors of production, like machinery, for labour. Thus the demand curve for labour slopes downwards.

Diagram (a) shows how an individual employer has to accept this wage rate. The supply of labour to that employer is infinitely elastic. In other words, at the market wage rate W_m, there is no limit to the number of workers available to that employer (but no workers at all will be available below it: they will all be working elsewhere). At the market wage rate W_m, the employer will employ Q_1 hours of labour.

Diagram (c) shows how an individual worker also has to accept this wage rate. In this case it is the demand curve for that worker that is infinitely elastic. In other words, there is as much work as the worker cares to do at this wage rate (but none at all above it).

We now turn to look at the supply and demand for labour in more detail.

The supply of labour

The supply of labour in each market will typically be upward sloping. The higher the wage rate offered in a particular type of job, the more people will want to do that job.

The *position* of the market supply curve of labour will depend on the number of people willing and able to do the job at each given wage rate. This depends on three things:

* The number of qualified people.
* The non-wage benefits or costs of the job, such as the pleasantness or otherwise of the working environment, job satisfaction or dissatisfaction, status, power, the degree of job security, holidays, perks and other fringe benefits.
* The wages and non-wage benefits in alternative jobs.

A change in the wage rate will cause a movement along the supply curve. A change in any of these other three determinants will shift the whole curve.

The elasticity of supply of labour

How *responsive* will the supply of labour be to a change in the wage rate? If the market wage rate goes up, will a lot more labour become available or only a little? This responsiveness (elasticity) depends on (a) the difficulties and costs of changing jobs and (b) the time period.

Another way of looking at the elasticity of supply of labour is in terms of the mobility of labour: the willingness and ability of labour to move to another job. The mobility of labour (and hence the elasticity of supply of labour) will be higher when there are alternative jobs in the same location, when alternative jobs require similar skills and when people have good information about these jobs. It is also much higher in the long run, when people have the time to acquire new skills and when the education system has had time to adapt to the changing demands of industry.

Definition

Mobility of labour
The willingness and ability of labour to move to another job.

The demand for labour: the marginal productivity theory

In the previous two chapters, when we were looking at the production of goods, we assumed that firms aim to maximise profits. The theory of labour demand is based on the same assumption. This theory is generally known as the marginal productivity theory.

The profit-maximising approach

How many workers should a firm employ in order to maximise profits? The firm will answer this question by weighing up the costs of employing extra labour against the benefits. It will use exactly the same principles as in deciding how much output to produce.

In the goods market, the firm will maximise profits where the marginal cost of producing an extra unit of a *good* equals the marginal revenue from selling it: $MC = MR$.

In the labour market, the firm will maximise profits where the marginal cost of employing an extra *worker* equals the marginal revenue that the worker's output earns for the firm: MC of labour = MR of labour. The reasoning is simple. If an extra worker adds more to a firm's revenue than to its costs, the firm's profits will increase. It will be worth employing that worker. But as more workers are employed, diminishing returns to labour will set in. Each extra worker will produce less than the previous one, and thus earn less revenue for the firm. Eventually the marginal revenue from extra workers will fall to the level of their marginal cost. At that point, the firm will stop employing extra workers. There are no additional profits to be gained. Profits are at a maximum.

Measuring the marginal cost and revenue of labour

Marginal cost of labour (MC_L). This is the extra cost of employing one more worker. Under perfect competition the firm is too small to affect the market wage. It faces a horizontal supply curve (see Figure 5.3(a)). Thus the additional cost of employing one more person will simply be the wage rate: $MC_L = W$.

Marginal revenue of labour (MRP_L). The marginal revenue that the firm gains from employing one more worker is called the marginal revenue product of labour (MRP_L). The MRP_L is found by multiplying two elements – the *marginal physical product* of labour (MPP_L) and the marginal revenue gained by selling one more unit of output (MR).

$$MRP_L = MPP_L \times MR$$

The MPP_L is the extra output produced by the last worker. Thus if the last worker produces 100 tonnes of output per week (MPP_L), and if the firm earns an extra £2 for each additional tonne sold (MR), then the worker's MRP is £200. This extra worker is adding £200 to the firm's revenue.

The profit-maximising level of employment for a firm

The MPP_L curve is illustrated in Figure 5.4. As more workers are employed, there will come a point when diminishing returns set in (point *x*). The MPP_L curve thus slopes down after this point. The MRP_L curve will be of a similar

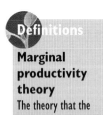

Marginal productivity theory
The theory that the demand for a factor depends on its marginal revenue product.

Marginal revenue product (of a factor)
The extra revenue a firm earns from employing one more unit of a variable factor: $MRP_{factor} = MPP_{factor} \times MR_{good}$.

FIGURE 5.4
Marginal physical product of labour curve

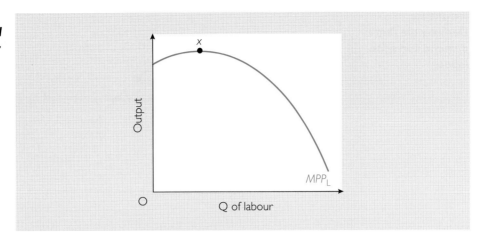

shape to the MPP_L curve, since it is merely being multiplied by a constant figure, MR. (Under perfect competition $MR = P$ and does not vary with output.) The MRP_L curve is illustrated in Figure 5.5, along with the MC_L 'curve'.

Profits will be maximised at an employment level of Q_e, where MC_L (i.e. W) = MRP_L. Why? At levels of employment below Q_e, MRP_L exceeds MC_L. The firm will increase profits by employing more labour. At levels of employment above Q_e, MC_L exceeds MRP_L. In this case the firm will increase profits by reducing employment.

Derivation of the firm's demand curve for labour

No matter what the wage rate, the quantity of labour demanded will be found from the intersection of W and MRP_L (see Figure 5.6). At a wage rate of W_1, Q_1, labour is demanded; at W_2, Q_2 is demanded; at W_3, Q_3 is demanded. Thus the MRP_L curve will show the quantity of labour employed at each wage rate. But this is just what the demand curve for labour shows. Thus the MRP_L curve is the demand curve for labour.

There are three determinants of the demand for labour:

FIGURE 5.5
The profit-maximising level of employment

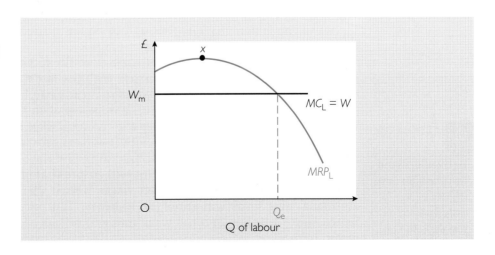

FIGURE 5.6
Deriving the firm's demand curve for labour

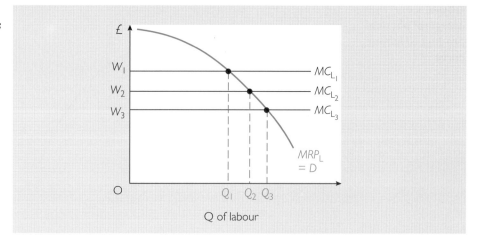

- The wage rate. This determines the position *on* the demand curve. (Strictly speaking we would refer here to the wage determining the 'quantity demanded' rather than the 'demand'.)
- The productivity of labour (MPP_L). This determines the position *of* the demand curve.
- The demand for the good. The higher the market demand for the good, the higher will be its market price, and hence the higher will be the MR, and thus the MRP_L. This too determines the position of the demand curve. It shows how the demand for labour (and other factors) is a derived demand: i.e. one derived from the demand for the good. The higher the demand for houses, and hence the higher their price, the higher will be the demand for bricklayers.

A change in the wage rate will be represented by a movement *along* the demand curve for labour. A change in the productivity of labour or in the demand for the good will *shift* the curve.

Wages and profits under perfect competition

The wage rate (W) will be determined by the interaction of demand and supply in the labour market. This will be equal to the value of the output that the last person produces (MRP_L).

Profits to the individual firm will arise from the fact that the MRP_L curve slopes downward (diminishing returns), with the last worker adding less to the revenue of firms than previous workers already employed.

If *all* workers in the firm receive a wage equal to the MRP of the *last* worker, everyone but the last worker will receive a wage less than their MRP. This excess of MRP_L over W of previous workers provides a surplus to the firm over its wages bill (see Figure 5.7).

Perfect competition between firms will ensure that profits are kept down to *normal* profits. If the surplus over wages is such that *supernormal* profits are made, new firms will enter the industry. The price of the good (and hence MRP_L) will fall, and the wage rate will be bid up, until only normal profits remain.

Definition

Derived demand
The demand for a factor of production depends on the demand for the good which uses it.

FIGURE 5.7
Wages and profits

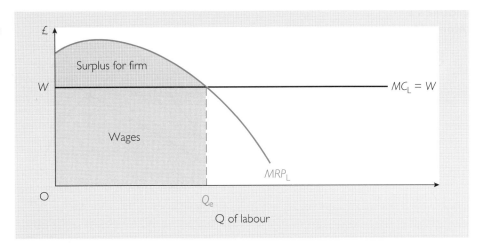

Summary

1. **Wage rates in a competitive labour market are determined by the interaction of demand and supply.**
2. **The market supply of labour curve will normally be upward sloping. Its elasticity will depend on the occupational and geographical mobility of labour. The more readily labour can transfer between jobs and regions, the more elastic will be the supply of labour.**
3. **The demand for labour is traditionally assumed to be based upon labour's productivity. Marginal productivity theory assumes that the employer will demand labour up to the point where the cost of employing one additional worker (MC_L) is equal to the revenue earned from the output of that worker (MRP_L).**

5.3   Wage determination in imperfect markets

How are wage rates affected by big business and by unions?

In the real world, many firms have the power to influence wage rates: they are not wage takers. This is one of the major types of labour market 'imperfection'.

When a firm is the only employer of a particular type of labour, this situation is called a **monopsony**. The Post Office is a monopsony employer of postal workers. Another example is when a factory is the only employer of certain types of labour in that district. It therefore has local monopsony power. When there are just a few employers, this is called oligopsony.

Monopsonists (and oligopsonists too) are 'wage setters' not 'wage takers'. Thus a large employer in a small town may have considerable power to resist wage increases or even to force wage rates down.

Such firms face an upward-sloping supply curve of labour. This is illustrated in Figure 5.8. If the firm wants to take on more labour, it will have to pay a higher wage rate to attract workers away from other industries. But conversely, by employing less labour it can get away with paying a lower wage rate.

Definitions

Monopsony
A market with a single buyer or employer.

Oligopsony
A market with just a few buyers or employers.

FIGURE 5.8
Monopsony

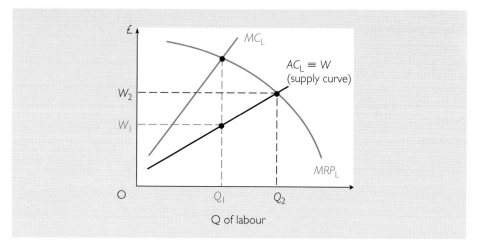

The supply curve shows the wage rate that must be paid to attract a given quantity of labour. The wage rate it pays is the *average cost* to the firm of employing labour (AC_L). The supply curve is also therefore the AC_L curve.

The *marginal* cost of employing one more worker (MC_L) will be above the wage (AC_L). The reason is that the wage rate has to be raised to attract extra workers. The MC_L will thus be the new higher wage paid to the new employee *plus* the small rise in the total wages bill for existing employees: after all, they will be paid the higher wage too.

The profit-maximising employment of labour would be at Q_1, where $MC_L = MRP_L$. The wage paid would thus be W_1.

If this had been a perfectly competitive labour market, employment would have been at the higher level Q_2, with the wage rate at the higher level W_2, where $W = MRP_L$. What in effect the monopsonist is doing, therefore, is forcing the wage rate down by restricting the number of workers employed.

The role of trade unions

Unions and market power
How can unions influence the determination of wages, and what might be the consequences of their actions?

The extent to which unions will succeed in pushing up wage rates depends on their power and militancy. It also depends on the power of firms to resist and on their ability to pay higher wages. In particular, the scope for unions to gain a better deal for their members depends on the sort of market in which the employers are producing.

Unions facing competitive employers
If the employers are producing under perfect or monopolistic competition, unions can raise wage rates only at the expense of employment. Firms are only earning normal profit. Thus if unions force up the wage rate, the marginal firms will go bankrupt and leave the industry. Fewer workers will be employed. The fall in output will lead to higher prices. This will enable the remaining firms to pay a higher wage rate.

Figure 5.9 illustrates these effects. If unions force the wage rate up from W_1 to W_2, employment will fall from Q_1 to Q_2. There will be a surplus of people

FIGURE 5.9
*Monopoly union
facing producers
under perfect
competition*

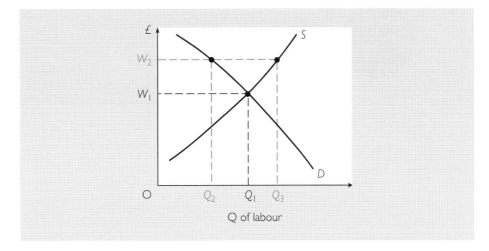

$(Q_3 - Q_2)$ wishing to work in this industry for whom no jobs are available.

The union is in a doubly weak position. Not only will jobs be lost as a result of forcing up the wage rate, but also there is a danger that these unemployed people will undercut the union wage, unless the union can prevent firms from employing non-unionised labour.

Wage rates can be increased without a reduction in the level of employment only if, as part of the bargain, the productivity of labour is increased. This is called a productivity deal. The *MRP* curve, and hence the *D* curve in Figure 5.9, shifts to the right.

In a competitive market, then, the union is faced with the choice between wages and jobs. Its actions will thus depend on its objectives.

If it wants to *maximise employment*, it will have to content itself with a wage of W_1 in Figure 5.9, unless productivity deals can be negotiated. At W_1, Q_1 workers will be employed. Above W_1, fewer than Q_1 workers will be *demanded*. Below W_1, fewer than Q_1 workers will be *supplied*.

If, on the other hand, it wants to *maximise the total amount of wages* paid by employers, it will continue pushing up the wage rate as long as the demand for labour is inelastic. As long as it is inelastic, the increase in the wage rate will be proportionately larger than the fall in employment, thereby causing total wage payments to rise. As the wage rate is raised, however, firms will increasingly be forced to cut back on labour. The elasticity of demand is likely to increase as the wage rate rises. When the elasticity has risen to equal unity, total incomes of workers will be at a maximum.

Definition

**Productivity
deal**
Where, in return for a
wage increase, a union
agrees to changes in
working practices that
will increase output per
worker.

Bilateral monopoly

What happens when a union monopoly faces a monopsony employer? What will the wage rate be? What will the level of employment be? Unfortunately, economic theory cannot give a precise answer to these questions. There is no 'equilibrium' level as such (see Box 5.1). Ultimately the wage rate and level of employment will depend on the relative bargaining strengths and skills of unions and management.

Unions may in fact be in a stronger position to make substantial gains for their members when they are facing a powerful employer. There is often

BOX 5.1 Wages under bilateral monopoly

All to play for?

There is no single equilibrium wage rate under bilateral monopoly. This box shows why.

Assume first that there is no union. The diagram shows that a monopsonist employer will maximise profits by employing Q_1 workers at a wage rate of W_1. (Q_1 is where $MRP_L = MC_L$).

Bilateral monopoly

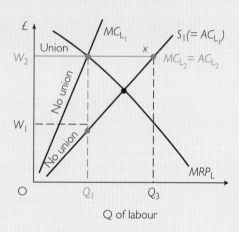

What happens when a union is introduced into this situation? Wages will now be set by negotiation between unions and management. Once the wage rate has been agreed, the employer can no longer drive the wage rate down by employing fewer workers. If it tried to pay less than the agreed wage, it could well be faced by a strike, and thus have a zero supply of labour!

considerable scope for them to increase wage rates *without* this leading to a reduction in employment, or even for them to increase both the wage rate *and* employment. The reason is that if firms have power in the *goods* market too, and are making supernormal profit, then there is scope for a powerful union to redistribute some of these profits to wages.

The actual wage rate under bilateral monopoly is usually determined through a process of negotiation or 'collective bargaining'. The outcome of this bargaining will depend on a wide range of factors, which vary substantially from one industry or firm to another.

Collective bargaining

Sometimes when unions and management negotiate, *both* sides can gain from the resulting agreement. For example, the introduction of new technology may allow higher wages, improved working conditions and higher profits. Usually, however, one side's gain is the other's loss. Higher wages

Definition

Picketing
Where people on strike gather at the entrance to the firm and attempt to dissuade workers or delivery vehicles from entering.

Similarly, if the employer decided to take on *more* workers, it would not have to *increase* the wage rate as long as the negotiated wage were above the free-market wage: as long as the wage rate were above that given by the supply curve S_1.

The effect of this is to give a new supply curve that is horizontal up to the point where it meets the original supply curve. For example, let us assume that the union succeeds in negotiating a wage rate of W_2. The supply curve will be horizontal at this level to the left of point x. To the right of this point it will follow the original supply curve S_1, since to acquire more than Q_3 workers it would have to raise the wage rate above W_2.

If the supply curve is horizontal to the left of point x at a level of W_2, so too will be the MC_L curve. The reason is simply that the extra cost to the employer of taking on an extra worker (up to Q_3) is merely the wage rate: no rise has to be given to existing employees. If MC_L is equal to the wage, the profit-maximising employment ($MC_L = MRP_L$) will now be where $W = MRP_L$. At a negotiated wage rate of W_2, the firm will therefore choose to employ Q_1 workers.

What this means, therefore, is that the union can push the wage right up from W_1 to W_2 and the firm will still *want* to employ Q_1. In other words, a wage rise can be obtained *without* a reduction in employment.

The union could go further still. By threatening industrial action, it may be able to push the wage rate above W_2 and still insist that Q_1 workers are employed (i.e. no redundancies). The firm may be prepared to see profits drop right down to normal level rather than face a strike and risk losses. The absolute upper limit to the wage rate will be that at which the firm is forced to close down.

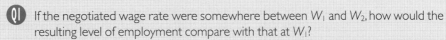 If the negotiated wage rate were somewhere between W_1 and W_2, how would the resulting level of employment compare with that at W_1?

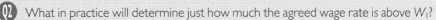 What in practice will determine just how much the agreed wage rate is above W_1?

mean lower profits. Either way, both sides will want to gain the maximum for themselves.

The outcome of the negotiations will depend on the relative bargaining strengths of both sides. In bargaining there are various threats or promises that either side can make. For these to be effective, of course, the other side must believe that they will be carried out.

Union *threats* might include strike action, **picketing, working to rule** or refusing to co-operate with management – for example, in the introduction of new technology. Alternatively, in return for higher wages or better working conditions, unions might *offer* no-strike agreements (or an informal promise not to take industrial action), increased productivity, reductions in the workforce, or long-term deals over pay.

In turn, employers might threaten employees with plant closure, **lock-outs**, redundancies or the employment of non-union labour. Alternatively, they might promise, in return for lower wage increases, various 'perks' such

Definition

Working to rule
Where union members are instructed to stick to the letter of their job description and to refuse to take on any extra duties.

as productivity bonuses, profit-sharing schemes, better working conditions, more overtime, better holidays or security of employment.

Strikes, lock-outs and other forms of industrial action impose costs on both unions and firms. Unions lose pay. Firms lose revenue. It is usually in both sides' interests, therefore, to settle by negotiation. Nevertheless to gain the maximum advantage, each side must persuade the other that it will carry out its threats if pushed.

The approach described so far has essentially been one of confrontation. The alternative is for both sides to concentrate on increasing the total net income of the firm by co-operating on ways to increase efficiency or the quality of the product. This approach is more likely when unions and management have built up an atmosphere of trust over time.

The role of government in collective bargaining

The government can influence the outcome of collective bargaining in a number of ways. One is to try to set an example. It may take a tough line in resisting wage demands by public-sector workers, hoping thereby to persuade employers in the private sector to do likewise.

Alternatively, it could act as an arbitrator. Past governments have attempted to mediate in pay disputes which they felt were damaging to the economy. 'Beer and sandwiches at No. 10 Downing Street' for the two sides in a dispute were not uncommon during the Labour government of the 1960s. More formally, the government can set up arbitration or conciliation machinery. For example, the Advisory Conciliation and Arbitration Service (ACAS) conciliates in over 1000 disputes each year. It also provides, on request by both sides, an arbitration service, where its findings will be binding.

Another approach is to use legislation. The government could pass laws that restrict the behaviour of employers or unions. It could pass laws that set a minimum wage rate, or prevent discrimination against workers on various grounds. Similarly, it could pass laws that curtail the power of unions. The UK Conservative governments between 1979 and 1997 put considerable emphasis on reducing the power of trade unions and making labour markets more 'flexible'. Several Acts of Parliament were passed. These included the following measures:

- Employees were given the right to join any union. This effectively ended **closed-shop agreements**.
- Secret postal ballots of the union membership were made mandatory for the operation of a political fund, the election of senior union officials, and strikes and other official industrial action.
- Political strikes, sympathy action and action against other non-unionised companies were made illegal.
- Lawful action was confined to that against workers' own direct employers, even to their own particular place of work. All **secondary action** was made unlawful.
- It was made unlawful for employers to penalise workers for choosing to join or refusing to join a trade union. It was also made unlawful for employers to deny employment on the grounds that an applicant does not belong to a union.

The effect of these measures was considerably to weaken the power of trade unions in the UK.

Definitions

Lock-out
Where workers are (temporarily) laid off until they are prepared to agree to the firm's conditions.

Closed shop
Where a firm agrees to employ only union members.

Secondary action
Industrial action taken against a firm not directly involved in the dispute.

The efficiency wage hypothesis

We have seen that a union may be able to force an employer to pay a wage above the market-clearing rate. But wage rates above the equilibrium are not just the result of union power. It may well be in firms' interests to pay higher wage rates, even in non-unionised sectors. The result may be that workers receive a wage rate above and beyond that which they would be prepared to accept. Even in times when unemployment is high, and it might be expected that wage levels would fall, many firms seem willing to maintain, or even increase, rates of pay (even after taking inflation into account).

One explanation for this phenomenon is the efficiency wage hypothesis. This states that the productivity of workers is affected by the wage rate that they receive. As a result, employers are frequently prepared to offer wage rates above the market-clearing level, attempting to balance increased wage costs against gains in productivity. But why may higher wage rates lead to higher productivity? Several explanations have been advanced.

Less 'shirking'. In many jobs it is difficult to monitor the effort that individuals put into their work. Workers may thus get away with shirking or careless behaviour. The business could attempt to reduce shirking by imposing a series of sanctions, the most serious of which would be dismissal, in which case the individual would have to find another job or rely on state benefits. The greater the wage rate currently received, the greater will be the cost to the individual of dismissal, and the less likely it is, therefore, that workers will shirk. The business will benefit not only from the additional output, but also from a reduction in the costs of having to monitor workers' performance. As a consequence, the efficient wage rate for the business will lie above the market-determined wage rate.

Reduced labour turnover. If workers receive on-the-job training or re-training, then to lose a worker once the training has been completed is a significant cost to the business. Labour turnover, and hence its associated costs, can be reduced by paying a wage above the market-clearing rate. By paying such a wage rate, the business is seeking a degree of loyalty from its employees.

Self-selection. A high wage rate will tend to attract the most productive workers. As such, it acts as a form of selection device, reducing the costs to the business of employing workers of lower quality.

Morale. A simple reason for offering wage rates above the market-clearing level is to motivate the workforce – to create the feeling that the firm is a 'good' employer that cares about its employees. As a consequence, workers might be more industrious and more willing to accept the introduction of new technology (with the reorganisation that it involves).

The paying of efficiency wages above the market-clearing wage will depend upon the type of work involved. Workers who occupy skilled positions, especially where the business has invested time in their training (thus

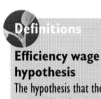

Definitions

Efficiency wage hypothesis
The hypothesis that the productivity of workers is affected by the wage rate that they receive.

Efficiency wage rate
The profit-maximising wage rate for the firm after taking into account the effects of wage rates on worker motivation, turnover and recruitment.

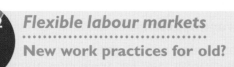

BOX 5.2

Flexible labour markets
·····································
New work practices for old?

The last two decades have seen sweeping changes in the ways that firms organise their workforce. Two world recessions combined with rapid changes in technology have led many firms to question the wisdom of appointing workers on a permanent basis to specific jobs. Instead, they want to have the greatest flexibility possible to respond to new situations. If demand falls, they want to be able to 'shed' labour without facing large redundancy costs. If demand rises, they want rapid access to additional labour supplies. If technology changes, say with the introduction of new computerised processes, they want to have the flexibility to move workers around, or to take on new workers in some areas and lose workers in others.

What many firms seek, therefore, is flexibility in employing and allocating labour. What countries are experiencing is an increasingly flexible labour market, as workers and employment agencies respond to the new 'flexible firm'.

There are three main types of flexibility in the use of labour:

Functional flexibility. This is where an employer is able to transfer labour between different tasks within the production process. It contrasts with traditional forms of organisation where people were employed to do a specific job, and then stuck to it. A functionally flexible labour force will tend to be multi-skilled and relatively highly trained.

Numerical flexibility. This is where the firm is able to adjust the size and composition of its workforce according to changing market conditions. To achieve this, the firm is likely to employ a large proportion of its labour on a part-time or casual basis, or even subcontract out specialist requirements, rather than employing such labour skills itself.

The flexible firm

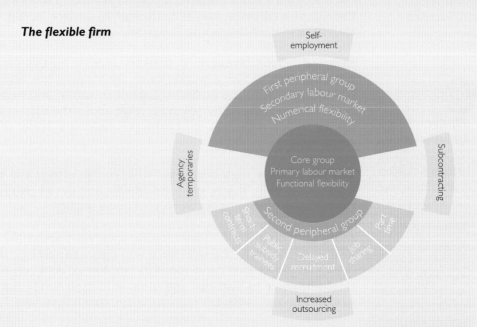

Source: Institute of Manpower Studies (1984).

Financial flexibility. This is where the firm has flexibility in its wage costs. In large part it is a result of functional and numerical flexibility. Financial flexibility can be achieved by rewarding individual effort and productivity rather than paying a given rate for a particular job. Such rates of pay are increasingly negotiated at the local level rather than being nationally set. The result is not only a widening of pay differentials between skilled and unskilled workers, but also growing differentials in pay between workers within the same industry but in different parts of the country.

The diagram shows how these three forms of flexibility are reflected in the organisation of a flexible firm, an organisation quite different from that of the traditional firm. The most significant difference is that the labour force is segmented. The core group, drawn from the *primary labour market*, will be composed of *functionally* flexible workers, who have relatively secure employment and are generally on full-time permanent contracts. Such workers will be relatively well paid and receive wages reflecting their scarce skills.

The periphery, drawn from the *secondary labour market*, is more fragmented than the core, and can be subdivided into a first and a second peripheral group. The first peripheral group is composed of workers with a lower level of skill than those in the core – skills that tend to be general rather than firm specific. Thus workers in the first peripheral group can usually be drawn from the external labour market. Such workers may be employed on full-time contracts, but they will generally face less secure employment than those workers in the core.

The business gains a greater level of numerical flexibility by drawing labour from the second peripheral group. Here workers are employed on a variety of short-term, part-time contracts. Workers in the second peripheral group have little job security.

As well as being able to supplement the level of labour in the first peripheral group, the second periphery can also provide high-level specialist skills that supplement the core. In this instance the business can subcontract or hire self-employed labour, minimising its commitment to such workers. The business thereby gains both functional and numerical flexibility simultaneously.

The Japanese model

The application of new flexible working patterns is becoming more prevalent in businesses in the UK and elsewhere in Europe, and in North America. In Japan, the practice of flexibility has been part of the business way of life for many years and has been crucial in shaping the country's economic success. In fact we now talk of a Japanese model of business organisation, which many of its competitors seek to emulate.

The model is based around four principles:

- Total quality management (TQM). This involves all employees working towards continuously improving all aspects of quality, both of the finished product and of methods of production.
- Elimination of waste. According to the 'just-in-time' (JIT) principle, businesses should take delivery of just sufficient quantities of raw materials and parts, at the right time and place. Stocks are kept to a minimum and hence the whole system of production runs with little, if any, slack. The adoption of JIT by western companies has not been as extensive so far as TQM. For JIT to work, deliveries must not be subject to disruptions or delays: something that cannot be relied upon by many western companies.

- A belief in the superiority of team work. Collective effort is a vital element in Japanese working practices. Team work is seen not only to enhance individual performance, but also to involve the individual in the running of the business and thus to create a sense of commitment.
- The use of functional and numerical flexibility within Japanese business is widely practised. Both are seen as vital components in maintaining high levels of productivity.

The principles of this model are now widely accepted as being important in creating and maintaining a competitive business in a competitive marketplace. It now appears that around these principles we are likely to see the convergence of the modern business organisation.

Q1 Is a flexible firm more likely or less likely to employ workers up to the point where their $MRP = MC_L$?

Q2 How is the advent of flexible firms likely to alter the gender balance of employment and unemployment?

Q3 What are the dangers of adopting a 'just-in-time' approach to managing production?

making them costly to replace) are likely to receive efficiency wages considerably above the market wage. By contrast, workers in unskilled positions, where shirking can be easily monitored, where little training takes place and where workers can be easily replaced, are unlikely to command an 'efficiency wage premium'. In such situations, rather than keeping wage rates high, the business will probably try to pay as little as possible.

Summary

1. **Where a firm has monopoly power in employing labour, it is known as a 'monopsonist'. Such a firm will employ workers to the point where $MRP_L = MC_L$. Since the wage is below MC_L, the monopsonist, other things being equal, will employ fewer workers at a lower wage than would be employed in a perfectly competitive labour market.**
2. **If a union has monopoly power, its power to raise wages will be limited if the employer operates under perfect or monopolistic competition in the goods market. A rise in wage rates will force the employer to cut back on employment, unless there is a corresponding rise in productivity.**
3. **In a situation of bilateral monopoly (where a monopoly union faces a monopsony employer) the union may have considerable scope to raise wage rates above the monopsony level. There is no unique equilibrium wage. The wage rate will depend on the outcome of a process of collective bargaining between union and management.**
4. **Collective bargaining is the process by which employers and unions negotiate wage levels and the terms and conditions of employment. Both sides can use threats and promises to determine the outcome of**

the negotiating process. The success of such threats and promises depends upon factors such as the power of the union or the employer; attitudes and the determination to win; scope for compromise; negotiating skills; information; and the role of government.

5. The efficiency wage hypothesis states that a firm might pay above the market-clearing wage rate so as to: reduce shirking; reduce labour turnover; improve the quality of labour recruited; and stimulate worker morale. The level of the efficiency wage rate will largely be determined by the type of job the worker does, and the level and scarcity of skill they possess.

Causes of inequality

Why are some people rich and others poor?

Inequality in the UK

FIGURE 5.10
Size distribution of UK income by quintile group of households: 1994/5
(a) Income before taxes and benefits
(b) Income after taxes and benefits

Figure 5.10 shows the distribution of income in the UK (from all sources). The population is placed into five equal-sized groups of households, from the poorest 20 per cent of households up to the richest 20 per cent. The following points can be drawn from these statistics:

- In 1995/6, the richest 20 per cent of households earned over 50 per cent of national income, and even after the deduction of taxes this was still 43 per cent.
- The poorest 20 per cent, by contrast, earned a mere 2.6 per cent of national income, and even after the receipt of benefits, this had risen to only 6.9 per cent.

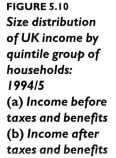

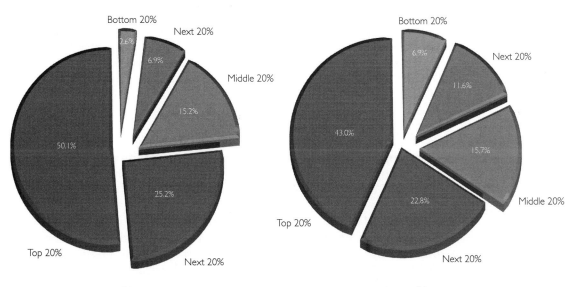

Source: *Economic Trends* (ONS, December 1995).

FIGURE 5.11
Sources of UK household income as a percentage of gross household income

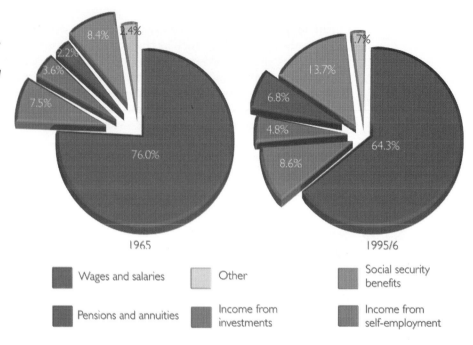

1965

1995/6

Wages and salaries

Other

Social security benefits

Pensions and annuities

Income from investments

Income from self-employment

Inequality has grown dramatically in the UK and many other countries in recent years. Between 1977 and 1995/6, the post-tax-and-benefits share of UK national income of the poorest 40 per cent of households fell from 23.3 per cent to 18.5 per cent; while the share of the top 20 per cent grew from 36.9 per cent to 43.0 per cent.

Distribution of income by source

Figure 5.11 shows the sources of household incomes in the UK. Wages and salaries constitute by far the largest element. However their share fell from 76.0 per cent to 64.3 per cent of national income between 1965 and 1995/6. Conversely, the share coming from social security benefits and pensions rose from 10.6 per cent to 20.5 per cent, reflecting the higher levels of unemployment in the 1990s and the growing proportion of the population past retirement age.

In contrast to wages and salaries, investment income (dividends, interest and rent) accounts for a very small percentage of household income – a mere 4.8 per cent in 1995/6.

With the growth of small businesses and the increased numbers of people being 'employed' on a freelance basis, so the proportion of incomes coming from self-employment has grown. It rose from 5.7 per cent in 1975 to 8.6 per cent in 1995/6.

Distribution of wages and salaries by occupation

The major cause of differences in incomes between individuals in employment is the differences in wages and salaries between different occupations. Differences in full-time wages and salaries are illustrated in Figure 5.12. This shows the average gross weekly earnings of full-time adult male workers in selected occupations in 1996. As can be seen, there are considerable differences in earnings between different occupations.

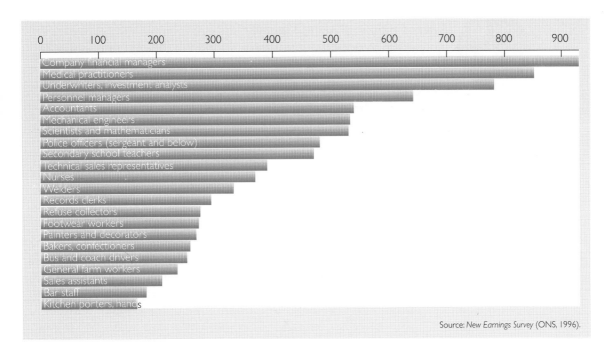

Source: *New Earnings Survey* (ONS, 1996).

FIGURE 5.12
Average gross weekly earnings of UK full-time adult male employees (£): selected occupations: 1996

About 10 per cent of the earnings in Figure 5.12 come from overtime (on average about 3 hours per week). The amount of overtime worked differs markedly, however, between occupations. Thus it is not just the basic hourly wage rate (or annual salary) that explains differences in earnings from one occupation to another, but also the number of hours worked and the overtime rate.

Since the late 1970s, wage differentials have widened. Part of the explanation lies in a shift in the demand for labour. Many firms have adopted new techniques which require a more highly educated workforce. Wage rates in some of these skilled occupations have increased substantially.

At the same time there has been a decline in the number of unskilled jobs in industry, and along with it, a decline in the power of unions to represent such people. Where low-skilled jobs remain, there will be intense pressure on employers to reduce wage costs if they are competing with companies based in developing countries, where wage rates are much lower.

As prospects for the unskilled decline in industry, so people with few qualifications increasingly compete for low-paid service-sector jobs (e.g. in supermarkets and fast-food outlets). The growth in people seeking part-time work has also kept wage rates down in this sector.

Distribution of wages and salaries by sex

Box 5.3 looks at some of the aspects of income inequality between the sexes. Figure 5.13 gives examples of average gross weekly earnings of full-time adult female workers in 1996. The average for all occupations was £283. This compares with £392 for men. There are three important factors to note:

- Women are paid less than men in the same occupations. You will see this if you compare some of the occupations in Figure 5.13 with the same ones in Figure 5.12.

BOX 5.3

Equal pay for equal work?
....
Wage inequalities between women and men

One of the key characteristics shown in Table (a) is that female gross hourly earnings relative to male gross hourly earnings increased substantially during the early 1970s. Having peaked at around 75 per cent in the late 1970s, they remained just under that level for the next ten years. They then rose again toward the 80 per cent mark by the late 1990s.

The inequality between male and female earnings can in part be explained by the fact that men and women are occupationally segregated. Seeing that women predominate in poorly paid occupations, the difference in earnings is somewhat to be expected. But if you consider Table (b), you can see that quite substantial earning differentials persist *within* particular occupations.

(a) Average gross hourly earnings, excluding the effects of overtime, for full-time UK employees, aged 18 and over, 1970–95 (pence per hour)

	1970	1974	1978	1980	1982	1984	1986	1988	1990	1992	1994	1996
Men	67	105	200	281	355	417	482	573	689	810	865	939
Women	42	71	148	206	262	306	358	429	528	638	688	750
Differential	25	34	52	74	93	111	124	144	161	172	177	189
Women's earnings as a % of men's	63.1	67.4	73.9	73.5	73.9	73.5	74.3	75.0	76.6	78.8	79.5	79.9

Source: *New Earnings Survey* (ONS).

So why has this inequality persisted? There are a number of possible reasons:

- The marginal productivity of labour in typically female occupations may be lower than in typically male occupations. This may in part be due to simple questions of physical strength. Very often, however, it is due to the fact that women tend to work in more labour-intensive occupations. If there is less capital equipment per female worker than there is per male worker, then it would be expected that the marginal product of a woman would be less than that of a man.
- Women may on average undertake less training than men. If, therefore, the resulting level of skills obtained by women is less than those obtained by men, women will have a lower marginal productivity.

  There are various reasons for differences in training and qualifications. In part it is due to an educational system which may favour boys rather than girls. Even if this is not deliberate policy, the attitudes of parents, teachers and pupils may be such as to give more encouragement to boys to think of qualifications for a future career. In part it is due to employers being more willing to invest money in training men, fearing that women may leave after a short time to have children.
- Women tend to be less geographically mobile than men. If social norms are such that the man's job is seen as somehow more 'important' than the woman's, then a couple will often move if that is necessary for the man to get promotion. The woman, however, will have to settle for whatever job she can get in the same locality as her partner.
- A smaller proportion of women workers are members of unions than men. Even when they are members of unions, these are often in jobs where unions are weak (e.g. clothing industry workers, shop assistants and secretaries).

(b) Average gross hourly earnings, excluding the effects of overtime, for selected occupations, full-time UK employees on adult rates, 1996

Occupation	Men	Women	Women's earnings as a % of men's
	(£ per hour)		
Nurses	9.58	9.06	94.6
Social workers	9.86	9.07	92.0
Police officers (below sergeant)	12.38	11.21	90.5
Bar staff	4.18	3.76	90.0
Secondary school teachers	15.45	13.78	89.2
Laboratory technicians	8.60	7.58	88.1
Medical practitioners	19.80	17.02	86.0
Sales assistants	5.17	4.37	84.5
Chefs/cooks	5.69	4.60	80.8
Computer operators	8.18	6.19	75.7
Assemblers and lineworkers	6.65	5.00	75.2
Personnel managers	17.32	12.65	73.0
Legal professionals	19.77	14.42	72.9
All occupations	9.39	7.50	79.9
Average gross weekly pay	391.60	283.00	72.3
Average weekly hours worked (incl. overtime)	41.7	37.6	
Average weekly overtime	3.1	0.9	

Source: *New Earnings Survey* (ONS).

- Part-time workers (mainly women) have less bargaining power, less influence and less chance of obtaining promotion.
- Custom and practice. Despite equal pay legislation, many jobs done wholly or mainly by women continue to be low paid, irrespective of questions of productivity.
- Prejudice. Some employers may prefer to give senior posts to men on grounds purely of sexual prejudice. This is very difficult to legislate against when the employer can simply claim that the 'better' person was given the job.

Which of the above reasons could be counted as economically 'irrational' (i.e. paying different wage rates to women and men for other than purely economic reasons)? Certainly the last two would classify. Paying different wage rates on these grounds would *not* be in the profit interests of the employer.

Some of the others, however, are more difficult to classify. The causes of the inequality in wage rates may be traced back beyond the workplace: perhaps to the educational system, or to a culture which discourages women from being so aggressive in seeking promotion or 'self-advertisement'. Even if it is a manifestation of profit-maximising behaviour by employers that women in some circumstances are paid less than their male counterparts (and is thus not an example of 'irrationality'), the reason *why* it is more profitable for employers to pay men more than women may indeed reflect discrimination elsewhere or at some other point in time.

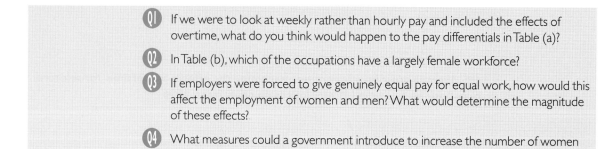

Q1 If we were to look at weekly rather than hourly pay and included the effects of overtime, what do you think would happen to the pay differentials in Table (a)?

Q2 In Table (b), which of the occupations have a largely female workforce?

Q3 If employers were forced to give genuinely equal pay for equal work, how would this affect the employment of women and men? What would determine the magnitude of these effects?

Q4 What measures could a government introduce to increase the number of women getting higher-paid jobs?

FIGURE 5.13
Average gross weekly earnings of full-time adult female employees (£): selected occupations: 1995

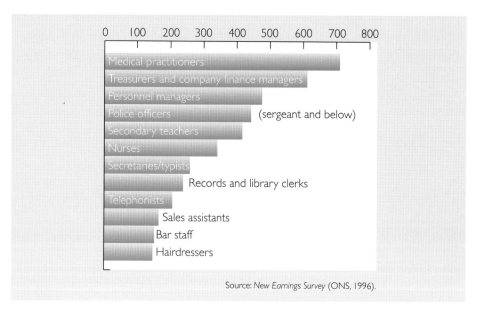

Source: *New Earnings Survey* (ONS, 1996).

- Women tend to be employed in lower-paid occupations than men.
- Women do much less overtime than men (on average just under 1 hour per week, compared with 3.1 for men).

Causes of inequality

We turn now to identify the major causes of inequality. The problem has many dimensions and there are many factors that determine the pattern and depth of inequality. It is thus wrong to try to look for a single cause, or even the major one. What follows then is a list of the possible determinants of inequality:

- Differences in ability. People differ in strength, intelligence, dexterity, etc. Some of these differences are innate and some are acquired through the process of 'socialisation'– education, home environment, peer group, etc.
- Differences in attitude. Some people are adventurous, willing to take risks, willing to move for better jobs, keen to push themselves forward. Others are much more cautious.

FIGURE 5.14
Weekly income for different types of UK household (£): 1994/5

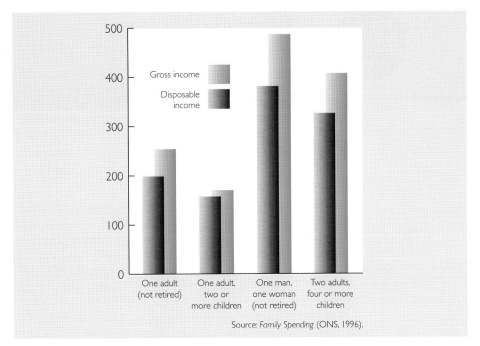

Source: *Family Spending* (ONS, 1996).

- Differences in qualifications. These are reflections of a number of things: ability, attitudes toward study, access to educational establishments, the quality of tuition, attitudes and income of parents, etc.

The above three sets of factors will cause differences in people's marginal productivity and hence differences in wage rates. Wages will also reflect the following:

- Differences in hours worked. Some people do a full-time job plus overtime, or a second job; others work only part time.
- Differences in the pleasantness/unpleasantness of jobs. Other things being equal, unpleasant, arduous or dangerous jobs will need to pay higher wage rates.
- Differences in power. Monopoly power in the supply of labour or goods, and monopsony power in the demand for labour, are unequally distributed in the economy.
- Differences in the demand for goods. Workers employed in expanding industries will tend to have a higher marginal revenue product because their output has a higher market value.
- Discrimination, whether by race, sex, age, social background, etc.

Inequality is not just the result of differences in wages. It is also caused by the following:

- Differences in household composition. Other things being equal, the more dependants there are in a household, the lower the income will be *per member* of that household. Figure 5.14 gives an extreme example of this. It shows the average household income in the UK in 1995/6 of four different categories of household.

   Households with two adults and four or more children had a lower average income than households with only one man and one woman.

BOX 5.4

Minimum wage legislation
....
A way of helping the poor?

It is a serious national evil that any class of His Majesty's subjects should receive less than a living wage in return for their utmost exertions. It was formerly supposed that the workings of the laws of supply and demand would naturally regulate or eliminate that evil, but whereas in what we call 'sweated trades' you have no parity of bargaining between employers and employed, when the good employer is continually undercut by the bad, and the bad again by the worse, there you have not a condition of progress, but of progressive degeneration.
Winston Churchill (1909)

One way of helping to relieve poverty is for the government to institute a legal minimum hourly wage. A form of minimum-wage legislation was introduced in Britain as long ago as 1909 by Winston Churchill, who was at the time President of the Board of Trade in the Liberal government. This involved the setting up of wages councils. These were independent bodies representing workers in low-pay industries which were poorly unionised. The councils set legally enforceable minimum hourly rates of pay for their respective industries.

In 1993, however, the government announced the abolition of wages councils, and today the UK is one of the few industrialised countries that does not have a legal minimum wage. The Council of Europe defines low pay as anything below two-thirds of the mean wage level. It refers to this as the 'decency threshold'. If a minimum hourly wage were to be based on this, then in the UK it would be set at just under £6, and would raise wages for over 9 million workers. Other studies have identified the low-pay threshold at two-thirds of *median* earnings of *male* workers. A minimum hourly wage set at this level would be about £3.75, and would raise wage rates for only 4 million workers, 70 per cent of whom would be women.

The call for a minimum wage from the political left has grown stronger as the number of low-paid workers has increased. Today there are many people working as cleaners, kitchen hands, garment workers, security guards and shop assistants, who are receiving pittance rates of pay, sometimes less than £2 per hour. Several factors explain the growth in the size of the low-pay sector.

- *Unemployment.* Very high rates of unemployment since the early 1980s have shifted the balance of power from workers to employers. Employers have been able to force many wage rates downwards, especially of unskilled and semi-skilled workers.
- *Growth in part-time employment.* Changes in the structure of the UK economy – in particular, the growth in the service sector and the growing proportion of women seeking work – have led to an increase in part-time employment. Many part-time workers do not receive the same rights, privileges and hourly pay as their full-time equivalents.
- *Changes in labour laws.* The abolition of the wages councils and the introduction of various new laws to reduce the power of labour (see page 156) have taken away what little protection there was for low-paid workers.

Assessing the arguments

The arguments against a national minimum wage were put forcibly by Michael Howard in 1992 when he was the Employment Secretary: 'There can be no conceivable justification for a policy which would, on its own, wreck our economy and devastate job prospects.'

So will the imposition of a minimum wage cause unemployment? At first sight the answer would seem to be yes. If it raises wage rates for the poor (and to be effective it must do), then surely the demand for labour will fall and the supply will rise?

Just what will happen to employment depends on two things: the competitiveness of individual labour markets and the elasticity of demand and supply of labour.

In a *competitive* labour market, the level of unemployment created will depend on how much the wage rate rises and on the elasticity of labour demand and supply. The more elastic the demand and supply of labour, the bigger the unemployment effect will be.

Evidence suggests that the demand for low-skilled workers by *individual* employers is likely to be relatively wage sensitive. Often such firms are operating in highly competitive goods/services markets. Any rise in wages, and hence prices, would lead to a large fall in sales and hence employment. But given that *all* firms would face the minimum wage, individual employers would be more able to pass on higher wages in higher prices, knowing that their competitors were doing the same.

When employers have a degree of *monopsony* power, however, it is not even certain that they would want to reduce employment. Remember what we argued in the diagram in Box 5.1 (on page 154) when we were examining the effects of unions driving up wages. The argument is the same with a minimum wage. The minimum wage can be as high as W_2 and the firm will still want to employ as many workers as at W_2. The point is that the firm can no longer drive down the wage rate by employing fewer workers, so the incentive to cut its workforce has been removed! Indeed, if the minimum wage rate were above W_1 but below W_2, the firm would now want to employ *more* workers (where the minimum wage rate ($= MC_L$) is equal to the MRP_L). What is effectively happening is that the minimum wage is redistributing the firm's income from profits to wages.

In the long run, the effect on unemployment will depend on the extent to which the higher wages are compensated by higher labour productivity. In several EU countries, where minimum wages have been in force for many years, unemployment has generally been no higher than in the UK, but investment and labour productivity are generally higher.

Recent findings in the USA have suggested that increases in the minimum wage have had a neutral effect upon employment. It has been found that there exists a 'range of indeterminacy' over which wages can fluctuate with little impact upon levels of employment. Even beyond this range, whereas some employers might reduce the quantity of labour they employ, others might respond to their higher wage bill, and hence higher costs, by improving productive efficiency.

Evidence on the employment effects of a national minimum wage appears far from conclusive, certainly where the minimum wage results in fairly modest rises in wage rates. The issue, then, seems to be: how *high* can the minimum wage be set before unemployment begins to rise?

Beyond the economic arguments, the potentially most powerful claim in favour of a legal minimum wage is the moral one: that people working hard in a job should be able to take home a fair wage. Being a moral justification, it is one on which economists can have little say, other than to consider whether in practice a minimum wage will indeed help to relieve poverty.

The biggest weakness of minimum wages as a means of relieving poverty is that they only affect the employed. One of the main causes of poverty is unemployment. Clearly the unemployed would not benefit from a minimum wage.

Another cause of poverty is a large number of dependants in a family. If there is only one income earner, he or she may be paid above the minimum wage and yet the family could be very poor. By contrast, many of those who would be helped by minimum wages are second income earners in a family.

These are not arguments against minimum wages. They merely suggest that minimum wages cannot be the sole answer to poverty.

Q1 If an increase in wage rates for the low paid led to their being more motivated, how would this affect the marginal revenue product and the demand for such workers? What implications does your answer have for the effect on employment in such cases?

Q2 If minimum wages encourage employers to substitute machines for workers, will this necessarily lead to higher long-term unemployment in (a) that industry and (b) the economy in general?

This means that they had a very much lower income *per member* of the household. There is a twin problem for many large households. Not only may there be relatively more children and old-age dependants, but also the total household income will be reduced if one of the adults stays at home to look after the family, or works only part time.

- Inequality of wealth. People with wealth are able to obtain an income other than from their own labour. The greater the inequality of wealth, the greater is the inequality of income likely to be.
- Degree of government support. The greater the support for the poor, the less will be the level of inequality in the economy.
- Unemployment. This has become one of the major causes of poverty and hence inequality in recent years.

Summary

1. **Wages and salaries constitute by far the largest source of income, and thus inequality can be explained mainly in terms of differences in wages and salaries. Nevertheless state benefits are an important moderating influence on inequality and constitute the largest source of income for the poorest 20 per cent of households. Investment earnings are only a minor determinant of income except for the richest 1 or 2 per cent.**
2. **Inequality is in large part the result of differences in wages. These differences reflect differences in the productivity of workers, consumer demand, power and discrimination.**
3. **Apart from differences in wages and salaries between occupations, other determinants of income inequality include differences in household composition, inequality of wealth, unemployment and the level of government benefits.**

The redistribution of income

How can income be redistributed from rich to poor? What will be the effects of doing so?

In this section we will look at policies to redistribute incomes more equally, and in particular we will focus on the use of government social security benefits and taxation.

Taxation

If taxes are to be used as a means of achieving greater equality, the rich must be taxed proportionately more than the poor. The degree of redistribution will depend on the degree of 'progressiveness' of the tax. In this context, taxes may be classified as follows:

- *Progressive tax*. As people's income (Y) rises, the percentage of their income paid in the tax (T) rises. In other words, the *average* rate of tax (T/Y) rises. Income taxes are progressive (but much less progressive in the UK than they used to be).
- *Regressive tax*. As people's income rises, the percentage of their income paid in the tax falls: T/Y falls. An extreme form of regressive tax is a lump-sum tax. This is levied at a fixed *amount* (not rate) irrespective of income. The 'poll tax', introduced in Scotland in 1989 and England in 1990 as the new form of local taxation, was an example of such a tax. But it proved massively unpopular with the electorate, and was replaced by the 'council tax' (based on property values) in 1993.
- *Proportional tax*. As people's income rises, the percentage of their income paid in the tax stays the same: T/Y is constant.

The more progressive a tax, the more it will redistribute incomes away from the rich. Regressive taxes will have the opposite effect, since they tax the rich proportionately less than the poor.

Problems with using taxes to redistribute incomes

Assuming that it is desirable to redistribute incomes from rich to poor, how successfully can taxes accomplish this, and at what economic cost?

Taxation takes away income. It can thus reduce the incomes of the rich. But no taxes, however progressive, can *increase* the incomes of the poor. This will require subsidies (i.e. benefits).

But what about tax cuts? Cannot bigger tax cuts be given to the poor? This is possible only if the poor are already paying taxes in the first place. Take the two cases of income tax and taxes on goods and services.

- Income tax. If the government cuts income tax, then anyone currently paying it will benefit. A cut in tax *rates* will give proportionately more to the rich, since they have a larger proportion of taxable income relative to total income. An increase in personal *allowances*, on the other hand, will give the same *absolute* amount to everyone above the new tax threshold. This will therefore represent a smaller proportionate gain to the rich. In either case, however, there will be no gain at all to those people below the tax threshold. They paid no income tax in the first place. These poorest of all people therefore gain nothing at all from income tax cuts.

- Taxes on goods and services. Since taxes such as VAT and excise duties on alcoholic drinks, tobacco, petrol and gambling are generally regressive, any cut in their rate will benefit the poor proportionately more than the rich. A more dramatic effect would be obtained by cutting the rate most on those goods consumed relatively more by the poor (e.g. on domestic fuel).

The government may not wish to cut the overall level of taxation, given its expenditure commitments. In this case, it can switch the burden of taxes from regressive to progressive taxes: it could cut taxes on certain goods and services and raise income taxes and taxes on company profits. That way, at least some benefit is gained by the very poor.

Taxation and incentives

One of the major justifications given by the Conservative governments after 1979 for cutting both the basic and higher rates of income tax was that it increased the incentive to work.

This whole question of incentives is highly charged politically. If the Conservatives are correct, then there is a trade-off between output and equity. High and progressive income taxes can lead to a more equal distribution of income, but a smaller national output. Alternatively, by cutting taxes there will be a bigger national output, but less equally divided. If many on the political left are correct, however, we can have both a more equal society and a bigger national output: there is no trade-off.

The key to analysing these arguments is to distinguish between the *income effect* and the *substitution effect* of raising taxes. Raising taxes does two things.

- It reduces incomes. People therefore are encouraged to work *more* in an attempt to maintain their consumption of goods and services. This is called the income effect. 'I have to work more to make up for the higher taxes', a person might say.
- It reduces the opportunity cost of leisure. An extra hour taken in leisure now involves a smaller sacrifice in consumption. Thus people may substitute leisure for consumption, and work *less*. This is called the substitution effect. 'What is the point of doing overtime', another person might say, 'if so much of the overtime pay is going in taxes?'

The relative size of the income and substitution effects is likely to differ for different types of people. For example, the *income* effect is likely to dominate for those people with a substantial proportion of long-term commitments: for example, people with families, with mortgages and other debts. Such people may feel forced to work more to maintain their disposable income. Clearly for such people, higher taxes are *not* a disincentive to work. The income effect is also likely to be relatively large for people on higher incomes, for whom an increase in tax rates represents a substantial cut in income.

The *substitution* effect is likely to dominate for those with few commitments: those whose families have left home, the single, and second income earners in families where that second income is not relied on for 'essential' consumption.

Definitions

Income effect of a tax rise
Tax increases reduce people's incomes and thus encourage people to work more.

Substitution effect of a tax rise
Tax increases reduce the opportunity cost of leisure and thus encourage people to work less.

Although high income earners may work more when there is a tax *rise*, they may still be discouraged by a steeply progressive tax *structure*. If they have to pay very high marginal rates of tax, it may simply not be worth their while seeking promotion or working harder.

The relative size of the income and substitution effects will also depend on the types of tax change. For example, if the government wishes to raise income taxes in order to redistribute incomes, there are three main ways it can do it: raising the higher rates of tax; raising the basic rate; reducing tax allowances.

Raising the higher rates of tax. This may seem the most effective way of redistributing incomes: after all, it is only the rich that will suffer. There may, however, be serious disincentives, especially if taxes are raised to very high levels:

- Except for those on *very* high incomes, the income effect will be relatively small, since it is only that part of incomes subject to the higher tax rates that will be affected. The substitution effect, however, could be relatively high. Rich people are likely to put more of a premium on leisure, and may well feel that it is not worth working so hard if a larger proportion of their income is taken in taxes.
- It may discourage risk taking by businesspeople. This may have a serious effect on future output and growth.
- The rich may be more mobile internationally. There may therefore be a 'brain drain'.

Raising the basic rate of tax. The income effect is likely to be relatively large for those with higher incomes. They will suddenly be faced with a substantial loss in income, for which they may feel the need to compensate by working harder, especially if they have substantial commitments like a large mortgage.

For those just above the tax threshold, there will be very little extra to pay on *existing* income, since most of it is tax free anyway. Thus there will be hardly any income effect. However, each *extra* pound earned will be taxed at the new higher rate. The substitution effect, therefore, is likely to outweigh the income effect. For these people, a rise in tax rates will act as a disincentive.

For those below the tax threshold, there will be no direct effect, since their 'tax rate' remains at zero. A rise in the basic rate might nevertheless deter them from undertaking training in order to get a better wage.

For those people who are not employed, a rise in tax rates may make them feel that it is no longer worth looking for a job.

Reducing tax allowances. For all those above the old tax threshold, there is no *substitution* effect at all. The rate of tax has not changed. However, there is an *income* effect. The effect is like a lump-sum tax. Everyone's take-home pay is cut by a fixed sum, and people will need to work harder to make up some of the shortfall. This type of tax change, however, is highly regressive. If everyone pays the same *amount* of extra tax, this represents a bigger percentage for poorer people than richer people. In other words, there may be no negative incentive effects, but it is not suitable as part of a policy to redistribute incomes more equally!

The conclusion from these arguments is that tax changes will have very different effects depending on (a) whom they affect and (b) the nature of the change.

One final point should be stressed. For many people there is no choice in the amount they work. The job they do dictates the number of hours worked, irrespective of changes in taxation.

Benefits

Benefits can be either cash benefits or benefits in kind.

Cash benefits

Means-tested benefits. Means-tested benefits are available only to those whose income (and savings in some instances) fall below a certain level. In order to obtain such benefits, therefore, people must apply for them and declare their personal circumstances to the authorities.

The benefits could be given as grants or merely as loans. They could be provided as general income support or for the meeting of specific needs, such as rents, fuel bills and household items.

Universal benefits. Universal benefits are those that everyone is entitled to, irrespective of their income, if they fall into a certain category. Examples include state pensions, and unemployment, sickness and invalidity benefits.

People who are working pay social security contributions (National Insurance Contributions in the UK), based on their earnings. When they retire, become unemployed or fall sick they are entitled to benefits (known as the jobseeker's allowance in the UK). In many countries, there is a time limit on unemployment benefits. After that, people have to accept whatever work is available or rely on a lower level of social security payments.

Benefits in kind

Individuals receive other forms of benefit from the state, not as direct monetary payments, but in the form of the provision of free or subsidised goods or services. These are known as benefits in kind. The two largest items in most countries are health care and education. They are very differently distributed, however. This difference can largely be explained on age grounds. Old people use a large proportion of health services, but virtually no education services.

Benefits in kind tend to be consumed roughly equally by the different income groups. Nevertheless they do have some equalising effect, since they represent a much larger proportion of poor people's income than rich people's. They still have a far smaller redistributive effect, however, than cash benefits.

Figure 5.15 shows the expenditure on social protection benefits in selected European countries. These include unemployment, sickness, invalidity, maternity, family, survivors' and housing benefits and state pensions. They are mainly cash benefits, but do include some benefits in kind. They exclude health and education. As you can see, the benefits vary significantly

Definitions

Means-tested benefits
Benefits whose amount depends on the recipient's income or assets.

Universal benefits
Benefits paid to everyone in a certain category irrespective of their income or assets.

Benefits in kind
Goods or services which the state provides directly to the recipient at no charge or at a subsidised price. Alternatively, the state can subsidise the private sector to provide them.

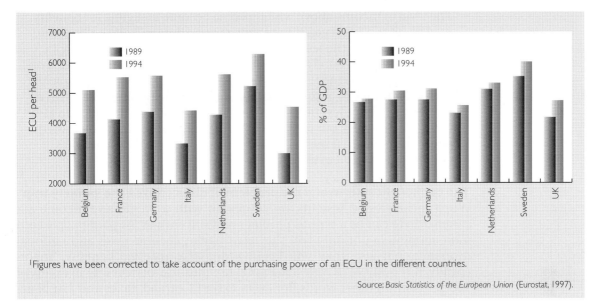

¹Figures have been corrected to take account of the purchasing power of an ECU in the different countries.

Source: *Basic Statistics of the European Union* (Eurostat, 1997).

FIGURE 5.15
Social protection benefits in various European countries

from one country to another. For example, Sweden provides 50 per cent more social protection than the UK. One note of caution: the expenditure on unemployment-related benefits depends on the level of unemployment, which depends on the state of the economy. Thus the expenditure on social protection in the UK rose from 21.7 per cent in 1989 (a time when the economy was booming) to 27.2 per cent in 1992 (a time of recession).

Benefits and the redistribution of income

It might seem that means-tested benefits are a much more efficient system of redistributing income from the rich to the poor: the money is directed to those most in need. With universal benefits, by contrast, many people may receive them who have little need for them. Do families with very high incomes need child benefit? Would it not be better for the government to redirect the money to those who are genuinely in need?

There are, however, serious problems in attempting to redistribute incomes by the use of means-tested benefits:

- Not everyone entitled to means-tested benefits actually receives them. This may be due to a number of factors:
  - Ignorance of the benefits available. This in turn may be due to the complexities of the system.
  - Difficulties in applying for the benefits. People may give up rather than having to face difficult forms or long queues or harassed benefit office staff.
  - Reluctance to reveal personal circumstances.
  - The perception that the benefits are 'charity' and therefore demeaning.
  Thus some of the poorest families may receive no support.
- Even when people do apply for benefits, the need first to disclose their personal circumstances may make the application procedure lengthy and unpleasant.

- The level of income above which people become ineligible for benefits may be set too low. Even if they were raised, there will always be some people just above the level who will still find difficulties.
- Means tests based purely on *income* (or even universal benefits based on broad categories) ignore the very special needs of many poor people. A person earning £80 a week living in a small, well-appointed flat with a low rent will have less need of assistance than another person who also earns £80 per week but lives in a cold, draughty and damp house with large bills to meet. If means tests are to be fair, then *all* of a person's circumstances need to be taken into account.

The tax/benefit system and the problem of disincentives: the 'poverty trap'

When means-tested benefits are combined with a progressive income tax system, there can be a serious problem of disincentives. As poor people earn more money, so not only will they start paying income taxes and national insurance, but also they will begin losing means-tested benefits. Theoretically, it is possible to have a marginal tax-plus-lost-benefit rate in excess of 100 per cent. In other words, for every extra £1 earned, taxes and lost benefits add up to more than £1. High marginal tax-plus-lost-benefit rates obviously act as a serious disincentive. What is the point of getting a job or trying to earn more money, if you end up earning little more or actually losing money?

This situation is known as the poverty trap. People are trapped on low incomes with no realistic means of bettering their position.

The problem of the poverty trap would be overcome by switching to a system of universal benefits unrelated to income. For example, *everyone* could receive a flat payment from the state fixed at a sufficiently high level to cover their basic needs. There would still be *some* disincentive, but this would be confined to an income effect: people would not have the same need to work if the state provided a basic income. But there would no longer be the disincentive to work caused by a resulting *loss* of benefits (a substitution effect).

The big drawback with universal benefits, however, is their cost. If they were given to everyone and were large enough to help the poor, their cost would be enormous. Thus although the benefits themselves would not create much disincentive effect, the necessary taxation to fund them almost certainly would.

There is no ideal solution to this conundrum. On the one hand, the more narrowly benefits are targeted on the poor, the greater the problem of the poverty trap. On the other hand, the more widely they are spread, the greater the cost of providing any given level of support to individuals.

Definition

Poverty trap
Where poor people are discouraged from working or getting a better job because any extra income they earn will be largely taken away in taxes and lost benefits.

Summary

1. **Taxes can be categorised as progressive, regressive or proportional. Progressive taxes have the effect of reducing inequality. The more steeply progressive they are, the bigger the reduction in inequality.**
2. **Taxes on their own cannot increase the incomes of the poor. Cutting taxes, however, *can* help the poor if the cuts are carefully targeted.**

3. Using taxes to redistribute incomes can cause disincentives. Raising taxes has two effects on the amount people wish to work. On the one hand, people will be encouraged to work more in order to maintain their incomes. This is the income effect. On the other hand, they will be encouraged to substitute leisure for income, since an hour's leisure now costs less in forgone income. This is the substitution effect. The relative size of the income and substitution effects will depend on the nature of the tax change. The substitution effect is more likely to outweigh the income effect for those with few commitments, for people just above the tax threshold of the newly raised tax and in cases where the highest rates of tax are increased.

4. Benefits can be cash benefits or benefits in kind. They can be universal or means tested. Universal benefits include child benefit, state pensions, unemployment benefits, and sickness and invalidity benefits. Benefits in kind include health care, education and free school meals.

5. Means-tested benefits can be specifically targeted to those in need and are thus more 'cost-effective'. However, there can be serious problems with such benefits including: limited take-up, time-consuming procedures for claimants, some relatively needy people falling just outside the qualifying limit and inadequate account taken of *all* relevant circumstances affecting a person's needs.

6. The poverty trap occurs when the combination of increased taxes and reduced benefits removes the incentive for poor people to earn more. The more steeply progressive this combined system is at low incomes, the bigger the disincentive effect.

Questions

1. If a firm faces a shortage of workers with very specific skills, it may decide to undertake the necessary training itself. If, on the other hand, it faces a shortage of unskilled workers, it may well offer a small wage increase in order to obtain the extra labour. In the first case it is responding to an increase in demand for labour by attempting to shift the supply curve. In the second case it is merely allowing a movement along the supply curve. Use a demand and supply diagram to illustrate each case. Given that elasticity of supply is different in each case, do you think that these are the best policies for the firm to follow?

2. For what types of reason does the marginal revenue product differ between workers in different jobs?

3. Why, do you think, are some of the lowest-paid jobs the most unpleasant?

4. The wage rate a firm has to pay and the output it can produce vary with the number of workers as follows (all figures are hourly):

Number of workers	1	2	3	4	5	6	7	8
Wage rate (AC_L) (£)	3	4	5	6	7	8	9	10
Total output (TPP_L)	10	22	32	40	46	50	52	52

Assume that output sells at £2 per unit.

(a) Copy the table and add additional rows for TC_L, MC_L, TRP_L and MRP_L. Put the figures for MC_L and MRP_L in the spaces between the columns.

(b) How many workers will the firm employ in order to maximise profits?

(c) What will be its hourly wage bill at this level of employment?

(d) How much hourly revenue will it earn at this level of employment?

(e) Assuming that the firm faces other (fixed) costs of £30 per hour, how much hourly profit will it make?

(f) Assume that the workers now formed a union and that the firm agreed to pay the negotiated wage rate to all employees. What is the maximum to which the hourly wage rate could rise without causing the firm to try to reduce employment below that in (b) above? (See the diagram in Box 5.1.)

(g) What would be the firm's hourly profit now?

5. The following are figures for a monopsonist employer:

Number of workers (1)	Wage rate (£) (2)	Total cost of labour (£) (3)	Marginal cost of labour (£) (4)	Marginal revenue product (£) (5)
1	100			230
2	105			240
3	110			240
4	115			230
5	120			210
6	125			190
7	130			170
8	135			150
9	140			130
10	145			

Fill in the missing figures for columns (3) and (4). How many workers should the firm employ if it wishes to maximise profits?

6. To what extent can trade unions be seen to be (a) an advantage, (b) a disadvantage to (i) workers in unions, (ii) employers bargaining with unions, (iii) non-union members in firms where there is collective bargaining, (iv) workers in non-unionised jobs?

7. Identify four groups of workers, two with very high wages and two with very low wages. Explain why they get the wages they do.

8. Do any of the following contradict marginal productivity theory: (a) wage scales related to length of service (incremental scales), (b) nationally negotiated wage rates, (c) discrimination, (d) firms taking the lead from other firms in determining this year's pay increase?

9. For what reasons is the average gross weekly pay of women only 72 per cent of that of men in the UK?

10. Does the existence of overtime tend to increase or decrease inequality?

11. Distinguish between proportional, progressive and regressive taxation. Could a progressive tax have a constant marginal rate?

12. If a person earning £5000 per year pays £500 in a given tax and a person earning £10 000 per year pays £800, is the tax progressive or regressive? Explain.

13. A proportional tax will leave the distribution of income unaffected. Why should this be so, given that a rich person will pay a larger absolute amount than a poor person?

14. Under what circumstances would a rise in income tax act as (a) a disincentive and (b) an incentive to effort?

15. Who is likely to work harder as a result of a cut in income tax rates – a person on a high income or a person on a low income? Why? Would your answer be different if personal allowances were zero?

16. What tax changes (whether up or down) will both have a positive incentive effect and also redistribute incomes more equally?

17. What is meant by the poverty trap? Would a system of universal benefits be the best solution to the problem of the poverty trap?

18. How would you go about deciding whether person A or person B gets more personal benefit from each of the following: (a) an electric fire; (b) a clothing allowance of £x; (c) draught-proofing materials; (c) child benefit? Do your answers help you in deciding how best to allocate benefits?

chapter six

Market failures and government policy

In recent years, governments throughout the world have tended to put more reliance on markets as the means of allocating resources. Policies of privatisation, deregulation, cutting government expenditure and taxes, and generally 'leaving things to the market' have been widely adopted, not only by conservative governments, but also by those of the centre and centre left.

But despite this increased reliance on markets, markets often fail. Despite our growing wealth and prosperity, our rivers are polluted, our streets are congested and often strewn with litter, our lives are dominated by the interests of big business and the quality of many of the goods we buy is very poor.

Governments are thus still expected to play a major role in the economy: from the construction and maintenance of roads, to the provision of key services such as education, health care and law and order, to social protection in the form of pensions and social security, to the regulation of businesses, to the passing of laws to protect the individual.

In this chapter we identify the various ways in which the market fails to look after society's interests (sections 6.1–6.3). Then we look at how the government can set about putting right these failings (sections 6.4–6.6). Finally, we look at some of the shortcomings of governments, and ask: should we have more or less intervention?

In order to decide the optimum amount of government intervention, it is first necessary to identify the various social goals that intervention is designed to meet. Two of the major objectives of government intervention identified by economists are social efficiency and equity.

Equity. Most people would argue that the free market fails to lead to a *fair* distribution of resources, if it results in some people living in great affluence whilst others live in dire poverty. Clearly what constitutes 'fairness' is a highly contentious issue: those on the political right generally have a quite different view from those on the political left. Nevertheless, most people would argue that the government does have some duty to redistribute incomes from the rich to the poor through the tax and benefit system, and perhaps to provide various forms of legal protection for the poor (such as a minimum wage rate). We looked at the causes of inequality and policies of redistribution in Chapter 5. In this chapter, therefore, we focus on the second issue: that of social efficiency.

Social efficiency. If the marginal benefits to society (MSB) of producing (or consuming) any given good or service exceed the marginal costs to society (MSC), then it is said to be socially efficient to produce (or consume) more. For example, if people's gains from having additional motorways exceed *all* the additional costs to society (both financial and non-financial), then it is socially efficient to construct more motorways. If, however, the marginal social costs of producing (or consuming) any good or service exceed the marginal social benefits, then it is socially efficient to produce (or consume) less. It follows that if the marginal social benefits of any activity are equal to the marginal social costs, then the current level is the optimum. To summarise: to achieve social efficiency in the production of any good or service, the following should occur:

$$MSB > MSC \rightarrow \text{produce more}$$
$$MSC > MSB \rightarrow \text{produce less}$$
$$MSB = MSC \rightarrow \text{keep production at its current level}$$

Similar rules apply to consumption. For example, if the marginal social benefits of consuming more of any good or service exceed the marginal social cost, then society would benefit from more of the good being consumed.

In the real world, the market rarely leads to social efficiency: the marginal social benefits of most goods and services do not equal the marginal social costs. Part of the problem is the existence of 'externalities', part is a lack of competition, part is a lack of knowledge on the part of both producers and consumers, and part is the fact that markets may take a long time to adjust to any disequilibrium, given the often considerable short-run immobility of factors of production.

In this chapter we examine these various 'failings' of the free market and what the government can do to rectify the situation. We also examine why the government itself may fail to achieve social efficiency.

Definitions

Social efficiency
Production and consumption at the point where $MSB = MSC$.

Equity
A fair distribution of resources.

Market failures: externalities and public goods
What will happen if certain markets are 'missing'?

Externalities

The market will not lead to social efficiency if the actions of producers or consumers affect people *other than themselves*. These effects on other people are known as externalities: they are the side-effects, or 'third-party' effects, of production or consumption. Externalities can be either desirable or undesirable. Whenever other people are affected beneficially, there are said to be external benefits. Whenever other people are affected adversely there are said to be external costs.

Thus the full costs to society (the social costs) of the production of any good or service are the private costs faced by firms plus any externalities of production. Likewise the full benefits to society (the social benefits) from the consumption of any good are the private benefits enjoyed by consumers plus any externalities of consumption.

There are four major types of externality.

External costs of production (MSC > MC)

When a chemical firm dumps waste into a river or pollutes the air, the community bears costs additional to those borne by the firm. The marginal *social* cost (*MSC*) of chemical production exceeds the marginal private cost (*MC*). Diagrammatically, the *MSC* curve is above the *MC* curve.

Figure 6.1 shows a firm which is operating under perfect competition and is thus a price taker. It will maximise profits at the output where price equals marginal cost (see section 4.2). It is assumed that there are no externalities on the demand side and that therefore the price that the firm faces is also equal to the marginal external benefit. In other words, the price that people are prepared to pay reflects the marginal benefit they get from consuming the good. The *socially* optimum output would be Q_2, where P (i.e. *MSB*) = *MSC*. The firm, however, produces Q_1 which is more than the optimum. Thus external costs lead to overproduction from society's point of view.

The problem of external costs arises in a free-market economy because no one has legal ownership of the air or rivers and can therefore prevent or charge for their use as a dump for waste. Such a 'market' is missing. Control must, therefore, be left to the government or local authorities.

Other examples of external costs of production include extensive farming that destroys hedgerows and wildlife, acid rain caused by smoke from coal-fired power stations, and nuclear waste from nuclear power stations.

External benefits of production (MSC < MC)

Imagine a bus company that spends money training its bus drivers. Each year some drivers leave to work for coach and haulage companies. These companies' costs are reduced as they do not have to train such drivers. Society has benefited from their training (including the bus drivers

---

Definitions

Externalities
Costs or benefits of production or consumption experienced by society but not by the producers or consumers themselves. Sometimes referred to as 'spillover' or 'third-party' costs or benefits.

External benefits
Benefits from production (or consumption) experienced by people *other* than the producer (or consumer).

External costs
Costs of production (or consumption) borne by people *other* than the producer (or consumer).

Social cost
Private cost plus externalities in production.

Social benefit
Private benefit plus externalities in consumption.

FIGURE 6.1
External costs in
production

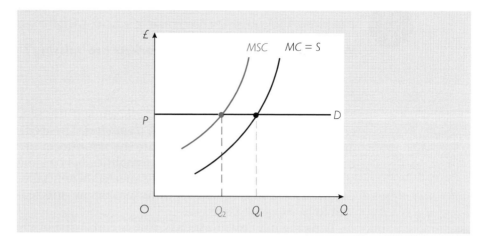

themselves, who have acquired marketable skills) even though the bus company has not. The marginal *social* cost of the bus service, therefore, is less than the marginal *private* cost to the company.

In a diagram like Figure 6.1, the *MSC* curve would be *below* the *MC* curve. The level of output (i.e. number of passenger miles) provided by the bus company would be where $P = MC$, a *lower* level than the social optimum where $P = MSC$.

Another example of external benefits in production is that of research and development. If other firms have access to the results of the research, then clearly the benefits extend beyond the firm which finances it. Given that the firm only receives the private benefits, it will conduct a less than optimal amount of research. Another example is the beneficial effect on the atmosphere from a forestry company planting new woodlands.

External costs of consumption (*MSB < MB*)

Figure 6.2 shows the marginal benefit and price to a motorist (i.e. the consumer) of using a car. It is assumed that the marginal benefit declines as the motorist travels more miles.[1] The optimal distance travelled for this motorist will be Q_1 miles: i.e. where marginal benefit (*MB*) = price (*P*) (where price is the cost of petrol, oil, wear and tear, etc. per mile). The reasoning is as follows: if the marginal benefit from the consumption of any good or service, measured in terms of what you are prepared to pay for it, exceeds its price (i.e. the marginal cost to the consumer), the consumer will gain by consuming more of it. If, however, the marginal benefit is less than the price, the consumer will gain by consuming less. The optimum level of

Definition

Principle of diminishing marginal utility
As more units of a good are consumed, additional units will provide less additional satisfaction than previous units.

[1]To understand this, consider your own position (assuming you had a car). If you had only a little money available for motoring, or if the price of petrol was very high, then you would only use your car for essential journeys: journeys with a high marginal private benefit (or 'marginal utility' as it is often referred to by economists). If your income increased, or if the price of petrol came down, you would use your car more (i.e. travel additional miles), but these additional journeys would be yielding you less additional benefit per mile than previous journeys, since they would be less essential to you. The more miles you travel, the less essential each *additional* mile: i.e. the marginal benefit diminishes. This is an example of the **principle of diminishing marginal utility**, which states that each additional unit of a good or service consumed yields you less additional utility than the last unit.

FIGURE 6.2
External costs in consumption

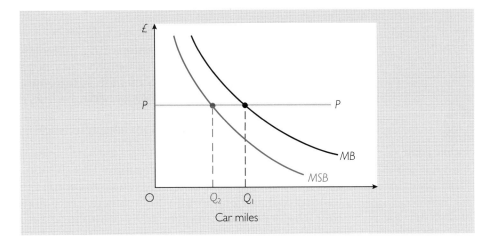

consumption from the motorist's point of view, therefore, will be where *MB* = *P*: i.e. Q_1 miles.

When people use their cars, however, other people suffer from their exhaust, the added congestion, the noise, etc. These 'negative externalities' make the marginal social benefit of using cars less than the marginal private benefit of the motorist. Thus the *MSB* curve is below the *MB* curve. Assuming that there are no externalities in *production*, and therefore that marginal social cost is given by the price, the *social* optimum will be where *MSB* = *P*: i.e. at Q_2. But this is less than the actual level of consumption, Q_1. Thus, when there are negative externalities in consumption, the actual level of consumption will be too great from society's point of view.

Other examples of negative externalities of consumption include the effects on other people of noisy radios in public places, the smoke from cigarettes, and litter.

External benefits of consumption (*MSB* > *MB*)
When people travel by train rather than by car, other people benefit by there being less congestion and exhaust and fewer accidents on the roads. Thus the marginal social benefit of rail travel is *greater* than the marginal private benefit to the rail passenger. There are external benefits from rail travel. In such circumstances, the *MSB* curve in Figure 6.2 will be *above* the private *MB* curve. The socially optimal level of consumption will thus be above the actual level of consumption. In other words, when there are 'positive externalities' in consumption, the actual level of consumption will be too low from society's point of view.

Other examples of positive externalities of consumption include the beneficial effects for other people of deodorants, vaccinations and attractive gardens in front of people's houses.

To summarise: whenever there are external benefits, there will be too little produced or consumed. Whenever there are external costs, there will be too much produced or consumed. The market will not equate *MSB* and *MSC*.

The above arguments have been developed in the context of perfect competition, with prices given to the producer or consumer by the market. Externalities also occur in all other types of market.

Public goods

There is a category of goods where the positive externalities are so great that the free market, whether perfect or imperfect, may not produce at all. They are called **public goods**. Examples include lighthouses, pavements, flood-control dams, public drainage, public services such as the police and even government itself.

Public goods have two important characteristics: *non-rivalry* and *non-excludability*.

Definitions

Public good
A good or service which has the features of non-rivalry and non-excludability and as a result would not be provided by the free market.

Non-rivalry
Where the consumption of a good or service by one person will not prevent others from enjoying it.

Non-excludability
Where it is not possible to provide a good or service to one person without it thereby being available for others to enjoy.

- If I consume a bar of chocolate, it cannot then be consumed by someone else. If, however, I walk along a pavement or enjoy the benefits of street lighting, it does not prevent you or anyone else doing the same. There is thus what we call **non-rivalry** in the consumption of such goods. These goods tend to have large external benefits relative to private benefits. This makes them socially desirable, but privately unprofitable. No one person on their own would pay to have a pavement built along his or her street. The private benefit would be too small relative to the cost. And yet the social benefit to all the other people using the pavement may far outweigh the cost.
- If I spend money erecting a flood-control dam to protect my house, my neighbours will also be protected by the dam. I cannot prevent them enjoying the benefits of my expenditure. This feature of **non-excludability** means that they would get the benefits free, and would therefore have no incentive to pay themselves. This is known as the **free-rider problem**.

When goods have these two features, the free market will simply not provide them. Thus these public goods can only be provided by the government or by the government subsidising private firms. (Note that not all goods and services produced by the public sector come into the category of 'public goods and services': thus education and health are publicly provided, but they *can* be, and indeed are, privately provided as well.)

Summary

1. Social efficiency will be achieved where *MSC* = *MSB* for each good and service. In practice, however, markets will fail to achieve social efficiency. One reason for this is the existence of externalities.
2. Externalities are spillover costs or benefits. Whenever there are external costs, the market will (other things being equal) lead to a level of production and consumption *above* the socially efficient level. Whenever there are external benefits, the market will (other things being equal) lead to a level of production and consumption *below* the socially efficient level.
3. Public goods will be underprovided by the market. The problem is that they have large external benefits relative to private benefits and without government intervention it would not be possible to prevent people having a 'free ride' and thereby escaping contributing to their cost of production.

Market failures: monopoly power

What problems arise from big business?

Whenever markets are imperfect, whether as pure monopoly or monopsony, or whether as some form of imperfect competition, the market will fail to equate *MSB* and *MSC*, even if there are no externalities.

Take the case of monopoly. A monopoly will produce less than the socially efficient output. This is illustrated in Figure 6.3. A monopoly faces a downward-sloping demand curve, and therefore marginal revenue is below average revenue ($= P$). Profits are maximised where marginal revenue equals marginal cost (at an output of Q_1 and at a price of P_1). But since price is above marginal revenue, price must also be above marginal cost (P_1 is above MC_1). If there are no externalities and thus $P = MSB$ and $MC = MSC$, the socially efficient output will be Q_2, where $MSB = MSC$. Since Q_2 is greater than Q_1, the firm is clearly producing less than the socially efficient output.

Deadweight loss under monopoly

Consumer and producer surplus

One way of analysing the welfare loss that occurs under monopoly is to use the concepts of *consumer* and *producer surplus*. Consumer surplus is the excess of consumers' total benefit (or 'utility') from consuming a good over their total expenditure on it. Producer surplus is just another name for profit. The two concepts are illustrated in Figure 6.4. The diagram shows an industry which is initially under perfect competition and then becomes a monopoly (but faces the same revenue and cost curves).

Consumer surplus. Under *perfect competition* the industry will produce an output of Q_{pc} at a price of P_{pc}, where $MC = P (= AR)$: i.e. at point *a* (see page 114).

Consumers' total benefit is given by the area under the demand curve (the sum of all the areas 1–7). The reason for this is that each point on the demand curve shows how much the last consumer is prepared to pay (i.e. the benefit to the marginal consumer). The area under the demand curve

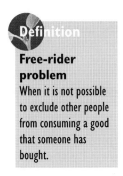

FIGURE 6.3
The monopolist producing less than the social optimum

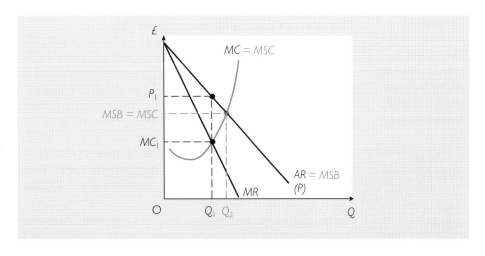

FIGURE 6.4
Deadweight loss from a monopoly

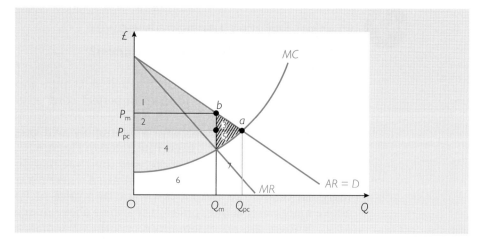

thus shows the total of all these marginal benefits from zero consumption to the current level: i.e. it gives total benefit.

Consumers' total expenditure is $P_{pc} \times Q_{pc}$ (areas 4 + 5 + 6 + 7).

Consumer surplus is the difference between total benefit and total expenditure: in other words, the area between the price and the demand curve (areas 1 + 2 + 3).

Producer surplus. Producer surplus (profit) is the difference between total revenue and total cost.

Total cost is the area under the *MC* curve (areas 6 + 7). The reason for this is that each point on the marginal cost curve shows what the last unit costs to produce. The area under the *MC* curve thus gives all the marginal costs starting from an output of zero to the current output: i.e. it gives total costs.[2]

Total revenue is $P_{pc} \times Q_{pc}$ (areas 4 + 5 + 6 + 7).

Producer surplus is thus the area between the price and the *MC* curve (areas 4 + 5).

Total (private) surplus. Total consumer plus producer surplus is therefore the area between the demand and *MC* curves. This is shown by the total shaded area (areas 1 + 2 + 3 + 4 + 5).

The effect of monopoly on total surplus

What happens when the industry is under *monopoly*? The firm will produce where *MC* = *MR*, at an output of Q_m and a price of P_m (at point *b* on the demand curve). Total revenue is $P_m \times Q_m$ (areas 2 + 4 + 6). Total cost is the area under the *MC* curve (area 6). Thus producer surplus is areas 2 + 4. This is clearly a *larger* surplus than under perfect competition (since area 2 is larger than area 5): monopoly profits are larger than profits under perfect competition.

Consumer surplus, however, will be much smaller. With consumption at Q_m, total benefit to consumers is given by areas 1 + 2 + 4 + 6, whereas consumer expenditure is given by areas 2 + 4 + 6. Consumer surplus, then, is

Definitions

Consumer surplus
The excess of what a person would have been prepared to pay for a good (i.e. the utility) over what that person actually pays.

Producer surplus
The excess of total revenue over total cost: i.e. profit.

[2]Strictly speaking, the sum of all marginal costs gives total *variable* costs. Producers' surplus is therefore total revenue minus total variable costs: i.e. total profit plus total fixed costs.

simply area 1. (Note that area 2 has been transformed from consumer surplus to producer surplus.)

Total surplus under monopoly is therefore areas 1 + 2 + 4: a smaller surplus than under perfect competition. 'Monopolisation' of the industry has resulted in a loss of total surplus of areas 3 + 5. The producer's gain is less than consumers' loss. This net loss of total surplus is known as the **deadweight welfare loss** of monopoly.

Conclusions

As was shown in section 4.3, there are possible social *advantages* from powerful firms; advantages such as economies of scale and more research and development. These advantages may outweigh deadweight loss from monopoly power. It can be argued that an ideal situation would be where firms are large enough to gain economies of scale and yet were somehow persuaded or compelled to produce where $P = MC$ (assuming no externalities).

Summary

1. Monopoly power will (other things being equal) lead to a level of output below the socially efficient level.
2. This will result in deadweight welfare loss, which is the loss in total producer and consumer surplus.
3. Consumer surplus is the excess of what consumers are prepared to pay (which is how we measure the benefit to consumers) over what they actually pay. Producer surplus is the excess of total revenue over total cost (i.e. total profit).
4. The effect of monopoly will be to give a higher producer surplus than under perfect competition, but a much lower consumer surplus. Thus total surplus is lower. This reduction in total surplus is known as 'deadweight welfare loss'.
5. There are potential gains from monopoly, such as economies of scale and higher investment. Such gains have to be offset against the deadweight loss.

6.3 Other market failures

In what other ways may a market fail to make the best use of scarce resources?

Definition

Deadweight welfare loss
The loss of consumer plus producer surplus in imperfect markets (when compared with perfect competition).

Ignorance and uncertainty

Perfect competition assumes that consumers, firms and factor suppliers have perfect knowledge of costs and benefits. In the real world there is often a great deal of ignorance and uncertainty. Thus people are unable to equate marginal benefit with marginal cost.

Consumers purchase many goods only once or a few times in a lifetime. Cars, washing machines, televisions and other consumer durables fall into this category. Consumers may not be aware of the quality of such goods until they have purchased them, by which time it is too late. Advertising may contribute to people's ignorance by misleading them as to the benefits of a good.

Firms are often ignorant of market opportunities, prices, costs, the productivity of labour (especially white-collar workers), the activity of rivals, etc.

Many economic decisions are based on expected future conditions. Since the future can never be known for certain, many decisions will be taken which, in retrospect, will be seen to have been wrong.

In some cases it may be possible to obtain the information through the market. There may be an agency which will sell you the information, or a newspaper or magazine that contains the information. In such cases you will have to decide whether the cost to you of buying the information is worth the benefit it will provide you. A problem here is that you may not have sufficient information to judge how reliable the information is that you are buying!

Immobility of factors and time-lags in response

Even under conditions of perfect competition, factors may be very slow to respond to changes in demand or supply. Labour, for example, may be highly immobile both occupationally and geographically. This can lead to large price changes and hence to large supernormal profits and high wages for those in the sectors of rising demand or falling costs. The long run may be a very long time coming!

In the meantime, there will be further changes in the conditions of demand and supply. Thus the economy is in a constant state of disequilibrium and the long run never comes. As firms and consumers respond to market signals and move towards equilibrium, so the equilibrium position moves and the social optimum is never achieved.

Whenever monopoly/monopsony power exists, the problem is made worse as firms or unions put up barriers to the entry of new firms or factors of production.

Protecting people's interests

Dependants
People do not always make their own economic decisions. They are often dependent on decisions made by others. Parents make decisions on behalf of their children; partners on each other's behalf; younger adults on behalf of old people; managers on behalf of shareholders, etc.

A free market will respond to these decisions, however good or bad they may be; whether they be in the interest of the dependant or not. Thus the government may feel it necessary to protect dependants.

The principal–agent problem
The problem of dependants is an example of a wider issue, known as the principal–agent problem. One of the features of a complex modern economy is that people (principals) have to employ others (agents) to carry out their wishes. If you want to go on holiday, it is easier to go to a travel

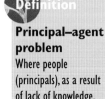

Definition

Principal–agent problem
Where people (principals), as a result of lack of knowledge, cannot ensure that their best interests are served by their agents.

agent to sort out the arrangements than to do it all yourself. Likewise, if you want to buy a house, it is more convenient to go to an estate agent. The point is that these agents have specialist knowledge and can save you, the principal, a great deal of time and effort. This is merely an example of the benefits of specialisation and the division of labour.

It is the same with firms. They employ people with specialist knowledge and skills to carry out specific tasks. Companies frequently employ consultants to give them advice, or engage the services of specialist firms such as an advertising agency. It is the same with the employees of the company. They can be seen as 'agents' of their employer. In the case of workers, they can be seen as the agents of management. Junior managers are the agents of senior management. Senior managers are the agents of the directors, who are themselves agents of the shareholders. Thus in large firms there is often a complex chain of principal–agent relationships. Indeed, it is often claimed that in large companies there tends to be a 'divorce' between the owners of the firm (the shareholders), who are the principals, and the controllers of the firm (the managers), who are the shareholders' agents.

These relationships have an inherent danger for the principal: there is asymmetric information between the two sides. The agent knows more about the situation than the principal – in fact, this is part of the reason why the principal employs the agent in the first place. The danger is that the agent may well not act in the principal's best interests, and may be able to get away with it because of the principal's imperfect knowledge. The estate agent trying to sell you a house may not tell you about the noisy neighbours or that the vendor is prepared to accept a much lower price. A second-hand car dealer may 'neglect' to tell you about the rust on the underside of the car or that it had a history of unreliability.

So how can principals tackle the problem? There are two elements in the solution:

- The principals must have some way of *monitoring* the performance of their agents. Thus a company might employ efficiency experts to examine the operation of its management.
- There must be *incentives* for agents to behave in the principals' interests. Thus managers' salaries could be more closely linked to the firm's profitability.

In a competitive market, managers' and shareholders' interests are more likely to coincide. Managers have to ensure that the company remains efficient or it may not survive the competition and they might lose their jobs. In monopolies and oligopolies, however, where supernormal profits can often be relatively easily earned, the interests of shareholders and managers are likely to diverge. Here it will be in shareholders' interests to institute incentive mechanisms that ensure that their agents, the managers, are motivated to strive for profitability.

Poor economic decision making by individuals on their own behalf

The government may feel that people need protecting from poor economic decisions that they make on their *own* behalf. It may feel that in a free market people will consume too many harmful things. Thus if the government wants to discourage smoking and drinking, it can put taxes on tobacco and alcohol. In more extreme cases it could make various activities

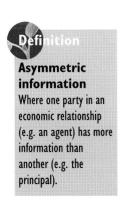

Definition

Asymmetric information
Where one party in an economic relationship (e.g. an agent) has more information than another (e.g. the principal).

illegal: activities such as prostitution, certain types of gambling, and the sale and consumption of drugs.

On the other hand, the government may feel that people consume too little of things that are good for them: things such as education, health care and sports facilities. Such goods are known as merit goods. The government could either provide them free or subsidise their production.

Macroeconomic goals

The free market is unlikely to achieve simultaneously the *macroeconomic* objectives of rapid economic growth, full employment, stable prices and a balance of international payments. These problems and the methods of government intervention to deal with them are examined in later chapters.

How far can economists go in advising governments?

It is not within the scope of economics to make judgements as to the relative importance of social goals. Economics can only consider means to achieving stated goals. First, therefore, the goals have to be clearly stated by the policy makers. Second, they have to be quantifiable so that different policies can be compared as to their relative effectiveness in achieving the particular goal. Certain goals, such as growth in national income, changes in the distribution of income and greater efficiency, are relatively easy to quantify. Others, such as enlightenment or the sense of community wellbeing, are virtually impossible to quantify. For this reason, economics tends to concentrate on the means of achieving a relatively narrow range of goals. The danger is that by economists concentrating on a limited number of goals, they may well influence the policy makers – the government, local authorities, various pressure groups, etc. – into doing the same, and thus into neglecting other perhaps important social goals.

Different objectives are likely to conflict. For example, economic growth may conflict with greater equality. In the case of such 'trade-offs', all the economist can do is to demonstrate the effects of a given policy, and leave the policy makers to decide whether the benefits in terms of one goal outweigh the costs in terms of another goal.

Where there are two or more alternative policies, economists can go further than this. They may be asked to consider the relative effectiveness of the various policies or even themselves to suggest alternative policies. In such cases it may be possible to say that policy A is preferable to policy B because its benefits are greater or its costs lower in terms of all stated goals. On the other hand, if policy A better achieves one goal and policy B better achieves another, once more all the economist can do is to point this out and leave the policy makers to decide.

Definition

Merit goods
Goods which the government feels that people will underconsume and which therefore ought to be subsidised or provided free.

Summary

1. **Ignorance and uncertainty may prevent people from consuming or producing the levels they would otherwise choose. Information may**

sometimes be provided (at a price) by the market, but it may be imperfect and in some cases not available at all.

2. Markets may respond sluggishly to changes in demand and supply. The time lags in adjustment can lead to a permanent state of disequilibrium and to problems of instability.

3. In a free market there may be inadequate provision for dependants and an inadequate output of merit goods.

4. Although economists cannot make ultimate pronouncements on the rights and wrongs of the market – that involves making moral judgements (and economists here are no different from any other person) – they can point out the consequences of the market and of various government policies, and also the trade-offs that exist between different objectives.

Government intervention: taxes and subsidies

Will taxing the bad and subsidising the good solve the problem of externalities?

Faced with all the problems of the free market, what is a government to do?

There are several policy instruments that the government can use. At one extreme it can totally replace the market by providing goods and services itself. At the other extreme it can merely seek to persuade producers, consumers or workers to act differently. Between the two extremes the government has a number of weapons it can use to change the way markets operate: weapons such as taxes, subsidies, laws and regulatory bodies. In this and the next two sections we examine these different forms of government intervention.

The use of taxes and subsidies

A policy instrument particularly favoured by many economists is that of taxes and subsidies. They can be used for two main purposes: (a) to promote greater social efficiency by altering the composition of production and consumption, and (b) to redistribute incomes. We examined their use for the second purpose in the last chapter. Here we examine their use to achieve greater social efficiency.

When there are imperfections in the market, social efficiency will not be achieved. Marginal social benefit (*MSB*) will not equal marginal social cost (*MSC*). A different level of output would be more desirable. Taxes and subsidies can be used to correct these imperfections. Essentially the approach is to tax those goods or activities where the market produces too much, and subsidise those where the market produces too little.

Taxes and subsidies to correct externalities

The rule here is simple: the government should impose a tax equal to the marginal external cost (or grant a subsidy equal to the marginal external benefit).

BOX 6.1 *Should health care provision be left to the market?*

A case of multiple market failures

When you go shopping you may well pay a visit to the chemist and buy a bottle of paracetamol, some sticking plasters or a tube of ointment. These health-care products are being sold through the market system in much the same way as other everyday goods and services such as food, household items and petrol.

But many health-care services and products are not allocated through the market in this way. In the UK, the National Health Service provides free hospital treatment, a free general practitioner service and free prescriptions for certain categories of people (such as pensioners and children). Their marginal cost to the patient is thus zero. Of course, these services use resources and they thus have to be paid for out of taxes. In this sense they are not free. (Have you heard the famous saying, 'There's no such thing as a free lunch'?)

But why are these services not sold directly to the patient, thereby saving the taxpayer money? Why is it considered that certain types of health care should be provided free, whereas food should not? After all, they could both be considered as basic necessities of life.

The advocates of free health-care provision argue that there are a number of fundamental objections to relying on a market system of allocation of health care, many of which do not apply in the case of food, clothing, etc. So what are the reasons why a free market would fail to provide the optimum amount of health care?

People may not be able to afford treatment

This is a problem connected with the distribution of income. Because income is unequally distributed, some people will be able to afford better treatment than others, and the poorest people may not be able to afford treatment at all. On grounds of equity, therefore, it is argued that health care should be provided free – at least for poor people.

The concept of equity that is usually applied to health care is that of treatment according to medical need rather than according to the ability to pay.

 Does this argument also apply to food and other basic goods?

Difficulty for people in predicting their future medical needs

If you were suddenly taken ill and required a major operation, or maybe even several, it could be very expensive indeed for you if you had to pay. On the other hand, you may go through life requiring very little if any medical treatment. In other words, there is great uncertainty about your future medical needs. As a result it would be very difficult to plan your finances and budget for possible future medical expenses if you had to pay for treatment. Medical insurance is a possible solution to this problem, but there is still a problem of equity. Would the chronically sick or very old be able to obtain cover, and if so, would the premiums be very high? Would the poor be able to afford the premiums? Also would insurance cover be comprehensive?

Externalities

Health care generates a number of benefits *external* to the patient. If you are cured of an infectious disease, for example, it is not just you who benefits but also others, since you will not infect them. Also your family and friends benefit from seeing you well; and if you have a job you will be able to get back to work, thus reducing the disruption there. These external benefits of health care could be quite large.

If the sick have to pay the cost of their treatment, they may decide not to be treated – especially if they are poor. They may not take into account the effect that their illness has on other people. The market, by equating *private* benefits and costs, would produce too little health care.

Patient ignorance

Markets only function well to serve consumer wishes if the consumer has the information to make informed decisions. If you are to buy the right things, you must know what you want and whether the goods you buy meet these wants. In practice, consumers do have pretty good knowledge about the things they buy. For example, when you go to the supermarket you will already have tried most of the items that you buy, and will therefore know how much you like them. Even with new products, provided they are the sort you buy more than once, you can learn from any mistakes.

In the case of health care, 'consumers' (i.e. patients) may have very poor knowledge. If you have a pain in your chest, it may be simple muscular strain, or it may be a symptom of heart disease. You rely on the doctor (the *supplier* of the treatment) to give you the information: to diagnose your condition. Two problems could arise here if there were a market system of allocating health care.

The first is that unscrupulous doctors might advise more expensive treatment than is necessary, or drugs companies might try to persuade you to buy a more expensive branded product rather than an identical cheaper version.

The second is that patients suffering from the early stages of a serious disease might not consult their doctor until the symptoms become acute, by which time it might be too late to treat the disease, or very expensive to do so. With a free health service, however, there is likely to be an earlier diagnosis of serious conditions. On the other hand, some patients may consult their doctors over trivial complaints.

Oligopoly

If doctors and hospitals operated in the free market as profit maximisers, it is unlikely that competition would drive down their prices. Instead it is possible that they would collude to fix standard prices for treatment, so as to protect their incomes.

Even if doctors did compete openly, it is unlikely that consumers would have the information to enable them to 'shop around' for the best value. Doctor A may charge less than doctor B, but is the quality of service the same? Simple bedside manner – the thing that may most influence a patient's choice – may be a poor indicator of the doctor's skill and judgement.

To argue that the market system will fail to provide an optimal allocation of health-care resources does not in itself prove that *free provision* is the best alternative. In the USA there is much more reliance on *private medical insurance*. Only the very poor get free treatment. Alternatively, the government may simply *subsidise* the provision of health care, so as to make it cheaper rather than free. This is the case with prescriptions and dental treatment in the UK, where many people have to pay part of the cost of treatment. Also the government can *regulate* the behaviour of the providers of health care, so as to prevent exploitation of the patient. Thus only people with certain qualifications are allowed to operate as doctors, nurses, pharmacists, etc.

Q2 Does the presence of external benefits from health care suggest that health care should be provided free?

Q3 If health care is provided free, the demand is likely to be high. How is this high demand dealt with? Is this a good way of dealing with it?

Q4 Go through each of the market failings identified in this box. In each case consider what alternative policies are open to a government to tackle them. What are the advantages and disadvantages of these alternatives?

FIGURE 6.5
Using taxes to correct a distortion: the first-best world

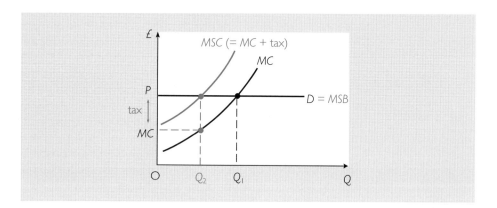

Assume, for example, that a chemical works emits smoke from a chimney and thus pollutes the atmosphere. This creates external costs for the people who breathe in the smoke. The marginal social cost of producing the chemicals thus exceeds the marginal private cost to the firm: $MSC > MC$.

This is illustrated in Figure 6.5. For simplicity, it is assumed that the firm is a price taker. It produces Q_1 where $P = MC$ (its profit-maximising output), but in doing so takes no account of the external pollution costs it imposes on society. If the government imposes a tax on production equal to the marginal pollution cost, it will effectively 'internalise' the externality. The firm will have to pay an amount equal to the external cost it creates. It will therefore now maximise profits at Q_2, which is the socially optimum output where $MSB = MSC$.

Taxes and subsidies to correct for monopoly

If the problem of monopoly that the government wishes to tackle is that of *excessive profits*, it can impose a lump-sum tax on the monopolist: that is, a tax of a fixed absolute amount irrespective of how much the monopolist produces, or the price it charges. Since a lump-sum tax is an additional *fixed* cost to the firm, and hence will not affect the firm's marginal cost, it will not reduce the amount that the monopolist produces (which *would* be the case with a per-unit tax). The 'windfall tax' imposed by the UK Labour government on the profits of various privatised utilities is an example of such a tax.

If the government is concerned that the monopolist produces *less* than the socially efficient output, it could give the monopolist a *per-unit subsidy* (which would encourage the monopolist to produce more). But would this not *increase* the monopolist's profit? The answer to this is to impose a harsh lump-sum tax in addition to the subsidy. The tax would not undo the subsidy's benefit of encouraging the monopolist to produce more, but it could be used to reduce the monopolist's profits below the original (i.e. pre-subsidy) level.

Advantages of taxes and subsidies

Many economists favour the tax/subsidy solution to market imperfections (especially the problem of externalities) because it still allows the market to operate. It forces firms to take on board the full social costs and benefits of their actions. It also has the flexibility of being adjustable according to the magnitude of the problem. For example, the bigger the external costs of a firm's actions, the bigger the tax can be.

What is more, when firms are taxed for *bad* practices, such as polluting, they are encouraged to find socially better ways of producing. The tax thus acts as an incentive over the longer term to reduce pollution: the more a firm can reduce its pollution, the more taxes it can save. Likewise, when *good* practices are subsidised, firms are given the incentive to adopt more good practices.

Disadvantages of taxes and subsidies

Infeasible to use different tax and subsidy rates. Each firm produces different levels and types of externalities and operates under different degrees of imperfect competition. It would be administratively very difficult and expensive, if not impossible, to charge every offending firm its own particular tax rate (or grant every relevant firm its own particular rate of subsidy). Even in the case of pollution, where it is possible to measure a firm's emissions, there would still have to be a different tax rate for each pollutant and even for each environment, depending on its ability to absorb the pollutant and the number of people affected.

Using combinations of lump-sum taxes and per-unit subsidies to correct monopoly distortions to price, output and profit would also probably be impractical. Given that cost and revenue curves differ substantially from one firm to another, separate tax and subsidy rates would be needed for each firm. An army of tax inspectors would be necessary to administer the system!

Lack of knowledge. Even if a government did decide to charge a tax equal to each offending firm's marginal external costs, it would still have the problem of measuring those costs and apportioning blame. The damage to lakes and forests from acid rain has been a major concern since the beginning of the 1980s. But just how serious is that damage? What is its current monetary cost? How long lasting is the damage? Just what and who are to

BOX 6.2

Green taxes
....
Their growing popularity in the industrialised world

Growing concerns over acid rain, the depletion of the ozone layer, industrial and domestic waste, traffic fumes and other forms of pollution have made the protection of the environment a major political issue. Governments round the world have responded in different ways, but increasingly it is the tax weapon that is being used to control polluting activities.

Taxes have the advantage of relating the size of the penalty to the amount of pollution. This means that there is a continuous pressure to cut down on production or consumption of polluting products or activities in order to save tax.

One approach is to modify *existing* taxes. In most developed countries, there are now higher taxes on leaded than unleaded petrol, and lower taxes on low-emission cars. Tax regimes can also be modified which currently *encourage* environmental degradation. For example, lower taxes on diesel could be abolished (given the higher pollution from diesel engines), as could tax relief for commuting expenses. Tax benefits which encourage the use of fertilisers and pesticides in farming, or the felling of trees or hedgerows, could also be abolished.

Increasingly, however, countries are introducing new 'green' taxes in order to discourage pollution as goods are produced, consumed or disposed of. The table shows the range of green taxes in use in 1995 in eight countries. As you can see, the Scandinavian countries have gone the furthest, reflecting the strength of environmental concerns in these countries.

There are various problems, however, with using the tax weapon in the fight against pollution.

Conflicts with revenue objectives

The more successful a tax is in reducing consumption, the less revenue it will earn for the government. In Denmark, where energy used in households has been taxed at higher rates than in most other countries, energy consumption fell by 25 per cent between 1973 and 1989. In Sweden, a sulphur tax reduced the sulphur content of fuel oils by 40 per cent between 1990 and 1992. Clearly, the reduced consumption reduces the tax revenue.

But the revenue will still be more than if no tax had been imposed! Provided green taxes are imposed on a wide range of products and at high enough rates, their revenue-earning potential can be considerable. After all, the aim is not to reduce the consumption of energy and many other potentially polluting activities to *zero*. If it were, it would be simplest just to ban the activity.

Redistributive effects

The poor spend a higher proportion of their income on domestic fuel than the rich. A 'carbon tax' on such fuel will, therefore, have the effect of redistributing incomes away from the poor. Thus, when the UK Conservative government in 1995 attempted to increase the rate of VAT on domestic fuel from 8 per cent to 17½ per cent (albeit primarily as a revenue-raising measure rather than as an environmental one), there was an outcry from groups representing the poor.

The poor also spend a larger proportion of their income on food than do the rich. Taxes on agriculture, designed to reduce intensive use of fertilisers and pesticides, will again tend to hit the poor proportionately more than the rich.

Taxes and charges with beneficial environmental effects: 1995

	Australia	Belgium	Denmark	Japan	Norway	Sweden	UK	USA
Motor fuel								
Leaded unleaded	•	•	•		•	•	•	•
Carbon/energy tax			•		•	•		
Sulphur tax			•		•	•		
Other excise duties	•	•	•		•	•	•	•
Other energy products								
Carbon/energy taxes			•		•	•		
Sulphur tax			•		•	•		
NO$_2$ charge					•			
Other excise duties	•	•	•	•	•	•	•	•
Vehicle-related								
Large cars>small cars	•	•	•	•	•		•	
Agricultural inputs								
Fertilisers					•	•		
Pesticides			•		•	•		
Other goods								
Batteries		•	•		•			
Plastic carrier bags			•					
Disposable containers			•		•			
Tyres					•			•
CFCs	•	•						•
Disposable razors/cameras			•					

	Australia	Belgium	Denmark	Japan	Norway	Sweden	UK	USA
Lubricant oil charge							•	
Oil pollution charge	•							
Air transport								
Noise charges	•	•				•		
Other taxes						•	•	•
Water charges and taxes								
Water charges	•	•				•	•	•
Sewerage charges	•	•			•	•	•	•
Water effluent charges	•							
Waste disposal								
Municipal waste	•	•			•	•	•	•
Waste-disposal charge	•	•	•			•	•	
Hazardous-waste charge	•	•				•		•
Direct tax provisions								
Tax relief on green investment	•		•		•			•
Employer-paid commuting expenses taxable	•	•				•		•
Employer-paid parking expenses taxable	•							•
Commuter use of public transport tax deductible								•

Source: J-P. Barde and J. Owens, 'The evolution of eco-taxes', *OECD Economic Observer* (Feb./March 1996).

Not all green taxes, however, are regressive. The rich spend a higher proportion of their income on motoring than the poor. Thus petrol and other motoring taxes could have a progressive effect. Also, other taxes, such as those on packaging, batteries and disposable items, are likely to be neutral in their impact, since their prime purpose is to encourage people to switch to non-polluting alternatives.

Where adverse redistribution does occur, a solution would be to make compensating payments to the poor, or to reduce other even more regressive taxes, such as VAT.

Problems with international trade

If a country imposes pollution taxes on its industries, its products will become less competitive in world trade. To compensate for this, the industries may need to be given tax rebates for exports. Also taxes would need to be imposed on imports of competitors' products from countries where there is no equivalent green tax.

Effects on employment

One of the worries about pollution taxes is that reduced output in the industries affected will lead to a reduction in employment. If, however, the effect was to encourage investment in new cleaner technology, employment might not fall. Where it did, there could be employment opportunities generated elsewhere if the extra revenues from the green taxes allowed reductions in taxes on labour (e.g. employers' national insurance contributions).

Given that much of the incidence of green taxes would fall on the consumer (e.g. the motorist), a reduction in employers' national insurance contributions would help to make industry *more* competitive. There could be a net *increase* in employment and exports.

 Is it a good idea to use the revenues from green taxes to subsidise green alternatives (e.g. using petrol taxes for subsidising rail transport)?

blame? These are questions that cannot be answered precisely. It is thus impossible to fix the 'correct' pollution tax on, say, a particular coal-fired power station.

Despite these problems, it is nevertheless possible to charge firms by the amount of a particular emission. For example, firms could be charged for chimney smoke by so many parts per million of a given pollutant. Although it is difficult to 'fine-tune' such a system so that the charge reflects the precise number of people affected by the pollutant and by how much, it does go some way to internalising the externality. As Box 6.2 shows, many countries in recent years have introduced 'green' taxes, seeing them as an effective means of protecting the environment.

Summary

1 Taxes and subsidies are one means of correcting market distortions.
2. Externalities can be corrected by imposing tax rates equal to the size of marginal external costs, and granting rates of subsidy equal to marginal external benefits.
3. Taxes and subsidies can also be used to affect monopoly price, output and profit. Subsidies can be used to persuade a monopolist to increase output to the competitive level. Lump-sum taxes can be used to reduce monopoly profits without affecting price or output.
4. Taxes and subsidies have the advantages of 'internalising' externalities and of providing incentives to reduce external costs. On the other hand, they may be impractical to use when different rates are required for each case, or when it is impossible to know the full effects of the activities that the taxes or subsidies are being used to correct.

6.5 Government intervention: laws and regulation

Should the government try to stop 'bad behaviour' by big business?

Laws prohibiting or regulating undesirable structures or behaviour

Laws are frequently used to correct market imperfections. Laws can be of three main types: those that prohibit or regulate behaviour that imposes external costs, those that prevent firms providing false or misleading information, and those that prevent or regulate monopolies and oligopolies.

Advantages of legal restrictions

- They are usually simple and clear to understand and are often relatively easy to administer. For example, various polluting activities could be banned or restricted.
- When the danger is very great, or when the extent of the danger is not as yet known, it might be much safer to ban various practices altogether (e.g. the use of various toxic chemicals) rather than to rely on taxes.
- When a decision needs to be taken quickly, it might be possible to invoke emergency action. For example, in a city like Athens it has been found to be simpler to ban or restrict the use of private cars during a chemical smog emergency than to tax their use.
- Because consumers suffer from imperfect information, consumer protection laws can make it illegal for firms to sell shoddy or unsafe goods, or to make false or misleading claims about their products.

Disadvantages of legal restrictions

The main problem is that legal restrictions tend to be a rather blunt weapon. If, for example, a firm were required to reduce the effluent of a toxic chemical to 20 tonnes per week, there would be no incentive for the firm to reduce it further. With a tax on the effluent, however, the more the firm reduced the effluent, the less tax it would pay. Thus with a system of taxes there is a *continuing* incentive to cut pollution, to improve safety, or whatever.

Regulatory bodies

Rather than using the blunt weapon of general legislation to ban or restrict various activities, a more 'subtle' approach can be adopted. This involves the use of various regulatory bodies. Having identified possible cases where action might be required (e.g. potential cases of pollution, misleading information or the abuse of monopoly power), the regulatory body would probably conduct an investigation and then prepare a report containing its findings and recommendations. It might also have the power to enforce its decisions. In the UK there are regulatory bodies for each of the major privatised utilities (see Box 6.3). Another example is the Office of Fair Trading (OFT) and the Monopolies and Mergers Commission (MMC), which investigate cases of suspected abuse of market power (see Box 4.3).

The advantage of this approach is that a case-by-case approach can be used. All the various circumstances surrounding a particular case can be taken into account, with the result that the most appropriate solution can be adopted.

BOX 6.3 *Regulating privatised industries*
....
Is it the best way of dealing with their monopoly power?

From the early 1980s, the Thatcher and Major governments engaged in extensive programmes of 'privatisation', returning most of the nationalised industries to the private sector. Nationalised industries, they claimed, were bureaucratic, inefficient, unresponsive to consumer wishes and often a burden on the taxpayer.

Other countries have followed similar programmes of privatisation in what has become a world-wide phenomenon. Privatisation has been seen by many governments as a means of revitalising ailing industries and raising revenues to ease budgetary problems.

However, privatisation has brought its own problems. Consumers have complained of poor service and high prices. The result is that governments have been increasingly concerned to *regulate* the behaviour of these industries, many of which have considerable market power.

The system of regulation in the UK

In each of the major privatised industries – telecommunications, gas, water, electricity and railways – there is a separate regulatory office, established at the time of privatisation. Their legal authority is contained in the Act of privatisation, but their real power lies in the terms of their licences and price-setting formulae.

The price-setting formulae are essentially of the '*RPI* minus *X*' variety. What this means is that the industries can raise their prices by the rate of increase in the retail price index (RPI) (i.e. by the rate of inflation) *minus* a certain percentage (X) to take account of expected increases in efficiency. The idea is that this will force the industry to pass cost savings on to the consumer.

The licence also permits the regulator to monitor other aspects of the behaviour of the industry and to require it to take various measures. For example, OFGAS (the gas industry regulator) has required the industry to allow other gas suppliers to use its pipelines and not to refuse to supply customers. Generally, however, the approach has been one of negotiation with the industry.

Assessing the system of regulation in the UK

The system that has evolved in the UK has various advantages over that employed in the USA and elsewhere (where regulation often focuses on the level of profits).

- It is a *discretionary* system, with the regulator able to judge individual examples of the behaviour of the industry on their own merits. The regulator has a detailed knowledge of the industry, which would not be available to government ministers or other bodies such as the Office of Fair Trading. The regulator could thus be argued to be the best person to decide on whether the industry is acting in the public interest.
- The system is *flexible*, since it allows for the licence and price formula to be changed as circumstances change.
- The '*RPI* minus *X*' formula provides an *incentive* for the privatised firms to be as efficient as possible. If they can lower their costs by more than X, they will, in theory, be able to make larger profits and keep them. If, on the other hand, they do not succeed in reducing costs sufficiently, they will make a loss. There is thus a continuing pressure on them to cut costs. (In the US system, where *profits* rather than *prices* are regulated, there is little incentive to increase efficiency, since any cost reductions must be passed on to the consumer in lower prices, and do not, therefore, result in higher profits.)

There are, however, some inherent problems with the way in which regulation operates in the UK.

- The '*RPI* minus *X*' formula was designed to provide an incentive for the firms to cut costs. But if *X* is too low, the firm might make excessive profits. Frequently regulators have underestimated the scope for cost reductions resulting from new technology and reorganisation, and have thus initially set *X* too low. As a result, instead of *X* remaining constant for five years, as intended, new higher values for *X* have been set after only one or two years. But this then leads to the same problem as with the US system. The incentive for the industry to cut costs will be removed. What is the point of being more efficient if the regulator is merely going to insist on a higher value for *X* and thus take away the extra profits?

- A large amount of power is vested in a regulator who is unelected and largely unaccountable. What guarantee is there that the regulator's perception of the public interest is the same as that of the government?

- Regulation is becoming increasingly complex. This makes it difficult for the industries to plan and may lead to a growth of 'short-termism'. One of the claimed advantages of privatisation was to give greater independence to the industries from short-term government interference, and allow them to plan for the longer term. In practice, one type of interference may have been replaced by another.

- There may also be the danger of **regulatory capture**. As regulators become more and more involved in their industry and get to know the senior managers at a personal level, so they are increasingly likely to see the managers' point of view. They will begin to adopt the values and modes of thinking of the industry and will become less and less tough. Commentators do not believe that this has happened yet: the regulators are generally independently minded. But it is a danger for the future.

Increasing competition in the privatised industries

Where natural monopoly exists (see page 112), competition is impossible in a free market. Of course, the industry *could* be broken up by the government, with firms prohibited from owning more than a certain percentage of the industry. But this would lead to higher costs of production. Firms would be operating further back up a downward-sloping long-run average cost curve.

But many parts of the privatised industries are *not* natural monopolies. Generally it is only the *grid* that is a natural monopoly. In the case of gas and water, it is the pipelines. It would be wasteful to duplicate these. In the case of electricity it is the power lines: the national grid and the local power lines. In the case of the railways it is the track. *Other* parts of these industries are potentially competitive. There could be many generators of electricity, provided they had access to the national and local grids. There could be many producers of gas, provided they had access to the pipelines. There could be many operators of trains, provided they could all use the same track with central timetabling and signalling.

Even for the parts where there *is* a natural monopoly, they could be made *contestable* monopolies. One way of doing this is by granting operators a licence for a specific period of time. This is known as **franchising**. This has been the approach used for the railways. Once a company has been granted a franchise, it has the monopoly of passenger rail services over specific routes. But the awarding of the franchise can be highly competitive, with rival companies putting in competitive bids, in terms of both price (or, in the case of railways, the level of government subsidy required) and the quality of service.

Another approach is to give all companies equal access to the relevant grid. Thus rival gas suppliers are by law given access to British Gas's pipelines at the same prices as the pipeline division of British Gas charges the supply division.

But despite attempts to introduce competition into the privatised industries, they are still dominated by giant companies. Even if they are no longer strictly monopolies, they still have considerable market power. Competition is far from being perfect! The scope for price leadership or other forms of oligopolistic collusion is great. However, regulation through the price formula has been progressively abandoned as elements of competition have been introduced. The intention is ultimately to confine regulation to the operation of the grids: the parts that are natural monopolies. But this assumes that competition really *will* be effective in protecting the public interest!

Q1 Should regulators of utilities that have been privatised into several separate companies allow (a) mergers between these companies or similar companies from abroad; (b) mergers with firms in other industries?

Q2 If an industry regulator adopts an *RPI − X* formula for price regulation, is it desirable that the value of *X* should be adjusted as soon as cost conditions change?

The problems with this approach, however, are that (a) investigations may be expensive and time consuming, (b) only a few cases may be examined and (c) offending firms may make various promises of good behaviour which, owing to a lack of follow-up by the regulatory body, may not in fact be carried out.

Summary

1. **Laws can be used to regulate activities that impose external costs, to regulate monopolies and oligopolies, and to provide consumer protection. Legal controls are often simpler and easier to operate than taxes, and are safer when the danger is potentially great. Nevertheless, legal controls tend to be rather a blunt weapon, although discretion can sometimes be allowed in the administration of the law.**
2. **Regulatory bodies can be set up to monitor and control activities that might be against the public interest (e.g. anti-competitive behaviour of oligopolists). They can conduct investigations of specific cases and can be very thorough. The investigations, however, may be expensive and time consuming, and may not be acted on by the authorities.**

Other forms of government intervention

What other weapons does the government have in its economic armoury?

Changes in property rights

One cause of market failure is the limited nature of property rights. If someone dumps a load of rubble in your garden, the law should protect you. It is *your* garden, *your* property, and you can thus insist that it is removed. If, however, someone dumps a load of rubble in his or her *own* garden, but which is next door to yours, what can you do? You can still see it from your window. It is still an eyesore. But you have no property rights over the next-door garden.

Property rights define who owns property, to what uses it can be put, the rights other people have over it and how it may be transferred. By *extending* these rights, individuals may be able to prevent other people imposing costs on them, or charge them for doing so.

The trouble is that in many instances this type of solution is totally impractical. It is impractical when *many* people are *slightly* inconvenienced, especially if there are many culprits imposing the costs. For example, if I were disturbed by noisy lorries outside my home, it would not be practical to negotiate with every haulage company involved. What if I wanted to ban the lorries from the street but my next-door neighbour wanted to charge them 10p per journey? Who gets their way?

Where the extension of private property rights becomes a more practical solution is when the culprits are few in number, are easily identifiable and impose clearly defined costs. Thus a noise abatement Act could be passed which allowed me to prevent my neighbours playing noisy radios, having noisy parties or otherwise disturbing the peace in my home. The onus would be on me to report them. Or if I chose, I could agree not to report them if they paid me adequate compensation.

But even in cases where only a few people are involved, there may still be the problem of litigation. I may have to incur the time and expense of taking people to court. Justice may not be free, and there is thus a conflict with equity. The rich can afford 'better' justice. They can employ top lawyers. Thus even if I have a right to sue a large company for dumping toxic waste near me, I may not have the legal muscle to win.

Finally there is the broader question of *equity*. The extension of private property rights may favour the rich (who tend to have more property) at the expense of the poor. Ramblers may get great pleasure from strolling across a great country estate, along public rights of way. This may annoy the owner. If the owner's property rights were now extended to exclude the ramblers, is this a social gain?

Of course, equity considerations can also be dealt with by altering property rights, but in a different way. *Public* property like parks, open spaces, libraries and historic buildings could be extended. Also the property of the rich could be redistributed to the poor. Here it is less a question of the rights that ownership confers, and more a question of altering the ownership itself.

Provision of information

When ignorance is a reason for market failure, the direct provision of information by the government or one of its agencies may help to correct that failure. An example is the information on jobs provided by job centres to those looking for work. They thus help the labour market to work better and increase the elasticity of supply of labour. Another example is the provision of consumer information – for example, on the effects of smoking, or of eating certain foodstuffs. Another is the provision of government statistics on prices, costs, employment, sales trends, etc. This enables firms to plan with greater certainty.

The direct provision of goods and services

In the case of public goods and services, such as streets, pavements, seaside illumination and national defence, the market may completely fail to provide. In this case the government must take over the role of provision. Central government, local government or some other public agency could provide these goods and services directly. Alternatively, they could pay private firms to do so. The public would pay through central and local taxation.

But just what quantity of the public good should be provided? How can the level of public demand or public 'need' be identified? Should any charge at all be made to consumers for each unit consumed?

With a pure public good, once it is provided the marginal cost of supplying one more consumer is zero. Take the case of a lighthouse. Once it is constructed and in operation, there is no extra cost of providing the service to additional passing ships. Even it were *possible* to charge ships each time they make use of it, it would not be socially desirable. Assuming no external costs, *MSC* is zero. Thus *MSB* = *MSC* at a price of zero. Zero is thus the socially efficient price.

But what about the construction of a new public good, like a new road or a new lighthouse? How can a rational decision be made by the government as to whether it should go ahead? This time the marginal cost is not zero: extra roads and lighthouses cost money to build. The solution is to identify all the costs and benefits to society from the project (private and external) and to weigh them up. This is known as cost–benefit analysis. If the social benefits of the project exceed the social costs, then it would be socially efficient to go ahead with it. Many proposed public projects are subjected to cost–benefit analysis in order to assess their desirability.

The government could also provide goods and services directly which are *not* public goods. Examples include health and education. There are four reasons why such things are provided free or at well below cost.

Social justice. Society may feel that these things should not be provided according to ability to pay. Rather they should be provided as of right: an equal right based on need.

Large positive externalities. People other than the consumer may benefit substantially. If a person decides to get treatment for an infectious disease,

Definition

Cost–benefit analysis
The identification, measurement and weighing-up of the costs and benefits of a project in order to decide whether or not it should go ahead.

other people benefit by not being infected. A free health service thus helps to combat the spread of disease.

Dependants. If education were not free, and if the quality of education depended on the amount spent, and if parents could choose how much or little to buy, then the quality of children's education would depend not just on their parents' income, but also on how much they cared. A government may choose to provide such things free in order to protect children from 'bad' parents. A similar argument is used for providing free prescriptions and dental treatment for all children.

Ignorance. Consumers may not realise how much they will benefit. If they had to pay, they may choose (unwisely) to go without. Providing health care free may persuade people to consult their doctors before a complaint becomes serious.

Summary

1. An extension of property rights may allow individuals to prevent others imposing costs on them, or to charge them for so doing. This is not practical, however, when many people are affected to a small degree, or where several people are affected but differ in their attitudes towards what they want doing about the 'problem'.
2. The government may provide information in cases where the private sector fails to provide an adequate level.
3. The government may also provide goods and services directly. These could be in the category of public goods or other goods where the government feels that provision by the market is inadequate.

6.7 More or less intervention?

Can the government always put things right?

Government intervention in the market can itself lead to problems. The case for non-intervention (*laissez-faire*) or very limited intervention is not that the market is the *perfect* means of achieving given social goals, but rather that the problems created by intervention are greater than the problems overcome by that intervention.

Drawbacks of government intervention

Shortages and surpluses. If the government intervenes by fixing prices at levels other than the equilibrium, this will create either shortages or surpluses (see section 2.6).

If the price is fixed *below* the equilibrium, there will be a shortage. For example, if the rent of council houses is fixed below the equilibrium in

BOX 6.4

The problem of urban traffic congestion
···
Does Singapore have the answer?

It takes only one hour to drive from one end of Singapore to the other. Yet the average Singaporean driver travels an estimated 18 600 km per year, more than the average US driver, and over 50 per cent more than the average Japanese driver. In Singapore in 1996 there were a little over 300 000 cars, giving a vehicle density of 200 motor vehicles per km of road. This compares with a vehicle density in the USA of only 27 motor vehicles per km. It is hardly surprising that traffic congestion has become a major focus of public debate, particularly as the demand for cars is set to increase as consumer affluence grows.

The problem of traffic congestion

Traffic congestion is a classic example of the problem of externalities. When people use their cars, not only do they incur private costs (petrol, wear and tear on the vehicle, tolls, the time taken to travel, etc.), but also they impose costs on *other* people. These external costs include the following:

Congestion costs: time. When a person uses a car on a congested road, it will add to the congestion. This will therefore slow down the traffic even more and increase the journey time of *other* car users.

Congestion costs: monetary. Congestion increases fuel consumption, and the stopping and starting increases the costs of wear and tear. When a motorist adds to congestion, therefore, there will be additional monetary costs imposed on other motorists.

Environmental costs. When motorists use a road they reduce the quality of the environment for others. Cars emit fumes and create noise. This is bad enough for pedestrians and other car users, but can be particularly distressing for people living along the road. Driving can cause accidents, a problem that increases as drivers become more impatient as a result of delays.

Exhaust gases cause long-term environmental damage and are one of the main causes of the greenhouse effect and of the increased acidity of lakes and rivers and the poisoning of forests. They can also cause long-term health problems (e.g. for asthma sufferers).

Actual and optimum road usage

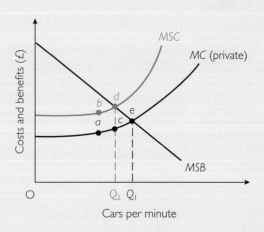

The socially efficient level of road usage

These externalities mean that road usage will be above the social optimum. This is illustrated in the diagram. Costs and benefits are shown on the vertical axis and are measured in money terms. Thus any non-monetary costs or benefits (such as time costs) must be given a monetary value. The horizontal axis measures road usage in terms of cars per minute passing a specified point on the road.

For simplicity it is assumed that there are no external benefits from car use and that therefore marginal private and marginal social benefits are the same. The MSB curve is shown as downward sloping. The reason for this is that different road users put a different value on any given journey. If the marginal (private) cost of making the journey were high, only those for whom the journey had a high marginal benefit would travel along the road. If the marginal cost of making the journey fell, more people would make the journey: people choosing to make the journey as long as the marginal cost of the journey was less than the marginal benefit. Thus the greater the number of cars, the lower the marginal benefit.

The marginal (private) cost curve (MC) is likely to be constant up to the level of traffic flow at which congestion begins to occur. This is shown as point a in the diagram. Beyond this point, marginal cost is likely to rise as time costs increase (i.e. journey times lengthen) and as fuel consumption rises.

The marginal *social* cost curve (MSC) is drawn above the marginal private cost curve. The vertical difference between the two represents the external costs. Up to point b, external costs are simply the environmental costs. Beyond point b, there are also external congestion costs, since additional road users slow down the journey of *other* road users. These external costs get progressively greater as traffic grinds to a halt.

The actual level of traffic flow will be at Q_1, where marginal private costs and benefits are equal (point e). The socially efficient level of traffic flow, however, will be at the lower level of Q_2 where marginal social costs and benefits are equal (point d). In other words, there will be an excessive level of road usage.

So what can governments do to 'internalise' these externalities?

The Singapore solution

In contrast to its neighbours, many of which are suffering more acute urban traffic congestion problems, Singapore has an integrated transport policy. This includes the following:

* Restricting the number of new car licences, and allowing their price to rise to the corresponding equilibrium. This makes car licences in Singapore among the most expensive in the world.
* Investment in a mass rail transit (MRT) system with subsidised fares. Trains are comfortable, clean and frequent. Stations are air-conditioned.
* A programme of building new estates near MRT stations.
* Cheap, frequent buses, serving all parts of the island.

In addition, a 1996 White Paper proposed:

* Building an extra 56 km of MRT lines running parallel to busy commuter routes.

- A light rail system to serve as feeders to the MRT.
- Private bus companies to operate all routes, including unprofitable ones, with prescribed fares and frequencies.
- 'Premium' buses offering greater comfort and service at higher fares.
- The construction of an extra 225 lane-km of motorways by 2001.
- The possible construction of underground roads in the city centre.

But it is in respect to road usage that the Singaporean authorities have been most innovative.

The first innovation was to make the city centre a restricted zone. Motorists who wish to enter this zone must buy a ticket (an 'area licence') at any one of 33 entry points. Police are stationed at these entry points and check that cars have paid and displayed.

With traffic congestion steadily worsening, however, it was realised that the Area Licensing Scheme had either to be widened, or to be replaced with some more flexible alternative. The decision was taken to introduce electronic road pricing. This alternative would not only save on police labour costs, but enable charge rates to be varied according to levels of congestion, times of the day and locality.

Under this system it is anticipated that all vehicles in Singapore will be fitted with an in-vehicle unit (IU). Every journey made will require the driver to insert a smart card into the IU. On specified roads, overhead gantries will first read the IU, deducting the road use charge, and at the same time take a photograph of the car's number plate. So long as there are no problems with the deduction from the smart card, the photograph is automatically overwritten. If a car does not have a smart card or the smart card has insufficient funds on it, the car's details will then be relayed to a control centre, and the necessary legal penalties imposed.

One of the major fears is that, if the system is abused, there will be no labour saving, with the police having to spend time tracking down motorists who have not paid.

In addition, the system is very expensive, given the need to avoid *creating* congestion. Several cheaper existing schemes, such as in Norway and parts of the United States, operate by funnelling traffic into a single lane in order to register the car. In Singapore the intention is to have the system operating on three-lane highways and not requiring the speed of traffic to slow. But despite the high set-up and running costs of the system, the Singapore government is quick to argue that the full social costs of doing nothing would be significantly greater, as would the direct cost of meeting all the potential extra demand by building new roads.

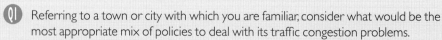 Referring to a town or city with which you are familiar, consider what would be the most appropriate mix of policies to deal with its traffic congestion problems.

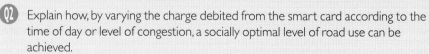 Explain how, by varying the charge debited from the smart card according to the time of day or level of congestion, a socially optimal level of road use can be achieved.

order to provide cheap housing for poor people, demand will exceed supply. In the case of shortages resulting from fixing prices below the equilibrium, either the government will have to adopt a system of waiting lists, or rationing, or giving certain people preferential treatment, or alternatively it will have to allow allocation to be on a first-come, first-served basis or allow queues to develop. Black markets are likely to occur.

If the price is fixed *above* the equilibrium price, there will be a surplus. For example, if the price of food is fixed above the equilibrium in order to support farmers' incomes, supply will exceed demand. Government will either have to purchase such surpluses and then perhaps store them, throw them away or sell them cheaply in another market, or it will have to ration suppliers by allowing them to produce only a certain quota, or allow them to sell to whom they can (see Box 2.4).

Poor information. The government may not know the full costs and benefits of its policies. It may genuinely wish to pursue the interests of consumers or any other group and yet may be unaware of people's wishes or misinterpret their behaviour.

Bureaucracy and inefficiency. Government intervention involves administrative costs. The more wide reaching and detailed the intervention, the greater the number of people and material resources that will be involved. These resources may be used wastefully.

Lack of market incentives. If government intervention removes market forces or cushions their effect (by the use of subsidies, welfare provisions, guaranteed prices or wages, etc.), it may remove certain useful incentives. Subsidies may allow inefficient firms to survive. Welfare payments may discourage effort. The market may be imperfect, but it does tend to encourage efficiency by allowing the efficient to receive greater rewards.

Shifts in government policy. The economic efficiency of industry may suffer if government intervention changes too frequently. It makes it difficult for firms to plan if they cannot predict tax rates, subsidies, price and wage controls, etc.

Lack of freedom for the individual. One of the major arguments put forward by those advocating *laissez-faire* is that government intervention involves a loss of freedom for individuals to make economic choices. The argument is not just that the pursuit of individual gain is seen to lead to the social good, but that it is desirable in itself that individuals should be as free as possible to pursue their own interests with the minimum of government interference: that minimum being largely confined to the maintenance of laws consistent with the protection of life, liberty and property.

Advantages of the free market

Although markets in the real world are not perfect, even imperfect markets can be argued to have positive advantages over government provision or even government regulation. These might include the following:

Automatic adjustments. Government intervention requires administration. A free-market economy, on the other hand, leads to automatic, albeit imperfect, adjustment to demand and supply changes.

Dynamic advantages of capitalism. The chances of making high monopoly/oligopoly profits will encourage capitalists to invest in new products and new techniques. The benefits to growth from such innovations may considerably outweigh any problem of resource misallocation.

A high degree of competition even under monopoly/oligopoly. Even though an industry at first sight may seem to be highly monopolistic, competitive forces may still work as a result of the following:

- A fear that excessively high profits might encourage firms to attempt to break into the industry.
- Competition from closely related industries (e.g. coach services for rail services, or electricity for gas).
- The threat of foreign competition.
- Countervailing powers. Large powerful producers often sell to large powerful buyers. For example, the power of detergent manufacturers to drive up the price of washing powder is countered by the power of supermarket chains to drive down the price at which they purchase it. Thus power is to some extent neutralised.
- The competition for corporate control (see page 115).

Should there be more or less intervention in the market?

No firm conclusions can be drawn in the debate between those who favour more and those who favour less government intervention, for the following reasons:

- Many moral, social and political issues are involved which cannot be settled by economic analysis. For example, it could be argued that freedom to set up in business and freedom from government regulation are desirable *for their own sake*. As a fundamental ethical point of view this can be disputed, but not disproved.
- In principle, the issue of whether a government ought to intervene in any situation could be settled by weighing up the costs and benefits of that intervention. However, such costs and benefits, even if they could be identified, are extremely difficult if not impossible to measure, especially when the costs are borne by different people from those who receive the benefits and when externalities are involved.
- Often the effect of more or less intervention simply cannot be predicted: there are too many uncertainties.

Nevertheless, economists can make a considerable contribution to analysing problems of the market and the effects of government intervention.

Summary

1. **Government intervention in the market may lead to shortages or surpluses; it may be based on poor information; it may be costly in terms of administration; it may stifle incentives; it may be disruptive if government policies change too frequently; it may not represent the majority of voters' interests if the government is elected by a minority, or**

if voters did not fully understand the issues at election time, or if the policies were not in the government's manifesto; it may remove certain liberties.
2. By contrast, a free market leads to automatic adjustments to changes in economic conditions; the prospect of monopoly/oligopoly profits may stimulate risk taking and hence research and development and innovation, and this advantage may outweigh any problems of resource misallocation; there may still be a high degree of actual or potential competition under monopoly and oligopoly.
3. It is impossible to draw firm conclusions about the 'optimum' level of government intervention. This is partly due to the moral/political nature of the question, partly due to the difficulties of measuring costs and benefits of intervention/non-intervention, and partly due to the difficulties of predicting the effects of government policies, especially over the longer term.

Questions

1. The following table gives the costs and benefits of an imaginary firm operating under perfect competition whose activities create a certain amount of pollution. (It is assumed that the costs of this pollution to society can be accurately measured.)
   (a) What is the profit-maximising level of output for this firm?
   (b) What is the socially efficient level of output?
   (c) Why might the marginal pollution costs increase in the way illustrated in this example?

Output (units)	Price per unit (MSB) (£)	Marginal (private) costs to the firm (MC) (£)	Marginal external (pollution) costs (MEC) (£)	Marginal social costs (MSC = MC + MEC) (£)
1	100	30	20	50
2	100	30	22	52
3	100	35	25	60
4	100	45	30	75
5	100	60	40	100
6	100	78	55	133
7	100	100	77	177
8	100	130	110	240

2. In Figure 6.1 (page 184) the *MSC* curve is drawn parallel to the *MC* curve. Under what circumstances would it have a steeper slope than the *MC* curve?

3. On diagrams similar to Figures 6.1 and 6.2, demonstrate that there will be a less than optimum output where there are external benefits in (a) production and (b) consumption.

4. Give some examples of public goods (other than those given on page 186). Does the provider of these goods or services (the government or local authority) charge for their use? If so, is the method of charging

based on the amount of the good people use? Is it a good method of charging? Could you suggest a better method?

5. Distinguish between publicly provided goods, public goods and merit goods.

6. Name some goods or services provided by the government or local authorities that are not public goods.

7. Some roads could be regarded as a public good, but some could be provided by the market. Which types of road could be provided by the market? Why? Would it be a good idea?

8. Assume that you have decided to buy a new video recorder. How do you set about ensuring that you make the right choice between the available makes?

9. Assume that you wanted the information given in (a)–(h) below. In which cases could you (i) buy perfect information; (ii) buy imperfect information; (iii) obtain information without paying for it; (iv) not obtain information?
   (a) Which washing machine is the most reliable?
   (b) Which of two jobs that are vacant is the most satisfying?
   (c) Which builder will repair my roof most cheaply?
   (d) Which builder will make the best job of repairing my roof?
   (e) Which builder is best value for money?
   (f) How big a mortgage would it be wise for me to take out?
   (g) What course of higher education should I follow?
   (h) What brand of washing powder washes whiter?
   In which cases are there non-monetary costs to you of finding out the information? How can you know whether the information you acquire is accurate or not?

10. Make a list of pieces of information a firm might want to know and consider whether it could buy the information and how reliable that information might be.

11. Assume that a country had no state education at all. For what reasons might the private education system not provide the optimal allocation of resources to and within education?

12. Assume that a firm discharges waste into a river. As a result, the marginal social costs (MSC) are greater than the firm's marginal (private) costs (MC). The following table shows how MC, MSC, AR and MR vary with output. Assume that the marginal private benefit (MB) is given by the price (AR). Assume also that there are no externalities on the consumption side, and that therefore $MSB = MB$.

Output	1	2	3	4	5	6	7	8
MC	23	21	23	25	27	30	35	42
MSC	35	34	38	42	46	52	60	72
TR	60	102	138	168	195	219	238	252
AR	60	51	46	42	39	36.5	34	31.5
MR	60	42	36	30	27	24	19	14

(a) How much will the firm produce if it seeks to maximise profits?
(b) What is the socially efficient level of output (assuming no externalities on the demand side)?
(c) How much is the marginal external cost at this level of output?
(d) What size tax would be necessary for the firm to reduce its output to the socially efficient level?
(e) Why is the tax less than the marginal externality?
(f) Why might it be equitable to impose a lump-sum tax on this firm?
(g) Why will a lump-sum tax not affect the firm's output (assuming that in the long run the firm can still make at least normal profit)?

13. On a diagram similar to Figure 6.5, demonstrate how a subsidy can correct for an external benefit.

14. Why might it be better to ban certain activities that cause environmental damage rather than to tax them?

15. To what extent could property rights (either public or private) be successfully extended and invoked to curb the problem of industrial pollution (a) of the atmosphere, (b) of rivers, (c) by the dumping of toxic waste, (d) by the erection of ugly buildings and (e) by the creation of high levels of noise?

16. What protection do private property rights in the real world give to sufferers of noise (a) from neighbours, (b) from traffic, (c) from transistor radios at the seaside?

17. How suitable are legal restrictions in the following cases?
    (a) Ensuring adequate vehicle safety (e.g. that tyres have sufficient tread or that the vehicle is roadworthy).
    (b) Reducing traffic congestion.
    (c) Preventing the abuse of monopoly power.
    (d) Ensuring that mergers are in the public interest.
    (e) Ensuring that firms charge a price equal to marginal cost.

18. How would you evaluate the following?
    (a) The external effects of building a reservoir in an area of outstanding natural beauty.
    (b) The external effects of acid rain pollution from a power station.

19. Many economists have argued that a form of 'congestion tax' ought to be imposed on motorists who use their cars on busy roads, to take account of the external costs they impose on other motorists and

pedestrians. Compare the relative advantages and disadvantages of the
following measures:
(a) Increasing the rate of duty on petrol.
(b) Increasing the annual road fund licence.
(c) Insisting that cars be fitted with an electronic device which allows
their account held in a central computer to be debited when the
car passes beacons installed at the roadside. Motorists would then
be sent a bill (like a telephone bill) every three or six months. The
charges could vary with the level of congestion.
(d) Setting up toll booths to charge motorists for using certain
stretches of road.
(e) The use of bus and cycle lanes at peak times.
(f) Subsidising public transport.

20. Give examples of how the government intervenes to protect the
interests of dependants from bad economic decisions taken on their
behalf.

21. What are the possible arguments in favour of fixing prices (a) below
and (b) above the equilibrium? Are there any means of achieving the
same social goals without fixing prices?

22. Make out a case for (a) increasing and (b) decreasing the role of the
government in the allocation of resources.

chapter seven

Aggregate demand and supply, and macroeconomic problems

We turn now to *macroeconomics*. This will be the subject for the second half of the book. As we have already seen, *microeconomics* focuses on *individual* markets. In macroeconomics we take a much loftier view. We examine the economy as a whole. We still examine demand and supply, but now it is the *total* level of spending in the economy and the *total* level of production. In other words, we examine *aggregate demand* and *aggregate supply*.

In particular, we will be examining four key issues. The first is national output. What determines the size of national output? What causes it to grow? Why do growth rates fluctuate? Why do economies sometimes surge ahead and at other times languish in recession?

The second is employment and unemployment. What causes unemployment? If people who are unemployed want jobs, and if consumers want more goods and services, then why does our economy fail to provide a job for everyone who wants one?

Then there is the issue of inflation. Why is it that the general level of prices always seems to rise, and virtually never to fall?

Finally there is the issue of a country's economic relationships with the rest of the world. What determines the level of its imports and exports? What determines the rate of exchange of its currency into other nations' currencies? How do these relationships with other countries affect the domestic economy?

7.1 Macroeconomic objectives

What are the major economic problems that economies as a whole suffer from?

Economic growth

Governments try to achieve high rates of economic growth over the long term: in other words, growth that is sustained over the years and is not just a temporary phenomenon. To this end, governments also try to achieve *stable* growth, avoiding both recessions and excessive short-term growth that cannot be sustained (governments are nevertheless sometimes happy to give the economy an excessive boost as an election draws near!).

Table 7.1 shows the average annual growth in output between 1960 and 1997 for selected countries. As you can see, the differences between countries are quite substantial.

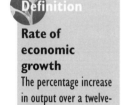

Definition

Rate of economic growth
The percentage increase in output over a twelve-month period.

Unemployment

Governments also aim to ensure that unemployment is as low as possible, not only for the sake of the unemployed themselves, but also because it represents a waste of human resources and because unemployment benefits are a drain on government revenues.

Unemployment in the 1980s and 1990s has been significantly higher than in the 1950s, 1960s and 1970s.

TABLE 7.1 *Economic growth (average % per annum), unemployment (average %) and inflation (average % per annum)*

	France	Germany (W)	Italy	Japan	UK	USA	EU (15)	OECD	Brazil	Malaysia	Singapore
Growth											
1960–9	7.5	4.4	5.3	10.9	2.9	4.3	3.5	4.6	5.4	6.5	8.8
1970–9	3.2	2.6	3.8	4.3	2.0	2.8	3.2	3.6	8.1	7.9	8.3
1980–9	2.2	1.8	2.4	4.0	2.4	2.5	2.2	2.6	3.0	5.8	6.1
1990–7	1.5	2.8	1.2	2.3	1.5	2.1	1.9	2.1	2.2	8.4	8.0
Unemployment											
1960–9	1.5	0.9	5.1	1.3	2.2	4.1	2.5	2.5	n.a.	n.a.	n.a.
1970–9	3.7	2.3	6.4	1.7	4.5	6.1	4.0	4.3	n.a.	n.a.	n.a.
1980–9	9.0	5.9	9.5	2.5	10.0	7.2	9.3	7.3	n.a.	6.8	4.0
1990–7	11.2	7.3	11.0	2.7	8.6	6.0	10.1	7.3	n.a.	3.9	2.3
Inflation											
1960–9	4.2	3.2	4.4	4.9	4.1	2.8	3.7	3.1	46.1	−0.3	1.1
1970–9	9.4	5.0	13.9	9.0	13.0	6.8	10.3	9.2	38.6	7.3	5.9
1980–9	7.3	2.9	11.2	2.5	7.4	5.5	7.4	8.9	227.8	2.2	2.5
1990–7	2.3	3.0	4.7	1.4	4.0	3.4	3.7	5.2	1100.3	3.8	2.6

Inflation

By inflation we mean a general rise in prices throughout the economy. Government policy here is to keep inflation both low and stable. One of the most important reasons for this is that it will aid the process of economic decision making. For example, businesses will be able to set prices and wage rates, and make investment decisions with far more confidence.

Today we are used to inflation rates of around 3 or 4 per cent, but it was not long ago that inflation in most developed countries was in double figures. In 1975, UK inflation reached 24 per cent.

The balance of payments

A country's balance of payments account records all transactions between the residents of that country and the rest of the world. These transactions enter as either debit items or credit items. The debit items include all payments *to* other countries: these include the country's purchases of imports, the investments it makes abroad and the interest and dividends paid to foreigners who have invested in the country. The credit items include all receipts *from* other countries: from the sales of exports, from investments made by foreigners in the country and interest and dividends earned from abroad.

The sale of exports and any other receipts earn foreign currency. The purchase of imports or any other payments abroad use up foreign currency. If we start to spend more foreign currency than we earn, one of two things must happen. Both are likely to be a problem.

The balance of payments will go into deficit. In other words, there will be a shortfall of foreign currencies. The government will therefore have to borrow money from abroad, or draw on its foreign currency reserves to make up the shortfall. This is a problem because, if it goes on too long, overseas debts will mount, along with the interest that must be paid; and/or reserves will begin to run low.

The exchange rate will fall. The exchange rate is the rate at which one currency exchanges for another. For example, the exchange rate of the pound into the dollar might be £1 = $1.60.

If the government does nothing to correct the balance of payments deficit, then the exchange rate must fall: for example, to $1.55 or $1.50, or lower. (We will show just why this is so in Chapter 12.) A falling exchange rate is a problem because it pushes up the price of imports and may fuel inflation. Also, if the exchange rate fluctuates, this can cause great uncertainty for traders and can damage international trade and economic growth.

In order to achieve the goals of high and sustainable economic growth, low unemployment and inflation and satisfactory balance of payments, the government may seek to control several 'intermediate' variables. These include interest rates, the supply of money, taxes, government expenditure and exchange rates. We will be looking at the relationship between all these in the coming chapters.

Definitions

Rate of inflation
The percentage increase in prices over a twelve-month period.

Balance of payments account
A record of the country's transactions with the rest of the world. It shows the country's payments to or deposits in other countries (debits) and its receipts or deposits from other countries (credits). It also shows the balance between these debits and credits under various headings.

Exchange rate
The rate at which one national currency exchanges for another. The rate is expressed as the amount of one currency that is necessary to purchase *one unit* of another currency (e.g. DM2.50 = £l).

Summary

1. Macroeconomics, like microeconomics, looks at issues such as output, employment and prices; but it looks at them in the context of the whole economy.
2. The four main macroeconomic goals that are generally of most concern to governments are economic growth, reducing unemployment, reducing inflation, and avoiding balance of payments and exchange rate problems.

The circular flow of income

Why does money go round and round from firms to consumers and back again?

Unfortunately, the pursuit of any one of the four objectives that we have identified may make at least one of the others worse. For example, attempts to increase the rate of economic growth by giving tax cuts so as to boost consumer spending, and thereby encourage investment, may lead to higher inflation. It is thus important to understand the relationship *between* the four objectives.

One way in which the objectives are linked is through their relationship with **aggregate demand** (*AD*). This is the total spending on goods and services made within the country ('domestically produced goods and services'). This spending consists of four elements: consumer spending on domestically produced goods and services (C_d), investment expenditure by firms (*I*), government spending (*G*) and the expenditure by foreign residents on the country's goods and services (i.e. their purchases of its exports and their new investments in the country) (*X*). Thus:

$$AD = C_d + I + G + X^1$$

To show how the four objectives are related to aggregate demand, we can use a simple model of the economy. This is the *circular flow of income*, and is shown in Figure 7.1. It is an extension of the model we looked at back in Chapter 1 (see Figure 1.1 on page 9).

In the diagram, the economy is divided into two major groups: *firms* and *households*. Each group has two roles. Firms are producers of goods and services; they are also the employers of labour and other factors of production. Households (which include all individuals) are the consumers of goods and services; they are also the suppliers of labour and various other factors of production. In the diagram there is an inner flow and various outer flows of incomes between these two groups.

Aggregate demand

Total spending on goods and services made in the economy. It consists of four elements, consumer spending (*C*), investment (*I*), government spending (*G*) and the expenditure on exports (*X*), less any expenditure on foreign goods and services (*M*): $AD = C + I + G + X - M$.

[1] Investment, government expenditure and export expenditure are also only on domestically produced goods and services (and thus strictly speaking should also be written with a subscript 'd'). If, alternatively, we were also to include in *C*, *I*, *G* and *X* any component of expenditure going on imports, we would then have to subtract imports again to get back to aggregate demand. Thus another way of writing aggregate demand is $AD = C + I + G + X - M$ (where each of *C*, *I*, *G* and *X* includes expenditure on both domestic *and* imported goods and services).

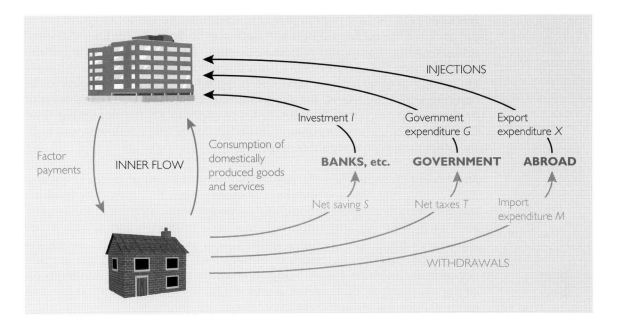

FIGURE 7.1
The circular flow of income

The inner flow, withdrawals and injections

The inner flow

Firms pay money to households in the form of wages and salaries, dividends on shares, interest and rent. These payments are in return for the services of the factors of production – labour, capital and land – that are supplied by households. Thus on the left-hand side of Figure 7.1 money flows directly from firms to households as 'factor payments'.

Households, in turn, pay money to domestic firms when they **consume domestically produced goods and services** (C_d). This is shown on the right-hand side of the inner flow. There is thus a circular flow of payments from firms to households to firms and so on.

If households spend *all* their incomes on buying domestic goods and services, and if firms pay out *all* this income they receive from consumers as factor payments to domestic households, and if the velocity at which money circulates does not change, the flow will continue at the same level indefinitely. The money just goes round and round at the same speed and incomes remain unchanged.

In the real world, of course, it is not as simple as this. Not all income gets passed on round the inner flow; some is *withdrawn*. At the same time, incomes are injected into the flow from outside. Let us examine these withdrawals and injections.

Withdrawals (W)

Only part of the incomes received by households will be spent on the goods and services of domestic firms. The remainder will be withdrawn from the inner flow. Likewise, only part of the incomes generated by firms will be paid to domestic households. The remainder of this will also be withdrawn. There are three forms of **withdrawals** (or 'leakages' as they are sometimes called).

Definitions

The consumption of domestically produced goods and services (C_d)
The direct flow of money payments from households to firms.

Withdrawals (W)
(or leakages) Incomes of households or firms that are not passed on round the inner flow. Withdrawals equal net savings (S) plus net taxes (T) plus import expenditure (M):
$W = S + T + M$.

Net saving (S). Saving is income that households choose not to spend but to put aside for the future. Savings will normally be deposited in financial institutions such as banks and building societies. This is shown in the bottom right of Figure 7.1. Money flows from households to 'banks, etc'. What we are seeking to measure here, however, is the *net* flow from households to the banking sector. We therefore have to subtract from saving any borrowing or drawing on past savings by households in order to get the net saving flow. Of course, if household borrowing exceeded saving, the net flow would be in the other direction: it would be negative.

Net taxes (T). When people pay taxes (to either central or local government), this represents a withdrawal of money from the inner flow in much the same way as saving: only in this case people have no choice. Some taxes, such as income tax and employees' national insurance contributions, are paid out of household incomes. Others, such as VAT and excise duties, are paid out of consumer expenditure. Others, such as corporation tax, are paid out of firms' incomes before being received by households as dividends on shares. (For simplicity, however, we show taxes being withdrawn at just one point. It does not affect the argument.)

When, however, people receive *benefits* from the government, such as unemployment benefits, child benefit and pensions, the money flows the other way. Benefits are thus equivalent to a 'negative tax'. These benefits are known as transfer payments. They transfer money from one group of people (taxpayers) to others (the recipients).

In the model, 'net taxes' (T) represent the *net* flow to the government from households and firms. It consists of total taxes minus benefits.

Definitions

Transfer payments
Moneys transferred from one person or group to another (e.g. from the government to individuals) without production taking place.

Injections (J)
Expenditure on the production of domestic firms coming from outside the inner flow of the circular flow of income. Injections equal investment (*I*) plus government expenditure (*G*) plus expenditure on exports (*X*).

Import expenditure (M). Not all consumption is of totally home-produced goods. Households spend some of their incomes on imported goods and services, or on goods and services using imported components. Although the money that consumers spend on such goods initially flows to domestic retailers, it will eventually find its way abroad, either when the retailers or wholesalers themselves buy the imports from abroad, or when domestic manufacturers purchase imported inputs to make their products. This expenditure on imports constitutes the third withdrawal from the inner flow. This money flows abroad.

Total withdrawals are simply the sum of net saving, net taxes and the expenditure on imports:

$$W = S + T + M$$

Injections (J)

Only part of the demand for firms' output (i.e. aggregate demand) arises from consumers' expenditure. The remainder comes from other sources outside the inner flow. These additional components of aggregate demand are known as injections (*J*). There are three types of injection.

Investment (I). This is the money that firms spend which they obtain from various financial institutions – either past savings or loans, or through a new issue of shares. They may invest in plant and equipment or may simply spend the money on building up stocks of inputs, semi-finished or finished goods.

Government expenditure (G). When the government spends money on goods and services produced by firms, this counts as an injection. Examples of such government expenditure include spending on roads, hospitals and schools. (Note that government expenditure in this model does not include state benefits. These transfer payments, as we saw above, are the equivalent of negative taxes and have the effect of reducing the T component of withdrawals.)

Export expenditure (X). Money flows into the circular flow from abroad when foreign residents buy our exports of goods and services.

Total injections are thus the sum of investment, government expenditure and exports:

$$J = I + G + X$$

The relationship between withdrawals and injections

There are indirect links between saving and investment, taxation and government expenditure, and imports and exports, via financial institutions, the government (central and local) and foreign countries respectively. If a greater proportion of income is saved, there will be more available for banks and other financial institutions to lend out. If tax receipts are higher, the government may be more keen to increase its expenditure. Finally, if imports increase, foreigners' incomes will increase, which will enable them to purchase more of our exports.

These links, however, do not guarantee that $S = I$ or $G = T$ or $M = X$. For a period of time, financial institutions can lend out (I) more than they receive from depositors (S) or vice versa; governments can spend (G) more than they receive in taxes (T) or vice versa; and exports (X) can exceed imports (M) or vice versa.

A major point here is that the decisions to save and invest are made by different people, and thus they plan to save and invest different amounts. Likewise the demand for imports may not equal the demand for exports. As far as the government is concerned, it may choose not to make $T = G$. It may choose not to spend all its tax revenues: to run a 'budget surplus' ($T > G$); or it may choose to spend more than it receives in taxes: to run a 'budget deficit' ($G > T$) – by borrowing or printing money to make up the difference.

Thus planned injections (J) may not equal planned withdrawals (W).

The circular flow of income and the four macroeconomic objectives

If planned injections are not equal to planned withdrawals, what will be the consequences? If injections exceed withdrawals, the level of expenditure will rise: there will be a rise in aggregate demand. This extra spending will increase firms' sales and thus encourage them to produce more. Total output in the economy will rise. Thus firms will pay out more in wages, salaries, profits, rent and interest. In other words, national income will rise.

The rise in aggregate demand will have the following effects upon the four macroeconomic objectives:

- There will be economic growth. The greater the initial excess of injections over withdrawals, the bigger will be the rise in national income.
- Unemployment will fall as firms take on more workers in order to meet the extra demand for output.
- Inflation will tend to rise. The greater the rise in aggregate demand relative to the capacity of firms to produce, the more will firms find it difficult to meet extra demand, and the more likely they will be to raise prices.
- The balance of payments will tend to deteriorate. The higher demand sucks more imports into the country, and higher domestic inflation makes exports less competitive and imports relatively cheaper compared with home-produced goods. Thus imports will tend to rise and exports will tend to fall.

If planned injections were *less* than planned withdrawals, then the converse of each of the above would occur.

Equilibrium in the circular flow

When injections do not equal withdrawals, a state of disequilibrium will exist. This will set in train a process to bring the economy back to a state of equilibrium where injections are equal to withdrawals.

To illustrate this, let us consider the situation again where injections exceed withdrawals. Perhaps there has been a rise in business confidence so that investment has risen. Or perhaps the government has decided to spend more on health or education. Or perhaps there has been a rise in foreign demand for the country's exports. Or perhaps one or more of the three withdrawals has fallen (e.g. a tax cut). As we have seen, the excess of injections over withdrawals will lead to a rise in national income. But as national income rises, so households will not only spend more on domestic goods (C_d), but also save more (S), pay more taxes (T) and buy more imports (M). In other words, withdrawals will rise. This will continue until they have risen to equal injections. At that point, national income will stop rising, and so will withdrawals. Equilibrium has been reached.

Summary

1. **The circular flow of income model depicts the flows of money round the economy. The inner flow shows the direct flows between firms and households. Money flows from firms to households in the form of factor payments, and back again as consumer expenditure on domestically produced goods and services.**

2. **Not all incomes get passed on directly round the inner flow. Some is withdrawn in the form of saving, some is paid in taxes, and some goes abroad as expenditure on imports.**
3. **Likewise not all expenditure on domestic firms is by domestic consumers. Some is injected from outside the inner flow in the form of investment expenditure, government expenditure and expenditure on the country's exports.**
4. **Planned injections and withdrawals are unlikely to be the same.**
5. **If injections exceed withdrawals, national income will rise, unemployment will tend to fall, inflation will tend to rise, imports will tend to rise and exports fall. The reverse will happen if withdrawals exceed injections.**
6. **If injections exceed withdrawals, the rise in national income will lead to a rise in withdrawals. This will continue until $W = J$. At this point the circular flow will be in equilibrium.**

Economic growth and the business cycle

Is a country's economic growth likely to be constant over time?

The distinction between actual and potential growth

Before examining the causes of economic growth, it is essential to distinguish between *actual* and *potential* economic growth.

Actual growth is the percentage annual increase in national output: the rate of growth in actual output. When statistics on growth rates are published, it is actual growth they are referring to.

Potential growth is the speed at which the economy *could* grow. It is the percentage annual increase in the economy's *capacity* to produce: the rate of growth in potential output. Two of the major factors contributing to potential economic growth are:

- An increase in resources – natural resources, labour or capital.
- An increase in the efficiency with which these resources can be used, through advances in technology, improved labour skills or improved organisation.

If the potential growth rate exceeds the actual growth rate, there will be an increase in spare capacity and an increase in unemployment: there will be a growing gap between potential and actual output. To close this gap, the actual growth rate would temporarily have to exceed the potential growth rate. In the long run, however, the actual growth rate will be limited to the potential growth rate.

There are thus two major issues concerned with economic growth: the short-run issue of ensuring that actual growth is such as to keep actual output as close as possible to potential output; and the long-run issue of what determines the rate of potential economic growth.

Definitions

Actual growth
The percentage annual increase in national output actually produced.

Potential growth
The percentage annual increase in the capacity of the economy to produce.

Potential output
The output that could be produced in the economy if there were a full employment of resources (including labour).

BOX 7.1 *Measuring national income and output*

Three routes: one destination

To assess how fast the economy has grown we must have a means of *measuring* the value of the nation's output. The measure we use is called **gross domestic product (GDP)**.

GDP can be calculated in three different ways, which should all result in the same figure. These three methods are illustrated in the simplified circular flow of income shown in Figure (a).

(a) *The circular flow of national income and expenditure*

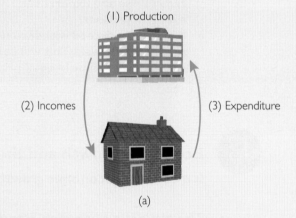

(1) Production

(2) Incomes

(3) Expenditure

(a)

The product method

This first method of measuring GDP is to add up the value of all the goods and services produced in the country, industry by industry. In other words, we focus on firms and add up all their production. Thus method number one is known as the *product method*.

In the national accounts these figures are grouped together into broad categories such as manufacturing, construction and distribution. The figures for the UK economy for 1996 are shown in Figure (b).

When we add up the output of various firms we must be careful to avoid *double counting*. For example, if a manufacturer sells a television to a retailer for £200 and the retailer sells it to the consumer for £300, how much has this television contributed to GDP? The answer is *not* £500. We do not add the £200 received by the manufacturer to the £300 received by the retailer: that would be double counting. Instead we either just count the final value (£300) or the value added at each stage (£200 by the manufacturer + £100 by the retailer).

The income method

The second approach is to focus on the incomes generated from the production of goods and services. A moment's reflection will show that this must be the same as the sum of all values added at each stage of production. Value added is simply the difference between a firm's revenue from sales and the costs of its purchases from other firms. This difference is made up of wages and salaries, rent, interest and profit. In other words, it consists of the incomes earned by those involved in the production process.

Since GDP is the sum of all values added, it must also be the sum of all incomes generated: the sum of all wages and salaries, rent, interest and profit.

Definition

Gross domestic product (GDP)
The value of output produced within the country over a twelve-month period.

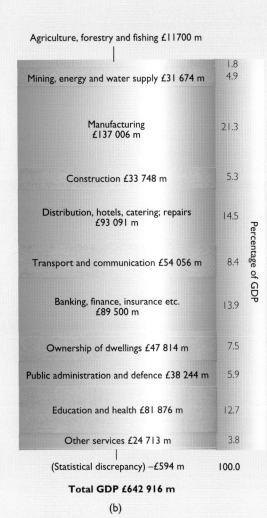

Agriculture, forestry and fishing £11700 m — 1.8

Mining, energy and water supply £31 674 m — 4.9

Manufacturing £137 006 m — 21.3

Construction £33 748 m — 5.3

Distribution, hotels, catering; repairs £93 091 m — 14.5

Transport and communication £54 056 m — 8.4

Banking, finance, insurance etc. £89 500 m — 13.9

Ownership of dwellings £47 814 m — 7.5

Public administration and defence £38 244 m — 5.9

Education and health £81 876 m — 12.7

Other services £24 713 m — 3.8

(Statistical discrepancy) −£594 m — 100.0

Percentage of GDP

Total GDP £642 916 m

(b)

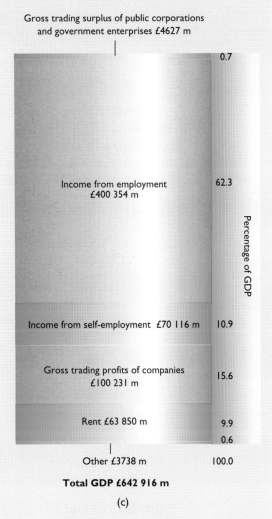

Gross trading surplus of public corporations and government enterprises £4627 m — 0.7

Income from employment £400 354 m — 62.3

Income from self-employment £70 116 m — 10.9

Gross trading profits of companies £100 231 m — 15.6

Rent £63 850 m — 9.9

Other £3738 m — 0.6 — 100.0

Percentage of GDP

Total GDP £642 916 m

(c)

Source: *UK National Income and Expenditure* (ONS, 1997).

(b) UK GDP product-based measure: 1995
(c) UK GDP by category of income: 1996

Figure (c) shows how these incomes are grouped together in the official statistics. As you can see, the total is the same as that in Figure (b), even though the components are quite different.

Note that we do not include *transfer payments* such as social security benefits and pensions. Since these are not payments for the production of goods and services, they are excluded from GDP. Conversely, part of people's gross income is paid in taxes. Since it is this *gross* (pre-tax) income that arises from the production of goods and services, we count wages, profits, interest and rent *before* the deduction of taxes.

On the other hand, we exclude taxes on goods and services (such as VAT), since the part of a firm's revenue that it pays in these 'indirect' taxes will *not* be available for wages, profits, rent or interest. We do include government subsidies to firms, however, since these *are* included in the incomes paid out by firms.

If we do *not* make these adjustments for indirect taxes and subsidies, and just look at the prices consumers pay – i.e. at the gross incomes of firms before they pay the taxes or obtain the subsidies – the figure we get is called *GDP at market prices*. The figure, however, that represents the true income to factors of production (i.e. after the *deduction* of indirect taxes from and the *addition* of subsidies to the market value of sales) is called *GDP at factor cost*. Thus:

GDP at factor cost = GDP at market prices – Indirect taxes + Subsidies

Figures (b) and (c) show GDP at *factor cost*.

The expenditure method

The final approach is to add up all expenditure on *final output*: i.e. consumer expenditure and the three injections – investment, government expenditure and the expenditure on exports. Again this will give us a figure for GDP at factor cost. To arrive at this figure, however, we have to go through a number of stages. Table (a) shows each of these stages in the calculation of the 1996 UK GDP at factor cost.

We start by measuring *total domestic expenditure (TDE)* at *market prices*.

TABLE (a) *UK GDP at market prices by category of expenditure: 1996*

	£million
Consumers' expenditure	473 509
Government final consumption	155 732
Gross domestic fixed capital formation (including new housing)	114 623
Value of physical increase in stocks and work in progress	2917
Total domestic expenditure	**746 781**
Plus Exports of goods and services	217 147
Total final expenditure	**963 928**
Less Imports of goods and services	–222 603
Statistical discrepancy	975
GDP at market prices	**742 300**
Less Taxes on expenditure	–108 484
Plus Subsidies	9100
GDP at factor cost	**642 916**

Source: *UK National Income and Expenditure* (ONS, 1997).

Total domestic expenditure (at market prices). This consists of the total expenditure on final goods and services by the residents of the country, whether these goods and services were produced at home or abroad. It thus includes consumer expenditure, government expenditure on final goods and services and investment. (Note that it excludes exports and includes imports.)

$$TDE = C + G + I$$

Total final expenditure (TFE) (at market prices). The next step is to add in exports. This gives the total expenditure that takes place within the country, whether by domestic residents or by people abroad. Note that it includes *both* imports *and* exports.

$$TFE = TDE + X$$
$$= C + G + I + X$$

Gross domestic product at market prices. The next step is to subtract imports. This gives us expenditure on *domestically produced goods.* In other words, we ignore that component of consumption, government expenditure and investment that goes on imports. We also exclude any imported component (e.g. raw materials) from exports.

$$GDP \text{ at market prices } = TFE - M$$
$$= C + G + I + X - M$$

Gross domestic product at factor cost. So far we have been using market prices: prices that have been increased by indirect taxes and reduced by any subsidies. If we are to have a true measure of the expenditure on actual *output,* we must correct for these taxes and subsidies. The final step to get to GDP at factor cost is thus to subtract indirect taxes and add subsidies. This gives us the formula we used above when looking at the income method of calculating GDP.

GDP at factor cost = GDP at market prices – Indirect taxes + Subsidies

From GDP to NNP

Gross national product. Some of the incomes earned in this country will go to shareholders abroad, or people with bank deposits in this country, but residing abroad. on the other hand, some of the incomes earned by domestic residents will come from shareholdings or accounts abroad. Gross *domestic* product, however, is concerned only with incomes generated *within* the country, irrespective of ownership. If, then, we are to take 'net property incomes' into account (i.e. the inflows minus the outflows of dividends and interest), we need a new measure. This is *gross national product (GNP)*. It is defined as follows:

GNP at factor cost = GDP at factor cost + Net property income from abroad

Net national product ('national income'). The measures we have used so far ignore the fact that each year some of the country's capital equipment will wear out or become obsolete: in other words, they ignore capital *depreciation*. If we subtract an allowance for depreciation (or 'capital consumption'), we are left with *net* national product (NNP).

NNP at factor cost (national income) = GNP at factor cost – Depreciation

Table (b) shows the 1995 GDP, GNP and NNP figures for the UK.

TABLE (b) *UK GDP, GNP and NNP at factor cost: 1996*

	£million
Gross domestic product	**642 916**
Plus Net property income from abroad	9652
Gross national product	**652 568**
Less Capital consumption (depreciation)	–77 372
Net national product (national income)	**575 196**

Source: *UK National Income and Expenditure* (ONS, 1997).

Personal disposable income

Finally, we come to a measure that is useful for analysing consumer behaviour. If we are to examine how consumption responds to changes in households' disposable income, the measure we require is called *personal disposable income*.

Let us start with GNP at factor cost. This measures the incomes generated by production. To get from this to personal disposable income, we must first subtract company incomes that are *not* paid to households: namely, company taxes, allowances for depreciation and undistributed profits. This gives us the incomes received by households from firms. To get from this to what is available for households to spend, we must subtract the money that households pay in income taxes and national insurance contributions, but add all benefits to households such as pensions and child benefit: in other words, we must *include* transfer payments.

Personal disposable income = GNP at factor cost − Company taxes − Depreciation − Undistributed profits − Personal taxes + Benefits

Q1 Should we include the sale of used items in the GDP statistics? For example, if you sell your car to a garage for £2000 and it then sells it to someone else for £2500, has this added £2500 to GDP, or nothing at all, or merely the value that the garage adds to the car: i.e. £500?

Q2 What items are excluded from national income statistics which would be important to take account of if we were to get a true indication of a country's standard of living?

Economic growth and the business cycle

Although growth in potential output will vary to some extent over the years – depending on the rate of advance of technology, the level of investment and the discovery of new raw materials – it will nevertheless tend to be much more steady than the growth in actual output.

Actual growth will tend to fluctuate. In some years there will be a high rate of economic growth: the country experiences a boom. In other years, economic growth will be low or even negative: the country experiences a recession. This cycle of booms and recessions is known as the business cycle or trade cycle.

There are four 'phases' of the business cycle. They are illustrated in Figure 7.2.

1. *The upturn*. In this phase, a stagnant economy begins to recover, and growth in actual output resumes.
2. *The boom*. During this phase there is rapid economic growth. A fuller use is made of resources and the gap between actual and potential output narrows.
3. *The peaking out*. During this phase, growth slows down or even ceases.
4. *The slowdown, recession or slump*. During this phase there is little or no growth or even a decline in output. Increasing slack develops in the economy.

Definition

Business cycle or trade cycle The periodic fluctuations of national output round its long-term trend.

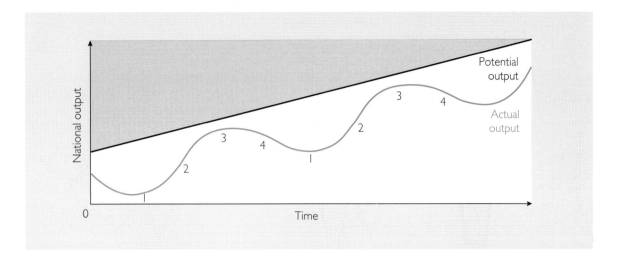

FIGURE 7.2
The business cycle

A word of caution: do not confuse a high *level* of output with a high *rate of growth* in output. The level of output is highest in phase 3. The rate of growth in output is highest in phase 2 (i.e. where the curve is steepest).

The business cycle in practice

The business cycle illustrated in Figure 7.2 is a 'stylised' cycle. It is nice and smooth and regular. Drawing it this way allows us to make a clear distinction between each of the four phases. In practice, however, business cycles are highly irregular. They are irregular in two ways.

The length of the phases. Some booms are short lived, lasting only a few months or so. Others are much longer, lasting perhaps three or four years. Likewise some recessions are short while others are long.

The magnitude of the phases. Sometimes in phase 2 there is a very high rate of economic growth, perhaps 5 per cent per annum or more. On other occasions in phase 2 growth is much gentler. Sometimes in phase 4 there is a recession, with an actual decline in output (e.g. in the early 1980s and early 1990s). On other occasions, phase 4 is merely a 'pause', with growth simply slowing down.

Nevertheless, despite the irregularity of the fluctuations, cycles are still clearly discernible, especially if we plot *growth* on the vertical axis rather than the *level* of output. This is done in Figure 7.3, which shows the business cycles in selected industrial countries from 1971 to 1997.

Causes of actual growth

The major determinants of variations in the rate of actual growth in the *short run* are variations in the growth of aggregate demand.

A rapid rise in aggregate demand will create shortages. This will tend to stimulate firms to increase output, thus reducing slack in the economy.

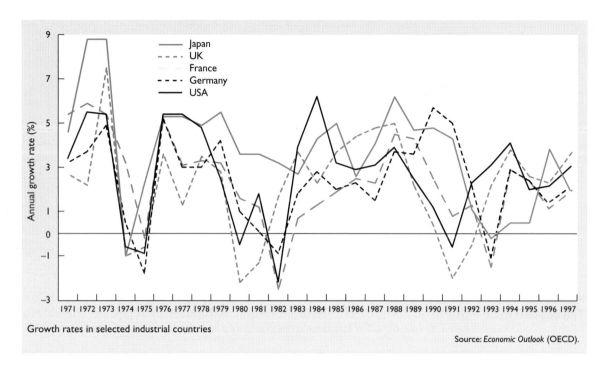

Growth rates in selected industrial countries

Source: *Economic Outlook* (OECD).

FIGURE 7.3
Growth rates in
selected industrial
countries

Likewise, a reduction in aggregate demand will leave firms with increased stocks of unsold goods. They will therefore tend to reduce output.

Aggregate demand and actual output, therefore, fluctuate together in the short run. A boom is associated with a rapid rise in aggregate demand: the faster the rise in aggregate demand, the higher the short-run rate of actual growth. A recession, by contrast, is associated with a reduction in aggregate demand.

A rapid rise in aggregate demand, however, is not enough to ensure a continuing high level of growth over a *number* of years. Without an expansion of potential output too, rises in actual output must eventually come to an end. Once spare capacity has been used up, once there is full employment of labour and other resources, the rate of growth of actual output will be restricted to the rate of growth of potential output. This is illustrated in Figure 7.2. As long as actual output is below potential output, the actual output curve can slope upward more steeply than the potential output curve. But once the gap between the two curves has been closed, the actual output curve can only slope as steeply as the potential output curve: the two curves cannot cross – actual output cannot be above potential output.

In the long run, therefore, there are two determinants of actual growth:

- The growth in aggregate demand. This determines whether potential output will be realised.
- The growth in potential output.

Causes of potential growth

We now turn to the *supply* question. Here we are concerned with the capacity of the economy to produce. There are two main determinants of potential output: (a) the amount of resources available and (b) their productivity.

Increases in the quantity of resources

Capital. The nation's output depends on its stock of capital (K). An increase in this stock will increase output. If we ignore the problem of machines wearing out or becoming obsolete and needing replacing, then the stock of capital will increase by the amount of investment. The rise in output that results will depend on the productivity of capital.

The rate of growth in potential output depends on the marginal capital/output ratio (k). This is the amount of extra capital (ΔK) divided by the extra annual output that it produces (ΔY). Thus $k = \Delta K/\Delta Y$. Potential growth also depends on the proportion of national income that is invested (i), which, assuming that all saving is invested, will equal the proportion of national income that is saved (s). The formula for growth becomes:

$$g = i/k \ (\text{or } g = s/k)$$

Thus if 20 per cent of national income went in new investment (i = 20 per cent), and if each £1 of new investment yielded 25p of extra income per year (k = 4), then the growth rate would be 5 per cent. A simple example will demonstrate this. If national income is £100 billion, then £20 billion will be invested (i = 20%). This will lead to extra annual output of £5 billion (k = 4). Thus national income grows to £105 billion: a growth of 5 per cent.

But what determines the rate of investment? There are a number of determinants. These include the confidence of businesspeople about the future demand for their products, the profitability of business, the tax regime, the rate of growth in the economy and the rate of interest.

Over the long term, if investment is to increase, then *saving* must increase in order to finance that investment. Put another way, people must be prepared to forgo a certain amount of consumption in order to allow resources to be diverted into producing more capital goods: factories, machines, etc.

Note that if investment is to increase, there may need to be an increase in *aggregate demand*. In other words, if firms are to be encouraged to increase their capacity by installing new machines or building new factories, they may need first to see the *demand* for their products growing. Here a growth in *potential* output is the result of a growth in aggregate demand and hence *actual output*.

Labour. If there is an increase in the working population, there will be an increase in potential output. This increase in working population may result from a larger 'participation rate': a larger proportion of the total population in work or seeking work.

Alternatively, a rise in the working population may be the result of an increase in total population. In this case, even though there will be growth in *total* output, there will only be an increase in output *per head* if the productivity of workers rises (see below).

Land and raw materials. Land is virtually fixed in quantity. Land reclamation schemes and the opening up of marginal land can only add tiny amounts to national output.

Whether new raw materials can be discovered is largely a matter of the luck of nature. If a country does discover new raw materials (e.g. oil), this will result only in *short-term* growth: i.e. while the rate of extraction is building up. Once the rate of extraction is at a maximum, economic growth will cease. Output will simply remain at the new higher level, until eventually the raw materials will begin to run out. This will cause output to fall.

The problem of diminishing returns. If a single factor of production increases in supply while others remain fixed, diminishing returns will set in (see pages 74–5). For example, if the quantity of capital increases with no increase in other factors of production, then diminishing returns to capital will set in. The rate of return on capital will fall. Unless *all* factors of production increase, therefore, the rate of growth is likely to slow down.

The solution to the problem of diminishing returns is for there to be an increase in the *productivity* of resources.

Increases in the productivity of resources

Technological improvements can increase the marginal productivity of capital. Much of the investment in new machines is not just in extra machines, but in superior machines producing a higher rate of return. Consider the microchip revolution of recent years. Modern computers can do the work of many people and have replaced many machines which were cumbersome and expensive to build. Improved methods of transport have reduced the costs of moving goods and materials. Improved communications (such as fax machines and the internet) have reduced the costs of transmitting information.

As a result of technical progress, the productivity of capital has tended to increase over time. Similarly, as a result of new skills, improved education and training, and better health, the productivity of labour has also tended to increase over time.

Policies to achieve growth

How can governments increase a country's growth rate? Policies differ in two ways.

First, they may focus on the demand side or the supply side of the economy. In other words, they may attempt to create sufficient *aggregate demand* to ensure that firms wish to invest and that potential output is realised. Alternatively, they may seek to increase *aggregate supply* by concentrating on measures to increase potential output: measures to encourage research and development, innovation and training.

Second, they may be market-orientated or have interventionist policies. Many economists and politicians, especially those on the political right, believe that the best environment for encouraging economic growth is one where private enterprise is allowed to flourish: where entrepreneurs are able to reap substantial rewards from investment in new techniques and new products. Such economists therefore advocate policies designed to free up the market. Others, however, argue that a free market will be subject to considerable cyclical fluctuations. The resulting uncertainty will discourage investment. Such economists, therefore, tend to advocate active intervention by the government to reduce these fluctuations.

Summary

1. Actual growth must be distinguished from potential growth. The actual growth rate is the percentage annual increase in the output that is actually produced, whereas potential growth is the percentage annual increase in the capacity of the economy to produce (whether or not it is actually produced).
2. Actual growth will fluctuate with the course of the business cycle. The cycle can be broken down into four phases: the upturn, the boom, the peaking out, and the slowdown or recession. In practice, the length and magnitude of these phases will vary: the cycle is thus irregular.
3. Actual growth is determined by potential growth and by the level of aggregate demand. If actual output is below potential output, actual growth can temporarily exceed potential growth, if aggregate demand is rising sufficiently. In the long term, however, actual output can grow only as fast as potential output will permit.
4. Potential growth is determined by the rate of increase in the *quantity* of resources: capital, labour, land and raw materials; and by the *productivity* of resources. The productivity of capital can be increased by technological improvements and the more efficient use of the capital stock; the productivity of labour can be increased by better education, training, motivation and organisation.
5. Whether governments can best achieve rapid growth through market-orientated or interventionist policies is highly controversial.

7.4 Unemployment

If people want to consume more goods, why are so many people out of work?

In Europe, in North America, in Australasia, and in many developing countries too, the problem of unemployment rapidly worsened in the early 1980s as the world plunged into the greatest recession since the Great Depression of the 1930s. But then, as the world economy recovered and sustained economic growth was experienced throughout the second half of the 1980s, so unemployment began to fall, only to rise again as the world once more experienced recession in the early 1990s. Then as the world slowly climbed out of recession in the mid-1990s, so unemployment rates once more began to fall. Figure 7.4 shows these cyclical movements in unemployment for selected countries.

As well as experiencing fluctuations in unemployment, most countries have experienced an increase in average unemployment rates from one cycle to another. This is illustrated in Table 7.2, which shows average unemployment in the UK, the OECD[2] and the EU for four unemployment cycles

[2]The Organisation for Economic Co-operation and Development: the 29 major industrialised countries including The Czech Republic, Hungary, Korea, Mexico, Poland and Turkey.

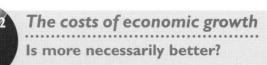

BOX 7.2 *The costs of economic growth*
....
Is more necessarily better?

For many developing countries economic growth is a necessity if they are to remove mass poverty. When the majority of their population is underfed, poorly housed, with inadequate health care and little access to education, few would quarrel with the need for an increase in productive potential. The main query is whether the benefits of economic growth will flow to the mass of the population, or whether they will be confined to the few who are already relatively well off.

For developed countries the case for economic growth is less clear cut. Economic growth is usually measured in terms of the growth in national output valued in prices as given by the market. The problem is that there are many 'goods' and 'bads' that are not included when measuring national output. Economic growth, therefore, is not the same as growth in a nation's *welfare*. True, there can be major advantages of economic growth, and certainly, other things being equal, the majority of the population wants higher levels of production and consumption. But it is important to recognise the costs of economic growth. Indeed, some people regard these costs as so serious that they advocate a policy of *zero economic growth*.

So, what are the benefits and costs of economic growth?

The benefits of growth

Increased levels of consumption

Provided economic growth outstrips population growth, it will lead to higher real income per head. This can lead to higher levels of consumption of goods and services. If human welfare is related to the level of consumption, then growth provides an obvious gain to society.

It can help avoid other macroeconomic problems

People have aspirations of rising living standards. Without a growth in productive potential, people's demands for rising incomes are likely to lead to higher inflation, balance of payments crises (as more imports are purchased), industrial disputes, etc. Growth in productive potential helps to meet these aspirations and avoid macroeconomic crises.

It can make it easier to redistribute incomes to the poor

If incomes rise, the government can redistribute incomes from the rich to the poor *without the rich losing*. For example, as people's incomes rise, they automatically pay more taxes. These extra revenues for the government can be spent on programmes to alleviate poverty.

Without a continuing rise in national income the scope for helping the poor is much more limited.

Society may feel that it can afford to care more for the environment

As people grow richer, they may become less preoccupied with their own private consumption and more concerned to live in a clean environment. The regulation of pollution tends to be tougher in developed countries than in the developing world.

The costs of growth

In practice, more consumption may not make people happier; economies may be no less crisis riven; income may not be redistributed more equally; the environment may not be

**High and low
growth paths**

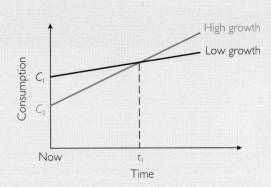

better protected. More than this, some people argue that growth may worsen these problems and create additional problems besides.

The current opportunity cost of growth

To achieve faster growth, firms will probably need to invest more. This will require financing. The finance can come from higher savings or higher taxes. Either way, there must be a cut in consumption. In the short run, therefore, higher growth leads to *less* consumption, not more.

In the diagram, assume that consumption is currently at a level of C_1. Its growth over time is shown by the line out from C_1. Now assume that the government pursues a policy of higher growth. Consumption has to *fall* to finance the extra investment. Consumption falls to, say, C_2. The growth in consumption is now shown by the line out from C_2. Not until time t_1 is reached (which may be several years into the future) does consumption overtake the levels it would have reached with the previous lower growth rate.

Growth may simply generate extra demands

'The more people have, the more they want.' If this is so, more consumption may not increase people's happiness at all. It is often observed that rich people tend to be miserable!

As people's incomes grow, they may become more materialistic and less fulfilled as human beings.

Social effects

Many people claim that an excessive pursuit of material growth by a country can lead to a more greedy, more selfish and less caring society. As society becomes more industrialised, violence, crime, loneliness, stress-related diseases, suicides, divorce and other social problems are likely to rise.

Environmental costs

A richer society may be more concerned for the environment, but it is also likely to do more damage to it. The higher the level of consumption, the higher is likely to be the level of pollution and waste. What is more, many of the environmental costs are likely to be underestimated due to a lack of scientific knowledge. Acid rain and the depletion of the ozone layer have been two examples.

Non-renewable resources

If growth involves using a greater amount of resources, rather than using the same amount of resources more efficiently, certain non-renewable resources will run out more rapidly. Unless viable alternatives can be found for various minerals and fossil fuels, present growth may lead to shortages for future generations.

Effects on the distribution of income

While some people may gain from a higher standard of living, others are likely to lose. If the means to higher growth are greater incentives (such as cuts in higher rates of income tax), then the rich might get richer, with little or no benefits 'trickling down' to the poor.

Growth involves changes in production: both in terms of the goods produced and in terms of the techniques used and the skills required. The more rapid the rate of growth, the more rapid the rate of change. People may find that their skills are no longer relevant. Their jobs may be replaced by machines. People may thus find themselves unemployed, or forced to take low-paid, unskilled work.

Conclusion

So should countries pursue growth? The answer depends on (a) just what costs and benefits are involved, (b) what weighting people attach to them, and (c) how opposing views are to be reconciled.

A problem is that the question of the desirability of economic growth is a normative one. It involves a judgement about what a 'desirable' society should look like.

A simpler point, however, is that the electorate seems to want economic growth. As long as that is so, governments will tend to pursue policies to achieve growth. That is why we need to study the causes of growth and the policies that governments can pursue.

One thing the government can do is to view the problem as one of *constrained optimisation*. It sets constraints: levels of environmental protection, minimum wages, maximum rates of depletion of non-renewable resources, etc. It then seeks policies that will maximise growth, while keeping within these constraints.

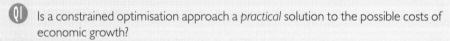 Is a constrained optimisation approach a *practical* solution to the possible costs of economic growth?

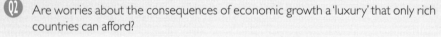 Are worries about the consequences of economic growth a 'luxury' that only rich countries can afford?

(minimum to minimum). Average unemployment rates in the 1980s and 1990s have been higher than in the 1970s, and average rates in the 1970s were, in turn, higher than in the 1950s and 60s.

The meaning of 'unemployment'

Unemployment can be expressed either as a number (e.g. 2.5 million) or as a percentage (e.g. 8 per cent). But just who should be included in the statis-

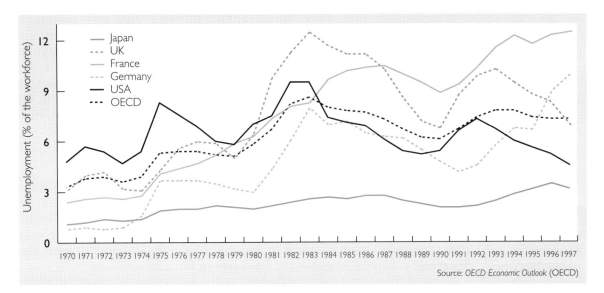

Source: *OECD Economic Outlook* (OECD)

FIGURE 7.4
Unemployment in selected industrial countries: 1970–97

TABLE 7.2 *Average unemployment for given cycles (%)*

Period	UK	EU	OECD
1964–73	3.0	2.7	3.0
1974–9	5.0	4.7	4.9
1980–9	10.0	9.3	7.3
1990–7	8.6	10.1	7.3

Definitions

Number unemployed (economist's definition)
Those of working age who are without work, but who are available for work at current wage rates.

Labour force
The number employed plus the number unemployed.

Unemployment rate
The number unemployed expressed as a percentage of the labour force.

tics? Should it be everyone without a job? The answer is clearly no, since we would not want to include children and pensioners. We would probably also want to exclude those who were not looking for work, such as parents choosing to stay at home to look after children.

The most usual definition that economists use for the number unemployed is: *those of working age who are without work, but who are available for work at current wage rates.* If the figure is to be expressed as a percentage, then it is a percentage of the total labour force. The labour force is defined as: *those in employment (including the self-employed, those in the armed forces and those on government training schemes) plus those unemployed.* Thus if 22.5 million people were employed and 2.5 million people were unemployed, the unemployment rate would be:

$$\frac{2.5}{22.5 + 2.5} \times 100 = 10 \text{ per cent}$$

Official measures of unemployment

Claimant unemployment
Two common measures of unemployment are used in official statistics. The first is claimant unemployment. This is simply a measure of all those in receipt of unemployment-related benefits. This is the method used in the UK official statistics. Claimants receive the 'job-seeker's allowance'.

Claimant statistics have the advantage of being very easy to collect. However, they exclude all those of working age available for work at current wage rates, but who are *not* eligible for benefits. If the government changes the eligibility conditions so that fewer people are now eligible, this will reduce the number of claimants and hence the official number unemployed, even if there has been no change in the numbers with or without work. In the UK, there have been some 30 changes to eligibility conditions since 1979, all but one of which have had the effect of reducing the claimant figures!

Standardised unemployment rates

Two international organisations that publish unemployment statistics for many countries are the International Labour Office (ILO) and the Organisation for Economic Co-operation and Development (OECD). They define the unemployed as persons of working age who are without work, available for work and *actively seeking employment* or waiting to take up an appointment. The figures are complied from the results of labour force *surveys*.

Because these international bodies use the same 'standardised' definition for all countries, it makes international comparisons easier. But is the **standardised unemployment rate** likely to be higher or lower than the claimant unemployment rate? The standardised rate is likely to be higher to the extent that it includes people seeking work who are nevertheless not entitled to claim benefits, but lower to the extent that it excludes those who are claiming benefits and yet who are not actively seeking work. Clearly, the tougher the benefit regulations, the lower the claimant rate will be relative to the standardised rate.

Table 7.3 shows standardised unemployment rates for different countries by age and sex.

Unemployment and the labour market

We now turn to the causes of unemployment. These causes fall into two broad categories: *equilibrium* unemployment and *disequilibrium* unemploy-

Definitions

Claimant unemployment
Those in receipt of unemployment-related benefits.

Standardised unemployment rate
The measure of the unemployment rate used by the ILO and OECD. The unemployed are defined as persons of working age who are without work, available for work and actively seeking employment.

TABLE 7.3 *Standardised unemployment rates in different sections of the labour market: March 1997*

Country	Total (all ages)	Women (all ages)	Men (all ages)	Total under 25 years old	Women under 25 years old	Men under 25 years old
Belgium	9.6	12.5	7.5	22.4	26.7	18.9
Germany	9.7	10.7	8.9	9.7	8.8	10.6
France	12.5	14.7	10.6	28.2	31.3	25.3
Ireland	11.1	11.8	10.7	16.3	15.8	16.8
Japan	3.2	3.3	3.2	6.4	6.3	6.6
Netherlands	5.5	7.1	4.3	9.0	10.1	7.8
Spain	21.0	28.2	16.4	39.5	46.3	33.7
UK	7.2	6.1	8.2	14.8	12.6	16.7
USA	5.2	5.3	5.1	11.7	11.2	12.2
EU15	10.8	12.6	9.5	21.2	22.9	19.7

Source: *Eurostatistics* (Eurostat).

BOX 7.3 *The costs of unemployment*

Is it just the unemployed who suffer?

The most obvious cost of unemployment is to the *unemployed themselves*. There is the direct financial cost of the loss in their earnings, measured as the difference between their previous wage and their unemployment benefit. Then there are the personal costs of being unemployed. The longer people are unemployed, the more dispirited they may become. Their self-esteem is likely to fall, and they are more likely to succumb to stress-related illness.

Then there are the costs to the *family and friends* of the unemployed. Personal relations can become strained, and there may be an increase in domestic violence and the number of families splitting up.

Then there are the *broader costs to the economy*. Unemployment represents a loss of output. In other words, actual output is below potential output. Apart from the lack of income to the unemployed themselves, this under-utilisation of resources leads to lower incomes for other people too:

- The government loses tax revenues, since the unemployed pay no income tax and national insurance, and, given that the unemployed spend less, they pay less VAT and excise duties. The government also incurs administrative costs associated with the running of benefit offices. It may also have to spend extra on health care, the social services and the police.
- Firms lose the profits that could have been made, had there been full employment.
- Other workers lose any additional wages that they could have earned from higher national output.

What is more, the longer people remain unemployed, the more deskilled they tend to become, thereby reducing *potential* as well as actual income.

Finally there is some evidence that higher unemployment leads to increased *crime and vandalism*. This obviously imposes a cost on the sufferers.

The costs of unemployment are to some extent offset by benefits. If workers voluntarily quit their jobs to look for a better one, then they must reckon that the benefits of a better job more than compensate for their temporary loss of income. From the nation's point of view, a workforce that is prepared to quit jobs and spend a short time unemployed will be a more adaptable, more mobile workforce – one that is responsive to changing economic circumstances. Such a workforce will lead to greater allocative efficiency in the short run and more rapid economic growth over the longer run.

Q1 How might an economist set about measuring the various costs of unemployment to family, friends and society at large?

ment. To make clear the distinction between the two, it is necessary to look at the working of the labour market.

Figure 7.5 shows the aggregate demand for labour and the aggregate supply of labour: that is, the total demand and supply of labour in the whole economy. The *real* wage is plotted on the vertical axis. This is the average wage expressed in terms of its purchasing power: in other words, after taking prices into account.

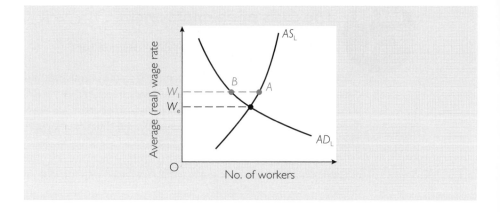

The **aggregate supply of labour curve** (AS_L) shows the number of workers *willing to accept jobs* at each wage rate. This curve is relatively inelastic, since the size of the workforce at any one time cannot change significantly. Nevertheless it is not totally inelastic because (a) a higher wage rate will encourage some people to enter the labour market (e.g. parents raising children), and (b) the unemployed will be more willing to accept job offers rather than continuing to search for a better-paid job.

The **aggregate demand for labour curve** (AD_L) slopes downward. The higher the wage rate, the more will firms attempt to economise on labour. They will be encouraged to substitute other factors of production for labour.

The labour market is in equilibrium at a wage of W_e, where the demand for labour equals the supply. If the wage were above W_e, the market would be in a state of disequilibrium. At a wage rate of W_1, there is an excess supply of labour of $A - B$. This is called **disequilibrium unemployment**.

For disequilibrium unemployment to occur, two conditions must hold:

- The aggregate supply of labour must exceed the aggregate demand.
- There must be a 'stickiness' in wages. In other words, the wage rate must not immediately fall to W_e.

Even when the labour market *is* in equilibrium, however, not everyone looking for work will be employed. Some people will hold out, hoping to find a better job. The curve N in Figure 7.6 shows the total number in the labour force. The horizontal difference between it and the aggregate supply of labour curve (AS_L) represents the excess of people looking for work over those actually willing to accept jobs. Q_e represents the equilibrium level of employment and the distance $D - E$ represents the **equilibrium level of unemployment**. This is sometimes known as the *natural level of unemployment*.

Types of disequilibrium unemployment

There are three possible causes of disequilibrium unemployment.

Real-wage unemployment

Real-wage unemployment is where trade unions use their monopoly power to drive wages above the market-clearing level. In Figure 7.5, the wage rate is

FIGURE 7.6
*Equilibrium
unemployment*

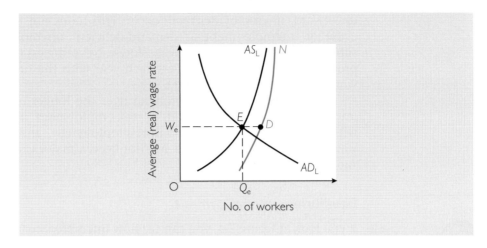

driven up above W_e. Excessive real wage rates were blamed by the Thatcher and Major governments for the high unemployment of the 1980s and 1990s. The possibility of higher real-wage unemployment was also one of the reasons for their rejection of a national minimum wage.

The solution to real-wage unemployment would seem to be a reduction in real wage rates. It may be very difficult, however, to prevent unions pushing up wages. Even if the government did succeed in reducing the average real wage rate, there would then be a problem of reduced consumer expenditure and a reduced demand for labour, with the result that unemployment might not fall at all.

Demand-deficient unemployment

Demand-deficient unemployment is associated with economic recessions. As the economy moves into recession, consumer demand falls. Firms find that they are unable to sell their current level of output. For a time they may be prepared to build up stocks of unsold goods, but sooner or later they will start to cut back on production and cut back on the amount of labour they employ. In Figure 7.5 the AD_L curved shifts to the left. The deeper the recession becomes and the longer it lasts, the higher will demand-deficient unemployment become.

As the economy recovers and begins to grow again, so demand-deficient unemployment will start to fall again. Because demand-deficient unemployment fluctuates with the business cycle, it is sometimes referred to as 'cyclical unemployment'. Figure 7.4 (on page 239) showed the fluctuations in unemployment in various industrial countries and for the OECD as a whole. If you compare this figure with Figure 7.3 (on page 232), you can see how unemployment tends to rise in recessions and fall in booms.

Demand-deficient unemployment can also exist in the longer term if the economy is constantly run at below full capacity and labour markets continue not to be in equilibrium. Even at the peak of the business cycle, actual output may be considerably below potential output.

Growth in the labour supply

If labour supply rises with no corresponding increase in the demand for labour, the equilibrium real wage rate will fall. If the real wage rate is 'sticky'

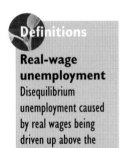

Definitions

Real-wage unemployment
Disequilibrium unemployment caused by real wages being driven up above the market-clearing level.

Demand-deficient or cyclical unemployment
Disequilibrium unemployment caused by a fall in aggregate demand with no corresponding fall in the real wage rate.

downward, unemployment will occur. This tends not to be such a serious cause of unemployment as demand-deficient unemployment, since the supply of labour changes relatively slowly. Nevertheless there is a problem of providing jobs for school leavers each year with the sudden influx of new workers on to the labour market.

There is also a potential problem over the longer term if social trends lead more women with children to seek employment. In practice, however, with the rapid growth of part-time employment, and the lower average wage rate paid to women, this has not been a major cause of excess labour supply.

Equilibrium unemployment

If you look at Figure 7.4, you can see how unemployment has been higher in the 1980s and 1990s than in the 1970s. Part of the reason for this has been the growth in equilibrium unemployment.

Although there may be overall *macro*economic equilibrium, with the *aggregate* demand for labour equal to the *aggregate* supply, and thus no disequilibrium unemployment, at a *micro*economic level supply and demand may not match. This is when equilibrium unemployment will occur. There are various types of equilibrium unemployment.

Frictional (search) unemployment

Frictional unemployment occurs when people leave their jobs, either voluntarily or because they are sacked or made redundant, and are then unemployed for a period of time while they are looking for a new job. They may not get the first job they apply for, despite a vacancy existing. The employer may continue searching, hoping to find a better-qualified person. Likewise, unemployed people may choose not to take the first job they are offered. Instead, they may continue searching, hoping that a better one will turn up.

The problem is that information is imperfect. Employers are not fully informed about what labour is available; workers are not fully informed about what jobs are available and what they entail. Both employers and workers, therefore, have to search: employers searching for the right labour and workers searching for the right jobs.

One obvious remedy for frictional unemployment is for there to be better job information. This could be provided by government job centres, by private employment agencies, or by local and national newspapers.

Structural unemployment

Structural unemployment is where the structure of the economy changes. Employment in some industries may expand while in others it contracts. There are two main reasons for this.

A change in the pattern of demand. Some industries experience declining demand. This may be due to a change in consumer tastes. Certain goods may go out of fashion. Or it may be due to competition from other industries. For example, consumer demand may shift away from coal and to other fuels. This will lead to structural unemployment in mining areas.

Definitions

Frictional (search) unemployment Unemployment that occurs as a result of imperfect information in the labour market. It often takes time for workers to find jobs (even though there *are* vacancies) and in the meantime they are unemployed.

Structural unemployment Unemployment that arises from changes in the pattern of demand or supply in the economy. People made redundant in one part of the economy cannot immediately take up jobs in other parts (even though there are vacancies).

Technological unemployment Structural unemployment that occurs as a result of the introduction of labour-saving technology.

A change in the methods of production (technological unemployment). New techniques of production often allow the same level of output to be produced with fewer workers. This is known as 'labour-saving technical progress'. Unless output expands sufficiently to absorb the surplus labour, people will be made redundant. This creates **technological unemployment**.

Structural unemployment often occurs in particular regions of the country. When it does, it is referred to as 'regional unemployment'. **Regional unemployment** is due to the concentration of particular industries in particular areas. For example, the decline in the South Wales coal mining industry led to high unemployment in the Welsh valleys.

The level of structural unemployment will depend on three factors:

- The degree of regional concentration of industry. The more that industries are concentrated in particular regions, the greater will be the level of structural unemployment if particular industries decline.
- The speed of change of demand and supply in the economy. The more rapid the rate of technological change or the shift in consumer tastes, the more rapid will be the rate of redundancies.
- The immobility of labour. The less able or willing workers are to move to a new job, the higher will be the level of structural unemployment.

Seasonal unemployment

Seasonal unemployment occurs when the demand for certain types of labour fluctuates with the seasons of the year. This problem is particularly severe in holiday areas, such as Cornwall, where unemployment can reach very high levels in the winter months.

Definitions

Regional unemployment
Structural unemployment occurring in specific regions of the country.

Seasonal unemployment
Unemployment associated with industries or regions where the demand for labour is lower at certain times of the year.

Summary

1. The two most common measures of unemployment are claimant unemployment (those claiming unemployment-related benefits) and ILO/OECD standardised unemployment (those available for work and actively seeking work or waiting to take up an appointment).
2. Unemployment can be divided into disequilibrium and equilibrium unemployment.
3. Disequilibrium unemployment occurs when the average real wage rate is above the level that will equate the aggregate demand and supply of labour. It can be caused by unions or government pushing up wages (real-wage unemployment), by a fall in aggregate demand (demand-deficient unemployment), or by an increase in the supply of labour.
4. Equilibrium unemployment occurs when there are people unable or unwilling to fill job vacancies. This may be due to poor information in the labour market and hence a time lag before people find suitable jobs (frictional unemployment), to a changing pattern of demand or supply in the economy and hence a mismatching of labour with jobs (structural unemployment – specific types being technological and regional unemployment), or to seasonal fluctuations in the demand for labour.

7.5 Aggregate demand and supply

What determines the level of output and the level of prices in an economy?

Before we examine the causes of inflation (the rate of increase in prices), we need to look at how the *level* of prices in the economy is determined. It is determined by the interaction of aggregate demand and aggregate supply. The analysis is similar to that of demand and supply in individual markets, but there are some crucial differences. Figure 7.7 shows an aggregate demand and an aggregate supply curve. Let us examine each in turn.

Aggregate demand curve
Remember what we said about aggregate demand earlier in the chapter. It is the total level of spending on the country's products: that is, by consumers, by the government, by firms on investment, and by people residing abroad. But why will the *AD* curve slope downwards: why will people demand fewer products as prices rise? There are three main reasons:

- If prices rise, people will be encouraged to buy fewer of the country's products and more imports instead (which are now relatively cheaper); the country will also sell fewer exports. Thus aggregate demand will be lower.
- As prices rise, people will need more money to pay for their purchases. With a given supply of money in the economy, this will have the effect of driving up interest rates (we will explore this in Chapter 9). The effect of higher interest rates will be to discourage borrowing and encourage saving. Both will have the effect of reducing spending and hence reducing aggregate demand.
- If prices rise, the value of people's savings will be eroded. They may thus save more (and spend less) to compensate.

Aggregate supply curve
The aggregate supply curve slopes upwards – at least in the short run. In other words, the higher the level of prices, the more will be produced. The

FIGURE 7.7
Aggregate demand and aggregate supply

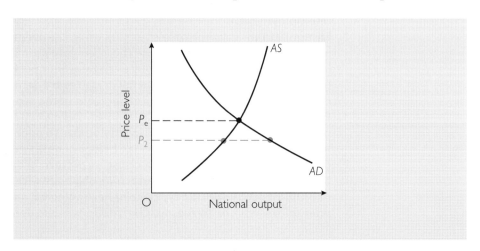

reason is simple: provided that factor prices (and in particular, wage rates) do not rise as rapidly as product prices, firms' profitability at each level of output will be higher than before. This will encourage them to produce more.

Equilibrium
The equilibrium price level will be where aggregate demand equals aggregate supply. To demonstrate this, consider what would happen if aggregate demand exceeded aggregate supply: for example, at P_2 in Figure 7.7. The resulting shortages throughout the economy would drive up prices. This would cause a movement up *along* both the *AD* and *AS* curves until *AD* = *AS* (at P_e).

Effect of a shift in the aggregate demand curve
If there is an increase in aggregate demand, the *AD* curve will shift to the right. This will lead to a combination of higher prices and higher output, depending on the elasticity of the *AS* curve. The more elastic the *AS* curve, the more will output rise relative to prices. We will consider the shape of the *AS* curve in more detail in Chapter 10.

Summary

1. Equilibrium in the economy occurs where aggregate demand equals aggregate supply.
2. A diagram can be constructed to show aggregate demand and aggregate supply, with price on the vertical axis and national output on the horizontal axis.
3. The *AD* curve is downward sloping, meaning that aggregate demand will be lower at a higher price level. The reason is that at higher prices: (a) there will be more imports and fewer exports; (b) interest rates will tend to be higher, resulting in reduced borrowing and increased saving; (c) people will be encouraged to save more to maintain the value of their savings.
4. The *AS* curve will be upward sloping because the higher prices resulting from higher demand will encourage firms to produce more (assuming that costs do not rise as rapidly as prices).
5. The amount that prices and output rise as a result of an increase in aggregate demand will depend on the shape of the *AS* curve.

Inflation

Why do prices have a tendency to rise?

The rate of inflation measures the annual percentage *increase* in prices. The most usual measure is that of *retail* prices. The government publishes an index of retail prices each month, and the rate of inflation is the percentage increase in that index over the previous twelve months. Figure 7.8 shows the rates of inflation for the USA, Japan, the UK, the EU and the OECD. As

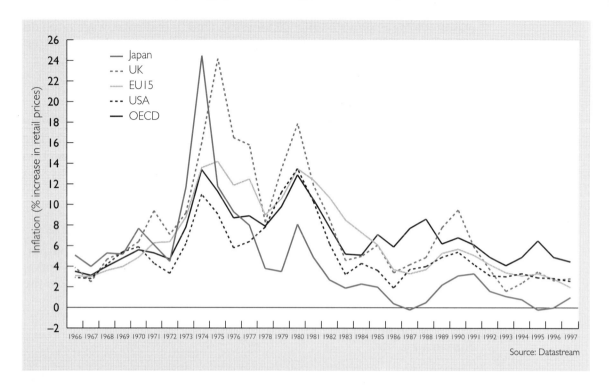

Source: Datastream

FIGURE 7.8
Inflation rates in selected industrial countries and groups of countries: 1966–97

you can see, inflation was particularly severe between 1973 and 1983, and relatively low in the late 1980s and mid-1990s.

It is also possible to give the rates of inflation for other prices. For example, indices are published for commodity prices, for food prices, for house prices (see Box 1.4), for import prices, for prices after taking taxes into account and so on. Their respective rates of inflation are simply their annual percentage increase. Likewise it is possible to give the rate of inflation of wage rates 'wage inflation').

Before we proceed, a word of caution: be careful not to confuse a rise or fall in *inflation* with a rise or fall in *prices*. A rise in inflation means a *faster* increase in prices. A fall in inflation means a *slower* increase in prices (but still an increase as long as inflation is positive).

Causes of inflation

Demand-pull inflation

Demand-pull inflation is caused by continuing rises in aggregate demand. In Figure 7.9, the *AD* curve shifts to the right (and continues doing so). Firms will respond to the rise in aggregate demand partly by raising prices and partly by increasing output (there is a move up along the *AS* curve). Just how much they raise prices depends on how much their costs rise as a result of increasing output. This in turn will depend upon how close actual output is to potential output. The less slack there is in the economy, the more will firms respond to a rise in demand by raising their prices (the steeper will be the *AS* curve).

Demand-pull inflation is typically associated with a booming economy. Many economists therefore argue that it is the counterpart of demand-

Definition

Demand-pull inflation
Inflation caused by persistent rises in aggregate demand.

FIGURE 7.9
Demand-pull inflation

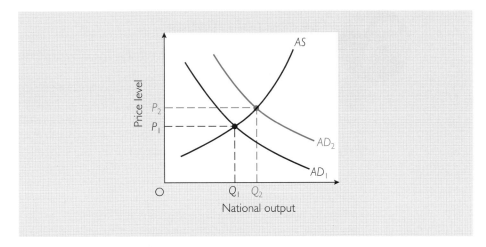

deficient unemployment. When the economy is in recession, demand-deficient unemployment will be high, but demand-pull inflation will be low. When, on the other hand, the economy is near the peak of the business cycle, demand-pull inflation will be high, but demand-deficient unemployment will be low.

Cost-push inflation

Cost-push inflation is associated with continuing rises in costs and hence continuing leftward (upward) shifts in the *AS* curve. Such shifts occur when costs of production rise *independently* of aggregate demand. If firms face a rise in costs, they will respond partly by raising prices and passing the costs on to the consumer, and partly by cutting back on production. This is illustrated in Figure 7.10. There is a leftward shift in the aggregate supply curve: from AS_1 to AS_2. This causes the price level to rise to P_3 and the level of output to *fall* to Q_3.

Just how much firms raise prices and cut back on production depends on the shape of the aggregate demand curve. The less elastic the *AD* curve, the less sales will fall as a result of any price rise, and hence the more will firms be able to pass on the rise in their costs to consumers as higher prices.

Note that the effect on output and employment will be the opposite of demand-pull inflation. With demand-pull inflation, output and hence employment will tend to rise. With cost-push inflation, however, output and employment will tend to fall.

It is important to distinguish between *single* shifts in the aggregate supply curve (known as 'supply shocks') and *continuing* shifts. If there is a single leftward shift in aggregate supply, there will be a single rise in the price level. For example, if the government raises the excise duty on oil, there will be a single rise in oil prices and hence in industry's fuel costs. This will cause *temporary* inflation while the price rise is passed on through the economy. Once this has occurred, prices will stabilise at the new level and the rate of inflation will fall back to zero again. If cost-push inflation is to continue over a number of years, therefore, the aggregate supply curve must *continually* shift to the left. If cost-push inflation is to *rise*, these shifts must get more rapid.

Rises in costs may originate from a number of different sources. As a result we can distinguish various types of cost-push inflation.

Definition

Cost-push inflation
Inflation caused by persistent rises in costs of production (independently of demand).

BOX 7.4 *The costs of inflation*
Is inflation more than a mere inconvenience?

A lack of growth is obviously a problem if people want higher living standards. Unemployment is obviously a problem, both for the unemployed themselves and also for society, which suffers a loss in output and has to support the unemployed. But why is inflation a problem? If prices go up by 10 per cent, does it really matter? Provided your wages kept up with prices, you would have no cut in your living standards.

If people could correctly anticipate the rate of inflation and fully adjust prices and incomes to take account of it, then the costs of inflation would indeed be relatively small. For us as consumers, they would simply be the relatively minor inconvenience of having to adjust our notions of what a 'fair' price is for each item when we go shopping. For firms, they would again be the relatively minor costs of having to change price labels, or prices in catalogues or on menus, or to adjust slot machines. These are known as **menu costs**.

In reality, people frequently make mistakes when predicting the rate of inflation and are not able to adapt fully to it. This leads to the following problems, which are likely to be more serious the higher the rate of inflation becomes and the more the rate fluctuates.

Redistribution. Inflation redistributes income away from those on fixed incomes and those in a weak bargaining position, to those who can use their economic power to gain large pay, rent or profit increases. It redistributes wealth to those with assets (e.g. property) which rise in value particularly rapidly during periods of inflation, and away from those with savings which pay rates of interest below the rate of inflation and hence whose value is eroded by inflation. Pensioners may be particularly badly hit by rapid inflation.

Uncertainty and lack of investment. Inflation tends to cause uncertainty among the business community, especially when the rate of inflation fluctuates. (Generally, the higher the rate of inflation, the more it fluctuates.) If it is difficult for firms to predict their costs and revenues, they may be discouraged from investing. This will reduce the rate of economic growth. On the other hand, as explained in the text, policies to reduce the rate of inflation may themselves reduce the rate of economic growth, especially in the short run. This may then provide the government with a policy dilemma.

Definition

Menu costs
The costs associated with having to adjust price lists or labels.

FIGURE 7.10
Cost-push inflation

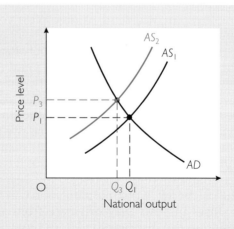

Balance of payments. Inflation is likely to worsen the balance of payments. If a country suffers from relatively high inflation, its exports will become less competitive in world markets. At the same time, imports will become relatively cheaper than home-produced goods. Thus exports will fall and imports will rise. As a result the balance of payments will deteriorate and/or the exchange rate fall. Both of these effects can cause problems. This is examined in more detail in the next chapter.

Resources. Extra resources are likely to be used to cope with the effects of inflation. Accountants and other financial experts may have to be employed by companies to help them cope with the uncertainties caused by inflation.

The costs of inflation may be relatively mild if inflation is kept to single figures. They can be very serious, however, if inflation gets out of hand. If inflation develops into 'hyperinflation', with prices rising perhaps by several hundred per cent or even thousand percent per year, the whole basis of the market economy will be undermined. Firms constantly raise prices in an attempt to cover their rocketing costs. Workers demand huge pay increases in an attempt to stay ahead of the rocketing cost of living. Thus prices and wages chase each other in an ever-rising inflationary spiral. People will no longer want to save money. Instead they will spend it as quickly as possible before its value falls any further. People may even resort to barter in an attempt to avoid using money altogether.

 Do you personally gain or lose from inflation? Why?

 Make a list of those who are most likely to gain and those who are most likely to lose from inflation. Explain.

- *Wage-push inflation.* This is where trade unions push up wage rates independently of the demand for labour.
- *Profit-push inflation.* This is where firms use their monopoly power to make bigger profits by pushing up prices independently of consumer demand.
- *Import-price-push inflation.* This is where import prices rise independently of the level of aggregate demand. An example is when OPEC quadrupled the price of oil in 1973/4.

In all these cases, inflation occurs because one or more groups are exercising economic power. The problem is likely to get worse, therefore, if there is an increasing concentration of economic power over time (for example, if firms or unions get bigger and bigger, and more monopolistic) or if groups become more militant.

Demand-pull and cost-push inflation can occur together, since wage and price rises can be caused both by increases in aggregate demand and by independent causes pushing up costs. Even when an inflationary process *starts* as either demand-pull or cost-push, it is often difficult to separate the two. An initial cost-push inflation may encourage the government to expand aggregate demand to offset rises in unemployment. Alternatively, an initial demand-pull inflation may strengthen the power of certain groups, who then use this power to drive up costs.

Structural (demand-shift) inflation

When the *pattern* of demand (or supply) changes in the economy, certain industries will experience increased demand and others decreased demand. If prices and wage rates are inflexible downwards in the contracting industries, and prices and wage rates rise in the expanding industries, the overall price and wage level will rise. The problem will be made worse, the less elastic is supply to these shifts.

Thus a more rapid structural change in the economy can lead to both increased structural unemployment and increased structural inflation. An example of this problem was the so-called north–south divide in the UK during the second half of the 1980s. The north experienced high structural unemployment as old industries declined, while the south experienced excess demand. This excess demand in the south, among other things, led to rapid house price inflation, and rapid increases in incomes for various groups of workers and firms. With many prices and wage rates being set *nationally*, the inflation in the south then 'spilt over' into the north.

Expectations and inflation

Workers and firms take account of the *expected* rate of inflation when making decisions.

Imagine that a union and an employer are negotiating a wage increase. Let us assume that both sides expect a rate of inflation of 5 per cent. The union will be happy to receive a wage rise somewhat above 5 per cent. That way, the members would be getting a *real* rise in incomes. The employers will be happy to pay a wage rise somewhat below 5 per cent. After all, they can put their price up by 5 per cent, knowing that their rivals will do approximately the same. The actual wage rise that the two sides agree on will thus be somewhere around 5 per cent.

Now let us assume that the expected rate of inflation is 10 per cent. Both sides will now negotiate around this benchmark, with the outcome being somewhere round about 10 per cent.

Thus the higher the expected rate of inflation, the higher will be the level of pay settlements and price rises, and hence the higher will be the resulting actual rate of inflation.

The importance of expectations in explaining the actual rate of inflation has been increasingly recognised by economists in recent years. As a result, economists have been concerned to discover just what determines people's expectations.

Summary

1. Demand-pull inflation occurs as a result of continuing increases in aggregate demand.
2. Cost-push inflation occurs when there are continuing increases in the costs of production independent of rises in aggregate demand. Cost-push inflation can be of a number of different varieties: wage-push, profit-push or import-price-push.
3. Inflation can also be caused by shifts in the pattern of demand in the economy, with prices rising in sectors of increasing demand but being reluctant to fall in sectors of declining demand.
4. Expectations play a crucial role in determining the level of inflation. The higher people expect inflation to be, the higher it will be.

Questions

1. The following table shows index numbers for real GDP (national output) for various countries (1990 = 100).

	1987	1988	1989	1990	1991	1992	1993	1994	1995	1996	1997
USA	92.7	96.4	98.8	100.0	99.4	101.7	104.8	109.1	112.7	115.7	119.5
Japan	85.5	90.8	95.2	100.0	104.0	105.1	105.2	105.7	106.5	108.1	110.3
Germany	87.9	91.1	94.4	100.0	104.6	105.8	103.8	107.4	108.5	111.1	113.8
France	89.5	93.8	97.6	100.0	100.8	102.1	100.6	103.5	106.0	108.3	110.7
UK	92.8	97.5	99.6	100.0	98.0	97.5	99.7	103.5	106.0	108.8	112.4

Sources: *Economic Trends* (ONS); *Economic Outlook* (OECD).

Using the formula $G = (Y_t - Y_{t-1})/Y_{t-1} \times 100$ (where G is the rate of growth, Y is the index number of output, t is any given year and $t-1$ is the previous year)
(a) Work out the growth rate for each country for each year from 1988 to 1997.
(b) Plot the figures on a graph. Describe the pattern that emerges.

2. For simplicity, taxes are shown as being withdrawn from the inner flow of the circular flow of income (see Figure 7.1) at just one point. In practice, different taxes are withdrawn at different points. At what point of the flow would the following be paid: (a) income taxes people pay on the dividends they receive on shares; (b) VAT; (c) business rates; (d) employees' national insurance contributions?

3. In terms of the UK circular flow of income, are the following net injections, net withdrawals or neither? If there is uncertainty, explain your assumptions.
(a) Firms are forced to take a cut in profits in order to give a pay rise.
(b) Firms spend money on research.
(c) The government increases personal tax allowances.

    (d) The general public invests more money in building societies.

    (e) UK investors earn higher dividends on overseas investments.

    (f) The government purchases US military aircraft.

    (g) People draw on their savings to finance holidays abroad.

    (h) People draw on their savings to finance holidays in the UK.

    (i) The government runs a budget deficit (spends more than it receives in tax revenues) and finances it by borrowing from the general public.

    (j) The government runs a budget deficit and finances it by printing more money.

4. Will the rate of actual growth have any effect on the rate of potential growth?

5. Figure 7.2 shows a decline in actual output in recessions. Redraw the diagram, only this time show a mere slowing down of growth in phase 4.

6. Why do cyclical swings seem much greater when we plot growth, rather than the level of output, on the vertical axis?

7. At what point of the business cycle is the country now? What do you predict will happen to growth over the next two years? On what basis do you make your prediction?

8. For what possible reasons may one country experience a persistently faster rate of economic growth than another?

9. Would it be desirable to have zero unemployment?

10. What major structural changes have taken place in the UK economy in the last ten years that have contributed to structural unemployment?

11. What are the causes of unemployment in the area where you live?

12. What would be the benefits and costs of increasing the rate of unemployment benefit?

13. Consider the most appropriate policy for tackling each of the different types of unemployment.

14. Do any groups of people gain from inflation?

15. If everyone's incomes rose in line with inflation, would it matter if inflation were 100 per cent or even 1000 per cent per annum?

16. Imagine that you had to determine whether a particular period of inflation was demand-pull, or cost-push, or a combination of the two. What information would you require in order to conduct your analysis?

chapter eight

The determination of national income and the role of fiscal policy

Macroeconomics is highly controversial. There is no universal agreement among economists as to how the economy functions at a macroeconomic level. Instead there are various schools of thought.

Although there are many of these schools, they are often grouped into two broad categories: *Keynesian* and *monetarist*.

In this chapter we focus on the theory developed by John Maynard Keynes back in the 1930s (see Box 8.1), a theory that has had a profound influence on economics. Keynes argued that, without government intervention to steer the economy, countries could lurch from unsustainable growth to deep and prolonged recessions.

In sections 8.1–8.4 we examine what determines the level of national output and why it tends to fluctuate (i.e. why there is a business cycle). As we shall see, Keynes placed particular emphasis on the role of aggregate demand in determining economic activity. If aggregate demand is too low, there will be a recession with high unemployment. On the other hand, if aggregate demand is too high, there will be inflation.

Then in the remainder of the chapter (sections 8.5–8.6), we look at the use of government policy, especially fiscal policy, to control aggregate demand so as to stabilise the level of output and keep the economy as close as possible to full employment.

Keynesianism had its birth in the 1920s and 1930s. The UK, like most of the rest of the world, was suffering from a deep and prolonged recession (the Great Depression). Governments seemed powerless to deal with the problem. The solution was found by the Cambridge economist John Maynard Keynes (see Box 8.1). He argued that the cause of the problem was a lack of spending: a lack of aggregate demand. The economy was caught in a vicious circle. People's spending was low because their income was low. Their income was low because wages and employment were low. Wages and employment were low because production was low. Production was low because consumer spending was low: there was no point in firms producing any more if it could not be sold.

The answer, argued Keynes, was for the government to break the vicious circle. It should deliberately seek to expand aggregate demand, either by increasing its own expenditure (for example, on public works such as roads, hospitals and schools), or by cutting taxes, thereby encouraging consumers to spend more. Either way, firms would be encouraged to produce more and take on more workers.

In general, Keynesians argue that free markets will fail to meet the macroeconomic objectives of rapid economic growth and low unemployment with simultaneously low inflation and the avoidance of balance of payments problems. They thus argue that the government should intervene to manage the economy.

In this chapter we examine the Keynesian theory of the determination of national income. We consider what determines the level of national income and whether there will be full employment, or a recession with high unemployment. We also examine the use of government policy to manage aggregate demand: to ensure that it is high enough to avoid a recession, but not so high as to cause demand-pull inflation.

In later chapters, and especially Chapter 10, we shall look at alternative views to those of Keynesians, and especially at monetarist views. Monetarists argue that government intervention generally does more harm than good. The role of government should be not to *manage* the economy, but simply to create a sound financial environment in which the free-enterprise economy can flourish. Primarily this means keeping inflation in check by not allowing the money supply to expand too rapidly.

Chapter 10 also examines a more extreme version of this school of thought: the 'new classical' school. New classicists argue that free markets work very well indeed in achieving the various macroeconomic goals.

8.1 The equilibrium level of national income

What determines the level of a country's output in the short run?

The Keynesian analysis of output and employment can be explained most simply in terms of the circular flow of income diagram. Figure 8.1 shows a simplified version of the circular flow that we looked at in section 7.2.

If injections (J) do not equal withdrawals (W), a state of disequilibrium exists. What will bring them back into equilibrium is a change in national income and employment.

FIGURE 8.1
The circular flow of income

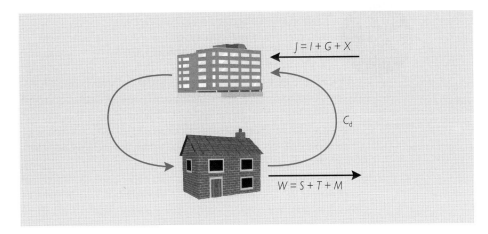

$$J = I + G + X$$

$$C_d$$

$$W = S + T + M$$

Start with a state of equilibrium, where injections equal withdrawals. If there is now a rise in injections – say, firms decide to invest more – aggregate demand ($C_d + J$) will be higher. Firms will respond to this increased demand by using more labour and other resources, and thus paying out more incomes (Y) to households. Household consumption will rise and so firms will sell more.

Firms will respond by producing more, and thus using more labour and other resources. Household incomes will rise again. Consumption and hence production will rise again, and so on. There will thus be a multiplied rise in incomes and employment. This is known as the **multiplier effect.**

The process, however, does not go on for ever. Each time household incomes rise, households save more, pay more taxes and buy more imports. In other words, withdrawals rise. When withdrawals have risen to match the increase in injections, equilibrium will be restored and national income and employment will stop rising. The process can be summarised as follows:

$$J > W \rightarrow Y\uparrow \rightarrow W\uparrow \text{ until } J = W$$

Similarly, an initial fall in injections (or rise in withdrawals) will lead to a multiplied fall in national income and employment:

$$J < W \rightarrow Y\downarrow \rightarrow W\downarrow \text{ until } J = W$$

Thus equilibrium in the circular flow of income can be at *any* level of output and employment.

Showing equilibrium with a Keynesian diagram

Definition

Multiplier effect
An initial increase in aggregate demand of £xm leads to an eventual rise in national income that is greater than £xm.

Equilibrium can be shown on a 'Keynesian' diagram. This plots various elements of the circular flow of income (such as consumption, withdrawals, injections and aggregate demand) against national income. There are two approaches to finding equilibrium: the withdrawals and injections approach; and the income and expenditure approach. Let us examine each in turn.

The withdrawals and injections approach
In Figure 8.2, national income (Y) is plotted on the horizontal axis. Withdrawals (W) and injections (J) are plotted on the vertical axis.

BOX 8.1

The Keynesian revolution

....

'In the long run we are all dead'

Up until the early 1920s, economists generally believed that there could be no such thing as mass unemployment. The reasoning of these 'classical' economists was simple: if there was unemployment in any given labour market, then all that was necessary was for a fall in real wage rates and the 'surplus' labour would disappear. In terms of Figure 7.5 (page 242), if unemployment is $A - B$, then a simple reduction in real wage rates from W_1 to W_e will eliminate the unemployment.

But in the early 1920s, Britain plunged into a deep recession that persisted until the outbreak of the Second World War in 1939. Britain was followed in 1929 by many other countries after the crash on the US stock exchange (the 'Wall Street Crash'). The world experienced the 'Great Depression'.

How did the classical economists explain what had seemed impossible? They argued that, as a result of growing unionisation, wage rates were not sufficiently flexible downwards. What was needed was a willingness on the part of workers to accept wage cuts, so as to 'price themselves into employment'. What would also help would be an increase in saving, so as to provide a greater fund of money for businesses to borrow for investment: investment which would get the economy growing again.

What was *not* needed, they argued, was an increase in government spending (a problem, given the growing expenditure on unemployment benefits as the number of unemployed rose). Increased government expenditure would mean more government borrowing (if higher taxes were to be avoided), and this would divert funds away from the private sector. Private investment would be 'crowded out' by increased government spending.

Keynes' response

This analysis was criticised by John Maynard Keynes. In 1936 his *General Theory of Employment, Interest and Money* was published. Probably no other economist and no other book has ever had such a profound influence on the subject of economics and on the policies pursued by governments. Indeed, throughout the 1950s and 1960s, governments in the UK and the USA, and many other countries too, considered themselves to be 'Keynesian'.

Full employment, maintained Keynes, was not a natural state of affairs. The economy could slide into a depression, and stay there. To achieve full employment, the government would have to intervene actively in the economy to ensure a sufficient level of aggregate demand. With government intervention, however, a depression would become merely a *short-term* problem – a problem that the intervention could cure.

The classical economists seemed more concerned with the *long* term: with issues of efficiency, productivity and *potential* output. Keynes was not particularly interested in the

As national income rises, so savings, taxes and imports will rise. Thus the withdrawals curve slopes upwards. But the amount that businesses plan to invest, that the government plans to spend and that overseas residents plan to import from the UK are all only slightly affected by the current level of UK national income. Thus injections, for simplicity, are assumed to be independent of national income. The injections line, therefore, is drawn as a horizontal straight line. (This does not mean that injections are constant long-run future of the world. 'Take care of the short run and the long run will look after itself' might have been Keynes' maxim. Keynes himself put it more succinctly: 'In the long run we are all dead.'

Keynes strongly criticised the classical economists' claim that the cause of the persistence of the Great Depression was a reluctance of real wage rates to fall. In Chapter 2 of the *General Theory*, he argues:

> … the contention that the unemployment which characterizes a depression is due to a refusal by labour to accept a reduction of money wages is not clearly supported by the facts. It is not very plausible to assert that unemployment in the United States in 1932 was due either to labour obstinately refusing to accept a reduction of money wages or to its obstinately demanding a real wage beyond what the productivity of the economic machine was capable of furnishing. Wide variations are experienced in the volume of employment without any apparent change either in the minimum real demands of labour or in its productivity. Labour is not more truculent in the depression than in the boom – far from it. Nor is its physical productivity less. These facts from experience are a *prima facie* ground for questioning the classical analysis.

Keynes also criticised the classical economists' arguments that increased saving would help to bring the economy out of depression. In fact, argued Keynes, it would do the reverse. An increase in saving would mean a decrease in consumer spending. Firms would sell fewer goods. They would thus cut back on production and also on their workforce.

Keynes' solution to mass unemployment

Keynes argued that the solution to mass unemployment was for the government to spend *more*, not less. Rather than raising taxes, or increasing borrowing from the general public, it could pay for the extra spending by expanding the money supply. Extra spending would stimulate firms to produce more and to take on more workers.

As more people were employed, so they would spend more. This would encourage firms to produce even more, and to take on even more workers. There would be a 'multiplied' rise in income and employment.

After the Second World War, 'Keynesianism' became the new orthodoxy. Governments of both parties accepted responsibility for ensuring that aggregate demand was kept at a sufficiently high level to maintain full, or near full, employment.

 How do you think a classical economist would reply to Keynes' arguments?

over time: merely that they are constant with respect to national income. If injections rise, the whole line will shift upwards.)

Withdrawals equal injections at point x in the diagram. Equilibrium national income is thus Y_e. If national income were below this level, say at Y_1, injections would exceed withdrawals (by an amount $a - b$). This additional net expenditure injected into the economy would encourage firms to produce more. This in turn would cause national income to rise. But as

FIGURE 8.2
Equilibrium national income: withdrawals equal injections

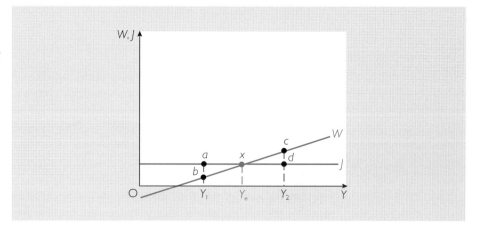

people's incomes rose, so they would save more, pay more taxes and buy more imports. In other words, withdrawals would rise. There would be a movement up along the W curve. This process would continue until $W = J$ at point x.

If, on the other hand, national income were at Y_2, withdrawals would exceed injections (by an amount $c - d$). This deficiency of demand would cause production and hence national income to fall. As it did so, there would be a movement down along the W curve until again point x was reached.

The income and expenditure approach

In Figure 8.3 two continuous lines are shown. The 45° line out from the origin plots $C_d + W$ against Y. It is a 45° line because by definition $Y = C_d + W$. To understand this, consider what can happen to national income: either it must be spent on domestically produced goods (C_d) or it must be withdrawn from the circular flow – there is nothing else that can happen to it. Thus if Y were £100 billion, then $C_d + W$ must also be £100 billion. If you draw a line such that whatever value is plotted on the horizontal axis (Y) is also plotted on the vertical axis ($C_d + W$), the line will at 45 degrees (assuming that the axes are drawn to the same scale).

The other continuous line plots aggregate demand. In this diagram it is known as the *national (or aggregate) expenditure line* (E). It consists of $C_d + J$: in other words, the total spending on domestic firms (see Figure 8.1).

To show how this line is constructed, consider the dashed line. This shows C_d. It is flatter than the 45° line. The reason is that for any given rise in national income, only *part* will be spent on domestic product, while the remainder will be withdrawn: i.e. C_d rises less quickly than Y. The E line consists of $C_d + J$. But we have assumed that J is constant with respect to changes in Y. Thus the E line is simply the C_d line shifted upward by the amount of J.

If national expenditure exceeded national income, at say Y_1, there would be excess demand in the economy (of $e - f$). In other words, people would be buying more than was currently being produced. Firms would thus find their stocks dwindling and would therefore increase their level of production. In doing so, they would employ more factors of production. National

FIGURE 8.3
Equilibrium national income: national income equals national expenditure

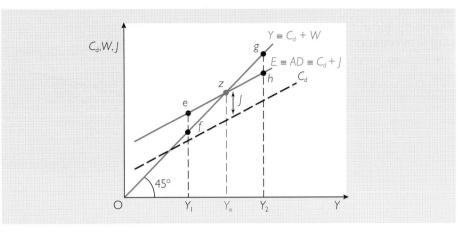

income would thus rise. As it did so, C_d and hence E would rise. There would be a movement up along the E line. But because not all the extra income would be consumed (i.e. some would be withdrawn), expenditure would rise less quickly than income: the E line is flatter than the Y line. As income rises towards Y_e, the gap between Y and E gets smaller. Once point z is reached, $Y = E$. There is then no further tendency for income to rise.

If national income exceeded national expenditure, at say Y_2, there would be insufficient demand for the goods and services currently being produced. Firms would find their stocks of unsold goods building up. They would thus respond by producing less and employing fewer factors of production. National income would thus fall and go on falling until Y_e was reached.

Note that if Y and E, and W and J were plotted on the same diagram, point z (in Figure 8.3) would be vertically above point x (in Figure 8.2).

Summary

1. In the simple Keynesian model, equilibrium national income is where withdrawals equal injections, and where national income equals the total expenditure on domestic products: where $W = J$ and where $Y = E$.
2. The relationships between national income and the various components of the circular flow of income can be shown on a diagram, where national income is plotted on the horizontal axis and the various components of the circular flow are plotted on the vertical axis.
3. Equilibrium national income can be shown on this diagram either at the point where the W and J lines cross, or where the E line crosses the 45° line (Y).

8.2 The multiplier

What will be the effect on output of a rise in spending?

When injections rise (or withdrawals fall), this will cause national income to rise. But by how much? The answer is that there will be a *multiplied* rise in

FIGURE 8.4
*The multiplier: a
shift in injections*

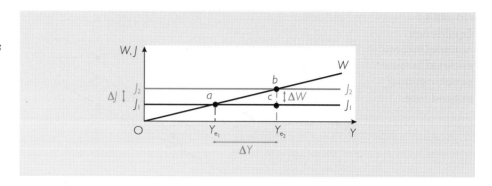

income: i.e. national income will rise by more than the rise in injections (or fall in withdrawals). The size of the **multiplier** is given by the letter k, where:

$$k = \Delta Y/\Delta J$$

Thus if injections rose by £10 million (ΔJ) and as a result national income rose by £30 million (ΔY), the multiplier would be 3.

The withdrawals and injections approach

Assume that injections rise from J_1 to J_2 in Figure 8.4. Equilibrium will move from point a to point b. Income will thus rise from Y_{e_1} to Y_{e_2}. But this rise in income (ΔY) is bigger than the rise in injections (ΔJ) that caused it. This is the multiplier effect. It is given by $(c - a)/(b - c)$ (i.e. $\Delta Y/\Delta J$).

It can be seen that the size of the multiplier depends on the *slope of the W curve*. The flatter the curve, the bigger will be the multiplier: i.e. the bigger will be the rise in national income from any given rise in injections. The slope of the W curve is given by $\Delta W/\Delta Y$. This is the proportion of a rise in national income that is withdrawn, and is known as the **marginal propensity to withdraw** (*mpw*).

The point here is that the less is withdrawn each time money circulates, the more will be recirculated and hence the bigger will be the rise in national income. The size of the multiplier thus varies inversely with the size of the *mpw*. The bigger the *mpw*, the smaller the multiplier; the smaller the *mpw*, the bigger the multiplier. In fact the **multiplier formula** is simply the inverse of the *mpw*:

$$k = 1/mpw$$

Thus if the *mpw* were $^1/_4$, the multiplier would be 4. So if J increased by £10 million, Y would increase by £40 million.

An alternative formula uses the concept of the marginal propensity to consume domestically produced goods (*mpc*$_d$). This is the proportion of a rise in national income that is spent on domestically produced goods, and thus is not withdrawn. Thus if a quarter of a rise in national income is withdrawn, the remaining three-quarters will recirculate as C_d. Thus:

$$mpw + mpc_d = 1$$
$$\text{and } mpw = 1 - mpc_d$$

Thus the alternative formula for the multiplier is:

Definitions

Multiplier
The number of times by which a rise in national income (ΔY) exceeds the rise in injections (ΔJ) that caused it: $k = \Delta Y/\Delta J$.

Marginal propensity to withdraw
The proportion of an increase in national income that is withdrawn from the circular flow of income: $mpw = \Delta W/\Delta Y$.

Multiplier formula
The formula for the multiplier is $k = 1/mpw$ or $1/(1 - mpc_d)$.

FIGURE 8.5
A shift in the expenditure line

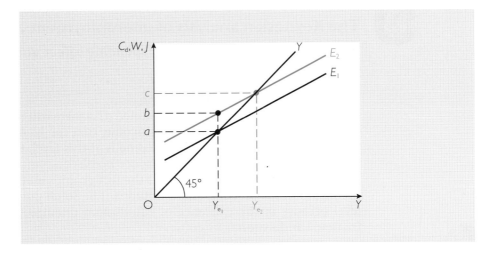

$$k = 1/(1 - mpc_d)$$

But why is the multiplier given by the formula $1/mpw$? This can be illustrated by referring to Figure 8.4. The mpw is the slope of the W line. In the diagram this is given by the amount $(b - c)/(c - a)$. The multiplier is defined as $\Delta Y/\Delta J$. In the diagram this is the amount $(c - a)/(b - c)$. But this is merely the inverse of the mpw. Thus the multiplier equals $1/mpw$.[1]

The income and expenditure approach

Assume in Figure 8.5 that the expenditure line shifts to E_2. This could be due either to a rise in one or more of the three injections, or to a rise in the consumption of domestically produced goods (and hence a fall in withdrawals). Equilibrium national income will rise from Y_{e_1} to Y_{e_2}.

What is the size of the multiplier? The initial rise in expenditure was $b - a$. The resulting rise in income is $c - a$. The multiplier is thus $(c - a)/(b - a)$.

Summary

1. If injections rise (or withdrawals fall), there will be a multiplied rise in national income. The multiplier is defined as $\Delta Y/\Delta J$. Thus if a £10 million rise in injections led to a £50 million rise in national income, the multiplier would be 5.
2. The size of the multiplier depends on the marginal propensity to withdraw (*mpw*). The smaller the *mpw*, the less will be withdrawn each time incomes are generated round the circular flow, and thus the more will go round again as *additional* demand for domestic product. The multiplier formula is $1/mpw$ or $1/(1 - mpc_d)$.

[1] In some elementary textbooks, the formula for the multiplier is given as $1/mps$ (where mps is the marginal propensity to save: the proportion of a rise in income saved). The reason for this is that it is assumed (for simplicity) that there is only one withdrawal, namely saving, and only one injection, namely investment. As soon as this assumption is dropped, $1/mps$ becomes the wrong formula.

8.3 The Keynesian analysis of unemployment and inflation

How will changes in the level of spending affect unemployment and inflation?

'Full-employment' national income

In simple Keynesian theory, it is assumed that there will be a maximum level of national output, and hence real income, that can be obtained at any one time. If the equilibrium level of income is at this level, there will be no deficiency of aggregate demand and hence no disequilibrium unemployment. This level of income is referred to as the **full-employment level of national income** (Y_F). (In practice, there would still be some unemployment at this level because of the existence of equilibrium unemployment – structural, frictional and seasonal.)

The deflationary gap

If the equilibrium level of national income (Y_e) is below the full-employment level (Y_F), there will be excess capacity in the economy and hence demand-deficient unemployment. There will be what is known as a **deflationary gap**. This situation is illustrated in Figure 8.6.

The gap is $a - b$: namely, the amount that the E line is below the 45° line at the full-employment level of national income (Y_F). It is also $c - d$: the amount that injections fall short of withdrawals at the full-employment level of income.

If national income is to be raised from Y_e to Y_F, injections will have to be raised and/or withdrawals lowered so as to close the deflationary gap.

Note that the size of the deflationary gap is *less* than the amount by which Y_e falls short of Y_F. This is another illustration of the multiplier. If injections are raised by $a - b$ (i.e. $c - d$), national income will rise by $Y_F - Y_e$. The multiplier is thus given by:

$$\frac{Y_F - Y_e}{a - b}$$

Definitions

Full-employment level of national income
The level of national income at which there is no deficiency of demand.

Deflationary gap
The shortfall of national expenditure below national income (and injections below withdrawals) at the full-employment level of national income.

FIGURE 8.6
The deflationary gap

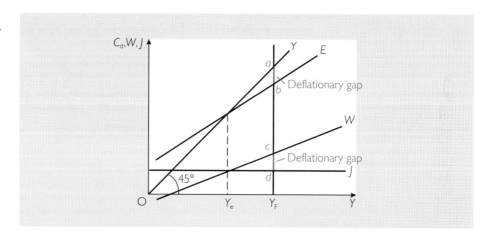

FIGURE 8.7
The inflationary gap

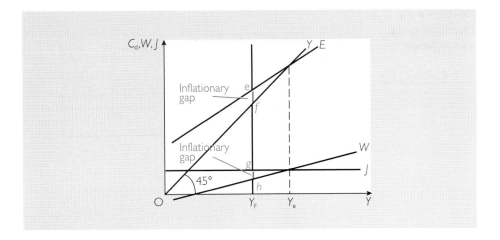

The inflationary gap
If at the full-employment level of income, national expenditure *exceeds* national income, there will be a problem of excess demand. Y_e will be above Y_F. The problem is that Y_F represents a real ceiling to output. In the short run, national income *cannot* expand beyond this point. Y_e cannot be reached. The result will therefore be demand-pull inflation.

This situation involves an **inflationary gap**. This is the amount by which expenditure exceeds income or injections exceed withdrawals at the full-employment level of national income. This is illustrated by the gaps $e - f$ and $g - h$ in Figure 8.7.

To eliminate this inflation, the inflationary gap must be closed, either by raising withdrawals or by lowering injections.

Policy implications
Keynesians advocate an active policy of demand management: raising aggregate demand (for example, by raising government expenditure or lowering taxes) to close a deflationary gap, and reducing aggregate demand to close an inflationary gap.

Unemployment and inflation at the same time

The simple analysis of deflationary and inflationary gaps implies that the aggregate supply curve looks like AS_1 in Figure 8.8. Up to Y_F, output and employment can rise with no rise in prices at all. The deflationary gap is being closed. At Y_F no further rises in output are possible. Any further rise in aggregate demand is entirely reflected in higher prices. An inflationary gap opens. In other words, this implies that either inflation *or* unemployment can occur, but not both simultaneously.

Two important qualifications need to be made to this analysis to explain the occurrence of both unemployment *and* inflation at the same time.

First, there are *other* types of inflation and unemployment not caused by an excess or deficiency of aggregate demand: for example, cost-push and expectations-generated inflation; frictional and structural unemployment.

Thus, even if a government could manipulate national income so as to get Y_e and Y_F to coincide, this would not eliminate all inflation and

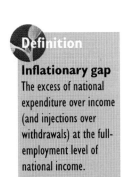

Definition

Inflationary gap
The excess of national expenditure over income (and injections over withdrawals) at the full-employment level of national income.

FIGURE 8.8
Unemployment
and inflation

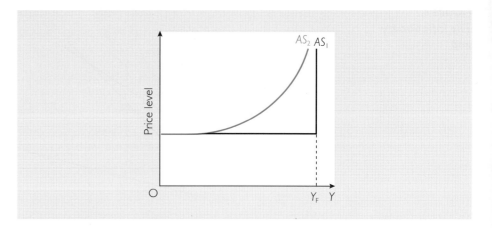

unemployment – only demand-pull inflation and demand-deficient unemployment. Keynesians argue, therefore, that governments should use a whole package of policies, each tailored to the specific type of problem. But certainly one of the most important of these policies will be the management of aggregate demand.

Second, not all firms operate with the same degree of slack. This may be due to different policies of firms over how much spare capacity to maintain and how many stocks to carry. It may be due to shifts in consumer demand away from some firms and towards others. The implication of this is that a rise in aggregate demand can lead to *both* a reduction in unemployment *and* a rise in prices: some firms responding to the rise in demand by taking up slack and hence increasing output; other firms, having little or no slack, responding by raising prices; others doing both. Similarly, labour markets have different degrees of slack and therefore the rise in demand will lead to various mixes of higher wages and lower unemployment. Thus the AS curve will look like AS_2 in Figure 8.8.

In Figure 8.9 aggregate demand curves have been added. If aggregate demand were initially at AD_1, equilibrium would be at Y_1, considerably below the full-employment potential. A rise in aggregate demand to AD_2 would lead to a rise in national income (to Y_2), but given the high level of unemployment and spare capacity, there is likely to be little in the way of price rises: the AS curve is virtually flat. But as slack is taken up, the AS curve becomes steeper. Firms, finding it increasingly difficult to raise output in the short run, simply respond to a rise in demand by raising prices. As Y_F is approached, so the AS curve becomes vertical: it is impossible in the short run to raise output beyond the capacity of firms.

In the longer term, if increased demand leads to more investment and increased capacity (potential output), the level of national income at which there is full employment will rise: the Y_F line will shift to the right, and with it the short-run AS curve. A long-run AS curve, in this view, therefore, would be more elastic than the short-term one (a view that monetarists strongly disagree with!).

The Phillips curve

The relationship between inflation and unemployment was examined in a famous article by A. W. Phillips back in 1958. He showed the statistical re-

FIGURE 8.9
The effects of increases in aggregate demand on national output

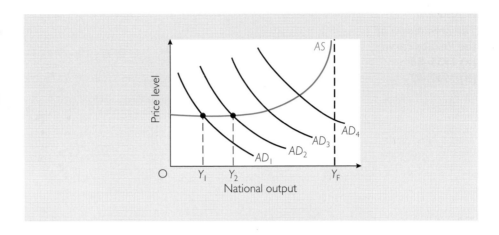

lationship between wage inflation and unemployment in the UK from 1861 to 1957. With wage inflation ($\dot{W}$) on the vertical axis and the unemployment rate (U) on the horizontal axis, a scatter of points was obtained. Each point represented the observation for a particular year. The curve that best fitted the scatter has become known as the **Phillips curve**. It is illustrated in Figure 8.10 and shows an inverse relationship between inflation and unemployment.

Given that wage increases over the period were approximately 2 per cent above price increases (made possible because of increases in labour productivity), a similar-shaped, but lower curve could be plotted showing the relationship between *price* inflation and unemployment.

The curve has often been used to illustrate the effects of changes in aggregate demand. When aggregate demand rose (relative to potential output), inflation rose and unemployment fell: there was a movement upward along the curve. When aggregate demand fell, there was a movement downward along the curve.

The Phillips curve was bowed in to the origin. The usual explanation for this is that as aggregate demand expanded, at first there would be plenty of

> **Definition**
>
> **Phillips curve**
> A curve showing the relationship between (price) inflation and unemployment. The original Phillips curve plotted *wage* inflation against unemployment for the years 1861–1957.

FIGURE 8.10
The Phillips curve

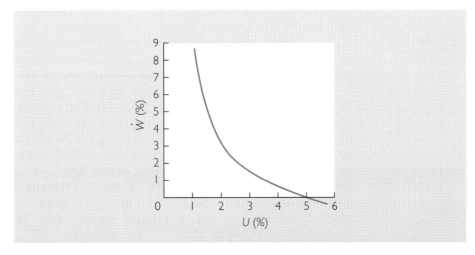

FIGURE 8.11
The breakdown of the Phillips curve
(a) 1955–66
(b) 1967–97

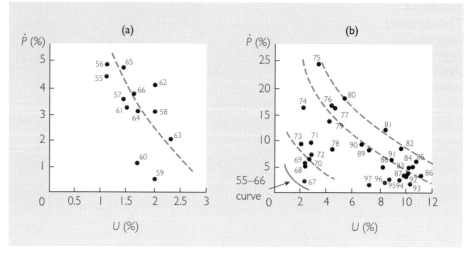

surplus labour, which could be employed to meet the extra demand without the need to raise wage rates very much. But as labour became increasingly scarce, firms would find that they had to offer increasingly higher wage rates to obtain the labour they required, and the position of trade unions would be increasingly strengthened.

The *position* of the Phillips curve depended on *non*-demand factors causing inflation and unemployment: frictional and structural unemployment; and cost-push, structural and expectations-generated inflation. If any of these non-demand factors changed so as to raise inflation or unemployment, the curve would shift outward to the right. The relative stability of the curve, over the 100 years or so observed by Phillips, suggested therefore that these non-demand factors had changed little.

The Phillips curve seemed to present governments with a simple policy choice. They could trade off inflation against unemployment. Lower unemployment could be bought at the cost of higher inflation, and vice versa. Unfortunately, the experience since the late 1960s has suggested that no such simple relationship exists beyond the short run.

From about 1966 the Phillips curve relationship seemed to break down. The UK, and many other countries in the western world too, began to experience growing unemployment *and* higher rates of inflation as well.

Figure 8.11 shows price inflation and unemployment in the UK from 1955 to 1997. From 1955 to 1966 a curve similar to the Phillips curve can be fitted through the data (diagram (a)). From 1967 to 1997, however, no simple picture emerges. Certainly the original Phillips curve can no longer fit the data; but whether the curve has shifted to the right, and, more recently, back to the left a little (the dotted lines), or whether the relationship has broken down completely, or whether there is some quite different relationship between inflation and unemployment, is not clear. There is much controversy among economists on this issue. We will examine the controversies in Chapter 10.

Summary

1. If equilibrium national income (Y_e) is below the full-employment level of national income (Y_F), there will be a deflationary gap. This gap is equal to $Y - E$ or $W - J$ at Y_F. This gap can be closed by increasing injections (or reducing withdrawals). This will then cause a multiplied rise in national income (up to a level of Y_F) and will eliminate demand-deficient unemployment.

2. If equilibrium national income exceeds the full-employment level of income, the inability of output to expand to meet this excess demand will lead to demand-pull inflation. This excess demand gives an inflationary gap, which is equal to $E - Y$ or $J - W$ at Y_F. This gap can be closed by reducing injections or increasing withdrawals.

3. This simple analysis tends to imply that the *AS* curve will be horizontal up to Y_F and then vertical. If allowance is made for other types of inflation and unemployment, the *AS* curve will be upward sloping but getting steeper as full employment is approached and as bottlenecks increasingly occur.

4. The Phillips curve showed the trade-off between inflation and unemployment. There seemed to be a simple inverse relationship between the two. After 1966, however, the relationship broke down as inflation *and* unemployment rose.

5. Although economists recognise that the relationships between inflation and unemployment are more complex than was thought back in the 1950s, there is considerable disagreement as to precisely what these relationships are.

8.4 Keynesian analysis of cyclical fluctuations in unemployment and inflation

Why do countries suffer from periodic booms and recessions?

Keynesians blame fluctuations in output and employment on fluctuations in aggregate demand. Theirs is therefore a 'demand-side' explanation of the business cycle. In the upturn (phase 1) aggregate demand starts to rise (see Figure 7.2 on page 231). It rises rapidly in the expansionary phase (phase 2). It then slows down and may start to fall in the peaking-out phase (phase 3). It then falls or remains relatively stagnant in the recession (phase 4).

Keynesians seek to explain why aggregate demand fluctuates, and then to devise appropriate stabilisation policies to iron out these fluctuations. A more stable economy, they argue, will provide a better climate for investment and the growth of both individual businesses and the economy as a whole.

Instability of investment: the accelerator

One of the major factors contributing to the ups and downs of the business cycle is the instability of investment.

BOX 8.2 The accelerator: an example
Demonstrating the instability of investment

The following example illustrates some important features of the accelerator. It looks at the investment decisions made by a firm in response to changes in the demand for its product. This firm is taken as representative of firms throughout the economy. The example is based on various assumptions:

- The firm's machines last exactly 10 years and then need replacing.
- At the start of the example, the firm has 10 machines in place, one 10 years old, one 9 years old, one 8 years old, one 7, one 6 and so on. Thus one machine needs replacing each year.
- Machines produce exactly 100 units of output per year. This figure cannot be varied.
- The firm always adjusts its output and its stock of machinery to match consumer demand.

The example shows what happens to the firm's investment over a six-year period when there is first a substantial rise in consumer demand, then a levelling off and then a slight fall. In year 2 consumer demand shoots up from 1000 units to 2000 units. In year 3 it goes up by a further 1000 units to 3000 units. In year 4 the rise slows down: demand goes up by 500 units to 3500 units. In year 5 there is no further rise in demand at all: demand is constant at 3500 units. In year 6 it falls slightly to 3400 units. This example illustrates the following features of the accelerator (see the table):

Investment will rise when the growth of national income (and hence consumer demand) is rising $(\Delta Y_{t+1} > \Delta Y_t)$. Years 1 to 2 illustrate this. The rise in consumer demand is zero in year 1 and 1000 units in year 2. Investment rises from 1 to 11 machines. The growth in investment may be considerably greater than the growth in consumer demand, giving a large accelerator effect. Between years 1 and 2, consumer demand doubles but investment goes up by a massive *eleven* times!

Investment will be constant even when national income is growing, if the increase in income this year is the same as last year: $(\Delta Y_{t+1} = \Delta Y_t)$. Years 2 to 3 illustrate this. Consumer demand continues to rise by 1000 units, but investment is constant at 11 machines.

The accelerator effect

	Year						
	0	1	2	3	4	5	6
Quantity demanded by consumers (sales)	1000	1000	2000	3000	3500	3500	3400
Number of machines required	10	10	20	30	35	35	34
Induced investment (I_i) (extra machines)		0	10	10	5	0	0
Replacement investment (I_r)		1	1	1	1	1	0
Total investment ($I_i + I_r$)		1	11	11	6	1	0

In a recession, investment in new plant and equipment can all but disappear. After all, what is the point in investing in additional capacity if you cannot even sell what you are currently producing?

When an economy begins to recover from a recession, however, and confidence returns, investment can rise very rapidly. In percentage terms, the rise in investment may be *several times that of the rise in income*. When

Investment will fall even if national income is still growing, if the rate of growth is slowing down ($\Delta Y_{t+1} < \Delta Y_t$). Years 3 to 4 illustrate this. Consumer demand rises now by 500 units (rather than the 1000 units last year). Investment falls from 11 to 6 machines.

If national income is constant, investment will be confined to replacement investment only. Years 4 to 5 illustrate this. Investment falls to the one machine requiring replacement.

If national income falls, even if only slightly, investment can be wiped out altogether. Years 5 to 6 illustrate this. Even though demand has fallen by only $^1/_{35}$, investment will fall to zero. Not even the machine that is wearing out will be replaced.

In practice, the accelerator will not be as dramatic and clear cut as this. The effect will be extremely difficult to predict for the following reasons:

- Many firms may have spare capacity and/or carry stocks. This will enable them to meet extra demand without having to invest.
- The willingness of firms to invest will depend on their confidence of *future* demand. Just because demand has currently risen, firms are not going to rush out and spend large amounts of money on machines that will last many years if it is quite likely that next year demand will fall back again.
- Firms may make their investment plans a long time in advance and may be unable to change them quickly.
- Even if firms do decide to invest more, the producer goods industries may not have the capacity to meet a sudden surge in demand for machines.
- Machines do not as a rule suddenly wear out. A firm could thus delay replacing machines and keep the old ones for a bit longer if it was uncertain about its future level of demand.

All these points tend to reduce the magnitude of the accelerator and to make it very difficult to predict. Nevertheless the effect still exists. Firms still take note of changes in consumer demand when deciding how much to invest. Evidence shows that fluctuations in investment are far more severe than fluctuations in national income.

 If there is an initial change in injections or withdrawals, then theoretically this will set off a chain reaction between the multiplier and accelerator. Assuming that there is an initial rise in injections, trace through the multiplier and accelerator effects. Why is it unlikely that national income will go on rising more and more rapidly?

the growth of the economy slows down, however, investment can fall dramatically. The point is that investment depends not so much on the *level* of national income and consumer demand, as on their *rate of change*. The reason is that investment (except for replacement investment) is to provide *additional* capacity, and thus depends on how much demand has risen, not on its level. But growth rates change by much more than the level of

Business expectations and their effect on investment

BOX 8.3

Recent European experience

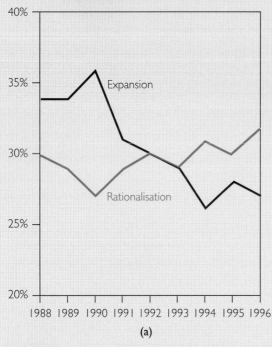

(a) Purposes of industrial investment (% of total investment)

In the boom years of the late 1980s, business optimism was widespread throughout Europe. Investment was correspondingly high, and with it there was a high rate of economic growth.

Surveys of European business expectations in the early 1990s, however, told a very different story. Pessimism was rife. Europe was in the grip of a recession, and output was falling (see Table (a)). Along with this decline in output and deteriorating levels of business and consumer confidence, there was a significant fall in investment.

Not only was the total level of investment falling, but the proportion of that investment used to expand capacity was also falling (see Figure (a)). By contrast, the proportion of investment devoted to rationalisation schemes had risen. Firms were increasingly having to look for ways of cutting their costs through restructuring their operations. One of the consequences of this was a growth in structural unemployment (as well as in demand-deficient unemployment).

But whereas these reductions in costs, and corresponding increases in labour productivity, provided a partial solution to the short-run difficulties faced by firms during the recession, in the long run productivity gains became increasingly difficult to achieve without investment in new capacity. This suggested that it was vital for firms to have confidence that their market *would* expand.

So were there any signs that confidence would pick up? As Table (b) and Figure (b) show, pessimism began to decrease after 1993, but it was not until the last quarter of 1994 that the average industrial confidence indicator for the EU as a whole became positive. (The figures in the table show the percentage excess of confident over pessimistic replies to business questionnaires: a negative figure meaning that there was a higher percentage of pessimistic responses.) Indeed, after mid-1995, the recovery in Europe began to slow down, and as a result industrial confidence waned, becoming negative once more.

(a) Macroeconomic indicators for the EU countries

	1989	1990	1991	1992	1993	1994	1995	1996
GDP growth (%)	3.5	2.9	1.5	0.9	−0.6	2.8	2.5	1.6
Investment (% change)	7.2	3.8	−0.5	−0.9	−6.5	2.5	3.5	2.2
Unemployment (%)	9.0	8.4	8.8	9.4	10.7	11.4	11.0	10.7
Inflation (%)	5.2	5.7	5.1	4.5	3.6	3.1	3.1	2.5
Net government borrowing (% of GDP)	−2.9	−4.1	−4.3	−5.1	−6.2	−5.5	−5.0	−4.4
Current account balance (% of GDP)	−0.3	−0.5	−1.3	−1.2	0.0	0.1	0.5	0.5

Source: *European Economy Annual Report* (Commission of the European Communities).

(b) Industrial confidence indicator

Country	Trough 1991–3	Peak 1988–90	1989	1991	1993	1995	1996
Belgium	−33	2	0	−15	−29	−9	−18
Denmark	−20	5	4	−8	−12	6	−8
France	−40	12	8	−20	−35	−2	−18
Germany	−36	11	5	0	−34	−3	−19
Ireland	−22	14	10	−9	−13	8	−1
Italy	−22	13	8	−13	−17	6	−12
Netherlands	−12	3	1	−5	−10	4	3
UK	−40	21	−2	−32	−11	3	−5
EU	−28	6	4	−14	−26	0	−14

Source: *European Economy Supplement B* (Commission of the European Communities).

(b) Confidence indicators in the EU

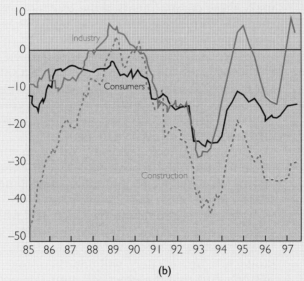

(b)

Source: *European Economy* (Commission of the European Communities).

As far as consumers were concerned, even with the recovery in Europe, which began in late 1993, the average EU consumer confidence indicator, although rising, remained negative. This was hardly the basis for a sustained rise in consumer expenditure and hence investment. From mid-1995 consumer confidence began falling again (see Figure (b)).

Q1 How is the existence of surveys of business confidence likely to affect firms' expectations and actions?

Q2 Why, if the growth in output slows down (but is still *positive*), is investment likely to *fall* (i.e. the growth in investment be *negative*)? If you look at Table (a) you will see that this happened in 1991 and 1992.

output. For example, if economic growth is 1 per cent in 1998 and 2 per cent in 1999, then in 1999 output has gone up by 2 per cent, but growth has gone up by 100 per cent! (i.e. it has doubled). Thus changes in investment tend to be much more dramatic than changes in national income. This is known as the accelerator theory. Box 8.2 gives an example of the accelerator effect.

These fluctuations in investment, being injections into the circular flow will then have a multiplied effect on national income and will thus magnify the upswings and downswings of the business cycle.

Fluctuations in stocks

Firms hold stocks of finished goods. These stocks tend to fluctuate with the course of the business cycle, and these fluctuations in stocks themselves contribute to fluctuations in output.

Imagine an economy that is recovering from a recession. At first, firms may be cautious about increasing production: doing so may involve taking on more labour or making additional investment. Firms may not want to make these commitments if the recovery could soon peter out. They may, therefore, run down their stocks rather than increase output. Initially the recovery from recession will be slow.

If the recovery does continue, however, firms will start to gain more confidence and will increase their production. Also they will find that their stocks have got rather low and will need building up. This gives a further boost to production, and for a time the growth in output will exceed the growth in demand. This extra growth in output will then, via the multiplier, lead to a further increase in demand.

Once stocks have been built up again, the growth in output will slow down to match the growth in demand. This slowing down in output will, via the accelerator and multiplier, contribute to the ending of the expansionary phase of the business cycle.

As the economy slows down, retailers will find themselves with unsold goods on their shelves. They will thus order less from the wholesalers, who in turn will order less from the manufacturers, who, unless they cut back production immediately, will find their stocks building up too. The increase in stocks cushions the effect of falling demand on output and employment.

If the recession continues, however, firms will be unwilling to go on building up stocks. But as firms attempt to reduce their stocks back to the desired level, production will fall *below* the level of sales, despite the fact that sales themselves are lower. This could therefore lead to a dramatic fall in output and, via the multiplier, to an even bigger fall in sales.

Eventually, once stocks have been run down to the minimum, production will have to rise again to match the level of sales. This will contribute to a recovery and the whole cycle will start again.

Determinants of the course of the business cycle

Keynesians seek to answer two key questions: why do booms and recessions last for several months or even years, and why do they eventually come to an end? Let us examine each in turn.

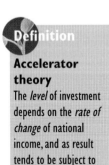

Definition

Accelerator theory
The *level* of investment depends on the *rate of change* of national income, and as result tends to be subject to substantial fluctuations.

Why do booms and recessions persist for a period of time?

Time lags. It takes time for changes in injections and withdrawals to be fully reflected in changes in national income, output and employment. The multiplier process takes time. Moreover, consumers, firms and government may not all respond immediately to new situations. Their responses are spread out over a period of time.

'Bandwagon' effects. Once the economy starts expanding, expectations become buoyant. People think ahead and adjust their expenditure behaviour: they consume and invest more *now*. Likewise in a recession a mood of pessimism may set in. The effect is cumulative.

The multiplier and accelerator interact: they feed on each other. A rise in income causes a rise in investment (the accelerator). This, being an injection into the circular flow, causes a multiplied rise in income. This then causes a further accelerator effect, and a further multiplier effect, and so on.

Why do booms and recessions come to an end? What determines the turning points?

Ceilings and floors. Actual output can go on growing more rapidly than potential output only as long as there is slack in the economy. As full employment is approached and as more and more firms reach full capacity, so a ceiling to output will be reached.

There is a basic minimum level of consumption that people will maintain. During a recession, people may not buy much in the way of luxury and durable goods, but they will still continue to buy food and other basic goods. There is thus a floor to consumption.

The industries supplying these basic goods will need to maintain their level of replacement investment. Also there will always be some minimum investment demand as firms, in order to survive competition, feel the need to install the latest equipment as it becomes available. There is thus a floor to investment too.

Echo effects. Durable consumer goods and capital equipment may last several years, but eventually they will need replacing. The replacement of goods and capital purchased in a previous boom may help to bring a recession to an end.

The accelerator. For investment to continue rising, consumer demand must rise at a *faster and faster* rate. If this does not happen, investment will fall back and the boom will break.

Random shocks. National or international political, social or natural events can affect the mood and attitudes of firms, governments and consumers, and thus affect aggregate demand.

Changes in government policy. In a boom, a government may become most worried by inflation and balance of payments deficits and thus pursue deflationary policies. In a recession it may become most worried by unemployment and lack of growth and thus pursue reflationary policies. These government policies, if successful, will bring about a turning point in the cycle.

Keynesians argue that governments should attempt to reduce cyclical fluctuations by the use of active stabilisation policies. A more stable economy will provide a better climate for long-term investment. It will help to reduce uncertainty about the future. Higher long-term investment will increase the growth in *potential* output and thus allow a faster growth in actual output to be maintained. The policy traditionally most favoured by Keynesians for stabilising the economy is *fiscal policy*. This is considered in the next section.

Summary

1. Keynesians explain cyclical fluctuations in the economy by examining the causes of fluctuations in the level of aggregate *demand*.
2. A major part of the Keynesian explanation of the business cycle is the instability of investment. The accelerator theory explains this instability. It relates the level of investment to *changes* in national income and consumer demand. An initial increase in consumer demand can result in a very large percentage increase in investment; but as soon as the rise in consumer demand begins to level off, investment will fall; and even a slight fall in consumer demand can reduce investment to virtually zero.
3. Keynesians identify other causes of cyclical fluctuations, such as cycles in the holding of stocks, time lags, 'bandwagon' effects, the *interaction* of the multiplier and accelerator, ceilings and floors to output, echo effects, swings in government policy and random shocks.

8.5 The role of fiscal policy

How can government expenditure and taxation be used to affect the level of economic activity?

Fiscal policy involves the government manipulating the level of government expenditure and/or rates of tax so as to affect the level of aggregate demand. An *expansionary* fiscal policy will involve raising government expenditure (an injection into the circular flow of income) or reducing taxes (a withdrawal from the circular flow). This will increase aggregate demand and lead to a *multiplied* rise in national income. A deflationary fiscal policy will involve cutting government expenditure and/or raising taxes.

During the 1950s and 1960s, when fiscal policy was seen by both governments and economists as the major way of controlling the economy, it was used to perform two main functions.

• To prevent the occurrence of *fundamental* disequilibria in the economy. In other words, expansionary fiscal policy could be used to prevent mass unemployment, and deflationary fiscal policy could be used to prevent excessive inflation.

- To smooth out the fluctuations in the economy associated with the business cycle. This would involve reducing government expenditure or raising taxes during the boom phase of the cycle. This would dampen down the expansion and prevent 'overheating' of the economy with its attendant rising inflation and deteriorating balance of payments. Conversely, during the recessionary phase, as unemployment grew and output declined, the government should cut taxes or raise government expenditure in order to boost the economy. If these stabilisation policies were successful, they would amount merely to fine tuning. Problems of excess or deficient demand would never be allowed to get severe. Any movement of aggregate demand away from a steady growth path would be immediately 'nipped in the bud'.

Deficits and surpluses

Central government deficits and surpluses

Since an expansionary fiscal policy will involve raising government expenditure and/or lowering taxes, this will have the effect of either increasing the budget deficit or reducing the budget surplus. A budget deficit in any one year is where central government's expenditure exceeds its revenue from taxation. A budget surplus is where tax revenues exceed central government expenditure. With the exception of short periods in 1969–70 and 1987–90, governments in the UK, like most governments around the world, have run budget deficits.

Public-sector deficits and surpluses

To get a complete view of the overall stance of fiscal policy – just how expansionary or contractionary it is – we would need to look at the deficit or surplus of the entire public sector: namely, central government, local government and public corporations. If the public sector spends more than it earns (through taxes and the revenues of public corporations, etc.) the amount of this deficit is known as the public-sector borrowing requirement (PSBR). The reason for the name 'public-sector borrowing requirement' is simple. If the public sector runs a deficit in the current year of, say, £1 billion, then it will have to borrow £1 billion this year in order to finance it (see Chapter 9 for methods of borrowing).

If the public sector runs a surplus, then this is called a public-sector debt repayment (PSDR), since the surplus will be used to reduce the accumulated debts from the past. The accumulated debts of central government are known as the national debt. The accumulated debts of the entire public sector are known as the *public-sector debt*. Table 8.1 shows the PSBR/PSDR, the national debt and the public-sector debt for the UK from 1985 to 1996.

Definitions

Budget surplus
The excess of central government's tax receipts over its spending.

Fiscal stance
How deflationary or reflationary the Budget is.

Public-sector borrowing requirement (PSBR)
The (annual) deficit of the public sector (central government, local government and public corporations), and thus the amount that the public sector must borrow.

Public-sector debt repayment (PSDR)
The (annual) surplus of the public sector, and thus the amount of debt that can be repaid.

National debt
The accumulated budget deficits (less surpluses) over the years: the total amount of government borrowing.

TABLE 8.1 *UK public-sector borrowing and debt (£bn)*

Year	1985	1986	1987	1988	1989	1990	1991	1992	1993	1994	1995	1996
PSBR(–) or PSDR(+)	–7.5	–2.4	+1.4	+11.6	+9.3	+2.1	–7.7	–28.7	–42.5	–37.9	–35.1	–24.9
National debt	146.6	158.4	169.3	178.1	167.2	160.0	163.7	180.4	225.8	274.7	305.9	343.9
Public-sector debt	189.0	196.6	204.1	212.0	198.6	189.2	193.2	208.4	254.6	306.8	337.7	374.6

Sources: *Financial Statistics* (ONS), *Annual Abstract of Statistics* (ONS).

BOX 8.4

Discretionary fiscal policy in Japan
....
An emergency package to stimulate the economy

Tokyo: 31 March 1992

The Japanese government early today approved a package of emergency economic measures that will increase public spending by at least ¥4000 billion (£17 billion) in the first half of the fiscal year, which begins tomorrow. The measures . . . are a response to rising concern at the slowdown of the Japanese economy. Industrial output is falling sharply and money supply growth is at an historic low.

Mr Masaru Yoshitomi, director-general of the Economic Planning Agency's co-ordination bureau, said the measures would give a strong stimulus to the economy, arrest further decline, and allow the government to reach its economic growth target of 3.5 per cent in 1992.[2]

In previous decades a fiscal expansion of this magnitude would have proved to be more than successful in getting the Japanese economy moving. Yet after an average growth rate of 5.0 per cent in the previous four years, growth in 1992 turned out to be only 1.0 per cent, followed by a mere 0.1 per cent in 1993 and 0.7 and 1.3 per cent in 1994 and 1995. This proved to be the longest recession experienced by the Japanese economy since the Second World War.

Yet over the four-year period 1992–5, the Japanese government had injected into the economy five public spending packages totalling ¥59 500 billion (£330 billion): an average increase in government spending of 7 per cent a year in real terms. There were also substantial cuts in taxes. This, combined with the economic slowdown, moved the public-sector finances massively into deficit. A public-sector surplus of 3 per cent of GDP in 1991 was transformed into a public-sector deficit of 4.4 per cent of GDP by 1996 (see Figure (a)). Japan's national debt rose from 63 per cent of GDP in 1991 to over 90 per cent by 1997.

In addition to this fiscal stimulus, the government reduced interest rates nine times, to a record low of 0.5 per cent by 1996. It also pursued a policy of business deregulation, especially within the service and financial sectors. Yet despite all these measures, the Ministry of International Trade and Industry feared that the Japanese economy might be unable to grow faster than 1 per cent per year for the rest of the decade.

Why did such an expansionary fiscal (and monetary) policy prove to be so ineffective? With a rise in G and a fall in T, why did the economy not expand? The answer can be found in the behaviour of the other components of aggregate demand.

Exports

In previous decades the prosperity of Japanese business was built upon an export-led growth strategy. If there was a lack of demand at home, surplus capacity in the economy could simply be exported. But this option was no longer so easy. Since 1985, as the graph shows, there had been a massive appreciation of the exchange rate: the yen rose by over 150 per cent against the US dollar in the ten years up to 1995. This, plus growing competition from other Asian exporters, meant that Japanese firms were finding it harder to export. The result was that by 1995 less than 70 per cent of productive capacity was being used.

Investment

The recession and the slowdown in export sales, plus high levels of debt from the expansion of the late 1980s, reduced profits to near record lows and created a climate of business

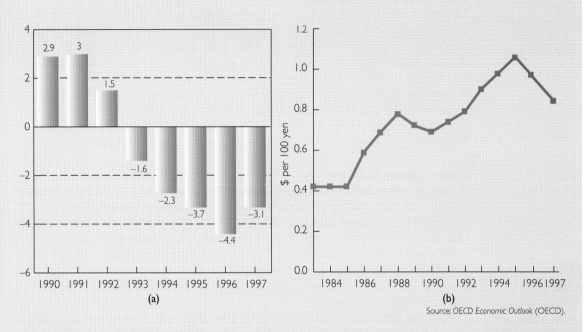

Source: OECD Economic Outlook (OECD).

(a) Japan's general government budget balance as % of GDP
(b) The US dollar/Japanese yen exchange rate

pessimism. After increases in investment averaging 10 per cent per year from 1987 to 1990, investment fell for three successive years after 1991.

Consumption

Consumers too were in a pessimistic mood. The salaries of many Japanese workers are heavily reliant upon bonuses and overtime payments. Such performance-related rewards can be as much as 50 per cent of total pay. The low profitability of Japanese business hit consumers hard. Even with a ¥5000 billion cut in taxation in 1994, consumer spending on domestic goods and services grew only marginally, whereas *saving* increased sharply, as did *imports*. Encouraged by the high yen, imports grew in real terms by an average of over 7 per cent per year between 1992 and 1995.

As deflationary pressure mounted (inflation became *negative* after 1994), so the criticisms of the Japanese government's fiscal policy grew stronger. The policy, said the critics, had been too little and too late. Even though the total fiscal stimulus over the years since 1992 had been large, the incremental nature of the government's action had failed on each occasion to stimulate business and consumer activity to any significant degree. What was needed, they claimed, was a more aggressive reflation to kick-start the economy, coupled with measures to support the banking sector and the further deregulation of industry.

 Would there have been any adverse consequences if the Japanese government had adopted a more reflationary fiscal policy?

[2]Steven Butler, *Financial Times*, 31 March 1992.

The use of fiscal policy

Automatic fiscal stabilisers

To some extent, government expenditure and taxation will have the effect of *automatically* stabilising the economy. For example, as national income rises, tax revenues automatically rise. This rise in withdrawals from the circular flow of income will help to dampen down the rise in national income. This effect will be bigger if taxes are progressive (i.e. rise by a bigger percentage than national income). Some government expenditure will have a similar effect. For example, total government expenditure on unemployment benefits will fall, if rises in national income cause a fall in unemployment. This again will have the effect of dampening the rise in national income.

Discretionary fiscal policy

If there is a fundamental disequilibrium in the economy or substantial fluctuations in national income, these automatic stabilisers will not be enough. The government may thus choose to *alter* the level of government expenditure or the rates of taxation. This is known as **discretionary fiscal policy**.

If government expenditure on goods and services (roads, health care, education, etc.) is raised, this will create a full multiplied rise in national income. The reason is that all the money gets spent and thus all of it goes to boosting aggregate demand.

Cutting taxes, however, will have a smaller effect on national income than raising government expenditure on goods and services by the same amount. The reason is that cutting taxes increases people's *disposable* incomes, of which only *part* will be spent. Part will be withdrawn into extra savings, imports and other taxes. In other words, not all the tax cuts will be passed on round the circular flow of income as extra expenditure. Thus if one-fifth of a cut in taxes is withdrawn and only four-fifths is spent, the tax multiplier will only be four-fifths as big as the government expenditure multiplier.

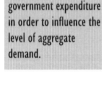

Definition

Discretionary fiscal policy
Deliberate changes in tax rates or the level of government expenditure in order to influence the level of aggregate demand.

Summary

1. A reflationary fiscal policy will involve raising government expenditure and/or reducing taxes. A deflationary fiscal policy will involve the reverse.
2. The government's fiscal policy will determine the size of the budget deficit or surplus and the size of the PSBR or PSDR.
3. Automatic fiscal stabilisers are tax revenues that rise and government expenditures that fall as national income rises. They have the effect of reducing the size of the multiplier and thus reducing cyclical upswings and downswings.
4. Discretionary fiscal policy is where the government deliberately changes taxes or government expenditure in order to alter the level of aggregate demand. Changes in government expenditure on goods and services will have a full multiplier effect. Changes in taxes and benefits will have a smaller multiplier effect as some of the tax/benefit changes will merely affect other withdrawals and thus have a smaller net effect on consumption of domestic product.

The effectiveness of fiscal policy

Is fiscal policy a reliable means of controlling the economy?

How successful will fiscal policy be? Will it be able to 'fine tune' demand? Will it be able to achieve the level of national income the government would like it to achieve? Will it be able to give full employment without inflation? Will the government know just how much to change taxes and/or government expenditure?

The effectiveness of fiscal policy will depend on a number of factors, including the following:

- The accuracy of forecasting. Governments would obviously like to act as swiftly as possible to prevent a problem of excess or deficient demand. The more reliable are the forecasts of what is likely to happen to aggregate demand, the more able will the government be to intervene quickly.
- The extent to which changes in government expenditure (*G*) and taxation (*T*) will affect total injections and withdrawals. Will changes in *G* or *T* be partly offset by changes in *other* injections and withdrawals? If so, are these changes predictable?
- The extent to which changes in injections and withdrawals affect national income. Will it be possible to predict the size of the multiplier and accelerator effects?
- The timing of the effects. It is no good simply being able to predict the *magnitude* of the effects of fiscal policy. It is also necessary to predict how long they will take. If there are long time lags with fiscal policy, it will be far less successful as a means of reducing fluctuations.
- The extent to which changes in aggregate demand will have the desired effects on output, employment, inflation and the balance of payments.
- The extent to which fiscal policy has undesirable side-effects, such as higher taxes reducing incentives.

Discretionary fiscal policy: problems of magnitude

Before changing government expenditure or taxation, the government will need to calculate the effect of any such change on national income, employment and inflation. The magnitude of these effects will depend on (a) the extent to which changes in *G* or *T* will affect *net* injections and withdrawals, and (b) the extent to which the changes in injections and withdrawals will affect final national income. If the magnitude of these effects can be forecast with relative accuracy, then fiscal policy could be a relatively powerful tool for controlling the economy. Forecasting, however, is often very unreliable for a number of reasons.

Predicting the effect of changes in government expenditure

A rise in government expenditure of £*x* may lead to a rise in total injections (relative to withdrawals) that is smaller than £*x*. This will occur if the rise in government expenditure *replaces* a certain amount of private expenditure. For example, a rise in expenditure on state education may dissuade some parents from sending their children to private schools. Similarly, an improvement in the national health service may lead to fewer people paying for private treatment.

Crowding out. Another reason for the total rise in injections being smaller than the rise in government expenditure is a phenomenon known as **crowding out** (something that monetarists see as being particularly significant). If the government relies on **pure fiscal policy** – that is, if it does not finance an increase in the budget deficit by increasing the money supply (which would make the policy a combination of fiscal and monetary policy) – it will have to borrow the money from individuals and firms. It will thus be competing with the private sector for finance and will have to offer higher interest rates. This will force the private sector too to offer higher interest rates, which may discourage firms from investing and individuals from buying on credit. Thus government borrowing *crowds out* private borrowing. In the extreme case, the fall in consumption and investment may completely offset the rise in government expenditure, with the result that aggregate demand does not rise at all.

Predicting the effect of changes in taxes

A reduction in taxes, by increasing people's real disposable income, will increase not only the amount they spend but also the amount they save. The problem is that it is not easy to predict just how much people will increase their spending and how much their saving. In part it will depend on whether people feel that the cut in tax is only temporary, in which case they may well simply save the extra and maintain their current level of consumption, or permanent, in which case they may well increase the level of their consumption.

Predicting the resulting multiplied effect on national income

Even if the government *could* predict the net *initial* effect on injections and withdrawals, the ultimate effect on national income will still be hard to predict for the following reasons:

- The size of the *multiplier* may be difficult to predict, since it is difficult to predict how much of any rise in income will be withdrawn. In other words, it is difficult to predict the size of the *mpw*. For example, the amount of a rise in income that households save or consume will depend on their expectations about future price and income changes. The amount of a rise in income spent on imports will depend on the exchange rate, which may fluctuate considerably.
- Induced investment through the *accelerator* is also extremely difficult to predict. It may be that a relatively small fiscal stimulus will be all that is necessary to restore business confidence, and that induced investment will rise substantially. In such a case, fiscal policy can be seen as a 'pump primer'. It is used to *start* the process of recovery, and then the *continuation* of the recovery is left to the market. But for pump priming to work businesspeople must *believe* that it will work. If they are cautious and fear that the recovery will falter, they may hold back from investing. This lack of investment will probably mean that the recovery *will* falter and that, therefore, the effects of the fiscal expansion will be very

Definitions

Crowding out
Where increased public expenditure diverts money or resources away from the private sector.

Pure fiscal policy
Fiscal policy which does not involve any change in money supply.

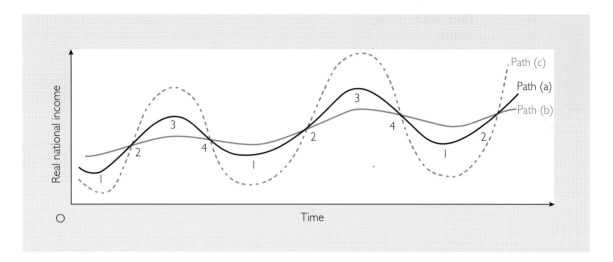

FIGURE 8.12
Fiscal policy: stabilising or destabilising?

modest. The problem is in predicting just how the business community will react. Business confidence can change very rapidly and in ways that could not have been foreseen a few months earlier.

Random shocks
Forecasts cannot take into account the unpredictable. For that you would have to consult astrologers or fortune tellers! Unfortunately, unpredictable events, such as a war or a major industrial dispute, do occur and may seriously undermine the government's fiscal policy.

Discretionary fiscal policy and the problem of timing

Fiscal policy can involve considerable time lags. If these are long enough, fiscal policy could even be *de*stabilising. Reflationary policies that are taken to cure a recession may only come into effect once the economy has *already* recovered and is experiencing a boom. Under these circumstances, reflationary policies will be quite inappropriate: they will simply worsen the problems of overheating. Similarly, deflationary policies that are taken to prevent excessive expansion may only start taking effect once the economy has peaked and is already plunging into recession. The deflationary policies will only deepen the recession.

This problem is illustrated in Figure 8.12. Path (a) shows the course of the business cycle without government intervention. Ideally, with no time lags, the economy should be deflated in stage 2 and reflated in stage 4. This would make the resulting course of the business cycle more like path (b), or even, if the policy were perfectly stabilising, a straight line. With the presence of time lags, however, deflationary policies taken in stage 2 may not come into effect until stage 4, and reflationary policies taken in stage 4 may not come into effect until stage 2. In this case the resulting course of the business cycle will be more like path (c). Quite obviously, in these circumstances 'stabilising' fiscal policy actually makes the economy less stable.

There are five possible lags associated with fiscal policy.

Time lag to recognition. Since the business cycle can be irregular and forecasting unreliable, governments may be unwilling to take action until they are convinced that the problem is serious.

Time lag between recognition and action. Most significant changes in government expenditure have to be planned well in advance. The government cannot increase spending on motorways overnight or suddenly start building new hospitals.

Changes in taxes and benefits cannot be introduced overnight either. They normally have to wait to be announced in the Budget and will not be instituted until the new financial year or at some other point in the future. As Budgets normally occur annually, there could be a considerable time lag if the problems are recognised a long time before the Budget.

Time lag between action and changes taking effect. A change in tax rates may not immediately affect tax payments. For example, income tax PAYE codings take two or three months to be changed by the Inland Revenue.

Time lag between changes in government expenditure and taxation and the resulting change in national income, prices and employment. The multiplier round takes time. Accelerator effects take time. The multiplier and accelerator go on interacting. It all takes time.

Consumption may respond slowly to changes in taxation. If taxes are cut, consumers may respond initially by saving the extra money. They may only later increase consumption.

If the fluctuations in aggregate demand can be forecast, and if the lengths of the time lags are known, then all is not lost. At least the fiscal measures can be taken early and their delayed effects can be taken into account.

Side-effects of discretionary fiscal policy

The purpose of fiscal policy is to control aggregate demand. In doing so, however, it may create certain undesirable side-effects. These include:

Cost inflation. If the economy is overheating and inflation is rising, the government may raise taxes. Although this will lower aggregate demand, a rise in expenditure taxes and corporation taxes will usually be passed on in full or in part to the consumer in higher prices. This in turn could lead to higher wage claims, as could a rise in income tax.

Welfare and distributive justice. The use of fiscal policy may conflict with various social programmes. The government may want to introduce cuts in public expenditure in order to reduce inflation. But where are the cuts to be made? Cuts will often fall on people who are relatively disadvantaged. After all, it is these people who are the most reliant on the welfare state and other public provision (such as state education).

Incentives. Both automatic stabilisers, in the form of steeply progressive income taxes, and discretionary rises in taxes could be a disincentive to effort (see section 5.5). What is the point in working more or harder, people might say, if so much is going to be taken in taxes? It could work the other way, however: faced with higher tax bills, people may feel the need to work more in order to maintain their living standards.

An alternative to using fiscal policy is to use monetary policy. This involves taking measures to control the money supply and interest rates. The role of money and monetary policy is the subject for the next chapter.

Summary

1. **The effectiveness of fiscal policy depends on the accuracy of forecasting. It also depends on the predictability of the outcome of the fiscal measures: the effect of changes in G and T on other injections and withdrawals, the size and timing of the multiplier and accelerator effects, the relative effects of changes in aggregate demand on the various macroeconomic objectives, and whether there are any side-effects. It also depends on whether there are any random shocks.**
2. **There are problems in predicting the magnitude of the effects of discretionary fiscal policy. Expansionary fiscal policy can act as a pump primer and stimulate increased private expenditure, or it can crowd out private expenditure. The extent to which it acts as a pump primer depends crucially on business confidence – something that is very difficult to predict beyond a few weeks or months. The extent of crowding out depends on monetary conditions and the government's monetary policy.**
3. **There are five possible time lags involved with fiscal policy: the time lag before the problem is diagnosed, the lag between diagnosis and new measures being announced, the lag between announcement and implementation, the lag while the multiplier and accelerator work themselves out, and the lag before consumption fully responds to new economic circumstances.**
4. **Discretionary fiscal policy can involve side-effects, such as disincentives, higher costs and adverse effects on social programmes.**

Questions

1. An economy is currently in equilibrium. The following figures refer to elements in its national income accounts.

	£bn
Consumption (total)	60
Investment	5
Government expenditure	8
Imports	10
Exports	7

(a) What is the current equilibrium level of national income?
(b) What is the level of injections?

(c) What is the level of withdrawals?

(d) Assuming that tax revenues are £7 billion, how much is the level of saving?

(e) If national income now rises to £80 billion and, as a result, the consumption of domestically produced goods rises to £58 billion, what is the mpc_d?

(f) What is the value of the multiplier?

(g) Given an initial level of national income of £80 billion, now assume that spending on exports rises by £4 billion, spending on investment rises by £1 billion, while government expenditure falls by £2 billion. By how much will national income change?

2. What is the relationship between the mpc_d and the mpw?

3. Assume that the multiplier has a value of 3. Now assume that the government decides to increase aggregate demand in an attempt to reduce unemployment. It raises government expenditure by £100 million with no increase in taxes. Firms, anticipating a rise in their sales, increase investment by £200 million, of which £50 million consists of purchases of foreign machinery. How much will national income rise? (Assume no other changes in injections.)

4. On a Keynesian diagram, draw three W lines of different slopes, all crossing the J line at the same point. Now draw a second J line above the first. Mark the original equilibrium and all the new ones corresponding to each of the W lines. Using this diagram, show how the size of the multiplier varies with the mpw.

5. Why does the slope of the E line in a Keynesian diagram equal the mpc_d? (Clue: draw an mpc_d line.)

6. On a Keynesian diagram, draw two E lines of different slopes, both crossing the Y line at the same point. Now draw another two E lines, parallel with the first two and crossing each other vertically above the point where the first two crossed. Using this diagram, show how the size of the multiplier varies with the mpc_d.

7. What factors could explain why some countries have a higher multiplier than others?

8. The present level of a country's exports is £12 000 billion; investment is £2000 billion; government expenditure is £4000 billion; total consumer spending (not C_d) is £36 000 billion; imports are £12 000 billion and expenditure taxes are £2000 billion. The economy is currently in equilibrium. It is estimated that an income of £50 000 billion is necessary to generate full employment. The mpw is 0.25.

(a) Is there an inflationary or deflationary gap in this situation?

(b) What is the size of the gap? (Don't confuse this with the difference between Y_e and Y_F.)

(c) What would be the appropriate government policies to close this gap?

9. The following table shows part of a country's national expenditure schedule (in £ billions).

National income (Y)	100	120	140	160	180	200	220
National expenditure (E)	115	130	145	160	175	190	205

    (a) What is the government expenditure multiplier?
    Assume that full employment is achieved at a level of national income of £200 billion.
    (b) Is there an inflationary or a deflationary gap, and what is its size?
    (c) By how much would government expenditure have to be changed in order to close this gap (assuming no shift in other injections or withdrawals)?

10. In what way will the nature of aggregate supply influence the effect of a change in aggregate demand on prices and real national income?

11. Why does investment in construction and producer goods industries tend to fluctuate more than investment in retailing and the service industries?

12. How can the interaction of the multiplier and accelerator explain cyclical fluctuations in national income?

13. Why is it difficult to predict the size of the multiplier and accelerator?

14. Assume that there is a trade-off between unemployment and inflation, traced out by a 'Phillips curve'. What could cause a leftward shift in this curve?

15. How does the size of (a) the budget deficit and (b) the national debt vary with the course of the trade cycle?

16. How would the withdrawals curve shift in each of the following cases? (a) A reduction in the basic rate of tax. (b) An increase in personal allowances.

17. Under what circumstances is a rise in taxes likely to have a disincentive effect?

18. What factors determine the effectiveness of discretionary fiscal policy?

19. Give some examples of changes in one injection or withdrawal that can affect others.

20. Why is it difficult to use fiscal policy to 'fine tune' the economy?

chapter nine

Money and monetary policy

I n this chapter we are going to look at the special role that money plays in the economy. Changes in the amount of money can have a powerful effect on all the major macroeconomic indicators, such as inflation, unemployment, economic growth, interest rates, exchange rates and the balance of payments.

But why do changes in the money supply affect the economy? The answer is that the supply of money and the demand for money between them determine the *rate of interest*, and this has a crucial impact on aggregate demand and the performance of the economy generally.

First we define what is meant by money (not as easy as it may seem), and examine its functions. Then in sections 9.2 and 9.3 we look at the operation of the financial sector of the economy and its role in determining the supply of money.

We then turn to look at the demand for money. Here we are not asking how much money people would like. The answer to that would probably be 'as much as possible'! What we are asking is: how much of people's assets do they want to hold in the form of money?

Then, in section 9.5, we put supply and demand together to show how interest rates are determined. Finally, we examine how money supply and interest rates are controlled by the authorities and the effect this has on the economy. In other words, we examine monetary policy: how it operates and how effective it is.

The meaning and functions of money

What is this thing called 'money'?

Before going any further we must define precisely what we mean by 'money'. Money is more than just notes and coin. It includes a number of other items as well. In fact, the main component of a country's money supply is not cash, but deposits in banks and other financial institutions. Only a very small proportion of these deposits are kept by the banks in their safes or tills in the form of cash. The bulk of the deposits appear merely as bookkeeping entries in the banks' accounts.

This may sound very worrying. Will a bank have enough cash to meet its customers' demands? The answer is yes. Only a small fraction of a bank's total deposits will be withdrawn at any one time, and banks always make sure that they have the ability to meet their customers' demands. The chances of banks running out of cash are practically nil. What is more, the bulk of all but very small transactions are not conducted in cash at all. With the use of cheques, credit cards and debit cards, most money is simply transferred from the purchaser's to the seller's bank account without the need for first withdrawing it in cash.

What items should be included in the definition of money? To answer this we need to identify the *functions* of money.

The functions of money

The main purpose of money is for buying and selling goods, services and assets: i.e. as a medium of exchange. It also has three other important functions. Let us examine each in turn.

A medium of exchange

In a subsistence economy where individuals make their own clothes, grow their own food, provide their own entertainments, etc., people do not need money. If people want to exchange any goods, they will do so by barter. In other words, they will do swaps with other people.

The complexity of a modern developed economy, however, makes barter totally impractical for most purposes. Someone else may have something you want, but there is no guarantee that they will want what you have to offer them in return. What is more, under a system of capitalism, where people are employed by others to do a specialist task, it would be totally impractical for people to be paid in food, clothes, cars, electrical goods, etc. What is necessary is a medium of exchange which is generally acceptable as a means of payment for goods and services and as a means of payment for labour and other factor services. 'Money' is any such medium.

Money may be in the form of some physical item that is actually handed from one person to another: for example, gold, silver, other coin, banknotes, or even something like cigarettes (used as money in prisoner of war camps in the Second World War). To be a suitable physical means of exchange, money must be light enough to carry around, must come in a number of denominations, large and small, and must not be easy to forge. Alternatively, money must be in a

Definition

Medium of exchange
Something that is acceptable in exchange for goods and services.

form that enables it to be transferred *indirectly* through some acceptable mechanism. For example, money in the form of bookkeeping entries in bank accounts can be transferred from one account to another by the use of such mechanisms as cheques, debit cards, standing orders and direct debits.

A means of storing wealth

Individuals and businesses need a means whereby income earned *today* can be used to purchase goods and services in the *future*. People need to be able to store their wealth: they want a means of saving. Money is one such medium in which to hold wealth. It can be saved.

A means of evaluation

Money is the unit used to value goods, services and assets. It allows the value of one good to be compared with another. In other words, the value of goods is expressed in terms of prices, and prices are expressed in money terms.

It also allows dissimilar things to be added up. Thus a person's wealth or a company's assets can best be expressed in money terms. Similarly, a country's national income is expressed in money terms.

A means of establishing the value of future claims and payments

People often want to agree *today* the price of some *future* payment. For example, workers and managers will want to agree the wage rate for the coming year. Firms will want to sign contracts with their suppliers specifying the price of raw materials and other supplies. The use of money prices is the most convenient means of measuring future claims.

What should count as money?

What items, then, should be included in the definition of money? Unfortunately, there is no sharp borderline between money and non-money.

Cash (notes and coin) obviously counts as money. It readily meets all the functions of money. Goods (fridges, cars and cabbages) do not count as money. But what about various financial assets such as bank and building society accounts, bonds and shares? Do they count as money? The answer is 'It depends': it depends on how narrowly money is defined.

Countries thus use several different measures of money supply. All include cash, but they vary according to what additional items are included. In order to understand their significance and the ways in which money supply can be controlled, it is first necessary to look at the various types of account in which money can be held and at the various financial institutions involved.

Summary

1. Money's main function is as a medium of exchange. In addition, it is a means of storing wealth, a means of evaluation and a means of establishing the value of future claims and payments.
2. What counts as money depends on how narrowly it is defined. All definitions include cash, but they vary according to what other financial assets are included.

The financial system in the UK

Where do banks and other financial institutions fit in?

In order to understand the role of the financial sector in determining the supply of money, it is important to distinguish different types of financial institution. Each type has a distinct part to play in determining the size of the money supply.

The key role of banks in the monetary system

By far the largest element of money supply is bank deposits. It is not surprising then that banks play an absolutely crucial role in the monetary system.

The most important of the banks in the UK for the functioning of the economy and for the implementation of monetary policy are the *retail banks*. These are the familiar high street banks, such as Barclays, Lloyds, Midland and National Westminster, and ex-building societies such as the Abbey National, Halifax and Woolwich. They specialise in providing branch banking facilities to members of the general public, but they do also lend to business, albeit often on a short-term basis. Their business is in retail deposits and loans. These are deposits and loans made through their branch network at published rates of interest. The branches are like 'retail outlets' for banking services.

The other major category of banks are the *investment banks*. These include *merchant banks* such as Kleinwort Benson, Morgan Grenfell, Rothschild and Hambro. They often act as 'brokers', arranging loans for companies from a number of different sources. They also offer financial advice to industry and provide assistance to firms in raising new capital through the issue of new shares. Investment banks also include many overseas banks, especially Japanese and American. These have expanded their business in the UK enormously in recent years, especially since the abolition of foreign exchange controls in 1979. Their major specialism is the finance of international trade and capital movements, and they deal extensively in the foreign exchange market. Most of their deposits are in foreign currencies.

Investment banks are also known as *wholesale* banks because they specialise in receiving large deposits from and making large loans to industry and other financial institutions: these are known as wholesale deposits and loans. These may be for short periods of time to account for the non-matching of the firm's payments and receipts from its business. They may be for longer periods of time, for various investment purposes. These wholesale deposits and loans are very large sums of money. Banks thus compete against each other for them and negotiate individual terms with the firm to suit the firm's particular requirements. The rates of interest negotiated will reflect the current market rates of interest and the terms of the particular loan/deposit. Very large loans to firms are often divided ('syndicated') between several banks.

Banks are in the business of deposit taking and lending. To understand this, we must distinguish between banks' liabilities and assets. The total liabilities and assets for the UK banks are set out in a balance sheet in Table 9.1.

Definitions

Retail deposits and loans
Deposits and loans made through bank/building society branches at published interest rates.

Wholesale deposits and loans
Large-scale deposits and loans made by and to firms at negotiated interest rates.

TABLE 9.1 *Balance sheet of UK banks: May 1997*

Sterling liabilities	£bn	%	Sterling assets	£bn	%
Sight deposits		(30.0)	Notes and coin	4.8	(0.5)
UK banks	34.0				
UK public sector	3.0		Balances with Bank of England		(0.2)
UK private sector	232.5		Operational deposits	0.2	
Overseas	17.3		Cash ratio deposits	2.1	
			Market loans		(25.7)
Time deposits		(42.2)	UK banks	129.5	
UK banks	103.2		UK banks CDs	49.9	
UK public sector	6.9		Building society CDs etc.	5.4	
UK private sector	226.8		UK local authorities	1.1	
Overseas	67.6		Overseas	60.1	
			Bills of exchange		(1.8)
			Treasury bills	1.7	
			Local authority bills	0.0	
Certificates of			Commercial bills	15.4	
deposit, etc.	100.6	(10.5)	Sale and repurchase	56.5	(5.9)
			agreements		
Sale and repurchase	55.4	(5.8)	Investments		(8.4)
agreements			Public sector	19.2	
			Building societies	4.1	
Items in suspense			Other	57.1	
and transmission	11.6	(1.2)	Advances		(53.9)
			UK public sector	2.9	
			UK private sector	496.2	
Capital and other			Overseas	16.7	
funds	95.4	(10.0)	Miscellaneous	33.8	(3.5)
Notes outstanding	2.5	(0.3)			
Total sterling	956.9	(100.0)	**Total sterling assets**	956.7	(100.0)
liabilities (Of which:					
Eligible liabilities)	(615.0)	(64.3)			
Liabilities in other			Assets in other		
currencies	1135.3		currencies	1135.5	
Total liabilities	2092.2		Total assets	2092.2	

Source: *Financial Statistics* (ONS).

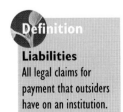

Definition

Liabilities
All legal claims for payment that outsiders have on an institution.

Liabilities

Customers' deposits in banks (and other deposit-taking institutions such as building societies) are **liabilities** to these institutions. This means simply that the customers have the claim on these deposits and thus the institutions are liable to meet the claims.

There are four major types of deposit: sight deposits, time deposits, certificates of deposit and 'repos'.

Sight deposits. Sight deposits are any deposits that can be withdrawn on demand by the depositor without penalty. In the past, sight accounts did not pay interest. Today, however, there are some sight accounts that do.

The most familiar form of sight deposits is current accounts at banks. Depositors are issued with cheque books and/or debit cards (e.g. Switch or Connect) which enable them to spend the money directly without first having to go to the bank and draw the money out in cash. In the case of debit cards, the person's account is electronically debited when the purchase is made and the card is 'swiped' across the machine. This process is known as EFTPOS (electronic funds transfer at point of sale).

An important feature of current accounts is that banks often allow customers to be overdrawn. That is, they can draw on their account and make payments to other people in excess of the amount of money they have deposited. This facility is a crucial ingredient in the process whereby the money supply expands. If person A is given an overdraft and then draws a cheque on the account and pays it to person B, person B's bank account has been credited and he or she can draw this money even though person A never deposited the money in the first place.

Sight deposits account for around 30 per cent of a bank's liabilities.

Time deposits. Time deposits require notice of withdrawal. However, they normally pay a higher rate of interest than sight accounts. With some types of account a depositor can withdraw a certain amount of money on demand, but there will be a penalty of so many days' lost interest. They are not cheque-book or debit-card accounts. The most familiar form of time deposits is the deposit and savings accounts in banks and the various savings accounts in building societies. No overdraft facilities exist with time deposits.

Certificates of deposit. Certificates of deposit (CDs) are certificates issued by banks to customers (usually firms) for large deposits of a fixed term (e.g. £100 000 for 18 months). They can be sold by one customer to another, and thus provide a means whereby the holders can get money quickly if they need it, without the banks which have issued the CD having to supply the money. (This makes them relatively 'liquid' to the depositor, but 'illiquid' to the bank: see below.) The use of CDs has grown rapidly in recent years. Their use by firms has meant that, at a wholesale level, sight accounts have become *less* popular.

Sale and repurchase agreements ('repos'). If banks have a temporary shortage of funds, they can sell some of their financial assets to other banks or to the Bank of England (see below), and later repurchase them on some agreed date, often about a fortnight later. These sale and repurchase agreements (repos) are in effect a form of loan, the bank borrowing for a period of time using some of its financial assets as the security for the loan. The most usual assets to use in this way are government bonds, normally called 'gilt-edged securities' or simply 'gilts' (see below). Sale and repurchase agreements involving gilts are known as *gilt repos*. As we shall see, gilt repos play a vital role in the operation of monetary policy.

Definitions

Sight deposits
Deposits that can be withdrawn on demand without penalty.

Time deposits
Deposits that require notice of withdrawal or where a penalty is charged for withdrawals on demand.

Certificates of deposit
Certificates issued by banks for fixed-term interest-bearing deposits. They can be resold by the owner to another party.

Sale and repurchase agreements (repos)
An agreement between two financial institutions whereby one in effect borrows from another by selling its assets, agreeing to buy them back (repurchase them) at a fixed price and on a fixed date.

Assets

Banks' financial **assets** are its claims on others. There are three main categories of assets.

Cash and balances in the Bank of England. Banks and certain other financial institutions, such as building societies, need to hold a certain amount of their assets as notes and coin. This is largely used as 'till money' to meet the day-to-day demands by customers for cash. They also keep 'operational balances' in the Bank of England. These are like the banks' own current accounts and are used for clearing purposes (i.e. for settling the day-to-day payments between the banks). They can be withdrawn in cash on demand.

Cash and balances in the Bank of England, however, earn no interest for banks. The vast majority of banks' assets are therefore in the form of various types of loan – to individuals and firms, to other financial institutions and to the government. These are 'assets' since they represent claims that the banks have on other people. Loans can be grouped into two types: short and long term.

Short-term loans. These are in the form of *market loans, bills of exchange* or *repos*.

- **Market loans** are made primarily to other financial institutions, such as discount houses (see below) or other banks. They consist of (a) money lent 'at call' (i.e. reclaimable on demand or at 24 hours' notice) and (b) money lent 'at short notice' (i.e. money lent for a few days).
- **Bills of exchange** are loans either to companies (commercial bills) or to the government (Treasury bills). These are, in effect, an IOU, with the company issuing them (in the case of commercial bills) or the Bank of England (in the case of Treasury bills) promising to pay the holder a specified sum on a particular date. Since bills do not pay interest, they are sold below their face value (at a 'discount') in order to enable the purchaser to earn a return.
- When a sale and repurchase agreement is made, the financial institution *making* the loan will temporarily acquire assets (e.g. gilts) in return.

Longer-term loans. These consist primarily of loans to customers, both personal customers and businesses. These loans, also known as *advances*, are of three main types: fixed-term (repayable in instalments over a set number of years – typically six months to five years), overdrafts (often for an unspecified term) and mortgages (typically for 25 years).

Banks also make *investments*. These are partly in gilts which are effectively loans to the government. The government sells bonds, which then pay a fixed sum each year as interest. Once issued, they can then be bought and sold on the stock exchange. Banks are normally only prepared to buy gilts that have less than five years to maturity (the date when the government redeems them). Banks also invest in various subsidiary financial institutions and in building societies.

Liquidity and profitability

As we have seen, banks keep a range of liabilities and assets. The balance of items in this range is influenced by two important considerations: profitability and liquidity.

Definitions

Assets
Possessions, or claims held on others.

Market loans
Short-term loans: e.g. money at call and short notice.

Bill of exchange
A certificate promising to repay a stated amount on a certain date, typically three months from the issue of the bill. Bills pay no interest as such, but are sold at a discount and redeemed at face value, thereby earning a rate of discount for the purchaser.

Profitability. Profits are made by lending money out at a higher rate of interest than that paid to depositors.

Liquidity. The liquidity of an asset is the ease with which it can be converted into cash without loss. Cash itself, by definition, is perfectly liquid.

Some assets, such as money lent at call to other financial institutions, are highly liquid. Although not actually cash, these assets can be converted into cash on demand with no financial penalty. Other assets, however, are much less liquid. Personal loans to the general public or mortgages for house purchase can only be redeemed by the bank as each instalment is paid. Other advances for fixed periods are only repaid at the end of that period.

Financial institutions must maintain sufficient liquidity in their assets to meet the demands of depositors.

Profitability is the major aim of banks and most other financial institutions. However, the aims of profitability and liquidity tend to conflict. In general, the more liquid an asset, the less profitable it is, and vice versa. Personal and business loans to customers are profitable to banks, but highly illiquid. Cash is totally liquid, but earns no profit.

Thus financial institutions like to hold a range of assets with varying degrees of liquidity and profitability.

The ratio of an institution's liquid assets to total assets is known as its liquidity ratio. For example, if a bank had £100 million of assets, of which £10 million were liquid and £90 million were illiquid, the bank would have a 10 per cent liquidity ratio. If a financial institution's liquidity ratio is too high, it will make too little profit. If the ratio is too low, there will be the risk that customers' demands may not be able to be met: this would cause a crisis of confidence and possible closure. Institutions thus have to make a judgement as to what liquidity ratio is best – one that is neither too high nor too low.

The Bank of England

The Bank of England is the UK's central bank. All countries have a central bank and they fulfil two vital roles in the economy.

The first is to oversee the whole monetary system and ensure that banks and other financial institutions operate as stably and as efficiently as possible.

The second is to act as the government's agent, both as its banker and in carrying out monetary policy. The Bank of England has traditionally worked in very close liaison with the Treasury, and there used to be regular meetings between the Governor of the Bank of England and the Chancellor of the Exchequer. Although the Bank may have disagreed with Treasury policy, it always carried it out. With the election of the Labour government in 1997, however, the Bank of England was given independence to decide the course of monetary policy. In particular, this meant that the Bank of England and not the government would now decide interest rates.

The degree of independence of central banks from government varies considerably from country to country (see Box 9.4). Germany's central bank, the Bundesbank, for example, has always been fiercely independent of the government. At the other extreme, the central banks of Australia, New

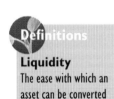

Definitions

Liquidity
The ease with which an asset can be converted into cash without loss.

Liquidity ratio
The proportion of a bank's total assets held in liquid form.

Zealand and Spain have been much more part of the whole government machinery.

As many countries in the EU prepare for a single European currency, one of the implications is that there will have to be a single European central bank responsible for managing the European currency (the Euro) and for setting interest rates. If the UK joins the single currency, this will mean a greatly reduced role for the Bank of England.

At present, within its two broad roles, the Bank of England has a number of different functions.

It issues notes

The Bank of England is the sole issuer of banknotes in England and Wales (in Scotland and Northern Ireland, retail banks issue banknotes). The amount of banknotes issued by the Bank of England depends largely on the demand for notes from the general public. If people draw more cash from their bank accounts, the banks will have to draw more cash from their balances in the Bank of England.

It acts as a bank

To the government. It keeps the two major government accounts: 'The Exchequer' and the 'National Loans Fund'. Taxation and government spending pass through the Exchequer. Government borrowing and lending pass through the National Loans Fund. The government tends to keep its deposits in the Bank of England to a minimum. If the deposits begin to build up (from taxation), the government will probably spend it on paying back government debt. If, on the other hand, it runs short of money, it will simply borrow more.

To the recognised banks. All recognised banks hold operational balances in the Bank of England. As we have seen, these are used for clearing purposes between the banks and to provide them with a source of liquidity.

To overseas central banks. These are deposits of sterling held by overseas authorities as part of their official reserves and/or for purposes of intervening in the foreign exchange market in order to influence the exchange rate of their currency.

It manages the government's borrowing programme

Whenever the government runs a budget deficit (i.e. spends more than it receives in tax revenue), it will have to finance that deficit by borrowing. It can borrow by issuing bonds (gilts), National Savings certificates or Treasury bills. The Bank of England organises this borrowing. Even when the government runs a budget surplus, the Bank of England will still have to manage the national debt (the accumulated borrowing from the past). The reason is that old bonds will be maturing and new issues of bonds will probably be necessary to replace them.

It supervises the activities of banks and other financial institutions

It advises banks on good banking practice. It discusses government policy with them and reports back to the government. It requires all recognised

Definition

Recognised banks
Banks licensed by the Bank of England. All financial institutions using the word 'bank' in their title have to be recognised by the Bank of England. This requires them to have paid-up capital of at least £5 million and to meet other requirements about their asset structure and range of services.

banks to maintain adequate liquidity: this is called prudential control. Since May 1997, the Bank of England has ceased to be responsible for the detailed supervision of banks' activities. This responsibility has passed to the Securities and Investment Board.

It provides liquidity, as necessary, to banks

It ensures that there is always an adequate supply of liquidity to meet the legitimate demands of depositors in recognised banks. As we shall see below, it does this through the discount and gilt repo markets.

It operates the government's monetary and exchange rate policy

Monetary policy. By careful management of the issue and repurchasing of gilts and Treasury bills, the Bank of England can thereby manipulate interest rates and influence the size of the money supply. This is explained in section 9.6.

Exchange rate policy. The Bank of England manages the country's gold and foreign currency reserves. This is done through the exchange equalisation account. As we shall see in Chapter 12, by buying and selling foreign currencies on the foreign exchange market, the Bank of England can affect the exchange rate.

The role of the London money market

It is through the London money market that the Bank of England exercises its control of the economy. The market deals in short-term lending and borrowing. It is normally divided into the 'discount' and 'repo' markets and the 'parallel' or 'complementary' markets.

The discount and repo markets

Traditionally this was simply the *discount market*. One of the main groups of institutions operating in this market are the discount houses. These specialise in borrowing and lending for very short periods of time. They lend money short-term to the government (through the Bank of England) and to firms by buying bills of exchange. To do this they obtain money from the banks by borrowing money at call and short notice and by selling them bills.

If the banks were short of liquid assets, they would call in money from the discount houses. But then the discount houses in turn would probably be short of liquid assets to meet this demand. What could they do?

In such circumstances, the Bank of England would always step in and lend to the discount houses or purchase bills of exchange from them before the bills had reached maturity. This process of purchasing bills by the Bank of England is known as rediscounting.

Since March 1997, the Bank of England has been willing to provide liquidity *directly* to banks and other financial institutions. The main way in which it does this is through *gilt repos*. How does the process work?

Assume that banks are short of liquidity. They make a repo agreement with the Bank of England, whereby the Bank of England buys gilts from the banks (thereby supplying them with money) on the condition that the banks buy the gilts back at a fixed price and on a fixed date, typically two weeks later.

Definitions

Prudential control
The insistence by the Bank of England that recognised banks maintain adequate liquidity.

Exchange equalisation account
The gold and foreign exchange reserves account in the Bank of England.

Discount houses
Institutions in London specialising in borrowing and lending for very short periods of time. They borrow primarily from banks and lend primarily through buying bills of exchange (at a discount).

Rediscounting bills of exchange
Buying bills before they reach maturity.

The repurchase price will be above the sale price. The difference is the equivalent of the interest that the banks are being charged for having what amounts to a loan from the Bank of England. The repurchase price (and hence the 'repo rate') will be set by the Bank of England ro reflect its chosen rate of interest.

In being prepared to rediscount bills or provide money through gilt repos, the Bank of England is thus the ultimate guarantor of sufficient liquidity in the monetary system and is known as **lender of last resort**.

The need for banks to acquire liquidity in this way is not uncommon: the 'last resort' occurs on most days! It is generally a deliberate policy of the Bank of England to create a shortage of liquidity in the economy to force banks to obtain liquidity from it. But why should the Bank of England do this? It does it as a means of controlling interest rates. If the banks are forced to obtain liquidity from the Bank of England, they will be borrowing at the Bank of England's *chosen rate* (i.e. the repo rate). The banks will then have to gear their other rates to it, and other institutions will gear their rates to those of the banks.

The way in which the Bank of England creates a shortage of liquidity and the way in which it forces through changes in interest rates are examined in section 9.6 and Box 9.2.

The parallel money markets

The parallel money markets include the following:

- The inter-bank market (wholesale loans from one bank to another from one day to up to several months).
- The market for certificates of deposit.
- The inter-companies deposit market (short-term loans from one company to another arranged through the market).
- The foreign currencies market (dealings in foreign currencies deposited short term in London).
- The finance house market (short-term borrowing to finance hire purchase).
- The building society market (wholesale borrowing by the building societies).
- The commercial paper market (borrowing in sterling by companies, banks and other financial institutions by the issue of short-term (less than one year) 'promissory notes'. These, like bills of exchange, are sold at a discount and redeemed at their face value.)

The parallel markets have grown in size and importance in recent years. The main reasons for this have been (a) the opening-up of markets to international dealing, given the abolition of exchange controls in 1979, (b) the deregulation of banking and money market dealing and (c) the volatility of interest rates and exchange rates, and thus the desire of banks to keep funds in a form that can be readily switched from one form of deposit to another, or from one currency to another. The main areas of growth have been in inter-bank deposits, certificates of deposit and the foreign currency markets.

Although the Bank of England does not deal directly in the parallel markets and does not provide 'last resort' lending facilities, it nevertheless closely monitors the various money market rates of interest and, if necessary, seeks to influence them, through its dealings in the discount and repo markets.

Definition

Lender of last resort
The role of the Bank of England as the guarantor of sufficient liquidity in the monetary system.

Summary

1. Banks' liabilities include both sight and time deposits. They also include certificates of deposit and repos. Their assets include: notes and coin, balances with the Bank of England, market loans (including money at call with the discount houses), bills of exchange (Treasury and commercial), advances to customers (the biggest item, including overdrafts, personal loans and mortgages) and investments (government bonds and inter-bank investments).

2. Banks aim to make profits, but they must also maintain sufficient liquidity. Liquid assets, however, tend to be relatively unprofitable, and profitable assets tend to be relatively illiquid. Banks therefore need to keep a balance of profitability and liquidity in their range of assets.

3. The Bank of England is the UK's central bank. It issues notes; it acts as banker to the government, to the commercial banks, to various overseas central banks and to certain private customers; it manages the government's borrowing programme; it provides support to prevent banks getting into difficulties; it operates monetary and exchange rate policy.

4. The money market is the market in short-term deposits and loans. It consists of the discount and repo markets and the parallel money markets.

5. The discount market centres on the activities of the discount houses, which buy bills (at a discount) from the government and firms. The repo market has grown rapidly in recent years. Repos are a means whereby banks obtain liquidity for short periods of time, by selling gilts or other securities, on the condition that they repurchase them on an agreed date in the near future. The Bank of England operates in these two markets. By buying (rediscounting) bills and through gilt repos, it provides liquidity to the banks. In the last resort it is always prepared to lend in this way in order to ensure adequate liquidity in the economy.

6. The parallel money markets consist of various markets in short-term finance between various financial institutions.

9.3 The supply of money

How is it measured and what determines its size?

If money supply is to be monitored and possibly controlled, it is obviously necessary to measure it. But what should be included in the measure? Here we need to distinguish between the *monetary base* and *broad money*.

The **monetary base** (or 'high-powered money') consists of cash (notes and coin) in circulation outside the central bank. It is sometimes referred to as the 'narrow monetary base' to distinguish it from the wide monetary base, which also includes banks' balances with the central bank. In the UK, the **wide monetary base** is known as *M0*.

Definition

Monetary base
Notes and coin outside the central bank.

TABLE 9.2 *Banks' original balance sheet*

Liabilities	£bn	Assets	£bn
Deposits	100	Balances with the B. of E.	10
		Advances	90
Total	100	Total	100

But the monetary base gives us a very poor indication of the effective money supply, since it excludes the most important source of liquidity for spending: namely, bank deposits. The problem is which deposits to include. There are three questions we need to answer:

- Should we include just sight deposits, or time deposits as well?
- Should we include just retail deposits, or wholesale deposits as well?
- Should we include just bank deposits, or building society deposits as well?

In the past there has been a whole range of measures, each including different combinations of these accounts. However, financial deregulation, the abolition of foreign exchange controls and the development of computer technology have led to huge changes in the financial sector throughout the world. This has led to a blurring of the distinctions between different types of account. It has also made it very easy to switch deposits from one type of account to another. For these reasons, the most usual measure that countries use for money supply is **broad money**, which in most cases includes both time and sight deposits, retail and wholesale deposits, and bank and building society (savings institutions) deposits.

In the UK, this measure of broad money is known as *M4*. In most other European countries and the USA, it is known as *M3*. There are, however, minor differences between countries in what is included.

As we have seen, bank deposits of one form or another constitute by far the largest component of (broad) money supply. To understand how money supply expands and contracts, and how it can be controlled, it is thus necessary to understand what determines the size of bank deposits. Banks can themselves expand the amount of bank deposits, and hence the money supply, by a process known as 'credit creation'.

The creation of credit

To illustrate this process in its simplest form, assume that banks have just one type of liability – deposits – and two types of asset – balances with the Bank of England (to achieve liquidity) and advances to customers (to earn profit).

Banks want to achieve profitability while maintaining sufficient liquidity. Assume that they believe that sufficient liquidity will be achieved if 10 per cent of their assets are held as balances with the Bank of England. The remaining 90 per cent will then be in advances to customers. In other words, the banks operate a 10 per cent liquidity ratio.

Assume initially that the combined balance sheet of the banks is as shown in Table 9.2. Total deposits are £100 billion, of which £10 billion (10

Definitions

Wide monetary base (*M0*)
Notes and coin outside the central bank plus banks' operational deposits with the central bank.

Broad money
Cash in circulation plus retail and wholesale bank and building society deposits.

BOX 9.1 *UK monetary aggregates*
··
How long is a piece of string?

In the recent past, measures of 'money supply' in the UK have included M0, non-interest-bearing M1, M1, M2, M3, M3H, M3c, M4, M4c, M5. This confusing array of measures reflected the many different types of deposit that might be considered to be part of money.

In the 1980s the business of banks and building societies became more and more similar, as banks increasingly became a source of mortgages, and building societies offered cheque-book accounts and cash machines. Those measures of money supply, that included bank deposits, but not building society deposits (M1 and M3), therefore ceased to provide a useful measure of liquidity in the economy. They were dropped as official measures in 1989 when the Abbey National Building Society changed its status to a bank, thereby increasing M1 and M3 at a stroke!

Today, there are just four official measures: M0, M2, M4 and M3H. The government regards M0 and M4 as the most important. M0 is referred to as the 'wide monetary base' and M4 is referred to as 'broad money' or simply as 'the money supply'. The definitions of these four aggregates are as follows:

M0. Cash in circulation with the public and held by banks and building societies, plus banks' operational balances with the Bank of England.

M2. Cash in circulation with the public (but not in banks and building societies), plus private-sector *retail* sterling deposits in banks and building societies. (This measure was designed to give an indicator of the amount of money available for transactions purposes.)

M4. M2 plus private-sector *wholesale* sterling deposits in banks and building societies, plus sterling certificates of deposit.

M3H. M4 plus private-sector foreign currency deposits in banks and building societies (in the UK), plus public corporations' sterling and foreign currency deposits in UK banks and building societies. (This measure of broad money is that adopted by the EU to allow comparisons between member countries.)

per cent) are kept in balances with the Bank of England. The remaining £90 billion (90 per cent) are lent to customers.

Now assume that the government spends more money – £10 billion, say, on roads or the National Health Service. It pays for this with cheques drawn on its account with the Bank of England. The people receiving the cheques deposit them in their banks. Banks return these cheques to the Bank of England and their balances correspondingly increase by £10 billion. The combined banks' balance sheet now is shown in Table 9.3.

But this is not the end of the story. Banks now have surplus liquidity. With their balances in the Bank of England having increased to £20 billion, they now have a liquidity ratio of 20/110. If they are to return to a 10 per cent liquidity ratio, they need only retain £11 billion as balances at the Bank of England (£11 billion/£110 billion = 10 per cent). The remaining £9 billion they can lend to customers.

When customers spend this £9 billion in shops, etc., and the shopkeepers deposit the cheques back in the banks, these new deposits of £9 billion in

The table gives the figures for all these aggregates for March 1997.

UK monetary aggregates, end March 1997

	£ million
Cash outside Bank of England	24 609
+ Banks' operational deposits with Bank of England	167
= M0	**24 776**
Cash outside banks (i.e. in circulation with the public and non-bank firms)	20 699
+ Private-sector retail bank and building society deposits	450 230
= M2	**470 929**
+ Private-sector wholesale bank and building society deposits + CDs	239 849
= M4	**710 778**

Source: *Financial Statistics* (ONS).

M5 was M4 plus various other holdings of liquid assets, such as bills of exchange. It was designed to give a broad measure of liquidity in the economy. The problem was that the list of liquid assets included in it was felt to be too arbitrary to give a true indication of general liquidity in the economy. As a result it is no longer published. Instead, figures for 'liquid assets outside M4' are published in official statistics.

 Q1 Why would the inclusion in any of the definitions of money deposited at call with the discount houses be a case of double counting?

 Q2 Why is cash in banks and building societies included in M0, but not in the other measures?

the shopkeepers' accounts can thus be used as the basis for *further* loans. 10 per cent (i.e. £0.9 billion) must be kept back in the Bank of England, but the remaining 90 per cent (i.e. £8.1 billion) can be lent out again. When this is deposited back in banks, again 10 per cent must be retained and the remaining 90 per cent can be lent out. This process goes on and on until eventually the position is as shown in Table 9.4.

TABLE 9.3 *The initial effect of an additional deposit of £10 billion*

Liabilities	£bn	Assets	£bn
Deposits (old)	100	Balances with the B. of E. (old)	10
Deposits (new)	10	Balances with the B. of E. (new)	10
		Advances	90
Total	110	Total	110

TABLE 9.4 *The full effect of an additional deposit of £10 billion*

Liabilities	£bn	Assets	£bn
Deposits (old)	100	Balances with the B. of E. (old)	10
Deposits (new: initial)	10	Balances with the B. of E. (new)	10
(new: subsequent)	90	Advances (old)	90
		Advances (new)	90
Total	200	Total	200

The initial increase in balances with the Bank of England of £10 billion has allowed banks to create new advances (and hence deposits) of £90 billion, making a total increase in money supply of £100 billion.

This effect is known as the **bank (or deposits) multiplier**. In this simple example, with a liquidity ratio of $1/10$ (i.e. 10 per cent), the deposits multiplier is 10. An initial increase in deposits of £10 billion allowed total deposits to rise by £100 billion. In this simple world, therefore, the deposits multiplier is the inverse of the liquidity ratio (L).

$$\text{Deposits multiplier} = 1/_L$$

The creation of credit: the real world

In practice, the creation of credit is not as simple as this. There are three major complications.

Banks' liquidity ratio may vary

Banks may choose a different liquidity ratio. At certain times, banks may decide that it is prudent to hold a larger proportion of liquid assets. If Christmas or the summer holidays are approaching and people are likely to make bigger cash withdrawals, banks may decide to hold more liquid assets. They may also do so if they anticipate that their liquid assets may soon be squeezed by government monetary policy.

Customers may not want to take up the credit on offer. Banks may wish to make additional loans, but customers may not want to borrow. There may be insufficient demand. But will the banks not then lower their interest rates, thus encouraging people to borrow? Possibly; but if they lower the rate they charge to borrowers, they must also lower the rate they pay to depositors. But then depositors may switch to other institutions such as building societies. Thus, just because banks have acquired additional liquid assets, it does not automatically follow that they will create credit on the basis of it.

Banks may not operate a simple liquidity ratio

The fact that banks hold a number of fairly liquid assets, such as money at call, bills of exchange and short-dated bonds, makes it difficult to identify a simple liquidity ratio. If the banks use extra cash to buy such liquid assets, can they then use *these* assets as the basis for creating credit? It is largely up to banks' judgements on their overall liquidity position.

Definition

Banks (or deposits) multiplier
The number of times greater the expansion of bank deposits is than the additional liquidity in banks that causes it: $1/L$ (the inverse of the liquidity ratio).

Some of the extra cash may be withdrawn from the banks

If extra cash comes into the banking system, and as a result extra deposits are created, part of them may be held by the public as cash *outside* the banks. In other words, some of the extra cash leaks out of the banking system. This will result in an overall **money multiplier** effect that is smaller than the full deposits multiplier.

What causes money supply to rise?

The money supply might rise as a consequence of the following.

Banks choose to hold a lower liquidity ratio

If banks collectively choose to hold a lower liquidity ratio, they will have surplus liquidity. The banks have tended to choose a lower liquidity ratio over time because of the increasing use of cheques and debit-card and credit-card transactions. Surplus liquidity can be used to expand advances, which will lead to a multiplied rise in the money supply.

An important trend in recent years has been the growth in *inter-bank lending*. These wholesale loans are often short term and are thus a liquid asset to the bank making them. Short-term loans to other banks and CDs are now the two largest elements in banks' liquid assets. Being liquid, these assets may be used by a bank as the basis for expanding loans and thereby starting a chain of credit creation. But although these assets are liquid to an *individual* bank, they do not add to the liquidity of the banking system *as a whole*. Thus by using them as the basis for credit creation, the banking system is in effect operating with a lower *overall* liquidity ratio.

An inflow of funds from abroad

Sometimes the Bank of England will intervene in the foreign exchange market. If the rate of exchange is rising too rapidly, the Bank of England may well buy foreign currencies by supplying extra pounds, thereby building up the foreign currency reserves. As we shall see in Chapter 12, this extra supply of sterling on the foreign exchange market will help to lower the exchange rate. When this extra sterling is used to pay for UK exports and is then deposited back in the banks by the exporters, credit will be created on the basis of it, leading to a *multiplied* increase in money supply.

A public-sector deficit: a PSBR

The public-sector borrowing requirement is the difference between public-sector expenditure and public-sector receipts. To meet this deficit the government has to borrow money by selling interest-bearing securities (Treasury bills and gilts). In general, the bigger the PSBR, the greater will be the growth in the money supply. Just how the money supply will be affected, however, depends on who buys the securities.

Such securities could be sold to the Bank of England. In this case the Bank of England credits the government's account to the value of the securities it has purchased. When the government spends the money, it pays with cheques drawn on its account with the Bank of England. When the recipients of these cheques pay them into their bank accounts, the banks will present the cheques to the Bank of England and their balances at

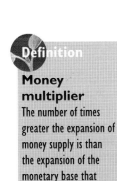

Definition

Money multiplier
The number of times greater the expansion of money supply is than the expansion of the monetary base that caused it: $\Delta M4/\Delta M0$.

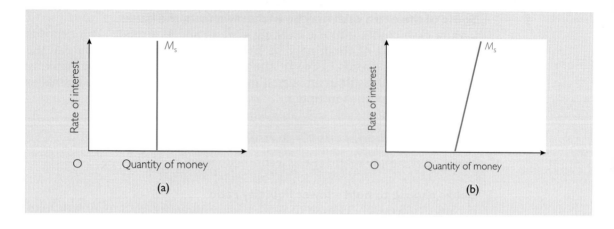

FIGURE 9.1
The supply of money curve
(a) Exogenous money supply
(b) Endogenous money supply

the Bank will be duly credited. These additional balances will then become the basis for credit creation. There will be a multiplied expansion of the money supply.

Similarly, if the government borrows through additional Treasury bills, and if these are purchased by the banking sector, there will be a multiplied expansion of the money supply. The reason is that, although banks' balances at the Bank of England will go down when the banks purchase the bills, they will go up again when the government spends the money. In addition, the banks will now have additional liquid assets (bills), which can be used as the basis for credit creation.

If, however, the government securities are purchased by the 'non-bank private sector' (i.e. the general public and non-bank firms), then the money supply will remain unchanged. When people buy the bonds or bills they will draw money from their banks. When the government spends the money it will be redeposited in banks. There is no increase in money supply. It is just a case of existing money changing hands.

The government could attempt to minimise the boost to money supply by financing the PSBR through the sale of gilts rather than Treasury bills.

The relationship between money supply and the rate of interest

Simple monetary theory often assumes that the supply of money is totally independent of interest rates. This is illustrated in Figure 9.1(a). The money supply is 'exogenous'. The supply of money is assumed to be determined by government: what the government chooses it to be, or what it allows it to be by its choice of the level and method of financing the PSBR.

Some economists, however, argue that money supply is 'endogenous', with higher interest rates leading to increases in the supply of money. This is illustrated in Figure 9.1(b). The argument is that the supply of money is responding to the demand for money. If people start borrowing more money, the resulting shortage of money in the banks will drive up interest rates. But if banks have surplus liquidity or are prepared to operate with a lower liquidity ratio, they will create extra credit in response to the increased demand and higher interest rates: money supply has expanded.

Summary

1. Money supply can be defined in a number of different ways, depending on what items are included. Except in the case of M0 (the narrowest definition in the UK) bank and building society deposits are the major proportion of money supply.
2. Bank deposits expand through a process of credit creation. If banks' liquid assets increase, they can be used as a base for increasing loans. When the loans are redeposited in banks, they form the base for yet more loans, and thus takes place a process of multiple credit expansion. The ratio of the increase of money to an expansion of the liquidity base is called the 'bank deposits multiplier'. It is the inverse of the liquidity ratio.
3. In practice, it is difficult to predict the precise amount by which money supply will expand if there is an increase in banks' liquidity. The reasons are that banks may choose to hold a different liquidity ratio; customers may not take up all the credit on offer; there may be no simple liquidity ratio, given the range of near money assets; and some of the extra cash may leak away into extra cash holdings by the general public.
4. Money supply will rise if (a) banks choose to hold a lower liquidity ratio and thus create more credit for an existing amount of liquidity; (b) there is an inflow of funds from abroad; (c) the government runs a PSBR and finances it by borrowing from the banking sector or from abroad.
5. Simple monetary theory assumes that the supply of money is independent of interest rates. In practice, a rise in demand for money and hence a rise in interest rates will often lead to an increase in money supply.

9.4 The demand for money

How much money do we want to hold at any one time?

The demand for money refers to the desire to *hold* money: to keep your wealth in the form of money, rather than spending it on goods and services or using it to purchase financial assets such as bonds or shares. It is usual to distinguish three reasons why people want to hold their assets in the form of money:

The transactions motive. Since money is a medium of exchange, it is required for conducting transactions. But since people only receive money at intervals (e.g. weekly or monthly) and not continuously, they require to hold balances of money in cash or in sight accounts.

The precautionary motive. Unforeseen circumstances can arise, such as a car breakdown. Thus individuals often hold some additional money as a precaution. Firms too keep precautionary balances because of uncertainties about the timing of their receipts and payments. If a large customer is late in making payment, a firm may be unable to pay its suppliers unless it has spare liquidity.

The speculative or assets motive. Certain firms and individuals who wish to purchase financial assets such as bonds, shares or other securities, may prefer to wait if they feel that their price is likely to fall. In the meantime they will hold idle money balances instead. This speculative demand can be quite high when the price of securities is considered certain to fall. Money when used for this purpose is a means of temporarily storing wealth.

The relationship between the demand for money and the rate of interest

The demand for money balances is called 'liquidity preference' (*L*). What determines liquidity preference and how is it related to the rate of interest?

Active balances

Money balances held for transactions and precautionary purposes are called active balances, since they are held to be used as a medium of exchange. The major determinant of active balances is the level of national income (*Y*). The bigger people's income, the more their purchases and the bigger their demand for active balances. The transactions and precautionary demands are also determined by the frequency with which individuals and businesses are paid. The less frequently they are paid, the greater the level of money balances that will be required to tide them over until the next payment. The rate of interest is another, albeit less important, determinant of active balances. At high rates of interest, people will be encouraged to risk reducing their holdings of money, and to keep their assets in a form that will earn the high interest.

Idle balances

Money balances held for speculative purposes are called idle balances. People who possess wealth, whether it be wealthy people or simply the small saver, have to decide the best form in which to hold that wealth. Do they keep it in cash or in a current account in a bank; or do they put it in some interest-bearing time account; or do they buy stocks and shares or government bonds; or do they buy some physical asset such as a car or property? The major determinant of speculative money balances is expectations of changes in the earning potential of securities and other assets. If the earning potential of an asset goes up, people will be likely to switch to that asset from others with a lower earning potential. Thus, for example, if people believe that the stock market is about to go through a period of 'boom', with share prices going up rapidly, they will switch some of their wealth into stocks and shares. Thus the greater the earning potential of non-money assets, the less will be the demand for money.

The price of assets is inversely related to interest rates. The higher the price of an asset (such as a government bond), the less will be any given interest payment as a percentage of its price (e.g. £10 as a percentage of £100 is 10 per cent, but as a percentage of £200 is only 5 per cent). Thus if the

Definitions

Active balances
Money held for transactions and precautionary purposes.

Idle balances
Money held for speculative purposes: money held in anticipation of a fall in asset prices.

FIGURE 9.2
The demand for money (liquidity preference) curve

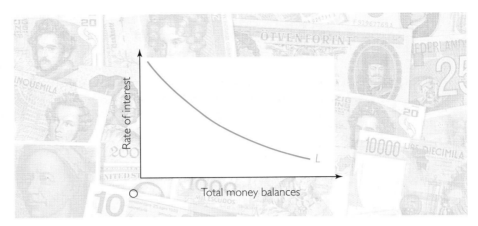

market price of securities is high, the rate of interest (i.e. the rate of return) on these securities will be low. Potential purchasers of these securities will probably wait until their prices fall and the rate of interest rises. In the meantime, therefore, large speculative balances of money will be held. If, on the other hand, the rate of interest is high, speculative demand is likely to be low. To take advantage of the high rate of return on securities, people buy them now instead of holding on to their money. Thus the speculative demand for money is inversely related to the rate of interest.

The speculative demand for money also depends on expectations about changes in the exchange rate. If businesses believe that the exchange rate is about to appreciate, they will hold idle balances of sterling in the meantime, hoping to exchange them when the rate has risen (since they will then get more foreign currency per pound).

The liquidity preference curve

The demand for money with respect to interest rates is given by a 'liquidity preference' curve. This is shown in Figure 9.2. It is downward sloping, showing that lower interest rates will encourage people to hold additional money balances (mainly for speculative purposes).

A change in interest rates is shown by a movement along the liquidity preference curve. A change in any other determinant of the demand for money (such as national income or expectations about exchange rate movements) will cause the whole curve to shift: a rightward shift representing an increase in demand; a leftward shift representing a decrease.

Summary

1. The three motives for holding money are the transactions, precautionary and speculative (or assets) motives.
2. The transactions-plus-precautionary demand for money (the demand for active balances) depends primarily on the level of national income, the frequency with which people are paid and institutional arrangements (such as the use of credit or debit cards). It also depends to some degree on the rate of interest.

3. **The speculative demand for money (the demand for idle balances) depends primarily on anticipations about future movements in security prices (and hence their rate of return) and future movements in exchange rates. If security prices are anticipated to fall or the exchange rate to rise, people will demand to hold more (domestic) money balances.**
4. **The demand for money with respect to interest rates is given by a 'liquidity preference' curve. It is downward sloping.**

9.5 Equilibrium

What effect do the demand and supply of money have on interest rates?

Equilibrium in the money market

Equilibrium in the money market will be where the demand for money (L) is equal to the supply of money (M_s). This equilibrium will be achieved through changes in the rate of interest.

In Figure 9.3 the equilibrium rate of interest is r_e and the equilibrium quantity of money is M_e. If the rate of interest were above r_e, people would have money balances surplus to their needs. They would use this to buy securities and other assets. This would drive up the price of securities and drive down the rate of interest. As the rate of interest fell, so there would be a contraction of the money supply (a movement down along the M_s curve) and an increase in the demand for money balances – especially speculative balances, since people would increasingly judge that, with lower interest rates, now was not the time to buy securities: there would be a movement down along the liquidity preference curve. The interest rate would go on falling until it reached r_e. Equilibrium would then be achieved.

Similarly, if the rate of interest were below r_e, people would have insufficient money balances. They would sell securities, thus lowering their prices and raising the rate of interest until it reached r_e.

FIGURE 9.3
Equilibrium in the money market

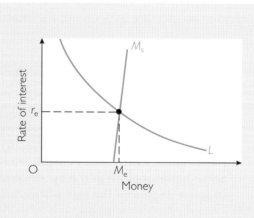

A shift in either the M_s or the L curve will lead to a new equilibrium quantity of money and rate of interest at the new intersection of the curves. For example, a rise in the quantity of money will cause the rate of interest to fall, whereas a rise in the demand for money will cause the rate of interest to rise.

Equilibrium in the foreign exchange market

Exchange rates are determined by the demand and supply of currencies. (We will examine this in detail in Chapter 12.) If the supply of sterling on the foreign exchange market (e.g. from importers to the UK wishing to buy foreign currencies in order to buy foreign goods) exceeds the demand (e.g. from foreign companies wishing to obtain sterling to buy UK exports), the exchange rate will fall ('depreciate'). For example, the pound might depreciate from $1.65 to $1.50, or from DM2.60 to DM2.40. Conversely, if the demand for sterling exceeds the supply, the exchange rate will rise ('appreciate').

Changes in the money supply will also affect the demand and supply of the currency and thus have an effect on exchange rates. Assume, for example, that the money supply increases. This has three direct effects:

- *Part* of the excess money balances will be used to purchase foreign assets. This will therefore lead to an increase in the supply of pounds coming on to the foreign exchange markets.
- The excess supply of money in the domestic money market will push down the rate of interest. This will reduce the return on UK assets below that on foreign assets. This, like the first effect, will lead to an increased demand for foreign assets and thus an increased supply of pounds on the foreign exchange market. It will also reduce the demand for UK assets by those outside the country, and thus reduce the demand for pounds.
- Speculators will anticipate that the higher supply of sterling will cause the exchange rate to depreciate. They will therefore sell sterling and buy foreign currencies now, before the depreciation takes place.

The effect of all three is to cause the exchange rate to depreciate.

The full effect of changes in the money supply

The effect of changes in the money supply on interest rates and exchange rates will in turn affect the level of economic activity in the economy. Assume that there is a rise in money supply. The sequence of events is as follows:

- A rise in money supply will lead to a fall in the rate of interest: this is necessary to restore equilibrium in the money market.
- The fall in the rate of interest will lead to a rise in investment and other forms of borrowing. (Since borrowing money will be cheaper, investment will cost less.)
- The fall in the domestic rate of interest and the resulting outflow of money from the country, plus the increased demand for foreign assets

resulting from the increased money supply, will cause the exchange rate to depreciate.
- The fall in the exchange rate will cause an increased demand for exports and a decreased demand for imports.
- The rise in investment and exports will mean increased injections into the circular flow of income (see section 7.2), and the fall in imports will mean reduced withdrawals from it. The effect will be a rise in aggregate demand and a resulting rise in national income and output, and possibly a rise in inflation too.

Summary

1. Equilibrium in the money market is where the supply of money is equal to the demand. Equilibrium is achieved through changes in the interest rate and the exchange rate.
2. The interest rate mechanism works as follows: a rise in money supply causes money supply to exceed money demand; interest rates fall; this causes investment to rise; this causes a multiplied rise in national income.
3. The exchange rate mechanism works as follows: a rise in money supply causes interest rates to fall; the rise in money supply plus the fall in interest rates causes an increased supply of domestic currency to come on to the foreign exchange market; this causes the exchange rate to depreciate; this will cause increased exports and reduced imports and hence a multiplied rise in national income.

9.6 Monetary policy

How can the government control the supply of money and interest rates?

Control of the money supply over the medium and long term

One of the major sources of monetary growth is government borrowing. If the government wishes to prevent excessive growth in the money supply over the longer term, therefore, it will have to be careful not to have an excessively high PSBR.

The precise effect of government borrowing on the money supply will depend on how the PSBR is financed. If it is financed by borrowing from the Bank of England or by the sale of Treasury bills to the banking sector, the money supply will increase. If, however, it is financed by selling bills or gilts outside the banking sector or by selling gilts to the banks, the money supply will not increase.

If there is no increase in money supply, however, the increased demand for loans by the government will 'crowd out' lending to the private sector. To attract money the government will have to offer higher interest rates on gilts. This will force up private-sector interest rates and reduce private-sector borrowing and investment. This is known as financial crowding out.

Definition

Financial crowding out Where an increase in government borrowing diverts money away from the private sector.

FIGURE 9.4
The demand for and supply of money

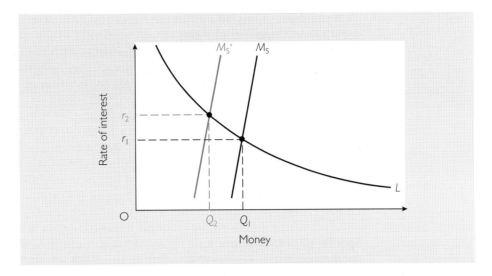

If governments wish to reduce monetary growth and yet avoid financial crowding out, they must therefore reduce the level of the PSBR.

Short-term monetary control

Monetary policy may be off target. Alternatively, the Bank of England may wish to alter its monetary policy. Assume, for example, that it wishes to operate a tighter monetary policy in order to reduce aggregate demand. What can it do?

There are various techniques for conducting monetary policy that the Bank of England could use. These can be grouped into three categories: (a) controlling the money supply; (b) controlling interest rates; (c) rationing credit.

Figure 9.4 shows the demand for and supply of money. Assume that the Bank of England wants to tighten monetary policy, such that the equilibrium quantity of money moves from Q_1 to Q_2. It could (a) seek to shift the supply of money curve to the left, from M_S to M_S' (resulting in the equilibrium rate of interest rising from r_1 to r_2), (b) raise the interest rate directly from r_1 to r_2, and then manipulate the money supply to reduce it to Q_2, or (c) keep interest rates at r_1, but reduce money supply to Q_2 by rationing the amount of credit granted by banks and other institutions.

Techniques to control the money supply

The possible techniques available to the authorities have one major feature in common: they involve manipulating the liquid assets of the banking system. The aim is to influence the total money supply by affecting the amount of credit that banks can create.

Open-market operations. Open-market operations are the sale or purchase by the Bank of England of government securities (gilts or Treasury bills) in the open market. These sales or purchases are *not* in response to changes in the PSBR, and are thus best understood in the context of an unchanged PSBR.

Open-market operations
The sale (or purchase) by the authorities of government securities in the open market in order to reduce (or increase) money supply.

If the Bank of England wishes to *reduce* the money supply, it will sell more securities. When people buy these securities, they pay for them with cheques drawn on banks. Thus banks' balances with the Bank of England are reduced. If this brings bank reserves below their prudent ratio, banks will reduce advances. There will be a multiple contraction of credit and hence of money supply.

Funding. Funding is where the Bank of England, if it wishes to reduce the money supply, sells more gilts, but at the same time fewer Treasury bills. Banks' balances with the Bank of England will be little affected, but to the extent that banks hold fewer bills, there will be a reduction in their liquidity. Funding is thus the conversion of one type of government debt (liquid) into another (illiquid).

Special deposits. Banks can be required to deposit a given percentage of their deposits in a special account at the Bank of England. These special deposits are frozen, and cannot be drawn on until the authorities choose to release them. They are thus illiquid. They provide a simple means of reducing banks' liquidity and hence their ability to create credit. Although still available to the Bank of England, this technique has not been used since 1981.

Techniques to control interest rates

The approach to monetary control today is to focus directly on interest rates. The Bank of England announces a change in interest rates, and this is backed up through its operations in the discount and gilt repo markets. Let us assume that the Bank of England decides to raise interest rates. What does it do?

In general the Bank of England seeks to keep banks short of liquidity. This will happen automatically on any day when tax payments by banks' customers exceed the money they receive from government expenditure. This excess is effectively withdrawn from banks and ends up in the government's account at the Bank of England. Even when this does not occur, sales of Treasury bills by the Bank of England will effectively keep the banking system short of liquidity.

This 'shortage' can then be used as a way of forcing through interest rate changes. Banks will obtain the necessary liquidity from the Bank of England through gilt repos or by selling it back bills. The Bank of England can *choose the rate of interest to charge* (i.e. the gilt repo rate or the bill rediscount rate). This will then have a knock-on effect on other interest rates throughout the banking system. (See Box 9.2 for more details on just how the Bank of England manipulates interest rates on a day-to-day basis.)

Techniques to ration credit

In the past, and particularly in the late 1960s, governments attempted to keep interest rates low so as not to discourage investment. This frequently meant that the demand for money exceeded the supply of money that the authorities were prepared to permit.

Faced with this excess demand, the authorities had to ration credit. There were two main ways in which credit was rationed. First, the Bank

Definition

Funding
Where the authorities alter the balance of bills and bonds for any given level of government borrowing.

BOX 9.2

The daily operation of monetary policy
....
What goes on at Threadneedle Street?

The Bank of England does not attempt to control money supply directly. Instead it seeks to control short-term interest rates by conducting open-market operations in the discount and gilt repo markets. These operations, as we shall see, will determine short-term interest rates, which will then have a knock-on effect on longer-term rates, as returns on different forms of assets must remain competitive with each other. A change in interest rates will then affect the demand for loans, which in turn will cause banks to respond by altering the amount of credit created, and hence altering the supply of money.

Let us assume that the Bank of England is worried that inflation is set to rise, perhaps because there is excessive growth in the money supply. It thus decides to raise interest rates. What does it do?

The first thing is that it will *announce* a rise in interest rates. But it must do more than this. It must back up the announcement by using open market operations to ensure that its announced interest rate is the *equilibrium rate*. In fact, it has to conduct open market operations every day to keep interest rates at the level it chooses.

How do these open market operations work? As we have seen, the Bank of England generally seeks to keep banks short of liquidity. It achieves this through its weekly sales of Treasury bills to the banks, discount houses and other financial institutions (collectively known as the Bank's 'counterparties').

The counterparties will thus have to borrow from the Bank of England. They do this by entering into sale and repurchase agreements (repos). This entails them selling gilts or bills to the Bank, with an agreement that they will repurchase them from the Bank at a fixed date in the future (typically about two weeks). The difference between the sale and repurchase prices will be set by the Bank of England to reflect its chosen rate of interest. By the Bank determining the repo rate in this way, there will then be a knock-on effect on other interest rates throughout the banking system.

Each morning at 9.45 the Bank of England forecasts that day's shortage (forecasts that are updated during the day). It then contacts its counterparties to offer them assistance. The assistance is provided at the published rate in two rounds of open market operations: at 12.00 noon and at 2.30 pm, with an additional 'early round' at 9.45 am if the predicted shortage of liquidity is large.

At about 3.45 pm the Bank publishes a final update for the day's liquidity shortage. If it is greater than was forecast earlier in the day, the Bank may make a further repo facility available, for which banks must apply by 3.55 pm.

Although there is usually a shortage of liquidity in the banking system, on some days there may be a *surplus*. To prevent this driving market interest rates down, the Bank will invite its counterparties to bid for outright purchase of short-dated Treasury bills (i.e. ones part-way through their life) at prices set by the Bank to reflect its current (above equilibrium) interest rate: i.e. at prices lower than the market would otherwise set. At such prices, the Bank has no difficulty in selling them and hence in 'mopping up' the surplus liquidity.

 Assume that the Bank of England wants to reduce interest rates. Trace through the process during the day by which it achieves this.

of England could ask banks to restrict their total lending to a certain amount, or to reduce lending to more risky customers or for non-essential purchases. The Bank of England had the power to order banks to obey, but in practice it always relied on persuasion. This was known as *suggestion and request* (or 'moral suasion'). Second, the authorities could restrict *hire-purchase credit*, by specifying minimum deposits or maximum repayment periods.

Summary

1. Control over the growth in the money supply over the longer term will normally involve governments attempting to restrict the size of the PSBR.
2. In the short term, the government can use monetary policy to restrict the growth in aggregate demand in one of three ways: (a) reducing money supply directly; (b) reducing the demand for money by raising interest rates; (c) rationing credit.
3. The money supply can be reduced directly by using open-market operations. This involves selling more government securities and thereby reducing banks' reserves when their customers pay for the securities from their bank accounts. Alternatively, funding can be used. This is where the government increases the ratio of gilts to bills. Since bills are a reserve of banks, this too will reduce banks' liquidity.
4. The current method of control involves the Bank of England influencing interest rates by its operations in the discount and gilt repo markets. It keeps banks short of liquidity, and then supplies them with liquidity, largely through gilt repos, at its chosen interest rate (gilt repo rate). This then has a knock-on effect on interest rates throughout the economy.
5. Credit rationing has not been used in the UK in the 1980s and 1990s.

9.7 The effectiveness of monetary policy

Is monetary policy a reliable means of controlling the economy?

Controlling the money supply over the medium and long term

A government committed to a sustained reduction in the growth of the money supply over a number of years will find this very difficult unless it restricts the size of the public-sector deficit. The Thatcher government in the 1980s recognised this and made reducing the PSBR the central feature of its 'medium-term financial strategy'. There are serious problems, however, in attempting to reduce the PSBR, principal among which is the difficulty in cutting government expenditure.

Cuts in government expenditure are politically unpopular. The Thatcher government as soon as it came into office met considerable opposition in Parliament, from public opinion, from local authorities and from various pressure groups, to 'cuts'. What is more, much of government expenditure is

The credit boom of the 1980s and decline of the early 1990s

The abandonment of all forms of credit rationing in the early 1980s contributed to a subsequent boom in consumer credit.

Between 1981 and 1989 consumer credit increased by some 17 per cent per year. Average earnings grew by only 8 per cent per year over the same period. By 1989 £48 billion was owed. This amounted to 14 per cent of total personal disposable income (compared with 7.5 per cent in 1981). The table highlights the massive credit expansion.

As the economy pulled out of the recession of the early 1980s, so this rapid rise in credit helped to fuel the recovery. But there were two macroeconomic problems with this credit boom. The first was that spending was going ahead of the ability to produce, and so inflation began to rise after 1986. The second was that a large proportion of the goods bought on credit were imported: foreign cars, Japanese hi-fi, Taiwanese sports goods and so on. Consequently, the balance of payments deteriorated rapidly.

The credit boom was a problem not only for the nation as a whole, but also for those individuals who, tempted by easy credit and the promise of instant consumption, found that they could not afford the repayments. Their problem was compounded in 1988 when there were substantial rises in the rate of interest. Many people were forced into borrowing more in order to pay the interest on existing loans, thus getting even deeper into debt.

Mortgages too were readily available, with various schemes to tempt the first-time buyer to enter the housing market. As more and more money was lent out, so this fuelled the demand for houses, and hence drove up their prices (see Box 1.4). People had to take out bigger and bigger mortgages, and when mortgage interest rates were then raised in 1988, many people had real difficulties in making ends meet.

But just as the boom in credit fuelled the expansion of the 1980s, so the recession of the early 1990s was aggravated by a *decline* in credit and hence a decline in spending.

But why was there a decline in credit? Households were faced with falling property prices, which for many people meant that their mortgage was now bigger than the value of their house (they had 'negative equity'). Many found themselves in mortgage arrears and were forced to sell their house. What is more, as real incomes fell and as unemployment rose, so many people found they could not afford any more to take on new personal loans or build up their credit-card debts. As a result, rather than spending, people now felt the need to pay off debts and to save as much as possible.

After 1993, consumer credit began to grow rapidly again, contributing to the recovery of the mid-1990s.

 How does the easy availability of credit affect the problem of inequality?

The rapid growth in credit (1981–9), slowdown and decline (1990–3) and growth again (1994–)

	1981	1982	1983	1984	1985	1986	1987	1988	1989	1990	1991	1992	1993	1994	1995	1996
Outstanding credit (£bn)	13.4	16.0	18.9	22.3	26.1	30.2	36.2	42.5	48.4	52.6	54.0	53.2	53.0	57.8	64.5	73.5
Growth of credit (%)	21.2	19.4	18.1	18.0	17.0	15.7	13.2	17.4	13.9	8.7	2.7	−1.6	−0.4	9.1	11.7	14.0
Disposable income growth (%)	10.6	7.9	7.8	8.7	8.9	8.6	8.3	11.1	10.6	7.9	6.4	7.2	5.2	3.2	5.6	6.1
Price inflation (%)	11.9	8.6	4.6	5.0	6.1	3.4	4.2	4.9	7.8	9.5	5.9	3.7	1.6	2.4	3.5	2.4

Sources: *Financial Statistics* and *Economic Trends* (ONS).

committed a long time in advance and cannot easily be cut. As a result the government may find itself forced into refusing to sanction *new* expenditure. But this will mean a decline in capital projects such as roads, housing, schools and sewers, with the net result that there is a decline in the country's infrastructure and long-term damage to the economy.

The less successful a government is in controlling the PSBR, the more it will have to borrow through gilt issue, to prevent money supply growing too fast. This will mean high interest rates and the problem of crowding out, and a growing burden of national debt with interest on it that has to be paid from taxation, from further cuts in government expenditure, or from further borrowing.

Short-term monetary control

In order to control the money supply, governments in the past, and particularly in the 1960s, resorted to various forms of credit rationing, such as ceilings on bank lending, requests to banks to discriminate between customers, and hire-purchase controls.

However, the problems of credit rationing can be serious:

- With credit rationing, there will be surplus liquidity that rationed banks are prevented from using for creating credit. To prevent business merely flowing from rationed banks (e.g. UK high street banks) to non-rationed banks (e.g. foreign banks, finance companies, retail banks' subsidiaries, etc.), credit rationing would have to extend to all institutions. The more complex is the banking system, and the more open is the banking system to international competition and international capital flows, the more difficult it is to do this.
- Banks might also resist the attempts at rationing. They would *like* to lend and have the liquidity to do so. They may thus find ways to get round the controls.
- Hire-purchase controls may have serious disruptive effects on certain industries (e.g. cars, furniture and other consumer durables), where products are bought largely on hire-purchase credit.

As long as people *want* to borrow, banks and other financial institutions will normally try to find ways of meeting the demand. In other words, in the short run at least, the supply of money is to a large extent demand determined. It is for this reason that the authorities prefer to control the *demand* for money by controlling interest rates.

The effectiveness of changes in interest rates

Even though this is the current preferred method of monetary control, it is not without its difficulties. The problems centre on the nature of the demand for loans. If this demand is (a) unresponsive to interest rate changes or (b) unstable because it is significantly affected by other determinants (such as anticipated income or foreign interest rates), then it will be very difficult to control by controlling the rate of interest.

Problem of an inelastic demand for loans. If the demand for loans is inelastic, any attempt to reduce demand will involve large rises in interest rates. The problem will be compounded if the demand has increased substantially, due, say, to a consumer spending boom. High interest rates lead to the following problems:

* They may discourage investment and hence long-term growth.
* They add to the costs of production, to the costs of house purchase and generally to the cost of living. They are thus cost inflationary.
* They are politically unpopular, since the general public do not like paying higher interest rates on overdrafts, credit cards and mortgages.
* The necessary gilt issue to restrain liquidity will commit the government to paying high rates on these gilts for the next twenty years or so.
* High interest rates encourage inflows of money from abroad. This drives up the exchange rate. This can be very damaging for export industries and industries competing with exports. Many firms suffered badly in 1997 when a policy of raising interest rates (among other things) caused the exchange rate to soar to over £1 = DM3.00 (from only £1 = DM2.30 some ten months earlier).

Evidence suggests that the demand for loans may indeed be quite inelastic. The reasons include the following:

* A rise in interest rates, particularly if it deepens a recession, may force many firms into borrowing merely to survive. This increase in 'distress borrowing' may largely offset any decline in borrowing by other firms or individuals.
* Although investment *plans* may be curtailed by high interest rates, *current* borrowing by many firms cannot easily be curtailed. Similarly, high interest rates may discourage householders from taking on *new* mortgages, but existing mortgages are unlikely to be reduced.
* High interest rates may discourage many firms from taking out long-term fixed-interest loans. But instead of reducing total borrowing, some firms may merely switch to shorter-term variable-interest loans. This will reduce the overall fall in demand for bank loans, thus making the demand less elastic.

Problem of an unstable demand. Accurate monetary control requires the authorities to be able to predict the demand curve for money (in Figure 9.4). Only then can they set the appropriate level of interest rates. Unfortunately, the demand curve may shift unpredictably, making control very difficult. The major reason is *speculation*:

* If people think interest rates will rise and gilt prices fall, in the meantime they will demand to hold their assets in liquid form. The demand for money will rise.
* If people think exchange rates will rise, they will demand sterling while it is still relatively cheap. The demand for money will rise.
* If people think inflation will rise, the transactions demand for money may rise. People plan to spend more while prices are still relatively low.
* If people think the economy is going to grow faster, the demand for loans will increase as firms seek to increase their investment.

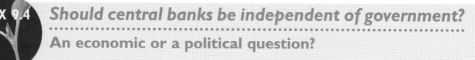

BOX 9.4 *Should central banks be independent of government?*

An economic or a political question?

In recent times there has been much discussion among both economists and politicians about whether the Bank of England should be independent. The Conservative governments under Margaret Thatcher and John Major felt that it was important for the government to retain control over monetary policy, if it was to achieve its macroeconomic objectives: a view also held by many on the left of the Labour Party.

In contrast to these views, the advocates of independence frequently cited the experience of Germany. The Bundesbank, Germany's central bank, is fiercely independent, and is credited with being instrumental in Germany's economic success. The Bundesbank's philosophy is simple: monetary and price stability are of overriding importance in the pursuit of growth. Inflation should be tightly controlled at all times.

The arguments in favour of an independent central bank are strong.

(a) Average annual inflation rate 1951–88
(b) Variability of inflation rate 1951–88

- An independent central bank is free from political manipulation. It can devote itself to attaining long-run economic goals, rather than to helping politicians achieve short-run economic success in time for the next election.
- Independence may strengthen the *credibility* of monetary policy. This may then play an important part in shaping expectations: workers may put in moderate wage demands and businesses may be more willing to invest.
- An independent central bank like the Bundesbank has a clear legal status and set of responsibilities. It is the 'protector of the currency' and as such it is not subordinate to

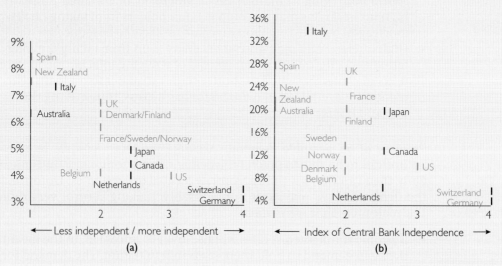

Source: *Financial Times*, 25 September 1992.

It is very difficult for the authorities to predict what people's speculation will be. Speculation depends so much on world political events, rumour and 'random shocks'.

If the demand curve shifts very much, and if it is inelastic, then monetary government. This is important given the political nature of economic policy making in both a domestic and an international context.

The diagram clearly illustrates that the greater the independence of a country's central bank, the lower and more stable is its rate of inflation. If this is the goal of economic policy, it would seem that more rather than less independence is desirable.

Certainly the incoming Labour government in 1997 was convinced of these arguments. Indeed, granting independence to the Bank of England was the very first act of the Chancellor, Gordon Brown. The decision could also have been affected by two other arguments.

The first was a political one: any blame for rises in interest rates would be deflected from the government.

The second was concerned with moves towards economic and monetary union (EMU) in the European Union. EMU will involve an independent European central bank to manage a single European currency (the euro) and to set the interest rates of the member states that adopt the single currency. The transition to a European central bank would be easier if the Bank of England were already independent: if the government had already reliquished control over monetary policy. We will examine the issues surrounding EMU in section 12.6.

One of the major arguments *against* having an independent central bank is that it makes it more difficult to integrate monetary management into wider economic policy objectives. On some occasions, for example, it might be desirable to accept a *higher* rate of inflation – if this were the consequence of a growth stimulus aimed at reducing unemployment. But with an independent central bank committed to monetary stability, it may be difficult for the government to achieve such economic policy goals. As Kenneth Clarke, the Chancellor in the outgoing Conservative government, argued: 'What you are going to see is tighter monetary policy than you might otherwise have got from a perfectly responsible Chancellor of the Exchequer.'

Another argument against having an independent central bank is that the government may pursue an overly lax fiscal policy. Governments like to be able to take the politically popular step of cutting taxes or increasing government expenditure (on, say, health or education). Doing this, however, can cause an excessive expansion of aggregate demand, with a resulting rise in inflation. This would then require the rate of interest to be raised to dampen demand again. Although this would itself be unpopular, it would be the central bank that would bear the brunt of criticism, not the government. In other words, by making the central bank independent, the political cost of pursuing an irresponsible fiscal policy would be reduced.

 Is there any case for an independent body to determine fiscal policy? If so, what would its role be?

control will be very difficult. Furthermore, the authorities will have to make frequent and sizeable adjustments to interest rates. These fluctuations can be very damaging to business confidence and may discourage long-term investment.

Using monetary policy

It is impossible to use monetary policy as a precise means of controlling aggregate demand. It is especially weak when it is pulling against the expectations of firms and consumers and when it is implemented too late. However, if the authorities operate a tight monetary policy firmly enough and long enough, they should eventually be able to reduce lending and aggregate demand. But there will inevitably be time lags and imprecision in the process.

An expansionary monetary policy is even less reliable. If the economy is in recession, no matter how low interest rates are driven, people cannot be forced to borrow if they do not wish to. Firms will not borrow to invest if they predict a continuing recession.

Despite these problems, changing interest rates can be quite effective. After all, they can be changed very rapidly. There are not the time lags of implementation that there are with fiscal policy. Indeed, during the 1990s, the government has used interest rate changes as its major means of keeping aggregate demand and inflation under control. Targets are set for the rate of inflation. If forecasts suggested that inflation is going to be above the target rate, the Bank of England will raise interest rates.

Since 1997, the Bank of England has had sole responsibility for changing interest rates and it does not have to answer to the government. The main objective of the Bank of England in controlling interest rates is to keep inflation within the target range (although it does also have regard to the exchange rate and other factors). The advantage of this is that it sends a very clear message to people that inflation *will* be kept under control. People will therefore be more likely to adjust their expectations accordingly and keep their borrowing in check.

Summary

1. It is difficult to control the growth of the money supply over the longer term without controlling the growth of the PSBR. This will be difficult to do in a period of recession.
2. All forms of short-term monetary policy involve problems. If the government is successful in controlling the money supply, there then arises the problem of severe fluctuations in interest rates if the demand for money fluctuates and is relatively inelastic.
3. Credit rationing provides a means of directly reducing aggregate demand without having to raise interest rates. It stifles competition between banks, however, and encourages banks to discriminate (maybe unfairly) between customers. Banks may also try to evade the controls, and business may simply flow to those institutions that are not controlled.
4. The form of monetary policy that has been favoured in recent years is the control of interest rates. Higher interest rates, by reducing the demand for money, effectively also reduce the supply. Nevertheless there are problems with this approach too. With an inelastic demand for loans,

interest rates may have to rise to very high levels in order to bring the required reduction in monetary growth. Controlling aggregate demand through controlling interest rates is made even more difficult as a result of *fluctuations* in the demand for money. These fluctuations are made more severe by speculation against changes in interest rates, exchange rates, the rate of inflation, etc.

5. Nevertheless, controlling interest rates is a way of responding rapidly to changing forecasts, and can be an important signal to markets that inflation will be kept under control.

Questions

1. How well could each of these fulfil the functions of money? Grain, strawberries, strawberry jam, gold, diamonds, luncheon vouchers, ICI share certificates, a savings account requiring one month's notice of withdrawal.

2. What is meant by the terms 'narrow money' and 'broad money'? Does broad money fulfil all the functions of money?

3. Which, if any, of the following count as (broad) money? (a) A credit card. (b) A debit card. (c) A cheque book. (d) A bank deposit account pass book. (e) A building society pass book.

4. If a bank has a surplus of cash, why might it choose to make a market loan with it rather than giving extra personal loans or mortgages to its customers?

5. Why do banks hold a range of assets of varying degrees of liquidity and profitability?

6. If a discount house buys a £50 000 Treasury bill for £48 000, at roughly what price will it sell it to a bank after 6 weeks?

7. Why should Bank of England intervention to influence rates of interest in the discount market also influence rates of interest in the parallel markets?

8. Would it be possible for an economy to function without (a) a central bank and (b) discount houses?

9. Imagine that the banking system receives additional deposits of £100 million and that all the individual banks wish to retain their current liquidity ratio of 20 per cent.
   (a) How much of the £100 million will banks choose to lend out initially?
   (b) What will happen to banks' liabilities when the money that is lent out is spent and the recipients of it deposit it in their bank accounts?
   (c) How much of these latest deposits will be lent out by the banks?

(d) By how much will total deposits (liabilities) eventually have risen, assuming that none of the additional liquidity is held outside the banking sector?

(e) How much of these are matched by (i) liquid assets; (ii) illiquid assets?

(f) What is the size of the bank multiplier?

(g) If one-half of any additional liquidity is held outside the banking sector, by how much less will deposits have risen compared with (d) above?

10. If banks choose to operate a 20 per cent liquidity ratio and receive extra cash deposits of £10 million, assuming that the general public does not wish to hold a larger total amount of cash balances outside the banks:

(a) How much credit will ultimately be created?

(b) By how much will total deposits have expanded?

(c) What is the size of the bank deposits multiplier?

11. Would the demand for securities be low if their price was high, but was expected to go on rising?

12. Which way will the liquidity preference curve shift if people believe that the pound is about to depreciate?

13. What effects will the following have on the equilibrium rate of interest? (You should consider which way the demand and/or supply curves of money shift.)

(a) Banks find that they have a higher liquidity ratio than they need.

(b) A rise in incomes.

(c) A growing belief that interest rates will rise from their current level.

14. Trace through the effect of a fall in the supply of money on aggregate demand. What will determine the size of the effect?

15. If the government reduces the size of its public-sector borrowing requirement, why might the money supply nevertheless increase more rapidly?

16. If the government ran a public-sector surplus (public-sector debt repayment, PSDR), could the money supply grow?

17. If the government borrows *but does not spend the proceeds*, what effect will this have on the money supply if it borrows from (a) the banking sector and (b) the non-bank private sector?

18. If the government buys back £1 million of maturing bonds from the general public and then, keeping the total amount of its borrowing the same, raises £1 million by selling Treasury bills to the discount houses, what will happen to the money supply?

19. Assume that a bank has the following simplified balance sheet, and is operating at its desired liquidity ratio.

Liabilities	(£m)	Assets	(£m)
Deposits	100	Balances with central bank	10
		Advances	90
	100		100

Now assume that the central bank repurchases £5 million of government bonds on the open market. Assume that the people who sell the bonds all have their accounts with this bank.

(a) Draw up the new balance sheet directly after the purchase of the bonds.

(b) Now draw up the eventual balance sheet after all credit creation has taken place.

(c) Would there be a similar effect if the central bank rediscounted £5billion of Treasury bills?

(d) How would such open-market operations affect the rate of interest?

20. What effect would a substantial increase in the sale of government bonds (gilts) and Treasury bills have on interest rates?

21. Why would it be difficult for the Bank of England to predict the precise effect on money supply of open-market operations?

22. What are the mechanics whereby interest rates are raised?

23. Why does an unstable demand for money make it difficult to control the supply of money?

24. If the Bank of England fixes interest rates at a low level and avoids credit rationing, what determines the supply of money?

chapter ten

Unemployment and inflation

Now that we have looked at money and interest rates, we are in a position to give a more complete explanation of the relationship between inflation and unemployment, and how they vary with the course of the business cycle. This is one of the most controversial areas of macroeconomics and there is considerable disagreement between Keynesians, monetarists and new classical economists. We will be examining their various viewpoints as the chapter progresses.

We start by having a look at the relationship between money supply and prices. If money supply rises, does this just lead to higher prices, or does it lead to higher output too? Is the answer to controlling inflation merely to restrict the growth of the money supply, or will doing so lead to a recession?

Then there is the issue of unemployment. If keeping inflation low involves running the economy at less than full capacity, does this mean that higher unemployment is the price of lower inflation? Is there a 'trade-off' between the two?

We will look at the views of the different schools (monetarist, new classical and Keynesian) about the relationship between inflation and unemployment: whether there is a trade-off between them. As we shall see, there is considerable disagreement. There is similar disagreement over the most appropriate policies to tackle the two problems. So let battle commence!

The link between money and prices

Will a rise in money supply cause output and employment to rise, or will it simply cause prices to rise?

Monetarists argue that inflation can be attributed entirely to increases in the money supply. The faster money supply expands, the higher will be the rate of inflation. Keynesians see a much looser association between money and prices. The debate can best be understood in terms of the quantity theory of money. The theory is simply that the level of prices in the economy depends on the quantity of money: the greater the supply of money, the higher will be the level of prices.

A development of the quantity theory is the *equation of exchange*. Focusing on this equation is the best way of understanding the debate over the relationship between money and prices.

The equation of exchange

The equation of exchange shows the relationship between national expenditure and national income. This identity may be expressed as follows:

$$MV = PQ$$

M is the supply of money in the economy. *V* is its velocity of circulation. This is the average number of times per year that money is spent on buying goods and services that have been produced in the economy that year (national output). *P* is the average level of prices. *Q* is the quantity of national output sold in that year.

PQ will thus be the money value of national output sold. For example, if 8 billion units of all the various goods and services produced were sold at an average price of £10 each, then the total value of these sales would be £80 billion.

MV will be the total spending on national output. For example, if money supply was £20 billion, and money, as it passed from one person to another, was spent on average 4 times a year on national output, then total spending (*MV*) would be £80 billion a year. But this *must* equal the value of goods sold (*PQ*).

The equation of exchange (or 'quantity equation') is true by definition. *MV* is *necessarily* equal to *PQ* because of the way the terms are defined. Thus a rise in *MV* *must* be accompanied by a rise in *PQ*. What a change in *M* alone does to *P* alone, however, is a matter of debate. The controversy centres on whether and how *V* and *Q* are affected by changes in the money supply (*M*). How a change in *M* affects *V* and *Q* will determine what happens to *P*.

How will a change in money supply affect aggregate demand? Assumptions about the velocity of circulation (V)

The Keynesian view

Keynesians argue that *V* tends to vary inversely with *M* (i.e. as one rises, the other falls). A rise in money supply will lead to a fall in interest rates and an increased holding of speculative balances, and hence a fall in the average speed at which money circulates (*V*). A rise in money supply might, there-

Definitions

Quantity theory of money
The price level (*P*) is directly related to the quantity of money in the economy (*M*).

The equation of exchange
MV = PQ. The total level of spending on GDP (*MV*) equals the total value of goods and services produced (*PQ*) that go to make up GDP.

Velocity of circulation
The number of times annually that money on average is spent on goods and services that make up GDP.

fore, have only a limited effect on total spending (*MV* and *PQ*). The effect is also rather unpredictable.

To understand their arguments, let us restate from the last chapter how an increase in money supply affects aggregate demand (see page 311 above):

1. A rise in money supply will lead to a fall in the rate of interest.
2. The fall in the rate of interest will lead to a rise in investment and other forms of borrowing. It will also lead to a fall in the exchange rate and hence a rise in exports and a fall in imports.
3. The rise in investment, and the rise in exports and fall in imports, will mean a rise in aggregate demand and a resulting rise in national income and output.

However, according to Keynesians, stages 1 and 2 are unreliable, and often weak.

Problems with stage 1: the money–interest rate link. According to Keynesians, the speculative demand for money is highly responsive to changes in interest rates. The speculative demand can be quite large. Keynesians point to the large sums of money that move around the money market as firms and financial institutions anticipate changes in interest rates. Thus only a small fall in interest rates may be necessary to persuade people to hold all the extra money as idle balances, thereby greatly slowing down the average speed at which money circulates. The fall in *V* may virtually offset the rise in *M*.

A more serious Keynesian criticism is that the demand for money is *unstable*. People hold speculative balances of money when they anticipate that interest rates will rise (security prices fall). But it is not just the current interest rate that affects people's expectations of the future direction of interest rates. There are many factors that could affect such expectations, such as changes in foreign interest rates, changes in exchange rates, statements of government intentions on economic policy, good or bad industrial news, or newly published figures on inflation or money supply. With an unstable demand for money, it is difficult to predict the effect on interest rates of a change in money supply.

Problems with stage 2: the interest rate–investment, exports and imports link. The problem here is that investment may be insensitive to changes in interest rates. Businesses are more likely to be influenced in their decision to invest by predictions of the future buoyancy of markets. Interest rates do have some effect on businesses' investment decisions, but the effect is unpredictable, depending on the confidence of investors.

Also the amount that the exchange rate will depreciate is uncertain, since exchange rate movements, as we shall see in Chapter 12, depend crucially on expectations about trade prospects and about future world interest rate movements. Thus the effects on imports and exports are also uncertain.

To summarise: the effects on total spending of a change in the money supply *might* be quite strong, but they could be weak. In other words, the effects are highly unpredictable.

$$M{\uparrow} \rightarrow V{\downarrow} \, (?) \rightarrow MV?$$

The monetarist view

Monetarists claim that in the long run V is determined *totally independently* of the money supply (M). Thus an increase in M will leave V unaffected and hence will directly increase in expenditure (MV):

$$M\uparrow, \rightarrow M\bar{V}\uparrow$$

where the bar over the V term means that it is exogenously determined: i.e. determined *independently* of M. But why do they claim this?

If money supply increases, people will have more money than they require to hold. They will spend this surplus. Much of this spending will go on goods and services, thereby directly increasing aggregate demand:

$$M_s\uparrow \rightarrow M_s > M_d \rightarrow AD\uparrow$$

The theoretical underpinning for this is given by the *theory of portfolio balance*. People have a number of ways of holding their wealth. They can hold it as money, or as financial assets such as bills, bonds and shares, or as physical assets such as houses, cars and televisions. In other words, people hold a whole portfolio of assets of varying degrees of liquidity – from cash to central heating.

If money supply expands, people will find themselves holding more money than they require: their portfolios are unnecessarily liquid. Some of this money will be used to purchase financial assets, and some to purchase *goods and services*. As more assets are purchased, this will drive up their price. This will effectively reduce their 'yield'. For bonds and other *financial* assets, this means a reduction in their rate of interest. For goods and services, this means an increase in their price relative to their usefulness. The process will stop when a balance has been restored in people's portfolios. In the meantime, there will have been extra consumption and hence an increase in aggregate demand.

Monetarists also argue that the interest rate and exchange rate mechanisms that we described above are relatively *strong*. Borrowing, they claim, whether for investment or by consumers, *will* be relatively responsive to changes in interest rates. For example, if interest rates go up, and mortgage rates follow suit, people will suddenly be faced with higher monthly repayments and will therefore have to cut down their expenditure on goods and services.

Short-run variability of V. Despite arguing that changes in money supply will have a strong effect on aggregate demand, monetarists do recognise that there will often be a time lag before these effects take place. In other words, they do admit to some variability of the velocity of circulation (V) in the short run. The demand for money can shift unpredictably in the short run with changing expectations of prices, interest rates and exchange rates. Thus V is unpredictable in the *short* run, and hence the effect of monetary policy on aggregate demand is also unpredictable in the short run. For these reasons monetarists argue that monetary policy cannot be used for short-run demand management. Here at least, then, there is a measure of agreement between Keynesians and monetarists.

How will a change in aggregate demand affect output and prices? Assumptions about Q

If there is a rise in aggregate demand (i.e. in MV), what will be the result? Will it simply result in a rise in prices (P)? This is the monetarist position (at

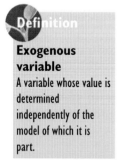

Definition

Exogenous variable
A variable whose value is determined independently of the model of which it is part.

FIGURE 10.1
Different aggregate supply curves

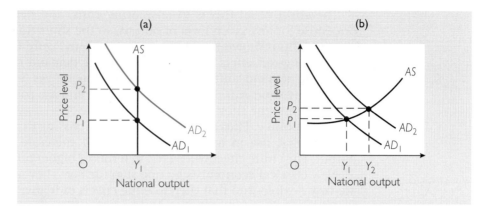

least in the long run). Or will it also (or even solely) result in a rise in national output (Q)? This is the Keynesian position. The argument here can best be understood in terms of the nature of the aggregate supply curve.

The monetarist and new classical views

Monetarists argue that aggregate supply is inelastic in the long run, and the new classicists argue that it is inelastic in the short run too (see Figure 10.1(a)), and therefore that output (Q) is determined independently of aggregate demand. Any rise in MV (i.e. in aggregate demand) will be totally reflected in a rise in prices (P):

$$MV\uparrow \rightarrow \bar{Q}), P\uparrow$$

They justify this by focusing on the *interdependence of markets*. Monetarists argue that a rise in aggregate demand will initially lead firms to raise both prices and output: the short-run aggregate supply curve is upward sloping (see Figure 10.2). This is consistent with all the models of perfect competition, imperfect competition and monopoly that we examined in Chapter 4. However, as raw material and intermediate goods producers raise their prices, so this will raise the costs of production further up the line. A rise in the price of steel will raise the costs of producing cars and washing machines. At the same time, workers, seeing the prices of goods rising, will demand higher wages. Firms will be relatively willing to grant these wage demands, given that they are experiencing a buoyant demand from their customers.

FIGURE 10.2
The long-run aggregate supply curve when firms are interdependent

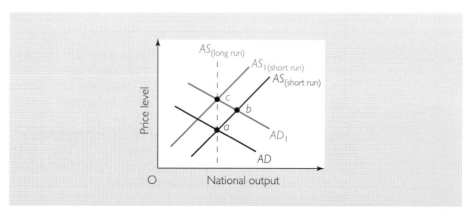

The effect of all this is to raise firms' *costs*, and hence their prices. As prices rise for any given level of output, so the short-run *AS* curve will shift upward. This is shown by a move to $AS_{1(\text{short run})}$ in Figure 10.2.

The long-run effect of a rise in aggregate demand can now be shown. Aggregate demand shifts to AD_1. The economy moves from point *a* to point *b* along the short-run *AS* curve. As costs rise and are passed on throughout the economy, the short-run *AS* curve shifts to $AS_{1(\text{short run})}$, and the economy moves to point *c*. Thus the long-run *AS* curve passing through points *a* and *c* is vertical. A rise in aggregate demand will therefore have no effect on output. The entire effect will be felt in terms of higher prices.

New classical economists go one step further. They assume that markets are very flexible, and that therefore the effects of higher costs will be passed through into higher prices virtually instantly. What is more, firms will anticipate this and hence take it into account *now*. For them, therefore, the *short-run aggregate supply curve is vertical also*.

We can now summarise the monetarist arguments about the effect of an increase in money supply. Because the velocity of circulation is independent of money supply, a rise in *M* will directly lead to a rise in *MV* (i.e. in aggregate demand). Because the aggregate supply curve is vertical (at least in the long run), the rise in aggregate demand will lead solely to an increase in prices (*P*). The stock of money therefore determines the price level, and the rate of increase in money supply determines the rate of inflation. Thus if inflation is to be reduced, it is important to keep a tight control of the money supply. This is why monetarists are given their name.

The Keynesian view

Keynesians argue that aggregate supply is relatively elastic except when full employment is approached (see Figure 10.1(b)). Thus *Q* is variable with respect to changes in aggregate demand. A rise in aggregate demand (i.e. a rise in *MV*) will lead to a rise in output *Q*. Conversely, a policy of restricting aggregate demand is likely to reduce *Q* as well as *P*, especially when there is resistance from monopolistic firms and unions to price and wage cuts:

$$MV\downarrow \rightarrow P\downarrow \text{ and } Q\downarrow$$

There are two parts to the Keynesian argument. Let us explain each in turn.

'Stickiness' of wages and prices. Wage rates are frequently determined by a process of collective bargaining and, once agreed, will typically be set for a whole year, if not two. Even if they are not determined by collective bargaining, wage rates often change relatively infrequently. So too with prices: except in perfect, or near perfect markets (such as commodity markets, or the markets for fresh fruit and vegetables), or at sale times or when there are special offers, firms tend to change their prices relatively infrequently. They do not immediately raise them when there is an increase in demand or lower them when demand falls. Thus there is a stickiness in both wage rates and prices.

FIGURE 10.3
Effect of investment on the long-run aggregate supply curve

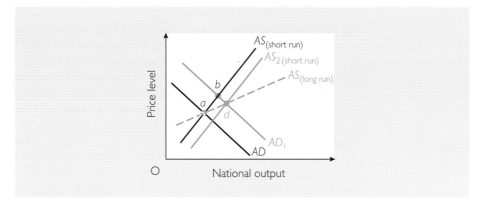

This will give an aggregate supply curve that is relatively flat (except as full employment is approached) (see Figure 10.1(b)): firms respond to a change in demand by changing output and employment.

Investment. With a rise in demand, firms may be encouraged to invest in new plant and machinery (the accelerator effect). In so doing they may well be able to increase output significantly in the long run with little or no increase in their prices. Their long-run *MC* curves are much flatter than their short-run *MC* curves.

In Figure 10.3 the short-run *AS* curve shifts to the right. Equilibrium moves from point *a* to *b* to *d*. In this case, the long-run *AS* curve joining points *a* and *d* is more elastic than the short-run curve. There is a relatively large increase in output and a relatively small increase in price.

The long-run *AS* curve will be flatter still and possibly even downward sloping if the investment involves the introduction of new cost-reducing technology. It will be steeper if the extra investment causes significant shortages of materials, machinery or labour. This is more likely when the economy is already operating near its full potential.

One very important dimension in the debate between monetarists, new classicists and Keynesians is the role of *expectations*. In order to see the effect on both inflation *and* unemployment of their different views on expectations, the analysis is best conducted in terms of the Phillips curve (see page 267 above).

Summary

1. The quantity equation $MV = PQ$ can be used to analyse the possible relationships between money and prices.
2. Keynesians argue that the velocity of circulation (*V*) varies inversely, but unpredictably, with the money supply (*M*). The reason is that changes in money supply will have unpredictable and probably rather weak effects on interest rates, and similarly changes in interest rates will have unpredictable and probably rather weak effects on aggregate demand. Thus spending (*MV*) will change by probably only a small and rather unpredictable amount.

3. Nevertheless, Keynesians argue that changes in aggregate demand (*MV*) *will* affect output (*Q*) according to the degree of slack in the economy. The aggregate supply curve, they argue, tends to be relatively elastic (except as full employment is approached). This is because both wage rates and prices tend to be relatively sticky. In the long run, the aggregate supply curve may be more elastic still, because of the effects of investment increasing the capacity of the economy to produce.
4. Monetarists argue that the velocity of circulation (*V*) and the level of output (*Q*) are independent of money supply (*M*) and that therefore increases in money supply will simply raise prices (*P*).
5. They argue that if people have an increase in money in their portfolios, they will attempt to restore portfolio balance by purchasing assets, including goods. Thus an increase in money supply is transmitted directly into an increase in aggregate demand. But given that the aggregate supply curve is vertical (at least in the long run), this will merely lead to an increase in prices, not output. The aggregate supply curve is argued to be vertical because of price increases being passed on from one firm to another.

The relationship between inflation and unemployment: monetarist views

What happens when people come to expect inflation?

The main contribution of monetarists to the theory of unemployment and inflation is the incorporation of expectations into the Phillips curve. This is then used to derive a *vertical* long-run Phillips curve. In other words, it is used to explain the monetarist contention that there is *no* trade-off between inflation and unemployment in the long run, and that therefore government policy to expand aggregate demand will not create more jobs (except perhaps in the very short term).

The monetarist theory of the vertical long-run Phillips curve is known as the *accelerationist theory*.

The expectations-augmented Phillips curve

In its simplest form, the expectations-augmented Phillips curve is given by the following:

$$\dot{P} = f(1/U) + \dot{P}^e$$

What this states is that inflation ($\dot{P}$) depends on two things:

- The inverse of unemployment ($1/U$). This is simply the normal Phillips curve relationship. The higher the rate of (demand-deficient) unemployment, the lower the rate of inflation.
- The expected rate of inflation ($\dot{P}^e$). The higher the rate of inflation that people expect, the higher will be the level of wage demands and the more willing will firms be to raise prices. Thus the higher will be the actual rate of inflation and thus the vertically higher will be the whole Phillips curve.

TABLE 10.1 *The accelerationist theory of inflation and inflationary expectations*

Year	Point on graph	$\dot{P}$	=	$f(1/U)$	+	$\dot{P}^e$
1	a	0	=	0	+	0
2	b	4	=	4	+	0
3	c	4	=	0	+	4
4	d	8	=	4	+	4
5	e	12	=	4	+	8
6	f	16	=	4	+	12

Let us assume, for simplicity, that the rate of inflation people expect this year ($\dot{P}^e_t$) (where t represents the current time period: i.e. this year) is the same rate that inflation actually was last year ($\dot{P}_{t-1}$).

$$\dot{P}^e_t = \dot{P}_{t-1}$$

Thus if unemployment is such as to push up prices by 4 per cent ($f(1/U) = 4\%$) and if last year's inflation was 6 per cent, then inflation this year will be 4 per cent + 6 per cent = 10 per cent.

The accelerationist theory

Let us trace the course of inflation and expectations over a number of years in an imaginary economy. To keep the analysis simple, assume there is no growth in the economy.

Year 1. Assume that at the outset, in year 1, there is no inflation at all; that none is expected; that $AD = AS$; and that equilibrium unemployment is 8 per cent. The economy will be at point a in Figure 10.4 and Table 10.1.

Year 2. Now assume that the government expands aggregate demand in order to reduce unemployment. Unemployment falls to 6 per cent. The economy moves to point b along curve I. Inflation has risen to 4 per cent, but people, basing their expectations of inflation on year 1, still expect a zero inflation. There is therefore no shift as yet in the Phillips curve. Curve I corresponds to an expected rate of inflation of zero.

FIGURE 10.4
The acceler-ationist theory of inflation and inflationary expectations

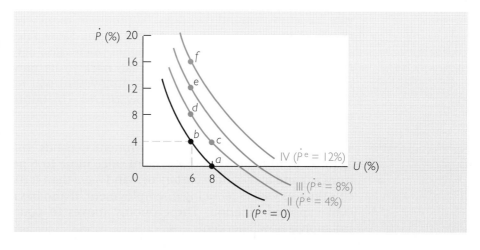

> **BOX 10.1** *The political business cycle*
> ....
> **The art of looping the loop**
>
> The accelerationist theory can be used to analyse the so-called political business cycle. This is where governments manipulate aggregate demand so that, by the time of the next general election, the economy will be growing nicely, with falling unemployment, but with inflation still relatively low.
>
> **Clockwise Phillips loops**
>
>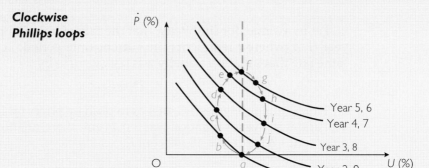
>
> Imagine that a politically naïve government has been fulfilling election promises to cure unemployment, cut taxes and increase welfare spending. In the diagram, this is shown by a move from point *a* to *b* to *c*.
>
> To its dismay, by the time the next election comes, inflation is accelerating and unemployment is rising again. The economy is moving from point *d* to *e* to *f*. You would hardly be surprised to learn that it loses the election!
>
> But now suppose a much more politically adroit government is elected. What does it do? The answer is that it does politically unpopular things first, so that before the next election it can do nice things and curry favour with the electorate.

Year 3. People now revise their expectations of inflation to the level of year 2. The Phillips curve shifts up by 4 percentage points to position II. If aggregate *monetary* demand (i.e. demand purely in money terms, irrespective of the level of prices) continues to rise at the same rate, the whole of the increase will now be absorbed in higher prices. *Real* aggregate demand (i.e. in terms of what it can buy) will fall back to its previous level and the economy will move to point *c*. Unemployment will return to 8 per cent. There is no *demand-pull* inflation now, $(f(1/U) = 0)$, but inflation is still 4 per cent due to expectations, $(\dot{P}^e = 4 \%)$.

Year 4. Assume now that the government expands *real* aggregate demand again so as to reduce unemployment once more to 6 per cent. This time it must expand aggregate *monetary* demand *more* than it did in year 2, because this time, as well as reducing unemployment, it also has to validate the 4 per cent expected inflation. The economy moves to point *d* along curve II. Inflation is now 8 per cent.

The first thing it does is to have a tough budget and to raise interest rates. 'We are having to clear up the economic mess left by the last government.' It thus engineers a recession and begins to squeeze down inflationary expectations. The economy moves from point *f* to *g* to *h*. In the meantime, unemployment has risen above the natural rate (U_n).

But people have very short memories (despite opposition attempts to remind them). After a couple of years of misery, the government announces that the economy has 'begun to turn the corner'. Things are looking up. Inflation has fallen and unemployment has stopped rising. The economy has moved from point *h* to *i* to *j*.

'Thanks to prudent management of the economy,' claims the Chancellor, 'I am now in a position to reduce taxes and to allow modest increases in government expenditure.' Unemployment falls rapidly; the economy grows rapidly; the economy moves from point *j* to *a* to *b*.

The government's popularity soars; the pre-election 'give-away' Budget is swallowed by the electorate, who trustingly believe that similar ones will follow if the government is returned to office. The government wins the election.

Then comes the nasty medicine again. But who will be blamed this time?

Q1 Why might a government sometimes 'get it wrong' and find itself at the wrong part of the Phillips 'loop' at the time of an election?

Q2 Which electoral system would most favour a government being re-elected – the US fixed-term system, with presidents being elected every four years, or the UK system, where the government can choose to hold an election any time within five years of the last one?

Year 5. *Expected* inflation is now 8 per cent (the level of actual inflation in year 4). The Phillips curve shifts up to position III. If at the same time the government tries to keep unemployment at 6 per cent, it must expand aggregate monetary demand 4 per cent faster in order to validate the 8 per cent expected inflation. The economy moves to point *e* along curve III. Inflation is now 12 per cent.

Year 6 onwards. To keep unemployment at 6 per cent, the government must continue to increase aggregate monetary demand by 4 per cent more than the previous year. As the expected inflation rate goes on rising, the Phillips curve will go on shifting up each year.

Thus in order to keep unemployment below the initial equilibrium rate, inflation must go on *accelerating* each year. For this reason, this theory of the Phillips curve is sometimes known as the **accelerationist theory**.

The more the government reduces unemployment, the greater the rise in inflation that year, and the more the rise in expectations the following year

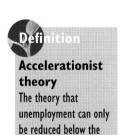

Definition

Accelerationist theory
The theory that unemployment can only be reduced below the natural rate at the cost of accelerating inflation.

and each subsequent year; and hence the more rapidly will price rises accelerate. Thus the true longer-term trade-off is between unemployment and the rate of *increase* in inflation.

Definition

Natural rate of unemployment or non-accelerating-inflation rate of unemployment (NAIRU)
The rate of unemployment consistent with a constant rate of inflation: the rate of unemployment at which the vertical long-run Phillips curve cuts the horizontal axis.

The long-run Phillips curve and the natural rate of unemployment

As long as there are demand-pull pressures ($f(1/U) > 0$), inflation will accelerate as the expected rate of inflation ($\dot{P}^e$) rises. In the long run, therefore, the Phillips curve will be vertical at the rate of unemployment where *real* aggregate demand equals *real* aggregate supply. This is the rate of unemployment that monetarists call the **natural rate** (U_n). It sometimes also known as the **non-accelerating-inflation rate of unemployment (NAIRU)**. In Figure 10.4 the NAIRU is 8 per cent.

The implication for government policy is that expansionary monetary and fiscal policy can only reduce unemployment below U_n in the *short* run. In the long run, the effect will be purely inflationary. On the other hand, a policy of restraining the growth in the money supply will *not* in the long run lead to higher unemployment: it will simply lead to lower inflation at the natural rate of unemployment. The implication is that governments should make it a priority to control money supply.

Summary

1. Monetarists argue that the introduction of expectations into the analysis of the Phillips curve implies that the curve must be vertical in the long run, at the 'natural rate of unemployment'.
2. The simplest analysis of expectations is that the expected rate of inflation this year is what it actually was last year:
$$\dot{P}^e_t = \dot{P}_{t-1}$$
3. If there is excess demand in the economy, producing upward pressure on wages and prices, initially unemployment will fall. The reason is that workers and firms will believe that wage and price increases represent *real* wage and price increases. Thus workers are prepared to take jobs more readily and firms choose to produce more. But as people's expectations adapt upward to these higher wages and prices, so ever increasing rises in demand will be necessary to maintain unemployment below the natural rate. Price and wage rises will accelerate: i.e. inflation will rise.
4. Thus a policy of expanding aggregate demand can only reduce unemployment below the natural rate in the short run. On the other hand, a policy of restraining the growth in the money supply in order to reduce inflation will not lead to unemployment higher than the natural rate in the long run.

10.3 The relationship between inflation and unemployment: new classical views

Can expanding aggregate demand have any effect on output and employment at all?

Rational expectations

New classical economists go further than the monetarist theory described above. They argue that even the short-run Phillips curve is vertical: that there is *no* trade-off between unemployment and inflation, even in the short run. They base their arguments on two key assumptions:

- Prices and wage rates are flexible and thus markets clear very rapidly. This means that there will be no disequilibrium unemployment. All unemployment will be equilibrium unemployment, or 'voluntary unemployment' as new classical economists prefer to call it.
- Expectations are 'rational', but are based on imperfect information.

In the accelerationist theory, expectations are based on *past* information and thus take a time to catch up with changes in aggregate demand. Thus for a short time a rise in aggregate demand will raise output, and reduce unemployment below the natural level, while prices and wages are still relatively low.

The new classical analysis is based on **rational expectations**. Rational expectations are not based on past rates of inflation. Instead they are based on the current state of the economy and the current policies being pursued by the government. Workers and firms look at the information available to them – at the various forecasts that are published, at various economic indicators and the assessments of them by various commentators, at government pronouncements, etc. Then, on the basis of this information, they predict as well as they can what the rate of inflation will be. It is in this sense that the expectations are 'rational': people use their reason to assess the future on the basis of current information.

But forecasters frequently get it wrong, and so do economic commentators! And the government does not always do what it says it will. Thus workers and firms will be basing expectations on *imperfect information*. The crucial point about the rational expectations theory, however, is that these errors in prediction are *random*. People's predictions of inflation are just as likely to be too high as too low.

If the government raises aggregate demand in an attempt to reduce unemployment, people will anticipate that this will lead to higher prices and wages, and that there will be *no* effect on output and employment. If their expectations of higher inflation are correct, this will thus *fully* absorb the increase in aggregate monetary demand, such that there will have been no increase in *real* aggregate demand at all. Firms will not produce any more output or employ any more people: after all, why should they? If they anticipate that people will spend 10 per cent more money, but that prices will rise by 10 per cent, their *volume* of sales will remain the same.

Output and employment will only rise, therefore, if people make an error in their predictions (i.e. if they underpredict the rate of inflation and

Rational expectations
Expectations based on the *current* situation. These expectations are based on the information people have to hand. While this information may be imperfect and therefore people will make errors, these errors will be random.

interpret an increase in money spent as an increase in *real* demand). But they are as likely to *over*predict the rate of inflation, in which case output and employment will fall! Thus there is no systematic trade-off between inflation and unemployment, even in the short run.

Real business cycles

If unemployment and output only fluctuate *randomly* from the natural level, and then only in the short run, how can the new classical economists explain booms and recessions? How can they explain the business cycle? Their answer, unlike Keynesians, lies not in fluctuations in aggregate demand, but rather in shifts in aggregate *supply*. In a recession, the vertical short- and long-run aggregate supply curves will shift to the left (output falls) and the vertical short- and long-run Phillips curves will shift to the right (unemployment rises). The reverse happens in a boom. Since the new classical theory of cyclical fluctuations focuses on supply, it is known as **real business cycle theory**.

But what causes aggregate supply to shift in the first place, and why, once there has been an initial shift, will the aggregate supply curve *go on* shifting, causing a recession or boom to continue?

The initial shift in aggregate supply could come from a structural change: say, a shift in demand from older manufacturing industries to new service industries. Because of the immobility of labour, not all those laid off in the older industries will find work in the new industries. Structural unemployment (part of equilibrium unemployment) rises and output falls.

Alternatively, the initial shift in aggregate supply could come from a change in technology. For example, a technological breakthrough in telecommunications could shift aggregate supply to the right. Or it could come from an oil price increase, shifting aggregate supply to the left.

But why, when a shift occurs, does the effect persist? Why is there not a single rise or fall in aggregate supply? There are two main reasons. The first is that several changes may take months to complete. For example, a decline in demand for certain older industries, perhaps caused by growing competition from abroad, does not take place overnight. Likewise, a technological breakthrough does not affect all industries simultaneously.

The second reason is that these changes will affect the profitability of investment. If investment rises, this will increase firms' capacity and aggregate supply will shift to the right. If investment falls (as a result, say, of the election of a government less sympathetic to industry), aggregate supply will shift to the left. In other words, investment is causing changes in output not through its effect on aggregate *demand* (through the multiplier), but rather through its effect on aggregate *supply*.

So far we have seen how the theory of real business cycles explains persistent rises or falls in aggregate supply. But how does it explain *turning points*? Why do recessions and booms come to an end? The most likely explanation is that, once a shock has worked its way through, aggregate supply will stop shifting. If there is then any shock in the other direction, aggregate supply will start moving back again. For example, after a period of recession, an eventual rise in business confidence will cause investment to rise and hence aggregate supply to shift back to the right. Since these 'reverse shocks' are

Real business cycle theory
The new classical theory which explains cyclical fluctuations in terms of shifts in aggregate supply, rather than aggregate demand.

likely to occur at irregular intervals, they can help to explain why real-world business cycles are themselves irregular.

Summary

1. **The new classical theory assumes flexible prices and wages in the short run as well as in the long run. It also assumes that people base their expectations of inflation on a rational assessment of the *current* situation.**
2. **People may predict wrongly, but they are equally likely to underpredict or to overpredict. On average over the years they will predict correctly.**

3. **The rational expectations theory implies that not only the long-run but also the short-run *AS* and Phillips curves will be vertical. If people correctly predict the rate of inflation, they will correctly predict that any increase in aggregate *monetary* demand will simply be reflected in higher prices. Total output and employment will remain the same: at the natural level.**
4. **With a vertical aggregate supply curve, cyclical fluctuations must arise from shifts in aggregate supply, not shifts in aggregate demand. Real business cycle theory thus focuses on aggregate supply shocks, which then persist for a period of time. Eventually their effect will peter out, and supply shocks in the other direction can lead to turning points in the cycle.**

10.4 The relationship between inflation and unemployment: Keynesian views

What will be the effect of expanding demand on business confidence and investment?

The Keynesian response

Keynesians today accept that the original analysis of the Phillips curve was an oversimplification and that expectations have to be taken into account. Nevertheless, Keynesians still maintain that output and employment depend on the level of aggregate demand, and that *excessive* expansion of aggregate demand will lead to inflation: in other words, that there *is* a trade-off between inflation and unemployment, even in the long run.

How is it then that both inflation *and* unemployment have generally been worse in the 1980s and 1990s than in the 1950s and 1960s? Keynesians argue that there is still a Phillips curve, but that it has shifted to the right. They give a number of explanations for this.

The growth in equilibrium unemployment: higher structural unemployment

Most Keynesians include growth in equilibrium unemployment (NAIRU) as part of the explanation of a rightward shift in the Phillips curve. In particular, Keynesians highlight the considerable structural rigidities in the economy in a period of rapid industrial change. The changes include the following:

- Dramatic changes in technology. The microchip revolution, for example, had led to many traditional jobs becoming obsolete.
- Competition from abroad. The introduction of new products from abroad, often of superior quality to domestic goods, or produced at lower costs, had led to the decline of many older industries: e.g. the textile industry.
- Shifts in demand away from the products of older labour-intensive industries to new 'high-tech' capital-intensive products.

Keynesians argue that the free market simply cannot cope with these changes without a large rise in structural/technological unemployment. Labour is not sufficiently mobile – either geographically or occupationally – to move to industries where there are labour shortages or into jobs where there are skill shortages. A particular problem here is the lack of investment in education and training, with the result that the labour force is not sufficiently flexible to respond to changes in demand for labour.

The growth in equilibrium unemployment: hysteresis
If a recession causes a rise in unemployment which is not then fully reversed when the economy recovers, there is a problem of hysteresis. This term, used in physics, refers to the lagging or persistence of an effect, even when the initial cause has been removed. In our context it refers to the persistence of unemployment even when the initial demand deficiency no longer exists.

The recessions of the early 1980s and early 1990s created a growing number of people who were both deskilled and demotivated. Many in their forties and fifties who had lost their jobs were seen as too old by prospective employers. Many young people, unable to obtain jobs, became resigned to 'life on social security' or to doing no more than casual work. What is more, many firms, in an attempt to cut costs, cut down on training programmes. In these circumstances, a rise in aggregate demand will not simply enable the long-term unemployed to be employed again. The effect has been a rightward shift in the Phillips curve: a rise in the NAIRU. To reverse this, argue Keynesians, the government should embark on a radical programme of retraining.

Recessions also cause a lack of investment. The reduction in their capital stock means that many firms cannot respond to a recovery in demand by making significant increases in output and taking on many more workers. Instead they are more likely to raise prices. Unemployment may thus fall only modestly and yet inflation may rise substantially. The NAIRU has increased: the Phillips curve has shifted to the right.

A rationale for the persistence of demand-deficient unemployment
If there is demand-deficient unemployment, why will there not be a long-run fall in real wage rates so as eliminate the surplus labour? Keynesians give two major explanations for the persistence of real wage rates above equilibrium.

Efficiency wages. The argument here is that wage rates fulfil two functions. The first is the traditional one of balancing the demand and supply of labour. To this Keynesians add the function of motivating workers. If real

Definition

Hysteresis
The persistence of an effect even when the initial cause has ceased to operate. In economics it refers to the persistence of unemployment even when the demand deficiency that caused it no longer exists.

wage rates are reduced when there is a surplus of labour (demand-deficient unemployment), then those workers already in employment may become dispirited and work less hard. If, on the other hand, firms keep wage rates up, then by maintaining a well-motivated workforce, by cutting down on labour turnover and by finding it easier to attract well-qualified labour, firms may find their costs are reduced: a higher real wage is thus more profitable for them. The maximum-profit real wage rate (the efficiency wage rate) is likely to be above the market-clearing real wage rate (see page 157). Demand-deficient unemployment is likely to persist.

Insider power. If those still in employment (the insiders) are members of unions while those out of work (the outsiders) are not, or if the insiders have special skills or knowledge that give them bargaining power with employers while the outsiders have no influence, then there is no mechanism whereby the surplus labour – the outsiders – can drive down the real wage rate and eliminate the demand-deficient unemployment.

These two features help to explain why real wage rates did not fall during the recessions of the early 1980s and early 1990s.

Keynesian analysis of expectations

Keynesians criticise the monetarist/new classical approach of focusing exclusively on price expectations. Expectations, argue Keynesians, influence *output* and *employment* decisions, not just pricing decisions.

Unless the economy is at full employment or very close to it, Keynesians argue that an expansion of demand *will* lead to an increase in output and employment, even in the long run after expectations have fully adjusted. If there is a gradual but sustained expansion of aggregate demand, firms, seeing the economy expanding and seeing their orders growing, will start to invest more and make longer-term plans for expanding their labour force. People will generally *expect* a higher level of output, and this optimism will cause that higher level of output to be produced. In other words, expectations will affect output and employment as well as prices.

Graphically, the increased output and employment from the recovery in investment will shift the *AS* curve to the right and the Phillips curve to the left, offsetting (partially, wholly or more than wholly) the upward shift from higher inflationary expectations.

The lesson here for governments is that a sustained, but moderate, increase in aggregate demand can lead to a sustained growth in aggregate supply. What should be avoided is an excessive and unsustainable expansion of aggregate demand, as occurred in the late 1980s. This will lead to a boom, only to be followed by a 'bust' and a consequent recession.

The Keynesian criticisms of non-intervention

Keynesians are therefore highly critical of the monetarist/new classical conclusion that governments should not intervene other than to restrain the growth of money supply. High unemployment may persist for many years and become deeply entrenched in the economy without a deliberate government policy of creating a steady expansion of aggregate demand.

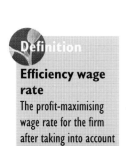

Definition

Efficiency wage rate
The profit-maximising wage rate for the firm after taking into account the effects of wage rates on worker motivation, turnover and recruitment.

Summary

1. Modern Keynesians argue that the Phillips curve has shifted to the right for various reasons.
2. There has been a growth in equilibrium unemployment. This has been the result of rapid changes in technology, greater competition from abroad and more rapid changes in demand patterns. It has also been the result of the persistence of unemployment beyond the recessions of the early 1980s and early 1990s, because of a deskilling of labour during the recessions (an example of hysteresis).
3. Demand-deficient unemployment may persist because real wage rates may be sticky downwards, even into the longer term. This stickiness may be the result of efficiency real wage rates being above market-clearing real wage rates and/or outsiders not being able to influence wage bargains struck between employers and insiders.
4. If expectations are incorporated into Keynesian analysis, the Phillips curve may become steeper in the long run (and steeper in the short run too, in the case of rational expectations). It will not become vertical, however, since people will expect changes in aggregate demand to affect output and employment as well as prices.
5. If people expect a rise in aggregate demand to be sustained, firms will invest more, thereby reducing unemployment in the long run and not just increasing the rate of inflation. The (short-run) Phillips curve will shift to the left.
6. Keynesians argue that it is important for governments to ensure that there is a sufficient level of aggregate demand.

10.5 Demand-side policy

What will be the effect of attempts by the government to control the level of spending in the economy?

Attitudes towards demand management

The debate over the management of demand has shifted ground somewhat in recent years. There is less debate today over the relative merits of fiscal and monetary policy. There is general agreement now that a *combination* of fiscal and monetary policies will have a more powerful effect on demand than just relying on one of the two policies. For example, a policy of cutting the size of the PSBR by reducing government expenditure and/or increasing taxes (fiscal policy) will enable the Bank of England much more easily to restrain the growth of the money supply (monetary policy), which in turn will help to reinforce the fiscal policy.

The debate today is much more concerned with whether the government ought to pursue an active demand management policy at all, or whether it ought merely to adhere to a set of policy rules. Keynesians prefer discretionary policy – changing policy as circumstances change. Monetarists prefer to set firm rules and then stick to them.

The monetarist case against discretion and in favour of rules

Monetarists are highly critical of discretionary policy, both fiscal and monetary. Such policy can involve long and variable time lags, which can make the policy at best ineffective and at worst destabilising. Taking the measures *before* the problem arises, and thus lessening the problem of lags, is no answer since forecasting tends to be unreliable.

Given the lags, the government may *over*correct the level of demand in order to speed up the effects of the policy. For example, it may give too big a boost to the economy if there is a recession. This may not create too much of a problem in the short term. Growth may rise and unemployment fall. But long-term effects will be undesirable as inflationary expectations rise. Governments may be tempted to ignore the long run, however, and, for example, engineer a pre-election boom in order to win votes.

By setting and sticking to rules, however, and then not interfering further, the government can provide a sound monetary framework in which firms are not cushioned from market forces, and are therefore encouraged to be efficient. By declaring medium-term targets either for a steady reduction in the growth of money supply, or for a low rate of inflation, and then resolutely sticking to these targets, people's expectations of inflation will be reduced. This will then help further to reduce inflation. This sound and stable monetary environment, with no likelihood of sudden deflations or reflations, will encourage firms to take a longer-term perspective, and plan ahead. This could then lead to increased capital investment and long-term growth.

The optimum situation is for all the major countries to adhere to mutually consistent rules, so that their economies do not get out of line. This will create more stable exchange rates and provide the climate for world growth.

The Keynesians case against rules and in favour of discretion

Keynesians reject one of the central points of the monetarist argument: that rules provide the environment for high and stable growth. Demand, argue Keynesians, is subject to many and sometimes violent shocks: e.g. changes in expectations, political events (such as an impending election), world economic factors (such as a change in US interest rates) or world political events (such as a war). The resulting shifts in injections or withdrawals cause the economy to deviate from a stable full-employment growth path.

Any change in injections or withdrawals will lead to a cumulative effect on national income via the multiplier and accelerator and via changing expectations. These effects take time and interact with each other, and so a process of expansion or contraction can last many months before a turning point is eventually reached.

Since shocks to demand occur at irregular intervals and are of different magnitudes, the economy is likely to experience cycles of irregular duration and of varying intensity.

Given that the economy is inherently unstable and is buffeted around by various shocks, Keynesians argue that the government needs actively to intervene to stabilise the economy. Otherwise, the uncertainty caused by unpredictable fluctuations would be very damaging to investment and hence to long-term economic growth (quite apart from the short-term effects of recessions on output and employment).

If demand fluctuates in the way Keynesians claim, and if the monetarist policy of having a money supply rule is adhered to, interest rates must fluctuate. But excessive fluctuations in interest rates will discourage long-term business planning and investment. What is more, the government may find it difficult to keep to its targets. This too may cause uncertainty and instability.

Economic circumstances may change. The rules adopted in the past may no longer be relevant. For example, a faster growth in productivity or a large increase in oil revenues may increase potential growth and thus warrant a faster growth in money supply. The government must have at least the discretion to *change* the rules, even if only occasionally.

The short-term costs of sticking to previously set rules may be too high. If expectations are slow to adjust downward and inflation remains high, then adherence to a tight monetary rule may lead to a very deep and unacceptable recession. This was a criticism made by many economists of monetarist policies between 1979 and 1982.

Improvements in forecasting, plus a willingness of governments to act quickly, plus the use of quick-acting policies can all help to increase the effectiveness of discretionary demand management.

Targeting the rate of inflation: the focus of demand-side policy in the 1990s

Targeting inflation was the main focus of Conservative monetary and fiscal policy in the UK after 1992. It was based on the belief that monetary policy cannot influence *real* variables such as output and employment in the long run. It can only influence inflation. It is better, therefore, to focus on achieving low inflation in order to provide the best environment for businesses to thrive. But to achieve an inflation target meant doing two things.

First, given the time lags between changing interest rates and their effect on inflation, interest rates would have to be changed in response to inflation *forecasts*, rather than the current rate of inflation. Second, people would have to be made to believe that the government could and would achieve the target. To this end, a number of steps were taken:

- The Bank of England published inflation forecasts, which the government publicly used to assess whether policy was on target.
- The Chancellor and the Governor of the Bank of England met monthly to consider the necessary interest rate policy to keep inflation within the target range. The Bank would then determine the *timing* of any agreed changes.
- Minutes of these meetings were published six weeks later, in order to give transparency to the process.
- Each time interest rates were changed, a press notice would be issued explaining the reasons. The idea here was to show the government's commitment to keeping to the target.

Was the policy a success? Inflation remained within the target bands, and the government claimed that this was the result of the policy. The government raised interest rates whenever inflationary forecasts were adverse. Thus monetary policy appeared to be successful within the goals set for it by the government.

As far as fiscal policy was concerned, with the PSBR for the year ending March 1993 being a massive £36.3 billion, there was a serious problem that, if monetary growth was kept in check, government borrowing would crowd out private-sector growth. The government thus saw the need to get a 'better' balance between fiscal and monetary policy. It therefore announced a series of tax increases to be phased in over the coming years. It also stated its intention to examine ways of reducing government expenditure.

In 1997, the incoming Labour government declared its commitment to stick to the previous government's expenditure targets and to continue bringing down the PSBR. That, plus a commitment not to raise taxes, prevented it from spending money on various social programmes advocated by many of its supporters.

As far as monetary policy was concerned, the government made the Bank of England independent. This allowed the Bank to focus on meeting inflation targets without political interference from the government (see Box 9.4.).

Summary

1. **The monetarist case against discretionary policy is that it involves unpredictable time lags, which can make the policy destabilising. The government may as a result overcorrect. Also the government may ignore the long-run adverse consequences of policies designed for short-run political gain.**
2. **The monetarist case in favour of rules is that they help to reduce inflationary expectations and thus create a stable environment for investment and growth.**
3. **The Keynesian case against sticking to money supply rules is that they may cause severe fluctuations in interest rates and thus create a less stable economic environment for business planning. Also, given the changing economic environment in which we live, rules adopted in the past may no longer be suitable for the present. Keynesians thus argue that the government must have the discretion to change its policy as circumstances demand.**
4. **Since 1992, UK governments have adopted a policy of targeting the rate of inflation, and have achieved success here, despite a very high PSBR.**

10.6 Supply-side policy

How might the government attempt to control the level of output and employment directly?

Supply-side policies, as the name suggests, focus on aggregate supply. If successful, they will shift the aggregate supply curve to the right, thus increasing output for any given level of prices (or reducing the price level for any given level of output). They may also shift the Phillips curve to the left, reducing the rate of unemployment for any given rate of inflation.

Unemployment and supply-side policies

Equilibrium unemployment – frictional, structural, etc. – is caused by various rigidities or imperfections in the market. There is a mismatching of aggregate supply and demand, and vacancies are not filled despite the existence of unemployment. Perhaps workers have the wrong qualifications, or are poorly motivated, or are living a long way away from the job, or are simply unaware of the jobs that are vacant. Generally, the problem is that labour is not sufficiently mobile, either occupationally or geographically, to respond to changes in the job market. Labour supply for particular jobs is too inelastic.

Supply-side policies aim to influence labour supply. They aim to make workers more responsive to changes in job opportunities. Alternatively, they may aim to make employers more adaptable and willing to operate within existing labour constraints.

Inflation and supply-side policies

If inflation is caused by cost-push pressures, supply-side policy can help to reduce these cost pressures in two ways:

- By reducing the power of unions and/or firms (e.g. by anti-monopoly legislation) and thereby encouraging more competition in the supply of labour and/or goods.
- By encouraging increases in productivity through the retraining of labour, or by investment grants to firms, or by tax incentives, etc.

Growth and supply-side policies

Supply-side economics focuses on *potential* income. Supply-side policies aim to increase the total quantity of factors of production (e.g. policies designed to encourage the building of new factories) or they can be used to encourage greater productivity of factors of production (e.g. policies to encourage the training of labour, or incentives for people to work harder).

The term 'supply-side policy' is often associated with monetarism. Monetarists advocate policies to 'free up' the market: policies that encourage private enterprise, risk taking and competition; policies that provide incentives and reward initiative, hard work and productivity.

Although the term 'supply-side policy' is often used to refer specifically to free-market-orientated policies, there are other supply-side policies which are *interventionist* in nature and are designed to counteract the deficiencies of the free market. Thus supply-side policies are advocated across the political and economic spectrum.

First we will examine market-orientated policies. Then we will turn to interventionist policies.

Market-orientated supply-side policies

Radical market-orientated supply-side policies were first adopted in the early 1980s by the Thatcher government in the UK and the Reagan administration in the USA. The essence of these supply-side policies was to encourage and reward individual enterprise and initiative, and to reduce the role of government; to

TABLE 10.2 *General government expenditure as a percentage of GDP at market prices*

	1961–70	*1971–80*	*1981–5*	*1986–90*	*1991–7*
Belgium	33.7	50.6	62.6	57.1	55.4
Germany	37.0	45.3	48.0	45.9	48.8
France	38.3	42.3	50.9	50.2	53.4
Japan	–	26.8	32.6	31.4	34.1
Netherlands	39.9	49.8	58.7	56.1	52.8
UK	36.5	41.3	44.5	39.7	42.3
USA	29.1	32.3	32.7	32.6	33.4

Source: *European Economy.*

put more reliance on market forces and competition, and less on government intervention and regulation. The policies were associated with the following:

- Reductions in government expenditure so as to release more resources for the private sector.
- Reductions in taxes so as to increase incentives.
- Reducing the monopoly power of trade unions so as to encourage greater flexibility in both wages and working practices, and to allow labour markets to clear.
- Reducing the automatic entitlement to certain welfare benefits so as to encourage greater self-reliance.
- Reducing red tape and other impediments to investment and risk taking.
- Encouraging competition through policies of deregulation and privatisation.
- Abolishing exchange controls and other impediments to the free movement of capital.

Such policies were increasingly copied by other governments around the world, so that by the late 1990s most countries had adopted some or all of the above measures.

Reducing government expenditure

The desire by many governments to cut government expenditure is not just to reduce the PSBR and hence reduce the growth of money supply, it is also an essential ingredient of their supply-side strategy.

In most countries the size of the public sector, relative to national income, grew substantially up until the mid-1980s (see Table 10.2). A major aim of Conservative governments throughout the world has been to reverse this trend. The public sector is portrayed as more bureaucratic and less efficient than the private sector. What is more, it is claimed that a growing proportion of public money has been spent on administration and other 'non-productive' activities, rather than on the direct provision of goods and services.

Two things are needed, it is argued: (a) a more efficient use of resources within the public sector and (b) a reduction in the size of the public sector. This would allow private investment to increase with no overall rise in aggregate demand. Thus the supply-side benefits of higher investment could be achieved without the demand-side costs of higher inflation.

In practice, governments have found it very difficult to cut their expenditure without cutting services and the provision of infrastructure.

Tax cuts: the effects on labour supply and employment

Cutting the marginal rate of income tax was a major objective of the Thatcher and Major governments. In 1979, the standard rate of income tax in the UK was 33 per cent and the top rate was 83 per cent. By 1997 the standard rate was only 23 per cent (with a starting rate of just 20 per cent), and the top rate was only 40 per cent. Cuts in the marginal rate of income tax have been claimed to have many beneficial effects: for example, people work longer hours; more people wish to work; people work more enthusiastically; unemployment falls; employment rises. The evidence regarding the truth of these claims, however, is less than certain.

For example, do more people wish to work? This applies largely to second income earners in a family, mainly women. A rise in after-tax wages may encourage more women to look for jobs. It may now be worth the cost in terms of transport, child minders, family disruption, etc. However, the effect of a 1 or 2 per cent cut in income tax rates is likely to be negligible. A more significant effect may be achieved by raising tax allowances: the amount of income that can be earned before taxes are paid. Part-time workers, especially, could end up paying no taxes. Then there is the question of whether the government will welcome more people seeking employment. This depends on the level of unemployment. If unemployment is already high, the government will not want to increase the labour force.

Whether people will be prepared to work longer hours is also questionable. On the one hand, each hour worked will be more valuable in terms of take-home pay, and thus people may be encouraged to work more and have less leisure time. On the other hand, a cut in income tax will make people better off, and therefore they may feel less need to do overtime than before (see pages 172–3). The evidence on these two effects suggests that they just about cancel each other out.

One of the main arguments is that tax cuts, especially at the lower end (by having a low starting rate of tax, or high personal allowances), will help to reduce unemployment. If income taxes are cut (especially if unemployment benefits are also cut), there will be a bigger difference between after-tax wage rates and unemployment benefit. More people will be motivated to take jobs rather than remain unemployed.

Despite the cuts in marginal rates of income tax, there have been significant tax *increases* elsewhere. In particular, VAT stood at only 8 per cent in 1979; in 1997 it was $17^{1}/_{2}$ per cent. The marginal rate of national insurance contributions was $6^{1}/_{2}$ per cent in 1979; in 1997 it was 10 per cent. The net effect was that taxes as a proportion of national income rose from 34.2 per cent in 1979 to over 36 per cent in 1997.

To the extent that tax cuts do succeed in increasing take-home pay, there is a danger of 'sucking in' imports. There tends to be a high income elasticity of demand for imports. Extra consumer incomes may be spent on Japanese videos and hi-fi, Japanese or European cars, holidays abroad, and so on. Tax cuts can therefore have a serious effect on the balance of payments.

Tax cuts for business and other investment incentives

A number of financial incentives can be given to encourage investment. Market-orientated policies seek to reduce the general level of taxation on profits, or to give greater tax relief to investment.

A cut in corporation tax (the tax on business profits) will increase after-tax profits. This will leave more funds for ploughing back into investment. Also the higher after-tax return on investment will encourage more investment to take place. In 1984 the main rate of corporation tax in the UK was reduced from 52 per cent of profits, the amount of the reduction depending on the size of the company. In 1997 the rate of corporation tax was 31 per cent for large companies and 21 per cent for small.

Reducing the power of labour

The argument here is that, if labour costs to employers are reduced, their profits will probably rise. This could encourage and enable more investment and hence economic growth. If the monopoly power of labour is reduced, then cost-push inflation will also be reduced.

The Thatcher government took a number of measures to weaken the power of labour. These included restrictions on union closed shops, restrictions on secondary picketing and enforced secret ballots on strike proposals (see page 156). It set a lead in resisting strikes in the public sector. Unlike Labour governments in the past, it did not consult with union leaders over questions of economic policy. It was publicly very critical of trade union militancy and blamed the unions for many of the UK's economic ills. As a result, unions lost a lot of political standing and influence.

Despite the legislation, it can be argued that the main factor that weakened the power of unions was the very high level of unemployment that existed throughout most of the period. When unemployment began to fall towards the end of the 1980s, and again in the mid-1990s, the level of industrial disputes increased.

Reducing welfare

Monetarists claim that a major cause of unemployment is the small difference between the welfare benefits of the unemployed and the take-home pay of the employed. This causes voluntary unemployment (i.e. frictional unemployment). People are caught in a 'poverty trap': if they take a job, they lose their benefits (see page 176).

A dramatic solution to this problem would be to cut unemployment benefits. Since 1979 the gap between take-home pay and welfare benefits to the unemployed has indeed widened. However, over the same period unemployment rose dramatically. This suggests that too high benefits have not been a significant cause of growing unemployment over this time. Nevertheless, the claim that there was too little incentive for people to work was still a major part of the Thatcher government's explanation of growing unemployment.

A major problem is that with changing requirements for labour skills, many of the redundant workers from the older industries are simply not qualified for new jobs that are created. What is more, the longer people are unemployed, the more demoralised they become. Employers would probably be prepared to pay only very low wages to such workers. To persuade these unemployed people to take low-paid jobs, the welfare benefits would have to be slashed. A 'market' solution to the problem, therefore, may be a very cruel solution. A fairer solution would be an interventionist policy: a policy of retraining labour.

Another alternative is to make the payment of unemployment benefits conditional on the recipient making a concerted effort to find a job. In the jobseeker's allowance introduced in 1996, claimants must be available for and actively seeking work, and must complete a Jobseeker's Agreement, which sets out the types of work the person is willing to do, and the plan to find work. Payment can be refused if the claimant refuses to accept the offer of a job.

Policies to encourage competition

If the government can encourage more competition, this should have the effect of increasing national output and reducing inflation. There were five major types of policy pursued under this heading.

Privatisation. If privatisation simply involves the transfer of a natural monopoly to private hands (e.g. the water companies), the scope for increased competition is limited. However, where there is genuine scope for increased competition (e.g. in the sale of telephones), privatisation can lead to increased efficiency, more consumer choice and lower prices.

Alternatively, privatisation can involve the introduction of private services into the public sector (e.g. private contractors providing cleaning services in hospitals, or refuse collection for local authorities). Private contractors may compete against each other for the franchise. This may well lower the cost of provision of these services, but the quality of provision may also suffer unless closely monitored. The effects on unemployment are uncertain. Private contractors may offer lower wages and thus may use more labour. But if they are trying to supply the service at minimum cost, they are likely to employ less labour.

Deregulation. This involves the removal of monopoly rights: again, largely in the public sector. The deregulation of the bus industry, opening it up to private operators, is a good example of this initiative. An example in the private sector was the so-called Big Bang on the Stock Exchange in 1986. Under this, the monopoly power of 'jobbers' to deal in stocks and shares on the Stock Exchange was abolished. In addition, stockbrokers now compete with each other in the commission rates they charge.

Introducing market relationships into the public sector. This is where the government tries to get different departments or elements within a particular part of the public sector to 'trade' with each other, so as to encourage competition and efficiency. The most well-known examples are within health and education.

The process often involves 'devolved budgeting'. For example, under the locally managed schools scheme (LMS), schools have become self-financing. Rather than the local authority meeting the bill for teachers' salaries, the schools have to manage their own budgets. The hope is that it will encourage them to cut costs, thereby reducing the burden on council tax payers. However, one result is that schools have tended to appoint inexperienced (and hence cheaper) teachers rather than those who can bring the benefits of their years of teaching.

Perhaps the most comprehensive introduction of market relationships has been in the field of health, where general practitioners who choose to control their own budgets purchase services directly from hospitals and have to cover the bill of the drugs prescribed to their patients. Hospitals depend for much of their income on attracting the business of GP purchasers. Hospitals can do this by periodically adjusting the price of treatment to make it competitive with other hospitals. Hospitals also compete using various non-price factors, such as the quality of care provided and the length of time patients must wait for treatment.

The Private Finance Initiative. In 1993 the government introduced its Private Finance Initiative (PFI). This became the new way in which public projects were to be financed and run. Instead of the government or local authority planning, building and then running a public project (such as a new toll bridge, a maintenance depot, a prison, a records office or a block of inner-city workshops), it merely decides in broad terms the service it requires, and then seeks tenders from the private sector for designing, building, financing and running such projects. The capital costs are borne by the private sector, but then, if the provision of the service is not self-financing, the public sector pays the private-sector firm for providing it. Thus instead of the public sector being a provider, it is merely an enabler, buying services from the private sector.

The aim of PFI is to introduce competition (through the tendering process) and private-sector expertise into the provision of public services. It is hoped that the extra burden to the taxpayer of the private-sector profits will be more than offset by gains in efficiency.

Free trade and capital movements. The opening-up of international trade and investment is central to a market-orientated supply-side policy. One of the first measures of the Thatcher government (in October 1979) was to remove all exchange controls, thereby permitting the free inflow and outflow of capital, both long term and short term. Most other industrialised countries also removed or relaxed exchange controls during the 1980s and early 1990s.

The Single European Act of 1986 which came into force in 1993 was another example of international liberalisation. As we shall see in section 11.5, it created a 'single market' in the EU: a market without barriers to the movement of goods, services, capital and labour.

Interventionist supply-side policies

For decades, the UK has had a lower level of investment relative to national income than other industrialised countries. This is illustrated in Table 10.3.

This low level of investment has been a major reason for the UK's poor growth performance. It has also meant that for many industries there has emerged a widening technological gap between the UK and its major competitors, such as Japan and Germany. This is reflected in the poor quality and high cost of many UK products. To some extent, however, this has been offset by the fact that wage rates in the UK have been lower than in competing countries. This has at least made the UK relatively attractive to inward investment, especially by Japanese, Korean and US companies seeking to set up production plants within the EU.

BOX 10.2 *Deregulating the bus industry*

Bus services were deregulated in the 1985 Transport Act, which came into effect on 26 October 1986. The Act privatised the National Bus Company and ended a system of strict route licensing which had been in existence for over 55 years.

For 30 years prior to deregulation the bus industry had been losing on average 4 per cent of its passengers per year. As a consequence the local authorities had been obliged to provide growing subsidies to the bus operators in order to keep loss-making services running. In 1985 such subsidies stood at £544 million at 1996 prices.

It was hoped that, following deregulation, greater competition in supply would lead to improved service efficiency, a growth in service provision and the number of passengers, lower fares, and the development of transport innovations, such as the new light-rail schemes (trams!) that had been proposed in many cities.

The impact of deregulation has, however, been mixed. On the positive side, the Department of Transport estimated that by 1993 operating costs per vehicle per mile had fallen by 36 per cent in real terms since deregulation, and that subsidies from local government to bus operators had fallen by over 50 per cent. Total bus mileage has increased since deregulation, along with the general frequency of service. Innovation in the form of minibuses has been significant. They now represent over 30 per cent of the total bus fleet.

However, many of the hoped-for benefits from deregulation have not materialised. Fares have increased by an average of 12 per cent in real terms. With direct income from fares falling by over 10 per cent from 1987 to 1993, the new bus operators have attempted to cut costs. Vehicles are being used more intensively and are not being replaced as frequently.

Other cost savings are being made by running services only on the busiest urban routes. Country routes and off-peak services have been progressively cut. The result is increased road congestion at peak periods on the most profitable city routes, as more buses compete for what is still a declining number of passengers.

Wages have also been subject to cost cutting. In 1993 the average bus driver's wage was 18 per cent below the average manual worker's full-time wage. In 1984 it had been a mere 2 per cent below.

The poor performance of UK manufacturing firms has resulted in a growing import penetration of the UK market. Imports of manufactured products have grown more rapidly than UK manufactured exports, and since 1983 the UK has become a net importer of manufactured products.

In many countries the approach to supply-side policy has been to pursue an interventionist industrial policy. Such policy has been extensively used in France, Germany and Japan, especially in the fields of research and development and of training (see Box 10.3).

Types of interventionist supply-side industrial policy

Nationalisation. This is the most extreme form of intervention. As in the cases of Rolls-Royce in 1971 and British Leyland (BL) in 1975, nationalisation may initially be a means of rescuing firms in financial difficulties – firms that are probably considered to be of strategic importance. Once they

Definition

Industrial policies
Policies to encourage industrial investment and greater industrial efficiency.

Passenger information has been very poor in many towns and cities. Companies form and collapse with such frequency that no reliable bus timetable is possible. Not only this, but the duplication of services leads to a massive waste of resources as well as congestion.

In cities where competition is more limited, such as Birmingham and Bristol, some economies of scale are possible from which both passengers and bus operators benefit. Services appear superior, being more organised and with up-to-date timetable information.

When companies have a monopoly on routes, however, fares are likely to rise unless the market remains contestable. With the establishment of large bus companies such as Stagecoach Holdings and FirstBus, contestability has tended to decline. Both companies were criticised by the Monopolies and Mergers Commission in August 1995 for their predatory behaviour. For example, when Stagecoach lost the bid to acquire the Darlington Transport Company (the town's former municipal bus company), Stagecoach decided to register a new bus service on all DTC routes. It announced that it would not wait the required six weeks before charging fares, but would offer a free service for the whole period. In addition it offered a £1000 signing-on fee to any qualified bus driver and wages 3 per cent higher than those at DTC. Predictably, DTC drivers left in droves to join the new bus company. Yorkshire Traction, the company that had won the DTC bid, subsequently pulled out as DTC faced the prospect of losing £30 000 per week for the six-week period. As a consequence, DTC went into liquidation.

Faced with aggressive business tactics like these, small operators would be unlikely to risk entering such a market: it would not be contestable. Responding to this situation, the MMC has suggested that it might become necessary to establish a bus regulator, OFBUS.

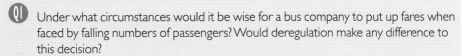 Under what circumstances would it be wise for a bus company to put up fares when faced by falling numbers of passengers? Would deregulation make any difference to this decision?

 Does the introduction of minibuses affect the case for or against deregulation?

are nationalised, however, the government may then choose to invest public money in them with the aim of making them profitable in the long run. By the time it was privatised in 1987, BL had become profitable again,

TABLE 10.3 *Gross fixed capital formation as a percentage of GDP: 1960–95*

Year (average)	UK	W. Germany[1]	Japan	EU (12)	OECD (total)
1960–7	17.7	25.2	31.0	22.8	21.0
1968–73	18.9	24.5	34.6	23.6	22.3
1974–80	19.2	21.0	31.8	22.2	22.2
1981–5	16.5	20.4	28.7	19.8	20.7
1986–90	18.9	19.9	29.8	20.1	20.8
1991–5	15.6	22.9	30.4	19.8	20.6

[1]All Germany from 1991.   Sources: *Historical Statistics 1960–87* (OECD, 1988); *Main Economic Indicators* (OECD).

BOX 10.3 *Alternative approaches to training and education*

It is generally recognised by economists and politicians alike that improvements in training and education can yield significant supply-side gains. Indeed, the UK's failure to invest as much in training as many of its major competitors is seen as a key explanation for the country's poor economic performance since the early 1970s. In the UK some 62 per cent of the manufacturing labour force have no qualifications. In Germany the figure is less than 30 per cent.

Training and economic performance are linked in three main ways:

- *Labour productivity*. In various studies comparing the productivity of UK and German industry, education and training was seen as the principal reason for the productivity gap between the two countries. In 1992 this gap was estimated at 22 per cent, of which nearly half was due to the superior skills of German workers.
- *Innovation and change*. A key factor in shaping a firm's willingness to introduce new products or processes will be the adaptability and skills of its workforce. If the firm has to spend a lot of money on retraining, or on attracting skilled workers away from other firms, the costs may prove prohibitive.
- *Costs of production*. A shortage of skilled workers will quickly create labour bottlenecks and cause production costs to increase. This will stifle economic growth.

If training is left to the employer, the benefits will become an externality if the workers leave to work elsewhere. Society has benefited from the training, but the firm has not. The free market, therefore, will provide a less than optimal amount of training. The more mobile the labour force, and the more 'transferable' the skills acquired from training, the more likely it is that workers will leave, and the less willing firms will be to invest in training.

In the UK, there is a high level of labour turnover. What is more, wage differentials between skilled and unskilled workers are narrower than in many other countries, and so there is less incentive for workers to train.

How can increased training be achieved? There are three broad approaches:

- Workers could be encouraged to stay with their employer so that employers would be more willing to invest in training. Externalities would be reduced.
- The government could provide subsidies for training. Alternatively, the government or some other agency could provide education and training directly.
- Firms could co-operate to prevent 'poaching' and set up industry-wide training programmes, perhaps in partnership with the government and unions.

As far as the first approach is concerned, most countries have seen a movement towards *greater* labour mobility. The rise in the 'flexible firm' has involved the employment of fewer permanent workers and more part-time and temporary workers. Some countries, such as Japan and Germany, however, have a generally lower rate of labour turnover than most. In Japan, in particular, it is common for workers to stay with one employer throughout their career. There the relationship between employer and employee extends well beyond a simple short-term economic arrangement. Workers give loyalty and commitment to their employer, which in return virtually guarantees long-term employment and provides various fringe benefits (such as housing, child care, holiday schemes and health care). It is not surprising that Japanese firms invest highly in training.

In the USA, labour turnover is very high and yet there is little in the way of industry-wide training. Instead, the US government hopes, by having a high percentage of young people in further and higher education, that sufficient numbers and quality of workers are available for industry. Almost 30 per cent of the US population graduates, and only just over 0.2 per cent of GDP is spent on training. The problem with the US approach is that many non-graduates are unskilled and receive no training at all.

In Germany the proportion of graduates is considerably lower (less than 14 per cent), but expenditure on training accounts for nearly 1.6 per cent of GDP. Most young people who do not enter higher education embark on some form of apprenticeship. They attend school for part of the week, and receive work-based training for the rest. The state, unions and employers' associations work closely in determining training provision, and they have developed a set of vocational qualifications based around the apprenticeship system. Given that virtually all firms are involved in training, the 'free-rider' problem of firms poaching labour without themselves paying for training is virtually eliminated. The result is that the German workforce is highly skilled. Many of the skills, however, are highly specific. This is a problem when the demand for particular skills declines.

In the UK, the Conservative government's attitude towards training was initially influenced by its free-market approach to supply-side policy. Training was to be left largely to employers. Government schemes such as the Youth Training Scheme (YTS), first introduced in 1983, were seen mainly as a means of reducing youth unemployment, rather than as a means of improving labour productivity. The 'training' element was often very limited or non-existent.

However, with growing worries over the UK's 'productivity gap', the government set up Training and Enterprise Councils (TECs) in 1988. The TECs were to be government funded, and to be responsible for identifying regional skill needs and the manner in which training was to be conducted.

Then in 1991, the National Vocational Qualification (NVQ) was launched. Students work for an employer, and receive on-the-job training. They also attend college on an occasional basis. The NVQ is awarded when they have achieved sufficient experience. In addition the government launched General National Vocational Qualifications (GNVQs). These further-education qualifications were aimed to bridge the gap between education and work, by ensuring that education was more work relevant.

The GNVQ system was modelled on that in France, where a clear vocational educational route is seen as the key to reducing skills shortages. At the age of fourteen, French students can choose to pursue academic or vocational education routes. The vocational route provides high-level, broad-based skills (unlike in Germany, where skills tend to be more job specific).

Critics of the UK strategy argue that it fails to address fundamental problems of funding, co-ordination and labour market flexibility. Employers still face the threat of having newly trained labour poached; the regional activities of the TECs fail to account for national, long-term training issues; and NVQs often provide too narrow forms of training. Most important, the funding devoted to training (0.5 per cent of GDP) is still low compared with most other industrialised countries. Critics claim that the UK system has the worst features of both the US and the German systems: too little training and too specific training.

Q1 Governments and educationalists generally regard it as desirable that trainees acquire transferable skills. Why may many employers disagree?

Q2 There are externalities (benefits) when employers provide training. What externalities are there from the undergoing of training by the individual? Do they imply that individuals will choose to receive more or less than the socially optimal amount of training?

thanks largely to a major programme of investment in new models and new production-line techniques.

Grants for research and development. The government may sponsor research and development in certain industries (e.g. aerospace) or in specific fields (e.g. microprocessors).

Rationalisation. The government may encourage mergers or other forms of industrial reorganisation that would lead to greater efficiency and/or higher levels of investment. This could be done through government agencies or government departments.

Advice and persuasion. The government may engage in discussions with private firms in order to find ways to improve efficiency and innovation. It may bring firms together to exchange information, so as to co-ordinate their decisions and create a climate of greater certainty. It may bring firms and unions together to try to create greater industrial harmony.

Information. The government may provide various information services to firms: technical assistance, the results of public research, information on markets, etc.

Direct provision. Improvements in infrastructure, such as a better motorway system, can be of direct benefit to industry. Alternatively, the government could provide factories or equipment to specific firms.

Training and education. The government may set up training schemes, or encourage educational institutions to make their courses more vocationally relevant, or introduce new vocational qualifications (such as the GNVQs and NVQs in the UK). Alternatively, the government can provide grants or tax relief to firms which themselves provide training schemes. The UK invests little in training programmes compared with most of its industrial competitors. However, Training and Enterprise Councils, which are run by local business and funded partly by the government, attempt to meet local training needs.

Summary

1. Market-orientated supply-side policies aim to increase the rate of growth of aggregate supply by encouraging private enterprise and the freer play of market forces.
2. Reducing government expenditure as a proportion of GDP is a major element of such policies. This involves measures such as the use of cash limits on government departments and local authorities, reducing grants and subsidies, reducing the number of public employees, resisting pay increases in the public sector, and reorganising public-sector industries and departments in order to achieve greater efficiency.

3. Tax cuts can be used to encourage more people to take up jobs, to work longer hours and to work more enthusiastically. The effects of tax cuts will depend on how people respond to incentives.

4. Reducing the power of trade unions and a reduction in welfare benefits, especially those related to unemployment, may force workers to accept jobs at lower wage rates, thereby decreasing equilibrium unemployment.

5. Other examples of market-orientated supply-side policy include privatisation, competitive tendering for public-sector contracts, deregulation, the Private Finance Initiative and free trade and capital movements.

6. Interventionist supply-side policy can take the form of nationalisation of ailing industries, grants for investment and research and development, the encouragement of mergers and other forms of rationalisation, advice and persuasion, the provision of information, the direct provision of infrastructure and the provision, funding or encouragement of various training schemes.

Questions

1. If V is constant, will (a) a £10 million rise in M give a £10 million rise in MV and (b) a 10 per cent rise in M give a 10 per cent rise in MV? (Test your answer by fitting some numbers to the terms.)

2. If both V and Q are constant, will (a) a £10 million rise in M lead to a £10 million rise in P and (b) a 10 per cent rise in M lead to a 10 per cent rise in P? (Again, try fitting some numbers to the terms.)

3. Compare Keynesian and monetarist assumptions about the V and Q terms in the quantity equation $MV = PQ$. What are the implications of these respective assumptions for the effectiveness of monetary policy to control inflation?

4. Assume that inflation depends on two things: the level of aggregate demand, indicated by the inverse of unemployment ($1/U$), and the expected rate of inflation ($\dot{P}^e{}_t$). Assume that the rate of inflation ($\dot{P}_t$) is given by the equation:

$$\dot{P}_t = (48/U - 6) + \dot{P}^e{}_t$$

Assume initially (year 0) that the actual and expected rate of inflation is zero.

(a) Now assume in year 1 that the government wishes to reduce unemployment to 4 per cent and continues to expand aggregate demand by as much as is necessary to achieve this. Fill in the rows for years 0 to 4 in the following table. It is assumed for simplicity that the expected rate of inflation in a given year ($\dot{P}^e{}_t$) is equal to the actual rate of inflation in the previous year ($\dot{P}_{t-1}$).

Year	U	48/U–6	+	$\dot{P}^e$	=	$\dot{P}$
0	...	...	+	...	=	...
1	...	...	+	...	=	...
2	...	...	+	...	=	...
3	...	...	+	...	=	...
4	...	...	+	...	=	...
5	...	...	+	...	=	...
6	...	...	+	...	=	...
7	...	...	+	...	=	...

    (b) Now assume in year 5 that the government, worried about rising inflation, reduces aggregate demand sufficiently to reduce inflation by 3 per cent in that year. What must the rate of unemployment be raised to in that year?

    (c) Assuming that unemployment stays at this high level, continue the table for years 5 to 7.

5. In the accelerationist model, if the government tries to maintain unemployment below the natural rate, what will determine the speed at which inflation accelerates?

6. For what reasons may the NAIRU increase?

7. Given the Keynesian explanation for the persistence of high levels of unemployment after the recession of the 1980s, what policies would you advocate to reduce unemployment?

8. Taking first a monetarist viewpoint and then a Keynesian one, explain each of the following:

    (a) Why there were simultaneously higher levels of inflation *and* unemployment in the 1970s and 1980s than in the 1950s and 1960s.

    (b) Why there were simultaneously lower levels of inflation *and* unemployment in the late 1990s than in the 1970s and 1980s?

In both cases consider the Keynesian and monetarist points of view.

9. For what reasons might the long-run aggregate supply curve be (a) vertical; (b) upward sloping?

10. What implications would a vertical short-run aggregate supply curve have for the effects of demand management policy?

11. (a) In the extreme Keynesian model (with a horizontal *AS* curve), is there any point in supply-side policies?

    (b) In the monetarist model (with a vertical *AS* curve), is there any point in using supply-side policies as a weapon against inflation?

12. Describe the effect of a contractionary monetary policy on national income from (a) a Keynesian perspective; (b) a monetarist perspective.

13. Imagine you are a Keynesian economist called in by the government to advise on whether it should adopt a policy of targeting the money supply. What advice would you give and how would you justify the advice?

14. Imagine you are a monetarist economist called in by the government to advise on whether it should attempt to prevent cyclical fluctuations by the use of fiscal policy. What advice would you give and how would you justify the advice?

15. Is there a compromise between purely discretionary policy and adhering to strict targets?

16. Under what circumstances would adherence to money supply targets lead to (a) more stable interest rates, (b) less stable interest rates than pursuing discretionary demand management policy?

17. Define *demand-side* and *supply-side* policies. Sometimes it is said that Keynesians advocate demand-side policies and monetarists advocate supply-side policies. Is there any accuracy in this statement?

18. Why might market-orientated supply-side policies have undesirable side-effects on aggregate demand?

19. If supply-side measures led to a 'shake-out' of labour and a resulting reduction in overstaffing, but also a resulting rightward shift in the Phillips curve, would you judge the policy as a success?

20. What types of tax cuts are likely to create the greatest (a) incentives, (b) disincentives to effort?

21. In what ways can interventionist industrial policy work *with* the market, rather than against it? What are the arguments for and against such policy?

chapter eleven

International trade

Trade between nations has the potential to benefit *all* participating countries (albeit to differing extents). This chapter explains why.

Totally free trade, however, may bring problems to countries or to groups of people within those countries. Many people argue strongly for restrictions on trade. Textile workers see their jobs threatened by cheap imported cloth. Car manufacturers worry about falling sales as customers switch to Japanese models or other east Asian ones. But are people justified in fearing international competition, or are they merely trying to protect some vested interest at the expense of everyone else? Section 11.2 examines the arguments for restricting trade.

If there are conflicting views as to whether we should have more or less trade, what has been happening on the world stage? Section 11.3 looks at the various moves towards making trade freer and at the obstacles that have been met.

A step on the road to freer trade is for countries to enter free-trade agreements with just a *limited* number of other countries. Examples include the EU and the North American Free Trade Association, NAFTA (the USA, Canada and Mexico). We consider such 'preferential trading systems' in section 11.4. Finally, we look in more detail at the EU and the development of a 'single European market'.

11.1 The gains from trade

Can international trade make all countries better off?

Specialisation as the basis for trade

Why do countries trade with each other and what do they gain out of it? The reasons for international trade are really only an extension of the reasons for trade *within* a nation. Rather than people trying to be self-sufficient and do everything for themselves, it makes sense to specialise.

Firms specialise in producing certain types of goods. This allows them to gain economies of scale and to exploit their entrepreneurial and management skills and the skills of their labour force. It also allows them to benefit from their particular location and from the ownership of any particular capital equipment or other assets they might possess. With the revenues that firms earn, they buy in the inputs that they need from other firms and the labour they require. Firms thus trade with each other.

Countries also specialise. They produce more than they need of certain goods. What is not consumed domestically is exported. The revenues earned from the exports are used to import goods which are not produced in sufficient amounts at home.

But which goods should a country specialise in? What should it export and what should it import? The answer is that it should specialise in those goods in which it has a *comparative advantage*. Let us examine what this means.

The law of comparative advantage

Countries have different endowments of factors of production. They differ in population density, labour skills, climate, raw materials, capital equipment, etc. These differences tend to persist because factors are relatively immobile between countries. Obviously land and climate are totally immobile, but even with labour and capital there tend to be more restrictions (physical, social, cultural or legal) on their international movement than on their movement within countries. Thus the ability to supply goods differs between countries.

What this means is that the relative costs of producing goods will vary from country to country. For example, one country may be able to produce 1 fridge for the same cost as 6 tonnes of wheat or 3 compact disc players, whereas another country may be able to produce 1 fridge for the same cost as only 3 tonnes of wheat but 4 CD players. It is these differences in relative costs that form the basis of trade.

At this stage we need to distinguish between *absolute advantage* and *comparative advantage*.

Absolute advantage

When one country can produce a good with less resources than another country it is said to have an **absolute advantage** in that good. If France can produce wine with less resources than the UK, and the UK can produce gin with less resources than France, then France has an absolute advantage in

Definition

Absolute advantage
A country has an absolute advantage over another in the production of a good if it can produce it with less resources than the other country.

TABLE 11.1 *Production possibilities for two countries*

		Kilos of wheat		Metres of cloth
Less developed country	Either	2	or	1
Developed country	Either	4	or	8

wine and the UK an absolute advantage in gin. Production of both wine and gin will be maximised by each country specialising and then trading with the other country. Both will gain.

Comparative advantage

The above seems obvious, but trade between two countries can still be beneficial even if one country could produce *all* goods with less resources than the other, providing the *relative* efficiency with which goods can be produced differs between the two countries.

Take the case of a developed country that is absolutely more efficient than a less developed country at producing both wheat and cloth. Assume that with a given amount of resources (labour, land and capital) the alternatives shown in Table 11.1 can be produced in each country.

Despite the developed country having an absolute advantage in both wheat and cloth, the less developed country (LDC) has a *comparative advantage* in wheat, and the developed country has a *comparative* advantage in cloth.

This is because wheat is relatively cheaper in terms of cloth in the LDC: only 1 metre of cloth has to be sacrificed to produce 2 kilos of wheat, whereas 8 metres of cloth would have to be sacrificed in the developed country to produce 4 kilos of wheat. In other words, the opportunity cost of wheat is 4 times higher in the developed country (8/4 compared with 1/2).

On the other hand, cloth is relatively cheaper in the developed country. Here the opportunity cost of producing 8 metres of cloth is only 4 kilos of wheat, whereas in the LDC 1 metre of cloth costs 2 kilos of wheat. Thus the opportunity cost of cloth is 4 times higher in the LDC (2/1 compared with 4/8).

If countries are to gain from trade, they should export those goods in which they have a comparative advantage and import those goods in which they have a comparative disadvantage. Given this we can state a *law of comparative advantage*: provided opportunity costs of various goods differ in two countries, both of them can gain from mutual trade if they specialise in producing (and exporting) those goods that have relatively low opportunity costs compared with the other country.

The gains from trade based on comparative advantage

Before trade, unless markets are very imperfect, the prices of the two goods are likely to reflect their opportunity costs. For example, in Table 11.1, since the less developed country can produce 2 kilos of wheat for 1 metre of cloth, the *price* of 2 kilos of wheat will roughly equal 1 metre of cloth.

Assume, then, that the pre-trade exchange ratios of wheat for cloth are as follows:

Definitions

Comparative advantage
A country has a comparative advantage over another in the production of a good if it can produce it at a lower opportunity cost: i.e. if it has to forgo less of other goods in order to produce it.

The law of comparative advantage
Trade can benefit all countries if they specialise in the goods in which they have a comparative advantage.

LDC: 2 wheat for 1 cloth
Developed country: 1 wheat for 2 cloth (i.e. 4 for 8)

Both countries will now gain from trade, provided the exchange ratio is somewhere between 2:1 and 1:2. Assume, for the sake of argument, that it is 1:1. In other words, 1 wheat trades internationally for 1 cloth. How will each country gain?

The LDC gains by exporting wheat and importing cloth. At an exchange ratio of 1:1, it now only has to give up 1 kilo of wheat to obtain a metre of cloth, whereas before trade it had to give up 2 kilos of wheat.

The developed country gains by exporting cloth and importing wheat. Again at an exchange ratio of 1:1, it now only has to give up 1 metre of cloth to obtain a kilo of wheat, whereas before it had to give up 2 metres of cloth.

Thus both countries have gained from trade.

The limits to specialisation and trade

Does the law of comparative advantage suggest that countries will completely specialise in just a few products? In practice, countries are likely to experience *increasing* opportunity costs. The reason for this is that, as a country increasingly specialises in one good, it will have to use resources that are less and less suited to its production and which were more suited to other goods. Thus ever increasing amounts of the other goods will have to be sacrificed. For example, as a country specialises more and more in grain production, it will have to use land that is less and less suited to growing grain.

These increasing costs as a country becomes more and more specialised will lead to the disappearance of its comparative cost advantage. When this happens, there will be no point in further specialisation. Thus whereas a country like Germany has a comparative advantage in capital-intensive manufactures, it does not produce only manufactures. It would make no sense not to use its fertile lands to produce food or its forests to produce timber. The opportunity costs of diverting all agricultural labour to industry would be very high.

Other reasons for gains from trade

Decreasing costs. Even if there are no initial comparative cost differences between two countries, it will still benefit both to specialise in industries where economies of scale can be gained, and then to trade. Once the economies of scale begin to appear, comparative cost differences will also appear, and thus the countries will have gained a comparative advantage in these industries.

This reason for trade is particularly relevant for small countries where the domestic market is not large enough to support large-scale industries. Thus exports form a much higher percentage of GNP in small countries such as Luxembourg than in large countries such as the USA.

Differences in demand. Even with no comparative cost differences and no potential economies of scale, trade can benefit both countries if demand conditions differ.

If people in country A like beef more than lamb, and people in country B like lamb more than beef, then rather than A using resources better suited for lamb to produce beef, and B using resources better suited for producing beef to produce lamb, it will benefit both to produce beef *and* lamb and to export the one they like less in return for the one they like more.

Increased competition. If a country trades, the competition from imports may stimulate greater efficiency at home. This extra competition may prevent domestic monopolies/oligopolies from charging high prices. It may stimulate greater research and development and the more rapid adoption of new technology. It may lead to a greater variety of products being made available to consumers.

Trade as an 'engine of growth'. In a growing world economy, the demand for a country's exports is likely to grow over time, especially when these exports have a high income elasticity of demand. This will provide a stimulus to growth in the exporting country.

Non-economic advantages. There may be political, social and cultural advantages to be gained by fostering trading links between countries.

Summary

1. Countries can gain from trade if they specialise in producing those goods in which they have a comparative advantage: i.e. those goods that can be produced at relatively low opportunity costs. This is merely an extension of the argument that gains can be made from the specialisation and division of labour.
2. If two countries trade, then, provided that the trade price ratio of exports and imports is somewhere between the pre-trade price ratios of these goods in the two countries, both countries can gain.
3. With increasing opportunity costs there will be a limit to specialisation and trade. As a country increasingly specialises, its (marginal) comparative advantage will eventually disappear. Trade can also be limited by transport costs, factor movements and government intervention.
4. Gains from trade also arise from decreasing costs (economies of scale), differences in demand between countries, increased competition from trade and the transmission of growth from one country to another. There may also be non-economic advantages from trade.

11.2 Arguments for restricting trade

If trade can benefit everyone, then why do countries attempt to limit trade?

We have seen how trade can bring benefits to all countries. But when we look around the world we often see countries erecting barriers to trade. Their politicians know that trade involves costs as well as benefits.

Do we exploit foreign workers by buying cheap foreign imports?

People sometimes question the morality of buying imports from countries where workers are paid 'pittance' wages. 'Is it right,' they ask, 'for us to support a system where workers are so exploited?' As is often the case with emotive issues, there is some truth and some misunderstanding in a point of view like this.

First the truth. If a country like the UK trades with a regime which denies human rights, and treats its workers very badly, then we may thereby be helping to sustain a corrupt system. We might also be seen to be lending it moral support. In this sense, therefore, trade may not help the cause of the workers in these countries. It is arguments like these that were used to support the imposition of trade sanctions against South Africa in the days of apartheid.

Now the misunderstanding. If we buy goods from countries that pay low wages, we are *not* as a result contributing to their low-wage problem. Quite the reverse. If countries like India export textiles to the West, this will help to *increase* the wages of Indian workers. If India has a comparative advantage in labour-intensive goods, these goods will earn a better price by being exported than by being sold entirely in the domestic Indian market. Provided *some* of the extra revenues go to the workers (as opposed to their bosses), they will gain from trade.

 Under what circumstances would a gain in revenues by exporting firms *not* lead to an increase in wage rates?

In looking at the costs and benefits of trade, the choice is not the stark one of whether to have free trade or no trade at all. Although countries may sometimes contemplate having completely free trade, typically countries limit their trade. However, they certainly do not ban it altogether.

Before we look at the arguments for restricting trade, we must first see what types of restrictions governments can employ.

Methods of restricting trade

Tariffs (customs duties). These are taxes on imports and are usually **ad valorem**: i.e. a percentage of the price of the import. Tariffs that are used to restrict imports will be most effective if demand is elastic (e.g. when there are close domestically produced substitutes). Tariffs can also be used as a means of raising revenue. Here they will be more effective if demand is inelastic. They can also be used to raise the price of imported goods to prevent 'unfair' competition for domestic producers.

Quotas. This is where a limit is imposed on the quantity of a good that can be imported. The quotas can be imposed by the government, or they can be negotiated with importing countries which agree 'voluntarily' to restrict the amount of imports.

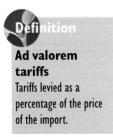

Ad valorem tariffs
Tariffs levied as a percentage of the price of the import.

Exchange controls. These include limits on the amount of foreign exchange made available to importers (financial quotas), or to citizens travelling abroad, or for investment. Alternatively, they can be in the form of charges made on people purchasing foreign currencies.

Import licensing. The imposition of exchange controls or quotas will often involve importers obtaining licences so that the government can better enforce its restrictions.

Embargoes. This is where the government completely bans certain imports (e.g. drugs) or exports to certain countries (e.g. to enemies during war).

Export taxes. These can be used to increase the price of exports when the country has monopoly power in their supply.

Subsidies. These can be given to domestic producers to prevent competition from otherwise lower-priced imports. They can also be given to exports in a process known as dumping. The goods are 'dumped' at artificially low prices in the foreign market. (This, of course, is a means of artificially *increasing* exports, rather than reducing imports.)

Administrative barriers. Regulations may be designed in such a way as to exclude imports. For example, all lagers that do not meet certain rigid purity standards could be banned. The Germans effectively excluded foreign brands by such measures. Other administrative barriers include taxes which favour locally produced products or ingredients.

Procurement policies. This is where governments favour domestic producers when purchasing equipment (e.g. defence equipment).

Arguments in favour of restricting trade

The infant industry argument. There may be industries in a country that are in their infancy, but which have a potential comparative advantage. This is particularly likely in developing countries. These industries are too small yet to have gained economies of scale; workers are as yet inexperienced; there is a lack of back-up facilities – communications networks, specialist research and development, specialist suppliers, etc. Without protection, these infant industries will not survive competition from abroad.

Protection from foreign competition, however, will allow them to expand and become more efficient. Once they have achieved a comparative advantage, the protection can then be removed to enable them to compete internationally.

Similar to the infant industry argument is the *senile industry* argument. This is where industries with a potential comparative advantage have been allowed to run down and can no longer compete effectively. They may have considerable potential, but be simply unable to make enough profit to be able to afford the necessary investment without some temporary protection from foreign competition. It is this argument that has been used to justify the use of special protection for the automobile and steel industries in the USA.

Definitions

Dumping
Where exports are sold at prices below marginal cost – often as a result of government subsidy.

Infant industry
An industry which has a potential comparative advantage, but which is as yet too underdeveloped to be able to realise this potential.

Changing comparative advantage and the inflexibility of markets. Comparative advantage can change over time, either naturally (e.g. new raw materials may be discovered) or as a result of deliberate policies (e.g. in the field of education, capital investment or technological research). Due to factor immobility, production may respond fairly slowly to these changing conditions. Thus free trade may reflect *past* comparative advantage rather than present. These industries could be regarded as infants and thus warranting protection.

To prevent 'dumping' and other unfair trade practices. A country may engage in dumping by subsidising its exports. Alternatively, firms may practise price discrimination by selling at a higher price in home markets and a lower price in foreign markets in order to increase their profits. Either way, prices may no longer reflect comparative costs. Thus the world would benefit from tariffs being imposed by importers to counteract the subsidy.

It can also be argued that there is a case for retaliating against countries which impose restrictions on your exports. In the *short* run, both countries are likely to be made worse off by a contraction in trade. But if the retaliation persuades the other country to remove its restrictions, it may have a longer-term benefit. In some cases, the mere threat of retaliation may be enough to get another country to remove its protection.

To prevent the establishment of a foreign-based monopoly. Competition from abroad could drive domestic producers out of business. The foreign company, now having a monopoly of the market, could charge high prices with a resulting misallocation of resources.

To reduce reliance on goods with little dynamic potential. Many developing countries have traditionally exported primaries: foodstuffs and raw materials. The world demand for these, however, is fairly income inelastic, and thus grows relatively slowly. In such cases, free trade is not an engine of growth. Instead, if it encourages countries' economies to become locked in to a pattern of primary production, it may prevent them from expanding in sectors like manufacturing which have a higher income elasticity of demand. There may thus be a valid argument for protecting or promoting manufacturing industry.

The above arguments are of general validity: restricting trade for such reasons could be of net benefit to the world. There are other arguments, however, that are used by individual governments for restricting trade, where their country will gain, but at the expense of other countries, such that there will be a net loss to the world. Such arguments include the following.

The exploitation of monopoly power. If a country, or a group of countries, has monopsony power in the purchase of imports (i.e. they are individually or collectively a very large economy, such as the USA or the EU), then they could gain by restricting imports so as to drive down their price. Similarly, if countries have monopoly power in the sale of some export (e.g. OPEC countries with oil), then they could gain by restricting exports, thereby forcing up the price (see Box 4.2).

To protect declining industries. The human costs of sudden industrial closures can be very high. In such circumstances, temporary protection may be warranted to allow the industry to decline more slowly, thus avoiding excessive structural unemployment. Such policies will be at the expense of the consumer, however, who will be denied access to cheaper foreign imports.

'Non-economic' arguments for restricting trade

A country may be prepared to forgo the direct economic advantages of free trade in order to achieve objectives that are often described as 'non-economic':

● It may wish to maintain a degree of self-sufficiency in case trade is cut off in times of war. This may apply particularly to the production of food and armaments.
● It may decide not to trade with certain countries with which it disagrees politically.
● It may wish to preserve traditional ways of life. Rural communities or communities built round old traditional industries may be destroyed by foreign competition.
● It may prefer to retain as diverse a society as possible, rather than one too narrowly based on certain industries.

Pursuing such objectives, however, will involve costs. Preserving a traditional way of life, for example, may mean that consumers are denied access to cheaper goods from abroad. Society must therefore weigh up the benefits against the costs of such policies.

Problems with protection

Protectionism will tend to push up prices, and restrict the choice of goods available. But apart from these direct costs to the consumer, there are several other problems. Some are a direct effect of the protection, others follow from the reactions of other nations.

Protection as 'second-best'. Many of the arguments for protection amount merely to arguments for some type of government intervention in the economy. Protection, however, may not be the best way of dealing with the problem, since protection may have undesirable side-effects. There may be a more direct form of intervention that has no side-effects. In such a case, protection will be no more than a *second-best* solution.

For example, using tariffs to protect old inefficient industries from foreign competition may help prevent unemployment in those parts of the economy, but the consumer will suffer from higher prices. A better solution would be to subsidise retraining and investment in those areas of the country in *new efficient* industries – industries with a comparative advantage. In this way, unemployment is avoided, but the consumer does not suffer.

World multiplier effects. If the UK imposes tariffs or other restrictions, imports will be reduced. But these imports are other countries' exports. A reduction in their exports will reduce the level of injections into the 'rest-of-the-world' economy, and thus lead to a multiplied fall in rest-of-the-world income. This in turn will lead to a reduction in demand for UK exports. This, therefore, tends to undo the benefits of the tariffs.

Retaliation. If the UK imposes restrictions on, say, Japan, then Japan may impose restrictions on the UK. Any gain to UK firms competing with Japanese imports is offset by a loss to UK exporters. What is more, UK consumers suffer, since the benefits from comparative advantage have been lost.

The increased use of tariffs and other restrictions can lead to a trade war, with each country cutting back on imports from other countries. In the end, everyone loses.

Protection may allow firms to remain inefficient. Tariffs and other forms of protection, by removing or reducing foreign competition, may reduce firms' incentive to reduce costs. Thus if protection is being given to an infant industry, the government must ensure that the lack of competition does not prevent it 'growing up'. Protection should not be excessive and should be removed as soon as possible.

Bureaucracy. If a government is to avoid giving excessive protection to firms, it should examine each case carefully. This can lead to large administrative costs. It could also lead to corrupt officials accepting bribes from importers to give them favourable treatment.

Summary

1. Countries use various methods to restrict trade, including tariffs, quotas, exchange controls, import licensing, export taxes, and legal and administrative barriers. Countries may also promote their own industries by subsidies.
2. Reasons for restricting trade that have some validity in a world context include the infant industry argument, the inflexibility of markets in responding to changing comparative advantage, dumping and other unfair trade practices, the danger of the establishment of a foreign-based monopoly, and the problems of relying on exporting goods whose market is growing slowly or even declining.
3. Countries may also have other objectives in restricting trade, such as remaining self-sufficient in certain strategic products, not trading with certain countries of which it disapproves, protecting traditional ways of life or simply retaining a non-specialised economy.
4. Even if government intervention to protect certain parts of the economy is desirable, restricting trade is unlikely to be a first-best solution to the problem, since it involves side-effect costs. What is more, restricting trade may have adverse world multiplier effects; it may encourage retaliation; it may allow inefficient firms to remain inefficient; it may involve considerable bureaucracy and possibly even corruption.

World attitudes towards trade and protection

Is trade becoming freer or less free?

Pre-war growth in protectionism

After the Wall Street crash of 1929 (when prices on the US stock exchange plummeted), the world plunged into the Great Depression (see Box 8.1). Countries found their exports falling dramatically and many suffered severe balance of payments difficulties. The response of many countries was to restrict imports by the use of tariffs and quotas. Of course, this reduced other countries' exports, which encouraged them to resort to even greater protectionism. The net effect of the Depression and the rise in protectionism was a dramatic fall in world trade. The volume of world trade in manufactures fell by more than a third in the three years following the Wall Street crash. Clearly there was a net economic loss to the world from this decline in trade.

Post-war reduction in protectionism and the role of GATT

After the Second World War there was a general desire to reduce trade restrictions, so that all countries could gain the maximum benefits from trade. There was no desire to return to the beggar-my-neighbour policies of the 1930s.

In 1947, 23 countries got together and signed the General Agreement on Tariffs and Trade (GATT). Today there are some 120 members of its successor organisation, the World Trade Organisation, which was formed in 1995. Between them, the members of the WTO account for over 90 per cent of world trade. The aims of GATT, and now the WTO, have been to liberalise trade. Periodically, member countries have met to negotiate reductions in tariffs and other trade restrictions. There have been eight 'rounds' of such negotiations since 1947. The three major ones were the Kennedy round (1964–7), the Tokyo round (1973–9) and the Uruguay round (1986–93).

The re-emergence of protectionist sentiments in the 1980s

Definition

Voluntary restraint arrangements (VRAs) or voluntary export restraints (VERs)
Where one country agrees to limit its imports to another to a particular quota.

The balance of payments problems that many countries experienced after the oil crisis of 1973 and the recession of the early 1980s led many politicians round the world to call for trade restrictions. Although a tariff war was averted, there was a gradual increase in non-tariff barriers, such as subsidies on domestic products, the prohibition of imports that do not meet precise safety or other specifications, administrative delays in customs clearance, limits on investment by foreign companies, and governments favouring domestic firms when purchasing supplies.

Quotas were increasingly used, especially against Japanese imports. In most cases these have been 'voluntary' agreements. Japan, on a number of occasions, agreed to restrict the number of cars it exported to the USA and various European countries. Similar restrictions applied to Japanese televisions and videos. Over 200 voluntary restraint arrangements (VRAs) (also known as voluntary export restraints (VERs)) were in force around the world in 1990.

The problem of increasing non-tariff barriers was recognised in the Uruguay round of GATT negotiations, and agreements were sought to dismantle many of them.

The Uruguay round

Aims of the negotiations

In September 1986 in the town of Punta del Este, in Uruguay,[1] the members of GATT began a new round of trade negotiations, but it was not until December 1993 that final agreement was reached between the 111 participating countries.

The major goals set for the Uruguay Round included: cutting tariffs on industrial products by one-third; substantially reducing non-tariff measures; liberalising trade in natural resources, textiles and tropical products; liberalising foreign investment; reducing agricultural support (such as that of the CAP); strengthening GATT rules and streamlining the procedure for settling disputes; strengthening voluntary codes against dumping and against technical and administrative barriers to trade; tightening the rules on the emergency protection of particular industries; agreements on fair trade in services and the protection of intellectual property rights (copyright, patents, etc.).

Problems in reaching agreement

These were an ambitious set of targets and it was soon clear that reaching agreement was not going to be easy. In particular, the USA and the EU were highly suspicious of each other and were unwilling to make concessions unilaterally without an equivalent concession from the other side. What is more, the USA was not prepared to liberalise its restrictions on imports while it saw other countries maintaining or increasing theirs.

The biggest stumbling block to agreement in the Uruguay round was agriculture, and it was not until the signing in London of the 'Blair House accord' in November 1992 that a breakthrough came. Under the agreement the EC agreed to cut subsidised farm exports by 21 per cent in volume and by 36 per cent in value within six years. Over the same period, support for domestic farmers would be cut by 20 per cent.

The agreement

An agreement was eventually reached in December 1993 and signed in April 1994. This involved a programme of phasing in substantial reductions in tariffs and other restrictions up to the year 2002.

The deal also led to the setting up in 1995 of the World Trade Organisation (WTO) as a successor to GATT. If there are disputes between member nations, these will be settled by the WTO, although there is provision for appeals, and the parties can agree to go to arbitration.

Was the Uruguay round a success? The answer must be a qualified yes: the net effect being to increase world GDP by about 1 per cent. The following are some of the main features of the agreement:

- Tariffs on industrial products cut by an average of 38 per cent (more than the original target) and eliminated entirely on certain products.

[1] Although the initial meeting was in Uruguay, subsequent meetings were in different locations around the world.

- Prohibition of export subsidies and voluntary export restraints (VERs).
- Non-tariff measures to be converted to tariffs.
- The Multifibre Agreement, which protected industrialised countries against imports of textiles from developing countries, to be phased out over ten years.
- Tariffs on agricultural products reduced by 36 per cent over six years in industrialised countries and ten years in developing countries.
- Protection of intellectual property rights strengthened (including patents, copyrights and trademarks).
- Adoption of voluntary codes limiting anti-dumping measures and the practice of government procurement favouring domestic suppliers.
- Stronger powers for the WTO than the old GATT to settle disputes and to enforce its rulings (e.g. against non-tariff barriers), with the new rules applying to *all* signatories, not just the industrialised countries, as was previously the case.
- Each country to have its trade policy periodically reviewed by the WTO.

But despite these successes, the cuts in agricultural protection were less than was originally hoped for. Although it was agreed to replace food import quotas into the EU and other industrialised countries by tariff equivalents, the degree of protection remains high, and the industrialised world continues to export food to many developing countries which have a comparative advantage in food production!

Summary

1. Most countries of the world are members of the WTO and in theory are in favour of moves towards freer trade.
2. The Uruguay round brought significant reductions in trade restrictions, both tariff and non-tariff.
3. In practice, however, countries have been very unwilling to abandon restrictions if they believe that they can gain from them, even though they might be at the expense of other countries.

Trading blocs

Why do some countries get together and trade more freely between themselves?

The world economy seems to have been increasingly forming into a series of trade blocs, based upon regional groupings of countries: a European region centred on the European Union, an Asian region on Japan, and a North American region on the United States. Although such trade blocs clearly encourage trade between their members, many countries outside these blocs complain that they benefit the members at the expense of the rest of the world. For many developing economies, in need of access to the most prosperous nations in the world, this represents a significant check on their ability to grow and develop.

Types of preferential trading arrangement

If a group of countries wish to become more open and trade more freely with each other, but do not want the vulnerability of facing unbridled global competition, they might attempt to remove trade restrictions between themselves, but maintain them with the rest of the world.

Such trading arrangements might take three possible forms.

Free trade areas

A free trade area is where member countries remove tariffs and quotas between themselves, but retain whatever restrictions *each member chooses* with non-member countries. Some provision will have to be made to prevent imports from outside coming into the area via the country with the lowest external tariff.

Customs unions

A customs union is like a free trade area, but in addition members must adopt *common* external tariffs and quotas with non-member countries.

Common markets

A common market is where member countries operate as a *single* market. Like a customs union there are no tariffs and quotas between member countries and there are common external tariffs and quotas. But a common market goes further than this. A full common market includes the following features.

A common system of taxation. In the case of a *perfect* common market, this will involve identical rates of tax in all member countries.

A common system of laws and regulations governing production, employment and trade. For example, in a perfect common market there would be a *single* set of laws governing issues such as product specification (e.g. permissible artificial additives to foods, or levels of exhaust emissions from cars), health and safety at work, the employment and dismissal of labour, the rights of trade unions and their members, mergers and takeovers, and monopolies and restrictive practices.

Free movement of labour, capital and materials, and of goods and services. In a perfect common market, this will involve a total absence of border controls between member states, the freedom of workers to work in any member country, and the freedom of firms to expand into any member state.

The absence of special treatment by member governments of their own domestic industries. Governments are large purchasers of goods and services. In a perfect common market, they should buy from whichever companies within the market offer the most competitive deal and not show favouritism towards domestic suppliers: they should operate a *common procurement policy*.

The definition of a common market is sometimes extended to include the following two features of *economic and monetary union*.

Definitions

Free trade area
A group of countries with no trade barriers between themselves.

Customs union
A free trade area with common external tariffs and quotas.

Common market
A customs union where the member countries act as a single market with free movement of labour and capital, common taxes and common trade laws.

A fixed exchange rate between the member countries' currencies. In the extreme case, this would involve a single currency for the whole market.

Common macroeconomic policies. To some extent this must follow from a fixed exchange rate, but in the extreme case it will involve a single macroeconomic management of the whole market, and hence the abolition of separate fiscal or monetary intervention by individual member states.

We will examine European economic and monetary union in section 12.6.

The direct effects of a customs union: trade creation and trade diversion

By joining a customs union (or free trade area), a country will find that its trade patterns change. Two such changes can be distinguished: trade creation and trade diversion.

Trade creation

Trade creation is where consumption shifts from a high-cost producer to a low-cost producer. The removal of trade barriers allows greater specialisation according to comparative advantage. Instead of consumers having to pay high prices for domestically produced goods in which the country has a comparative disadvantage, the goods can now be obtained more cheaply from other members of the customs union. In return, the country can export to them goods in which it has a comparative advantage.

Trade diversion

Trade diversion is where consumption shifts from a lower-cost producer outside the customs union to a higher-cost producer within the union.

Assume that the most efficient producer in the world of a particular good is New Zealand – outside the EU. Assume that before membership of the EU (EC), the UK paid a similar tariff on this good from any country, and thus imported the product from New Zealand rather than from the EC.

After joining the EC, however, the removal of the tariff made the EC product cheaper, since the tariff remained on the New Zealand product. Consumption thus switched to a higher-cost producer. There was thus a net loss in world efficiency. As far as the UK was concerned, consumers still gained, since they were paying a lower price than before. There was a loss, however, to domestic producers (from the reduction in protection, and hence reduced prices and profits) and to the government (from reduced tariff revenue). These losses may have been smaller or larger than the gain to consumers: in other words, there may still have been a net gain to the UK, but there could have been a net loss, depending on the circumstances.

Dynamic effects of a customs union

Over the longer term, there may be other gains and losses from being a member of a customs union.

Definitions

Trade creation
Where a customs union leads to greater specialisation according to comparative advantage and thus a shift in production from higher-cost to lower-cost sources.

Trade diversion
Where a customs union diverts consumption from goods produced at a lower cost outside the union to goods produced at a higher cost (but tariff free) within the union.

Longer-term advantages

- Increased market size may allow a country's firms to exploit *(internal) economies of scale*. This argument is more important for small countries, which have therefore more to gain from an enlargement of their markets.
- *External economies of scale*. Increased trade may lead to improvements in the infrastructure of the members of the customs union (better roads, railways, financial services, etc.). This in turn could bring bigger long-term benefits from trade between members, and from external trade too, by making the transport and handling of imports and exports cheaper.
- The bargaining power of the whole customs union with the rest of the world may allow member countries to gain *better terms of trade*. This, of course, will necessarily involve a degree of political co-operation between the members.
- *Increased competition* between member countries may stimulate efficiency, encourage investment and reduce monopoly power. Of course, a similar advantage could be gained by the simple removal of tariffs with any competing country.
- Integration may encourage a *more rapid spread of technology*.

Longer-term disadvantages

- Resources may flow from the country to more efficient members of the customs union, or to the geographical centre of the union (so as to minimise transport costs). This can be a major problem for a *common market* (where there is free movement of labour and capital). The country could become a depressed 'region' of the community.
- If integration encourages greater co-operation between firms in member countries, it may also encourage *greater oligopolistic collusion*, thus keeping prices higher to the consumer. It may also encourage mergers and takeovers which would increase monopoly power.
- *Diseconomies of scale*. If the union leads to the development of very large companies, they may become bureaucratic and inefficient.
- The *costs of administering* the customs union may be high. This problem is likely to be worse, the more intervention there is in the affairs of individual members.

Preferential trading in practice

Preferential trading has the greatest potential to benefit countries whose domestic market is too small, taken on its own, to enable them to benefit from economies of scale, and where they face substantial barriers to their exports. Most developing countries fall into this category and as a result many have attempted to form preferential trading arrangements.

Examples in Latin America include the Latin American Integration Association (LAIA), the Andean Pact and the Central American Common Market (CACM). A Southern Common Market (MerCoSur) was formed in 1995, consisting of Argentina, Brazil, Paraguay and Uruguay. It has a common external tariff and most of its internal trade is free of tariffs.

In 1993, the Asian Free Trade Area (AFTA) was formed. This plans to achieve a reduction in internal tariffs to a maximum of 5 per cent by 2008,

BOX 11.2   *The North American Free Trade Association (NAFTA)*

A bloc to rival the EU?

Along with the EU, NAFTA is one of the two most powerful trading blocs in the world. The North American Free Trade Association (NAFTA) was formed in 1993 and consists of the USA, Canada and Mexico. These three countries have agreed to abolish tariffs between themselves in the hope that increased trade and co-operation will follow. Tariffs between the USA and Canada will be phased out by 1999 and tariffs between Mexico and the other two countries by 2009. New non-tariff restrictions will not be permitted either, but many existing ones can remain in force, thus preventing the development of true free trade between the members. Indeed, some industries, such as textiles and agriculture, will continue to have major non-tariff restrictions.

NAFTA members hope that, with a market similar in size to the EU (a combined GDP of $7 trillion and over 360 million consumers), they will able to rival the EU's economic power in world trade. Other countries may join in the future, so NAFTA may eventually develop into a Western Hemisphere free trade association.

NAFTA is, however, at most only a free trade area and not a common market. Unlike the EU, it does not seek to harmonise laws and regulations, except in very specific areas such as environmental management and labour standards. Member countries are permitted total legal independence, subject to the one proviso that they must treat firms of other member countries equally with their own firms. Nevertheless, NAFTA has encouraged a growth in trade between its members, most of which is trade creation rather than trade diversion.

Of the three countries in NAFTA, Mexico potentially has the most to gain from the agreement. With easier access to US and Canadian markets, and the added attractiveness it now has to foreign investors, especially US multinationals looking to reduce labour costs, the Mexican economy could reap huge benefits. Studies have estimated that the Mexican economy might benefit by anything from a 0.1 per cent to an 11.4 per cent rise in real GDP. Estimates of gains for the USA and Canada are more modest: typically a 0.5 per cent rise in real GDP. The estimated employment gains from NAFTA are also subject to some variation. Optimistic estimates anticipate that 600 000 new jobs might be created in Mexico, and 130 000 new jobs in the USA. Pessimistic estimates, in contrast, suggest that the USA might suffer a net loss in employment of up to 500 000 jobs.

Even given the largely positive effects of NAFTA, the Mexican economy faces a number of real and potential threats from the agreement. For example, as trade barriers fall, Mexican companies will suddenly be faced with competition from potentially bigger and more efficient US and Canadian rivals. This is particularly likely in the case of 'hi-tech' sectors, such as telecommunications, which will probably become dominated, if not exclusively run, by foreign business.

Q1   What problems would be likely to occur if the member countries of NAFTA sought to make it a full common market?

with many products being tariff free. In Africa, the Economic Community of West African States (ECOWAS) has been attempting to create a common market between its members.

The most significant and advanced trade blocs, however, are to be found not in the developing world but in the developed, notably in Europe and North America. In Box 11.2 we look at the North American Free Trade Association (NAFTA) between the USA, Canada and Mexico. Then in the remainder of this chapter we consider the development of the EU, the longest established and most comprehensive of the world's preferential trading arrangements.

Summary

1. Countries may make a partial movement towards free trade by the adoption of a preferential trading system. This involves free trade between the members, but restrictions on trade with the rest of the world. Such a system can be either a simple free trade area, or a customs union (where there are common restrictions with the rest of the world) or a common market (where in addition there is free movement of capital and labour, and common taxes and trade laws).
2. A preferential trading area can lead to trade creation, where production shifts to low-cost producers within the area, or to trade diversion, where trade shifts away from lower-cost producers outside the area to higher-cost producers within the area.
3. Preferential trading may bring longer-term advantages of increased economies of scale (both internal and external), improved terms of trade from increased bargaining power with the rest of the world, increased efficiency from greater competition between member countries and a more rapid spread of technology. On the other hand, it can lead to increased regional problems for members, greater oligopolistic collusion and various diseconomies of scale. There may also be large costs of administering the system.
4. There have been several attempts around the world to form preferential trading systems.

11.5   The European Union

What have been the effects of the creation of a 'single market' in the EU?

The European Economic Community (EEC) was formed by the signing of the Treaty of Rome in 1957 and came into operation on 1 January 1958.

The original six member countries of the EEC (Belgium, France, Italy, Luxembourg, Netherlands and West Germany) had already made a move towards integration with the formation of the European Coal and Steel Community in 1952. This had removed all restrictions on trade in coal, steel and iron ore between the six countries. The aim had been to gain economies of scale and allow more effective competition with the USA and other foreign producers.

The EEC extended this principle and aimed eventually to be a full common market with completely free trade between members in all products, and with completely free movement of labour, enterprise and capital.

By uniting many of the countries of western Europe, it was hoped too that the conflicts of the two world wars would never be repeated, and that acting together the countries of the EEC could be an effective political and economic force in a world dominated by political giants such as the USA and the USSR, and economic giants such as the USA (and later Japan).

All internal tariffs between the six members had been abolished and common external tariffs established by 1968. But this still only made the EEC a *customs union*, since a number of restrictions on internal trade remained (legal, administrative, fiscal, etc.). Nevertheless the aim was eventually to create a full common market.

In 1973 the UK, Denmark and Ireland joined the EEC. Greece joined in 1981, Spain and Portugal in 1986, and Sweden, Austria and Finland in 1995.

From customs union to common market

The European Union is clearly a customs union. It has common external tariffs and no internal tariffs. But is it also a common market?

For many years there have been *certain* common economic policies.

Common Agricultural Policy (CAP). The Union sets common high prices for farm products. This involves charging variable import duties to bring foreign food imports up to EU prices and intervention to buy up surpluses of food produced within the EU at these above-equilibrium prices (see Box 2.4).

Regional policy. EU regional policy provides grants to firms and local authorities in depressed regions of the Union.

Monopoly and restrictive practice policy. EU policy here has applied primarily to companies operating in more than one member state. For example, Article 85 of the Treaty of Rome prohibits agreements between firms (e.g. over pricing or sharing out markets) which will adversely affect competition in trade between member states.

Harmonisation of taxation. VAT is the standard form of indirect tax throughout the EU. There are, however, substantial differences in VAT rates between member states, as there are with other tax rates.

Social policy. Articles 117–28 refer to social policy, and include calls for collaboration between member states on laws relating to employment, health and safety at work and collective bargaining rights, and equal pay for women and men for doing the same work.

In 1989 the European Commission presented a *social charter* to the EC heads of state. This spelt out a series of worker and social rights that should apply across the whole Community. These rights were grouped under twelve headings covering areas such as the guarantee of decent levels of income for both the employed and the non-employed, freedom of movement of labour between EC countries, freedom to belong to a trade union and equal treatment of women and men in the labour market. The social charter was only a recommendation and each element had to be approved separately by the Council.

BOX 11.3 *Features of the single market*

Since 1 January 1993 trade within the EU has operated very much like trade within a country. In theory there should be no more difficulty for a firm in Birmingham to sell its goods in Paris than in London. At the same time, the single market allows free movement of labour and involves the use of common technical standards.

The features of the single market are summed up in two EC publications:[2]

- Elimination of border controls on goods within the EU: no more long waits.
- Free movement of people across borders.
- Common security arrangements.
- No import taxes on goods bought in other member states for personal use.
- The right for everyone to live in another member state.
- Recognition of vocational qualifications in other member states: engineers, accountants, medical practitioners, teachers and other professionals able to practise throughout Europe.
- Technical standards brought into line, and product tests and certification agreed across the whole EU.
- Common commercial laws – making it attractive to form Europe-wide companies and to start joint ventures.
- Public contracts to supply equipment and services to state organisations now open to tenders across the EU.

Of the 282 proposals in the Internal Market Programme established in the Single European Act of 1986, 91 per cent had been adopted by the beginning of 1993 and 96 per cent by the end of that year.

So what does the single market mean for individuals and for businesses?

VAT rates (%) in the EC/EU: 1988 and 1996

	1988 Standard rate	High rates	1996 Standard rate
Austria			20
Belgium	19	25, 33	20.5
Denmark	22	–	25
Finland			22
France	18.6	33.3	20.6
Germany	14	–	15
Greece	18	36	18
Ireland	25	–	21
Italy	18	38	19
Luxembourg	12	–	15
Netherlands	20	–	17.5
Portugal	16	30	17
Spain	12	33	16
Sweden			25
UK	15	–	17.5

The social chapter of the Maastricht Treaty (1991) attempted to move the Community forward in implementing the details of the social charter in areas such as maximum hours, minimum working conditions, health and safety

Individuals

Before 1993, if you were travelling in Europe, you had a 'duty-free allowance'. This meant that you could only take goods up to the value of ECU600 across borders within the EC without having to pay VAT in the country into which you were importing them. Now you can take as many goods as you like from one EU country to another, provided they are for your own consumption. But to prevent fraud, member states may ask for evidence that the goods have been purchased for the traveller's own consumption if they exceed specified amounts (e.g. 800 cigarettes, 10 litres of spirits, 90 litres of wine, 110 litres of beer).

The one exception to the free import of goods for personal consumption is means of transport, such as cars, boats and planes. If a person imports a car from another member state which has been driven for less than 3000 km and is less than three months old, VAT must be paid in the person's home country. No VAT is levied on second-hand means of transport, however.

Individuals have the right to live and work in any other member state. Qualifications obtained in one member state must be recognised by other member states.

Firms

Before 1993 all goods traded in the EC were subject to VAT at every internal border. This involved some 60 million customs clearance documents at a cost of some ECU70 (about £50) per consignment.[3]

This has all now disappeared. Goods can cross from one member state to another without any border controls: in fact the concepts of 'importing' and 'exporting' within the EU no longer officially exist. All goods sent from one EU country to another will be charged VAT only in the country of destination. They are exempt from VAT in the country where they are produced.

One of the important requirements for fair competition in the single market is the convergence of tax rates. Although income tax rates, corporate tax rates and excise duties still differ between member states, there has been some narrowing in the range of VAT rates. There is now a lower limit of 15 per cent on the standard rate of VAT. What is more, the member states have agreed to abolish higher rates of VAT on luxury goods, and to have no more than two lower rates of at least 5 per cent on 'socially necessary' goods, such as food and water supply. The table shows VAT rates in 1988 and 1996.

 In what ways would competition be 'unfair' if VAT rates differed widely between member states?

[2] *A Single Market for Goods* (Commission of the European Communities, 1993); *10 Key Points about the Single European Market* (Commission of the European Communities, 1992).
[3] See *A Single Market for Goods* (Commission of the European Communities, 1993).

protection, information and consultation of workers, and equal opportunities.

The UK Conservative government refused to sign this part of the Maastricht Treaty. It maintained that such measures would increase costs of production and would, therefore, make EU goods less competitive in world trade and increase unemployment. If there was any truth in these arguments, then the non-adoption of the social chapter would have progressively given the UK a competitive advantage over its EU partners. Critics of the UK position argued that the refusal to adopt minimum working conditions (and also a minimum wage rate) would help to make the UK the 'cheap labour sweat-shop' of Europe. One of the first acts of the incoming Labour government in 1997 was to sign up to the social chapter.

Despite these various common policies, in other respects the Community of the 1970s and 1980s was far from a true common market: there were all sorts of non-tariff barriers. The Single European Act of 1986, however, sought to remove these barriers and to form a genuine common market by the end of 1992 (see Box 11.3).

The benefits and costs of the single market

It is difficult to quantify the benefits and costs of the single market, given that many occur over a long period, and that it is difficult to know to what extent the changes that are taking place are the direct result of the single market. Nevertheless it is possible to identify the *types* of benefit and cost that have resulted. The benefits have included the following.

Trade creation. Costs and prices have fallen as a result of a greater exploitation of comparative advantage. Member countries are now able to specialise further in those goods and services that they can produce at a comparatively low opportunity cost.

Reduction in the direct costs of barriers. This category includes administrative costs, border delays and technical regulations. Their abolition or harmonisation has led to substantial cost savings.

Economies of scale. With industries based on a Europe-wide scale, many firms can now be large enough, and their plants large enough, to gain the full potential economies of scale. Yet the whole European market is large enough for there still to be adequate competition. Such gains vary from industry to industry, depending on the minimum efficient scale of a plant or firm.

Greater competition. More effective competition from other EU countries has (a) squeezed profit margins and thus brought prices more in line with costs, and (b) encouraged more efficient use of resources and thus reduced costs. In the long run, greater competition can stimulate greater innovation, the greater flow of technical information and the rationalisation of production.

Despite these gains, the single market has not received universal welcome within the EU. Its critics argue that, in a Europe of oligopolies, unequal ownership of resources, rapidly changing technologies and industrial practices, and factor immobility, the removal of internal barriers to trade has merely exaggerated the problems of inequality and economic power. More specifically, the following criticisms are made.

Radical economic change is costly. Substantial economic change is necessary to achieve the full economies of scale and efficiency gains from a single European market. These changes necessarily involve redundancies – from bankruptcies, takeovers, rationalisation and the introduction of new technology. The severity of this 'structural' and 'technological' unemployment (see section 7.4) depends on (a) the pace of economic change and (b) the mobility of labour – both occupational and geographical.

Adverse regional effects. Firms are likely to locate as near as possible to the 'centre of gravity' of their markets and sources of supply. If, before barriers are removed, a firm's prime market was the UK, it might well have located in the Midlands or the north of England. If, however, when barriers are removed, its market has now become Europe as a whole, it may choose to locate in the south of England or in France, Germany or the Benelux countries instead. The creation of a single European market thus tends to attract capital and jobs away from the edges of the Union to its geographical centre.

In an ideal market situation, areas like the west of Ireland, the south of Italy and Portugal should attract resources from other parts of the Union. Being relatively depressed areas, wages and land prices are lower. The resulting lower industrial costs should encourage firms to move into the areas. In practice, however, as capital and labour (and especially young and skilled workers) leave the extremities of the Union, so these regions are likely to become more depressed. If, as a result, their infrastructure is neglected, they then become even less attractive to new investment.

The development of monopoly/oligopoly power. The free movement of capital is likely to lead to the development of giant 'Euro-firms' with substantial economic power. Indeed, the period both before and after 1992 saw some very large European mergers. This can lead to higher, not lower prices, and less choice for the consumer. It all depends on just how effective competition is, and how effective EU competition policy is in preventing monopolistic and collusive practices.

Trade diversion. Just as increased trade creation has been a potential advantage of completing the internal market, so trade diversion has been a possibility too. This is more likely if *external* barriers remain high (or are even increased) and internal barriers are *completely* abolished.

Loss of sovereignty. One of the biggest objections raised against the single European market is a political one: the loss of national sovereignty. Governments find it much more difficult to intervene at a microeconomic level in their own economies.

Soon after the implementation of the Single European Act, clear evidence emerged that it was beginning to bring benefits. The narrowing of price differences between countries for many manufactured products, especially cars, was one of the first signs that the Single European Act was having an impact. The elimination of border controls for goods has reduced costs and shortened delivery times. The simplification of VAT arrangements on cross-border transactions has also reduced costs. Several national government contracts have been won by firms from other member states. Many of Europe's larger retailers, such as Marks and Spencer and Carrefour, are taking advantage of the single market by expanding across Europe and hope to gain economies of scale from so doing. The financial services sector in individual countries is also facing increased competition from other member states (and non-member states too, such as the USA and Japan).

Although the elimination of trade barriers has brought initial benefits, the development of the internal market is now seen as vital if the gains so far achieved are to be built upon. Although there has been some adoption of common technical standards, separate national standards still exist in several industries. There is no truly single market for labour, with differences in employment and remuneration regulations between countries. There are still significant differences in VAT rates across the EU. Government procurement contracts are still awarded predominantly to domestic companies. Environmental measures still differ substantially from one member country to another.

Probably the biggest barrier to the future development of the internal market is the existence of multiple currencies – the costs of changing money and the uncertainties associated with currency fluctuations. Many argue that, without greater monetary union and ultimately the creation of a single European currency, the single European market will remain incomplete. Section 12.6 explores these arguments further, and considers the case both for and against greater monetary union.

Summary

1. The European Union is a customs union, in that it has common external tariffs and no internal ones. But virtually from the outset it has also had elements of a common market, particularly in the areas of agricultural policy, regional policy, monopoly and restrictive practice policy, and to some extent in the areas of tax harmonisation and social policy.

2. Nevertheless, there have been substantial non-tariff barriers to trade within the Community: e.g. customs formalities, various regulations over product quality, licensing, state procurement policies, educational qualification requirements, subsidies or tax relief to domestic producers.

3. The Single European Act of 1986 sought to sweep away these restrictions and to establish a genuine free market within the EC: to establish a full common market. Benefits from completing the internal market have included trade creation, cost savings from no longer having to administer barriers, economies of scale for firms now able to operate on a Europe-wide scale, and greater competition leading to reduced costs and prices and greater flows of technical information and more innovation.

4. Critics of the single market point to the costs of radical changes in industrial structure, the attraction of capital away from the periphery of

the **EU** to its geographical centre, to possible problems of market power with the development of giant 'Euro-firms', and to the possibilities of trade diversion.

5. The actual costs and benefits of **EU** membership to the various countries vary with their particular economic circumstances. These costs and benefits in the future will depend on just how completely the barriers to trade are removed, on the extent of monetary union and on any enlargements to the Union.

 Questions

1. Referring to Table 11.1, show how each country could gain from trade if the LDC could produce (before trade) 3 wheat for 1 cloth and the developed country could produce (before trade) 2 wheat for 5 cloth, and if the exchange ratio (with trade) was 1 wheat for 2 cloth. Would they both still gain if the exchange ratio was (a) 1 wheat for 1 cloth and (b) 1 wheat for 3 cloth?

2. Imagine that two countries, Richland and Poorland, can produce just two goods, computers and coal. Assume that for a given amount of land and capital, the output of these two products requires the following constant amounts of labour:

	Richland	Poorland
1 computer	2	4
100 tonnes of coal	4	5

Assume that each country has 20 million workers.

(a) If there is no trade, and in each country 12 million workers produce computers and 8 million workers produce coal, how many computers and tonnes of coal will each country produce? What will be the total production of each product?

(b) What is the opportunity cost of a computer in (i) Richland; (ii) Poorland?

(c) What is the opportunity cost of 100 tonnes of coal in (i) Richland; (ii) Poorland?

(d) Which country has a comparative advantage in which product?

(e) Assuming that price equals marginal cost, which of the following would represent possible exchange ratios? (i) 1 computer for 40 tonnes of coal; (ii) 2 computers for 140 tonnes of coal; (iii) 1 computer for 100 tonnes of coal; (iv) 1 computer for 60 tonnes of coal; (v) 4 computers for 360 tonnes of coal.

(f) Assume that trade now takes place and that 1 computer exchanges for 65 tonnes of coal. Both countries specialise completely in the product in which they have a comparative advantage. How much does each country produce of its respective product?

(g) The country producing computers sells 6 million domestically. How many does it export to the other country?

(h) How much coal does the other country consume?

3. Why doesn't the USA specialise as much as General Motors or Texaco? Why doesn't the UK specialise as much as ICI? Is the answer to these questions similar to the answer to the questions, 'Why doesn't the USA specialise as much as Luxembourg', and 'Why doesn't ICI or Unilever specialise as much as the local florist?'

4. To what extent are the arguments for countries specialising and then trading with each other the same as those for individuals specialising in doing the jobs at which they are relatively well suited?

5. The following are four items that are traded internationally: wheat; computers; textiles; insurance. In which one of the four is each of the following most likely to have a comparative advantage? India; the UK; Canada; Japan. Give reasons for your answer.

6. Would it be possible for a country with a comparative disadvantage in a given product at *pre*-trade levels of output to obtain a comparative advantage in it by specialising in its production and exporting it?

7. Go through each of the arguments for restricting trade and provide a counter-argument for not restricting trade.

8. It is often argued that if the market fails to develop infant industries, then this is an argument for government intervention, but not necessarily in the form of restricting imports. What *other* ways could infant industries be given government support?

9. How would you set about judging whether an industry had a genuine case for infant/senile industry protection?

10. Does the consumer in the importing country gain or lose from dumping? (Consider both the short run and the long run.)

11. What is fallacious about the following two arguments? Is there any truth in either?
    (a) 'Imports should be reduced because money is going abroad which would be better spent at home.'
    (b) 'We should protect our industries from being undercut by imports produced using cheap labour.'

12. Make out a case for restricting trade between the UK and Japan. Are there any arguments here that could not equally apply to a case for restricting trade between Scotland and England or between Liverpool and Manchester?

13. In what ways may free trade have harmful cultural effects on developing countries?

14. If countries are so keen to reduce the barriers to trade, why do many countries frequently attempt to erect barriers?

15. What factors will determine whether a country's joining a customs union will lead to trade creation or trade diversion?

16. How would you set about assessing whether or not a country had made a net dynamic gain by joining a customs union? What sort of evidence would you look for?

17. What would be the economic effects of (a) different rates of VAT; (b) different rates of personal income tax; (c) different rates of company taxation between member states, if in all other respects there were no barriers to trade or factor movements between the members of a customs union?

18. Is trade diversion in the EU more likely or less likely in the following cases?
    (a) European producers gain monopoly power in world trade.
    (b) Modern developments in technology and communications reduce the differences in production costs associated with different locations.
    (c) The development of the internal market produces substantial economies of scale in many industries.

19. Why is it difficult to estimate the magnitude of the benefits of completing the internal market of the EU?

20. Look through the costs and benefits that we identified from the single European market. Do the same costs and benefits arise from a substantially enlarged EU?

chapter twelve

Balance of payments and exchange rates

In this chapter we will first explain what is meant by the balance of payments. In doing so we will see just how the various monetary transactions between the domestic economy and the rest of the world are recorded.

Then (in sections 12.2 and 12.3) we will examine how rates of exchange are determined, and how they are related to the balance of payments. We will see what causes exchange rate fluctuations, and how the government can attempt to prevent these fluctuations.

The government could decide to leave exchange rates entirely to market forces (a free-floating exchange rate). Alternatively, it could attempt to fix its currency's exchange rate to some other currency (e.g. the US dollar). Or it could simply try to reduce the degree to which its currency fluctuates. In section 12.4, we look at the relative merits of different degrees of government intervention in the foreign exchange market: of different 'exchange rate regimes'.

Finally, we look at attempts to achieve greater currency stability between the members of the EU. Section 12.5 looks at the European exchange rate mechanism (the ERM), which has sought to limit the amount that member currencies are allowed to fluctuate against each other. Then section 12.6 examines the moves towards the adoption of a common currency, the euro.

12.1 The balance of payments account

What is meant by a balance of payments deficit or surplus?

In Chapter 7 we identified balance of payments deficits as one of the main macroeconomic problems that governments face. But what precisely do we mean by 'balance of payments deficits' (or surpluses), and what is their significance?

A country's balance of payments account records all the flows of money between residents of that country and the rest of the world. *Receipts* of money from abroad are regarded as *credits* and are entered in the accounts with a positive sign. *Outflows* of money from the country are regarded as *debits* and are entered with a negative sign.

There are two main parts of the balance of payments account: the *current account* and the *capital account*. Each part is then subdivided. We shall look at each part in turn, and take the UK as an example. Table 12.1 gives a summary of the UK balance of payments for 1996.

Definitions

Current account of the balance of payments
The record of a country's imports and exports of goods and services, plus incomes and transfers of money to and from abroad.

Balance of trade in goods or **balance of visible trade** or **merchandise balance**
Exports of goods minus imports of goods.

Services balance
Exports of services minus imports of services.

Balance of trade in goods and services or **balance of trade**
Exports of goods and services minus imports of goods and services.

The current account

The current account records payments for imports and exports of goods and services, plus incomes from property flowing into and out of the country, plus net transfers of money into and out of the country. It is normally divided into three subdivisions.

The trade in goods account. This records imports and exports of physical goods (previously known as 'visibles'). Exports result in an inflow of money and are therefore a credit item. Imports result in an outflow of money and are therefore a debit item. The balance of these is called the balance of trade in goods or balance of visible trade or merchandise balance. A *surplus* is when exports exceed imports. A *deficit* is when imports exceed exports.

The trade in services account. This records imports and exports of services (such as transport, tourism and insurance). Thus the purchase of a foreign holiday would be a debit, whereas the purchase by an overseas resident of a UK insurance policy would be a credit to the UK services account. The balance of these is called the services balance.

The balance of both the goods and services accounts together is known as the balance of trade in goods and services or simply the balance of trade.

Other current flows. There are two items here:

- Investment incomes. These consist of interest, profit and dividends flowing into and out of the country. For example, interest earned by a foreign resident from shares in a UK company would be an outflow of money (a debit item).
- Transfers of money. These include government grants to developing countries (aid), government contributions to the EU Budget and to international organisations, and international transfers of money by private individuals and firms. For example, a birthday gift of money received by a British student from an aunt in Australia would be a credit item.

TABLE 12.1 *UK balance of payments: 1996*

		£ million	
Current account			
1. Trade in goods			
(a) Exports		+166 340	
(b) Imports		−178 938	
Balance on trade in goods		−12 598	
2. Trade in services			
(a) Exports		+50 807	
(b) Imports		−43 665	
Balance on trade in services		+7142	
Balance on trade in goods and services			−5456
3. Other income flows			
Investment income balance			+9652
Transfers balance			−4631
Current account balance			**−435**
Capital account			
(transactions in UK external assets and liabilities)			
4. Long-term capital transactions			
(a) Net investment in UK from abroad		+48 459	
(b) Net UK investment abroad		−89 251	
Long-term capital balance			−40 792
5. Short-term capital flows			
(a) Net deposits in UK from abroad and borrowing from abroad by UK residents		+168 636	
(b) Net deposits abroad by UK residents and UK lending to overseas residents		−130 551	
Short-term capital balance			+38 085
6. Reserves (drawing on + adding to −)			+509
Net transactions in external assets and liabilities (capital account balance)			**−2198**
Total current + capital accounts			−2633
7. (Balancing item)			+2633
			0

Sources: *Economic Trends* (ONS); *Financial Statistics* (ONS).

Definitions

Capital account of the balance of payments (or transactions in external assets and liabilities)
The record of all changes in the country's ownership of foreign assets and foreign ownership of this country's assets.

The current account balance is the overall balance of all the above three subdivisions.

The capital account

The official title for the capital account of the balance of payments is the *transactions in external assets and liabilities*. It records cross-border changes in the holding of shares, property, bank deposits and loans, government securities, etc. In other words, unlike the current account which is concerned with money *incomes*, the capital account is concerned with the purchase and sale of *assets*. There are three main sections in this part of the balance of payments.

The long-term capital account. This records capital investments. There are two categories here.

- Direct investment. If a foreign company invests in the UK (e.g. acquires a new factory), this represents an inflow of money when the investment is made and is thus a credit item. (Any subsequent profit from this investment that flows abroad will be a debit on the investment income part of the *current* account.) UK investment abroad represents an outflow of money when the investment is made. It is thus a debit item.
- Portfolio investment. This is changes in the holding of paper assets, such as company shares. Thus if a UK resident buys shares in an overseas company, this will be a debit item.

Short-term capital flows. These consist of various types of short-term monetary movement between the UK and the rest of the world. Deposits by overseas residents in banks in the UK and loans to the UK from abroad are credit items, since they represent an inflow of money. Deposits by UK residents in overseas banks and loans by UK banks to overseas residents are debit items. They represent an outflow of money.

Short-term monetary flows are common between international financial centres to take advantage of differences in countries' interest rates and changes in exchange rates.

Flows to and from the reserves. The UK, like all other countries, holds reserves of gold and foreign currencies. From time to time the Bank of England (acting as the government's agent) will sell some of these reserves to purchase sterling on the foreign exchange market. It does this normally as a means of supporting the rate of exchange (as we shall see below). Drawing on reserves represents a *credit* item in the balance of payments accounts: money drawn from the reserves represents an *inflow* to the balance of payments (albeit an outflow from the reserves account). The reserves can thus be used to support a deficit elsewhere in the balance of payments.

Conversely, if there is a surplus elsewhere in the balance of payments, the Bank of England can use it to build up the reserves. Building up the reserves counts as a debit item in the balance of payments, since it represents an outflow from it (to the reserves).

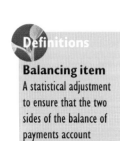

Definitions

Balancing item
A statistical adjustment to ensure that the two sides of the balance of payments account balance. It is necessary because of errors in compiling the statistics.

When all the components of the balance of payments account are taken together, the balance of payments should exactly balance: credits should equal debits. As we shall see below, if they were not equal, the rate of exchange would have to adjust until they were, or the government would have to intervene to make them equal.

When the statistics are compiled, however, a number of errors are likely to occur. As a result there will not be a balance. To 'correct' for this, a balancing item is included in the accounts. This ensures that there will be an exact balance. The main reason for the errors is that the statistics are obtained from a number of sources, and there are often delays before items are recorded and sometimes omissions too.

Summary

1. The balance of payments account records all payments to and receipts from foreign countries.
2. The current account records payments for the imports and exports of goods and services, plus property incomes and transfers of money to and from abroad.
3. The capital account (transactions in external assets and liabilities) records changes in foreign ownership of domestic assets and domestic ownership of foreign assets. It also includes dealings in the country's foreign exchange reserves.
4. The whole account must balance, but surpluses or deficits can be recorded on any specific part of the account. Thus the current account could be in deficit, but it would have to be matched by an equal and opposite capital account surplus.

Exchange rates

What causes exchange rates to change?

An exchange rate is the rate at which one currency trades for another on the foreign exchange market.

If you want to go abroad, you will need to exchange your pounds into francs, dollars, pesetas or whatever. To do this you will go to a bank. The bank will quote you that day's exchange rates: for example, 9 francs to the pound, or $1.50 to the pound. It is similar for firms. If an importer wants to buy, say, some machinery from Japan, it will require yen to pay the Japanese supplier. It will thus ask the foreign exchange section of a bank to quote it a rate of exchange of the pound into yen. Similarly, if you want to buy some foreign stocks and shares, or if companies based in the UK want to invest abroad, sterling will have to be exchanged into the appropriate foreign currency.

Likewise, if Americans want to come on holiday to the UK or to buy UK assets, or American firms want to import UK goods or to invest in the UK, they will require sterling. They will be quoted an exchange rate for the pound in the USA: say, £1 = $1.54. This means that they will have to pay $1.54 to obtain £1 worth of UK goods or assets.

Exchange rates are quoted between each of the major currencies of the world. These exchange rates are constantly changing. Minute by minute dealers in the foreign exchange dealing rooms of the banks are adjusting the rates of exchange. They charge commission when they exchange currencies. It is important for them, therefore, to ensure that they are not left with a large amount of any currency unsold. What they need to do is to balance the supply and demand of each currency: to balance the amount they purchase to the amount they sell. To do this they will need to adjust the price of each currency – namely, the exchange rate – in line with changes in supply and demand.

One of the problems in assessing what is happening to a particular currency is that its rate of exchange may rise against some currencies (weak currencies) and fall against others (strong currencies). In order to gain an overall picture of its fluctuations, therefore, it is best to look at a weighted average exchange rate against all other currencies. This is known as the *exchange rate index*. The weight given to each currency in the index depends on the proportion of transactions done with that country. Table 12.2 shows exchange rates between the pound and various currencies and the sterling exchange rate index from 1980 to 1997.

The determination of the rate of exchange in a free market

In a free foreign exchange market, the rate of exchange is determined by demand and supply. Thus the sterling exchange rate is determined by the demand and supply of pounds. This is illustrated in Figure12.1.

For simplicity, assume that there are just two countries: the UK and the USA. When UK importers wish to buy goods from the USA, or when UK residents wish to invest in the USA, they will *supply* pounds on the foreign exchange market in order to obtain dollars. The higher the exchange rate, the more dollars they will obtain for their pounds. This will effectively make

TABLE 12.2 *Sterling exchange rates: 1980–96*

	US dollar	French franc	Japanese yen	German mark	Italian lira	Sterling exchange rate index (1990 = 100)
1980	2.33	9.83	526	4.23	1992	124.4
1981	2.03	10.94	445	4.56	2287	127.9
1982	1.75	11.48	435	4.24	2364	123.2
1983	1.52	11.55	360	3.87	2302	115.6
1984	1.34	11.63	317	3.79	2339	111.4
1985	1.30	11.55	307	3.78	2463	111.3
1986	1.47	10.16	247	3.18	2186	101.4
1987	1.64	9.84	237	2.94	2123	99.3
1988	1.78	10.60	228	3.12	2315	105.4
1989	1.64	10.45	226	3.08	2247	102.3
1990	1.79	9.69	257	2.88	2133	100.0
1991	1.77	9.95	238	2.93	2187	100.8
1992 Q1	1.77	9.75	228	2.87	2155	99.4
Q2	1.81	9.83	235	2.92	2198	101.2
Q3	1.90	9.45	238	2.79	2154	99.4
Q4	1.58	8.30	194	2.45	2145	87.7
1993	1.50	8.51	167	2.48	2360	88.9
1994	1.53	8.49	156	2.48	2467	89.2
1995	1.58	7.87	148	2.26	2571	84.8
1996	1.56	7.99	170	2.35	2408	86.3
1997 Q1	1.63	9.11	197	2.70	2666	96.9
Q2	1.64	9.45	196	2.80	2765	99.6
Q3	1.60	10.13	190	3.01	2942	103.9

Source: *Economic Trends* (ONS).

Definition

Exchange rate index
A weighted average exchange rate expressed as an index, where the value of the index is 100 in a given base year. The weights of the different currencies in the index add up to 1.

BOX 12.1

The sterling index
....
What goes into the basket?

The UK's *effective* exchange rate measures the value of the pound against a group or 'basket' of other currencies. Each currency's exchange rate with the pound enters with a weight somewhere between 0 and 1. The size of each currency's weight depends on the relative importance of that country as a competitor to the UK. The more important it is, the bigger its weight. All the weights must add up to 1.

The effective exchange rate is expressed as an index with the base year equal to 100. The effective increase or decrease in the value of the pound can thus be expressed in terms of the percentage increase or decrease in this index.

The current official sterling index was introduced in February 1995. It is a weighted average of the sterling exchange rates with twenty other currencies. The weights are chosen to reflect the importance of UK trade with the various countries. The table shows the current and previous weights. The changes in these weights reflect the changing pattern of the UK's international trade and are based on 1989–91 trade flows.

The weights of foreign currencies in the sterling exchange rate index

	Previous	Current		Previous	Current
Germany	0.2001	0.2249	Ireland	0.0242	0.0308
USA	0.2044	0.1649	Finland	0.0145	0.0141
France	0.1175	0.1259	Canada	0.0190	0.0138
Italy	0.0766	0.0827	Denmark	0.0145	0.0138
Japan	0.0883	0.0700	Norway	0.0131	0.0119
Netherlands	0.0500	0.0571	Austria	0.0124	0.0119
Belgium	0.0525	0.0539	Portugal	–	0.0084
Spain	0.0202	0.0385	Australia	–	0.0048
Sweden	0.0379	0.0345	Greece	–	0.0031
Switzerland	0.0548	0.0327	New Zealand	–	0.0021

Q1 What are the current and previous total weights of the EU countries? Comment.

American goods cheaper to buy, and investment more profitable. Thus the *higher* the exchange rate, the *more* pounds will be supplied. The supply curve of pounds will therefore typically slope upwards.

When US residents wish to purchase UK goods or to invest in the UK, they will require pounds. They *demand* pounds by selling dollars on the foreign exchange market. The lower the dollar price of the pound (the exchange rate), the cheaper it will be for them to obtain UK goods and assets, and hence the more pounds they are likely to demand. The demand curve for pounds, therefore, will typically slope downwards.

The equilibrium exchange rate will be where the demand for pounds equals the supply. In Figure 12.1 this will be at an exchange rate of £1 = $1.60. But what is the mechanism that equates demand and supply?

If the current exchange rate were above the equilibrium, the supply of pounds being offered to the banks would exceed the demand. For example, in Figure 12.1 if the exchange rate were $1.80, there would be an excess

FIGURE 12.1
*Determination
of the rate of
exchange*

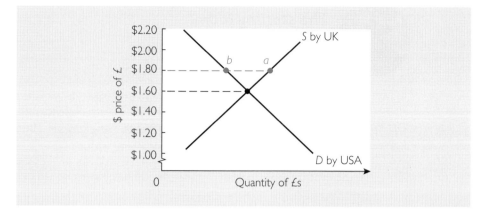

supply of pounds of $a - b$. The banks, wishing to make money by *exchanging* currency, would have to lower the exchange rate in order to encourage a greater demand for pounds and reduce the excessive supply. They would continue lowering the rate until demand equalled supply.

Similarly, if the rate were below the equilibrium, say at $1.40, there would be a shortage of pounds. The banks would find themselves with too few pounds to meet all the demand. At the same time they would have an excess supply of dollars. The banks would thus raise the exchange rate until demand equalled supply.

In practice, the process of reaching equilibrium is extremely rapid. The foreign exchange dealers in the banks are continually adjusting the rate as new customers make new demands for currencies. What is more, the banks have to watch closely what each other is doing. Banks are constantly in competition with each other and thus have to keep their rates in line. The dealers receive minute-by-minute updates on their computer screens of the rates being offered round the world.

Shifts in the currency demand and supply curves

If the currency demand and/or supply curves shift, the exchange rate will change. Thus in Figure 12.2 (which this time shows the DM exchange rate for the £), if the demand and supply curves shifted from D_1 and S_1 to D_2 and S_2 respectively, the exchange rate would fall from DM2.75 to DM2.50.

The following are the major factors which could cause the exchange rate to fall.

Definitions

Depreciation
A fall in the free-market exchange rate of the domestic currency with foreign currencies.

Appreciation
A rise in the free-market exchange rate of the domestic currency with foreign currencies.

- A rise in domestic aggregate demand. People would buy more imports. The supply of the domestic currency would shift to the right.
- Higher inflation in the domestic economy than abroad. Imports would now be relatively cheaper and thus the supply curve of the domestic currency would shift to the right. Exports would be relatively more expensive, and thus their sales would probably fall. If it resulted in less being spent on exports, the demand curve for the domestic currency from abroad would shift to the left.
- A fall in domestic interest rates. This would cause an outflow of currency as money was deposited abroad where it could earn a higher rate of interest.
- Speculation that the exchange rate will fall. If businesses involved in importing and exporting, and also banks and other foreign exchange

FIGURE 12.2
Floating exchange rates: movement to a new equilibrium

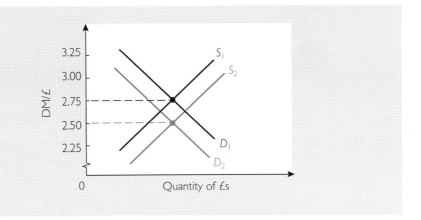

dealers, believed that the exchange rate would fall in the near future, they would sell the domestic currency before the rate did fall.

The exchange rate would rise if the opposite of each of the above occurred. When the exchange rate falls, we call this a depreciation of the currency. When the exchange rate rises, we call this an appreciation of the currency.

Summary

1. The rate of exchange is the rate at which one currency exchanges for another. Rates of exchange are determined by demand and supply in the foreign exchange market. Demand for the domestic currency consists of all the credit items in the balance of payments account. Supply consists of all the debit items.
2. The exchange rate will depreciate (fall) if the demand for the domestic currency falls or the supply increases. These shifts can be caused by increases in aggregate demand, higher inflation than abroad, reductions in domestic interest rates relative to foreign ones, or the belief by speculators that the exchange rate will fall.
3. The opposite in each case would cause an appreciation (rise).

Exchange rates and the balance of payments

How does the balance of payments affect the exchange rate?

Exchange rates and the balance of payments: no government intervention

In a free foreign exchange market the balance of payments will *automatically* balance. But why?

The credit side of the balance of payments constitutes the demand for sterling. For example, when foreigners buy UK exports they will demand sterling in order to pay for them. The debit side constitutes the supply of sterling. For example, when UK residents buy foreign goods, the importers of these

BOX 12.2 *Dealing in foreign currencies*

A daily juggling act

Imagine that a large car importer in the UK wants to import 5000 cars from Germany costing DM75 million. What does it do?

It will probably contact a number of banks' foreign exchange dealing rooms in London and ask them for exchange rate quotes. It thus puts all the banks in competition with each other. Each bank will want to get the business and thereby obtain the commission on the deal. To do this it must offer a higher rate than the other banks, since the higher the DM/£ exchange rate, the more DM the firm will get for its money. (For an importer a rate of, say, DM2.72 to £1 is better than a rate of, say, DM2.70.)

Now it is highly unlikely that any of the banks will have a spare DM75 million. But a bank cannot say to the importer 'Sorry, you will have to wait before we can agree to sell them to you.' Instead the bank will offer a deal and then, if the firm agrees, the bank will have to set about obtaining the DM75 million. To do this it must offer Germans who are *supplying* DM to obtain pounds at a sufficiently *low* DM/£ exchange rate. (The lower the DM/£ exchange rate, the fewer DM the Germans will have to pay to obtain pounds.)

The banks' dealers thus find themselves in the delicate position of wanting to offer a *high* enough exchange rate to the car importer in order to gain its business, but a *low* enough exchange rate in order to obtain the required amount of DM. The dealers are thus constantly having to adjust the rates of exchange in order to balance the demand and supply of each currency.

In general, the more of any foreign currency that dealers are asked to supply (by being offered sterling), the lower will be the exchange rate they will offer. In other words, a higher supply of sterling pushes down the foreign currency price of sterling.

 Assume that an American firm wants to import Rolls-Royces from the UK. Describe how foreign exchange dealers will respond.

goods will require foreign currency to pay for them. They will thus supply pounds. A **floating exchange rate** will ensure that the demand for pounds is equal to the supply. It will thus also ensure that the credits on the balance of payments are equal to the debits: that the balance of payments balances.

This does not mean that each part of the balance of payments account will separately balance, but simply that any current account deficit must be matched by a capital account surplus and vice versa.

For example, suppose initially that each part of the balance of payments *did* separately balance. Then let us assume that aggregate demand expanded rapidly (the economy was experiencing a boom). Consumers would buy more goods and services, including more imports. The current account would begin to move into deficit. The supply of sterling in Figure 12.2 would shift to the right. The exchange rate would fall.

As the exchange rate fell, so there would be a movement along the demand curve for sterling: among other things, the lower exchange rate would attract long-term foreign investment into the UK. The capital

Definition

Floating exchange rate
When the government does not intervene in the foreign exchange markets, but simply allows the exchange rate to be freely determined by demand and supply.

account would thus move into surplus and would exactly offset any deficit on the current account.

Exchange rates and the balance of payments: with government intervention

The government may be unwilling to let the country's currency float freely. Frequent shifts in the demand and supply curves would cause frequent changes in the exchange rate. This, in turn, might cause uncertainty for businesses, which might curtail their trade and investment.

The government may thus intervene in the foreign exchange market. But what can it do? The answer to this will depend on its objectives. It may simply want to reduce the day-to-day fluctuations in the exchange rate, or it may want to prevent longer-term, more fundamental shifts in the rate.

Reducing short-term fluctuations

Assume that the government believes that an exchange rate of DM2.75 to the pound is approximately the long-term equilibrium rate. Short-term left-ward shifts in the demand for sterling and rightward shifts in the supply, however, are causing the exchange rate to fall below this level (see Figure 12.2). What can the government do to keep the rate at DM2.75?

Using reserves. The Bank of England can sell gold and foreign currencies from the reserves to buy pounds. This will shift the demand for sterling back to the right.

Borrowing from abroad. The government can negotiate a foreign currency loan from other countries or from an international agency such as the International Monetary Fund. It can then use these moneys to buy pounds on the foreign exchange market, thus again shifting the demand for sterling back to the right.

Raising interest rates. If the government raises interest rates, it will encourage people to deposit money in the UK and encourage UK residents to keep their money in the country. The demand for sterling will increase and the supply of sterling will decrease.

Maintaining a fixed rate of exchange over the longer term

Governments may choose to maintain a fixed rate over a number of months or even years. The following are possible methods it can use to achieve this (we are assuming that there are downward pressures on the exchange rate: e.g. as a result of higher aggregate demand and higher inflation).

Deflation. This is where the government deliberately curtails aggregate demand by either *fiscal policy* or *monetary policy* or both.

Deflationary fiscal policy will involve raising taxes and/or reducing government expenditure. Deflationary monetary policy will involve reducing the supply of money and raising interest rates. Note that in this case we are talking about not just the temporary raising of interest rates to prevent a short-term outflow of money from the country, but the use of higher interest rates to reduce borrowing and hence dampen aggregate demand.

A reduction in aggregate demand will work in two ways:

● It will reduce the level of consumer spending. This will directly cut imports, since there will be reduced spending on Japanese videos, German cars, Spanish holidays and so on. The supply of sterling coming on to the foreign exchange market thus decreases.
● It will reduce the rate of inflation. This will make UK goods more competitive abroad, thus increasing the demand for sterling.

Supply-side policies. This is where the government attempts to increase the long-term competitiveness of UK goods by encouraging reductions in the costs of production and/or improvements in the quality of UK goods. For example, the government may attempt to improve the quantity and quality of training and research and development.

Controls on imports and/or foreign exchange dealing. This is where the government restricts the outflow of money, either by restricting people's access to foreign exchange, or by the use of tariffs (customs duties) and quotas.

Summary

1. In a free foreign exchange market, the balance of payments will automatically balance, since changes in the exchange rate will balance the demand for the currency (credits on the balance of payments) with the supply (debits on the balance of payments).
2. There is no guarantee, however, that there will be a balance on each of the separate parts of account.
3. The government can attempt to prevent the rate of exchange falling by central bank purchases of the domestic currency in the foreign exchange market, either by selling foreign currency reserves or by using foreign loans. Alternatively, the government can raise interest rates. The reverse actions can be taken if it wants to prevent the rate from rising.
4. In the longer term, it can attempt to prevent the rate from falling by pursuing deflationary policies, protectionist policies, or supply-side policies to increase the competitiveness of the country's exports.

12.4 Fixed versus floating exchange rates

Should exchange rates be 'left to the market'?

Are exchange rates best left free to fluctuate and be determined purely by market forces, or should the government intervene to fix exchange rates, either rigidly or within bands? Unfortunately, the answer is not clear cut. Both floating and fixed exchange rates have their advantages and disadvantages.

Advantages of fixed exchange rates

Surveys reveal that most businesspeople prefer relatively rigid exchange rates: if not totally fixed, then at least pegged for periods of time. The following arguments are used to justify this preference.

Certainty. With fixed exchange rates, international trade and investment become much less risky, since profits are not affected by movements in the exchange rate.

Assume that a firm correctly forecasts that its product will sell in the USA for $1.50. It costs 80p to produce. If the rate of exchange is fixed at £1 = $1.50, each unit will earn £1 and hence make a 20p profit. If, however, the rate of exchange were not fixed, exchange fluctuations could wipe out this profit. If, say, the rate appreciated to £1 = $2, and if units continued to sell for $1.50, they would now earn only 75p each, and hence make a 5p loss.

Little or no speculation. Provided the rate is *absolutely* fixed – and people believe that it will remain so – there is no point in speculating. If there is no speculative pressure on the pound, the Bank of England will need to intervene less to maintain the rate.

Prevents governments pursuing 'irresponsible' macroeconomic policies. If a government deliberately and excessively expands aggregate demand – perhaps in an attempt to gain short-term popularity with the electorate – the resulting balance of payments deficit will force it to constrain demand again (unless it resorts to import controls).

Governments cannot allow their economies to have a persistently higher inflation rate than competitor countries without running into balance of payments crises, and hence a depletion of reserves. Fixed rates thus force governments (in the absence of trade restrictions) to keep the rate of inflation roughly to world levels.

Disadvantages of fixed exchange rates

Exchange rate policy may conflict with the interests of domestic business and the economy as a whole. A balance of payments deficit can occur even if the economy is not 'overheating'. For example, there can be a fall in the demand for the country's exports as a result of an external shock (such as a recession in other countries) or because of increased foreign competition. If protectionism is to be avoided, and if supply-side policies work only over the long run, the government will be forced to deflate the economy. This is likely to have two adverse effects on the domestic economy:

- Deflationary policy normally involves higher interest rates. These, however, may discourage business investment. This in turn will lower firms' profits in the long term and reduce the country's long-term rate of economic growth. The country's capacity to produce will be restricted and businesses are likely to fall behind in the competitive race with their international rivals to develop new products and improve existing ones.

- Deflationary policy can lead to a recession. If real wage rates and prices are sticky downward, the deflation may have to be severe if the deficit is to be corrected. Reliance will have to be placed largely on lower *incomes* reducing the demand for imports. A severe recession, with high unemployment, may thus result.

The problem is that, with fixed exchange rates, domestic policy is entirely constrained by the balance of payments. Any attempt to reflate and cure unemployment will simply lead to a balance of payments deficit and thus force governments to deflate again.

Competitive deflations leading to world depression. If deficit countries deflated, but surplus countries *reflated*, there would be no overall world deflation or reflation. Countries may be quite happy, however, to run a balance of payments surplus and build up reserves. Countries may thus competitively deflate – all trying to achieve a balance of payments surplus. But this is beggar-my-neighbour policy. Not all countries can have a surplus! Overall the world must be in balance. The result of these policies is to lead to general world deflation and a restriction in growth.

Problems of international liquidity. If trade is to expand, there must be an expansion in the supply of currencies acceptable for world trade (dollars, pounds, marks, gold, etc.): there must be adequate international liquidity. Countries' reserves of these currencies must grow if they are to be sufficient to maintain a fixed rate at times of balance of payments disequilibrium. Conversely, there must not be excessive international liquidity. Otherwise the extra demand that would result would lead to world inflation. It is important under fixed exchange rates, therefore, to avoid too much or too little international liquidity. The problem is whether there is adequate control of international liquidity. The supply of dollars, for example, depends largely on US policy, which may be dominated by its internal economic situation rather than by a concern for the well-being of the international community.

Inability to adjust to shocks. With sticky prices and wage rates, there is no swift mechanism for dealing with sudden balance of payments crises – like that caused by a sudden increase in oil prices. In the short run, countries will need huge reserves or loan facilities to support their currencies. There may be insufficient international liquidity to permit this. In the longer run, countries may be forced into a depression, by having to deflate. The alternative may be to resort to protectionism, or to abandon the fixed rate and devalue.

Speculation. If speculators believe that a fixed rate simply cannot be maintained, speculation is likely to be massive. If, for example, there is a large balance of payments deficit, speculative selling will worsen the deficit, and may itself force a devaluation.

Advantages of a free-floating exchange rate

The advantages and disadvantages of free-floating rates are to a large extent the opposite of fixed rates.

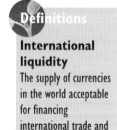

Definitions

International liquidity
The supply of currencies in the world acceptable for financing international trade and investment.

Devaluation
Where the government repegs the exchange rate at a lower level.

Automatic correction. The government simply lets the exchange rate move freely to the equilibrium. In this way, balance of payments disequilibria are automatically and instantaneously corrected without the need for specific government policies.

No problem of international liquidity and reserves. Since there is no central bank intervention in the foreign exchange market, there is no need to hold reserves. A currency is automatically convertible at the current market exchange rate.

Insulation from external economic events. A country is not tied to a possibly unacceptably high world inflation rate, as it is under a fixed exchange rate. It is also to some extent protected against world economic fluctuations and shocks.

Governments are free to choose their domestic policy. Under a floating rate the government can choose whatever level of domestic demand it considers appropriate, and simply leave exchange rate movements to take care of any balance of payments effect. This is a major advantage, especially when the effectiveness of deflation under fixed exchange rates is reduced by downward wage and price rigidity, and when competitive deflation between countries may end up causing a world recession.

Disadvantages of a free-floating exchange rate

Despite these advantages there are still a number of serious problems with free-floating exchange rates:

Unstable exchange rates. The less elastic are the demand and supply curves for the currency in Figure 12.2, the greater the change in exchange rate that will be necessary to restore equilibrium following a shift in either demand or supply. In the long run, in a competitive world with domestic substitutes for imports and foreign substitutes for exports, demand and supply curves are relatively elastic. Nevertheless, in the short run, given that many firms have contracts with specific overseas suppliers or distributors, the demands for imports and exports are less elastic.

Speculation. In an uncertain world, where there are few restrictions on currency speculation, where the fortunes and policies of governments can change rapidly, and where large amounts of short-term deposits are internationally 'footloose', speculation can be highly destabilising in the short run. If people think that the exchange rate will fall, then they will sell the currency, and this will cause the exchange rate to fall even further, perhaps overshooting the eventual equilibrium. At times of international currency turmoil (see Box 12.4), such speculation can be enormous. Worldwide, over a trillion dollars on average passes daily across the foreign exchanges: greatly in excess of countries' foreign exchange reserves!

Uncertainty for traders and investors. The uncertainty caused by currency fluctuations can discourage international trade and investment. To some

BOX 12.3 *The importance of capital movements*

How a current account deficit can coincide with an appreciating exchange rate

The era of dirty floating exchange rates has seen a huge increase in short-term capital movements. Vast amounts of moneys transfer from country to country in search of higher interest rates or a currency that is likely to appreciate. This can have a bizarre effect on exchange rates.

If a country pursues a reflationary fiscal policy, the current account will tend to go into deficit as extra imports are 'sucked in'. What effect will this have on exchange rates? You might think that the answer is obvious: the higher demand for imports will create an extra supply of domestic currency on the foreign exchange market and hence drive down the exchange rate.

In fact the opposite is likely. The higher interest rates resulting from the higher domestic demand can lead to a massive inflow of short-term capital. The capital account can thus move sharply into surplus. This is likely to outweigh the current account deficit and cause an *appreciation* of the exchange rate.

Exchange rate movements, especially in the short term, are largely brought about by changes on the capital rather than the current account.

 Why do high international capital mobility and an absence of exchange controls severely limit a country's ability to choose its interest rate?

extent the problem can be overcome by using the **forward exchange market**. Here traders agree with a bank *today* the rate of exchange for some point in the *future* (say, six months' time). This allows traders to plan future purchases of imports or sales of exports at a known rate of exchange. Of course, banks charge for this service, since they are taking on the risks themselves of adverse exchange rate fluctuations.

But dealing in the futures market only takes care of short-run uncertainty. Banks will not be prepared to take on the risks of offering forward contracts for several years hence. Thus firms simply have to live with the uncertainty over exchange rates in future years. This will discourage long-term investment. For example, the possibility of exchange rate appreciation may well discourage firms from investing abroad, since a higher exchange rate will mean that foreign exchange earnings will be worth less in the domestic currency.

Figure 12.3 shows the fluctuations in the dollar/pound exchange rate and the exchange rate index from 1976 to 1997. As you can see, there have been large changes in exchange rates. Such changes do not only make it difficult for exporters. Importers too will be hesitant about making long-term deals. For example, a UK manufacturing firm signing a contract to buy US components in 1980, when $2.40 worth of components could be purchased for £1, would find a struggle to make a profit some four years later when only just over $1.00 worth of US components could be purchased for £1!

Definition

Forward exchange market
Where contracts are made today for the price at which a currency will be exchanged at some specified future date.

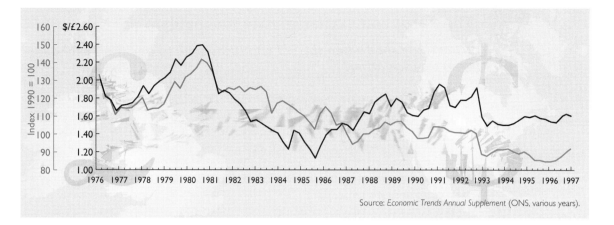

Source: *Economic Trends Annual Supplement* (ONS, various years).

FIGURE 12.3
Dollar/sterling exchange rate and sterling exchange rate index: 1976–97

Lack of discipline on the domestic economy. Governments may pursue irresponsibly inflationary policies (for short-term political gain, say). This will have adverse effects over the longer term as the government will at some point have to deflate the economy again, with a resulting fall in output and rise in unemployment.

Summary

1. Fixed exchange rates bring the advantage of certainty for the business community, which encourages trade and foreign investment. They also help to prevent governments from pursuing irresponsible macroeconomic policies.

2. However, with fixed rates domestic policy is entirely constrained by the balance of payments. What is more, they can lead to competitive deflation world-wide; there may be problems of excessive or insufficient international liquidity; there may be difficulty in adjusting to external shocks; and speculation could be very severe if people came to believe that a fixed rate was about to break down.

3. The advantages of free-floating exchange rates are that they automatically correct balance of payments disequilibria; they eliminate the need for reserves; and they give governments a greater independence to pursue their chosen domestic policy.

4. On the other hand, a completely free exchange rate can be highly unstable, especially when the elasticities of demand for imports and exports are low; also speculation may be destabilising. This may discourage firms from trading and investing abroad. What is more, a flexible exchange rate, by removing the balance of payments constraint on domestic policy, may encourage governments to pursue irresponsible domestic policies for short-term political gain.

12.5 The European exchange rate mechanism

What happened when the EU countries tried to peg their exchange rates to each other?

There have been many attempts to regulate exchange rates since 1945. By far the most successful was the Bretton Woods system, which was adopted worldwide from the end of the Second World War until 1971. This was a form of **adjustable peg** exchange rate, where exchange rates were pegged (i.e. fixed) to the US dollar, but could be repegged at a lower or higher level ('devalued' or 'revalued') if there was a persistent and substantial balance of payments deficit or surplus.

With growing world inflation and instability from the mid-1960s, the system was abandoned in the early 1970s. What followed was a period of exchange rate management known as **dirty floating**. In this system, exchange rates are not pegged, but allowed to float. However, central banks intervened from time to time to prevent excessive exchange rate fluctuations. It is thus a form of 'managed flexibility'. This system largely continues to this day.

However, on a regional basis, especially within Europe, there have been attempts to create greater exchange rate stability by establishing exchange rate bands: upper and lower limits within which exchange rates are allowed to fluctuate. The name given to the EU system is the **exchange rate mechanism (ERM)**.

The origins of the ERM

At the Bremen Summit of EC members in 1978, it was agreed to set up a *European Monetary System* (EMS). The aim of the EMS was to create currency stability, monetary co-operation between the member states and the convergence of their economic policies. The central feature of the EMS would be an exchange rate mechanism.

The EMS and the ERM duly came into existence in March 1979. Although the UK became a formal member of the EMS, it chose not to join the exchange rate mechanism. When Greece joined the EC in 1984, it too joined the EMS, but stayed outside the ERM. Spain and Portugal joined the EC in 1986, but it was not until 1989 that Spain joined the ERM. The UK eventually joined in 1990. Finally Portugal joined in April 1992. Then in September 1992, the UK and Italy indefinitely suspended their membership of the ERM, but Italy rejoined in November 1996 as part of its bid to join the single European currency (see section 12.6).

Features of the ERM

The exchange rate mechanism is a 'parity grid' system. Each currency is denominated in terms of the other ERM currencies in a grid. The grid specifies the central parity rates for each pair of currencies, and fluctuations are allowed within specified limits. The parities can be adjusted from time to time by agreement, thus making the ERM an 'adjustable peg' system. All the currencies float jointly with currencies outside the ERM.

Definitions

Adjustable peg
A system whereby exchange rates are fixed for a period of time, but may be devalued (or revalued) if a deficit (or surplus) becomes substantial.

Dirty floating (managed flexibility)
A system of flexible exchange rates, but where the government intervenes to prevent excessive fluctuations or even to achieve an unofficial target exchange rate.

ERM (the exchange rate mechanism)
A semi-fixed system whereby participating EU countries allow fluctuations against each other's currencies only within agreed bands. Collectively they float freely against all other currencies.

Each currency's fluctuations are limited to a certain percentage either side of each other currency. These bands were set at $\pm2^1/_4$ per cent in 1979 for all countries except Italy, which was given a ±6 per cent band. It moved to the narrow band in 1990. Spain, then the UK, and then Portugal all joined at the ±6 per cent band. Then in 1993, the bands were widened for all the nine remaining countries in the ERM to ±15 per cent (except for Germany and the Netherlands, which maintained the $\pm2^1/_4$ per cent band between their two currencies). Despite this, countries have attempted to maintain their currencies within much narrower limits.

If a currency approaches the upper or lower limit against *any* other ERM currency, the two countries must intervene to maintain their currencies within the band. This can take the form of their central banks selling the stronger currency and buying the weaker one, or reducing interest rates in the case of the strong currency and raising interest rates in the case of the weak currency. Thus any currency's limit to appreciation is determined by the weakest currency in the band, and any currency's limit to depreciation is determined by the strongest currency in the band.

The ERM in practice

The ERM in the 1980s

In a system of pegged exchange rates, countries should harmonise their policies to avoid excessive currency misalignments and the need for large devaluations or revaluations. In the early 1980s, however, French and Italian inflation rates were persistently higher than German rates. At first there were approximately two realignments per year. This was frequent enough to prevent severe balance of payments disequilibria from building up, and thus helped to reduce speculation. It was also frequent enough to allow the realignments to be relatively small.

After 1983 realignments became less frequent, and then from 1987 to 1992 they ceased altogether. This was due to a growing convergence of members' internal policies. France, Italy and the other members increasingly adopted exchange rate stability as their major monetary goal. This disciplined them into adopting the lower inflation rates experienced in Germany, especially as it was the DM exchange rate with their currencies that had become the major target.

By the time the UK joined in 1990, the ERM was generally seen by its existing members as being a great success. It had created a zone of currency stability in a world of highly unstable exchange rates, and had provided the necessary environment for the establishment of a truly common market by the end of 1992.

Crisis in the ERM

For most of the period 1990–2, there was optimism that convergence could continue in the enlarged ERM and would remove the need for realignments. After all, there had been no realignments since 1987, and there seemed a genuine collective commitment to defend the agreed parities. The anchor was the German economy, with its history of monetary stability and low inflation.

It might have been expected that, with the abolition of restrictions on capital movements between ERM members (achieved by 1991), there would

BOX 12.4

Currency turmoil in 1995
····························
A problem of a lack of international convergence

For many years now the leaders of the Group of Seven' countries (USA, Japan, Germany, France, Italy, UK and Canada) have met once a year at an economic summit conference (and more frequently if felt necessary). Top of the agenda in most of these G7 meetings has been how to generate world economic growth without major currency fluctuations. But to achieve this it is important that there is a *harmonisation* of economic policies between nations. In other words, it is important that all the major countries are pursuing consistent policies aiming at common international goals.

But how can policy harmonisation be achieved? As long as there are significant domestic differences between the major economies, there is likely to be conflict not harmony. For example, if one country, say the USA, is worried about the size of its budget deficit, it may be unwilling to respond to world demands for a stimulus to aggregate demand to pull the world economy out of recession. What is more, speculators, seeing differences between countries, are likely to exaggerate them by their actions, causing large changes in exchange rates.

Currency turmoil in March 1995

A good example of exchange rate volatility resulting from a lack of international harmonisation occurred in 1995. On 6 March the dollar reached post-war lows against the DM and the yen, standing at DM1.386 and ¥92.40 respectively. The fall in value against the yen represented a 32 per cent depreciation since 1992.

In Europe, the knock-on effect of the strong DM was felt in some measure by all the currencies, especially those within the ERM. The Spanish peseta, under pressure prior to the DM's rise, was devalued by 7 per cent, and the Portuguese escudo by 3.5 per cent. Both the French and Swedish governments, with their currencies reaching record lows against the DM, were forced to put up interest rates to prevent further depreciation.

The high yen and DM proved to be equally problematic for the Japanese and German governments. The Japanese economy, which is highly dependent on the US economy for its export earnings (over a third of its foreign sales go to the USA, amounting to 15 per cent of its GDP), found its competitive position significantly eroded. On top of this, a surge in cheap imports reduced many Japanese companies' share of their home market and subsequently stifled the recovery of business growth. Such growth was also being undermined by the sustained high value of the yen, which was encouraging many Japanese businesses to shift production facilities overseas, reducing domestic investment still further.

In Germany too, concern was being expressed about the high exchange rate and its impact upon the economy's faltering economic recovery. It was suggested that if the 13 per cent appreciation of the DM since December 1994 were not to be reversed, economic growth could be reduced by as much as 1 per cent.

But why had there been such a large appreciation of the DM and yen? The speculative pressure on the dollar began in late December following an economic crisis in Mexico.

have been the danger of increased speculation. But speculation will occur only if the speculators believe that realignments are likely – and they did not.

But despite the apparent strength of the ERM, there were underlying weaknesses that were eventually to lead to a crisis:

Not only did the USA quickly arrange a $20 billion aid package, but more significantly, the prospect of a large decline in Mexican imports was seen by many speculators as a severe blow to the USA's export recovery. On top of this, market analysts were predicting that US interest rates, which had previously been rising, would now fall as US economic growth slowed. In contrast, interest rates in Germany looked set to rise, as the German authorities faced growing inflationary pressures. Faced by all this, many investors moved out of dollars and into the more stable DM. This merely intensified a process that had been occurring throughout 1994, whereby US and Asian investors, seeking to diversify their portfolios and invest in non-US equities and bonds, sold dollars.

The US Federal Reserve seemed unconcerned about the falling dollar and took no steps to support it. This expression of total indifference led speculators to believe that the dollar's fall was not yet over, encouraging yet further selling of dollar balances.

Such was the strength of this speculative wave driving the dollar down, that many investment banks began to argue that the dollar had significantly overshot its long-term equilibrium value. By early March the investment bank Goldman Sachs estimated that the dollar was anywhere between 40 and 50 per cent undervalued against the yen and DM.

The currency crisis of March trailed on into April and was the main topic of discussion at the IMF summit held in Washington on the 26th of that month. Blame for the volatility in currency markets was squarely levelled at the USA for being far too slow to raise domestic interest rates to halt the dollar's slide. Both France and Japan (the one keen to push its currency up, the other down) argued that greater international co-operation was vital if the dollar's slide was to be halted and currency speculation stabilised.

The future?

Such problems are unlikely to diminish in the future as international interdependence continues to grow. The G7 nations have responded to the problem of co-ordination by seeking to expand and reform the responsibilities of the world's leading international financial and trade institutions. For example, the key reform proposed at the 1995 G7 summit in Halifax, Canada was that the IMF, the WTO and the World Bank should work more closely together, offering advice to borrowing countries and help with economic adjustment and trade liberalisation.

The G7 nations hope that greater co-operation between these international institutions will enable the world economy to be more successfully managed in the future.

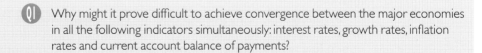

?1 Why might it prove difficult to achieve convergence between the major economies in all the following indicators simultaneously: interest rates, growth rates, inflation rates and current account balance of payments?

- The removal of capital controls had made the ERM currencies vulnerable to speculative attack, were such an attack ever to occur.
- The German economy was becoming subject to increasing strains from the reunification process. The finance of reconstruction in the eastern part of Germany was causing a growing budget deficit. The Bundesbank

thus felt obliged to maintain high interest rates in order to keep inflation in check.

- The UK had entered the ERM at a rate that many commentators felt was unsustainably high without considerable deflation. Indeed, with a massive current account deficit, and high German interest rates, the UK was obliged to keep interest rates high in order to protect the pound, despite the fact that the economy was sliding rapidly into recession.
- The French franc was perceived to be overvalued, and there were the first signs of worries as to whether its exchange rate within the ERM could be retained. For much of the period 1990–3 it was the weakest of the ERM currencies.
- The US economy was moving into recession and, as a result, US interest rates were cut. This led to a large outflow of capital from the USA. With high German interest rates, much of this capital flowed to Germany. This pushed up the value of the DM and with it the other ERM currencies.
- The likelihood of a successful move towards European economic and monetary union was diminishing with the rejection of the Maastricht Treaty by the Danes in the referendum of June 1992, and with the possibility that the French might also reject the treaty. Fears were expressed that exchange rate instability might re-emerge.

As the summer of 1992 progressed, these tensions increased. Then in September 1992, with a further fall in US interest rates and further buying of the DM, things reached crisis point. First the lira was devalued. Then two days later, on 'Black Wednesday' (16 September), the UK and Italy were forced to suspend their membership of the ERM: the pound and the lira were floated. At the same time, the Spanish peseta was devalued by 5 per cent.

After this turmoil a period of relative calm ensued. Even so, the peseta and the escudo were devalued twice (in November 1992 and May 1993) and the Irish punt was devalued once in January 1993. Thus the ERM that had survived the departure of Italy and the UK was no longer one of fixed rates.

Turmoil returned in the summer of 1993. The French economy was moving into recession and there were calls for cuts in French interest rates. But this was possible only if Germany was prepared to cut its rates too, and it was not. Speculators began to sell francs and it became obvious that the existing franc/DM parity could not be maintained. In an attempt to rescue the ERM, the EC finance ministers agreed to adopt wide ±15 per cent bands. The result was that the franc and the Danish krone depreciated against the mark.

An ERM with ±15 per cent bands is a quite different system from one with ±2$^1/_4$ per cent bands. There is considerable scope for fluctuations and much less need for intervention. Nevertheless, the remaining ERM members have attempted to minimise fluctuations by harmonising, where possible, their interest rates. For most of the time since 1993, the currencies have remained within much narrower limits.

Summary

1. One means of achieving greater currency stability is for a group of countries to peg their internal exchange rates and yet float jointly with the rest of the world. The exchange rate mechanism of the EU is an example. Members' currencies are allowed to fluctuate against other member currencies within a band. The band was ±2¼ per cent for the majority of the ERM countries, but originally Italy (until 1990) and then the new members, Spain, the UK and Portugal, adopted a wider ±6 per cent.
2. The need for realignments seemed to have diminished in the late 1980s as greater convergence was achieved between the members' economies. However, growing strains in the system, in the early 1990s, led to a crisis in September 1992. The UK and Italy left the ERM and realignments of the peseta, escudo and punt followed. There was a further crisis in July 1993 and the bands were widened to ±15 per cent.
3. The ERM has been seen as an important first stage on the road to complete economic and monetary union in the EU.

12.6 EMU and the single European currency

Is monetary union a good idea?

The ERM was conceived as a stage on the road to complete economic and monetary union (EMU). If achieved, this will involve the complete economic and financial integration of the EU countries. It will be not just a common market, but a market with a single currency, a single central bank and a single monetary policy. This European monetary union will be like the current 'British monetary union' – the economic union of England, Scotland, Wales and Northern Ireland – or the economic and monetary union of the United States of America.

The Maastricht Treaty

In December 1991 the leaders of the twelve EC countries met at Maastricht in the Netherlands to negotiate a treaty on European Union. The treaty was signed in February 1992 and was subsequently ratified by the individual member countries

The Maastricht Treaty was a major move towards full economic, political and social union. It sought to develop a common European foreign policy and defence policy, a common security policy (to encourage greater co-operation between the police) and in its social chapter it set out a common social policy. It also made all EU nationals 'citizens of the Union', thereby granting them total freedom to live and work wherever they chose in the EU.

It also set out a detailed programme for economic and monetary union (EMU). The timetable for EMU was divided into three stages.

Stage 1. This was to be a preliminary stage, during which a 'Monetary Committee' of the European Union would monitor monetary policy in the member states and provide advice to the Council of Ministers on monetary convergence. During this stage preparations would be made for the establishment of a European Monetary Institute (EMI), an institution which would be the forerunner of a European central bank.

It was hoped that stage 1 would start on 1 January 1993, but it could not begin until all twelve member states had ratified the treaty. As it turned out, it was not until the autumn of 1993 that the last country (Germany) completed the ratification process.

Stage 2. This would begin on 1 January 1994, at which point the EMI would be established. It would seek to co-ordinate monetary policy and encourage greater co-operation between EU central banks. It would also monitor the operation of the ERM and would prepare the ground for the establishment of a European central bank in stage 3.

During stage 2 the member states would seek to achieve convergence of their economies. In order to progress to full economic and monetary union in stage 3, a country would have to meet five convergence criteria:

- Inflation: this should be no more than $1^{1}/_{2}$ per cent above the average inflation rate of the three lowest inflation countries in the EU.
- Interest rates: the rate on long-term government bonds should be no more than 2 per cent above the average of the three countries with the lowest interest rates.
- Budget deficit: this should be no more than 3 per cent of GDP at market prices.[1]
- National debt: this should be no more than 60 per cent of GDP at market prices.
- Exchange rates: the currency should have been within the normal bands of the ERM for at least two years with no realignments or excessive intervention.

By the end of 1996, the EMI would have to specify the details of the central banking system to be established in stage 3. Also by this date the Council of Ministers would have to decide whether the conditions had been met for the start of stage 3. The conditions specify that at least seven countries must have met the five convergence criteria. If they had, then the Council of Ministers would specify the date on which these countries would commence stage 3, the stage of full EMU.

Stage 3. It would commence at the earliest in 1997. If a date were not set by the end of 1997, a review would take place during 1998 and stage 3 would commence on 1 January 1999.

At the beginning of this stage, the countries which met the five criteria would fix their currencies permanently to a single European currency (which was subsequently named the 'Euro'). Their national currencies would therefore effectively disappear.

At the same time a European System of Central Banks (ESCB) would be created, consisting of a European Central Bank (ECB) and the central banks of the member states. Like the Bundesbank (and unlike the Bank of England)

---

[1]See Box 7.1 for a definition of GDP at market prices.

the ECB would be independent: independent from governments and also from EU political institutions. Its board members would be appointed by the Council of Ministers for an eight-year term.

The ECB would operate the monetary policy on behalf of the countries which had adopted full EMU. It would be the sole issuer of banknotes (denominated in euros) and would distribute them through the individual central banks. It would control the money supply and determine interest rate policy. It would take over the reserves of the member states and would use them to support the euro on the foreign exchange markets.

Any member state not initially meeting the convergence criteria would proceed to full EMU when the criteria had subsequently been met.

The UK and Denmark negotiated an 'opt-out' from the Maastricht Treaty. They do not have to proceed to stage 3 if they so choose.

As 1999 drew closer, concerns were raised as to whether even a limited number of 'core' countries, such as Germany, France and the Netherlands, would be ready to move to full EMU with a single currency. Germany's budget deficit was edging above the 3 per cent of GDP ceiling, and France's, although falling, was still over 4 per cent in 1996. What is more, other countries that had expressed an eagerness to join fell well short of meeting the convergence criteria. Several countries had higher than permitted inflation rates or national debt. Belgium and Italy, for example, both had a national debt of more than twice the permitted level.

Supporters of EMU were quick to point out that states which were eligible to proceed with EMU would not be identified until early 1998, and both the French and German governments were confident that by this date all of the Maastricht convergence criteria would be met. What is more, there is some flexibility built into the criteria. A budget deficit in excess of 3 per cent of GDP would be permitted if it were declining and 'close' to 3 per cent, or if an excess of 3 per cent were 'exceptional and temporary'; and a national debt in excess of 60 per cent of GDP would be permitted, if it were 'sufficiently diminishing and approaching the reference value at a satisfactory rate'. In other words, membership of EMU would be permitted for countries making satisfactory progress towards meeting these two criteria: and what constitutes 'satisfactory' is clearly open to interpretation and negotiation.

On a loose interpretation, most of the EU countries could be eligible for progressing to stage 3. Countries only meeting the convergence criteria on this loose interpretation, however, would not *have* to join. They would effectively have an opt-out, like the UK and Denmark.

But even if some countries in 1999 did more to full EMU and the adoption of a single currency, other countries would not. There would thus be a 'two-speed Europe'. Capital and trade could be attracted to the inner core of stable countries, while the peripheral countries, such as Portugal, Greece and the UK (if it chose not to join), would suffer from greater instability and a loss of influence.

How desirable is EMU?

EMU has the potential to bring several major advantages.

Elimination of the costs of converting currencies. With separate currencies in each of the EU countries, these transaction costs can be very large, especially when the various parts of a good are made in several different countries. By 1993 each of the twelve EU countries already did more trade with each other than with non-EU countries. With the further encouragement of trade and factor movements that the single market will continue to bring, these transaction coss are likely to rise as long as separate currencies remain.

Nevertheless, the elimination of these costs is probably the least important benefit from a single currency. The European Commission has estimated that the effect would be to increase the GDP of the countries concerned by an average of only 0.4 per cent. The gains to countries like the UK, which have well-developed financial markets, would be even smaller.

Increased competition and efficiency. Despite the advent of the single market, large price differences have remained between member states. A single currency would not only eliminate the need to convert one currency into another (a barrier to competition), but it would bring more transparency in pricing, and put greater downward pressure on prices in high-cost firms and countries.

Elimination of exchange rate uncertainty (between the members). Even with a narrow-banded ERM, realignments may still occur from time to time if separate currencies remain. As the events of 1992 and 1993 showed, this can cause massive speculation if it is believed that currencies are out of line. Removal of this uncertainty would help to encourage trade between member countries. Perhaps more importantly, it would encourage investment by firms that trade between these countries, given that exchange rate uncertainty is a major deterrent to long-term investment by such firms.

Increased inward investment. Investment from the rest of the world would be likely to increase, attracted to a single market of up to 200 million customers, where there would be no fear of internal currency movements. EU countries which did not join, by contrast, could find that inward investment was diverted away from them to the common-currency countries.

Lower inflation and interest rates. A single monetary policy would force convergence in inflation rates (just as inflation rates are very similar between the different regions *within* a country). Provided the European central bank is independent from short-term political manipulation, this is likely to result in a lower average inflation rate in the EU. This, in turn, would help to convince markets that the euro would be strong relative to other currencies. The result would be less need to manipulate short-term interest rates to defend the currency and a lower long-term rate of interest. This, in turn, would further encourage investment in the single-currency countries, both by member states and by the rest of the world.

Opposition to EMU

Monetary union has been bitterly opposed, however, by certain groups. Many 'Eurosceptics' see within it a surrender of national political and economic sovereignty. The lack of an independent monetary and exchange rate policy is a serious problem, they argue, if an economy is at all out of harmony with the rest of the Union. For example, if countries like the UK, Italy and Spain have higher endemic rates of inflation (due, say, to greater cost-push pressures – perhaps caused by a lower growth in productivity than in other EU countries), then how are they to make their goods competitive with the rest of the Union? With separate currencies these countries could devalue or run a deflationary monetary policy. With a single currency, however, they could become depressed 'regions' of Europe, with rising unemployment and all the other regional problems of depressed regions *within* a country. This may then require significant regional policies – policies which may not be in place or, if they were, would be seen as too interventionist by the political right.

The answer given by proponents of EMU is that it is better to tackle the problem of high inflation in such countries by the disciplines of competition from other EU countries, than merely to feed that inflation by keeping separate currencies and allowing repeated devaluations, with all the uncertainty that that brings. If such countries become depressed, they argue, it is better to have a fully developed *fiscal* policy for the Union which will divert funds into investment in such regions. What is more, the high-inflation countries tend to be the poorer ones with lower wage levels (albeit faster wage *increases*). With the high mobility of labour and capital that will accompany the development of the single market, resources are likely to be attracted to such countries. This could help to narrow the gap between the richer and poorer member states. Nevertheless, with separate languages and cultures, it is unlikely that labour mobility would ever be as high as in the USA (whose single currency area has been compared with the EU). If there was high unemployment in Tyneside, would many people there migrate to Turin, say, if there was plenty of work there?

Another problem for members of a single currency occurs in adjusting to a shock when that shock affects members to different degrees. For example, a sudden change in the price of oil would affect an oil-exporting country like the UK differently from oil-importing countries. This problem is more serious, the less the factor mobility between member countries and the less the price flexibility within member countries.

This problem, however, should not be overstated. The divergences between economies are often the result of a lack of harmony between countries in their demand management policies: something that would be impossible in the case of monetary policy, and more difficult in the case of fiscal policy, for countries with a single currency. Also, many of the shocks that face economies today are global and have similar (albeit not identical) effects on all countries. Adjustment to such shocks would often be better with a single co-ordinated policy, which would be much easier with a single currency and a single central bank.

Even when shocks are uniformly felt in the member states, however, there is still the problem that policies adopted centrally will have different impacts on each country. For example, in the UK, a large proportion of borrowing is at variable interest rates. In Germany, by contrast, much is at fixed rates. Thus if the European Central Bank were to raise interest rates, the deflationary effects would be felt disproportionately in the UK. Of course, were this balance to change – and there is some evidence that types of borrowing are becoming more uniform across the EU – this problem would diminish.

The problem for economists is that the issue of monetary union is a very emotive one. 'Europhiles' often see monetary union as a vital element in their vision of a united Europe. Many Eurosceptics, however, see EMU as a surrender of sovereignty and a threat to nationhood. In such an environment, a calm assessment of the arguments and evidence is very difficult.

Summary

1. The Maastricht Treaty set out a timetable for achieving EMU. This would culminate in stage 3 with the creation of a currency union: a single European currency with a common monetary policy operated by an independent European Central Bank.
2. The advantages claimed for EMU are that it will eliminate the costs of converting currencies and the uncertainties associated with possible changes in inter-EU exchange rates. What is more, a common central bank, independent from domestic governments, will provide the stable monetary environment necessary for a convergence of the EU economies and lower long-term interest rates, the effect of which would be the encouragement of investment and inter-Union trade.
3. Critics claim, however, that it might make adjustment to domestic economic problems more difficult. The loss of independence in policy making is seen by such people to be a major issue, not only because of the loss of political sovereignty, but also because domestic economic concerns may be at variance with those of the Union as a whole. Countries and regions at the periphery of the Union may become depressed unless there is an effective regional policy.

Questions

1. Which of the following items are credits on the UK balance of payments and which are debits?
   (a) The expenditure by UK tourists on holidays in Greece.
   (b) The payment of dividends by foreign companies to investors resident in the UK.
   (c) Foreign residents taking out insurance policies with UK companies.
   (d) Drawing on reserves.
   (e) Investment by UK companies overseas.

2. The following are the items in the UK's 1994 balance of payments. Calculate the following (a) the balance of trade in goods; (b) the balance of trade in goods and services; (c) the balance of payments on current account; (d) the long-term capital account balance; (e) net transactions in external assets and liabilities (the capital account balance); (f) the balancing item.

	£ billions
Exports of goods	152.7
Imports of goods	164.2
Net services	+5.7
Net investment income	+6.6
Net transfers	−7.5
Overseas investment in UK	38.6
UK investment overseas	63.6
Other capital inflows	83.1
Other capital outflows	53.5
Reserves	+0.1

3. Explain how the current account of the balance of payments is likely to vary with the course of the business cycle.

4. Is it a 'bad thing' to have a deficit on the long-term capital account?

5. Why may credits on the UK's short-term capital account create problems for the UK economy in the future?

6. List some factors that could cause an increase in the credit items of the balance of payments and a decrease in the debit items. What would be the effect on the exchange rate (assuming that it is freely floating)? What effect would these exchange rate movements have on the balance of payments?

7. What policy measures could the government adopt to prevent the exchange rate movements in question 6?

8. Using the concept of income elasticity of demand, explain why many developing countries have chronic balance of payments problems.

9. What adverse effects on the domestic economy may follow from (a) a depreciation of the exchange rate and (b) an appreciation of the exchange rate?

10. What will be the effects on the domestic economy under free-floating exchange rates if there is a rapid expansion in world economic activity? What will determine the size of these effects?

11. Why would banks not be prepared to offer a forward exchange rate to a firm for, say, five years' time?

12. Under what circumstances would the demand for imports be likely to be inelastic? How would an inelastic demand for imports affect the magnitude of fluctuations in the exchange rate?

13. Why are the price elasticities of demand for imports and exports likely to be lower in the short run than in the long run?

14. Assume that the government pursued an expansionary fiscal policy and that the resulting budget deficit led to higher interest rates. What would happen to (a) the current account and (b) the capital account of

the balance of payments? What would be the likely effect on the exchange rate, given a high degree of international capital mobility?

15. Consider the argument that in the modern world of large-scale short-term international capital movements, the ability of individual countries to affect their exchange rate is very limited.

16. Why does high international capital mobility and an absence of exchange controls severely limit a country's ability to choose its interest rate?

17. What practical problems are there in achieving a general harmonisation of economic policies between (a) EU countries; (b) the major industrialised countries?

18. Do the exchange rate difficulties experienced by countries under the ERM strengthen or weaken the arguments for progressing to a single European currency?

19. Under what circumstances may a system such as the ERM (a) help prevent speculation; (b) aggravate the problem of speculation?

20. Assume that just some of the members of a common market like the EU adopt full economic and monetary union, including a common currency. What are the advantages and disadvantages to those members joining the full EMU and to those not?

21. By what means would a depressed country in an economic union with a single currency be able to recover? Would the market provide a satisfactory solution to its problems or would (Union) government intervention be necessary, and if so, what form could that intervention take?

Answers to odd numbered end-of-chapter questions

Chapter 1

1. For most people it would certainly be eased! But it would not be solved. As the old saying goes, money can't buy everything. Many things would still be scarce. For example, you would still have only a finite amount of time to enjoy what the money could buy: there are only 24 hours in a day, and we do not live for ever. Then, for many lottery winners, happiness has proved illusive. Friendships and family relationships may become strained or even be destroyed and it may be very difficult to trust people's motives. Do they really want to be my friend, or are they merely after my money?

3. If people specialise in jobs in which they are relatively able, total production (and hence consumption) in the economy will be larger than if everyone tried to do a little of everything. Part of the reason is that people would be spending much of their time doing things in which they had little or no ability; part is that a lot of time would be wasted in moving from job to job; part is that concentrating on just one job allows people to develop skills. It is the same for countries: total world production and consumption can be higher if countries specialise in producing those goods at which they are relatively efficient and then trading with other countries (see the 'law of comparative advantage' in section 11.1).

5. The reduction in supply will cause a shortage of oil at current prices. This will cause the price of oil to rise. This will then have a twin effect: it will reduce demand and it will also make it profitable to use more expensive extraction methods, thereby increasing supply. The effect of the higher price, therefore, will be to eliminate the shortage.

7. (a) Equilibrium is where quantity demanded equals quantity supplied:
$$P = £5; Q = 12 \text{ million}.$$

(b) The schedules are shown in the following table:

Price (£)	8	7	6	5	4	3	2	1
Quantity demanded	10	12	14	16	18	20	22	24
Quantity supplied	18	16	14	12	10	8	6	4

Equilibrium price and quantity are now as follows:
$$P = £6; Q = 14 \text{ million}$$
Demand has risen by 4 million but equilibrium quantity has only risen by 2 million (from 12 million to 14 million). The reason why quantity sold has risen by less than demand is that price has risen. This has choked off some of the extra demand (i.e. 2 of the 4 million).

(c) See Figure A1.1.

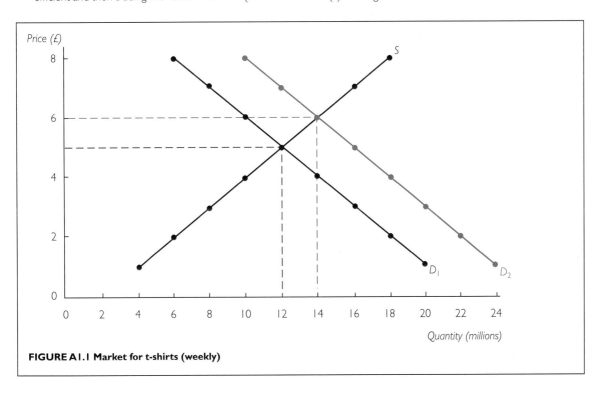

FIGURE A1.1 Market for t-shirts (weekly)

9. • A rise in the price of air travel (supply).
   • A fall in the exchange rate, giving less foreign currency for the pound (supply – tour operators' costs abroad rise when measured in pounds).
   • The economy booms (demand – more people can afford to go on holiday; supply – inflation raises tour operators' costs).
   • The price of domestic holidays increases (demand – a rise in the price of a substitute).
   • Certain tour operators go out of business or cut down on the number of holidays on offer (supply).
   • Poor weather at home (demand – more people decide to take their holidays abroad).

11. (a) Price rises, quantity rises (demand shifts to the right: butter and margarine are substitutes).
   (b) Price falls, quantity rises (supply shifts to the right: butter and yoghurt are in joint supply).
   (c) Price falls, quantity falls (demand shifts to the left: bread and butter are complementary goods).
   (d) Price rises, quantity rises (demand shifts to the right: bread and butter are complementary goods).
   (e) Price rises, quantity rises or falls depending on relative sizes of the shifts in demand and supply (demand shifts to the right as people buy now before the price rises; supply shifts to the left as producers hold back stocks until the price does rise).
   (f) Price rises, quantity falls (supply shifts to the left).
   (g) Price rises, quantity rises or falls depending on the relative size of the shifts in demand and supply (demand shifts to the right as more health-conscious people start buying butter; supply shifts to the left as a result of the increased cost of production).

Chapter 2

1. With the flatter of the two supply curves, the price will rise less and the quantity rise more than in the case of the steeper supply curve.

3. Because there has been a *rightward shift* in the demand curve for oil. This is likely to be the result of rising incomes. Car ownership and use increase as incomes increase. Also tastes may have changed so that people want to drive more. There may also have been a decline in substitute modes of transport such as rail transport and buses. Finally, people may travel longer distances to work as a result of a general move to the suburbs.

5. As long as demand remains inelastic, the firm should go on raising its price if it wants to increase revenue. Eventually consumers will stop buying the good: even if there is no close substitute, the income effect will become large – people will simply not be able to afford to buy the good. This illustrates the fact that a demand curve is likely to have different elasticities along its length.

7. Two brands of coffee, because they are closer substitutes than coffee and tea.

9. Generally, stabilising speculation will benefit both consumers and firms as it will create a more stable market environment in which it is easier to plan purchases, production or investment. Generally people prefer certainty to uncertainty. Destabilising speculation, on the other hand, by exaggerating the upswings and downswings in markets, will make it more difficult to plan – something that will be unpopular with consumers and producers alike.

   Of course, to the extent that the consumers or producers are themselves taking part in the speculation, they will gain from it, whether it is stabilising or destabilising, provided that they predict correctly. For example, if you are thinking of buying a house and, correctly, predict that house prices will rise in the near future, then you will gain by buying now before they do.

11. (a) Equilibrium is where quantity demanded equals quantity supplied: where
      $P = £2.00$ per kilo; $Q = 50\,000$ kilos
   (b) (i) There will be a surplus of 22 000 kilos (i.e. 62 000 – 40 000).
      (ii) No effect. The equilibrium price of £2.00 is above the minimum.
   (c) (i) With the £1.00 subsidy, producers will supply at each price the amount that they were previously willing to supply for £1.00 more. The schedules will now be as follows:

Price (£ per kilo)	4.00	3.50	3.00	2.50	2.00	1.50	1.00	0.50	0.00
Qd (000 kilos)	30	35	40	45	50	55	60		
Qs (000 kilos)			80	68	62	55	50	45	38

      (ii) The new equilibrium price will be £1.50 (where quantity demanded and the new quantity supplied are equal).
      (iii) The cost will be £1 × 55 000 = £55 000.
   (d) (i) At a price of £2.50, (original) supply exceeds demand by 10 000 kilos. The government would therefore have to buy this amount in order to ensure that all the tomatoes produced were sold.
      (ii) £2.50 × 10 000 = £25 000
   (e) (i) It would have purchased 55 000. To dispose of all these, price would have to fall to £1.50.
      (ii) The cost of this course of action would be (£2.50 – £1.50) × 55 000 = £55 000.

13. Two examples are:
   • Rent controls. Advantages: makes cheap housing available to those who would otherwise have difficulty in affording reasonable accommodation. Disadvantages: causes a reduction in the supply of private rented accommodation; causes demand to exceed supply and thus some people will be unable to find accommodation.
   • Tickets for a concert. Advantages: allows the price to be advertised in advance and guarantees a full house;

makes seats available to those who could not afford the free-market price. Disadvantages: causes queuing or seats being available only to those booking well in advance.

Chapter 3

1. (a) Two or three days: the time necessary to acquire new equipment or DJs.
   (b) Two or more years: the time taken to plan and build a new power station.
   (c) Several weeks: the time taken to acquire additional premises.
   (d) One or two years: the time taken to plan and build a new store.
3. (a) Variable.
   (b) Fixed (unless the fee negotiated depends on the success of the campaign).
   (c) Variable (the more that is produced, the more the wear and tear).
   (d) Fixed.
   (e) Fixed if the factory will be heated and lit to the same extent irrespective of output, but variable if the amount of heating and lighting depends on the amount of the factory in operation, which in turn depends on output.
   (f) Variable.
   (g) Variable (although the basic wage is fixed *per worker*, the cost will still be variable because the total cost will increase with output if the number of workers is increased).
   (h) Variable.
   (i) Fixed (because it does not depend on output).
5. Because economies of scale, given that most arise from increasing returns to scale, will be fully realised after a certain level of output (see Box 3.4 on page 88), whereas diseconomies of scale, given that they largely arise from the managerial problems of running large organisations, are only likely to set in beyond a certain level of output.
7. Diagram (a) The long-run marginal cost curve would be falling (and below the *LRAC* curve) and thus the long-run total cost would be rising less and less steeply.
   Diagram (b) The long-run marginal cost curve would be rising (and above the *LRAC* curve) and thus the long-run total cost curve would be rising more and more steeply.
   Diagram (c) The long-run marginal cost curve would be horizontal and (equal to the *LRAC* curve) and thus the long-run total cost curve would be rising at a constant rate: i.e. it would be a straight line up from the origin.
9. The diagram should look something like Figure 3.9. The table should be set out like Table 3.5. Total revenue (*TR*) is simply *P* × *Q* and marginal revenue (*MR*) is the rise in *TR*

per 1 unit rise in *Q*. (The *MR* figures are plotted *between* the values for *Q*: i.e. between 1 and 2, 2 and 3, 3 and 4, etc.) The figures for *MR* should then be simply read off the table and plotted on your diagram.
11. The slopes are the same.
    Given that the slope of the total curve gives the respective marginal, this means that marginal revenue will be equal to marginal cost.
13. Normal profit is the opportunity cost of capital for owners. It is the return they could have earned on their capital elsewhere, and is thus the minimum profit they must make to persuade them to continue producing in the long run and not to close down and move into some alternative business.
15. Its fixed costs have already been incurred. Provided, therefore, that it can cover its variable costs, anything over can be used to help pay off these fixed costs. Once the fixed costs come up for renewal, however (and thus cease to be fixed costs), the firm will close down if it cannot cover these also. It will thus be willing to make a loss only as long as the fixed costs have been paid (or committed).

Chapter 4

1. (a)

Output	0	1	2	3	4	5	6	7	8
TC (£)	10	18	24	30	38	50	66	91	120
AC (£)	–	18	12	10	9½	10	11	13	15
MC (£)		8	6	6	8	12	16	25	29

   (b) See Figure A4.1.
   (c) Profit is maximised where *MC = MR* (point *b*): i.e. at an output of 5.
   (d) £20
       Profit per unit is given by *AR − AC*.
       AR (=*MR*) is constant at £14; *AC* at an output of 5 units is £10.
       Thus profit per unit = 14 − 10 = 4
       Total profit is then found by multiplying this by the number of units sold:
       i.e. £4 × 5 = £20.
       This is shown by the area *abcd*.
   (e) Supernormal profit would encourage new firms to enter the industry. This would cause price to fall until it was equal to the minimum point of the *long-run* average cost curve (at that point, there would be no supernormal profit remaining and hence firms would stop entering and the price would stop falling).
3. This is illustrated in Figure A4.2. The long-run equilibrium is shown where the *AR* curve is tangential to the *LRAC* curve (and where, therefore, there is no supernormal profit). If the demand curve now shifts from D_1 to D_2, the equilibrium price will fall to P_2. Less than normal profit will now be made. Firms will therefore leave the industry. As they do, so the industry supply curve will shift to the

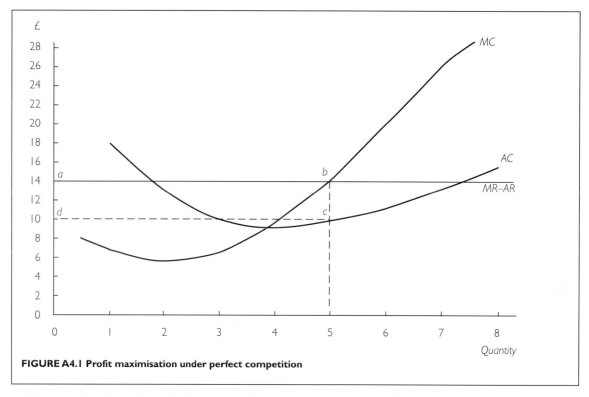

FIGURE A4.1 Profit maximisation under perfect competition

left, causing the price to rise again. Once the supply curve has reached S_2 and price has risen back to P_1, long-run equilibrium will have been restored, with the remaining firms making normal profit again.

5. The criticism should really be directed at the market system as a whole: that where significant economies of scale exist, markets are bound to be imperfect. Of course, there may be significant *benefits* to consumers and society generally from such imperfect markets (see pages 114–15): there are advantages as well as disadvantages of imperfect markets. What is more, if the market is highly contestable, many of the advantages of perfect competition may be achieved even though the industry is actually a monopoly (or oligopoly).

7. Demand is elastic at the point where $MR = MC$. The reason is that MC must be positive and therefore MR must also be positive. But if MR is positive, demand must be elastic. Nevertheless, at any given price a monopoly will face a less elastic demand curve than a firm producing the same good under monopolistic competition or oligopoly. This enables it to raise price further before demand becomes elastic (and before the point is reached where $MR = MC$).

9. (a) High. The plant cannot be used for other purposes.
   (b) Relatively low. The industry is not very capital intensive, and the various tools and equipment could be sold or transferred to producing other crops.
   (c) Very high. The plant cannot be used for other

purposes and decommissioning costs are very high.
   (d) Low. The capital costs are low and offices can be sold.
   (e) Relatively low. The plant and machinery can probably be adapted to producing other toys.
   (f) Low to moderate. It is likely that a pharmaceutical company can relatively easily switch to producing alternative drugs. Substantial exit costs are only likely to arise if the company is committed to a long-term research and development programme or if equipment is not transferable to producing alternative drugs.
   (g) Low to moderate. Exit costs from one particular client are likely to be low if the firm can easily transfer to supplying alternative clients. Costs will be higher if there are penalties for breaking contracts, or if the firm wishes to exit from catering altogether. In this latter case the costs will depend on the second-hand value of its equipment.
   (h) Low to moderate. The exit costs again will depend on the second-hand value of the equipment.
   (i) Relatively low if the ships can be transferred to other routes. Much higher if the company wishes to move out of shipping entirely and if the market for second-hand ships is depressed.

11. You will see when you think about this question that it is often difficult to identify the boundaries of a market. Take a product like chocolate. If the product is defined as bars

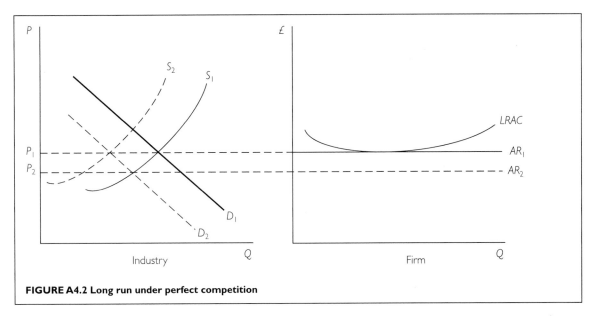

FIGURE A4.2 Long run under perfect competition

of chocolate, then there are probably about three or four different makes available, but maybe only one or two in any one shop. If, however, the product is defined to include filled chocolate bars, then there are many more varieties available, but, of course, several made by each individual company (such as Cadbury's, Mars, Nestlé, etc). You will also notice for many products that there are one or two large producers, and many small producers, making the market a hybrid form of oligopoly if the large producers dominate the market.

The sorts of competition to look out for are: price competition, advertising, product specification, product availability, after sales service, etc.

13. The first type of customer will have a lower price-elasticity of demand, since they will not have the time to shop around, and will thus be prepared to pay a higher price than at the supermarket. It is this type of customer that the small shop relies on. The other type of customer will probably simply wait until they next visit the supermarket. For such customers, the supermarket provides a substitute service.

15. No. Demand would become less elastic and the lack of competition may enable remaining petrol stations to make supernormal profits in the long run as well as the short run. If, with a reduced number of firms, there was still sufficient competition to allow profits to be kept at a normal level, cost conditions would have to change so that the LRAC would now continue sloping downward for longer (so that the point of tangency is at a higher output): this would require changes in technology such as new computerised systems which allow one cashier to handle a larger number of customers.

17. In all cases collusion is quite likely: check out the factors favouring collusion on pages 129–30. In some cases it is

more likely than others: for example, in the case of cement, where there is little product differentiation and a limited number of producers, collusion is more likely than in the case of carpets, where there is much more product differentiation.

19. (a) and (c) are examples of effective countervailing power, because the individual purchasing firms are large relative to the total market for the product.

21. Examples include: a firm charging different prices for the same product in different countries; a supermarket chain charging higher prices in more affluent areas; airlines charging different prices for the same flight with the same booking conditions through different tour operators; cheaper travel for particular categories of person (children, students, elderly people).

Generally consumers gain if they buy in the low-price market and lose if they buy in the high-price market. If the discrimination were first degree, however, no-one would gain, since everyone would be charged the highest price they were prepared to pay.

The use of price discrimination, by enabling the firm to make higher profits, may also enable it to compete more effectively with its rivals. This could help consumers if competition thereby increased (e.g. if a firm used price discrimination to enable it to compete more effectively against a powerful rival), but could be against consumers' interests if firms used it to drive rivals out of business.

In order to form a judgement, it is necessary to know the extent of the gains and losses to consumers. It is also important to know to what extent differences in prices are the result of genuine price discrimination, rather than merely a reflection of the different costs that firms incur in different markets, or a reflection of a *different* service. For example, it is not price discrimination to charge a higher price for a better seat at a concert: the price difference is, at least in part, a reflection of the *quality* of the seat.

Chapter 5

1. In the first case (skilled workers), the supply curve is less elastic. A rightward shift in demand would mean that the firm would have to give a substantial rise in wages (the second policy) in order to attract sufficient workers from outside. Thus it may be profitable for the firm to undertake the expense of training itself to avoid having to pay these high wages. There is a danger, however, that once it has trained its workers they could now get a higher wage elsewhere. The effect would be a vertical shift in the supply curve, and the firm may end up having to pay the higher wages anyway.

   In the second case (unskilled workers), supply is more elastic: workers can readily transfer from and to other jobs. Thus a rightward shift in demand will only lead to a relatively small rise in wages.

   If it used the second policy (of offering a wage rise) in the first case (that of a shortage of *skilled* workers), the wage rise is likely to have to be substantial in order to recruit the necessary extra labour. The less elastic the supply of labour, the higher the rise in wages will have to be.

3. Because they require fewer qualifications, and thus there is a plentiful supply of labour available to do them.

5.

Number of workers (1)	Wage rate (£) (2)	Total cost of labour (£) (3)	Marginal cost of labour (£) (4)	Marginal revenue product (£) (5)
1	100	100		
2	105	210	110	230
3	110	330	120	240
4	115	460	130	240
5	120	600	140	230
6	125	750	150	210
7	130	910	160	190
8	135	1080	170	170
9	140	1260	180	150
10	145	1450	190	130

The figures have been filled in in the above table. The firm should employ workers up to the point where $MC_L = MRP_L$: it should employ seven or eight workers.

7. You would need to look at the following factors: (a) differences in the productivity of workers in each group; (b) whether the demand for each type of worker is expanding or contracting, and in that context, the elasticity of supply of labour (since the less elastic the supply, the bigger will be the change in the wage rate for any shift in the demand for labour); (c) the price of the good that they produce (which will determine the workers' marginal *revenue* product); (d) whether the workers are members of unions and, if so, how strong are the unions; (e) whether their employers have monopsony power; (f) whether there are any other factors, such as custom and practice or discrimination, that determine their wage rate.

9. See the reasons given in Box 5.2: 'Equal Pay for Equal Work!'

11. See page 168 in the text.

   A progressive tax is defined as one whose *average* rate with respect to income rises as income rises. It is possible for this to happen even when the marginal rate is constant. For example, if people can earn a certain proportion of their income tax-free, and above that pay at a constant marginal rate, then the average rate will go on rising as income rises because the tax-free element will account for a smaller and smaller proportion of the total.

13. An example will illustrate why. Assume that before tax one person earns £20 000 and the other earns £10 000: the first person's income is twice that of the second. Now assume that a 50 per cent income tax is imposed on every pound (a proportional tax). The first person now has a disposable (after tax) income of £10 000, and the second of £5000. The distribution is unaffected: the first person's income is still twice that of the second.

15. A person on low income. There would be little income effect to offset the substitution effect. With a person on high income, however, a cut in income tax rates would lead to a substantial windfall income. The income effect is therefore likely to be large and may outweigh the substitution effect (causing the rich person to work less).

   In the case of people on *very* low incomes, however, who are below the tax threshold, a cut in income tax will have no effect at all. If personal allowances were zero, however, this would not apply. The substitution effect would outweigh the income effect.

17. This is when poor people have little or no incentive to get a job, because the combined effect of paying taxes and losing benefits would make them virtually no better off than before (or even worse off).

   Universal benefits would help because, not being means tested, they would not be lost as a person's income increased: the marginal tax-plus-lost-benefit rate would be lower. The problem is that they are less narrowly targeted, and therefore are paid to people who are less needy. This means that it costs the taxpayer a lot more to help the poor through universal benefits than through means-tested ones. The result would be either less help for the poor or higher taxes (which could themselves act as a disincentive).

Chapter 6

1. (a) 7 units (where marginal revenue (= P) equals marginal cost).

(b) 5 units (where marginal social benefit ($= P$) equals marginal social cost.

(c) Because the environment becomes ever less able to cope with additional amounts of pollution.

3. (a) The *MSC* curve will be *below* the *MC* curve. The actual level of production (where $MC = P$) will thus be below the optimum level.

(b) The *MSB* curve will be *above* the *MU* curve. The actual level of consumption (where $MU = P$) will thus be *below* the optimum level (where $MSB = P$).

5. *Publicly provided goods* are merely goods that the government or some other public agency provides, whether or not they could be provided by the market. *Public goods* are the much narrower category of goods that the market would fail to provide because of their characteristics of non-rivalry and non-excludability. Thus a local government might provide both street lighting and public libraries: they are both publicly provided goods, but only street lighting is a public good.

A *merit good* is either publicly provided or subsidised. It is one that the government feels that people would otherwise underconsume (e.g. health care). It is not normally a public good, however, because it *would* be provided by the market: it is just that people would consume too little of it.

7. Roads where there are relatively few access points and where therefore it would be practical to charge tolls. Charges could be regarded as a useful means of restricting use of the roads in question, or, by charging more at peak times, of encouraging people to travel at off-peak times. Such a system, however, could be regarded as unfair by those using the toll roads, and might merely divert congestion onto the non-toll roads.

9. (a) (i) or (ii) (e.g. *Which* magazine);

(b (iii) (by asking people currently doing the job) or (iv);

(c) (iii) (by obtaining estimates);

(d) (iii) (albeit imperfect, by inspecting other work that the different builders have done) or (iv);

(e) as (d);

(f) (iii);

(g) (iii);

(h) (i) or (ii) (as in (a)) or (iii) by experimenting.

All could involve the non-monetary costs of the time involved in finding out.

If the information is purely factual (as in (c) above), and you can trust the source of your information, there is no problem. If you cannot trust the source, or if the information is subjective (such as other people's experiences in (b) above), then you will only have imperfect information of the costs and/or benefits until you actually experience them.

11. Virtually all the categories of market failure (except public goods) apply to a free-market system of educational provision.

- In any given area there may be oligopolistic collusion to keep fees high.
- There are positive externalities from education: for example, the benefits to other members of society from a well-educated workforce. Thus too few resources would be allocated to education.
- Education can be seen as a merit good: something that the government feels that people are entitled to and should not depend on ability to pay.
- Access to education would depend on parents' income: this could be argued to be unfair.
- Children would also be dependent on their parents' *willingness* to pay. Parents differ in the amount that they care for their children's welfare.
- Parents and potential students may be ignorant of the precise benefits of particular courses, something that an unscrupulous educational establishment might exploit, by pushing the 'merits' of their establishment.

13. Assuming that the external benefit was in production, the *MSC* curve in Figure 6.5 would be *below* the *MC* curve. The optimum subsidy would be equal to the gap between *MSC* and *MC* at the point where the *MSC* curve crossed the $D = MSB$ line.

15. (a) This would be very difficult given that large numbers of people are affected by the pollution. One possible answer would be to legislate such that if specific health problems could be traced to atmospheric pollution, then those affected would have rights to sue.

(b) If tracts of the river were privately owned, then as relatively few owners would be involved, it would be relatively easy to pursue polluters through the courts, provided they could be clearly identified (i.e. it would be easier to pursue factories for specific toxic emissions than individuals for dumping litter).

(c) Again if the dumpers could be identified and the dumping were on private ground, then the owners could use the courts to prevent it. The problem here is that the owners may be quite happy to charge the company for dumping, not caring about the effects on other people of polluting, say, the water table.

(d) This is more difficult, given that the ugly buildings are on land owned by owners of the buildings! The law would have to give people the right to sue for *visual* pollution. This could be difficult to prove, as it involves aesthetic judgments.

(e) There would have to be laws prohibiting noise above a certain level within the hearing of residents. Then it would be a relatively simple case of the affected residents demonstrating to the satisfaction of the courts that a noise offence had been committed. It would be easier if the summons could be brought by an environmental inspectorate.

It should be clear from these answers that the boundaries between legal controls and exercising property rights are rather blurred. The ability of people to exercise property rights depends on the laws of property.

17. (a) Very suitable, provided that periodic tests and possibly spot checks are carried out.

(b) Good in certain cases: e.g. one-way systems, banning lorries of a certain size from city centres during certain parts of the day, bus lanes.

(c) Not very, given that the main problem is excessive profits, which would be difficult to define legally and relatively easy to evade even if they were defined. Various types of unsafe or shoddy goods (which are possibly more likely to be produced by firms not facing competition) could be made illegal, however.

(d) Good. The law could give the government or some other body the right to ban any merger it considered not to be in the public interest. (See Chapter 12, section 12.2.)

(e) Not. It would require an army of inspectors to identify marginal costs, or to check that a firm's reported marginal costs were what it claimed. The scope for evasion and ambiguity would be immense.

19. (a) This increases the marginal cost of motoring and thus does discourage people from using their cars. But it affects everyone, including those driving their cars on uncongested roads.

(b) This is not very effective at all, since it is not a marginal charge related to congestion. You do not pay more, the more you use your car: the marginal cost is zero. In fact it may even have the perverse effect of encouraging people to use their cars more. After all, if they are paying a large annual fee, they may feel that they want to get 'full value for money' by using their cars as much as possible. The only positive effect is that it may discourage people from owning a car or a second car, and for that reason may encourage the increased use of public transport.

(c) 'Road pricing', as it is called, is the system most favoured by economists, since the charge is directly related to the level of congestion. It is quite expensive, however, to install and operate the system.

(d) This is quite effective, especially if the tolls can vary according to the amount of congestion. They have the disadvantage, however, of causing possible tailbacks from the booths. There is also the problem that traffic may simply be diverted onto other roads where there are no tolls, thus worsening the problem of congestion elsewhere.

(e) These may encourage the use of bicycles and buses, but they can increase the level of congestion for cars, as they are forced into one lane.

(f) This can be effective, provided that public transport is fast, efficient, frequent and clean. They are especially useful when applied to city centre transport, or transport from park-and-ride car parks to city centres.

21. Fixing prices

(a) (i) to enable those on low incomes to be able to afford the good.

(ii) to prevent firms with market power from exploiting their position.

(iii) to help in the fight against inflation.

(b) (i) to protect the incomes of producers (e.g. farmers).

(ii) to increase profits and thereby encourage investment.

(iii) (in the case of wages) to protect workers' incomes.

(iv) to create a surplus in times of glut which can be stored in preparation for possible future shortages.

Alternatives to fixing prices

(a) (i) cash benefits and benefits in kind; subsidising the good.

(ii) anti-monopoly legislation; lump-sum taxes.

(iii) fiscal, monetary and supply-side policies (see macro half of the book).

(b) (i) subsidies and tax relief.

(ii) subsidies and tax relief.

(iii) benefits and progressive taxation.

(iv) state acting as purchaser or seller on the open market.

Chapter 7

1. (a) See Table A7.1

In each case the growth rate (G) is found by using the following formula:

$$G = (Y_t - Y_{t-1})/Y_{t-1} \times 100$$

TABLE A7.1

	1988	1989	1990	1991	1992	1993	1994	1995	1996	1997
USA	3.99	2.49	1.21	−0.60	2.31	3.05	4.10	3.30	2.13	2.17
Japan	6.20	4.85	5.04	4.00	1.06	0.10	0.48	0.76	2.44	2.29
Germany	3.64	3.62	5.93	4.60	1.15	−1.89	3.46	1.02	0.83	2.47
France	4.80	4.05	2.46	0.80	1.29	−1.47	2.88	2.42	1.32	2.70
UK	5.06	2.15	0.40	−2.00	−0.51	2.25	3.81	2.42	2.26	3.04

(b) See Figure A7.1

3. (a) Neither; there is merely a redistribution of factor payments on the left-hand side of the inner flow. (The only exception to this would be if a smaller proportion of wages were saved than of profits. In this case there would be a net reduction in withdrawals.)

(b) Increase in injections (investment).

(c) Decrease in withdrawals (taxes).

(d) Increase in withdrawals (saving). Note that 'investing'

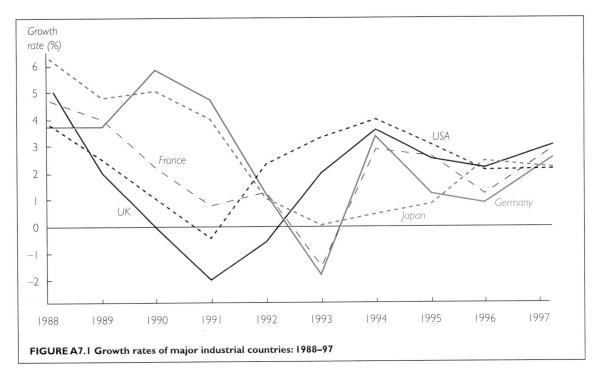

FIGURE A7.1 Growth rates of major industrial countries: 1988–97

in building societies is really *saving* not investment.

(e) Fall in withdrawals (a reduction in net outflow abroad from the household sector).

(f) Neither. The inner flow is unaffected. If, however, this were financed from higher taxes, it would result in an increase in withdrawals.

(g) Neither. The inner flow is unaffected. The consumption of domestically produced goods and services remains the same.

(h) Decrease in withdrawals (saving).

(i) Neither. An increase in government expenditure (or decrease in taxes, or both) is offset by an increase in saving (i.e. people buying government securities).

(j) Net injections. An increase in government expenditure (or decrease in taxes, or both) is not offset by changes elsewhere. Extra money is printed to finance the net injection.

5. The curve would still slope upwards during phase 4, but its slope would be less than in the other phases. Its slope would also be less than that of the potential output curve, with the result that the gap between actual and potential output would widen.

7. Look back over the last few years and see what pattern emerges. What predictions are currently being made for output growth over the next two years in the press by various forecasting organisations and commentators?

9. On the surface it would seem desirable that nobody would be suffering from being unemployed. But for an economy to be able to absorb everyone looking for a job, one of three conditions would have to hold, each of

which brings serious problems. Either the economy would have to be suffering from such a huge shortage of labour that firms were providing all sorts of inducements to keep labour. The shortage of labour could be a serious constraint on some firms' ability to expand and it would probably lead to considerable inflation, which itself brings problems. Alternatively, unemployment benefits would have to be so low (or non-existent) that people would be forced to accept work at pittance wages. Alternatively, the government would have to provide work for everyone who would otherwise be unemployed: such schemes, unless carefully devised and managed, could prove an expensive way of reducing unemployment, might not be seen as 'real work' and could be demoralising to those involved.

11. First you will need to see to what extent changes in employment in your area reflect national trends. If they do, then the causes may be cyclical fluctuations in demand or longer-term changes in the labour market (such as changes in trade union power or patterns of part-time working), or in the competitiveness of the national economy, or in work practices or in unemployment benefits. Then you will need to see whether there are any factors in your area that cause unemployment to be different from the national average: e.g. certain industries that are concentrated in your area either declining or expanding.

13. Generally economists argue that an economic problem should be tackled at source: i.e. that it is better to tackle the root of a problem than merely treating its symptoms.

This means that if unemployment is caused by a deficiency of aggregate demand, then the most appropriate policy would be to ensure that demand is sufficient. Economists disagree, however (as we shall see in later chapters), as to whether it is better to manage aggregate demand over the short term (say, by increasing government expenditure or reducing taxes) or to provide a more stable environment over the longer term in which the economy will be less subject to recessions.

If unemployment is caused by structural or technological change, or by too many 'frictions' in the economy, the best approach is to make the economy adapt more rapidly to these changing conditions. This involves what are called 'supply-side policies'. These could involve 'freeing up' markets to remove impediments to labour and capital mobility (e.g. deregulation or reducing the power of trade unions). Such policies tend to be favoured by the political right. The alternative would be to have interventionist supply-side policy. For example, the government could invest in education and training in order to create a more flexible workforce, or provide better job information, or invest in the transport infrastructure.

15. Most of the costs of inflation would disappear, but menu costs would still remain. Investment, balance of payments and speculation costs would only disappear if everyone correctly anticipated *future* inflation.

Chapter 8

1. (a) In equilibrium, income (Y) = expenditure (E)

   $E = C + I + G + X - M$
   $= £60bn + £5bn + £8bn + £7bn - £10bn$
   $= £70bn$

   (b) $J = I + G + X$
   $= £5bn + £8bn + £7bn$
   $= £20bn$

   (c) In equilibrium, $W = J$. As this economy is in equilibrium, withdrawals will equal current injections.
   $W = £20bn$

   (d) $W = S + T + M$
   $= S + £7bn + £10bn$
   $\therefore S = £20bn - £7bn - £10bn$
   $= £3bn$

   (e) $C_d = C - M = £50bn$
   $mpc_d = \Delta C_d/\Delta Y = (£58bn - £50bn)/(£80bn - £70bn)$
   $= £8bn/£10bn$
   $= 0.8$ or $^4/_5$

   (f) Multiplier $= 1/(1 - mpc_d)$
   $= 1/^1/_5$
   $= 5$

   (g) Injections have risen by £4bn + £1bn - £2bn = £3bn
   $\therefore$ national income will rise by 5 times this amount
   = increase of £15bn

3. Injections rise by £100m + (£200m - £50m) = £250m. Therefore, with a multiplier of 3, national income will rise by £750m.

5. The E line is parallel with the C_d line (assuming that the J 'curve' is a horizontal straight line). Thus the slope of the E line is the same as the slope of the C_d line, which is given by the mpc_d ($\Delta C_d/\Delta Y$).

7. • The lower a country's national income, the higher will tend to be its mpc and thus the higher will be its multiplier.
   • In some countries there is much more of a 'savings culture' and thus the mps is higher. Those with less of a savings culture will tend to have a lower mps and hence a higher multiplier.
   • In some countries, especially large ones, trade accounts for a relatively small proportion of national income. In such countries the mpm will be lower and hence the multiplier will be higher than in countries with a higher proportion of trade relative to national income.
   • The marginal tax rate, the mpt, differs from one country to another. The lower the mpt the higher the multiplier.

9. (a) For each £20bn rise in Y there is a £15bn rise in E.
   $\therefore mpc_d = ^3/_4$
   $\therefore$ multiplier $= 1/(1 - ^3/_4) = 4$.

   (b) The current equilibrium national income is £160bn (where $Y = E$)
   Thus national income is £40bn below the full-employment national income.
   With a multiplier of 4, there is a deflationary gap of £10bn.

   (c) It would have to be increased by £10bn.

11. Because demand for the output of these industries (which are 'investment' goods industries) fluctuates much more – the accelerator effect.

13. Multiplier
   The proportion of a rise in income that people spend on domestic goods (mpc_d) will vary in ways that are difficult to predict. It depends on:
   • Exchange rates, since these determine the proportion of a rise in income that will go on imports.
   • Consumer expectations about price rises. If consumers think that prices will rise in the near future, they are likely to increase their spending now, in order to beat the price increases.
   • Consumer confidence about future incomes and employment prospects. The more 'up-beat' consumers are, the more they are likely to spend out of any given rise in income.
   • Changes in interest rates, since these determine the cost of credit and the attractiveness of saving.
   Accelerator
   • Many firms may have spare capacity and/or carry stocks. This will enable them to meet extra demand without having to invest.

- The willingness of firms to invest will depend on their confidence in *future* demand. Firms will only respond to a rise in demand by investing if they think that the rise in demand will persist.
- Firms may make their investment plans a long time in advance and may be unable to change them quickly.
- Even if firms do decide to invest more, the producer goods industries may not have the capacity to meet a sudden surge in demand for machines.
- Machines do not as a rule suddenly wear out. A firm could thus delay replacing machines and keep the old ones for a bit longer if it was uncertain about its future level of demand.

15. (a) Assuming that the government does not alter tax or benefit rates, then the budget deficit is likely to increase as the economy moves into recession. Tax revenues will fall because people are earning and spending less. The payment of benefits, on the other hand, is likely to increase as more people claim unemployment benefit. In a boom, the budget deficit is likely to decrease and there may even be a budget surplus.

(b) Since the budget deficit tends to increase in a recession, so the size of the national debt will increase more rapidly, as government debts are built up more rapidly. In a boom, the national debt will rise more slowly as the budget deficit falls. If there is a budget surplus, the national debt will fall.

17. A rise in income tax has an income and a substitution effect. Higher taxes reduce people's incomes: this is the income effect. Being poorer they have to work more to make up for some of their lost income. The income effect, therefore, makes income tax increases an incentive to work more. Higher taxes, however, also mean that work is worth less than before, and therefore people might well substitute leisure for work: there is no point in working so much if you bring home less. This is the substitution effect, and makes income tax increases a disincentive.

(i) If the substitution effect is bigger than the income effect, then a rise in income tax will act as a net *disincentive* to work. As is shown on pages 306–7, this is likely for those people with few commitments and for second income earners in families where the second income is not relied on for 'essential consumption'. It is also likely for those who are only currently paying a small amount of tax, and for whom, therefore, the income effect is likely to be small; and also for those just in a higher tax bracket when that higher tax rate is raised.

(ii) If the income effect is bigger than the substitution effect, a rise in tax will act as a net *incentive*. This is most likely for those currently paying a large amount of tax and who would suddenly be faced with a

substantial increase in their tax bill. It is also likely if the tax increase takes the form of a cut in tax allowances. Except for those having to pay tax for the first time, or those pushed into a higher tax band, cutting allowances has no substitution effect since it does do not alter the marginal rate.

19. • A rise in government expenditure on research and development or training may make firms feel less need to invest in these areas themselves.
- A rise in taxes may make people feel less able to save such a large proportion of their income.
- A rise in exports may stimulate firms to invest more in the export sector.

Chapter 9

1. • Acceptability: most are not currently acceptable as a medium of exchange, with the possible exception of gold under certain circumstances. Most, however, *could* be acceptable, if society chose. Strawberries would be a clear exception! Clearly the degree of acceptability would depend on the extent to which the item met the other six requirements.
- Durability: gold, diamonds and a savings account have almost perfect durability; luncheon vouchers and share certificates have moderately high durability; grain and strawberry jam have moderate durability; strawberries clearly have very low durability (unless frozen).
- Convenience: luncheon vouchers and share certificates would be very convenient; gold and diamonds would be moderately convenient for *large* transactions; again, strawberries would be very inconvenient.
- Divisibility: a savings account scores highest here (assuming that any amount can be withdrawn or transferred); share certificates and luncheon vouchers also score highly (especially if they come in different 'denominations'); gold and diamonds are divisible down to moderately low levels; strawberries are also good in this respect (mind you, it's about the only one!); strawberry jam would be quite good, if it came in small-sized jars as well as normal-sized ones; grain is virtually perfectly divisible.
- Uniformity: the paper assets are the best in this respect; the others are only suitable here if there is a means of identifying quality.
- Hard for individuals to produce themselves. In the case of the commodities, there would be no problem here providing that their value as money was no higher than their market value as a commodity. As far as the other assets are concerned, a savings account would also be good, providing it was not possible for people to get unauthorised access to the account; the suitability of share certificates and luncheon vouchers would depend on how easy they were to forge.

- Stability of value: a savings account is as good as the currency in which it is denominated; luncheon vouchers could be good, but only if their supply were tightly controlled; share certificates are bad, given that share prices fluctuate with the fortunes of the company; diamonds and gold are good, as their supply is relatively constant; grain and especially strawberries are bad, given that their supply fluctuates with the harvest; strawberry jam is not very good either, given that its cost of production also fluctuates – with the price of strawberries.

3. None. They are all means of obtaining access to the money held in accounts, but they are not the money itself.

5. So that they can balance the two objectives of liquidity and profitability and also spread their risks, given that the relative profitability and security of different types of assets may change. For reasons of profitability the banks will want to minimise their holdings of cash; but to avoid the risks of insufficient liquidity, they hold a whole range of other liquid assets (such as money at call), which, although they are highly liquid, do, nevertheless, earn some interest for the bank.

7. Because market forces will ensure that interest rates in the two markets will move together: otherwise deposits would flow to the higher interest rate market and loans would be sought in the lower interest rate market. The higher interest rate market would thus have a glut of funds and the lower interest rate market would have a shortage of funds. These shortages and surpluses would act to eliminate the interest rate differential.

9. (a) £80 million (retaining £20 million as reserves). In other words, banks retain $1/5$ and lend out the remaining $4/5$.
    (b) Increase by a further £80 million.
    (c) £64 million (i.e. $4/5$ of £80 million).
    (d) £500 million (given a bank multiplier of $5 = 1/L = 1/^1/_5$).
    (e) (i) £100 million; (ii) £400 million.
    (f) 5
    (g) £250 million, since initial new deposits (and hence extra liquid assets) in the banking sector will have only been £50 million.

11. No. The demand would be high. People would want to hold the securities, so that they could benefit from the anticipated capital gain.

13. (a) They will increase credit and hence the money supply. M_s will shift to the right. The equilibrium rate of interest will therefore fall.
    (b) Higher incomes will increase the transactions plus precautionary demand for money (L_1). L will shift to the right. The equilibrium rate of interest will therefore rise.
    (c) If people believe that interest rates will rise, the speculative demand for money (L_2) will rise. L will shift to the right. The equilibrium rate of interest will therefore rise.

15. Because one of the other determinants of money supply may cause it to grow more rapidly even though the reduction in the PSBR, other things being equal, is causing the growth in the money supply to slow down. For example, if the economy is experiencing a boom, the growth in national income will increase the level of tax receipts and reduce the amount paid out in government benefits, thereby reducing the PSBR. At the same time, however, the buoyant demand for bank loans is likely to increase bank lending.

17. (a) Little or no effect, if it simply replaces one liquid asset by another; but reduce it, if it involves reducing the liquidity of the banking sector (e.g. by the sale of *bonds*).
    (b) Reduce it. The liquidity of the banking sector will be reduced (when people pay for the securities with cash withdrawn from the banks, or cheques drawn on the banks).

19. (a) Balance sheet directly after purchase of bonds

Liabilities	(£m)	Assets	(£m)
Old deposits	100	Old balances with central bank	10
New deposits	5	New balances with central bank	5
		Advances	90
	105		105

(b) Eventual balance sheet after credit creation has taken place (assuming a 10% liquidity ratio)

Liabilities	(£m)	Assets	(£m)
Old deposits	100	Old balances with central bank	10
New deposits	5	New balances with central bank	5
Further deposits	45	Old advances	90
		Further advances	45
	150		150

(c) No. To the extent that the holding of Treasury bills by the banking sector was reduced, this would reduce the size of the increase in banks' liquidity and hence reduce the size of the increase in advances. Only if all the bills purchased by the central bank came from *outside* the banking sector would the effect be the same as in (b) above. If *all* the bills came from the banking sector, there would be little or no increase in liquidity, and hence little or no increase in advances.

(d) The extra demand for bills by the central bank would increase their price and hence reduce their rate of rediscount. The effect would be to drive down interest rates.

21. (a) Banks may vary their liquidity ratio.
    (b) It is difficult to predict how much the holding of Treasury bills by the banks will vary, and how much the banks will take this into account when deciding how much credit to grant.

23. Because the supply of money depends in part on the demand for money.

Chapter 10

1. (a) No (unless $V = 1$)
   (b) Yes

3. Monetarists assume that both V and Q are exogenously (independently) determined (at least over the longer term) and relatively stable. Thus changes in money supply (M) have a direct effect on prices (P). This makes control of the growth in the money supply essential for controlling inflation.

   Keynesians argue that both V and Q are endogenously determined (i.e. dependent on M), but subject to exogenous shocks). This means that changes in M will affect both V and Q. A rise in money supply, by leading to lower interest rates is likely to increase speculative balances and therefore reduce the velocity of circulation (V). On the other hand, to the extent that a rise in money supply does affect MV and hence aggregate demand, then it could be output (Q) that is affected, rather than prices. The effects on both V and Q, however, are rather unpredictable. This makes monetary policy a very unreliable weapon for controlling inflation, especially over the short term.

5. The amount the unemployment is held below the natural rate. The lower the level of unemployment that the government tries to maintain, the faster must it increase the level of aggregate demand and thus the faster will inflation accelerate.

7. A careful management of demand so as to avoid recessions, and thus encouraging more investment and more training and preventing people being forced into long-term unemployment (and thereby becoming de-skilled); supply-side policies, involving increased government expenditure on training and education and improved infrastructure.

9. (i) All the following must apply: (a) long-run equilibrium can only be at the natural rate of unemployment (i.e. there can be non long-run deficiency of demand); (b) perfectly flexible wages and prices in the long run; (c) no long-run money illusion; (d) no increase in capacity as a result of investment stimulated by a rise in demand, or decrease in capacity caused by lack of investment during a recession.
   (ii) If (a), (b), (c) and especially (d) above do not hold.

11. (a) Yes. Successful supply-side policies, by increasing potential output, will shift the vertical portion of the AS curve to the right. As a result, expansionary demand management policies could now increase output to a higher level than before.
    (b) No. Demand-side policy must be used to control inflation (which for a monetarist means monetary policy). Supply-side policy will be the policy to use to reduce unemployment. If successful, it will shift the (vertical) AS curve to the right, and shift the (vertical) Phillips curve to the left by reducing the equilibrium level of unemployment.

13. Targeting the money supply could involve large changes in interest rates, given the unstable and interest-inelastic nature of the demand for money. This, in turn, could be very damaging to investment and reduce long-term growth. It is therefore better to avoid targeting the money supply. Instead, a discretionary approach should be adopted, with policies changed according to the changing nature of the real economy.

15. Yes. Targets could be set, but reassessed periodically in the light of the evidence of the success of policy and of changing circumstances. Alternatively loose targets for a number of different objectives could be set, and then the government could seek to achieve the best compromise between them if there were any apparent conflict.

17. Demand-side policies (like fiscal and monetary policy) shift the aggregate demand curve, whereas supply-side policies shift the aggregate supply curve.

    It is a 'half-truth' to say that Keynesians advocate demand-side policies and monetarists advocate supply-side policies. It is true to the extent that Keynesians argue that demand-side policies will usually be necessary to ensure that 'full-employment' output is achieved, and that disequilibrium unemployment is eliminated; whereas monetarists argue that (at least in the long run) this will occur automatically through the market, and that any attempt to reduce unemployment below the natural level by expanding aggregate demand will only lead to accelerating inflation. According to monetarists, the only way of reducing unemployment below the natural level and of increasing output in the long run is to adopt supply-side policies.

    The statement is, in fact, not accurate, because Keynesians advocate supply-side policy to increase potential output, reduce *equilibrium* unemployment and reduce cost-push inflation. What is more, monetarists advocate demand-side policy in the form of monetary policy as the *only* means of curing inflation.

19. Clearly there are costs and benefits. The benefits are an increase in efficiency and an increase in potential output in the economy. The costs are the increase in unemployment and the wastes associated with it. An important question is whether the government (or the market) can eventually reduce the equilibrium level of unemployment again, and thereby shift the Phillips curve back to the left. This could be done, for example, by policies of retraining and improved information on job opportunities.

21. By providing various forms of modern infrastructure (roads, railways, telecommunications, etc.) to help private-sector firms operate more effectively; by subsidising or giving tax relief for private-sector investment and training.

    By relying on such measures, rather than on regulation, the government is still allowing the market to continue providing the incentives to firms to innovate and invest, and at the same time the government can use the policy to correct for various market failures (such as externalities). However, when there is a serious problem of the abuse of monopoly power or serious externalities, regulation or direct government provision (e.g. educational establishments) may be more appropriate (see the arguments developed in sections 6.5 and 6.6).

Chapter 11

1. The LDC still gains by exporting wheat and importing cloth. At an exchange ratio of 1:2, it now only has to give up 1 kilo of wheat to obtain 2 metres of cloth, whereas without trade it would have to give up 3 kilos of wheat to obtain just 1 metre of cloth.

   The developed country still gains by importing wheat and exporting cloth. At an exchange ratio of 1:2, it can now import 1 kilo of wheat for only 2 metres of cloth, whereas without trade it would have to give up 5 metres of cloth for 2 of wheat (i.e. 2½ of cloth for 1 of wheat).

   (a) Yes. (This ratio is between their two pre-trade ratios.)

   (b) No. The LDC would gain, but the DC would lose. It would now have to give 3 metres of cloth for 1 kilo of wheat, whereas before trade it only had to give 2½ metres of cloth for 1 kilo of wheat. Thus the developed country would choose not to trade at this ratio.

3. There are two elements to the answer. One concerns costs, one concerns demand and revenue.

   In terms of costs, as a firm or country specialises and increases production, so the opportunity costs of production are likely to fall at first, due to economies of scale, and then rise as resources become increasingly scarce. The butcher's shop may not have reached the point of rising long-run opportunity costs. Also it is too small to push up the price of inputs as it increases its production. It is a price taker. ICI and Texaco, however, probably will have reached the point of rising opportunity costs. Countries certainly would have if they specialized in only one product. Thus the larger the organisation or country, the more diversified they are likely to be.

   Turning to the demand side: the butcher's shop supplies a relatively small market and faces a relatively elastic demand. It is therefore likely to find that complete specialisation in just one type of product is unlikely to lead to market saturation and a highly depressed price. Large companies, however, may find that complete specialisation in one product restricts their ability to expand. The market simply is not big enough. Countries would certainly find this. The USA could hardly just produce one product! The world market would be nowhere near big enough for it. The general point is that

overspecialisation would push the price of the product down and reduce profits.

5. India: textiles
   UK: insurance
   Canada: wheat
   Japan: computers
   The reason in each case is that the products are intensive in factors that are relatively abundant in that country (e.g. Canada has an abundance of land that is suited to growing wheat; India has an abundance of labour and land suited to growing cotton).

7. *The infant industry argument.* Infants may never 'grow up': the support may allow them to remain inefficient; not all those industries claiming and receiving infant-industry protection are genuine infants (i.e. those which have a potential comparative advantage); infants may be better promoted through subsidies or other support, rather than by restricting trade – imposing tariffs, by raising prices, cuts down on the consumption not only of imported substitutes, but also of the goods produced by the infant itself.

   Changing comparative advantage and the inflexibility of markets. Factor immobility is better tackled directly, rather than by protecting industries which have growth potential in export markets. Examples of schemes to encourage greater factor mobility are: retraining schemes, investment grants, tax relief for companies' relocation expenses and government advice on exporting.

   To prevent dumping and other unfair trade practices. In the short run, consumers will *gain* from cheap imports. Even if the country loses in the long run from the dumping, the use of protection to stop the dumping may contribute to growing world-wide protectionism. It would be better to try to negotiate an end to the dumping, perhaps through the auspices of the World Trade Organization.

   To prevent the establishment of a foreign-based monopoly. There might be *international* competition to prevent individual foreign companies gaining monopoly power. Also, in practice it would be very difficult to decide when protection is warranted, given that many domestic companies would want to make a case for protection for themselves.

   To reduce reliance on goods with little dynamic potential. In many cases, world market conditions change relatively slowly, and thus most firms will be able to adjust to new opportunities and declining old ones without the need for intervention.

   To spread the risks of fluctuating markets. If countries are vulnerable to fluctuations in international markets, then individual companies trading in such markets will also be vulnerable, and therefore may themselves decide to diversify.

   To reduce the influence of trade on consumer tastes. Given the global nature of mass communication, it is very difficult in practice to prevent people's tastes being influenced by the products and marketing of multinational companies.

To prevent the importation of harmful goods. If it is agreed that the goods are harmful (e.g. certain drugs), then attempting to stop imports may well be desirable, but should probably be part of a much broader strategy to stop the production, sale and consumption of such products.

To take account of externalities. If the externalities are within the country, then they are better dealt with by tackling them at source: e.g. taxing production or consumption that involves negative externalities and subsidising production or consumption that involves positive externalities.

To improve a country's terms of trade by exploiting its market power. Although the export monopoly argument is valid in a static context for certain products, it is likely that export taxes will erode the country's monopoly power over the longer term. By driving up the price of exports in which the country has monopoly power, other firms in other countries are likely to break into the international market. In practice there are few goods in which individual countries do have significant monopoly power (except for a few raw materials). There are even fewer where countries have significant monopsony power in importing: with a growing process of globalisation, companies have many alternative markets in which to sell.

To protect declining industries. There are various ways of helping individuals cope with the adjustment costs of economic change that are not as drastic as cutting down on trade. For example, retraining and special redundancy settlements could help workers who lose their jobs in declining industries.

To improve the balance of payments. In virtually all cases, there are other methods of dealing with balance of payments problems, both short term and long term.

9. Whether it can be demonstrated that, with appropriate investment, costs can be reduced sufficiently to make the industry internationally competitive.

11. (a) Imports are consumed and thus add directly to consumer welfare. Also, provided they are matched by exports there is no net outflow of money. Trade, because of the law of comparative advantage, allows countries to increase their standard of living: to import products that could only have been produced relatively inefficiently at home.

(b) Importing cheap goods from, say, Hong Kong, allows more goods to be consumed. The UK uses less resources by buying these goods through the production and sale of exports, than by producing them at home. However, there will be a cost to *certain* UK workers whose jobs are lost through foreign competition. Policy makers must weigh up the benefits of trade to consumers and export industries against the costs to specific workers.

13. The products and the lifestyles which they foster could be seen as alien to the values of society. For example, many developing countries have complained about the 'cocacolonisation' of their economies, whereby traditional values are being overcome by Western materialist values.

15. • The size of the external tariff. The higher the external tariff, the more likely it is that trade diversion will take place.
    • The difference in costs of production between countries inside and outside the union. The smaller the cost differences, the more likely it is that trade diversion will take place.

17. (a) Consumers would buy items in those countries that charged the lower rates of VAT. This would push up the prices in these countries and thus have the effect of equalising the tax-inclusive prices between member countries. This effect will be greater with expensive items (such as a car), where it would be worthwhile for the consumer to incur the costs of travelling to another country to purchase it.

(b) Workers would move to countries with lower income taxes, thus depressing gross wage rates there and equalising after-tax wages. This effect would be greater, the greater is the mobility of labour between member countries.

(c) Capital would move to countries with lower rates of company tax, thus depressing the rate of profit in the low tax countries and equalising the after-tax rate of profit. This effect will be greater, the greater is the mobility of capital between member countries.

In these last two cases, there will be an opposite effect caused by the multiplier. Workers or capital moving into a country will generate incomes there and hence increase the demand for factors and push *up* wages and profits.

19. • Removing barriers to trade creates opportunities. The degree to which firms and individuals will take advantage of those opportunities is uncertain.
    • It depends on whether any barriers remain (e.g. administrative barriers), and on whether there will be a single currency, and if so when and for which countries.
    • It depends on the rate of economic growth and other macroeconomic factors. The macroeconomy is difficult to forecast more than a few months ahead.
    • It is difficult to predict the degree to which the increased competition in the single market will stimulate increased technical progress and the increased spread of skills and information.

Chapter 12

1. (a) debit; (b) credit; (c) credit; (d) credit; (e) debit.

3. During the boom, the current account will tend to deteriorate. There are two reasons. The first is the direct result of higher incomes. Part of the extra incomes will be spent on imports. The second is the result of higher inflation. Higher prices of domestic goods and services relative to foreign ones will lead to both an increase in imports and a decrease in exports.

   The opposite effects are likely to occur during a recession. Lower incomes and relative prices of domestic goods and services will cause a fall in imports and a rise in exports: the current account will improve.

   In both cases we are assuming that other countries are not at the same time experiencing similar effects. If other countries were at the same phase of their business cycle, the above effects could be neutralised. For example, any fall in demand for imports by country A from country B could be offset by a fall in demand for imports by country B from country A. Imports and exports of both countries would fall (but not necessarily by the same amount).

5. Inward investment in the UK (a credit on the capital account when it is made) will yield profits for the overseas investors in the future. This will enter as a *debit* on the investment income part of the current account.

7. Reduction in interest rates; the central bank buying in foreign currencies into the reserves by selling domestic currency on the foreign exchange market; lending abroad or paying back loans from abroad by the government/central bank; reflationary fiscal and monetary policy; lifting or reducing controls on imports or access to foreign exchange.

9. (a) It may fuel inflation by increasing the price of imported goods and reducing the need for export industries to restrain cost increases.

   (b) It may damage export industries and domestic import-competing industries, which would now find it more difficult to remain competitive.

11. It would involve too much risk. The longer the time period the greater the scope for movements in the exchange rate and the more unpredictable they become. (Look at Figure 12.3 on page 405 of the text and see what happened to the exchange rate over the five year period from 1980 to 1985!)

13. Both consumers and firms (when buying inputs) may take a time to change their consumption patterns. Thus the shorter the time period, the less will be the response to a change in the prices of imports and exports, and therefore the less price elastic will be their demand.

15. The answer is that it depends on the effect of government policy on the views of speculators. The point is that the power of speculation to influence the exchange rate is likely to exceed the power of governments. The reason is that the exchange rate is dependent on the demand for and supply of the domestic currency on the foreign exchange market. If there are very large-scale short-term international capital movements, these will be the major short-term determinant of the rate of exchange – far more important than central bank intervention from the reserves. If speculators believe that the government is not going to be able to maintain the current exchange rate at such a high level, no matter how much it intervenes on the foreign exchange market or raises interest rates, then their actions will virtually ensure that the government will fail. This is why the UK was forced out of the ERM in September 1992.

   If, however, the government can convince speculators that it intends to maintain interest rates above international ones and that therefore the current rate of exchange is not too high, then speculators will not sell the currency and the rate of exchange *will* be maintained.

   The main conclusion is that speculative movements in international capital are normally too hard to resist merely by the government trying to create flows in the opposite direction by intervention from the reserves or by changing interest rates. What is necessary is to stop the speculation itself. This is as much an art as a science: persuading speculators that the current rate will remain the equilibrium rate.

17. They have little bearing on the debate between those advocating a single currency and those advocating flexible exchange rates between members. They do highlight the dangers, however, of fixed exchange rates when economies are not in harmony. There is therefore a problem in *progressing* to a single currency if it involves an intermediate stage of fixed exchange rates. Once sufficient harmony has been achieved, it is better to move *directly* to a single currency: there can be no speculation between the members if they all have the same currency (any more than there can be between the English pound and the Scottish or Welsh pounds, or the Californian and Maryland dollar).

19. Trade is likely to be attracted to those countries which join, and they may have greater influence in determining future EU policy. Those that do not join, however, will be able to take advantage of exchange rate movements to deal with any economic shocks that have a different effect on them from other members. They may be vulnerable, however, to speculative international capital movements between their currency and others, including the euro: movements which are not merely a reflection of their *trade* account divergences.

Index